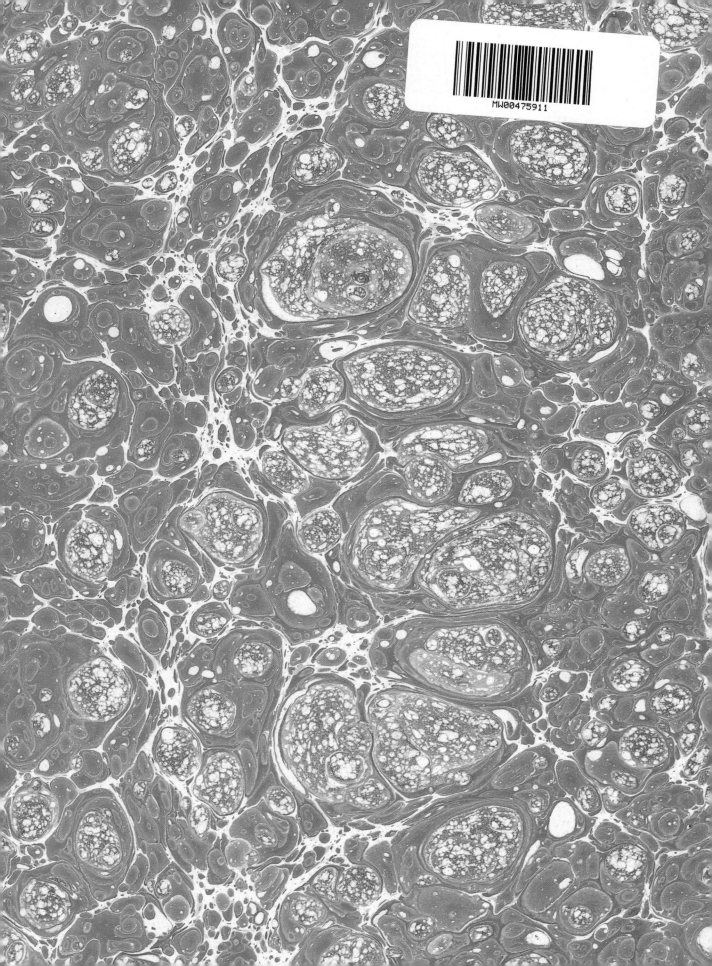

# THE
# WAFFEN-SS

## by HERBERT WALTHER

# THE WAFFEN-SS

## A PICTORIAL DOCUMENTATION

BY
HERBERT WALTHER

WITH GENERALFELDMARSCHALL von MANSTEIN,
GENERAL von MANTEUFFEL and HEINZ HOHNE

Schiffer Publishing Ltd

1469 Morstein Road
West Chester, PA 19380 U.S.A.

Originally published under the title "Die Waffen SS", copyright
Podzun-Pallas-Verlag, 6360 Friedberg 3 (Dorheim).

Translated from the German by Dr. Edward Force.

Copyright © 1990 by Schiffer Publishing.
Library of Congress Catalog Number: 89-063358.

Printed in the United States of America.
ISBN: 0-88740-204-6

Published by Schiffer Publishing, Ltd.
1469 Morstein Road
West Chester, Pennsylvania 19380
Please write for a free catalog.
This book may be purchased from the publisher.
Please include $2.00 postage.
Try your bookstore first.

# CONTENTS

# PREFACE

This book is made up of photographs which should have been burned in 1945. All of the photographic negatives taken by the war reporters of the Waffen-SS, were completely destroyed on highest order shortly before the end of the war. Luckily, a large cache of the small contact prints were saved.

Of the 100,000 contact prints (24mm x 36mm), most are without captions and dates. It was thus necessary to interpret them only by painstaking research, reconstruction, comparisons and by identifying people and places. Naturally, here and there errors are inevitable, but these can be accepted. On the other hand it has been possible to give a comprehensive survey of the fighting Waffen-SS by using these impressive photographs. We are indebted to Fotomeister Werner Held for making these optimal photo reproductions possible.

When the publishers produced this book, they were conscious of the fact that a portrayal of the Waffen-SS in battle will always be incomplete, although we were able to use hitherto unpublished photographs. Amidst the falling of bombs during the Normandy invasion, the battles in the Italian Campaign and the final battles in Germany, photos were rarely taken. The available material from the period is scarce.

Of course we could easily have fallen back on pictures which have been frequently published. We did not want to do this, especially as in other volumes we had a great number of absolutely unique and so far unpublished photographs at our disposal. We have therefore used more of these unknown new pictures, and at the same time we have dropped some photos which certainly would have rounded up the history of the war, but which are far too well known.

This book shows the Waffen-SS in battle, exploring those who stood and fought in the forward front line, and who gave their best during military actions. We emphatically disassociate ourselves from those who within the special units carried out the tragic business, from the "desk murderers", and from the Highest Command of the Waffen-SS. The men of the Waffen-SS, however, their officers and commanders, fully deserve fair judgement. They were soldiers like their brothers in arms of the Army and their sacrifice of killed, wounded and those missing in action do not count any less than those of the other soldiers and their former opponents.

We are grateful to Mr. Herbert Walther for his work. We thank Generalfeldmarschall von Manstein, General von Manteuffel and Mr. Heinz Höhne for their kind collaboration. We also thank the Bundesarchiv, Coblenz, especially Herrn Regel the Archivrat, Herrn Held and the Weltkriegbücherei in Stuttgart, which supplied us with most of the pictures.

L.B. Ahnert, Editor

**"...Extraordinary Bravery..."**

A collective condemnation of the SS cannot destroy the feeling of solidarity the former soldiers of the Army have with the Waffen-SS, whom they fought with shoulder to shoulder, especially as "...crimes against humanity..." in every single case were gone into and tried by the International Military Tribunal in Nuremberg, or by German courts. Our assessment of the majority of the combat units of the Waffen-SS, as far as an evaluation of their engagements is concerned, can be neither spoilt nor shaken by this condemnation.

As the commander of the 7th Panzer-Division and later as the commander of the Panzergrenadier-Division "Grossdeutschland", I often fought side by side with the combat units of the Waffen-SS. Also, as commander-in-chief of the 5th Panzer-Division and later of the 3rd Panzer Army, numerous units of the Waffen-SS were under my command. I never had any "difficulties" with them, as was very often said by others.

Because of their good equipment, these combat units were usually used in especially heavy fighting, and serious crises areas as the so called "emergency reserve". The commanders of the Army liked to use them, as their units were fully motorized and therefore, extremely mobile. The units of the Waffen-SS distinguished themselves by their discipline and excellent morale in battle, they proved successful during attack and defensive undertakings. Their "esprit de corps" within their divisions resulted in outstandingly good comradeship in these units: in action all elements co-operated, producing a very high standard of reliability. Their readiness for action was excellent. Their super-human bravery was fully acknowledged by the enemy, too. This courage was seen at the Wolchow River, in Moscow, in Charkow, in Kowel and Tscherkassy, in Normandy 1944 and on many other battlefields.

The fighting units of the Army, which fought shoulder to shoulder with these brave soldiers of the Waffen-SS, remember them and their fallen comrades gratefully-they were fighting for Germany-they too suffered and were killed.

General Hasso von Manteuffel

# THE YEARS 1933-1938

In the year 1933, the "Leibstandarte" Adolf Hitler was founded. Uniforms and rank designations are the same as those of the common SS.

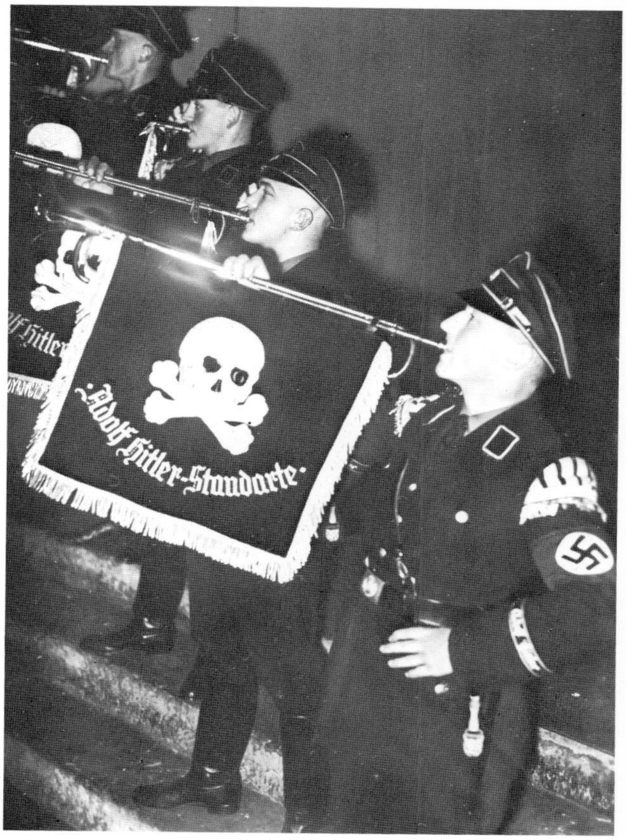
Adolf Hitler-Standarte

Combat practice takes place in the Army training area, The 1. company of the LAH under the command of Lieutenant Fritz Witt in Jüterbog (February 1934).

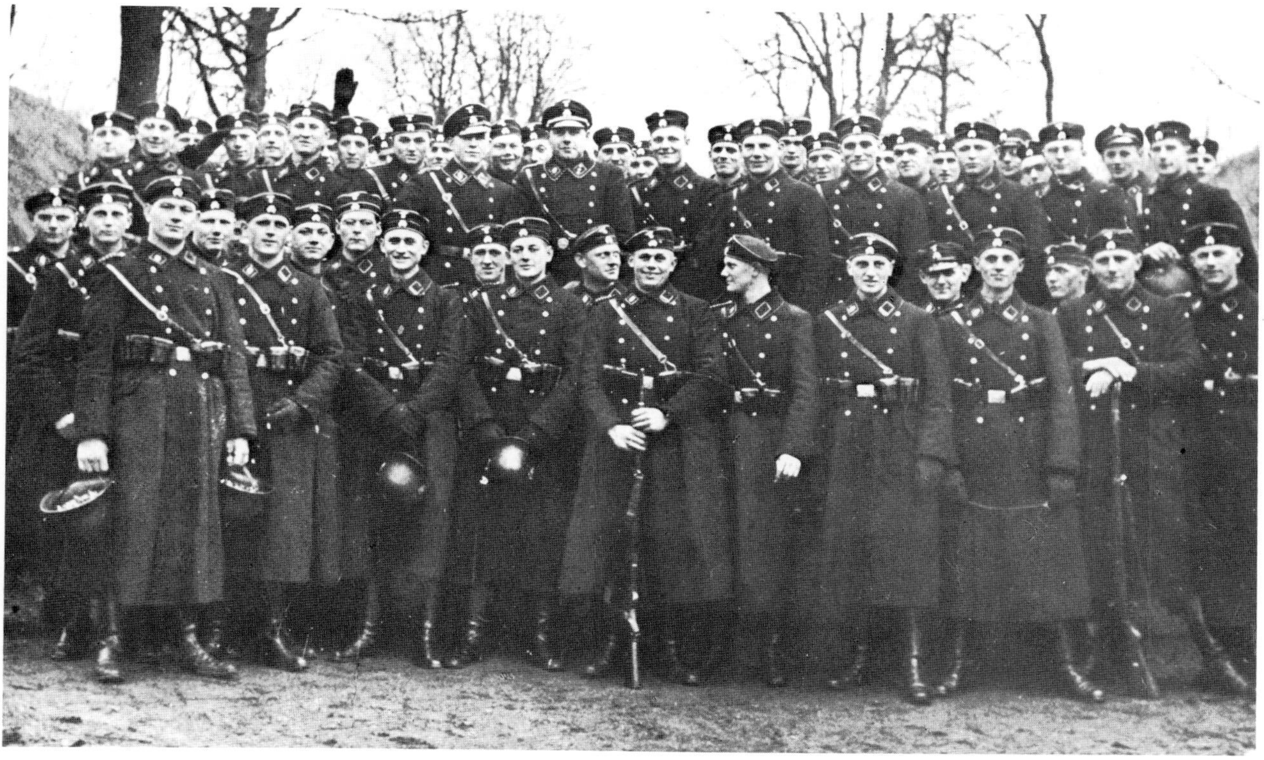

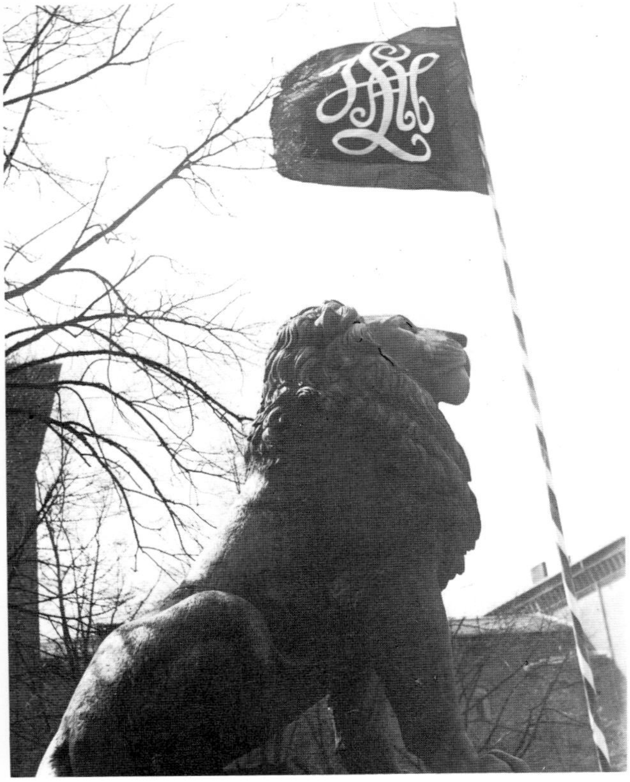

The banner of the "Leibstandarte" Adolf Hitler (LAH) in the barracks of Berlin-Lichterfelde-a former military academy.

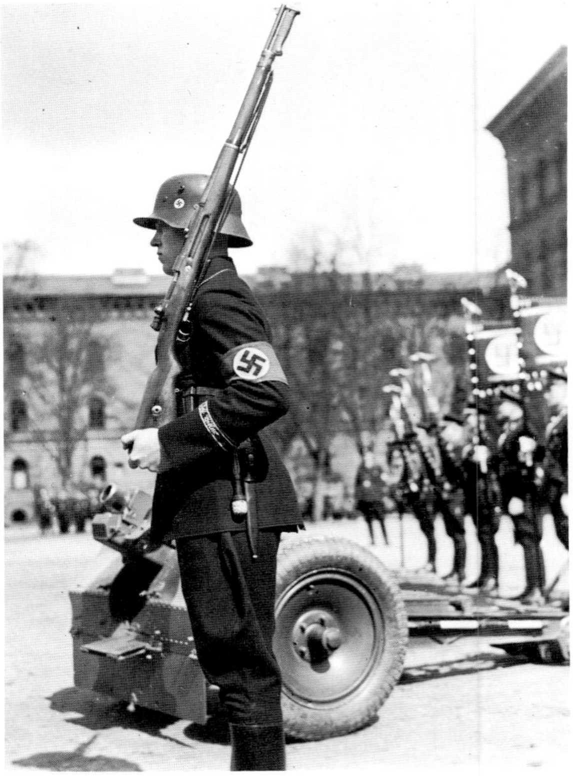

Swearing in of new recruits on 19 April, 1936.

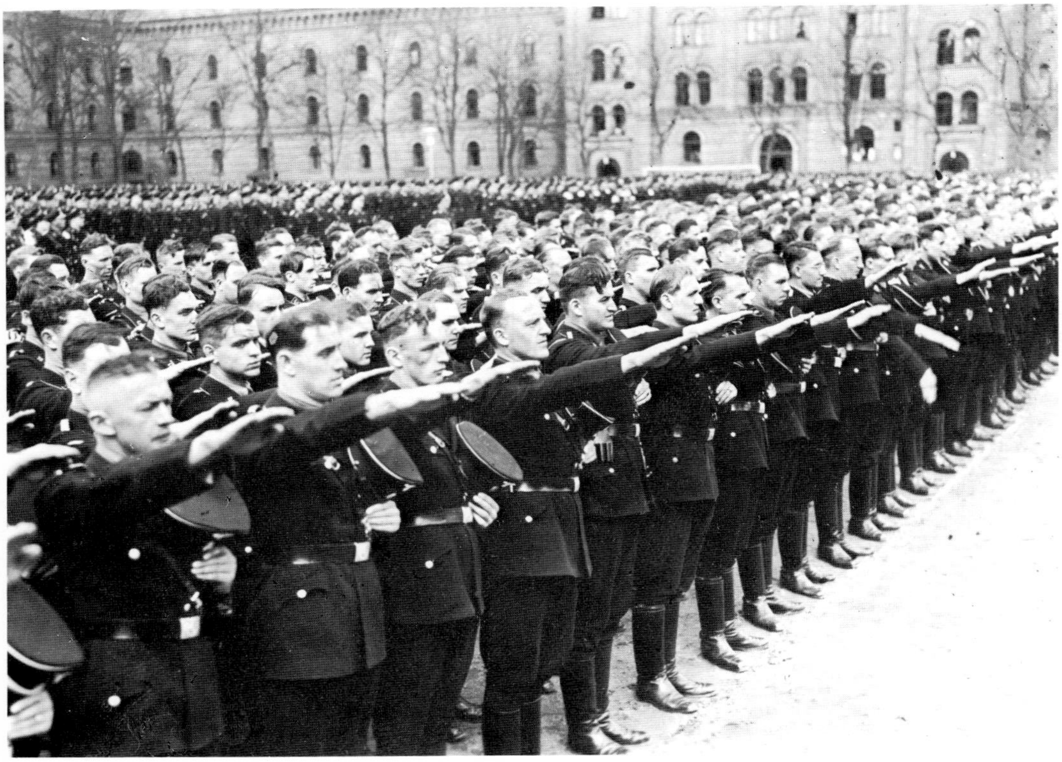

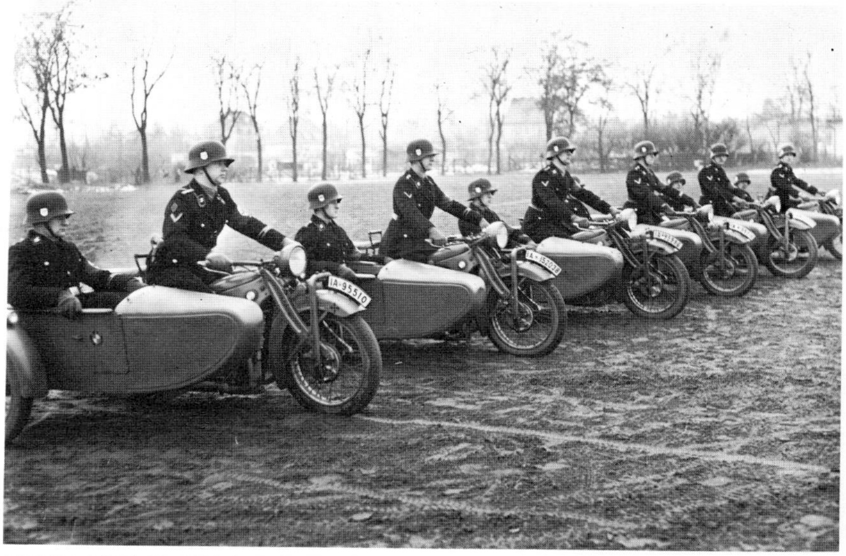

Training of motorcycle riflemen-still wearing the black uniforms.

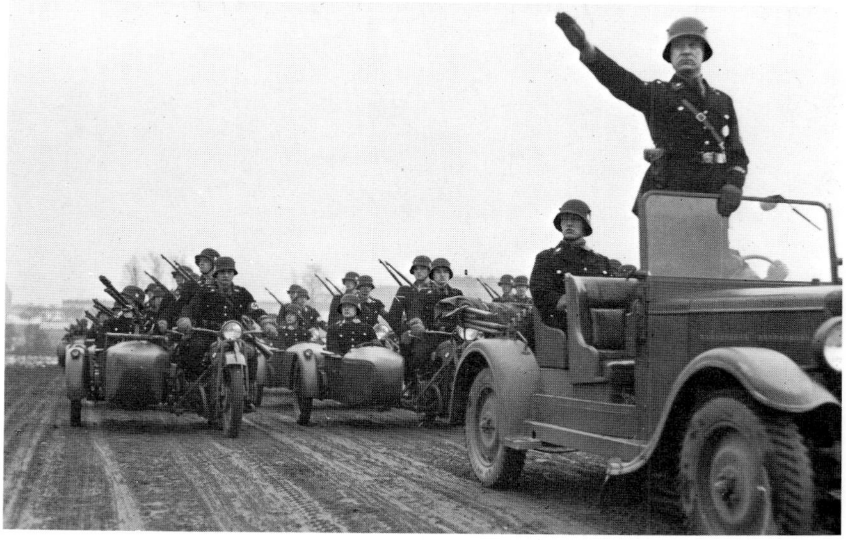

Inspection of the LAH by Adolf Hitler. Beside him is commander Lt. General Sepp Dietrich and Major Jürgen Wagner. (Dec. 12, 1934)

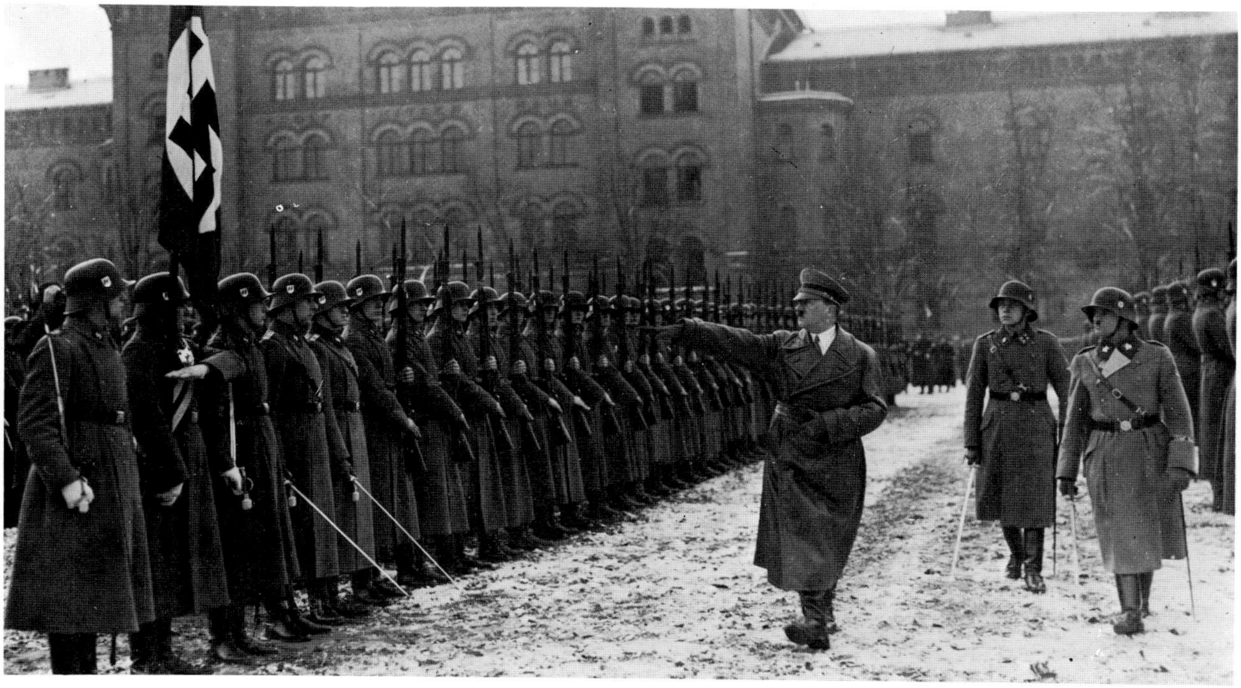

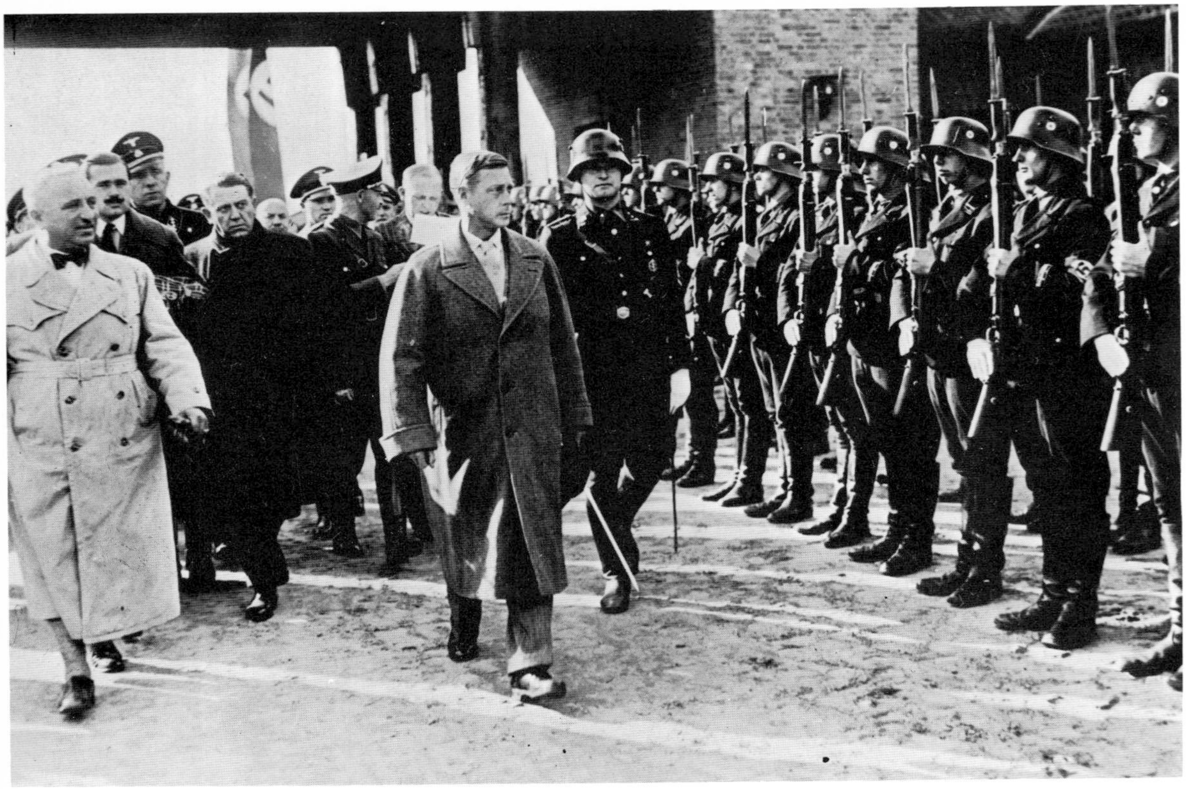

The Duke of Windsor taking the review of an honor formation of the regiment "Germania" at the "Crössinee" castle. (October 13, 1937)

Honor formation of the LAH in front of the Kroll opera in Berlin. (February 20, 1938)

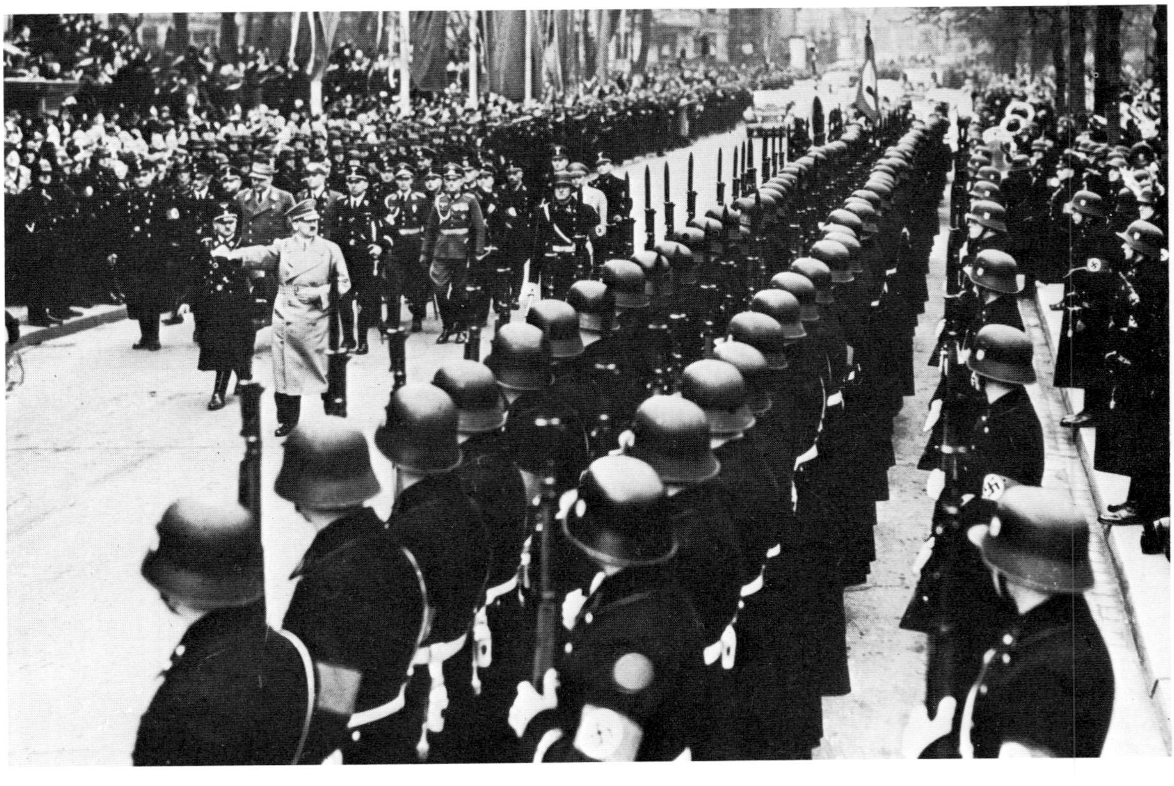

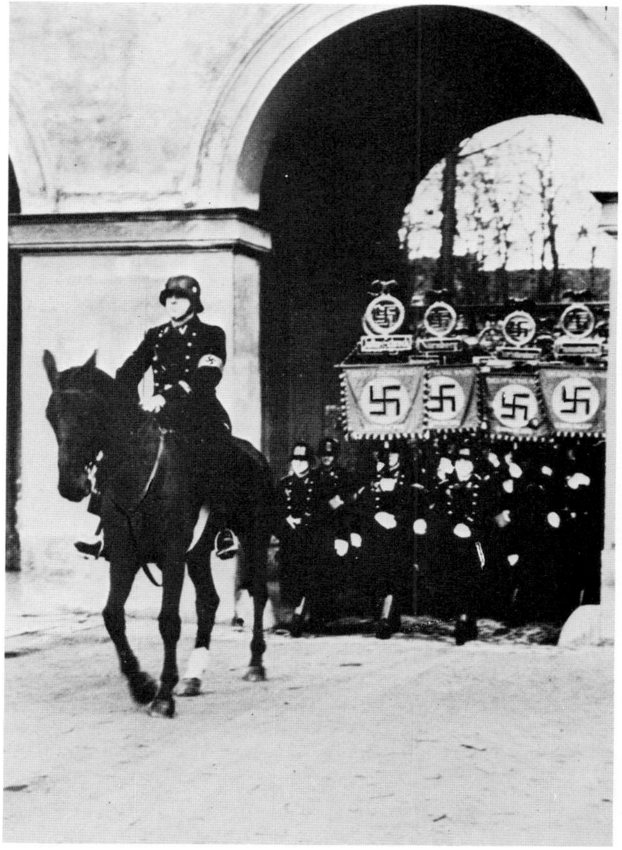

The LAH and the regiments of the support unit which has been newly formed, were used as review formations for official occasions. Fritz Witt leading an honor formation of the regiment "Deutschland".

The banner of the regiment "Deutschland".

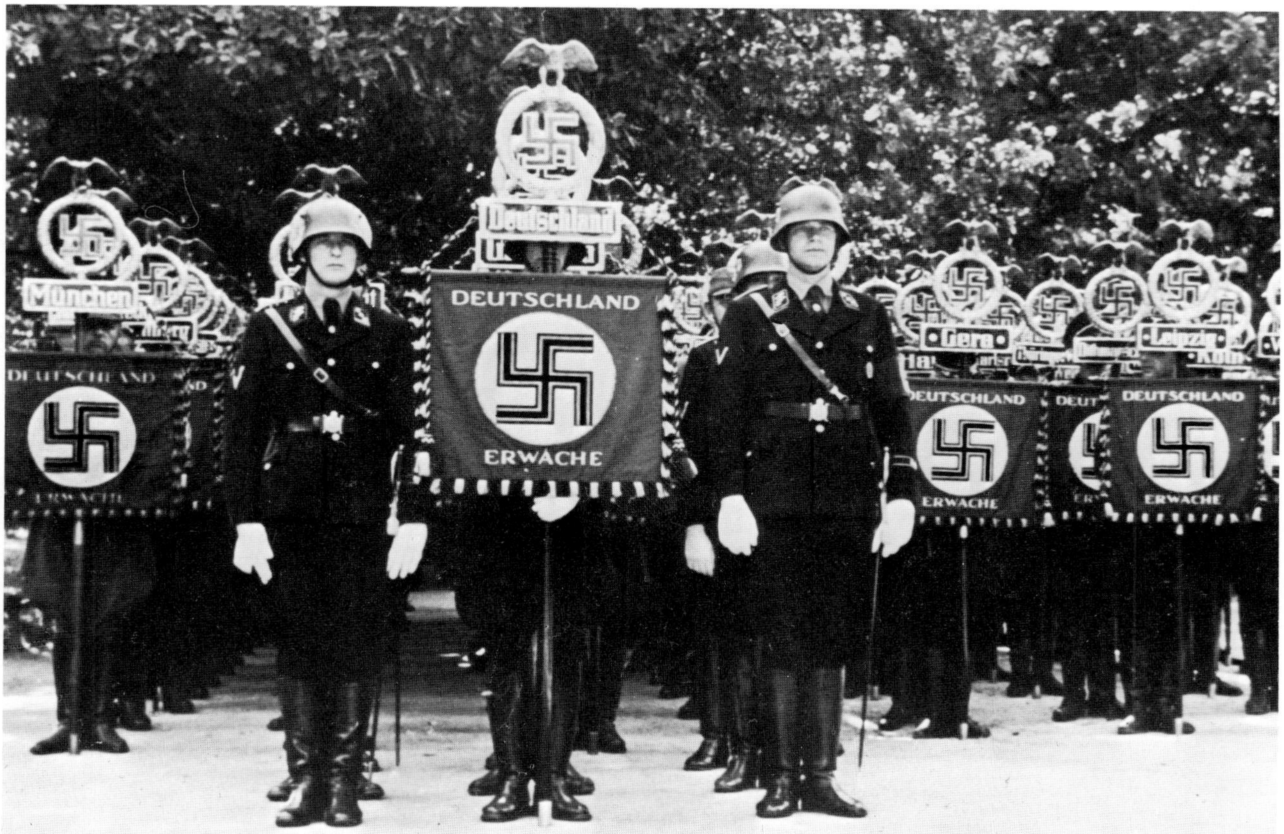
München
Deutschland
DEUTSCHLAND
ERWACHE
Gera
Leipzig
DEUTSCHLAND
ERWACHE
DEUTSCHLAND
ERWACHE

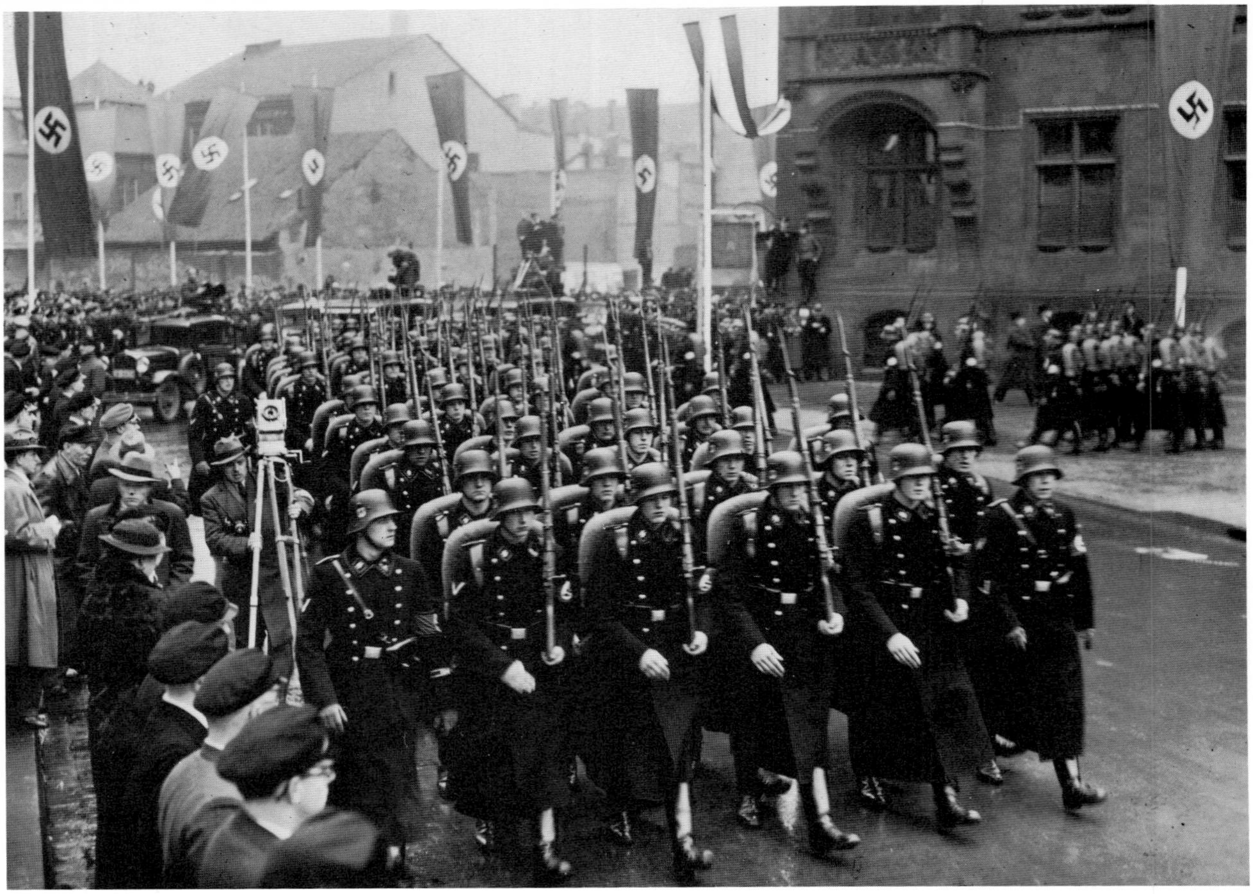

After the plebiscite in the Saarland, the LAH invades the city of Saarbrücken.

Birthday parade for Adolf Hitler in Berlin 1937.

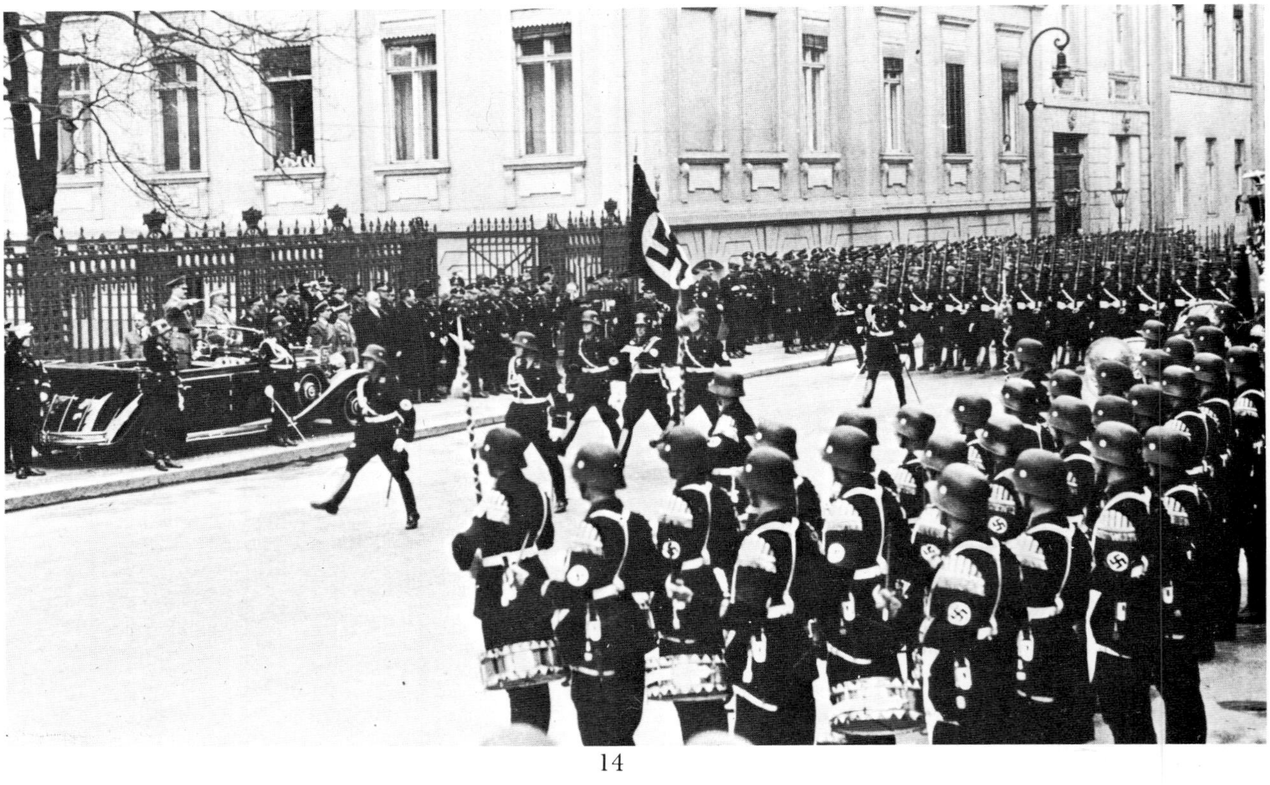

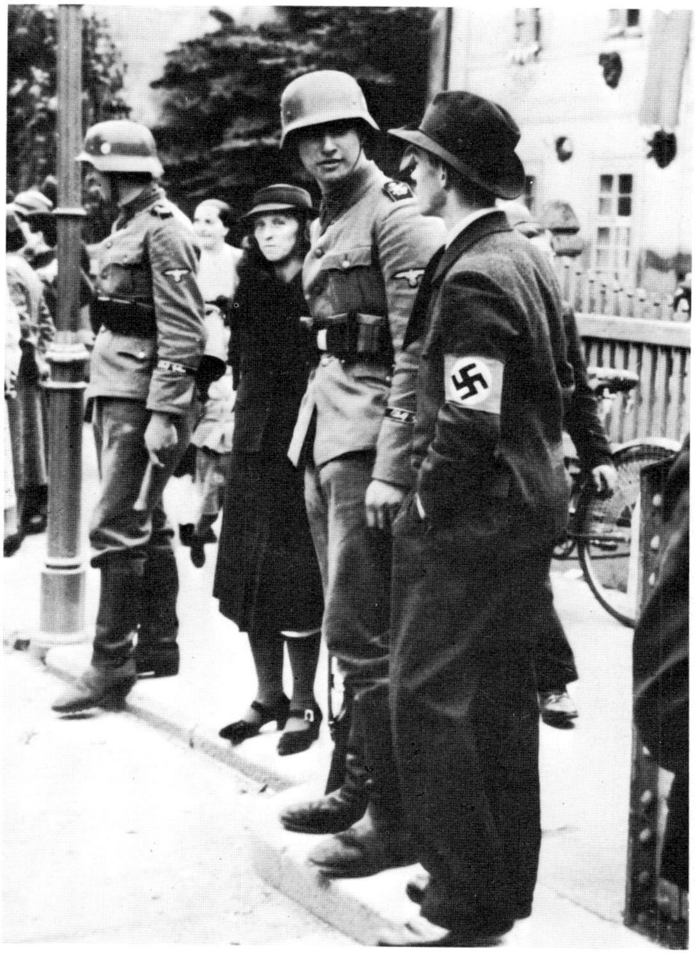

After the treaty of Munich, elements of the LAH also invade the Sudetenland.

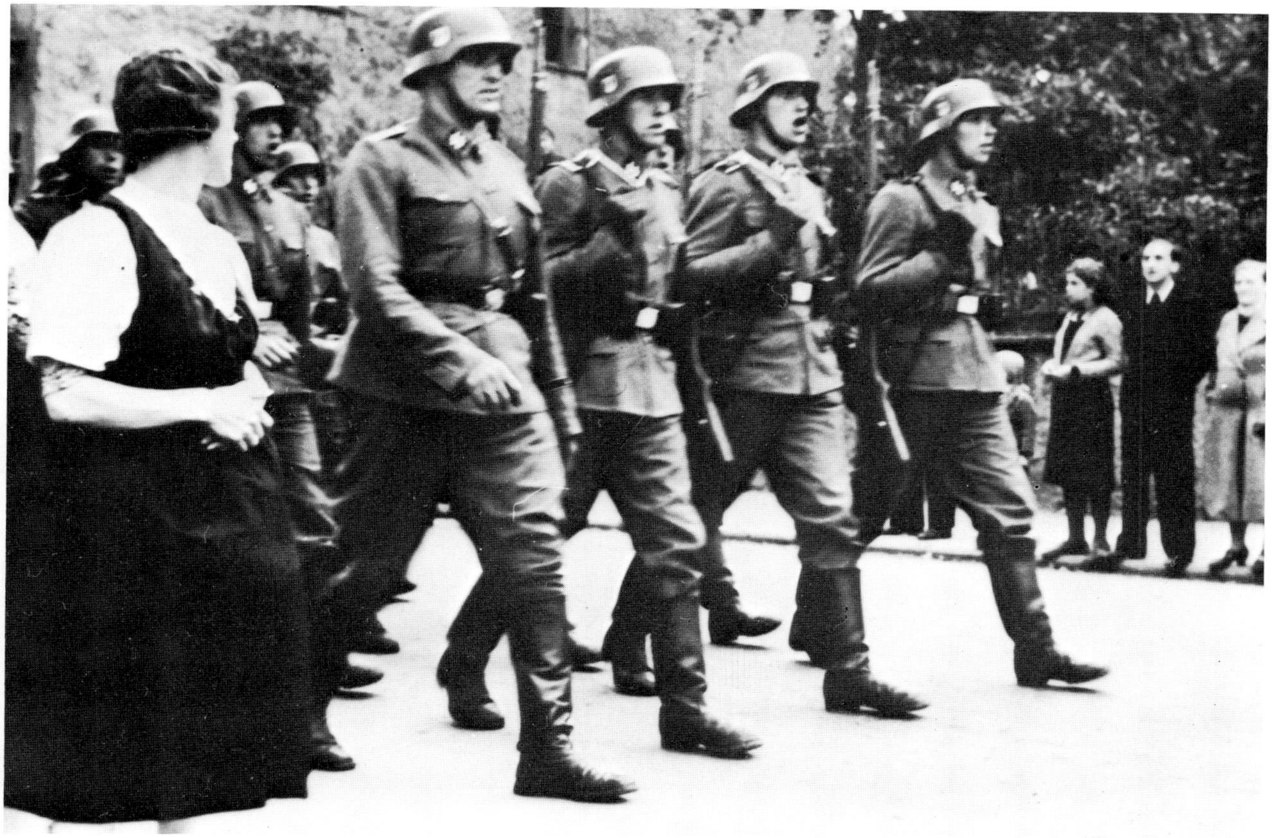

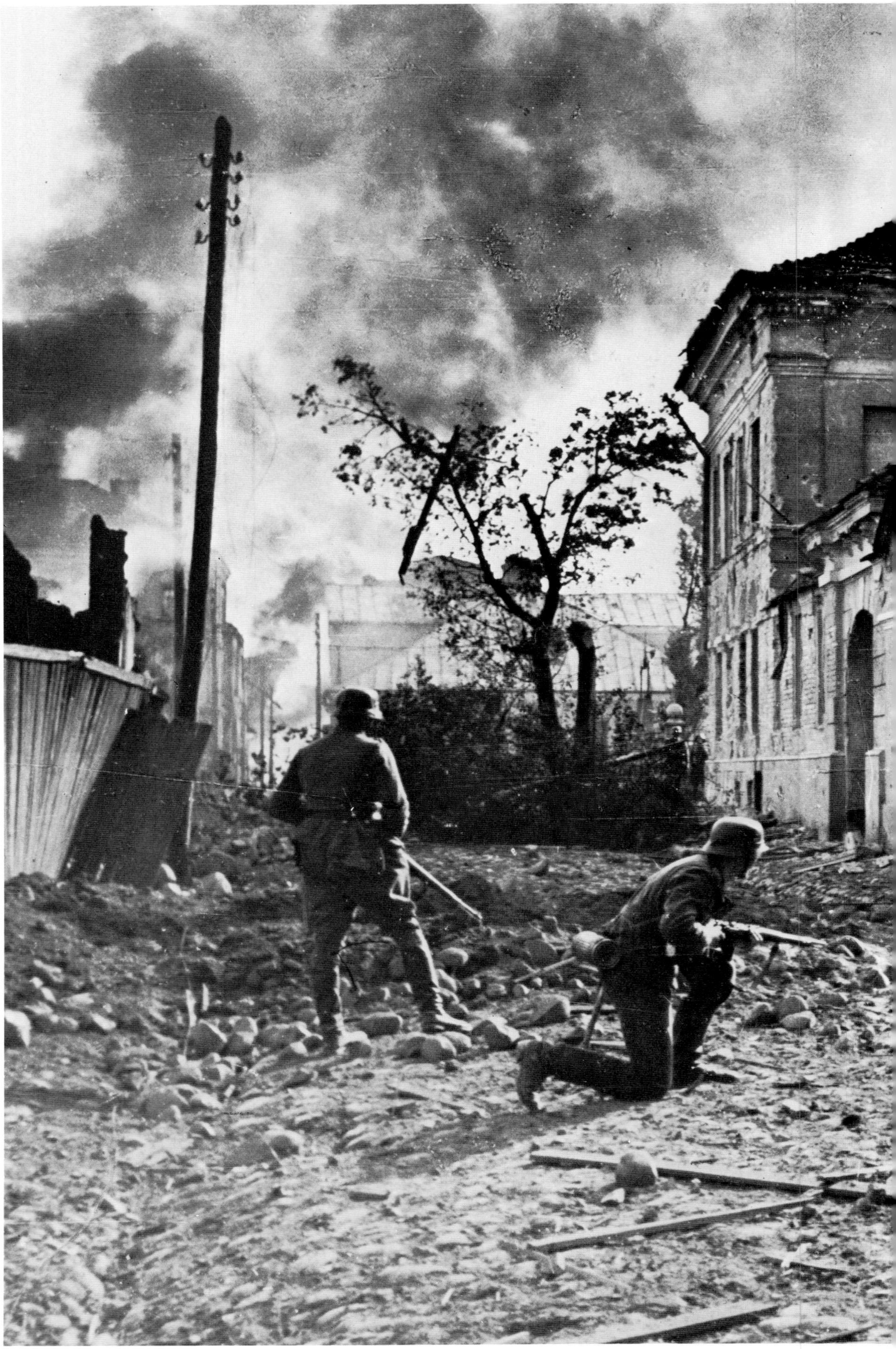

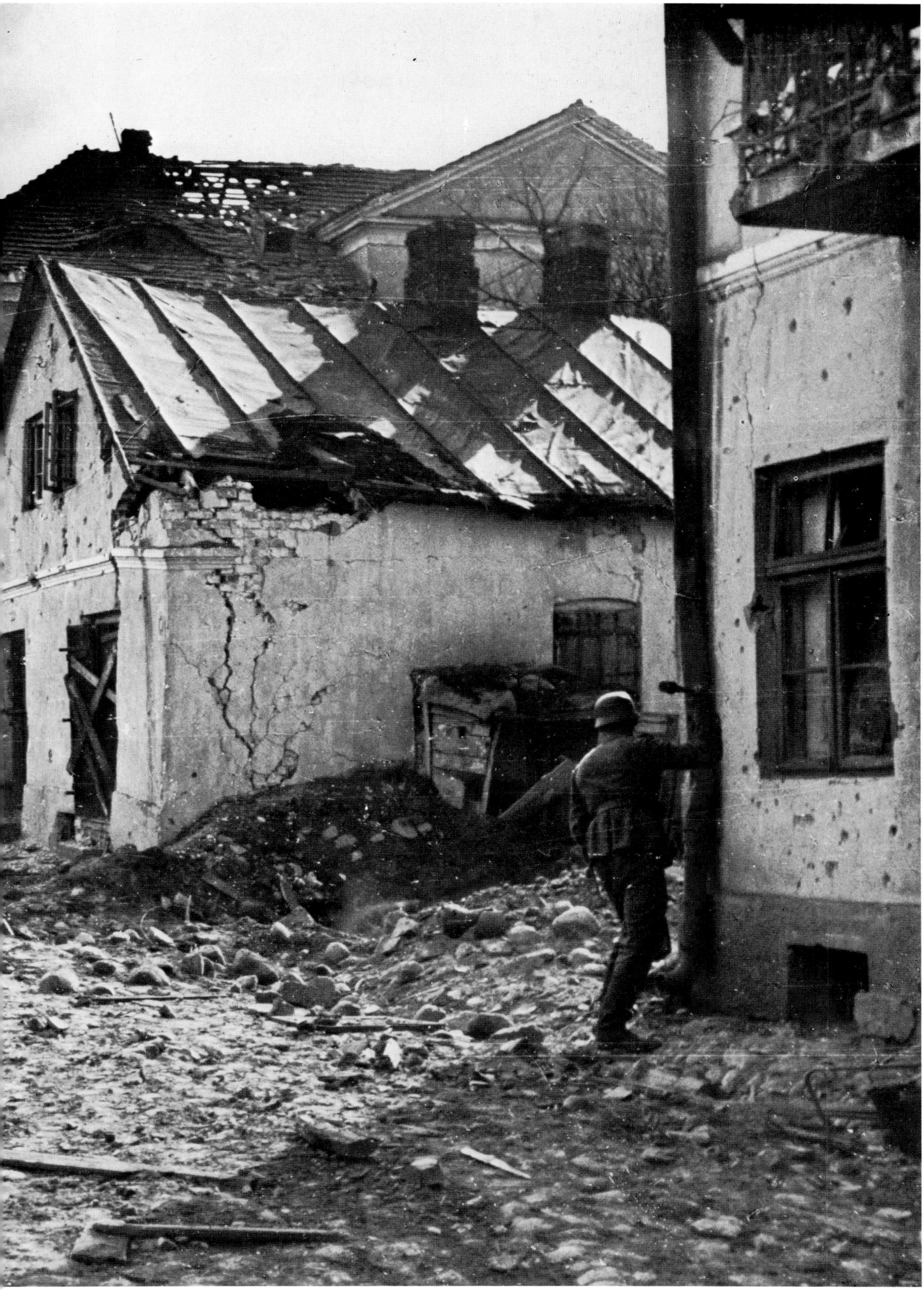

# THE POLISH CAMPAIGN, 1939

The first of the "Lightning Campaigns", it introduced both the strength and the functioning of the German war machine to a frightened world.

This 18-day war resulted in the growth of Hitler's pride in his invincibility and his military leadership.

Against the 36 infantry divisions, 11 cavalry divisions, 1 mountain brigade and 2 armored brigades that Poland possessed, there were 7 armored divisions (including the army units and O.K.H. reserve) and 55 infantry, mountain or light divisions. They smashed the Polish army, supported by the superiority of the Luftwaffe. Units of SS troops fought on many sectors of the front within the North and South Army Groups.

The Polish campaign was a shattering event in the history of war. Within four weeks, in battle against an opponent approximately equal in manpower, a gigantic slaughter took place, with 700,000 prisoners taken and a loss of only 10,000 German dead and 30,000 wounded. This victory was largely the work of the German armored troops, gained along with the Luftwaffe, which won sovereignty in the air and thus made the armored troops' movements possible. The decisive role of the infantry had now passed to the armored troops. Germany did not begin the "war of yesterday".

Firing at a Polish post office in Danzig.

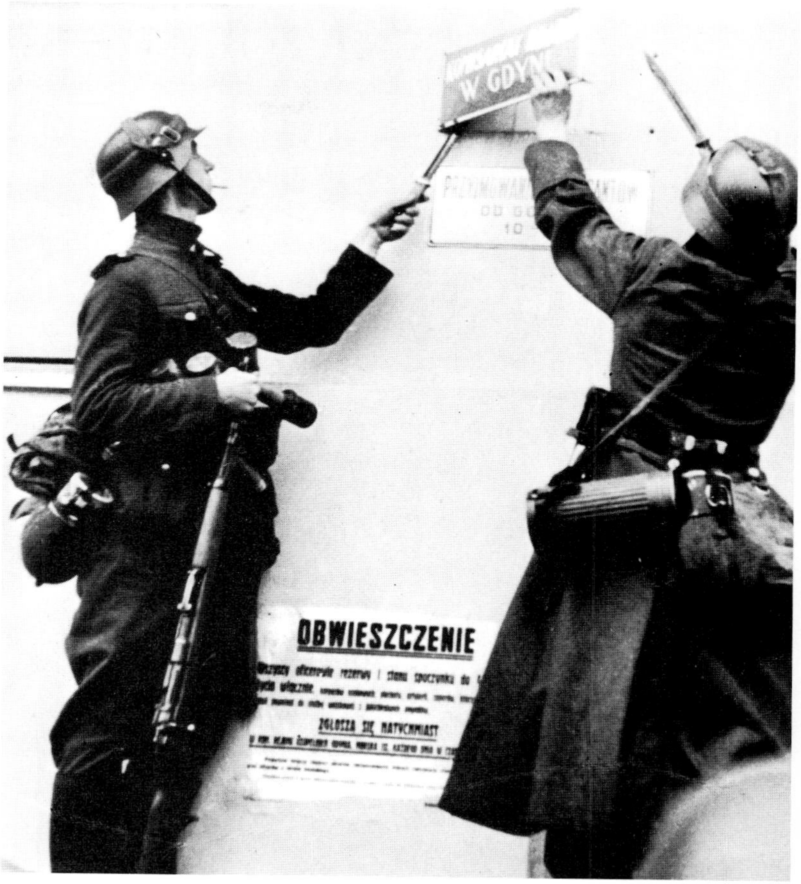
OBWIESZCZENIE

The removal of Polish street signs.

State Secretary Greiser inspects the post office in Danzig, which has been destroyed.

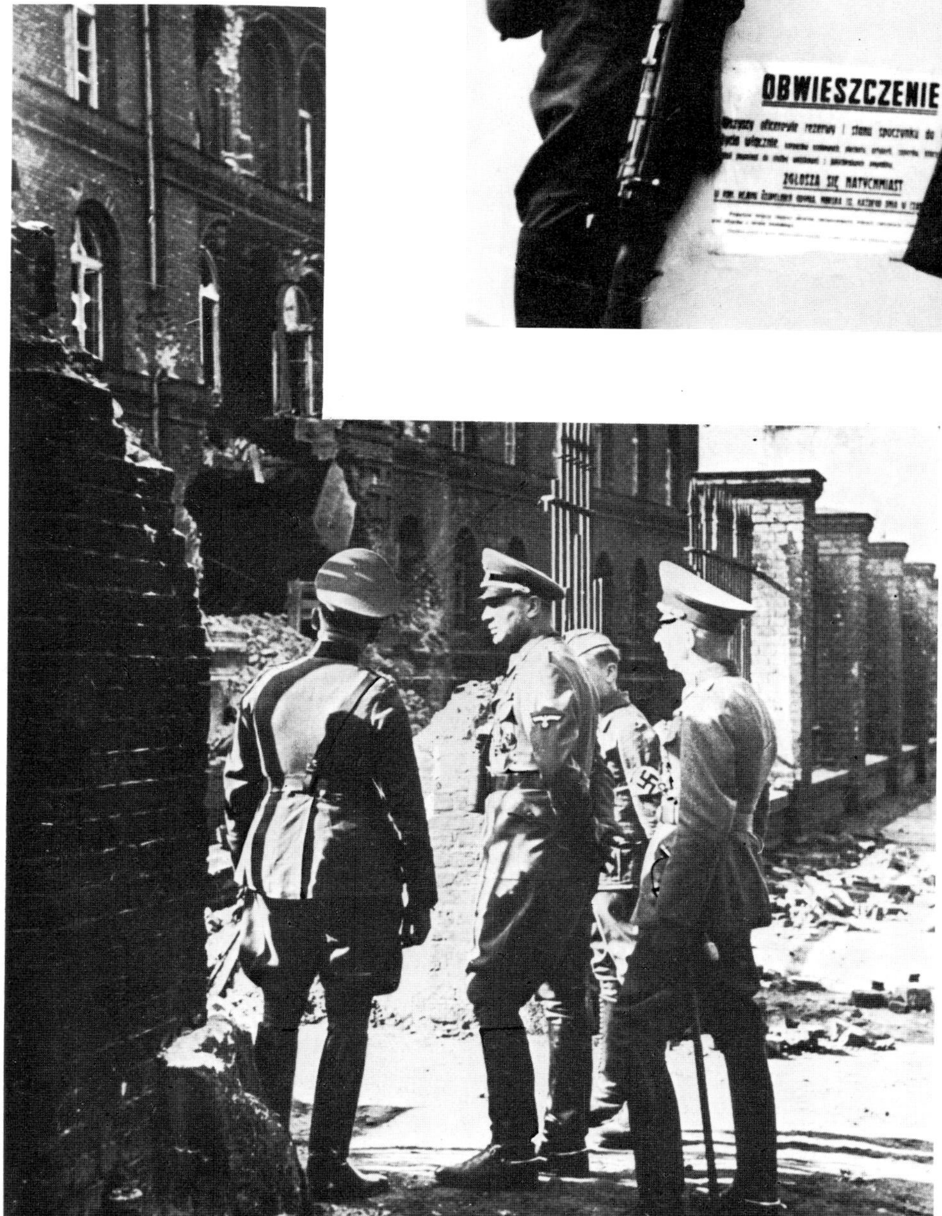

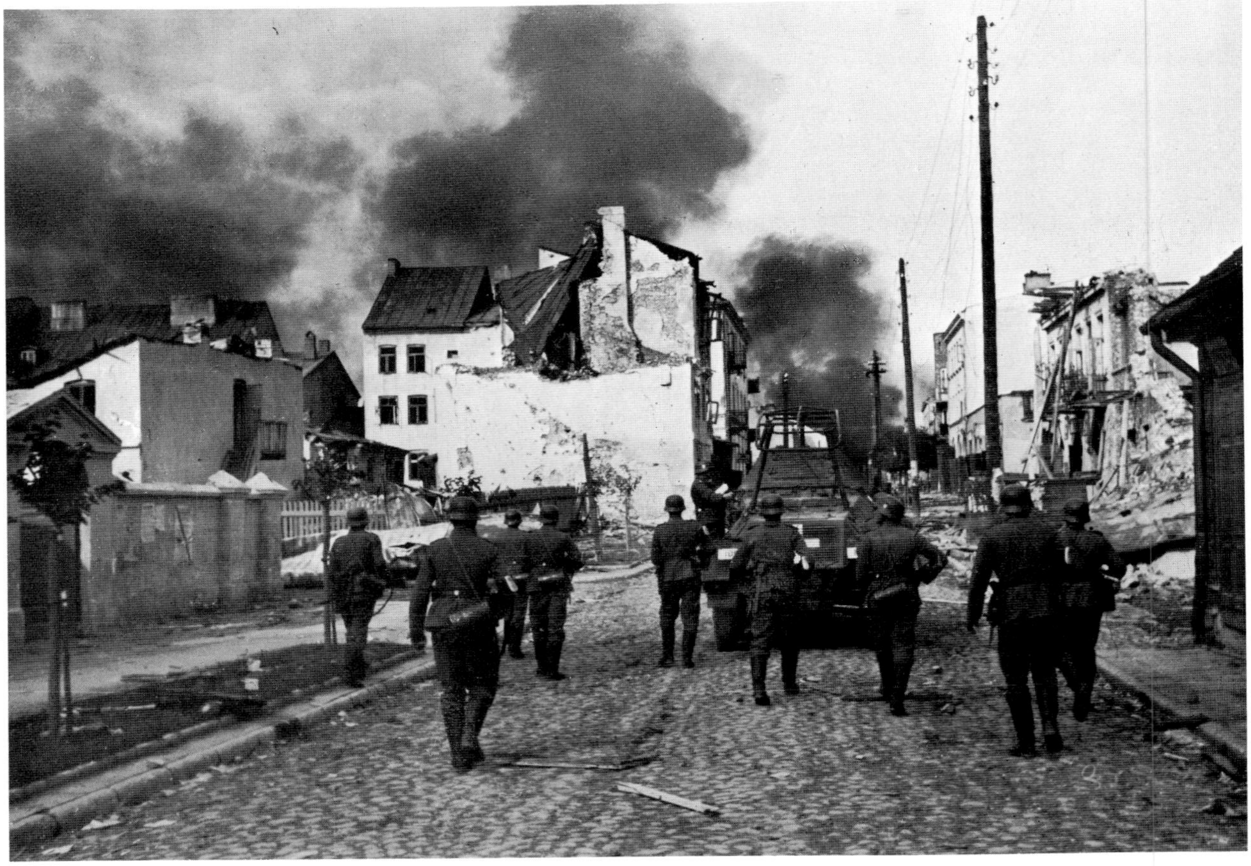

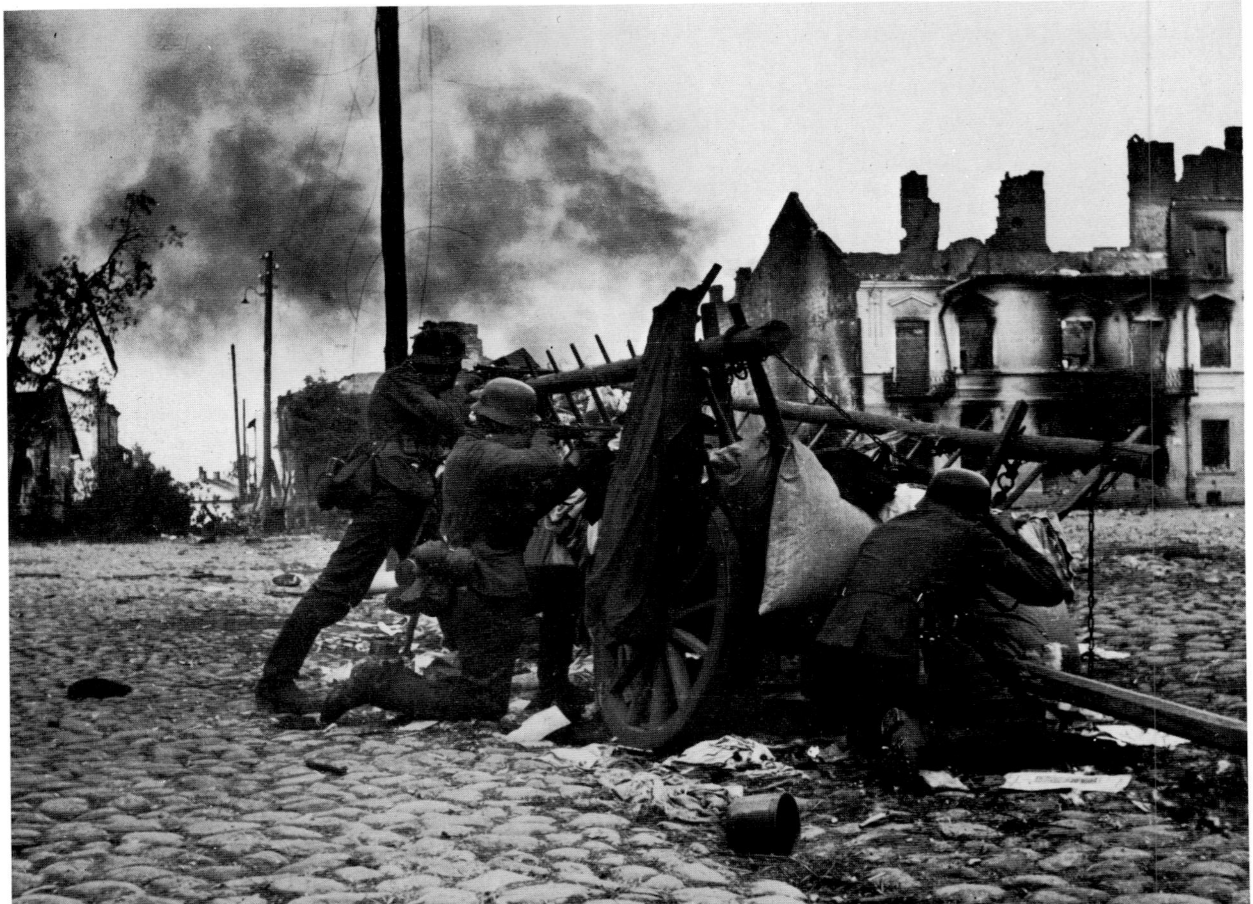

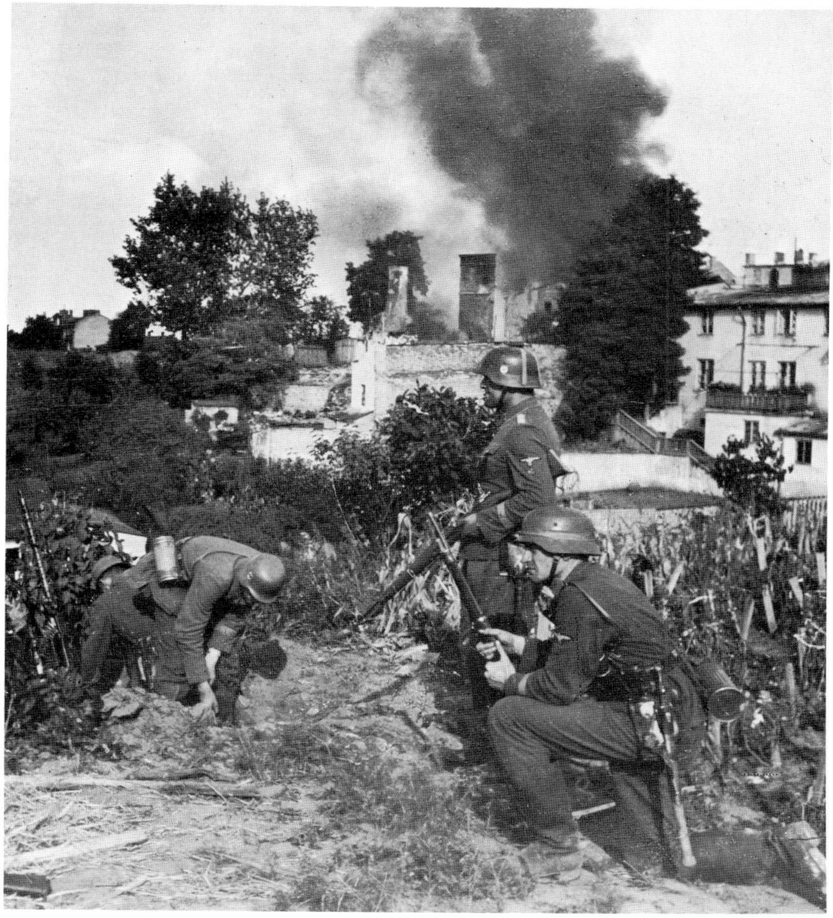

Heavy resistance is offered only locally by the Polish regiments. Formations of SS support units attempting to seize a Polish village.

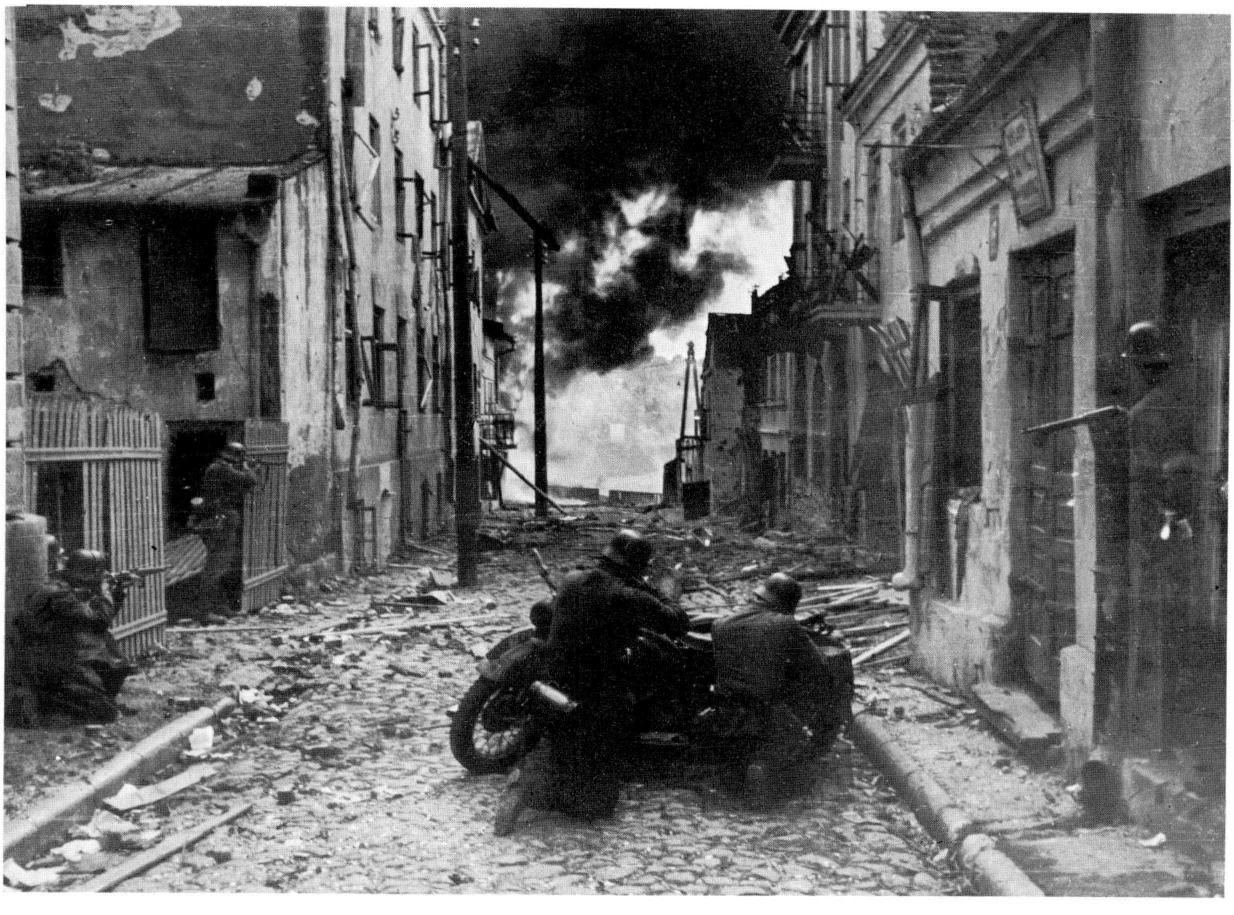

# THE WESTERN CAMPAIGN

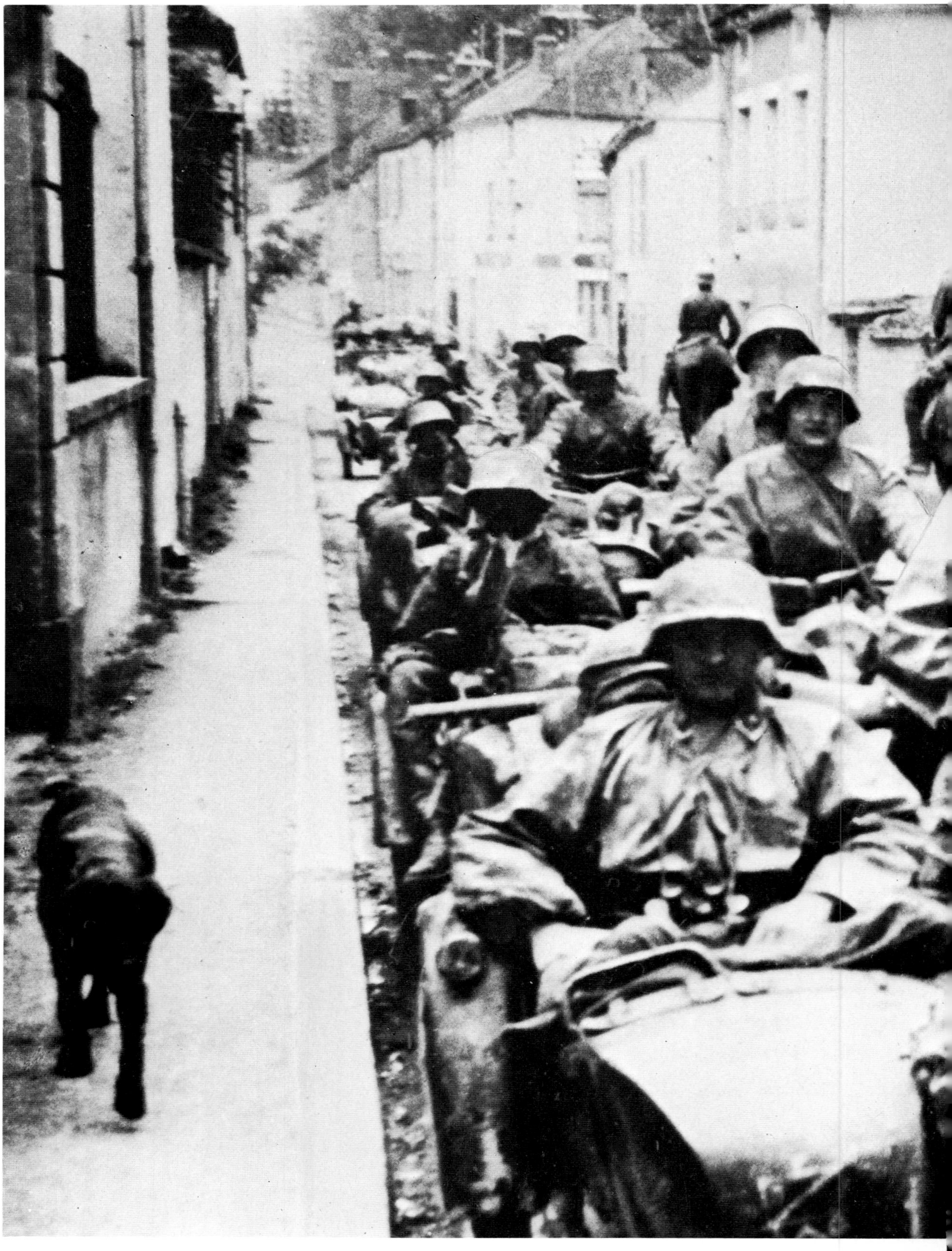

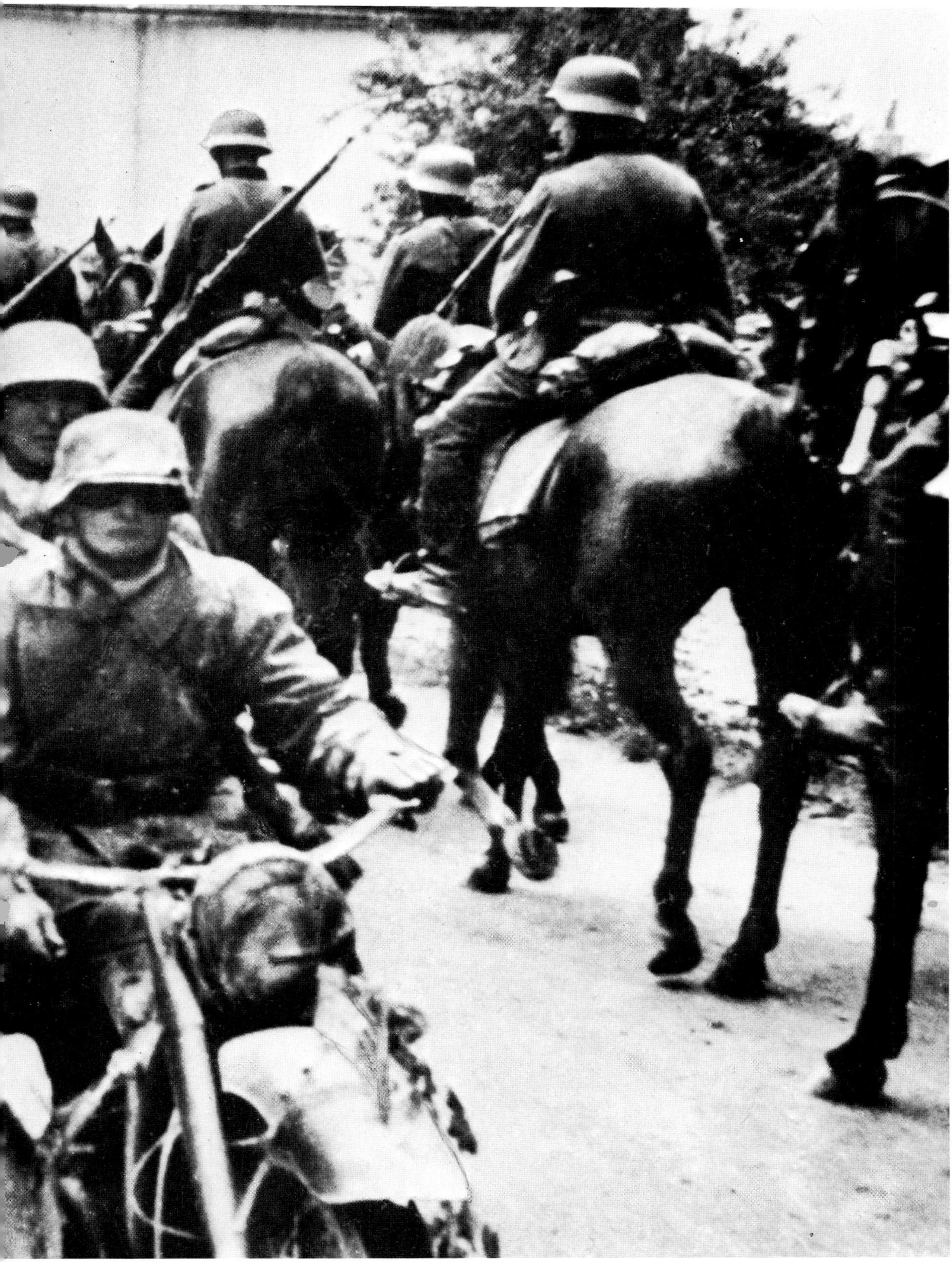

After months of inaction on the fronts, at 5:30 AM on May 10, 1940 the attack began, led by 122 infantry and mountain divisions, 10 armored divisions with 2500 tanks, 1 cavalry division and, for the first time, also 2 SS divisions (motorized). One SS division advanced in the direction of Holland (Rotterdam), the other SS division, as part of the 12th Army and the "Sickle Cut" column, toward Dunkirk. The Dutch, Belgian, English and French units were overrun, surrounded or wiped out within a few weeks, so that Hitler saw himself confirmed as a "genius of leadership". The SS divisions under Hausser and Eicke proved themselves as battle units to a particularly high degree.

The German views of the fighting principles of large armored units, developed against a world where different ideas of military science prevailed, were correct. Opposed to the warning voice of de Gaulle, whose ideas resembled those of Guderian, the Allies, as at the end of World War I, had spread their armored divisions equally along the entire front. The German leadership, though, had now all learned that armored troops had to be deployed together, with distant goals, separated from the slower troops.

Two days before the beginning of hostilities the Upper Rhine front seems "quiet". Members of an SS-Police unit wave to their adversaries on the opposite side of the river. This photograph was classified "top secret" at this time. It was available for publication until after the end of the war.

The preparation for combat was checked and improved by continuous training.

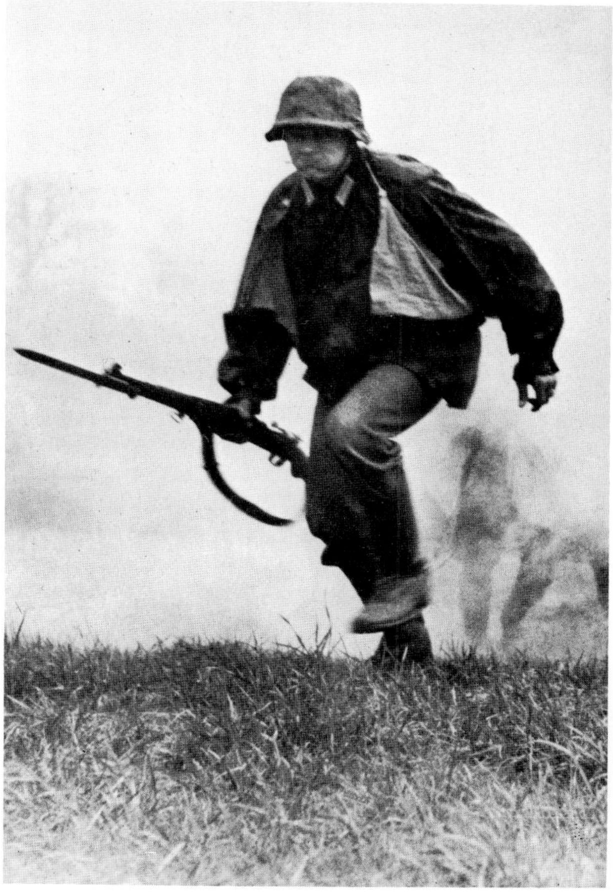

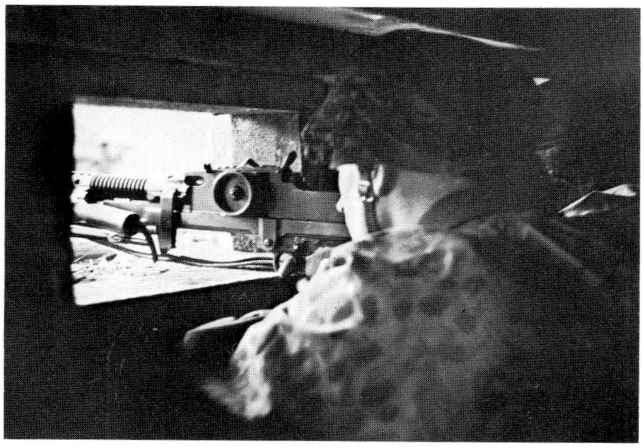

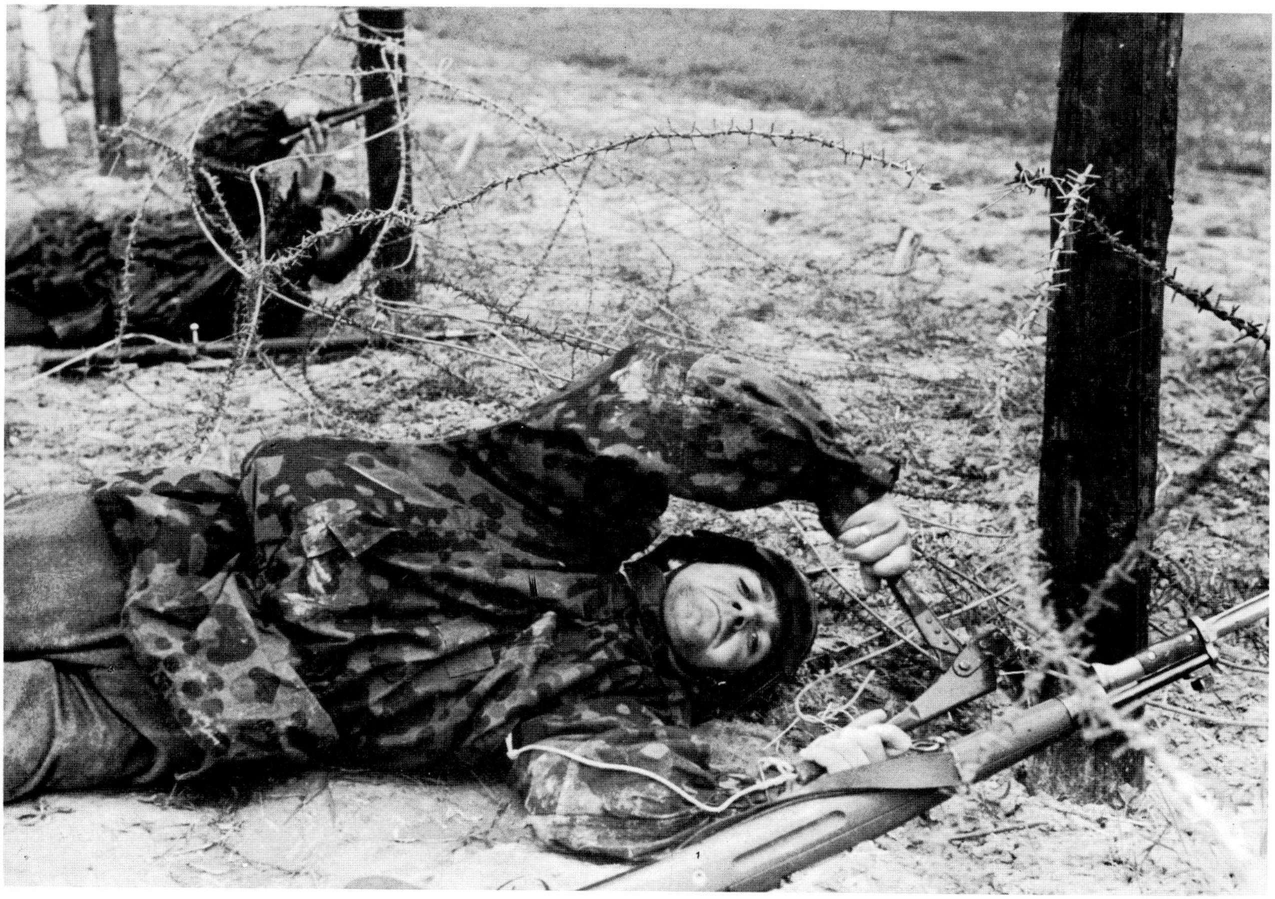

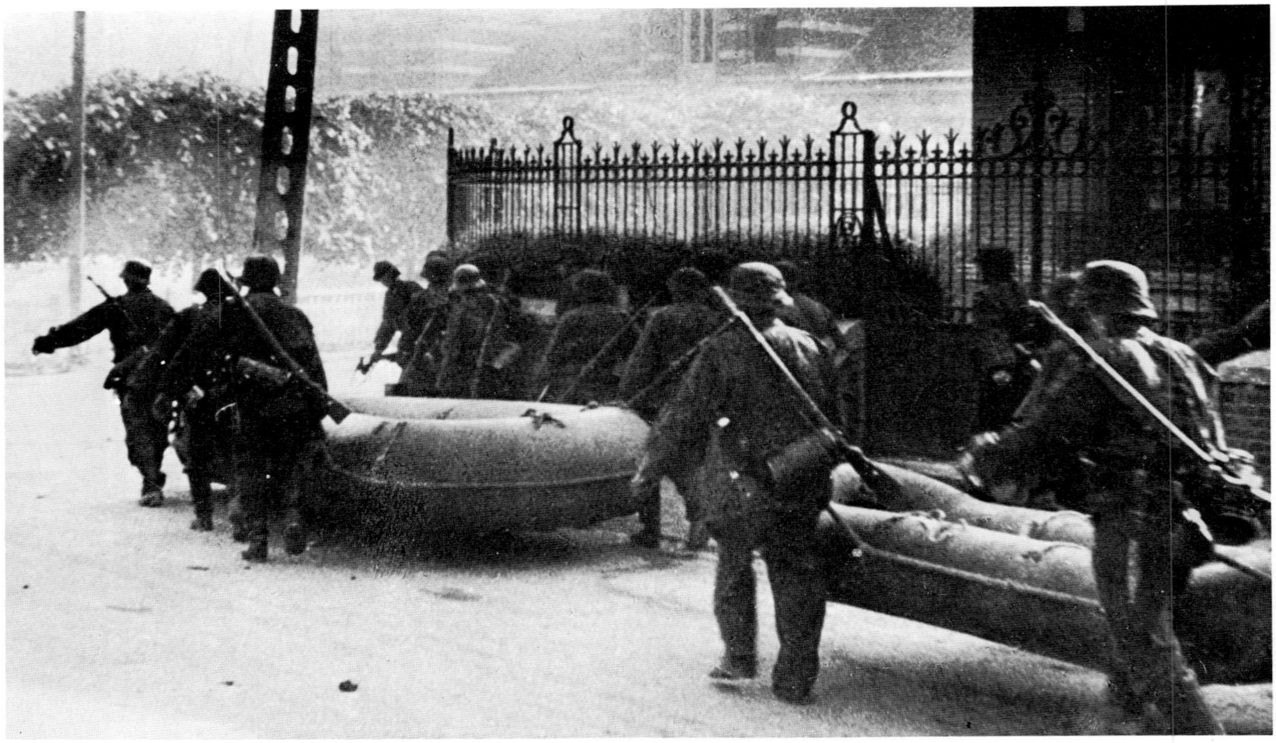

Preparations are made for the river crossing in rafts. Still, the enemy does not move...until suddenly, there is heavy firing from the French defenses, forcing the men to take cover.

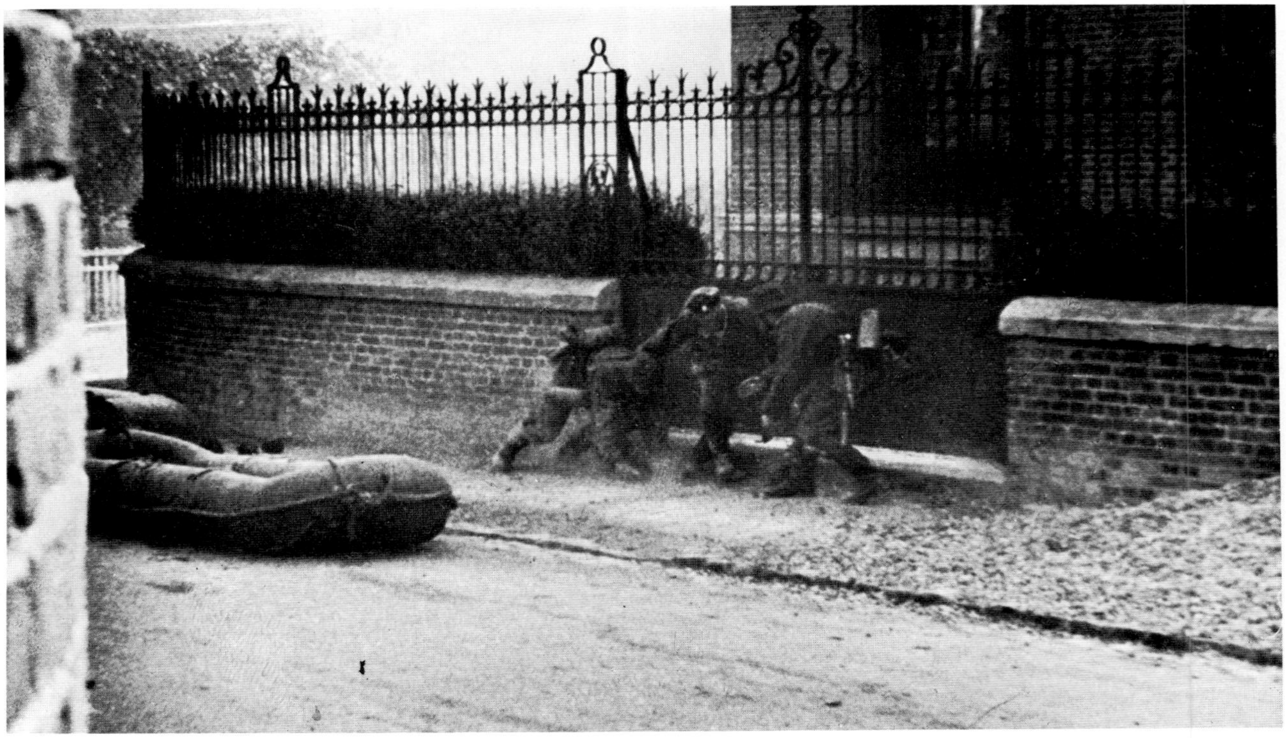

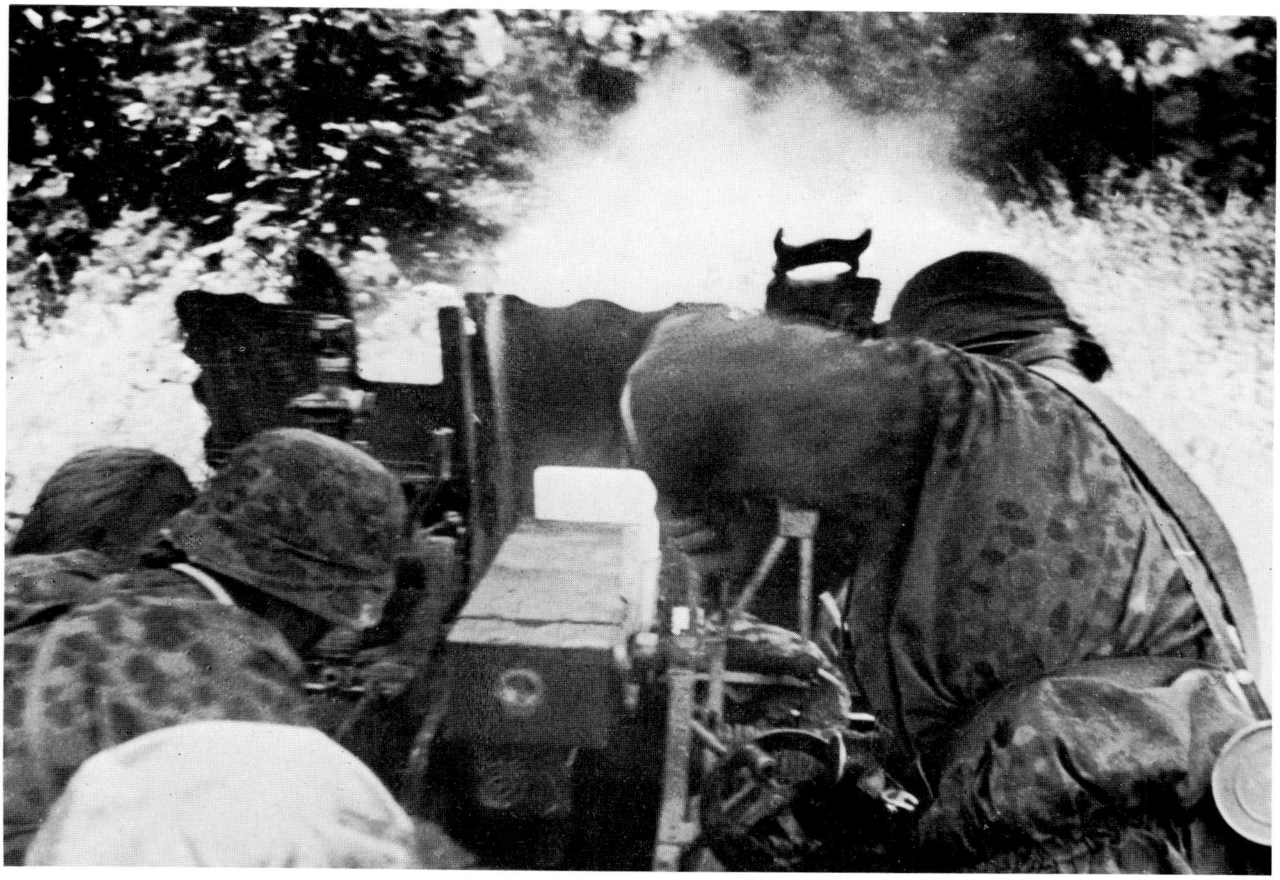

The resistance was broken with only light infantry guns. Infantrymen searching the abandoned village.

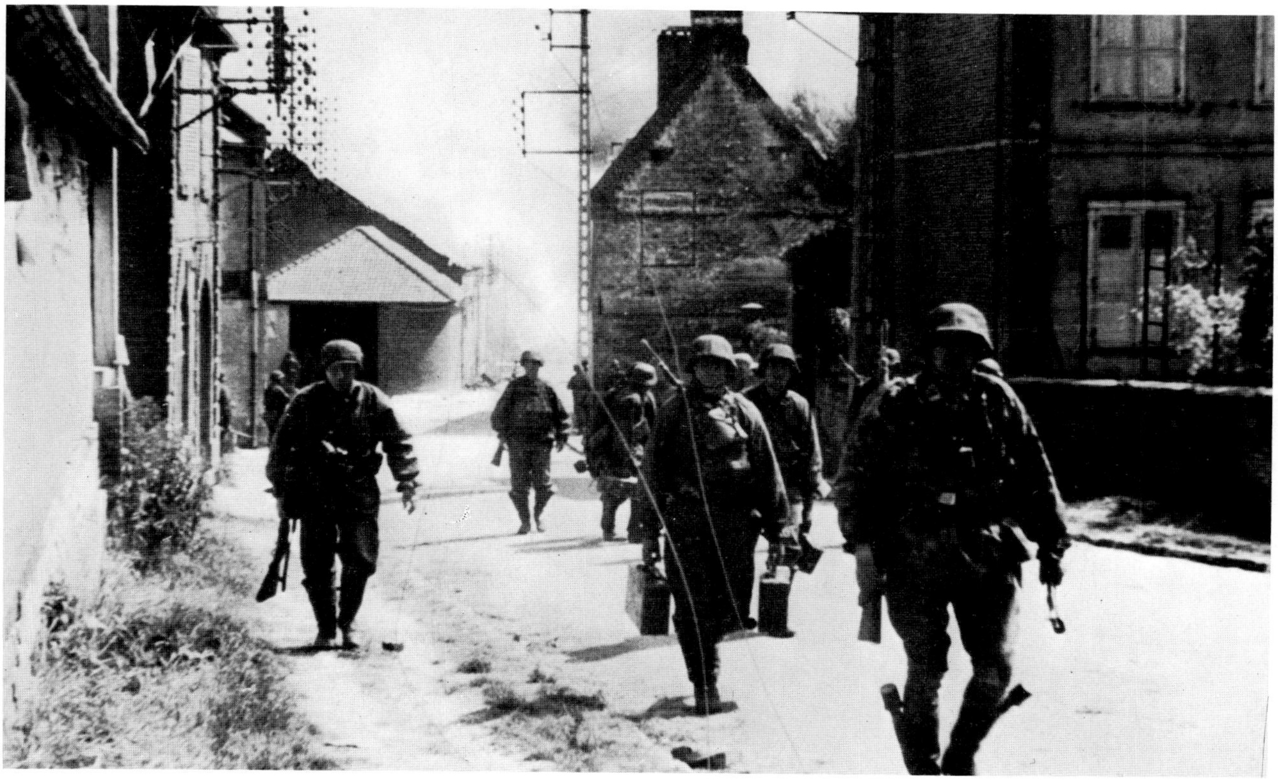

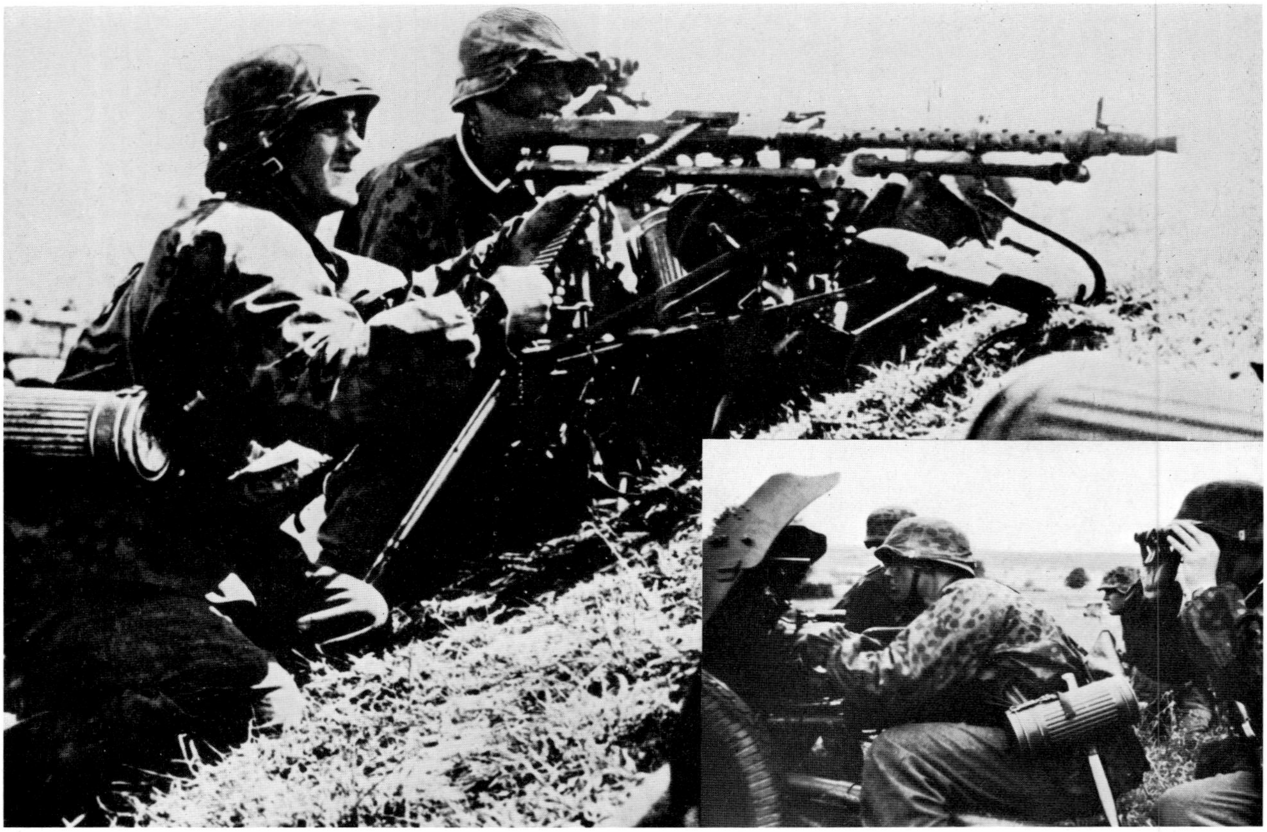

SMG in position. A 37 mm anti-tank gun. A river crossing under enemy fire.

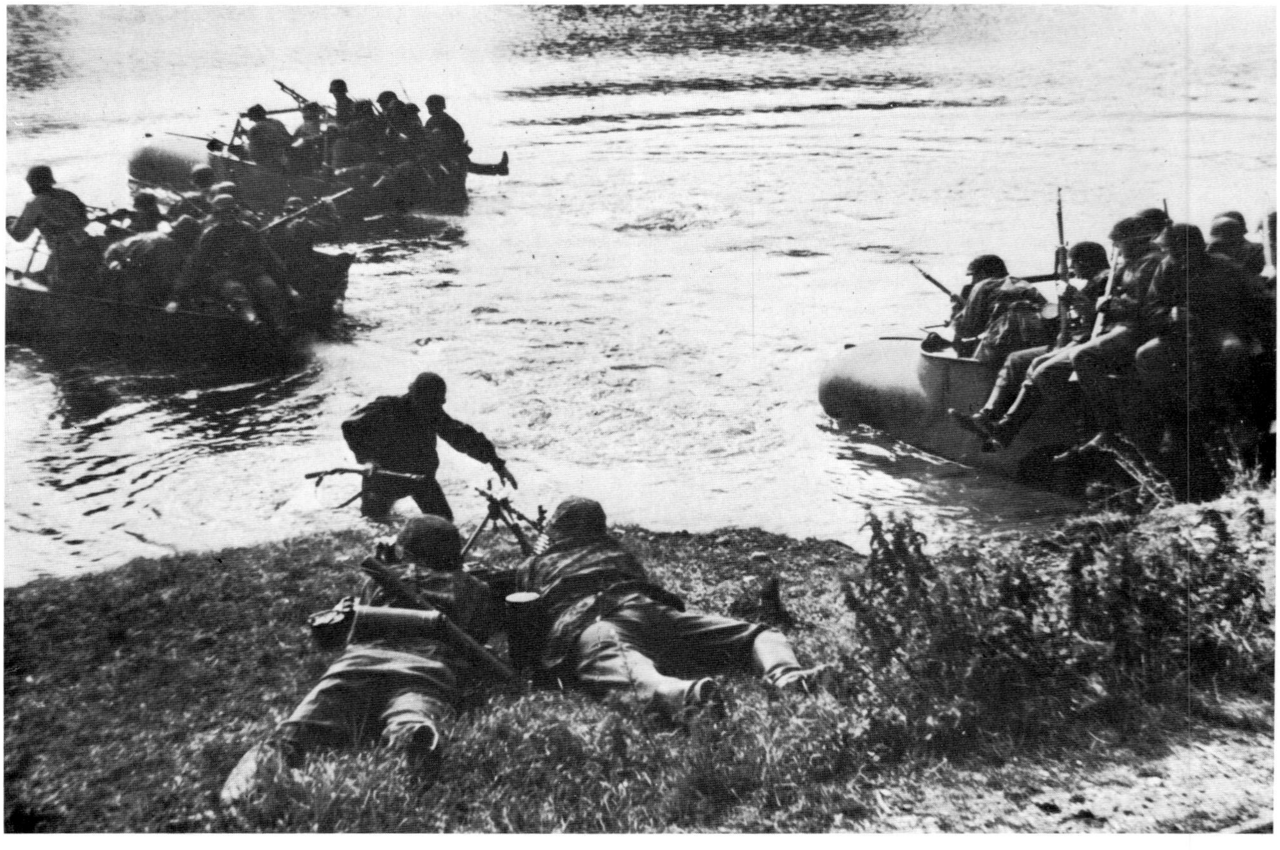

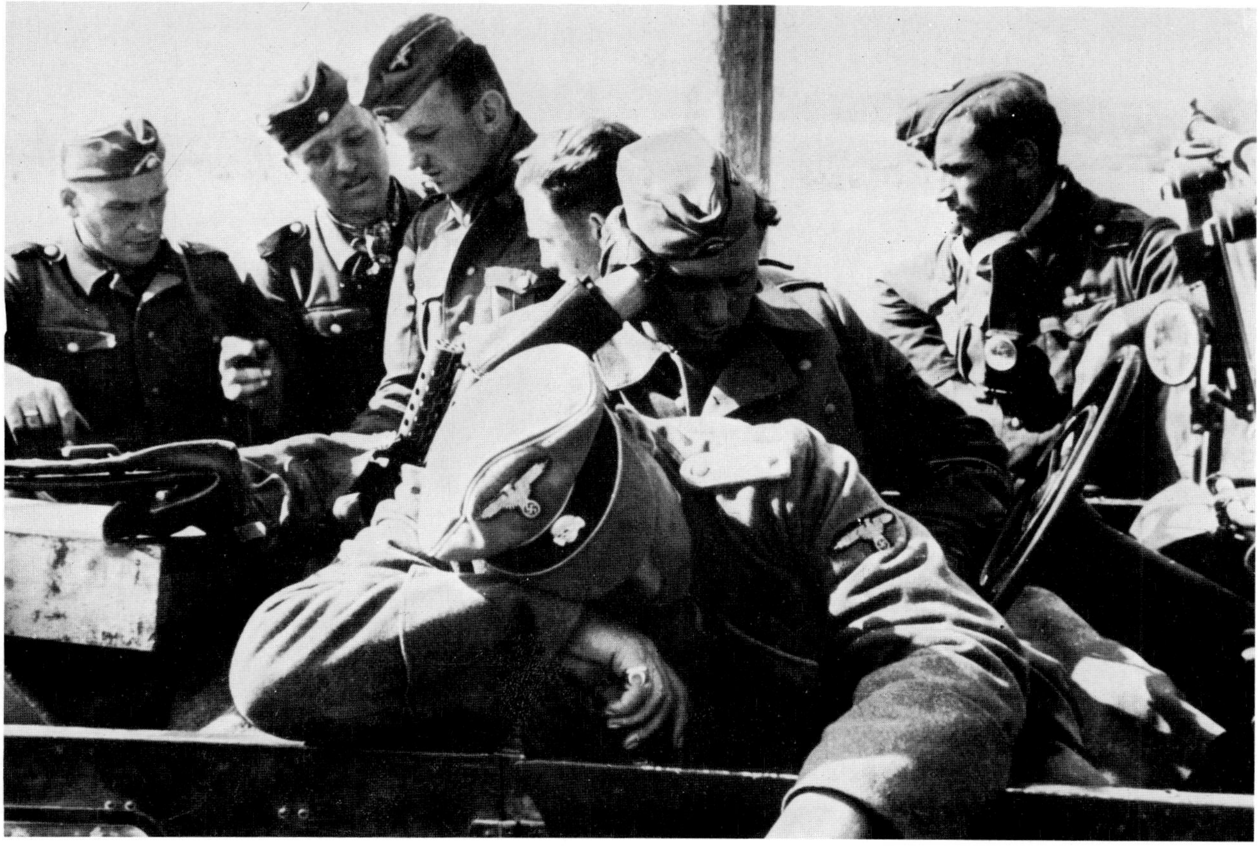

During the rapid armored thrusts, motorized formations of the SS support unit were put into action. They experience long road marches and continuous fighting, up to the point of exhaustion.

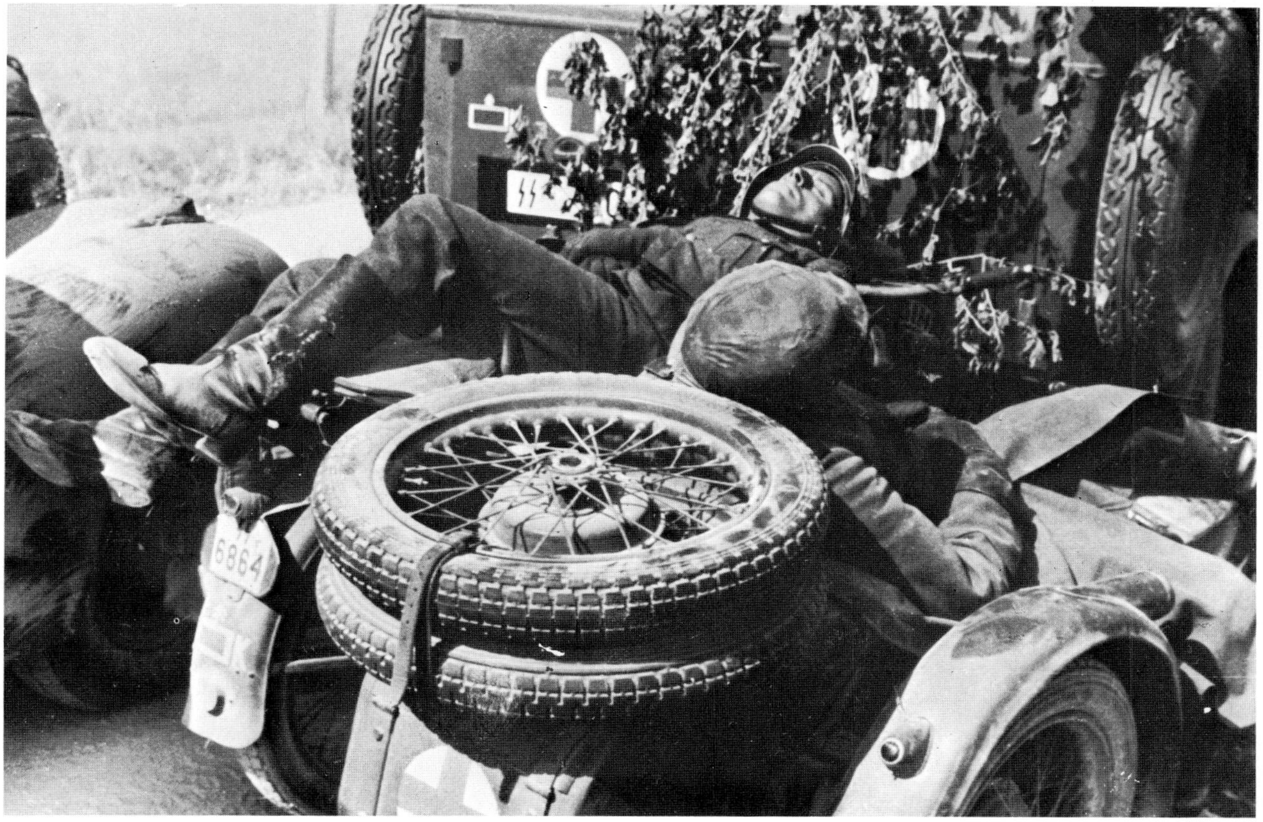

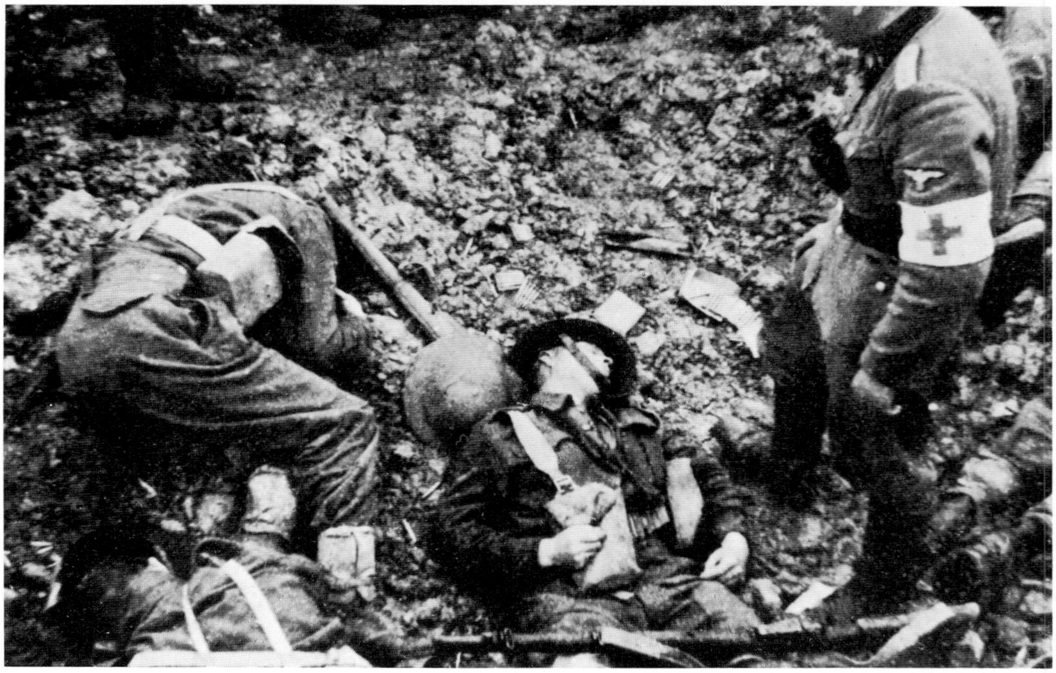

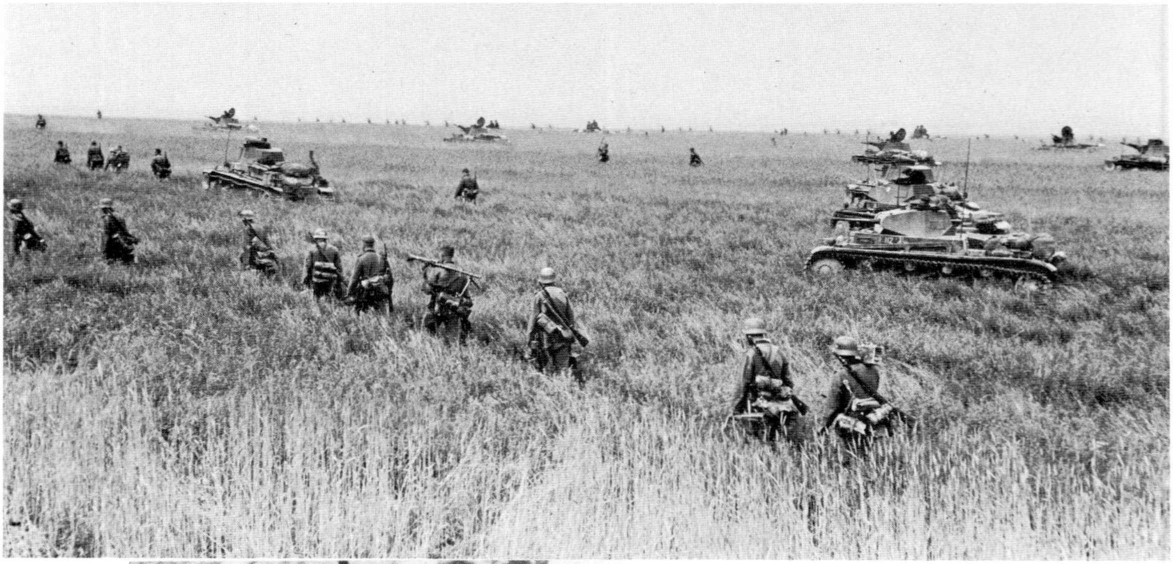

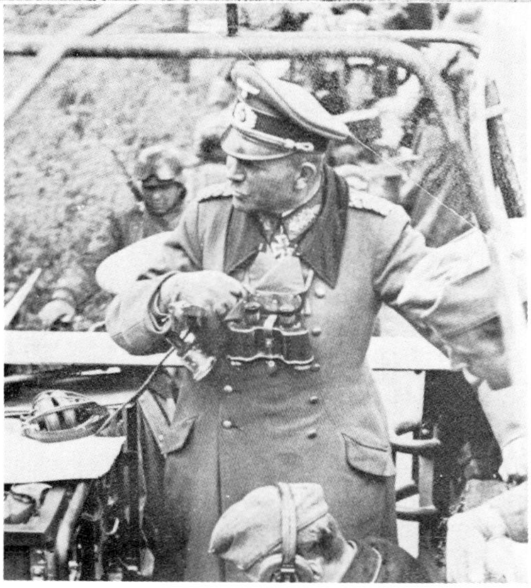

A medical officer of the "Totenkopf" units, care for injured English soldiers.

General Guderian, Commander of the Armored Troops, led parts of the LAH and the VT during the thrust on Dunkirk.

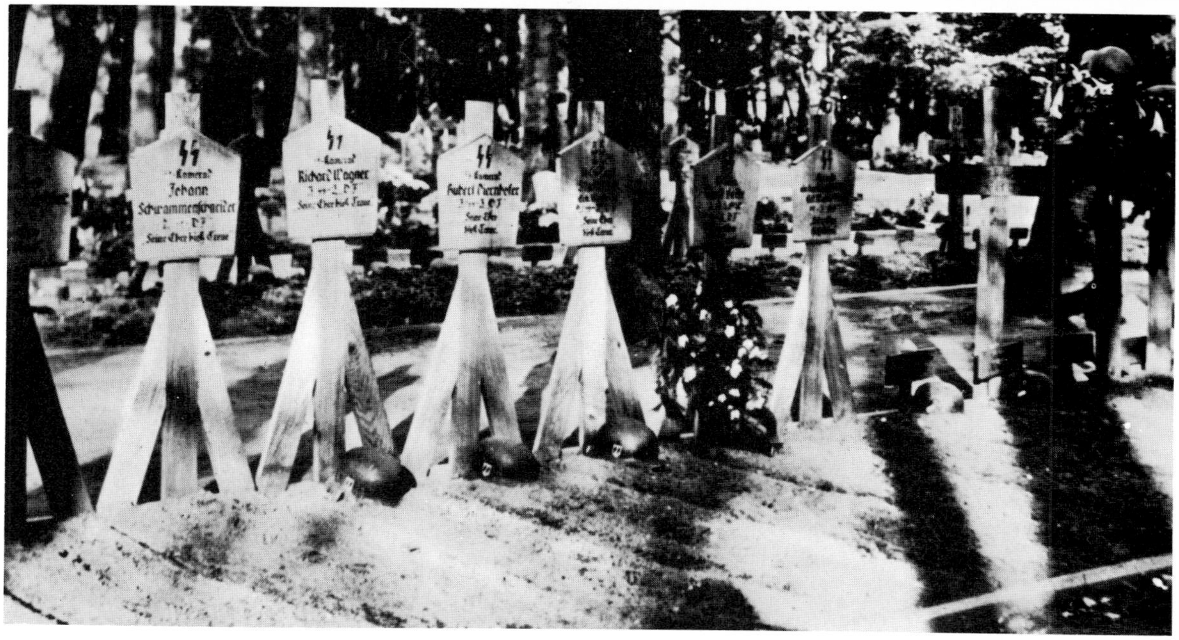

An SS-cemetery on the Grebbe-Berg, Holland where heavy fighting took place.

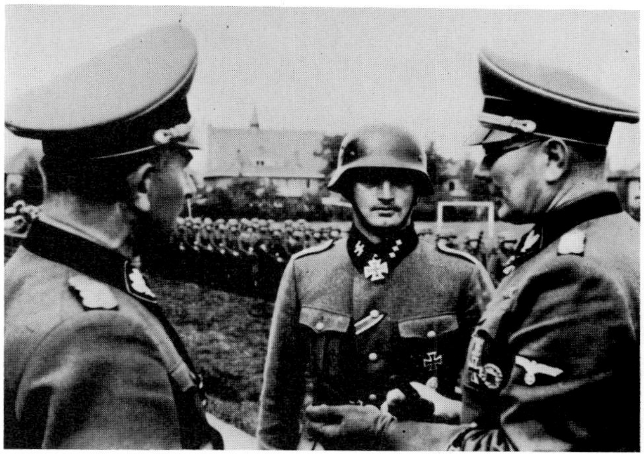

Lieutenant Kepplinger was awarded the Ritterkreuz for his participation in the conquering of the Grebbe-Berg. (Hausser, Kepplinger, Keppler)

After the Western Campaign the LAH takes part in the victory parade in Berlin.

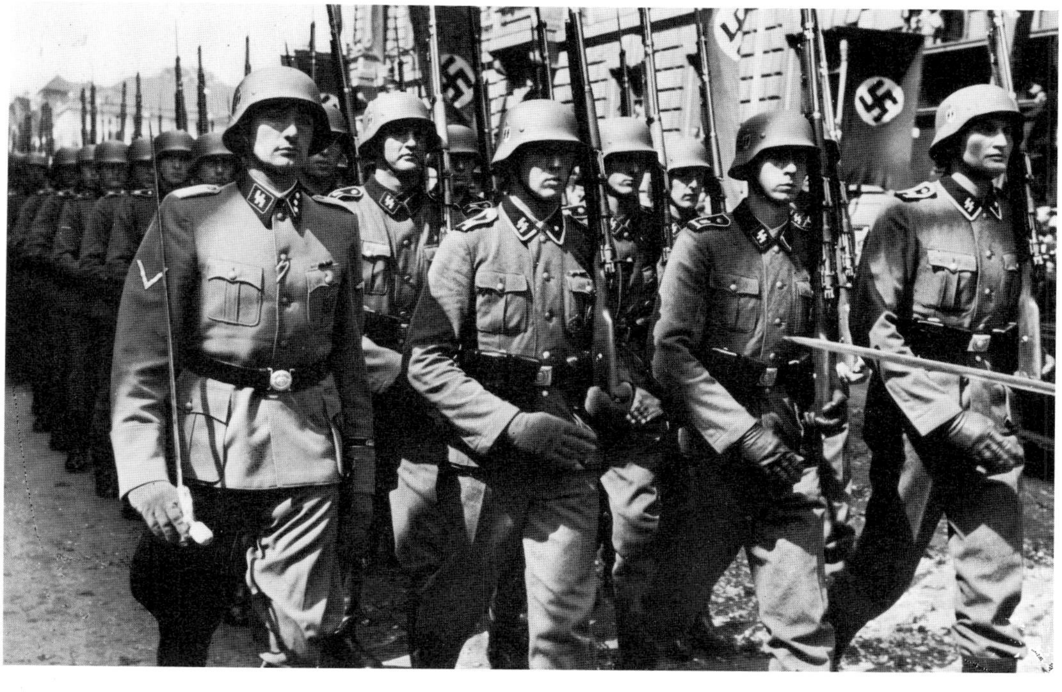

# THE BALKANS CAMPAIGN

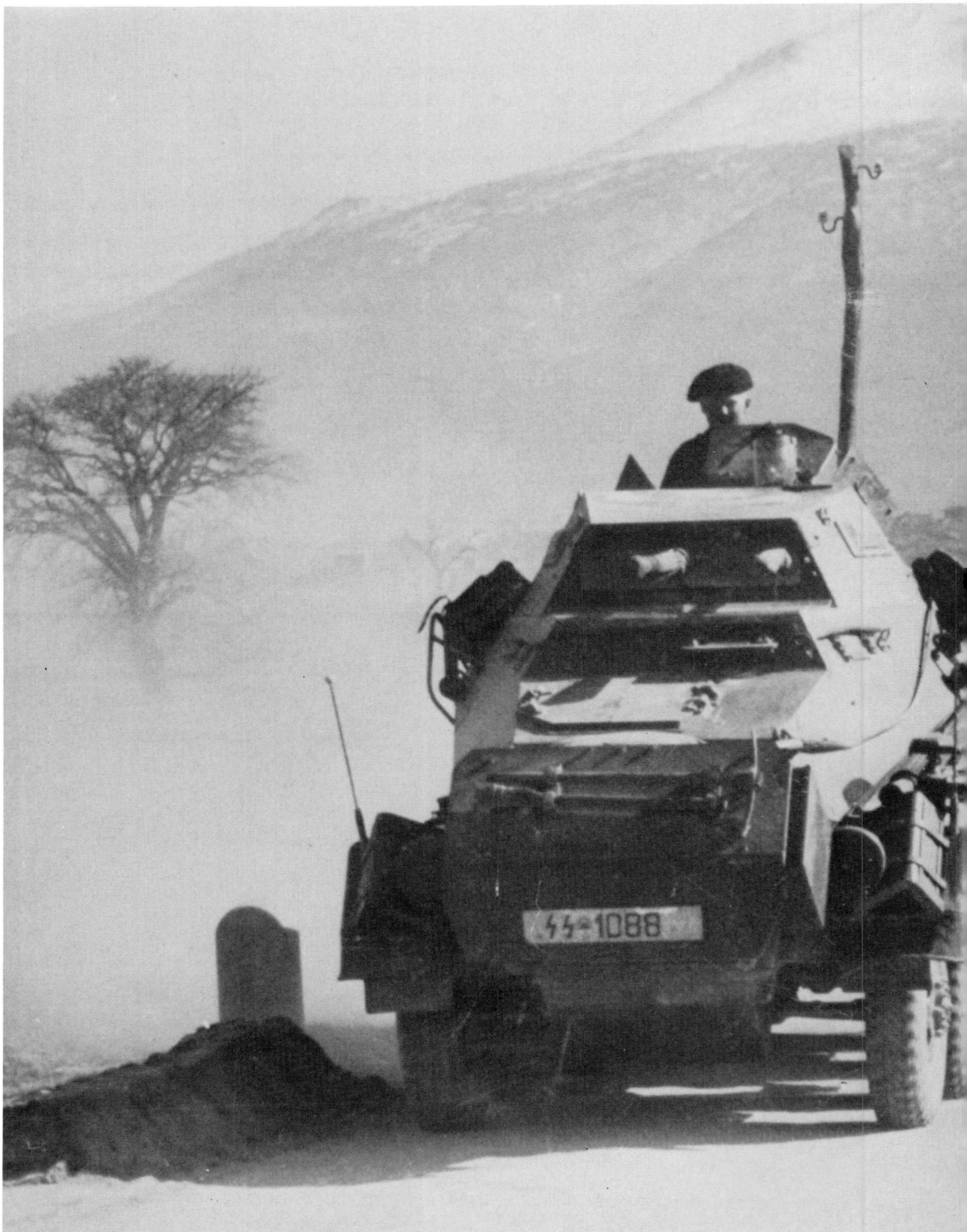

SS-1088

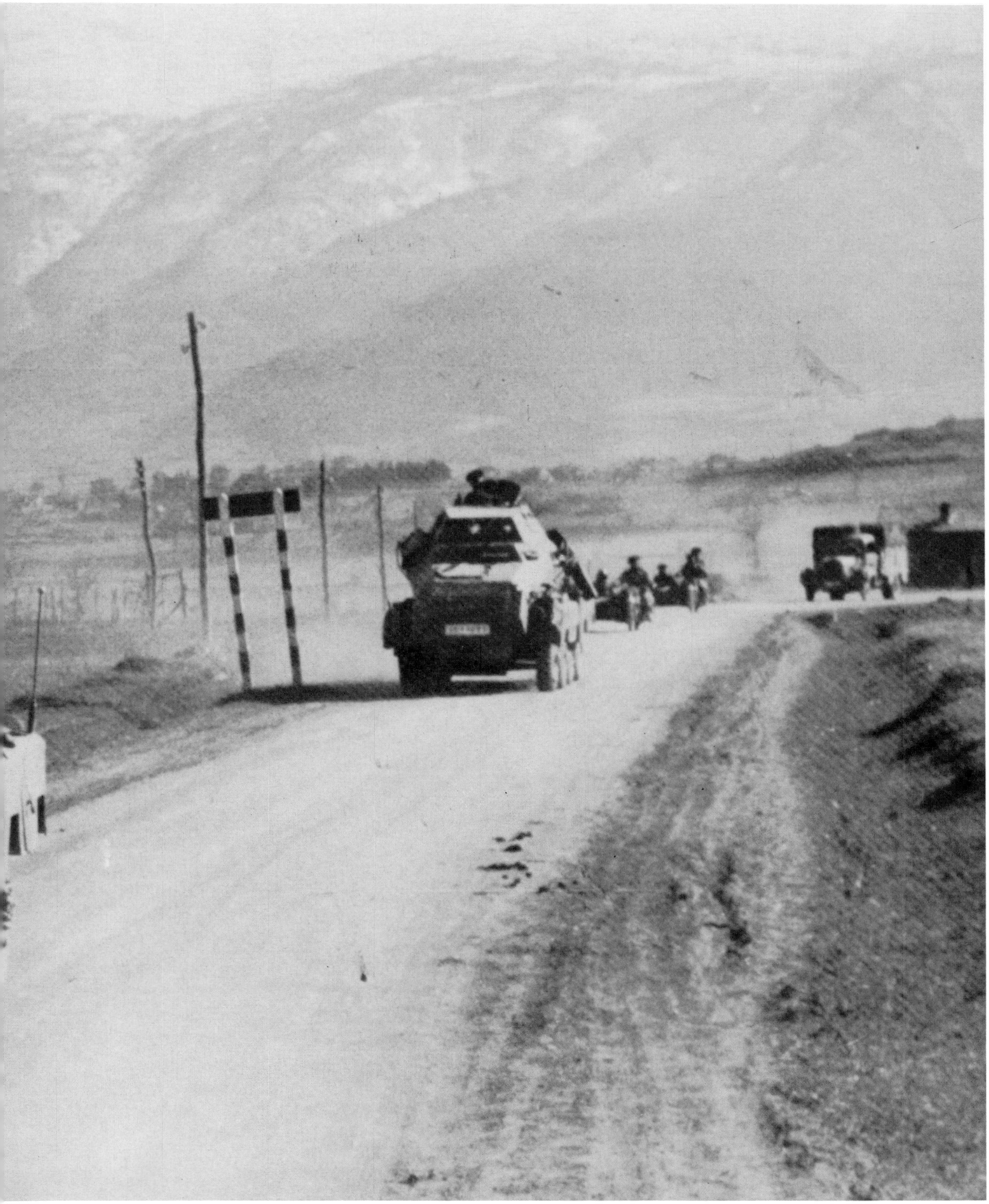

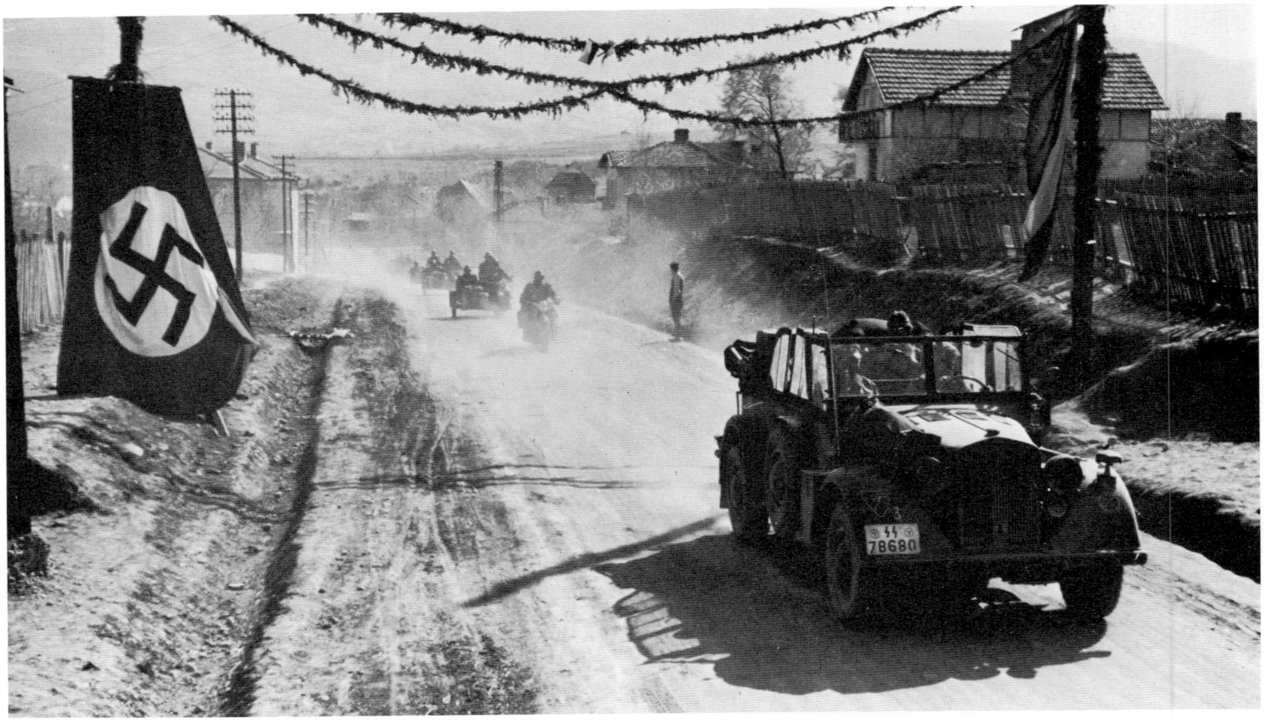
78680

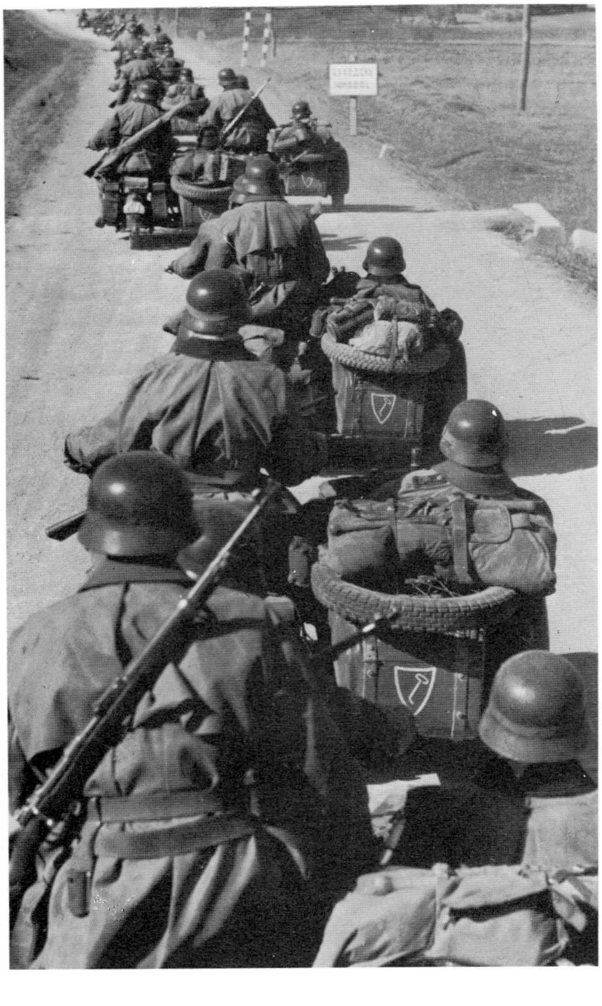

After the conquest of Romania, the LAH invades Greece. Motorcycle riflemen of the LAH during their advance. The tactical signs of the LAH, the "Dietrich", now appear on the vehicles.

The Balkan campaign, not originally foreseen by Hitler and only carried out to close out the mounting flank attack cleverly forced by the English, was to push the attack against Russia, long foremost in Hitler's mind, from his view for many, and surely decisive, weeks.

The SS divisions "Leibstandarte Adolf Hitler" (Sepp Dietrich) and "Das Reich" (Hausser) played a major part in the quick end of the campaign. In penetrating the Metaxas line, moving against Belgrade, capturing the Klidi Pass and smashing the positions of the British troops west of Mount Olympus, the SS divisions played a decisive role.

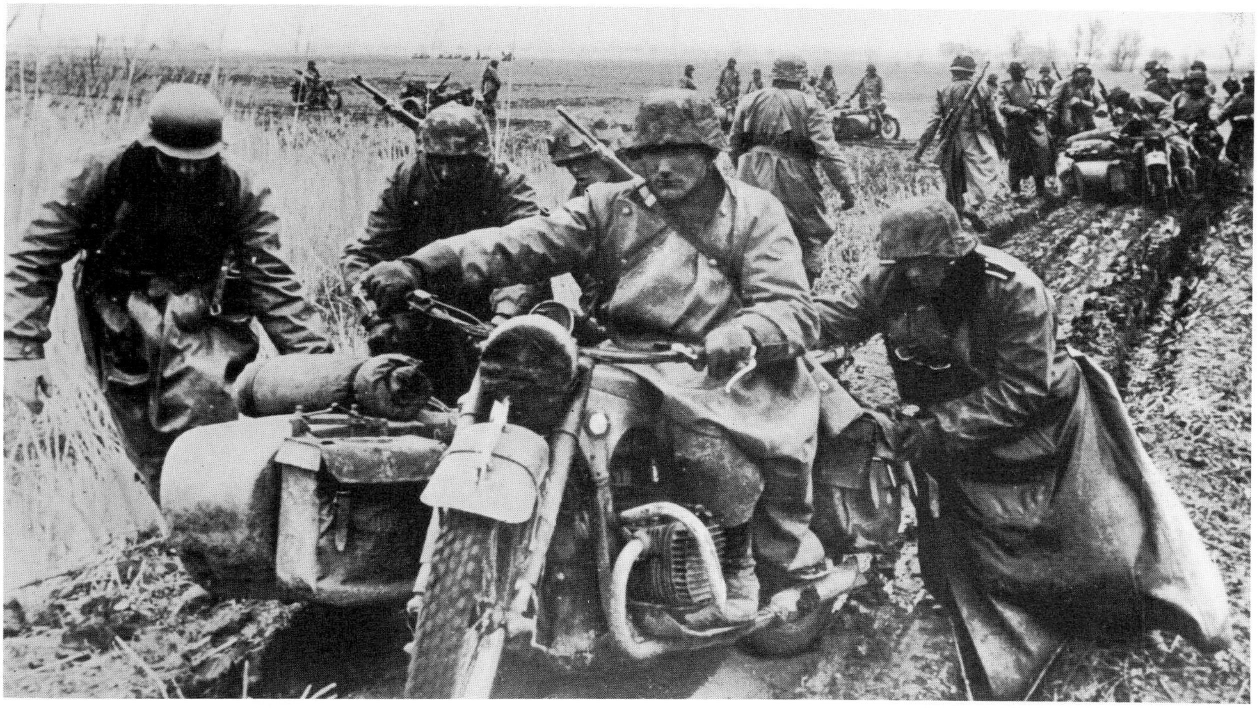

Difficult terrain conditions are extremely demanding of the motorized units.

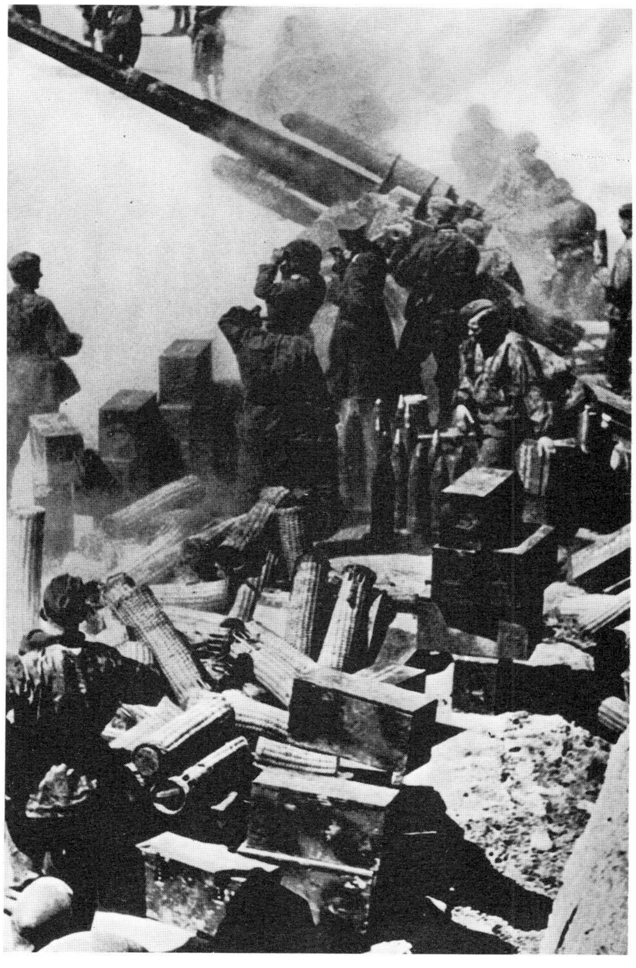

The heavy artillery of the LAH fires on English positions in the Klidi-Pass.

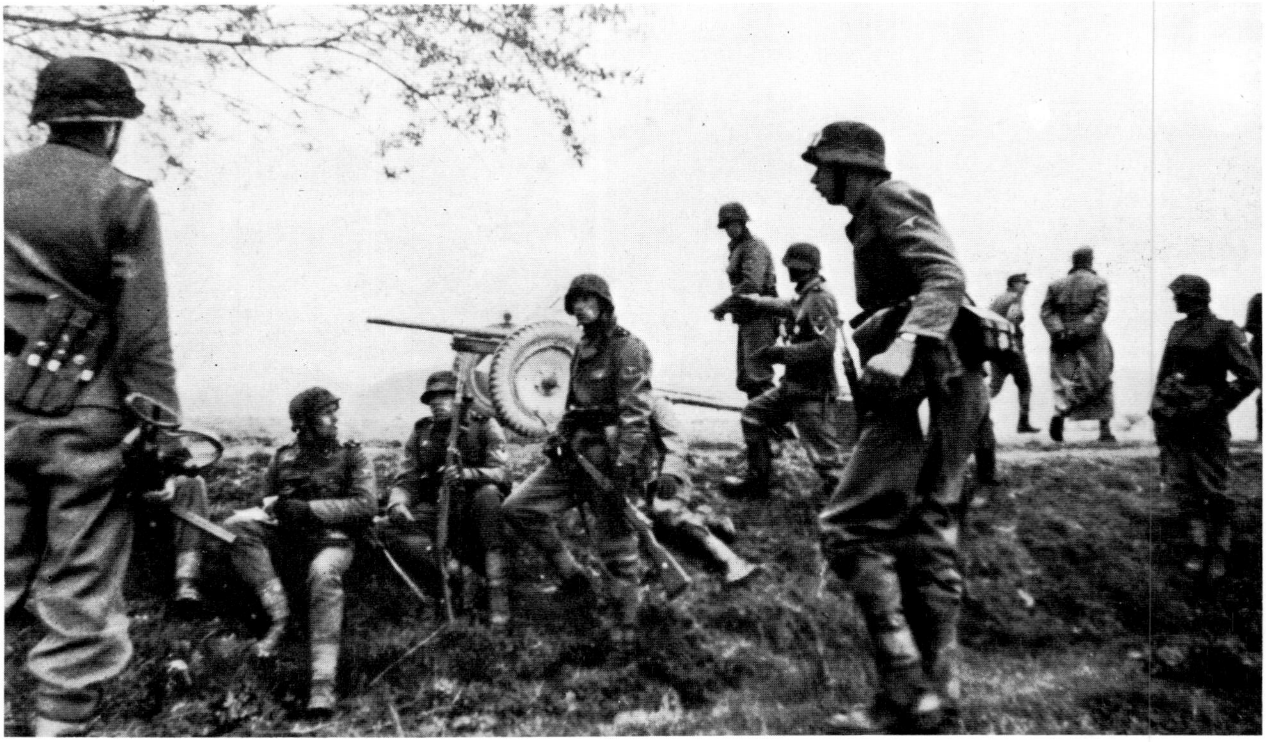

After conquering the heavily fought for Klidi-Pass, the Germans look after the English prisoners and injured soldiers.

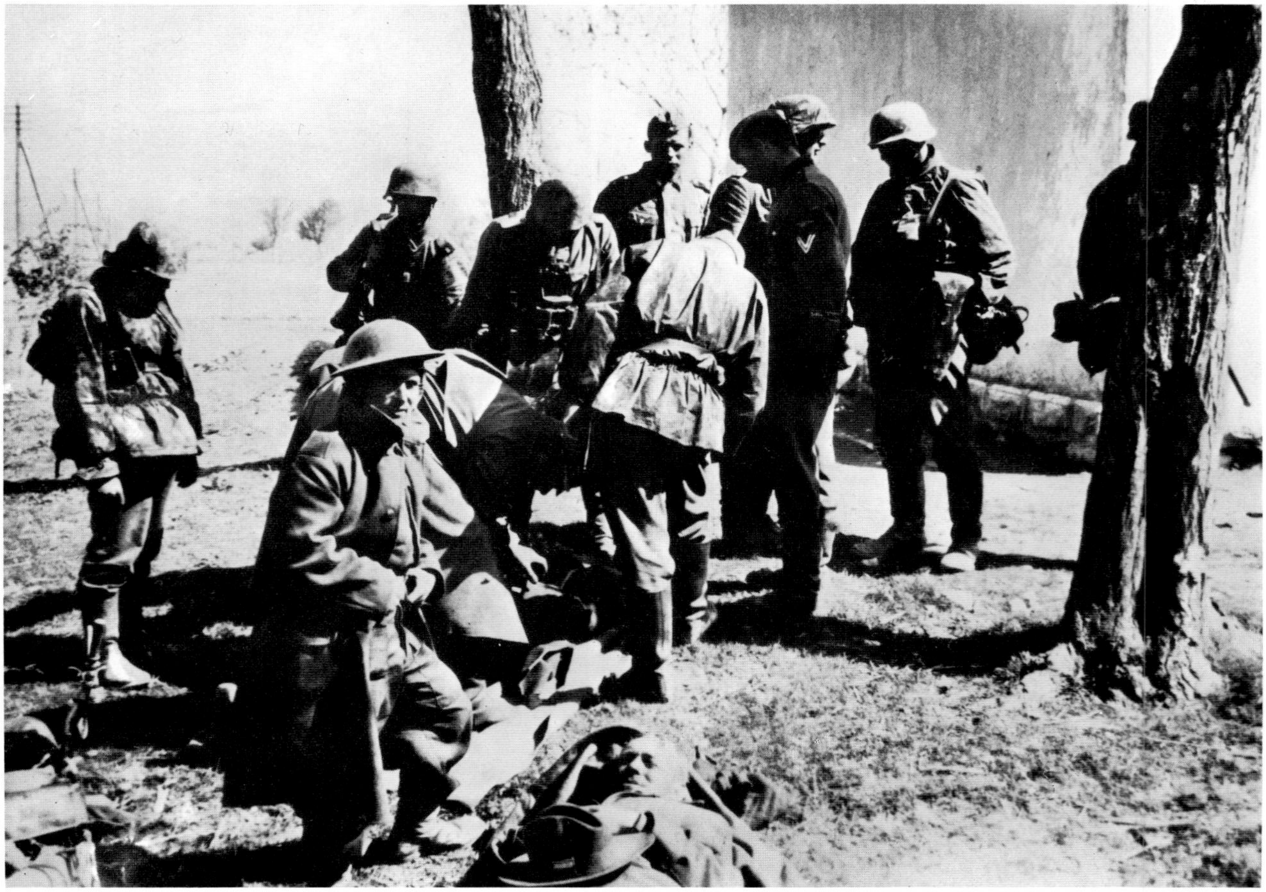

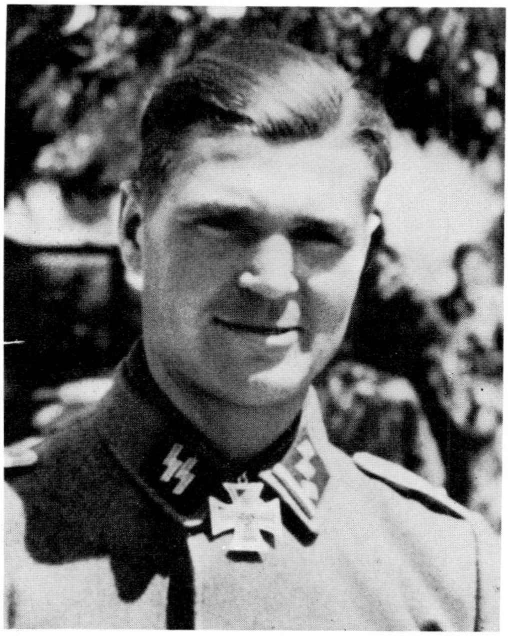

Lieutenant Gerd Pleiss, the conqueror of the Klidi-Pass.

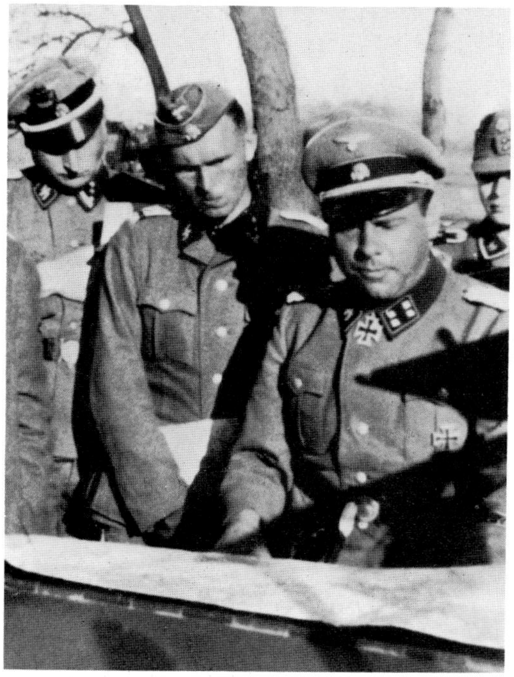

Major Fritz Witt, whose brother died during the battle for the Klidi-Pass (photo below), gives orders.

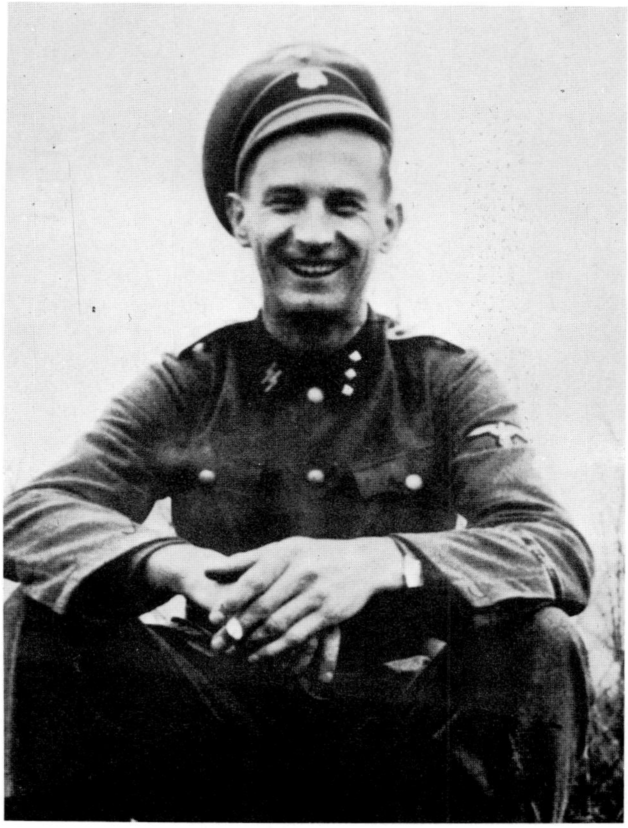

Graves of the LAH in the Klidi-Pass.

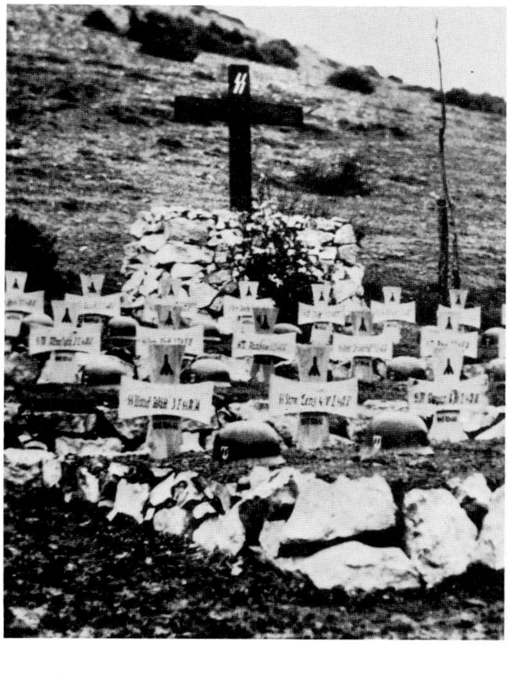

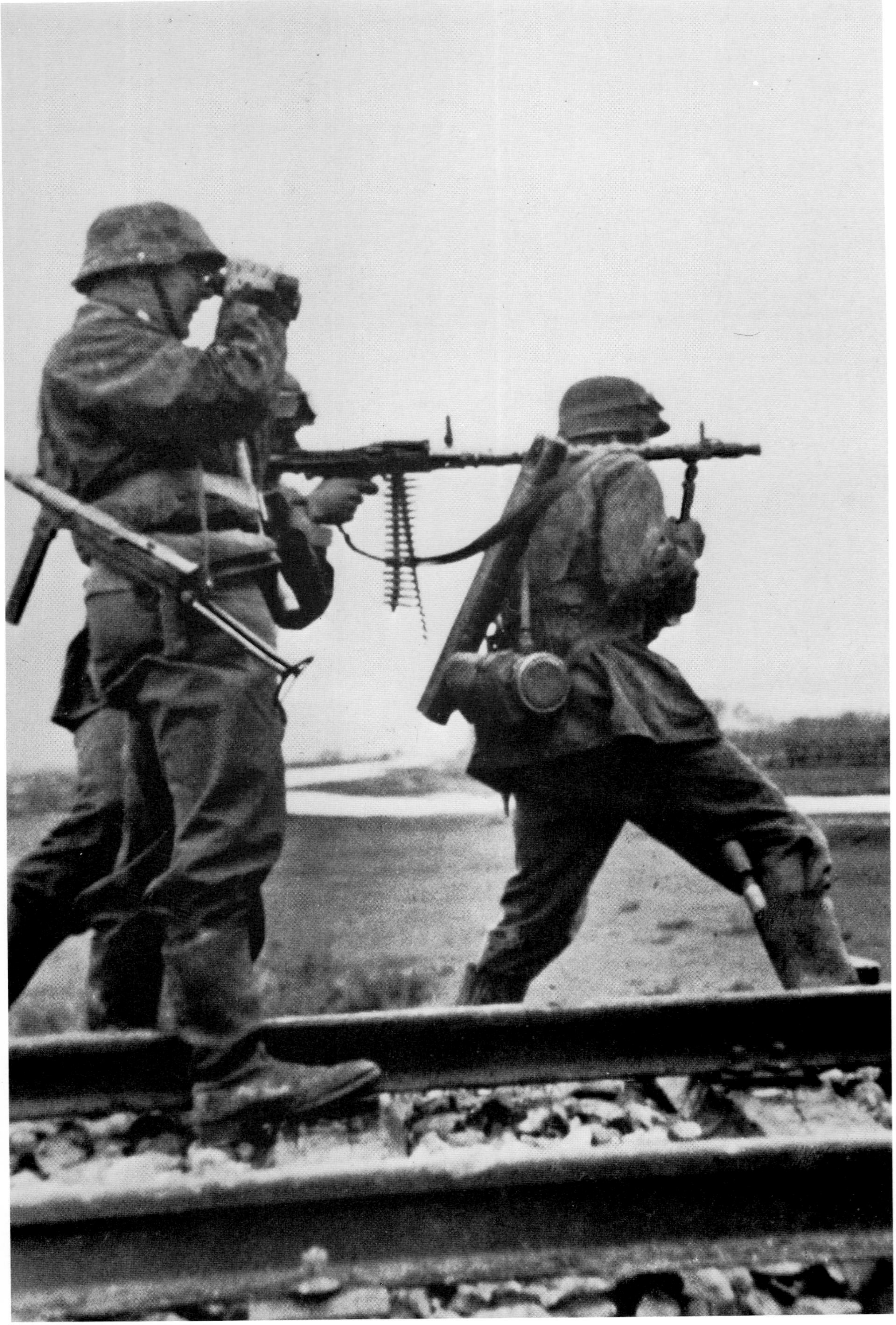

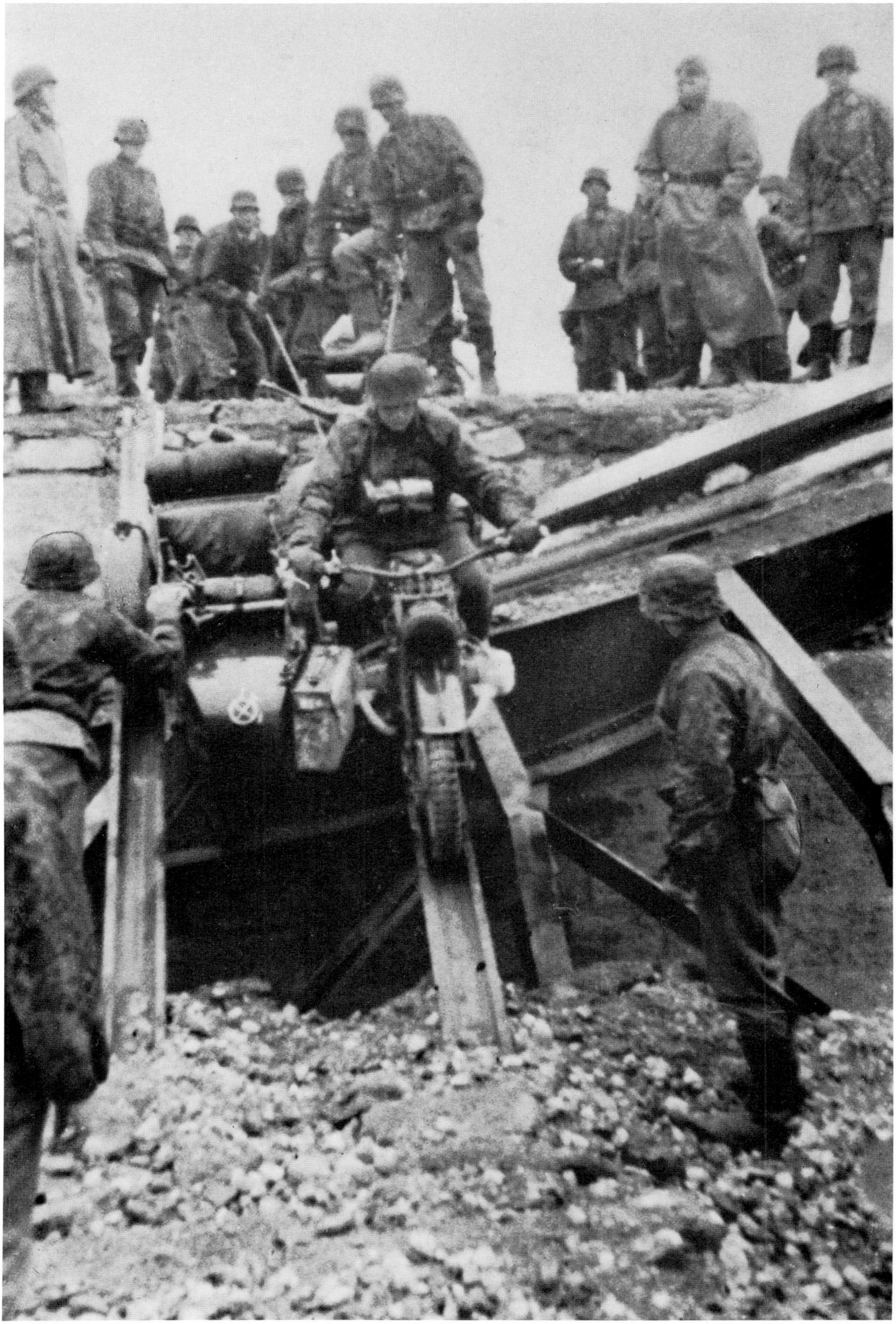

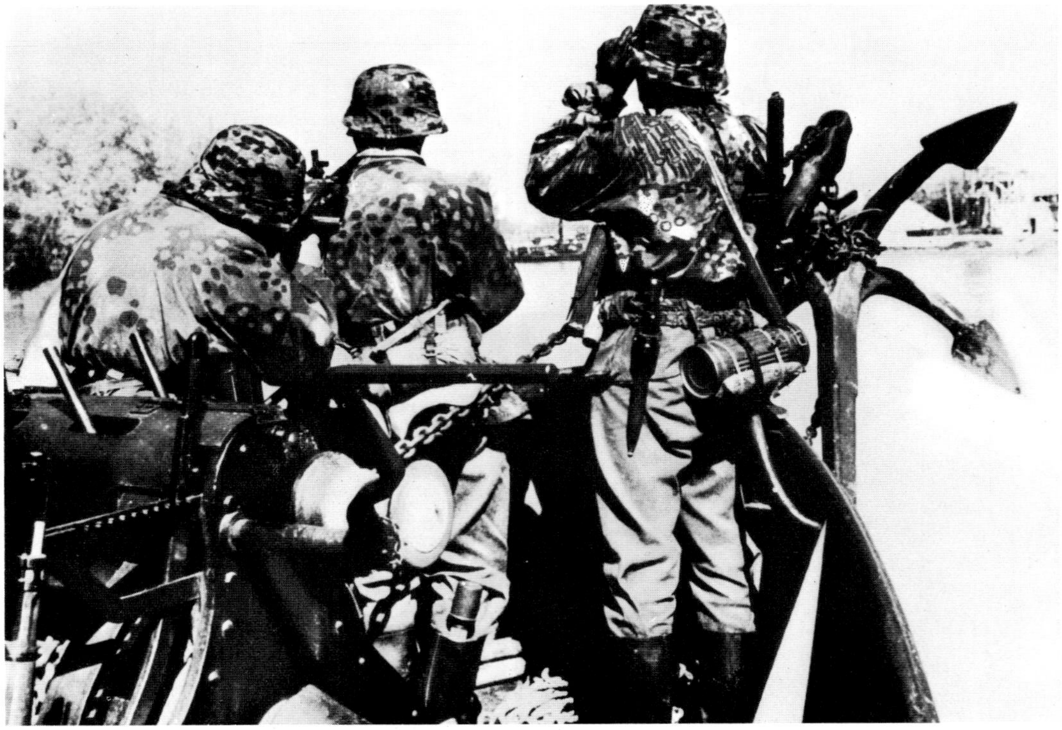

An advance troop of the division "Das Reich" conquers Belgrade on April 13, 1941.

In a bold thrust, a reconnaissance unit of the LAH cross over to Patras.

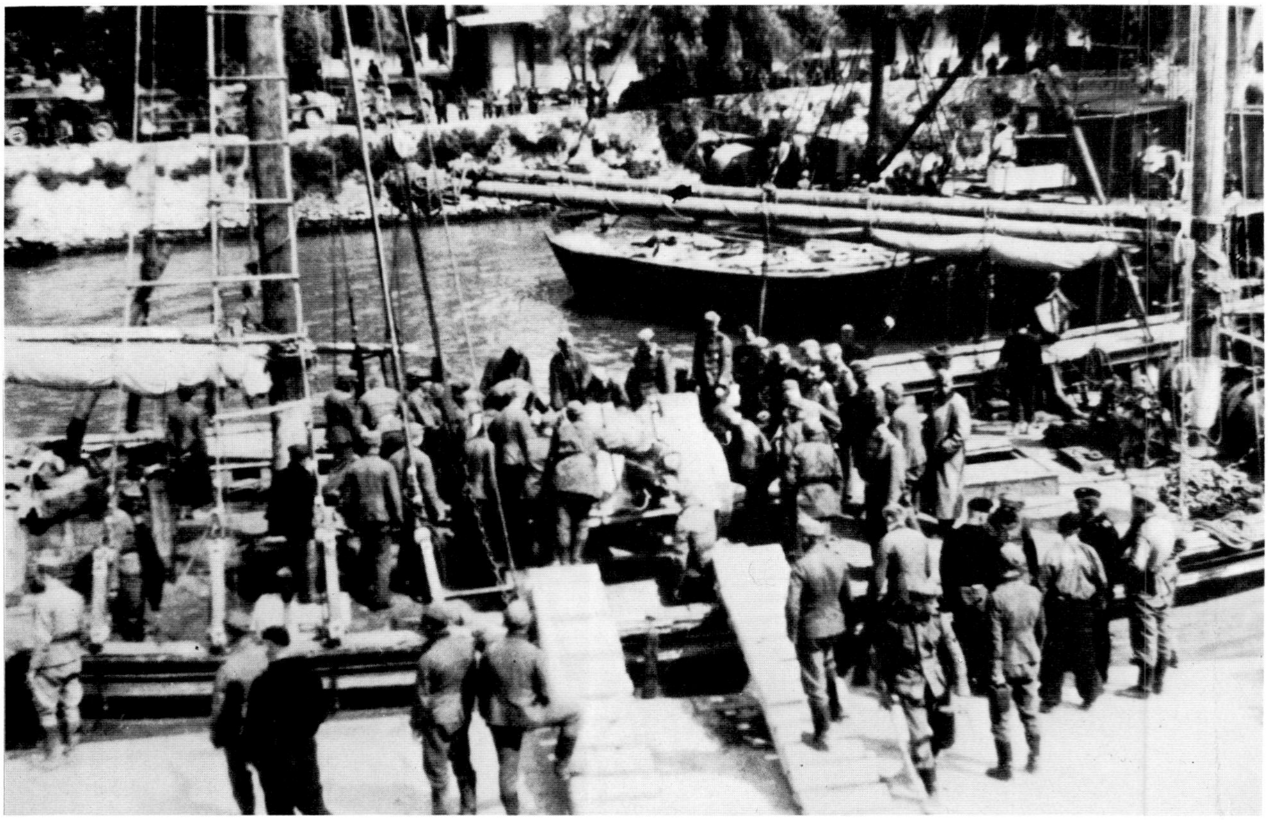

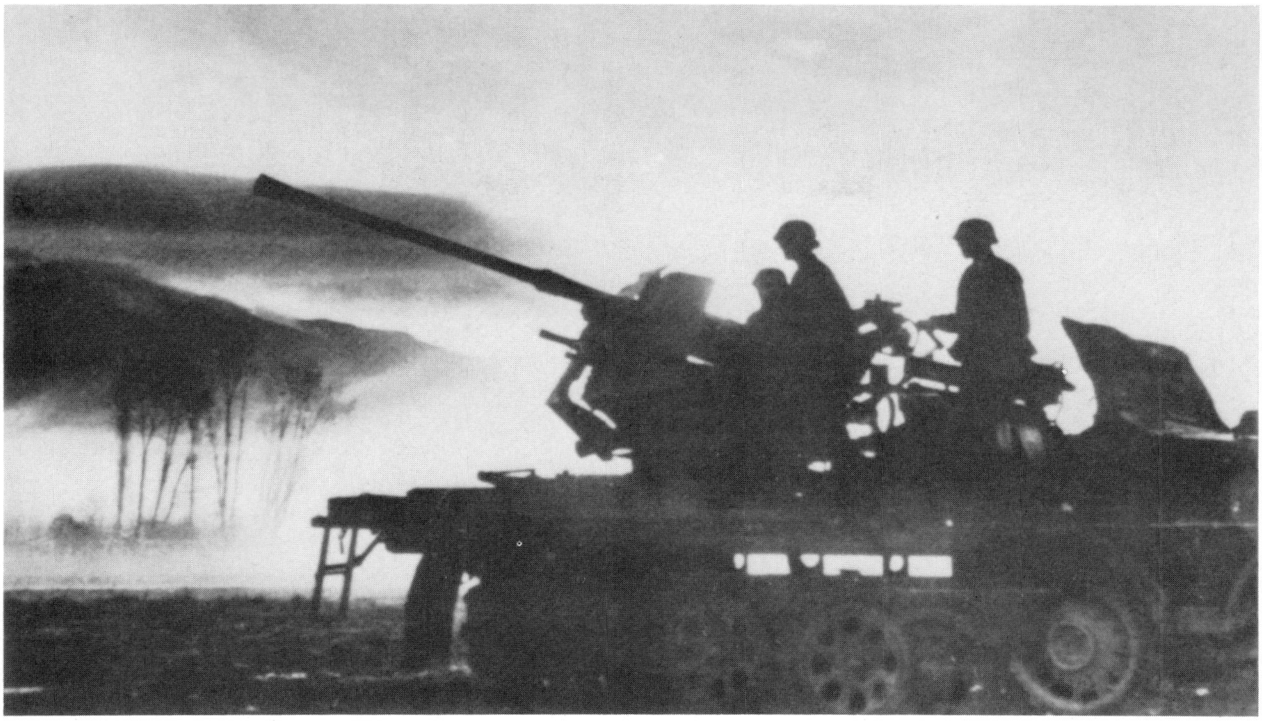

A 37 mm anti-aircraft gun in position.

During their advance, motorized units of the division "Das Reich" pass the defeated enemy.

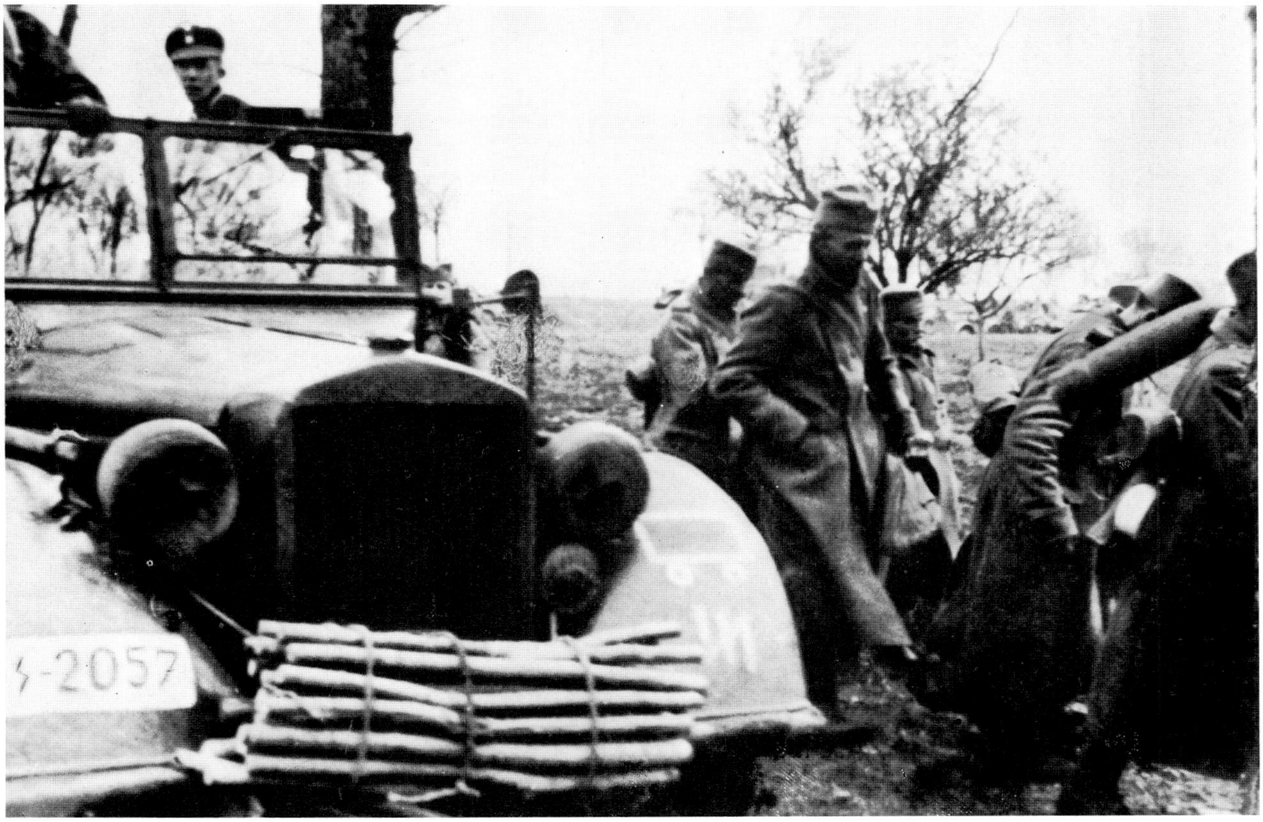
-2057

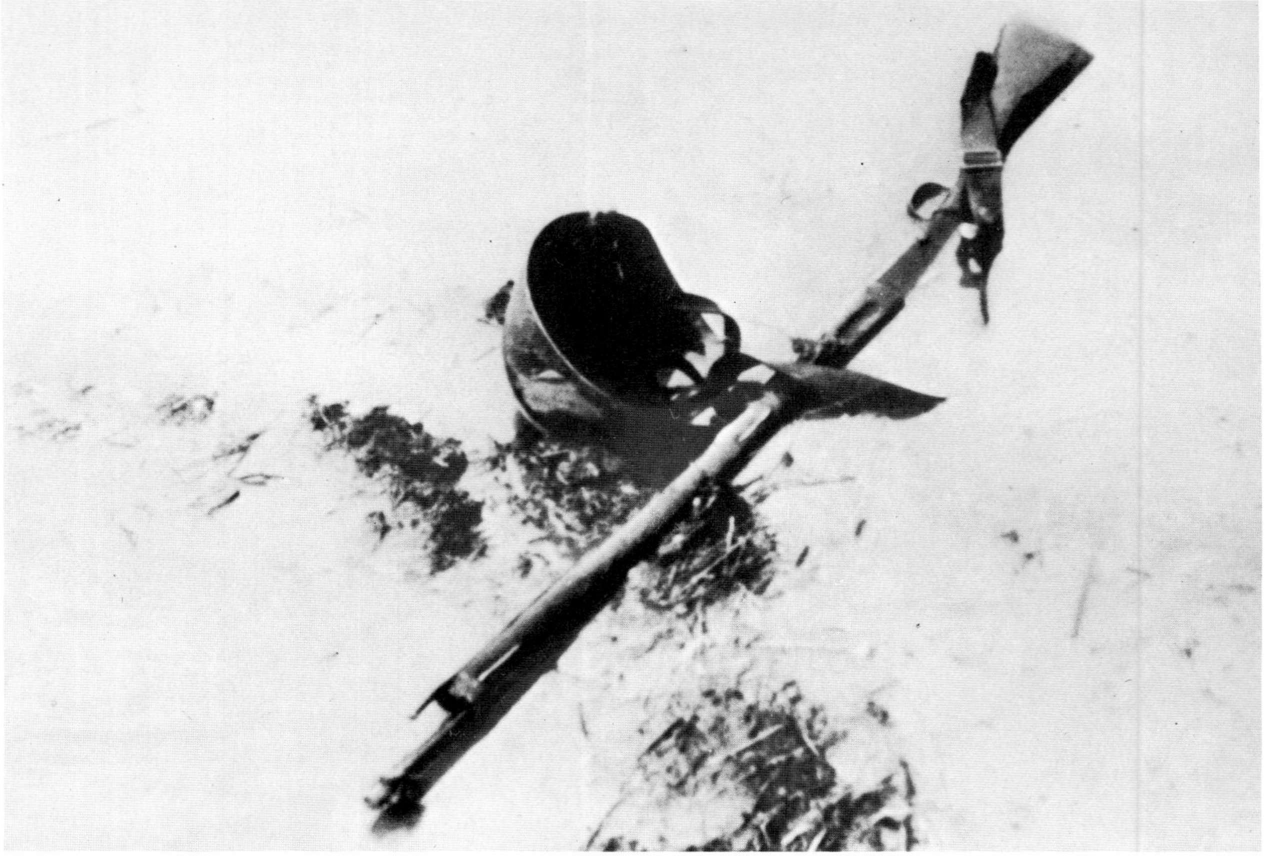

The end of the campaign in Greece: The enemy is defeated. Sepp Dietrich, the commander of the LAH, delivers an address in the ruins of Olympia.

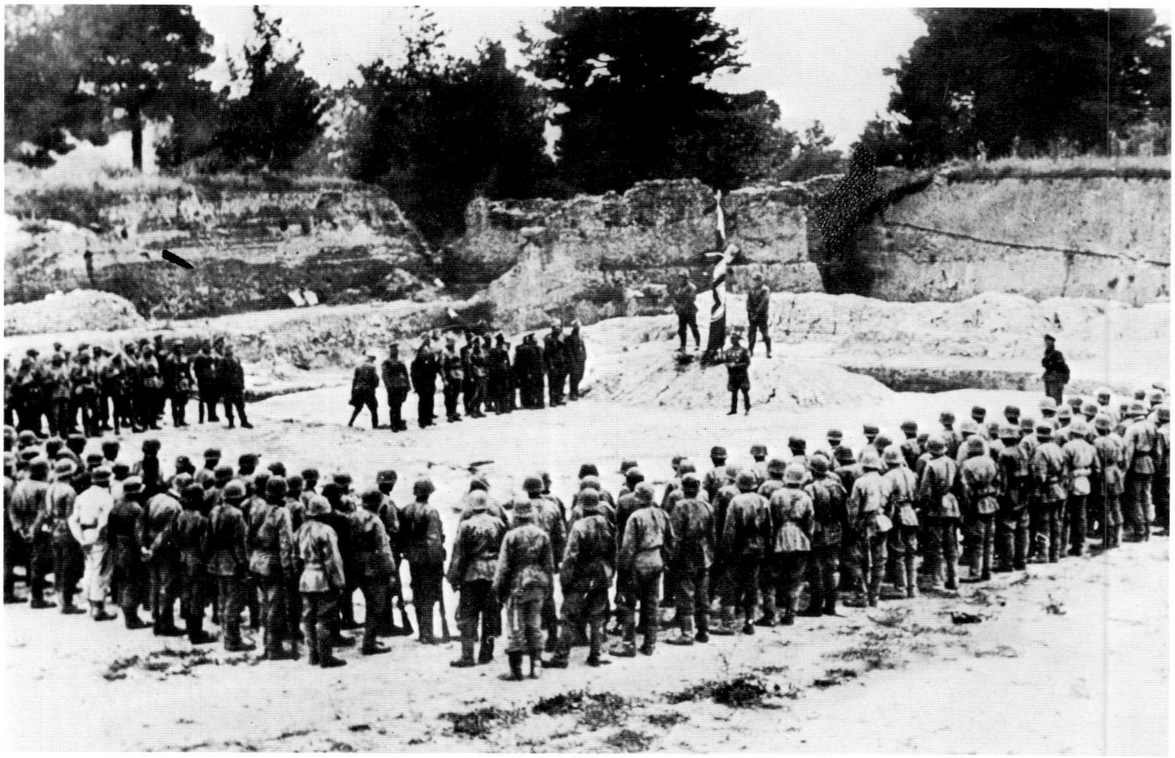

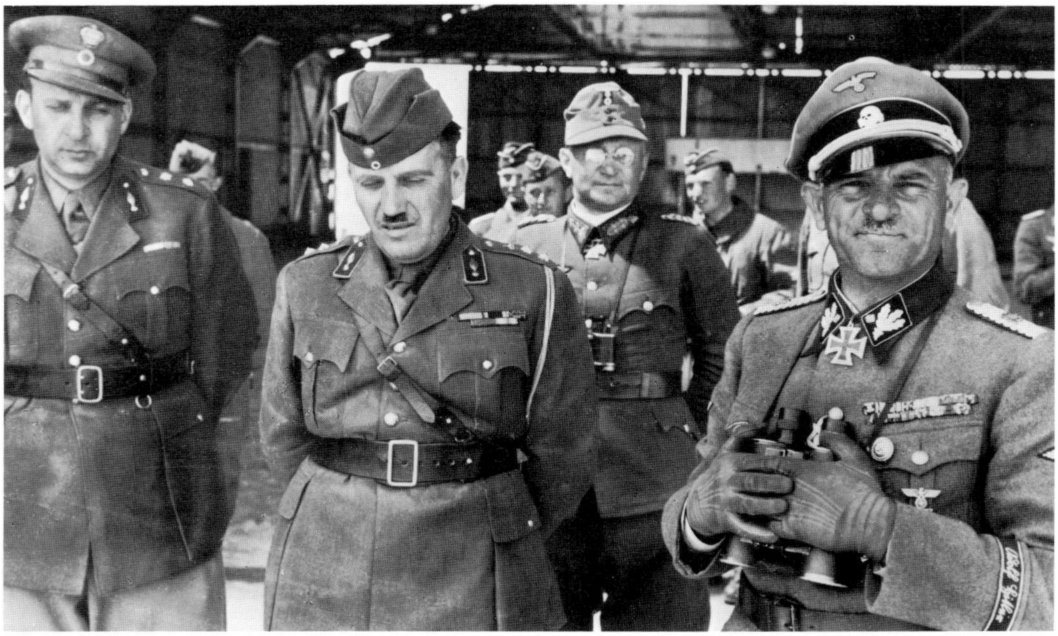

Negotiations with Greek officers on the terms of surrender. On the right: Sepp Dietrich.

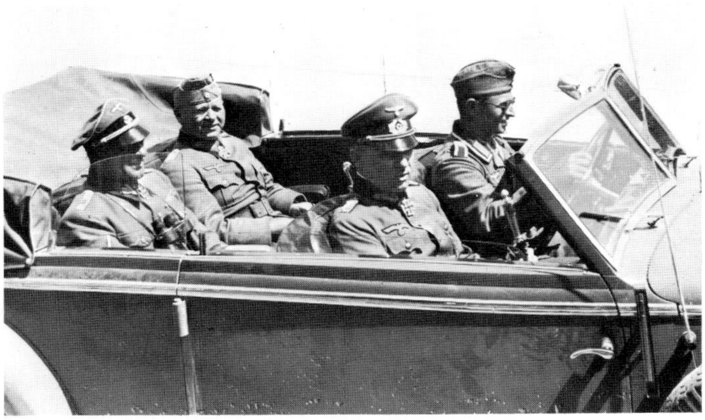

From the left: SS-General Sepp Dietrich, General Stumme, Generalfeldmarschall List.

Sepp Dietrich leading the victory parade in front of Generalfeldmarschall List in Athens.

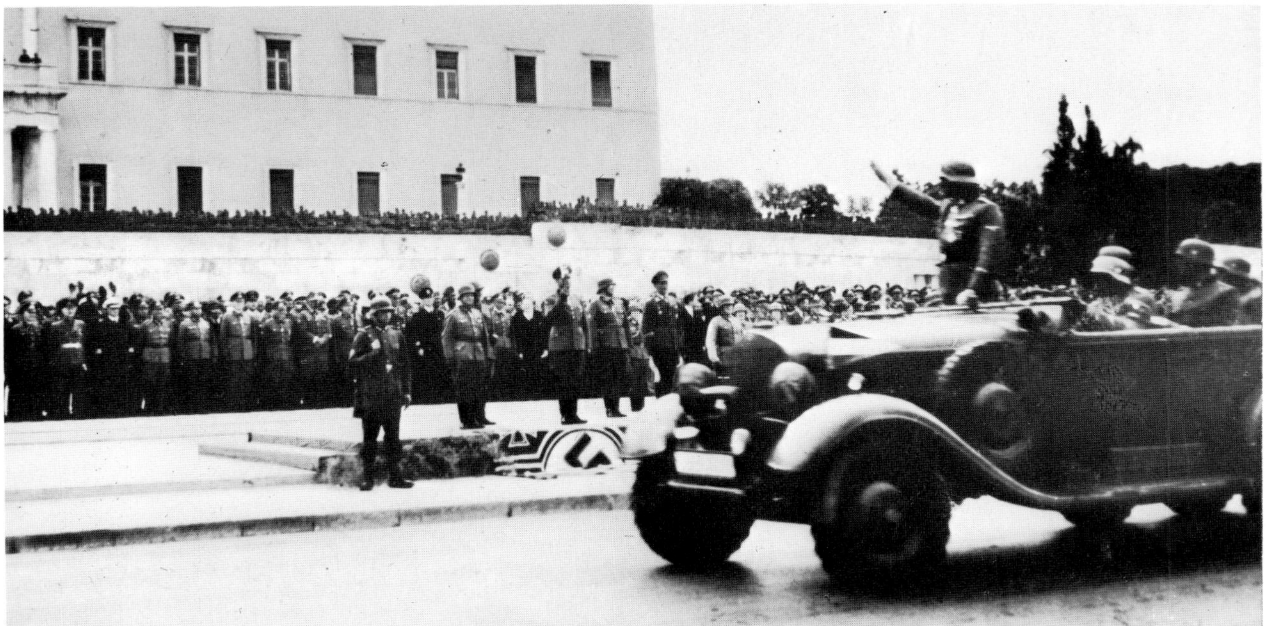

# THE RUSSIAN CAMPAIGN, 1941

The SS divisions, and the SS armored divisions from 1942 on, were chosen to serve at the focal points of the fighting during the whole campaign. The bravery of the Waffen-SS men, their readiness for unconditional service and their spirit of self-sacrifice soon made them the feared, indeed the most hated opponents of the Russian troops. What with the two sides' attitudes to each other, it was inevitable that the hardness of the fighting and the irreconcilable spirit of their service always found bitter expression. But if one strips this fighting of all preconceived and seemingly proven opinions, there remains-on both sides-the sacrifice of young men who fought for their country with all they had to give, convinced that they were doing right, without wish and will to understand the motivation of the other side. And why should they? They were going at each other in a fight for life and death, and only much later could many of them on the German side begin to be aware of what was really going on in this strange land, Russia. But at that time the German soldier had seen vast numbers of his comrades fall and be buried in Russian soil.

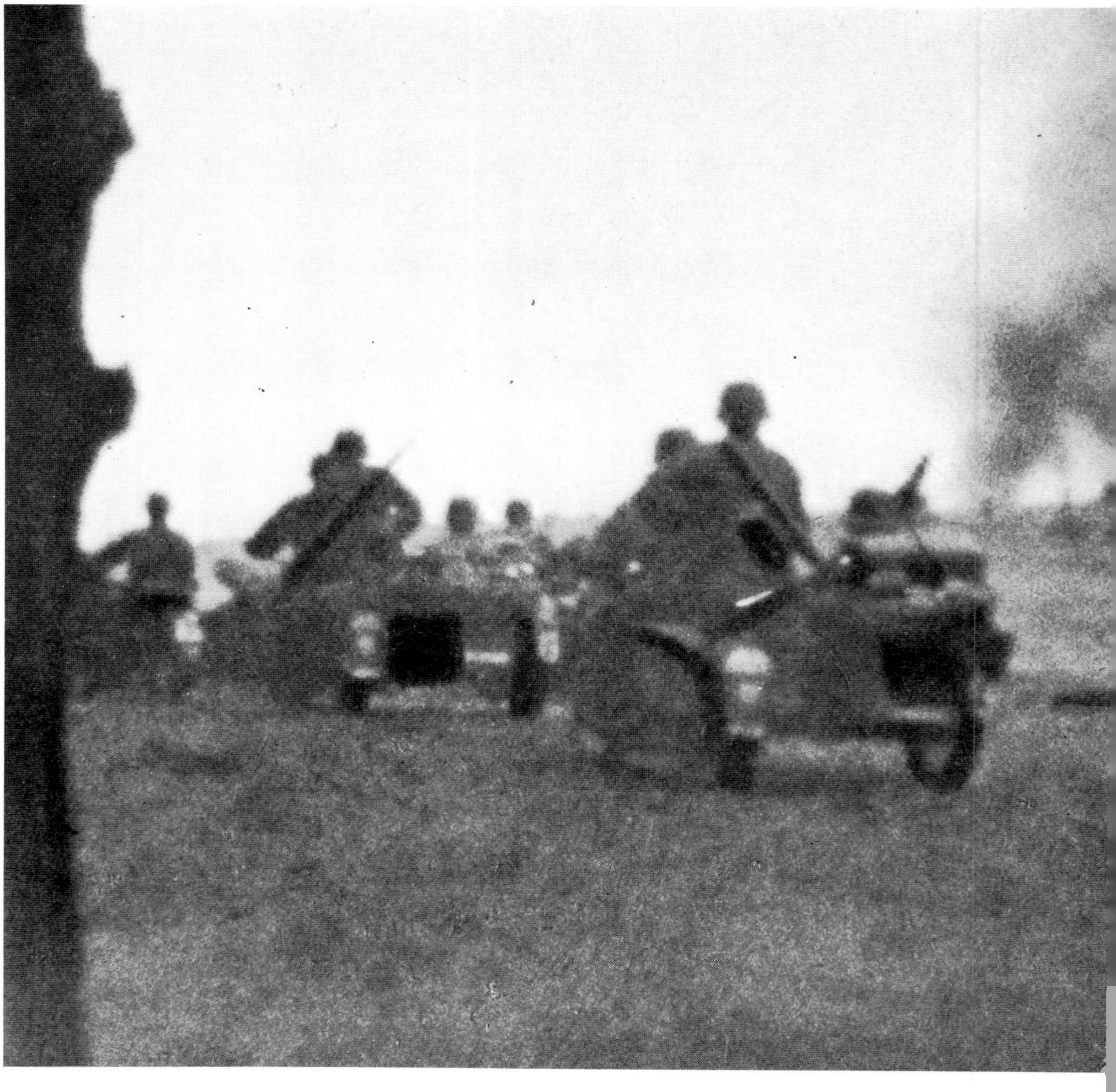

Since this book does not concern the highest leadership of the SS or the special units, from whose sad work every decent person must distance himself, we are speaking only from the combat soldiers of the Waffen-SS. They, like their comrades of the Army and the Luftwaffe, fought on the vast Russian plains, in the swamps or the Russian cities, against an opponent who grew ever stronger, in the days of the stormy advance and the hard times of the retreat, in good faith, abandoned and forgotten in the end, when Hitler, Himmler and other responsible parties escaped through suicide. They had to taste the bitterness of defeat to the end. Many were shot, falling victim to the Red Army's revenge, many remained in Russian captivity. The survivors, though, despised and scorned in the first years after the war, learned only much later that, in evaluating their military achievements, one should not throw political considerations, mistakes, errors and crimes of National Socialism into the balance.

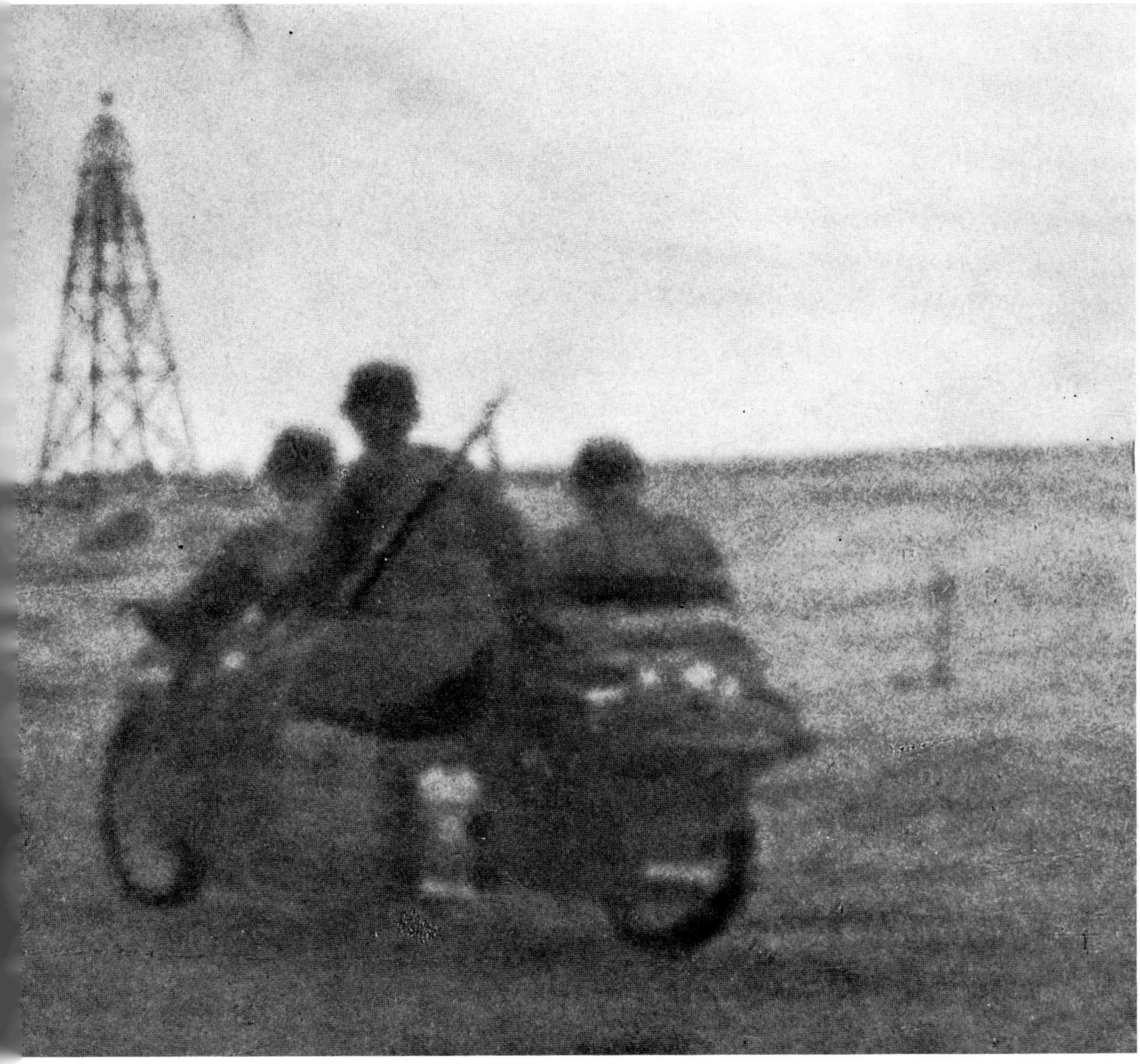

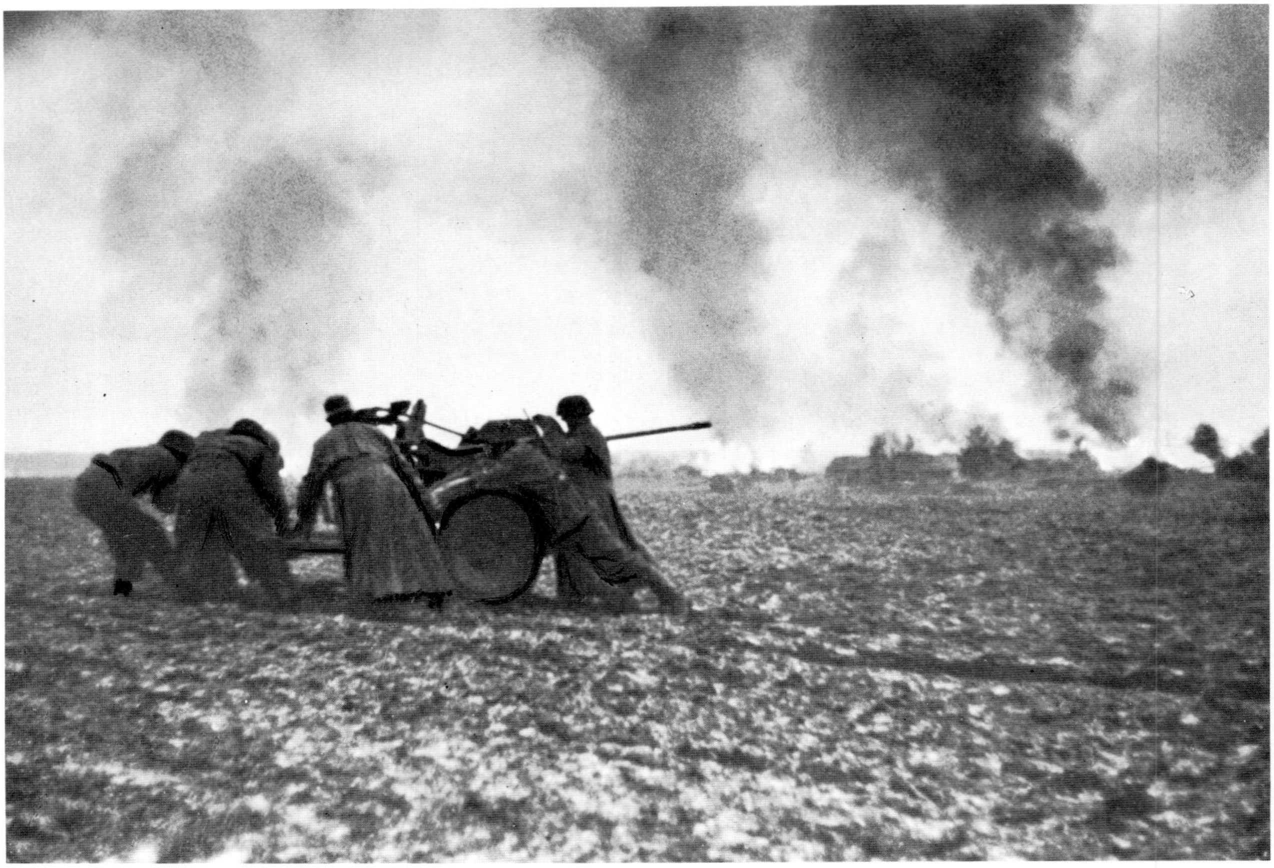

Among the lead elements of the attack troops are men of the Waffen-SS. As they pass the Russian border, they immediately encounter very heavy fighting.

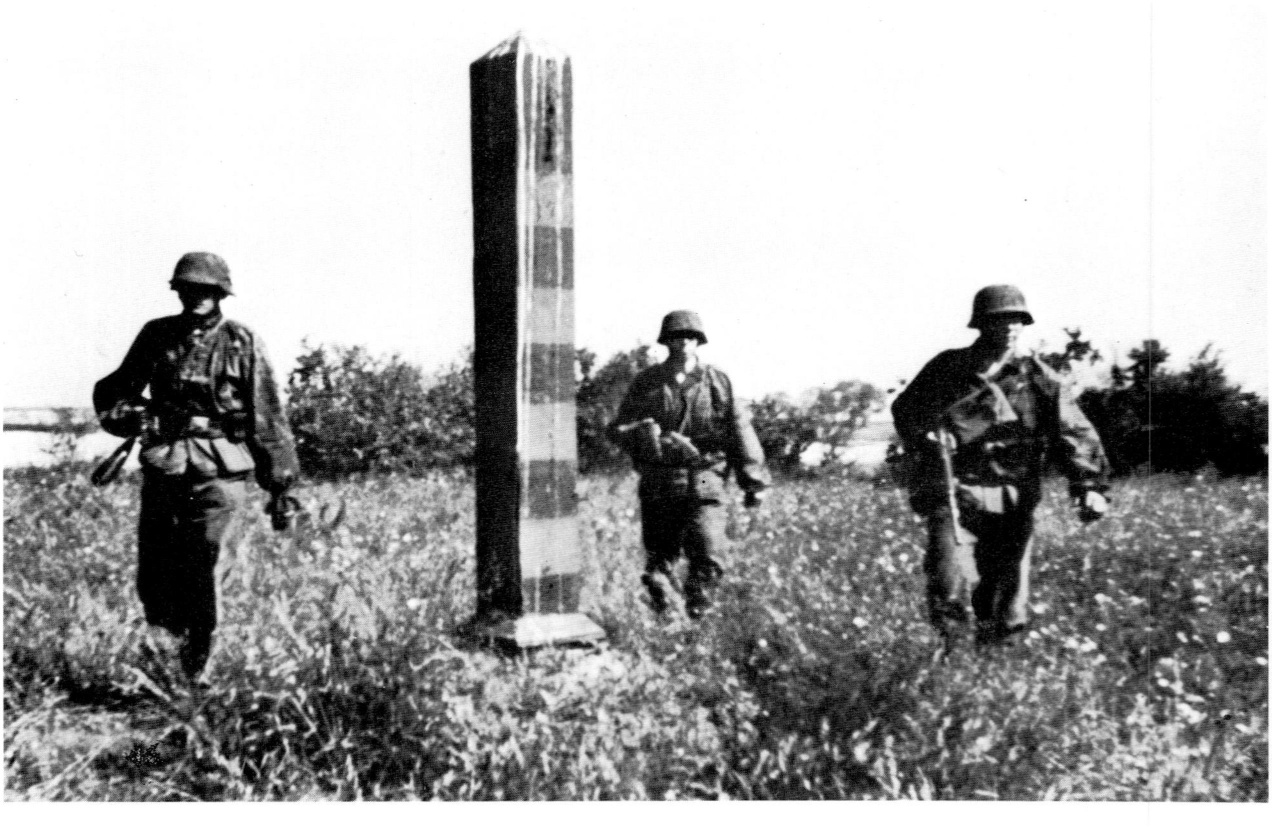

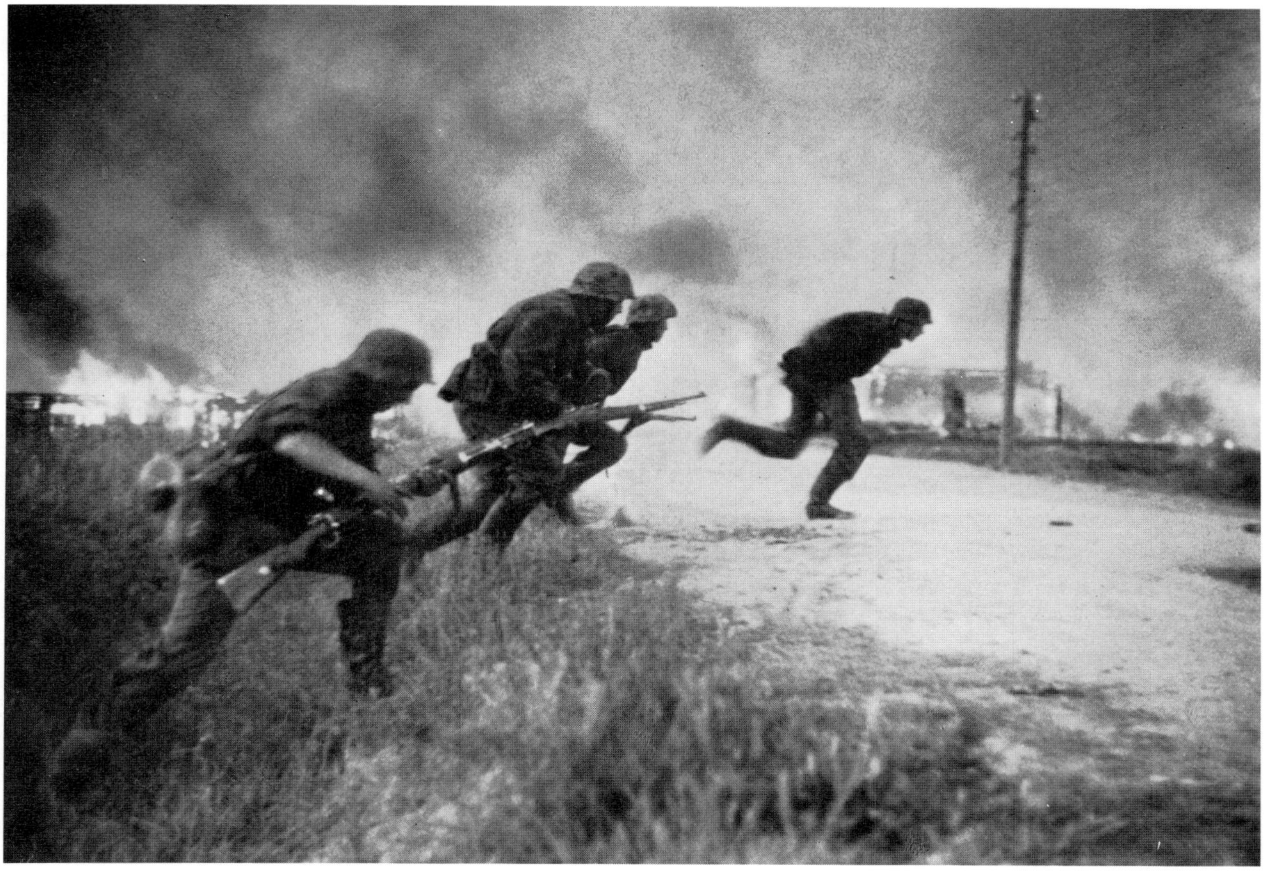

From the outset, the Russian troops offer stubborn resistance which very often must be broken in hand-to-hand combat.

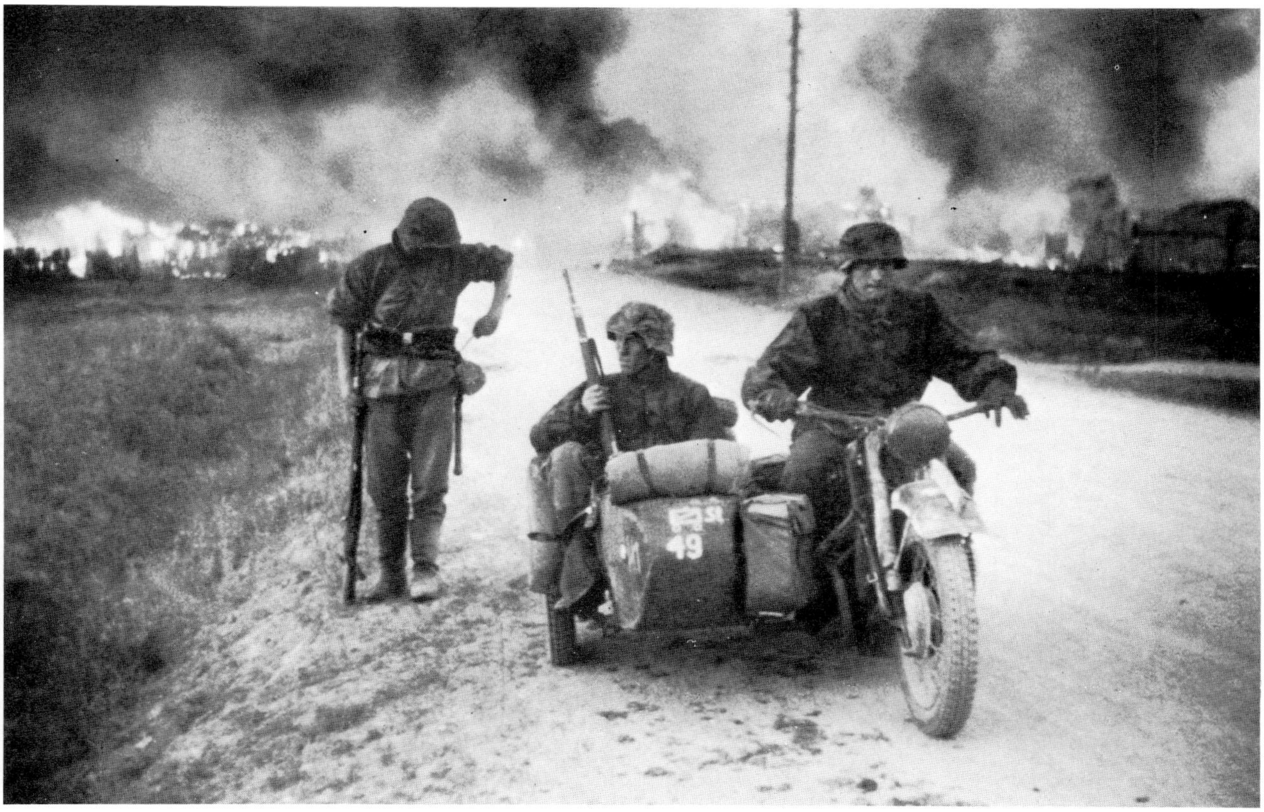
49

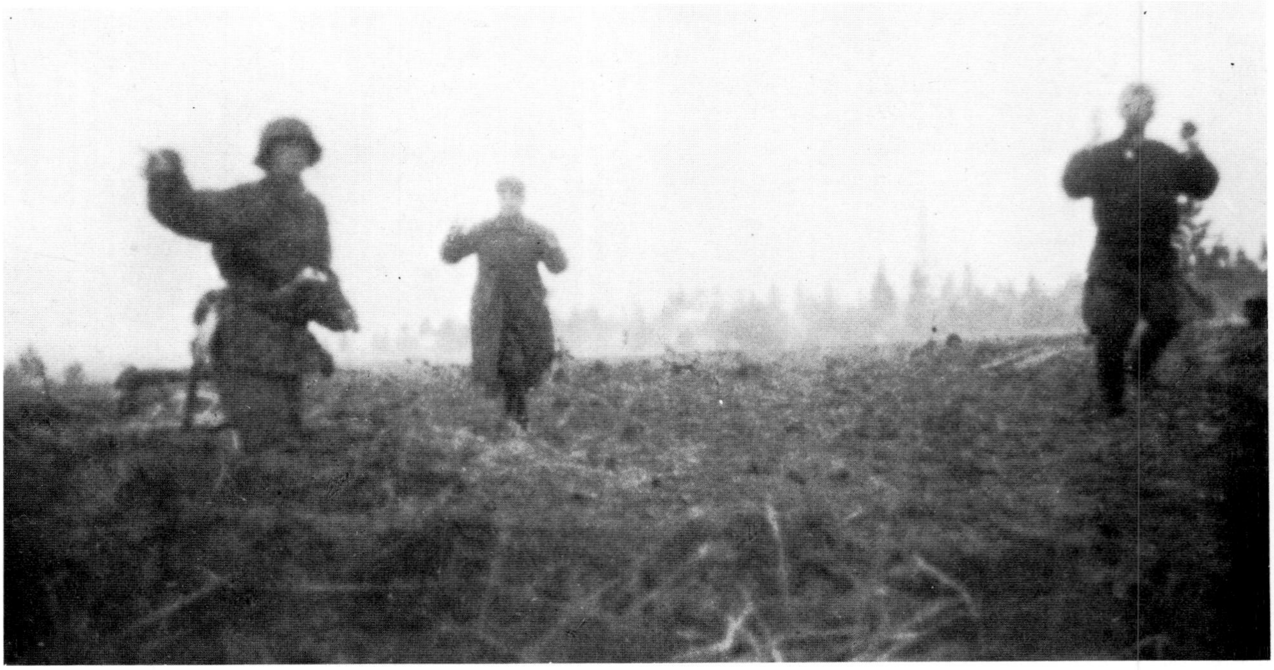

The bringing in of the first prisoners. Immediate interrogations are supposed to give a better impression of the enemy situation.

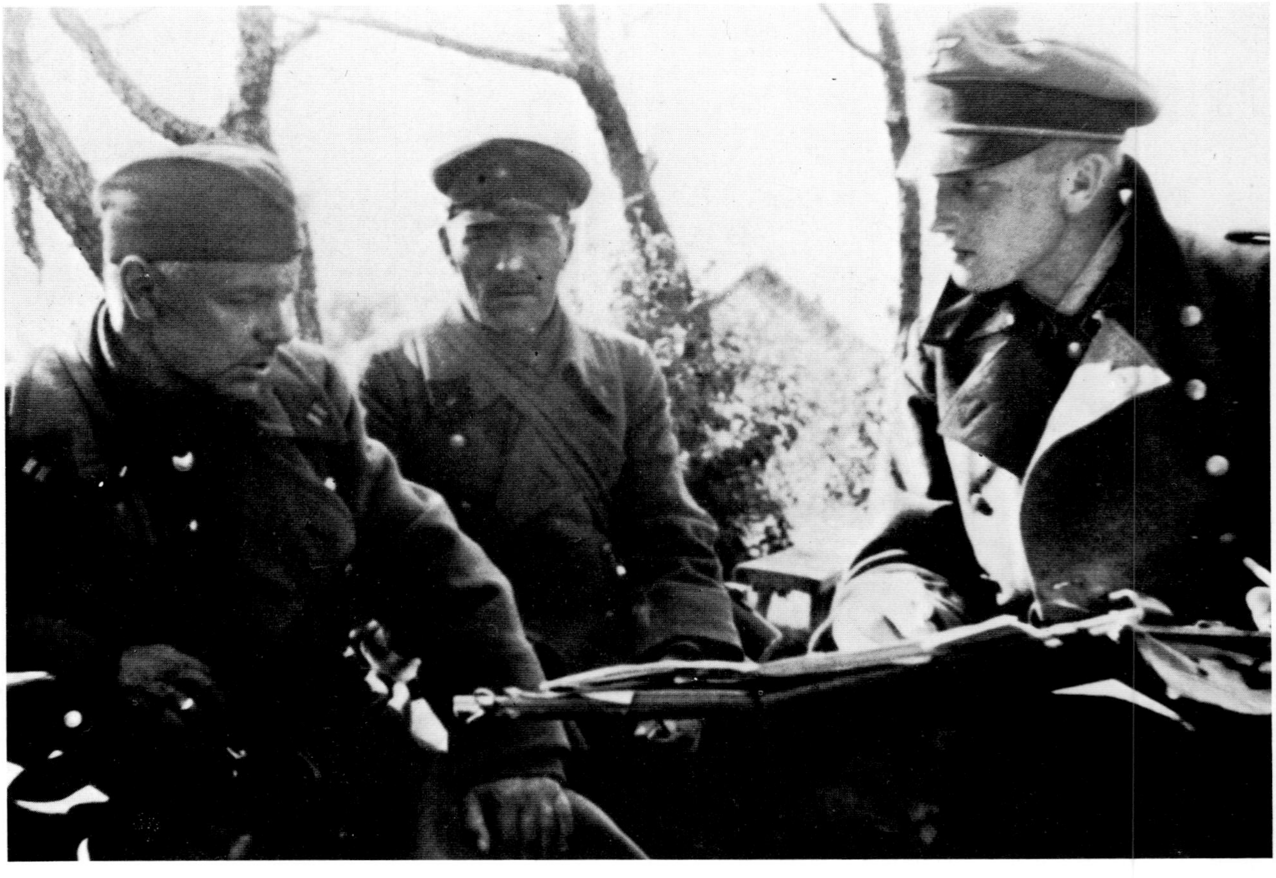

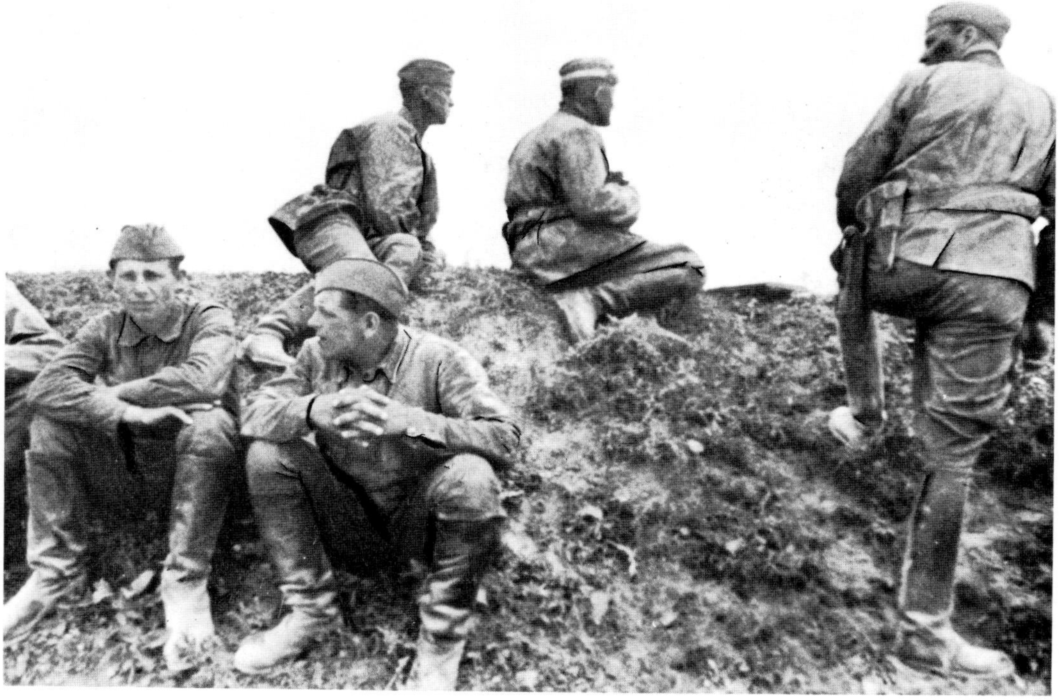

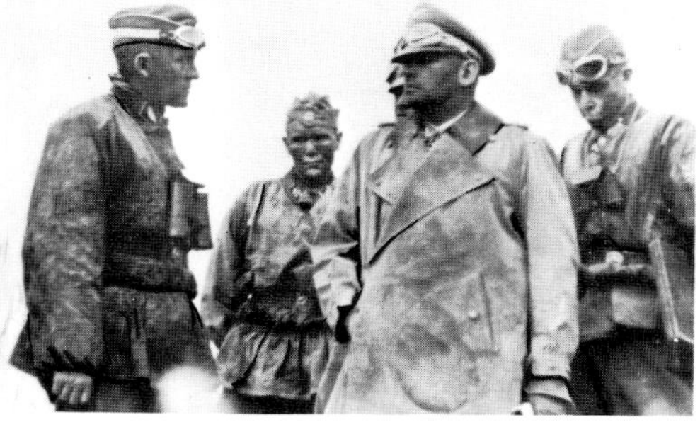

The first combat headquarters of the regiment "Westland", east of Lemberg on July 1, 1941.

From the left: Colonel Wäckerle, Captain Paetsch (Ic), Captain von Schalburg (01), Brig. General Steiner, Captain Ziemsen (Adj. Westland).

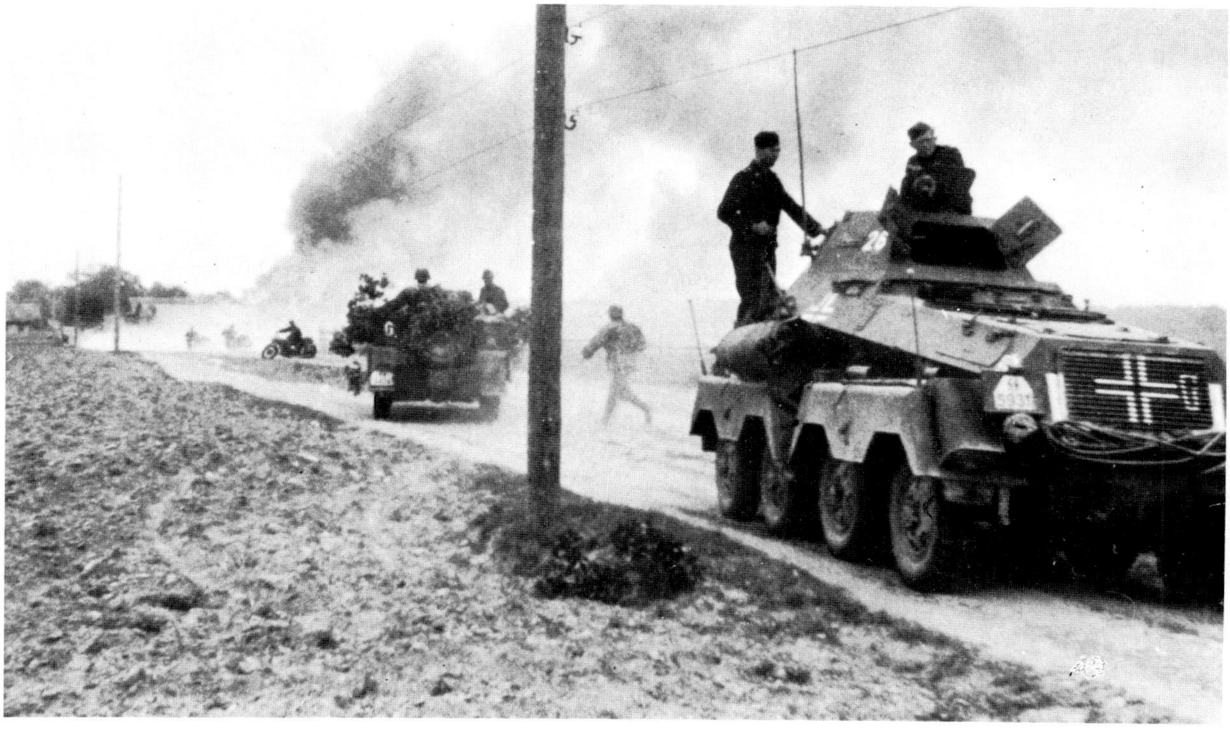

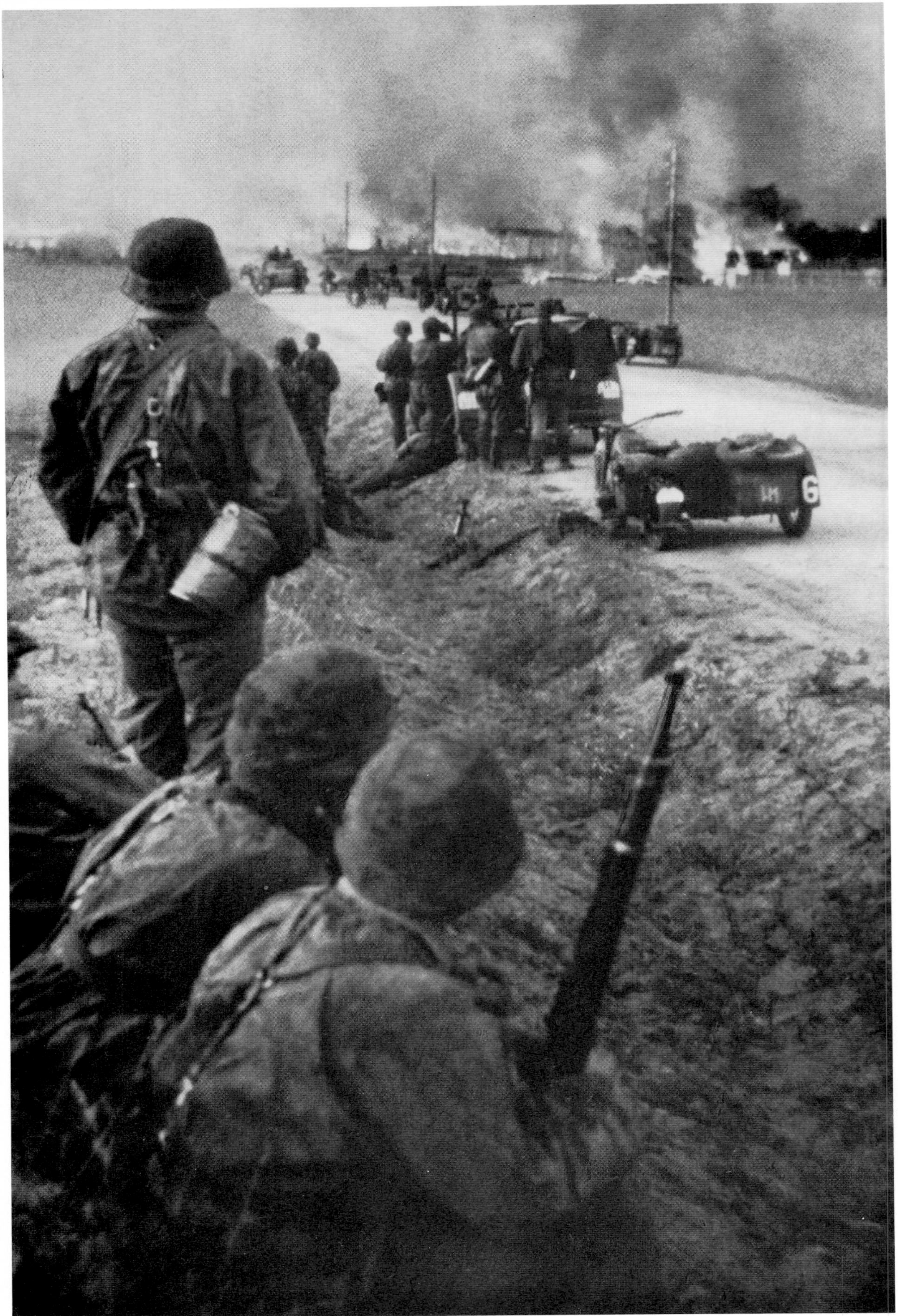

The enemy is pursued by motorized units of the division "Das Reich", supported by army tanks.

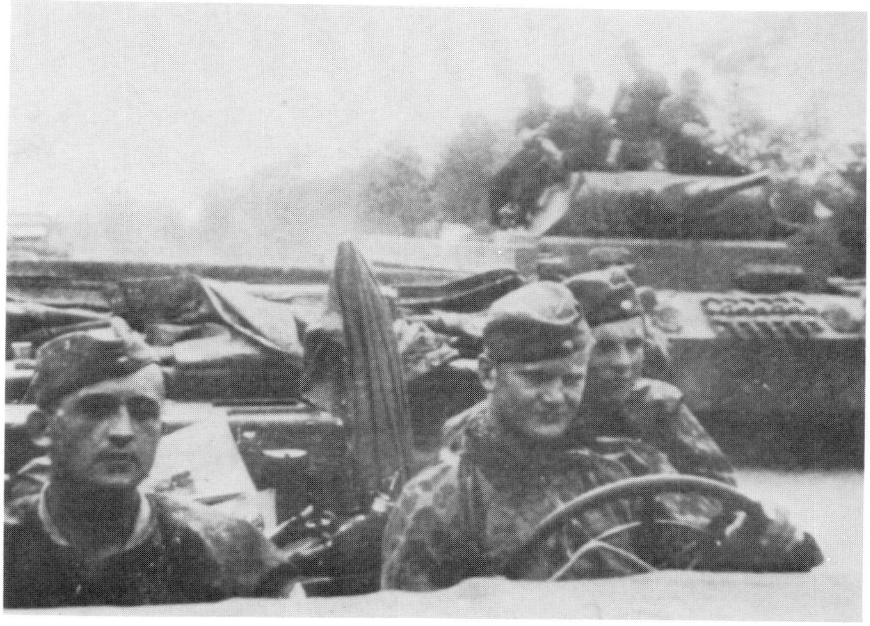

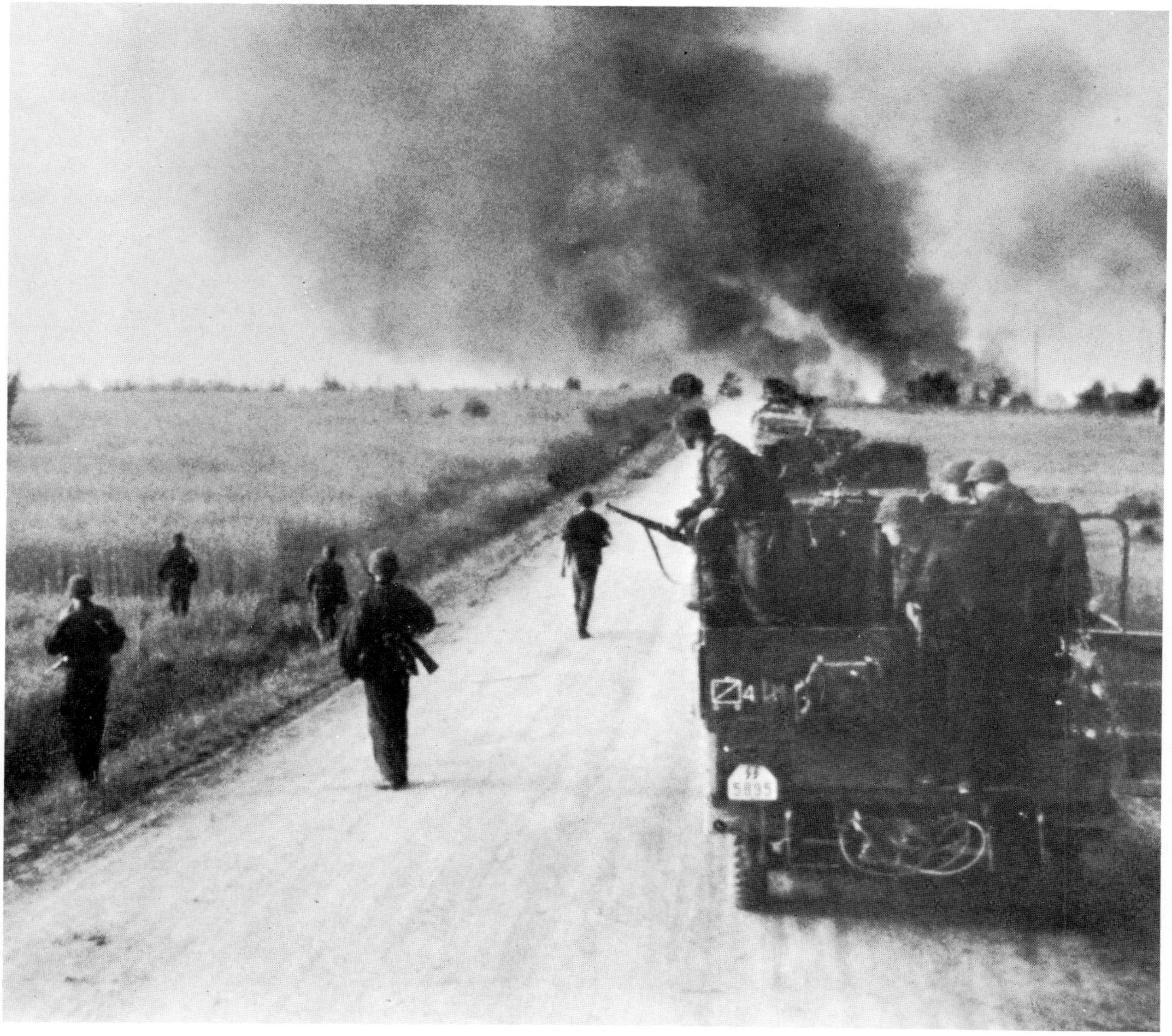

From the left: Fritz Mühlenkamp of the reconnaissance unit "Das Reich".

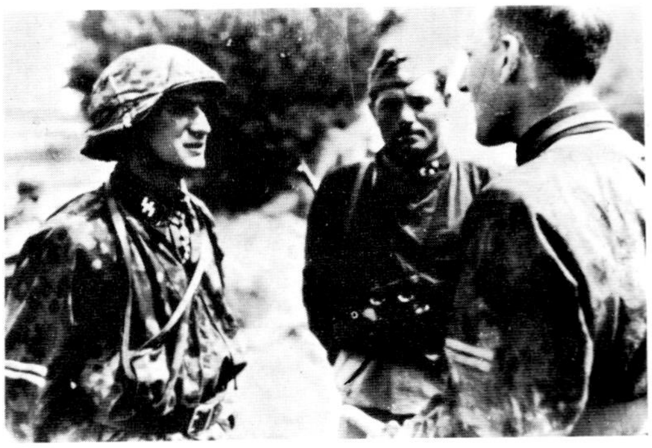

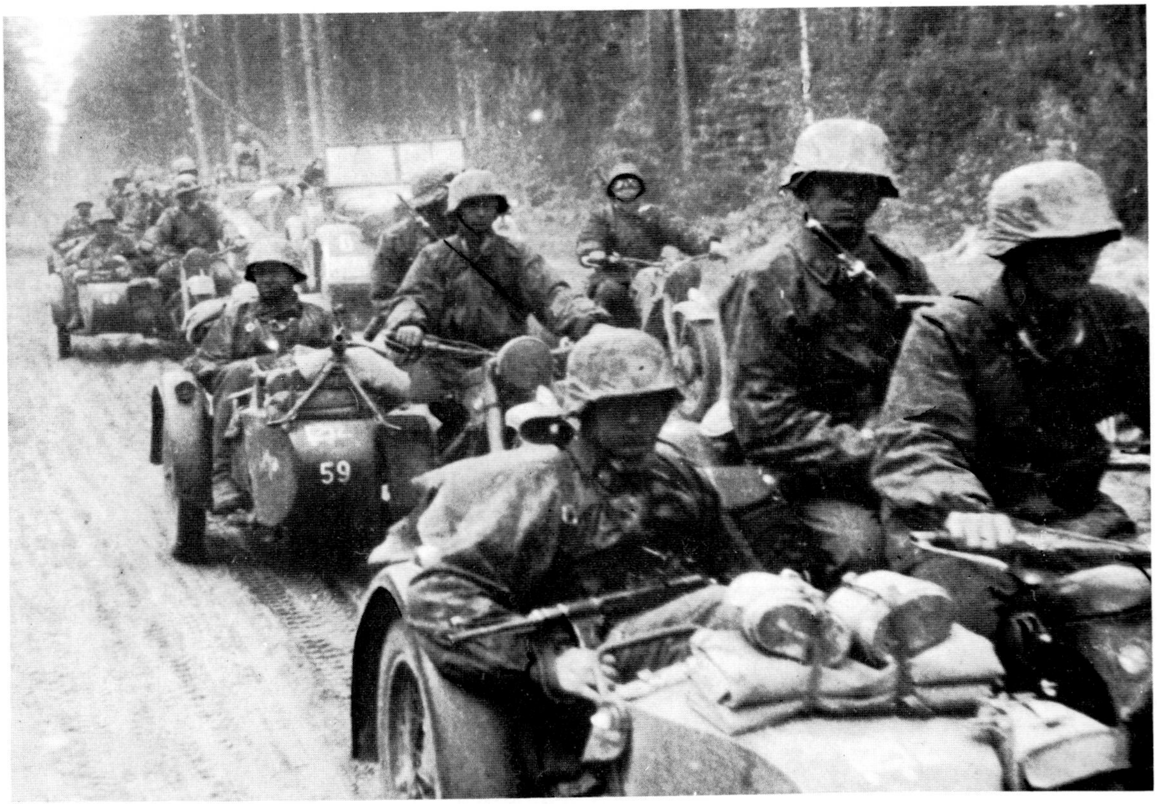
59

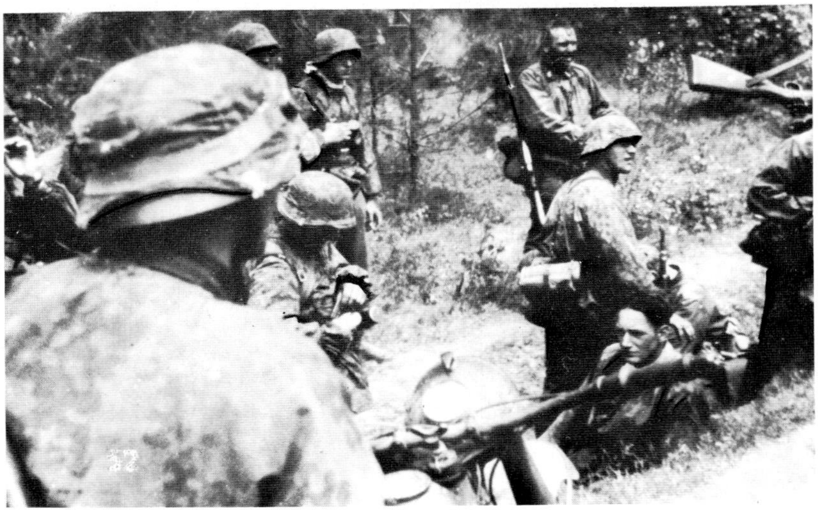

The reconnaissance unit of the division "Das Reich" is always at the front of the Guderian Panzer Group.

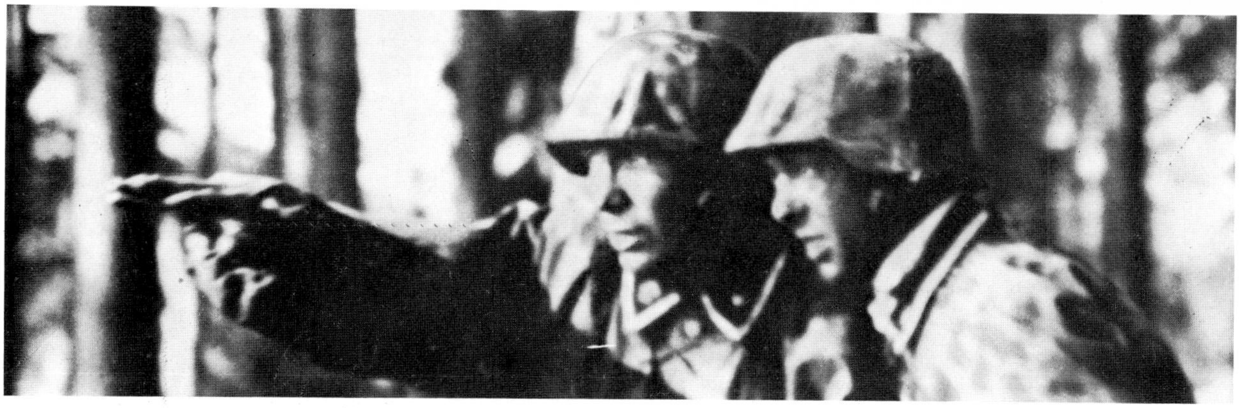

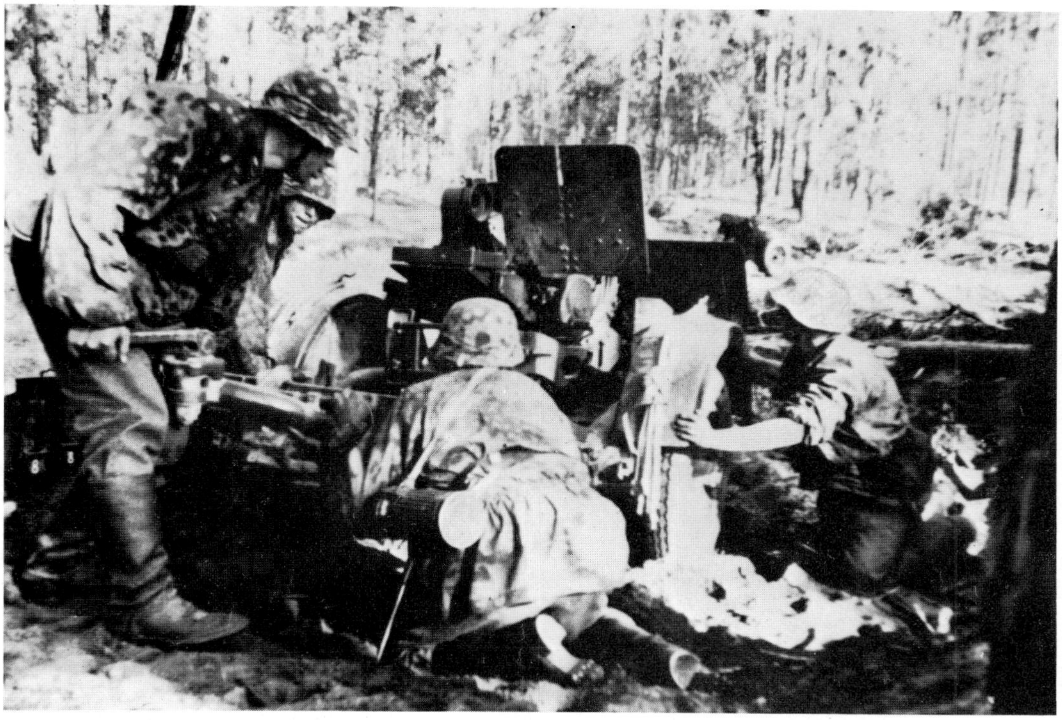

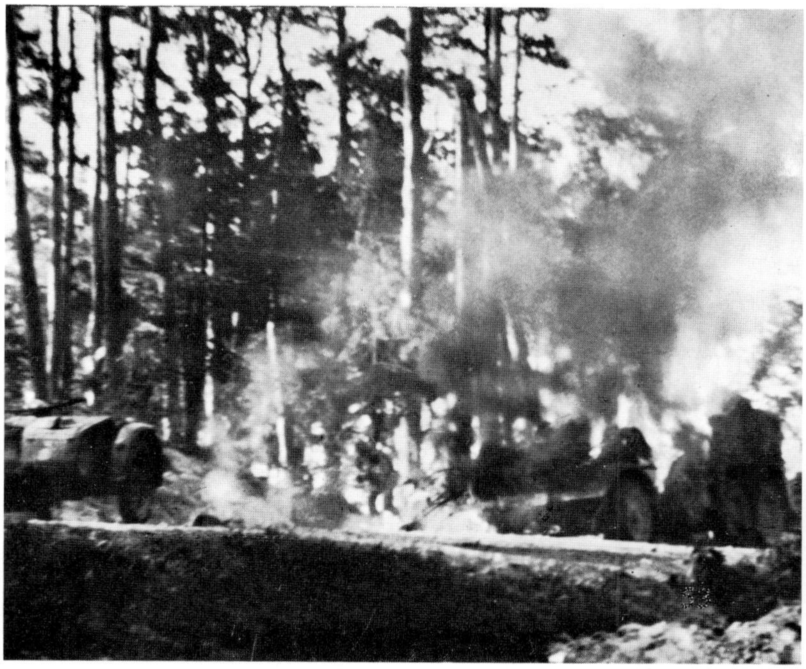

Russian armored cars-identified and destroyed by the infantry guns of the "Totenkopf" Division.

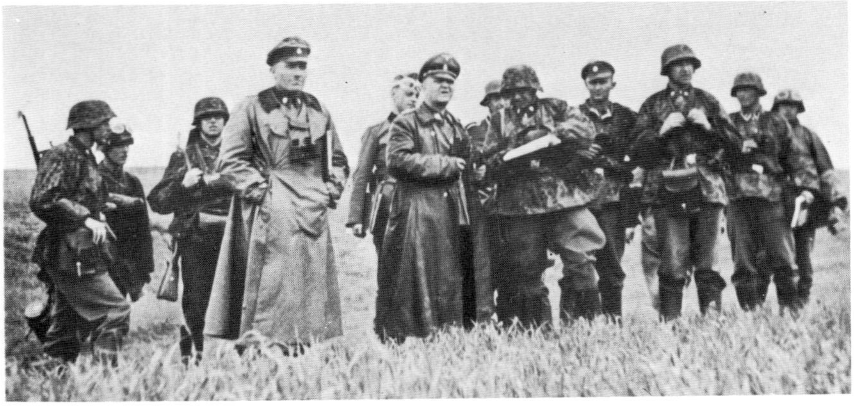

Command post of the T-Division. In the center: Priess, Eicke, Becker.

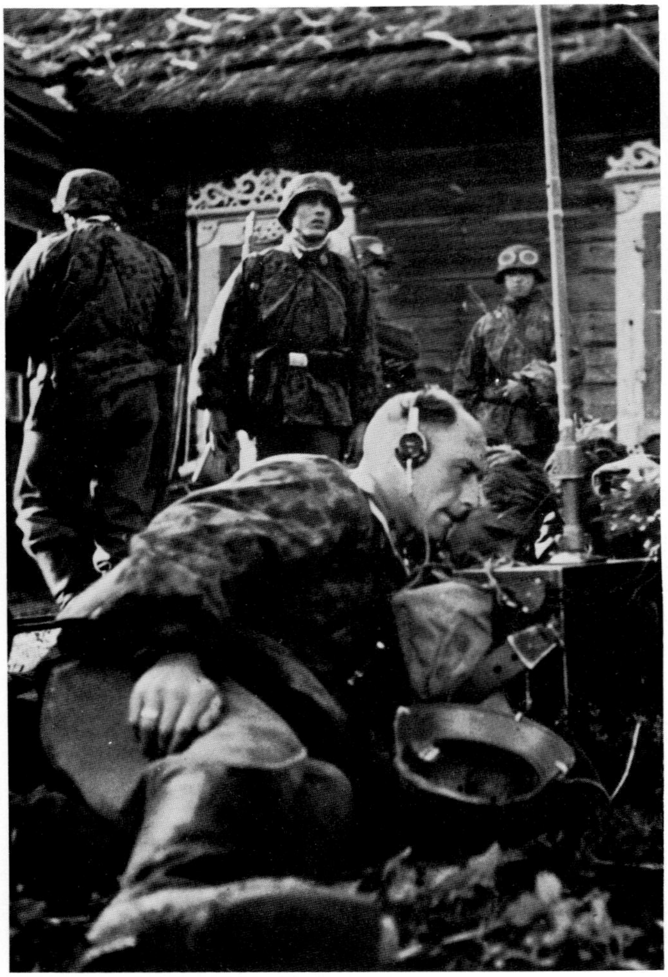

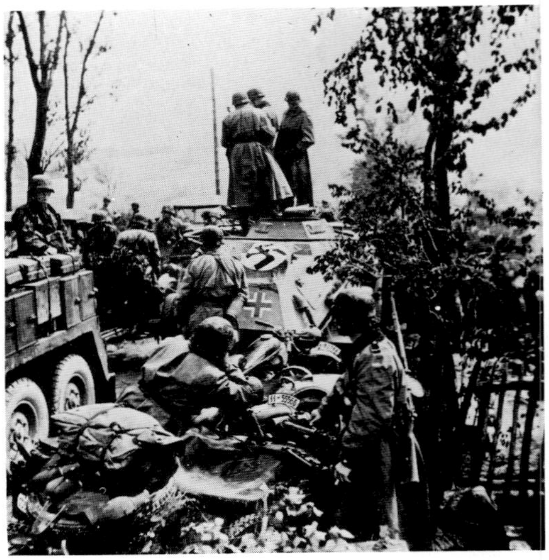

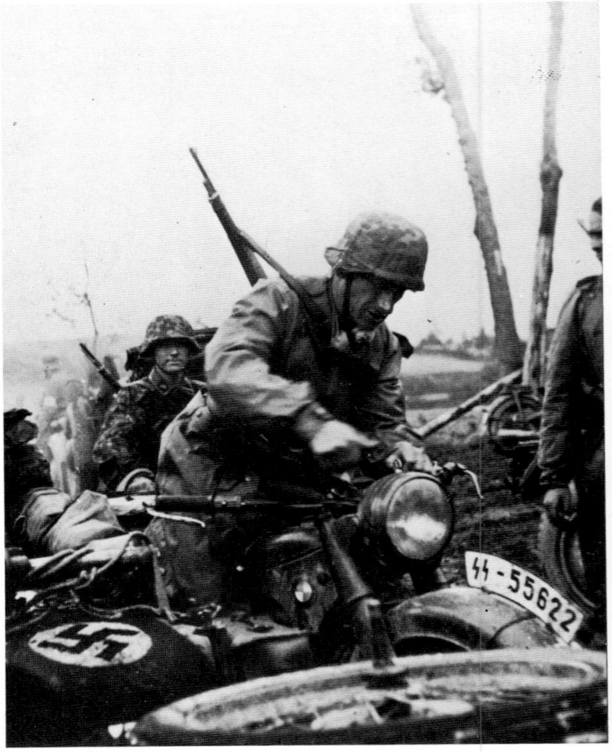
55622

After a short rest and a reorientation, the advance is continued.

Eicke and Preiss in a VW-command car.

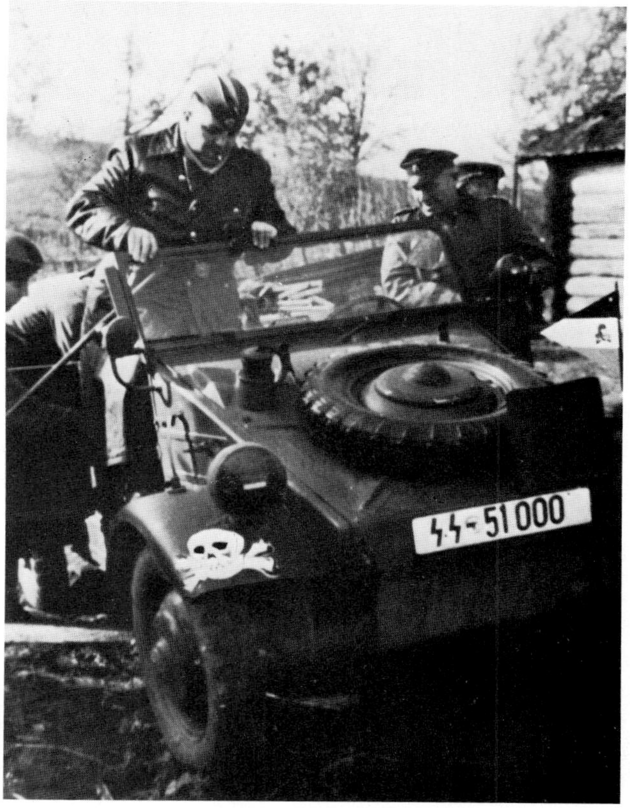
ϟϟ-51 000

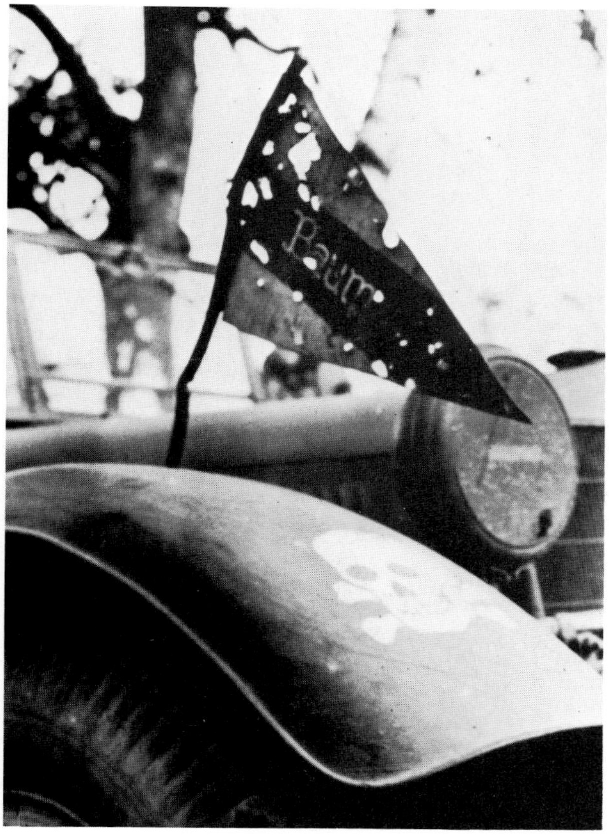
Baum

Captain Otto Baum-his banner shows signs of the heavy fighting of the past few days-in the lead element with General Eicke.

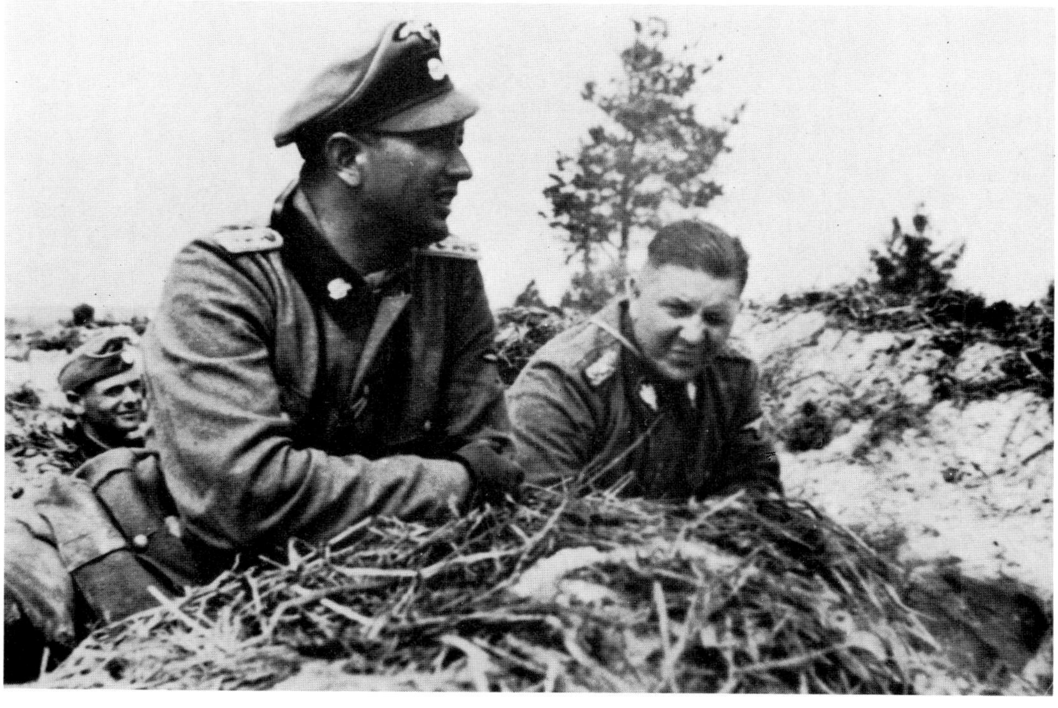

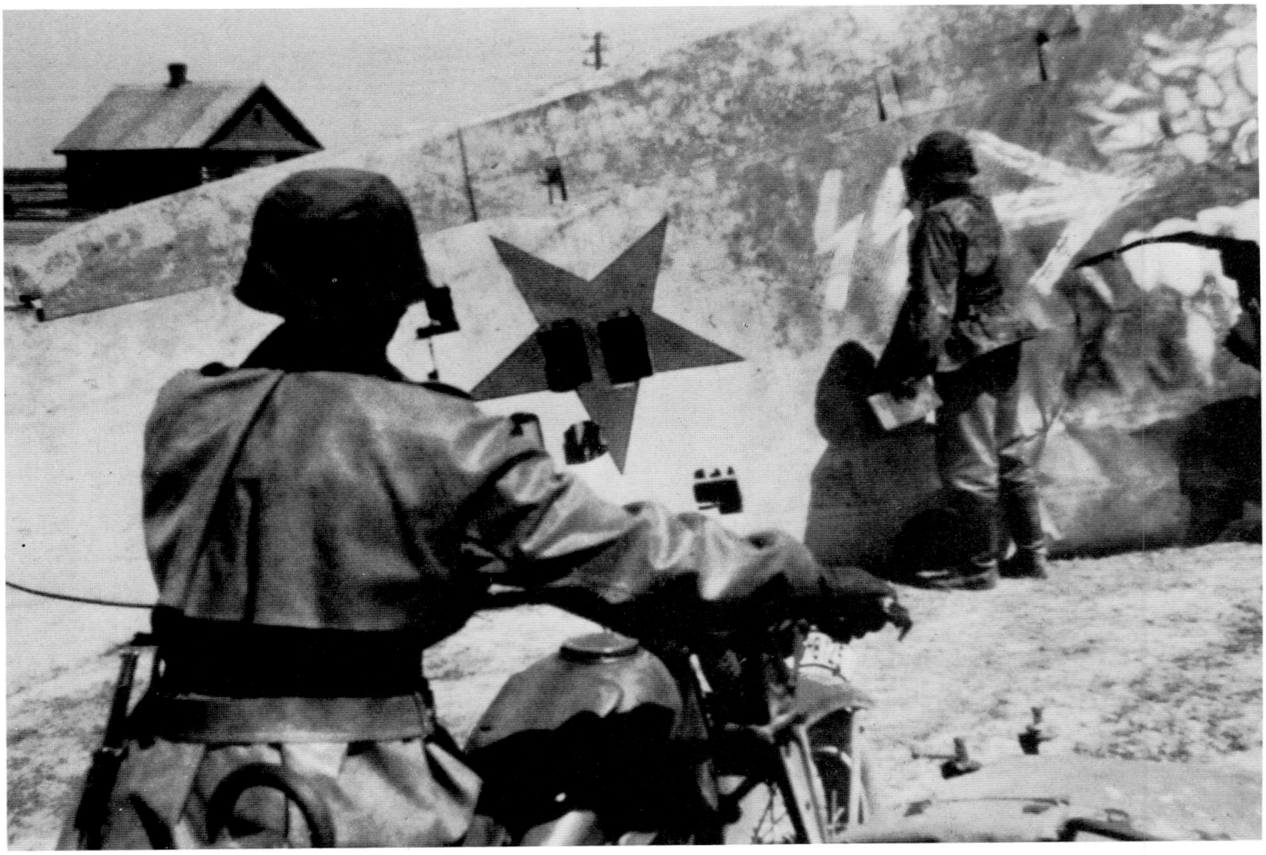

The advance goes on supported by tanks. The men are fully committed time and time again.

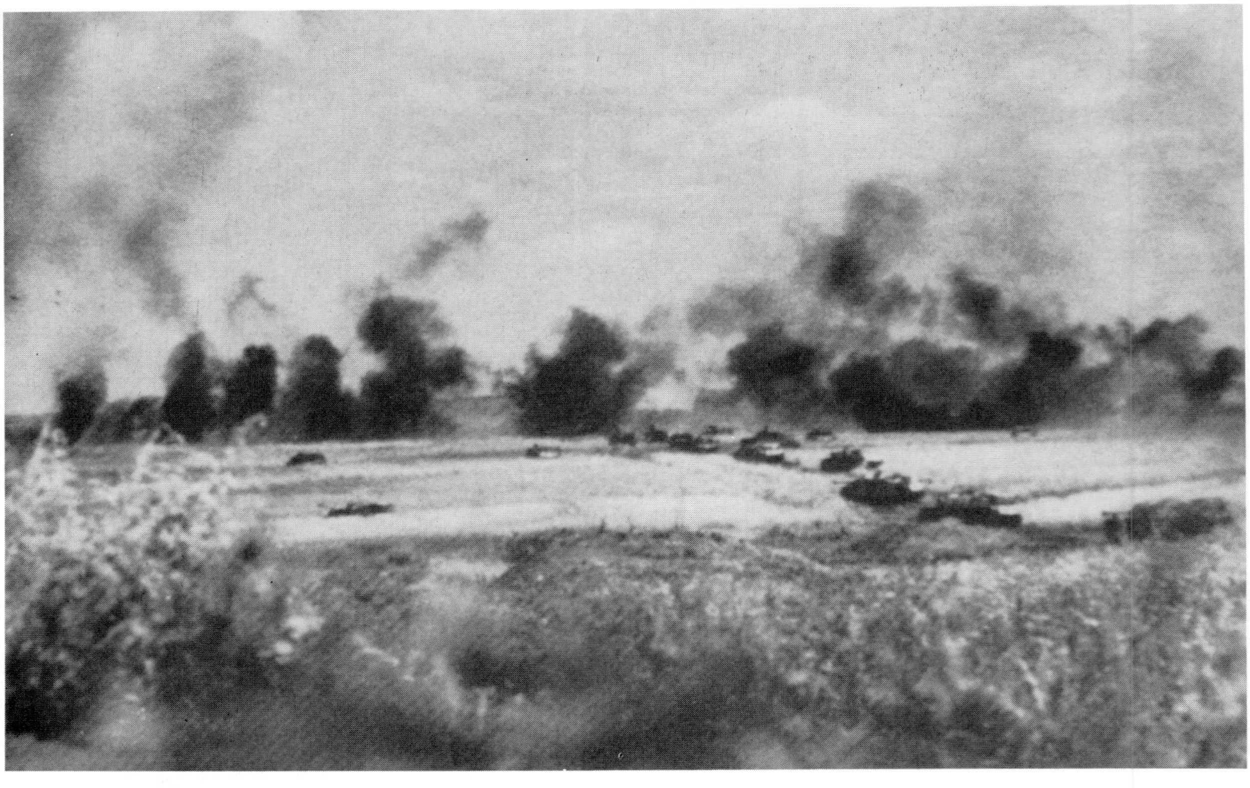

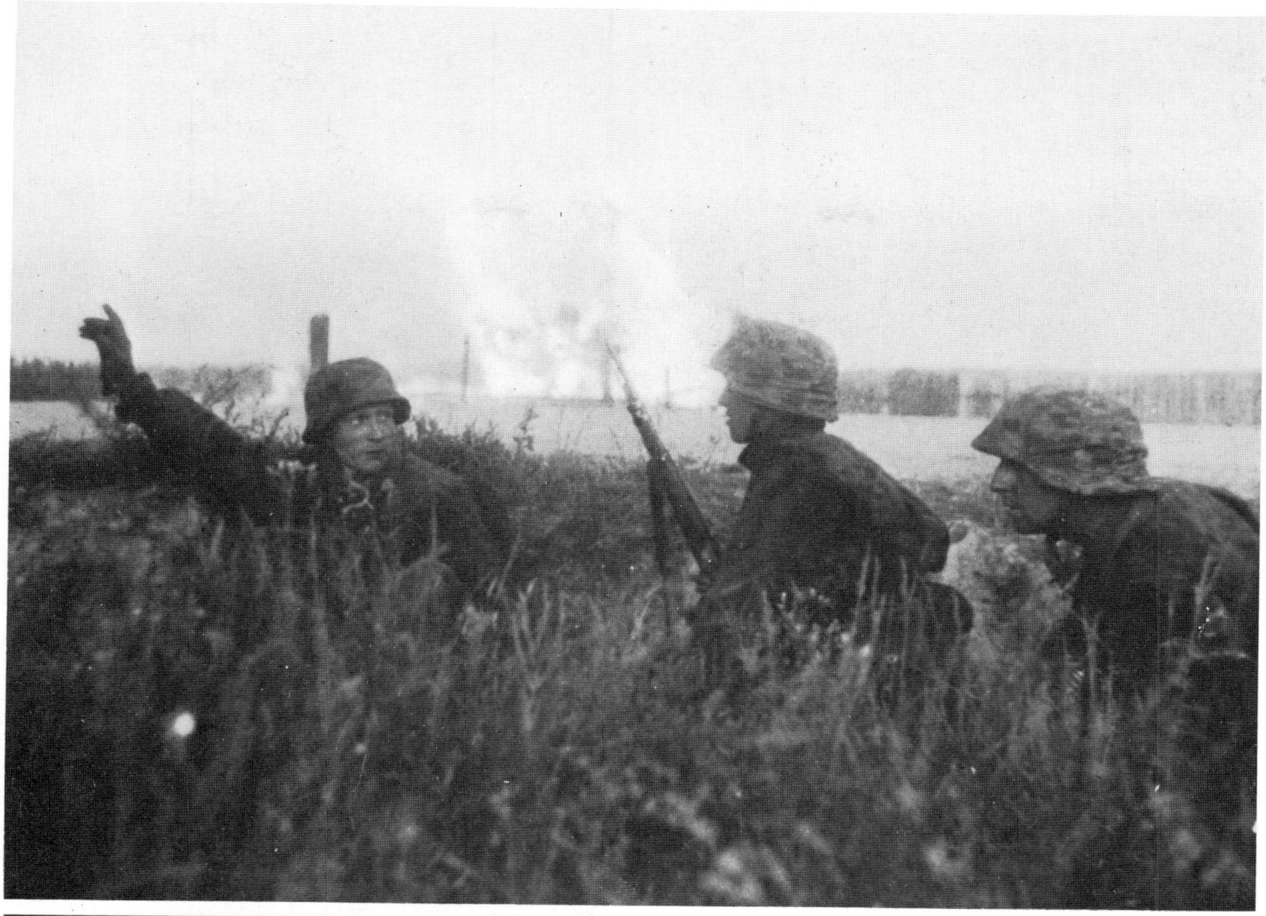
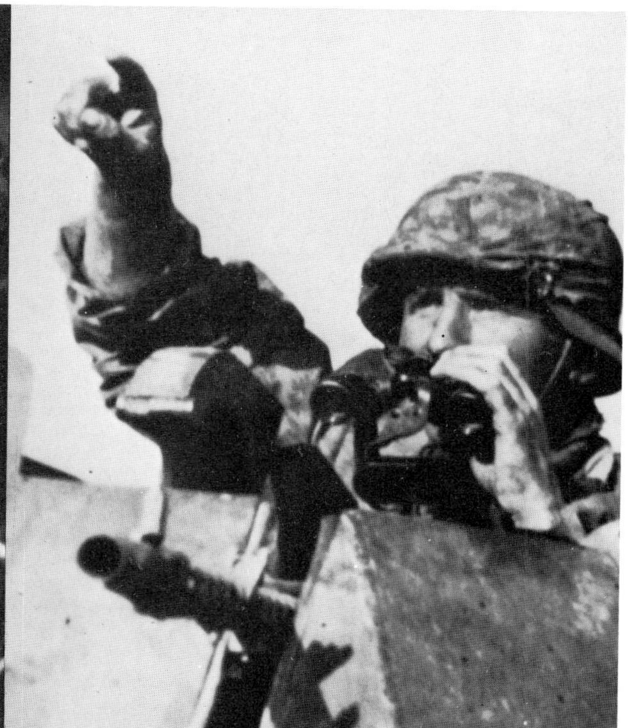
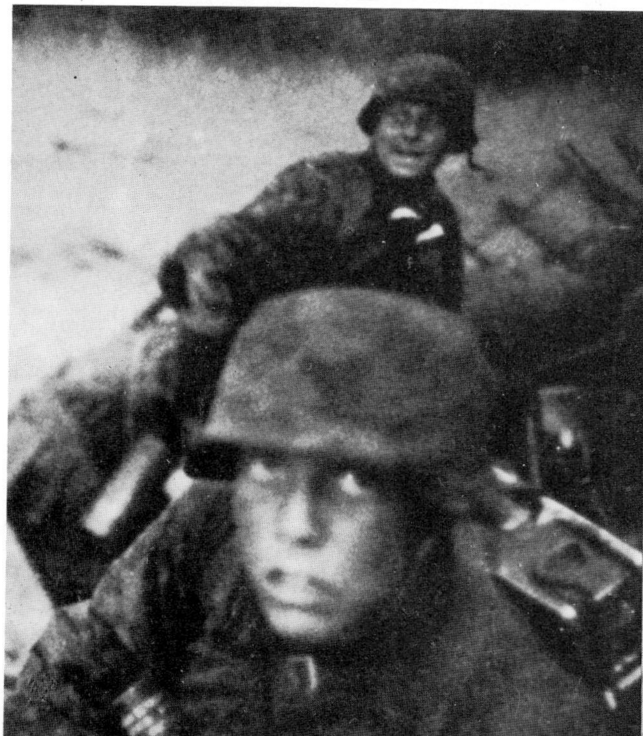

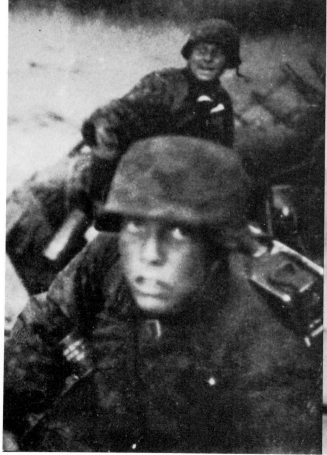

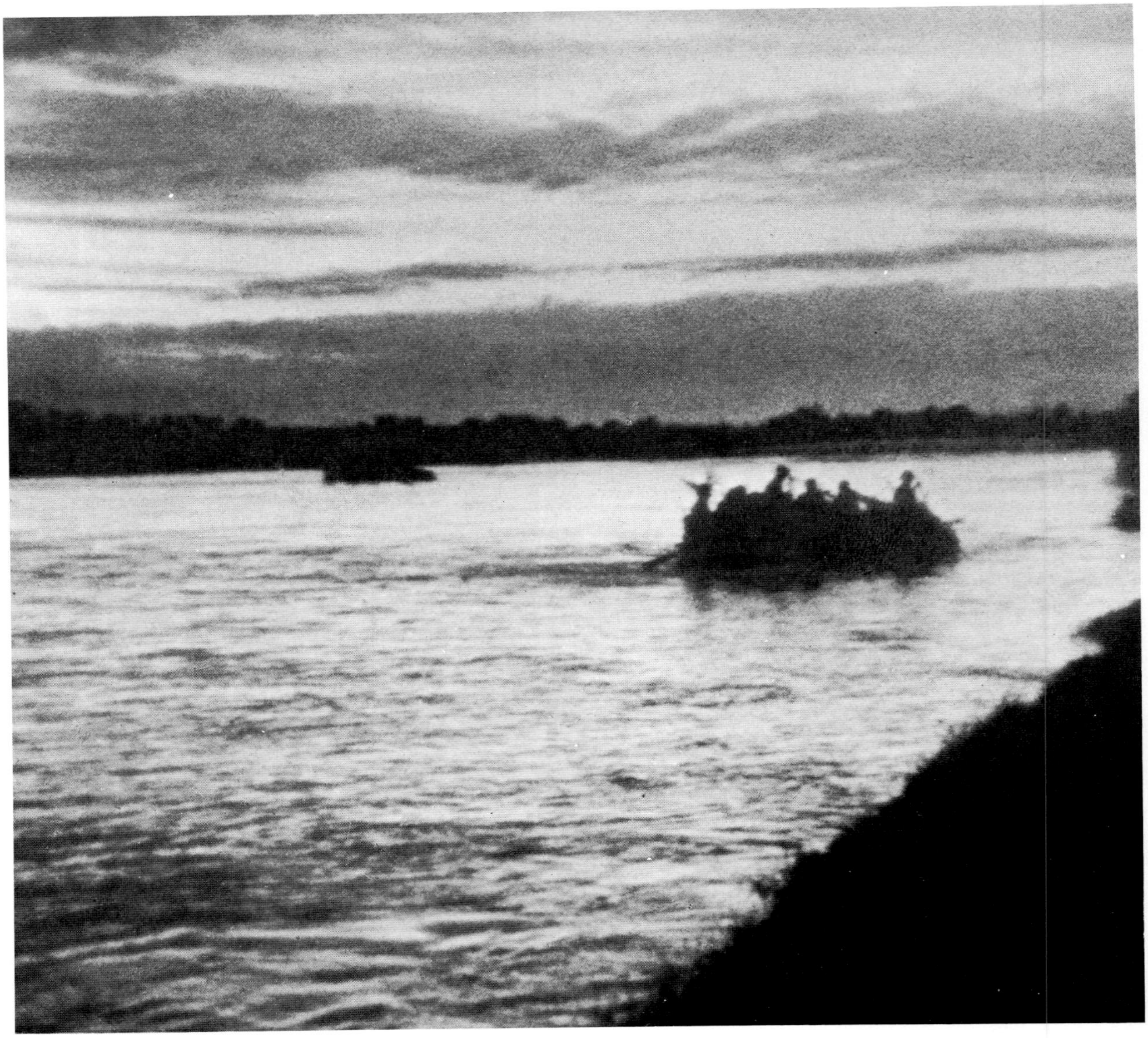

At dawn the Dneiper is passed. This photo depicts one of the many hard fought river crossings which time and again demanded many sacrifices.

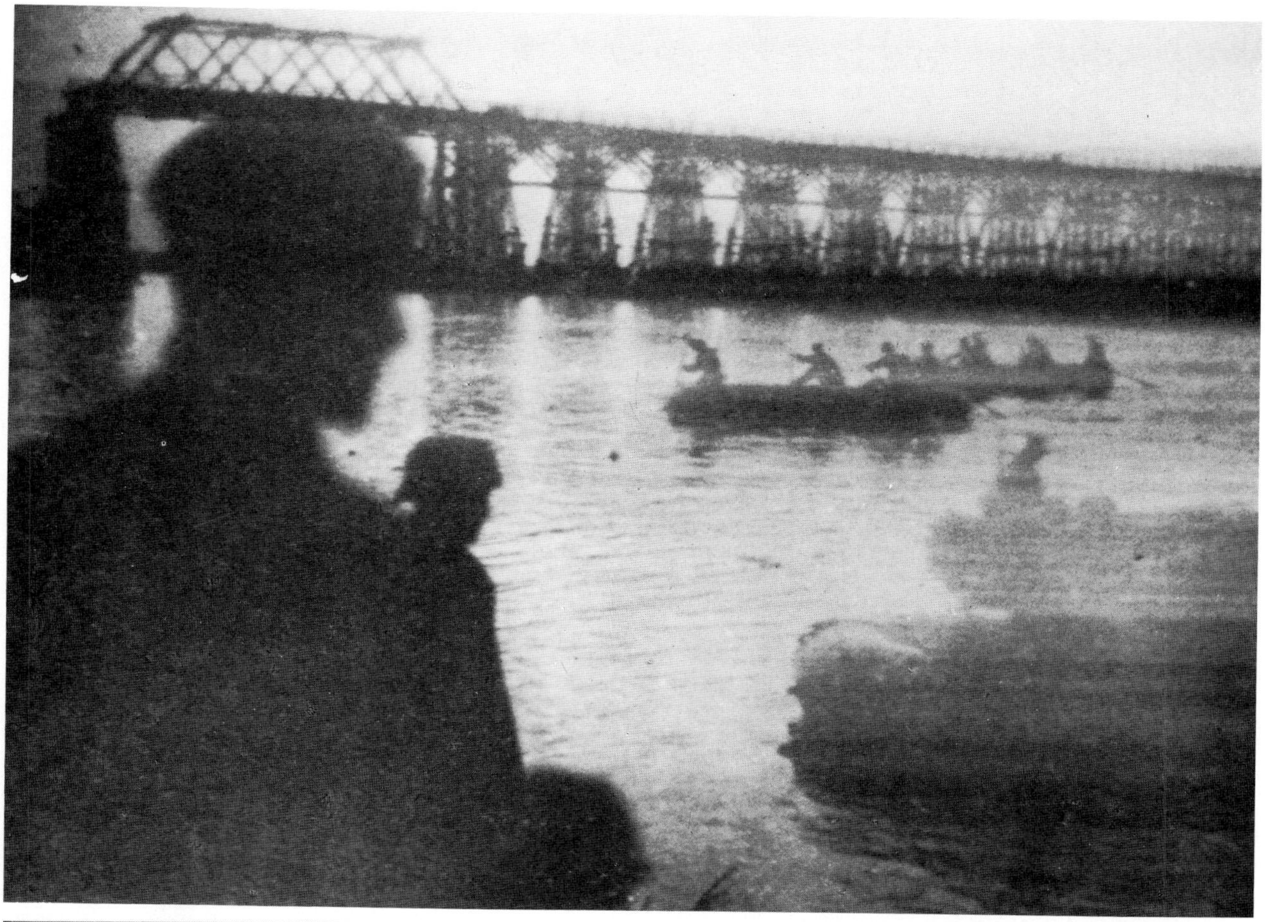

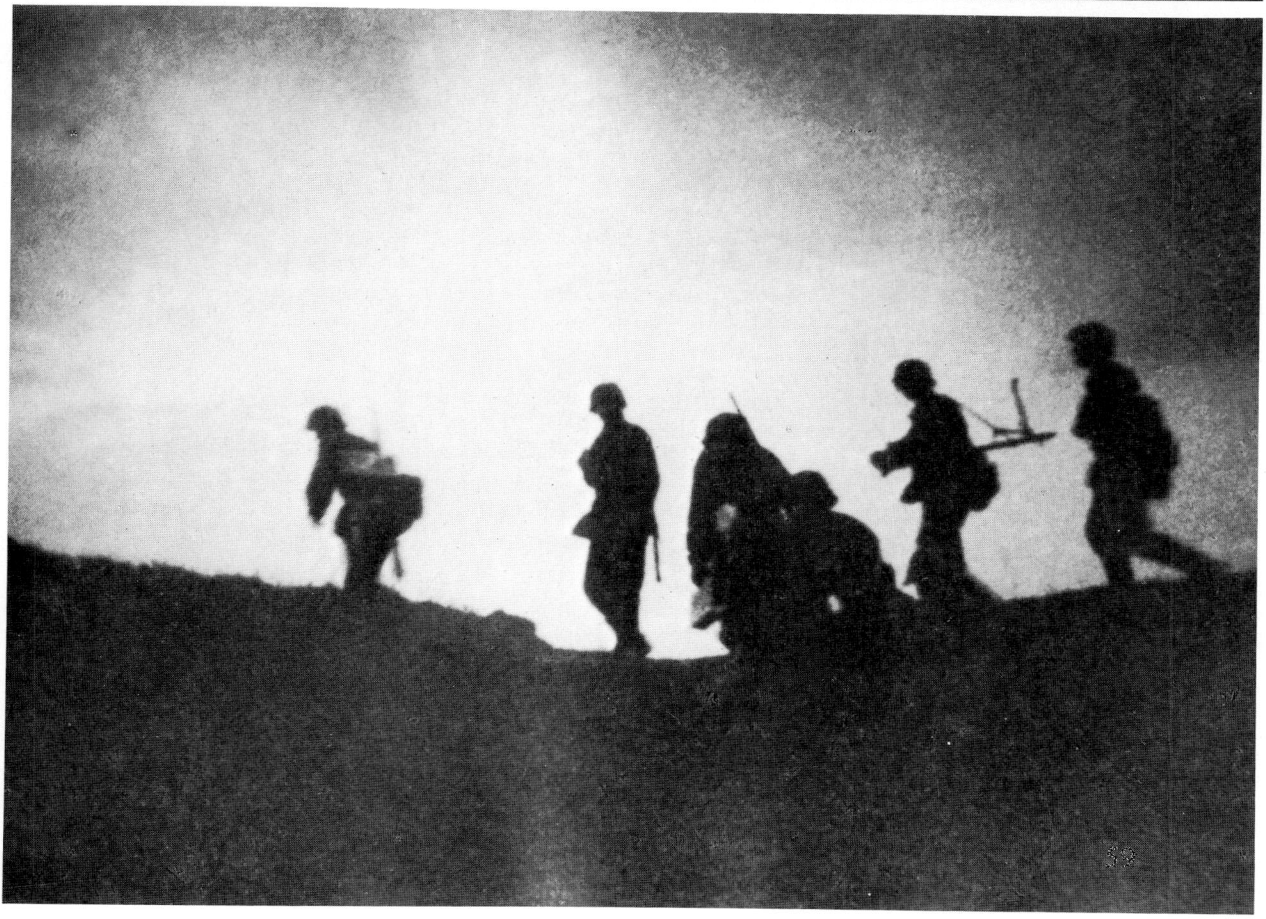

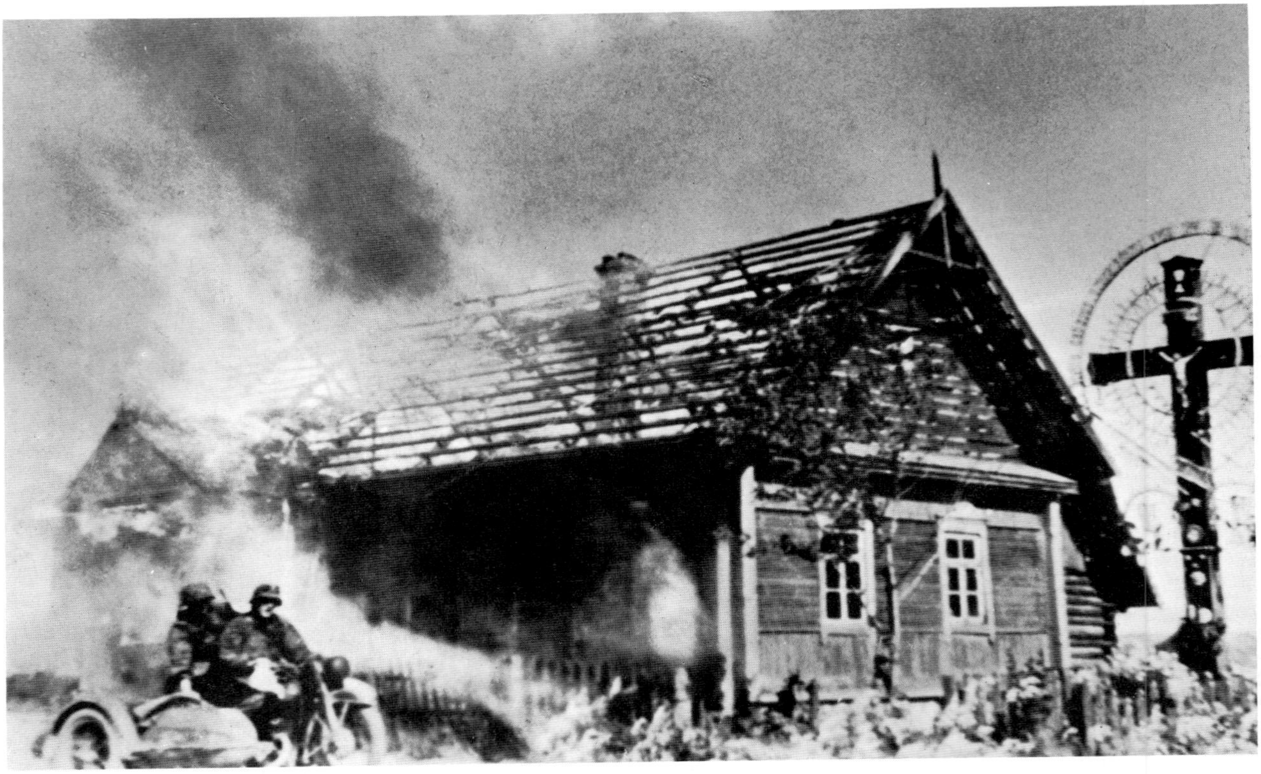

In the Ukraine. In spite of the heavy fighting, the relations with the inhabitants are still good...

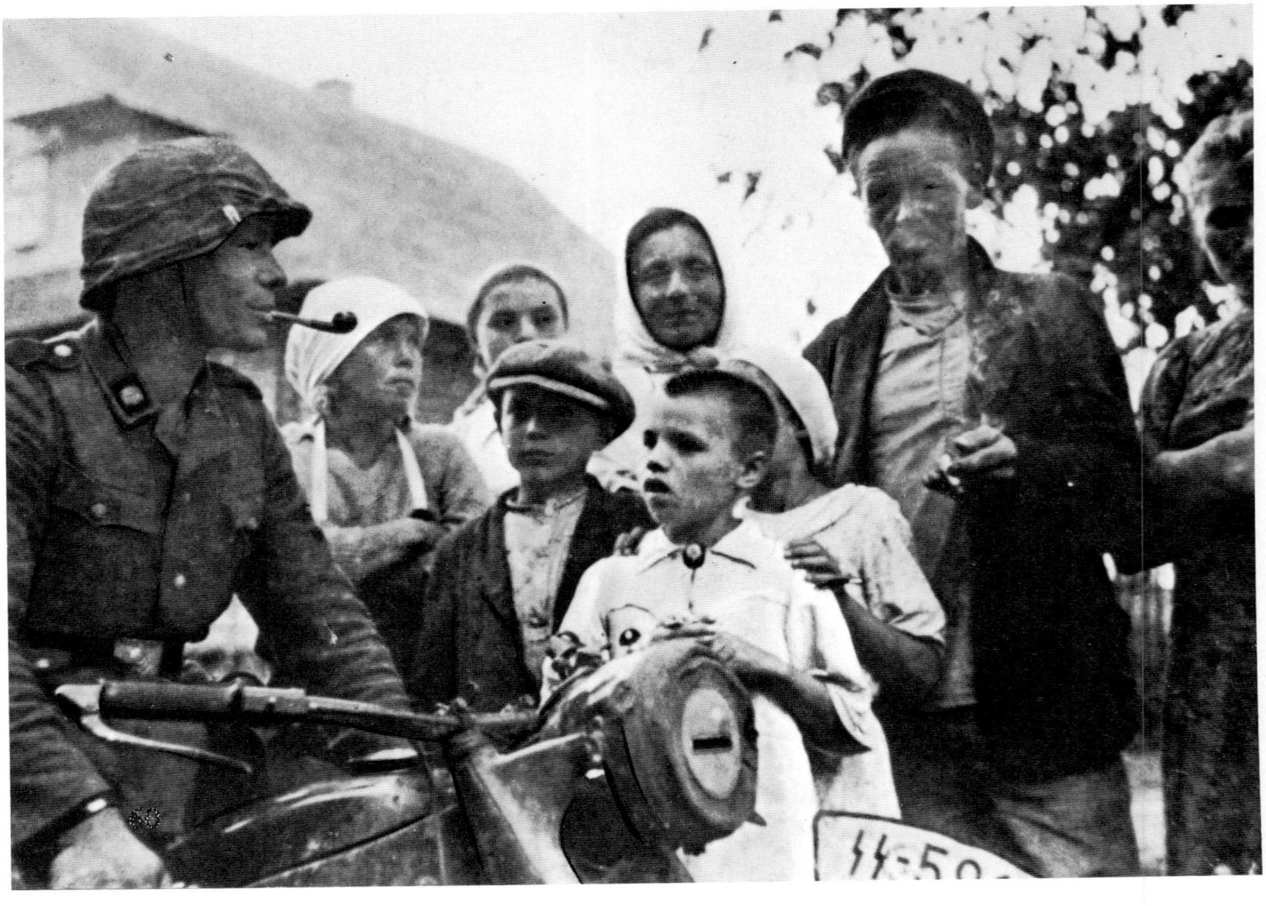

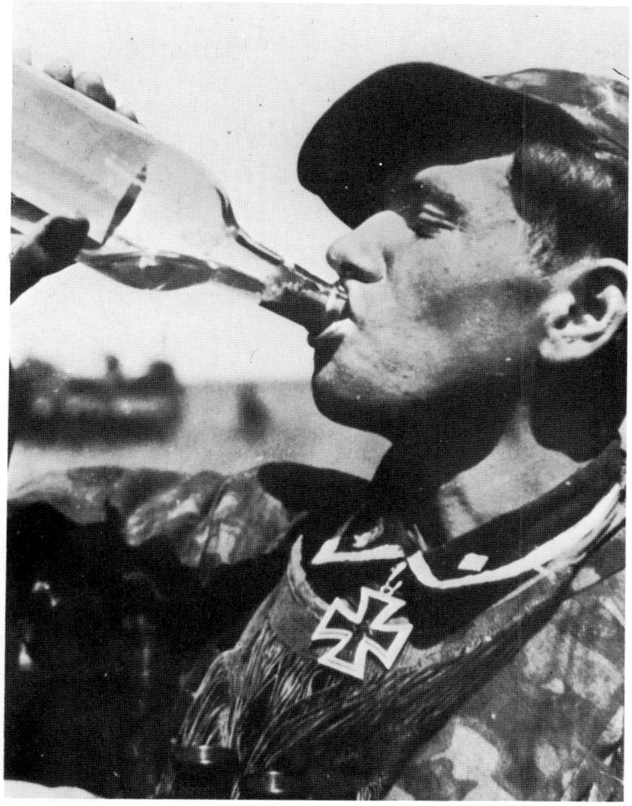
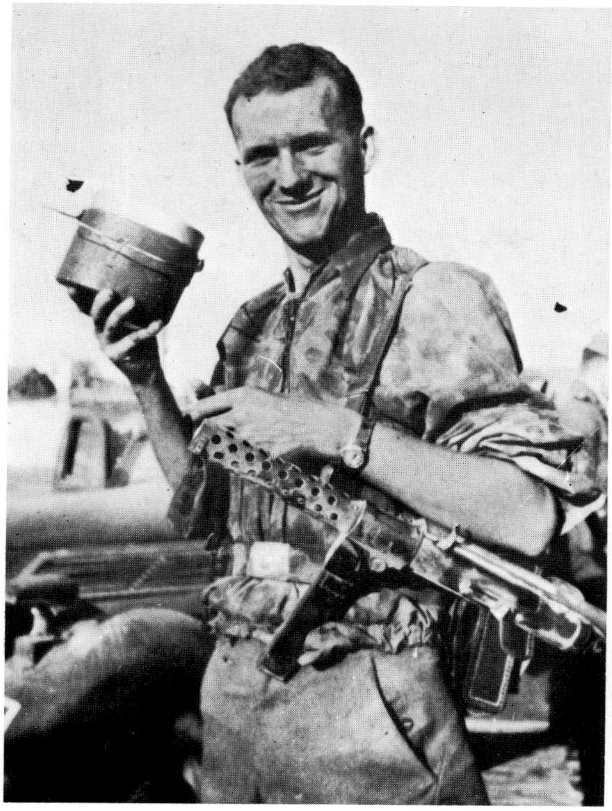

During the advance, when the heat becomes unbearable, the soldiers only desire is to quench his  thirst.

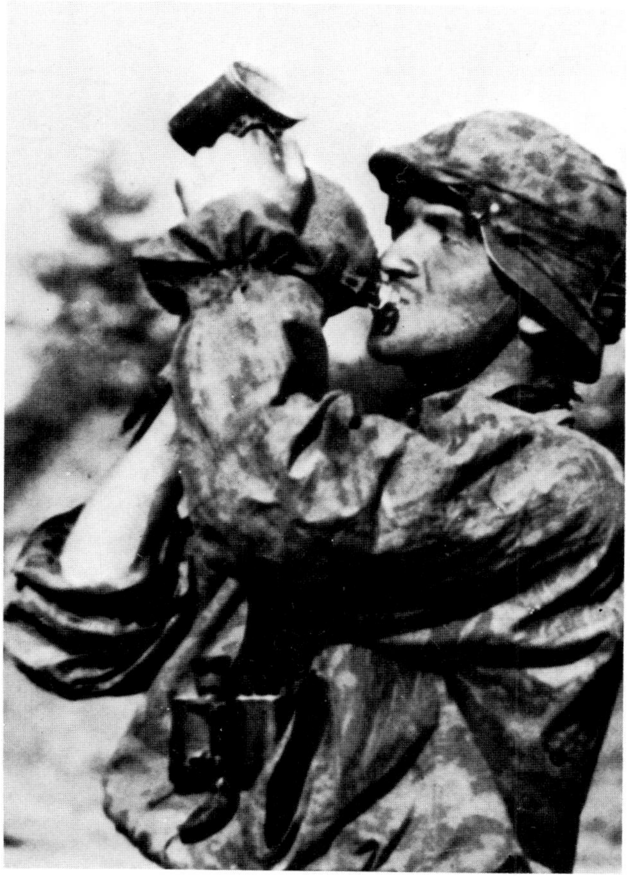
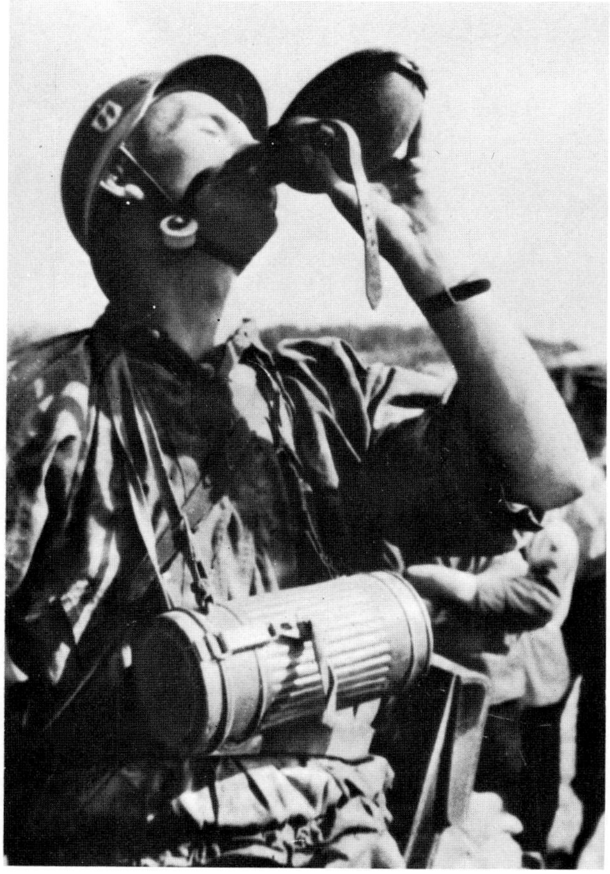

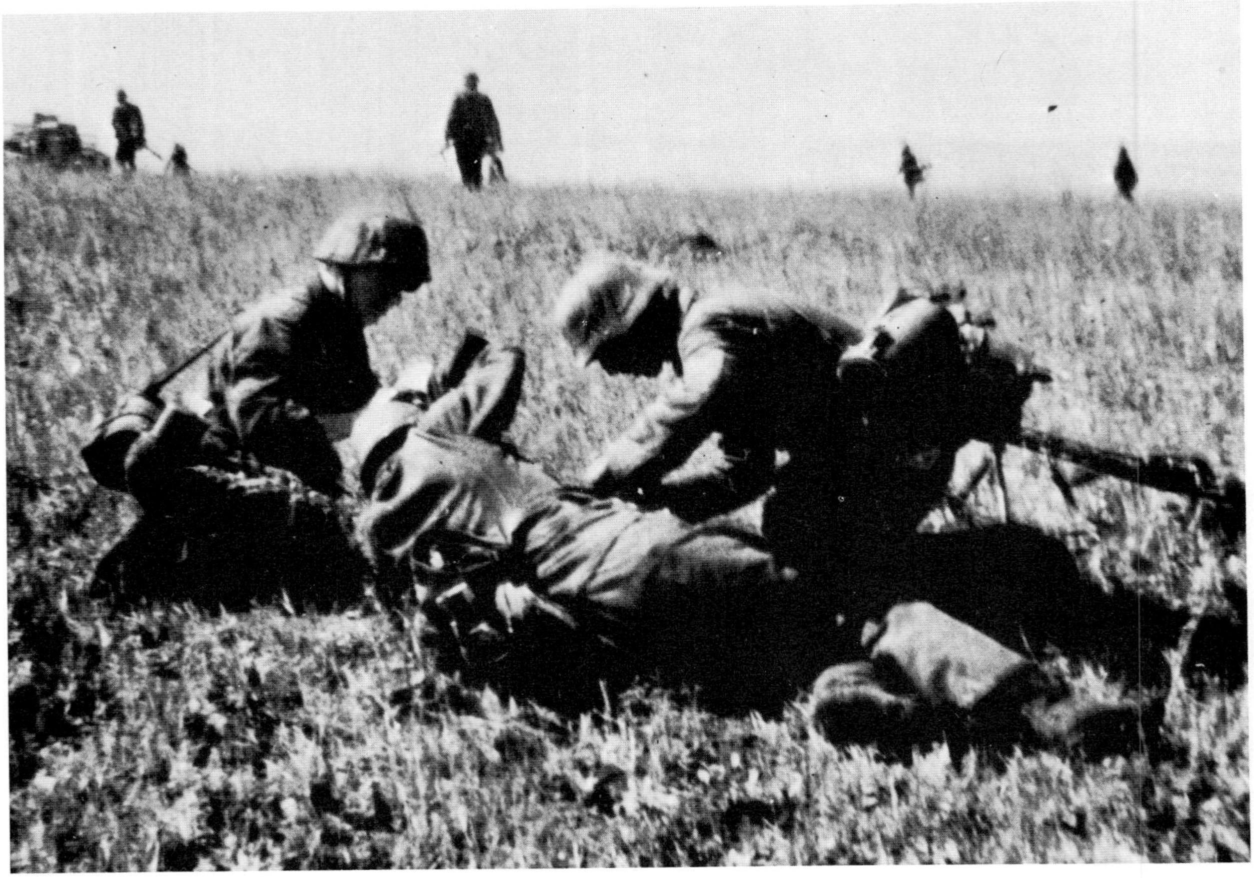

The resistance of the Red Army stiffens and causes heavy losses. First aid for the injured soldiers on the battlefield.

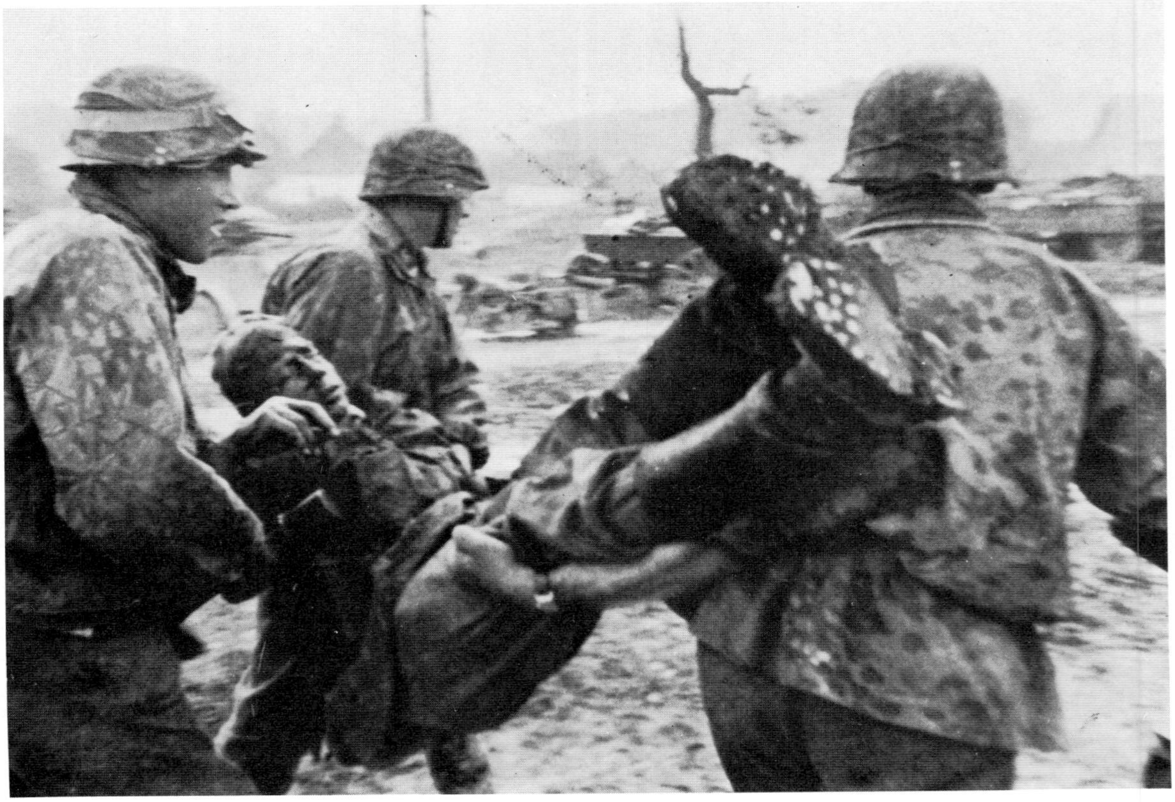

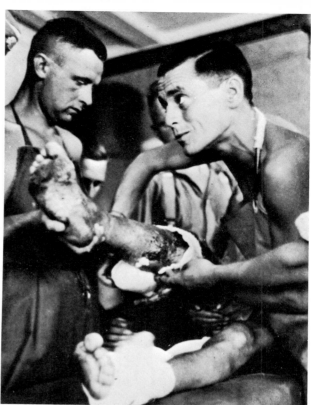

Medical treatment in the clearing station.

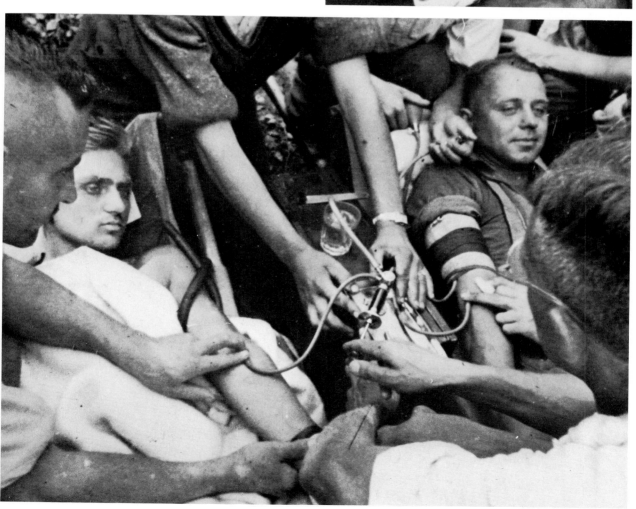

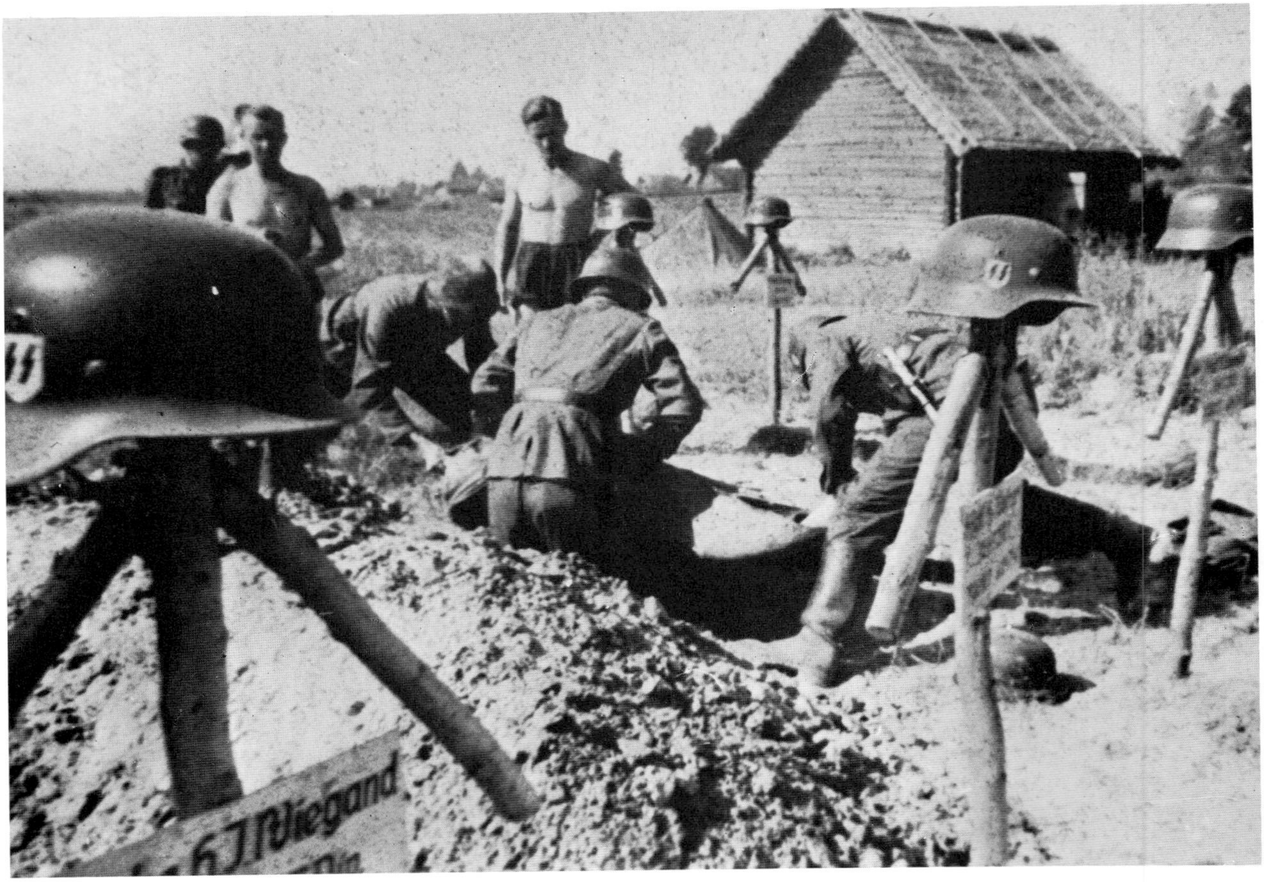
Wiegand

More and more men of the Waffen-SS are buried in Russian soil.

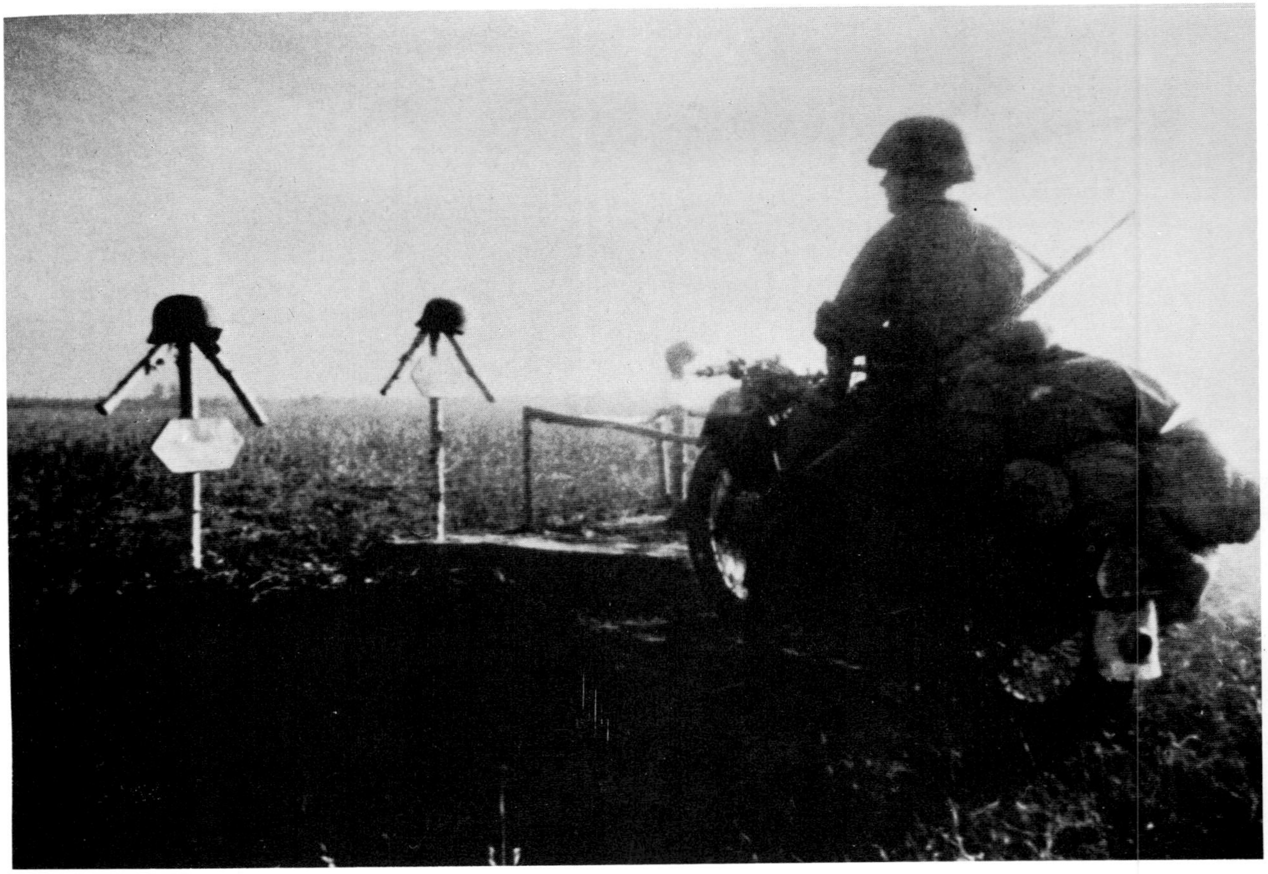

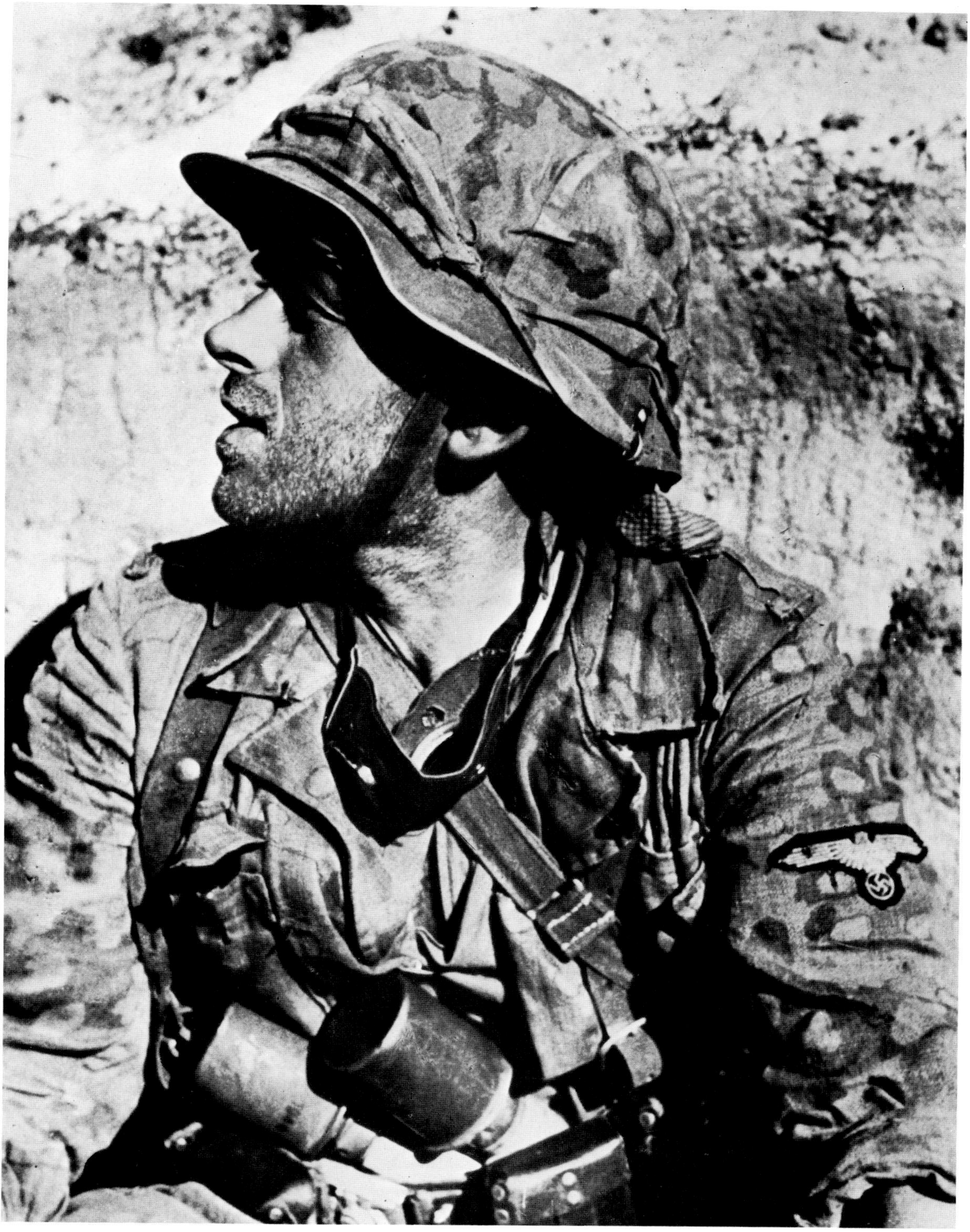

The brunt of the fight is carried by the Landser (doughboys), the legendary "Rottenführer" among them deserve special mention.

"The Rottenführer is the backbone of the Waffen-SS. Their number and their mission is to be kept absolutely secret".

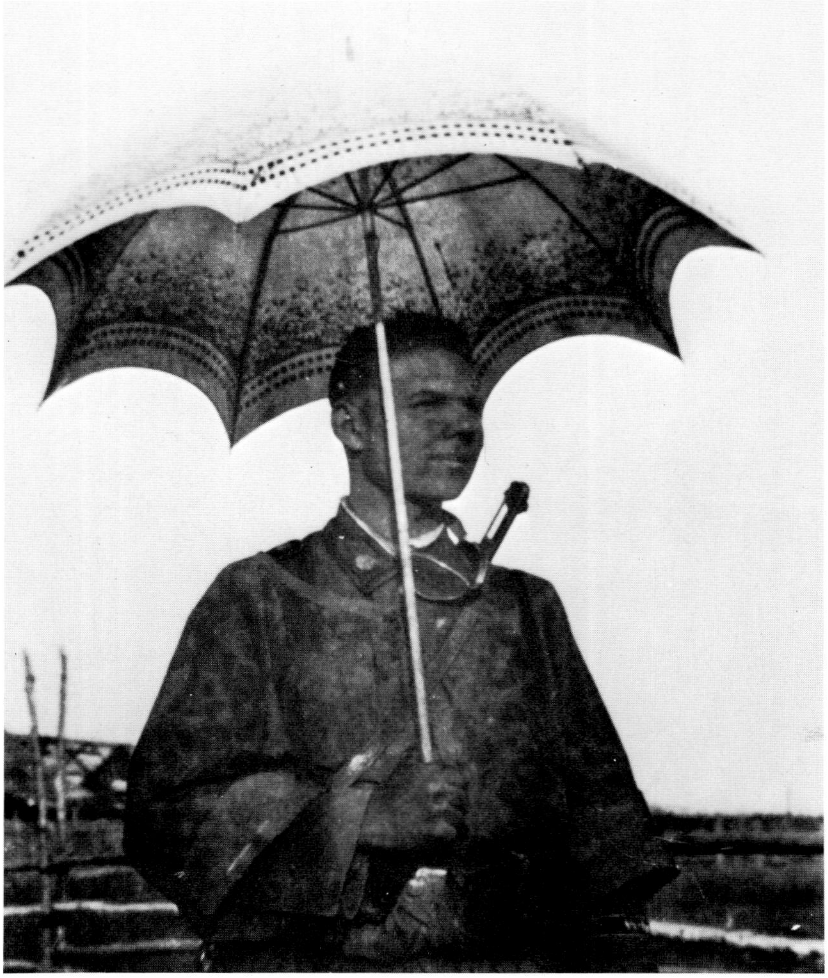

As the heavy rain begins to fall, men and vehicles are engaged to their maximum extent. The advance slows down.

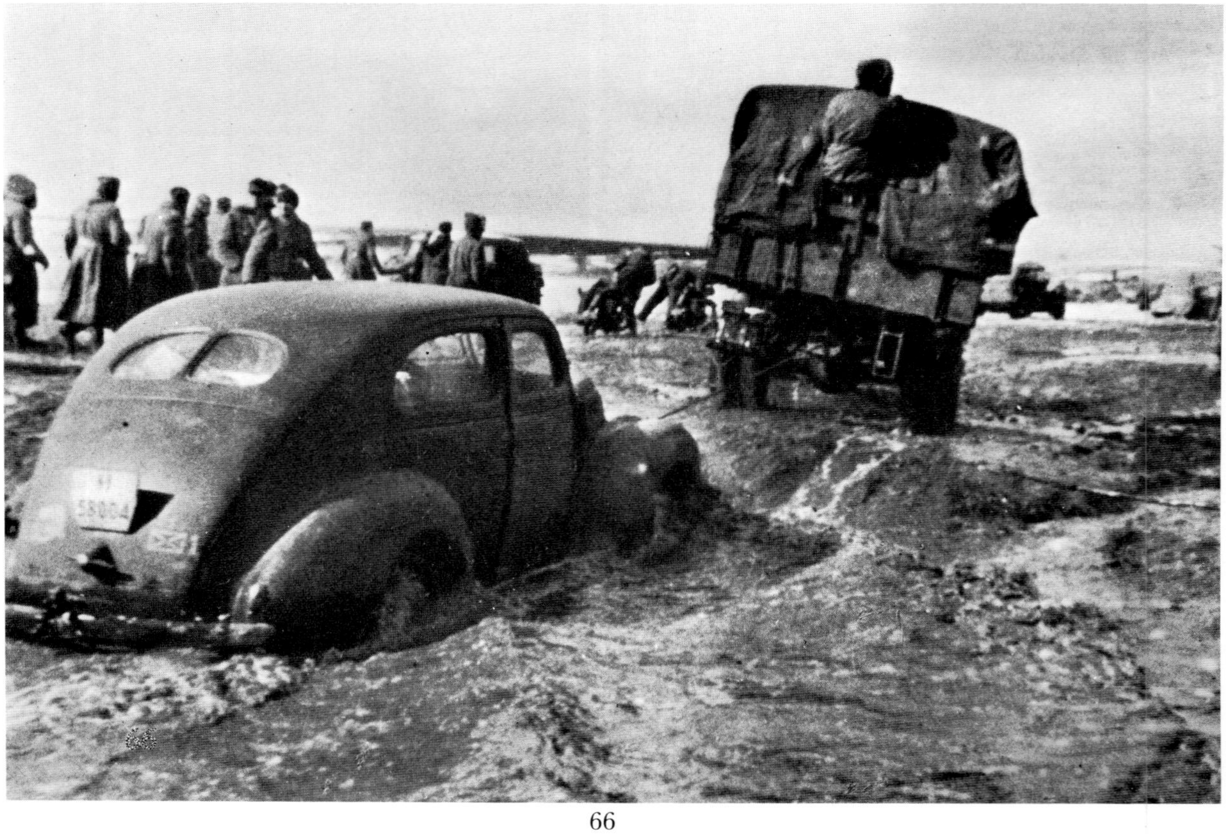

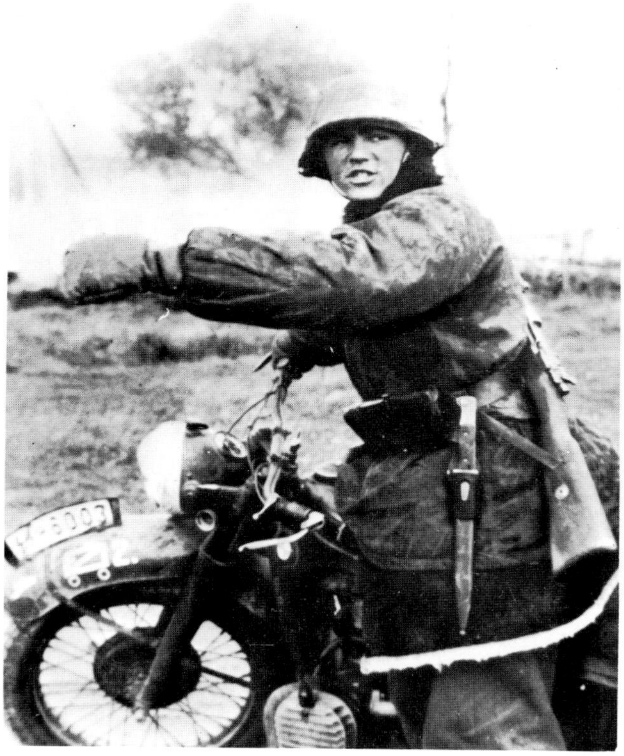

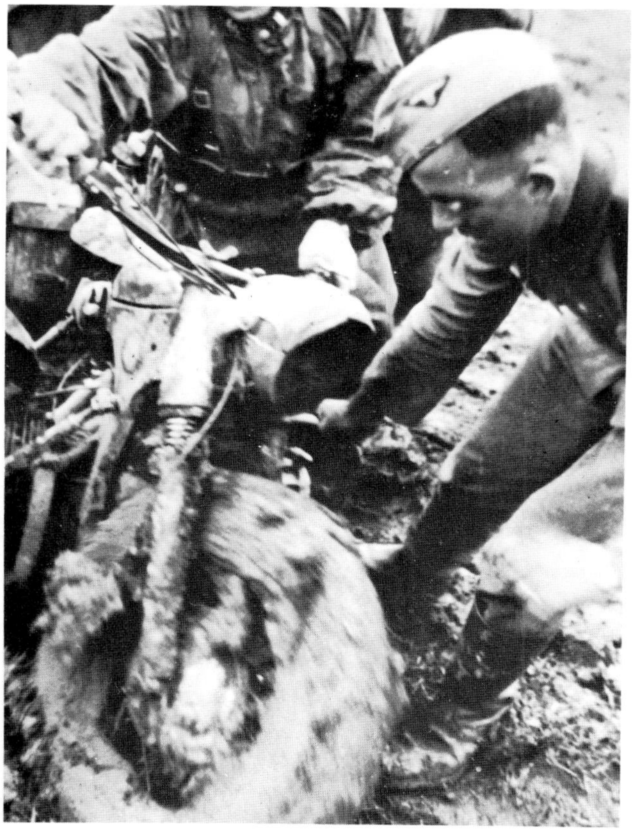

Motorcyclists especially suffered from the disastrous weather.

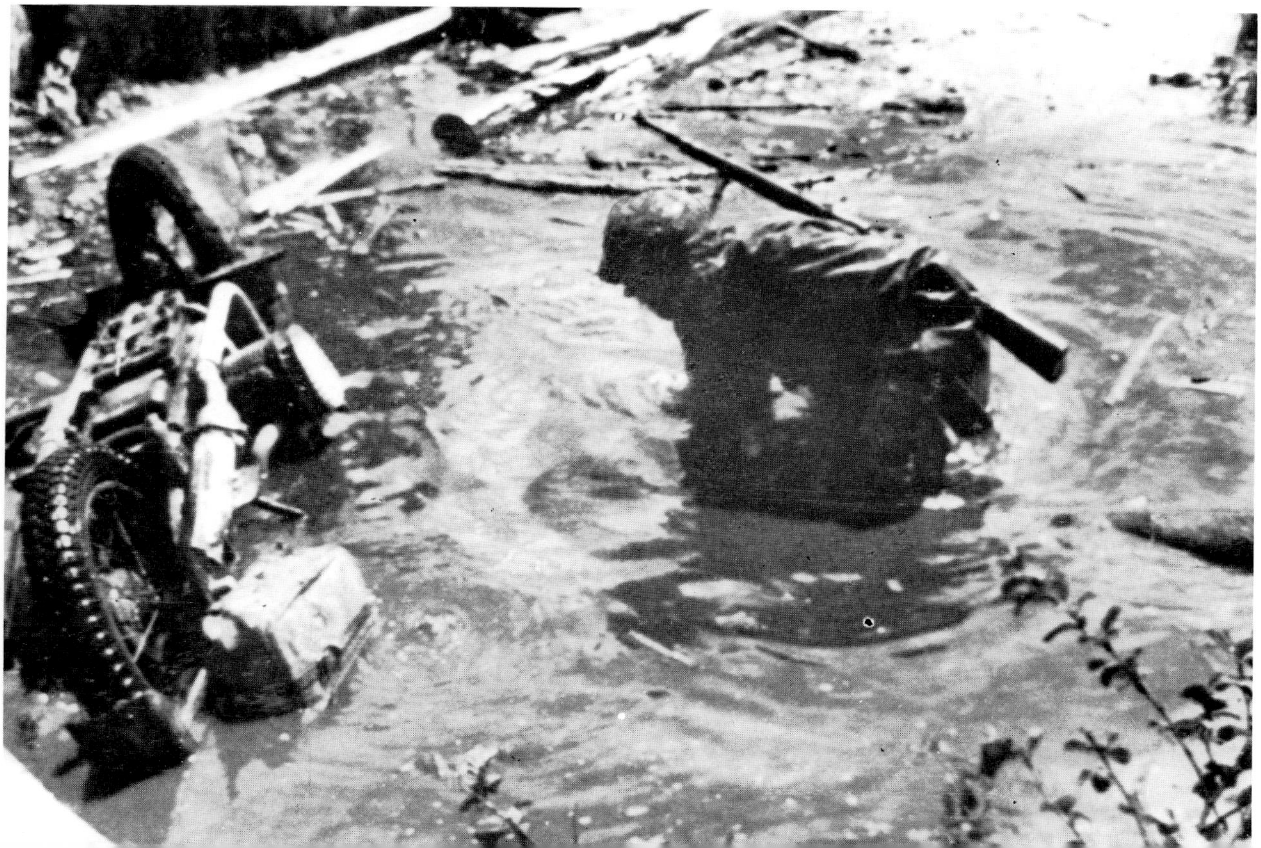

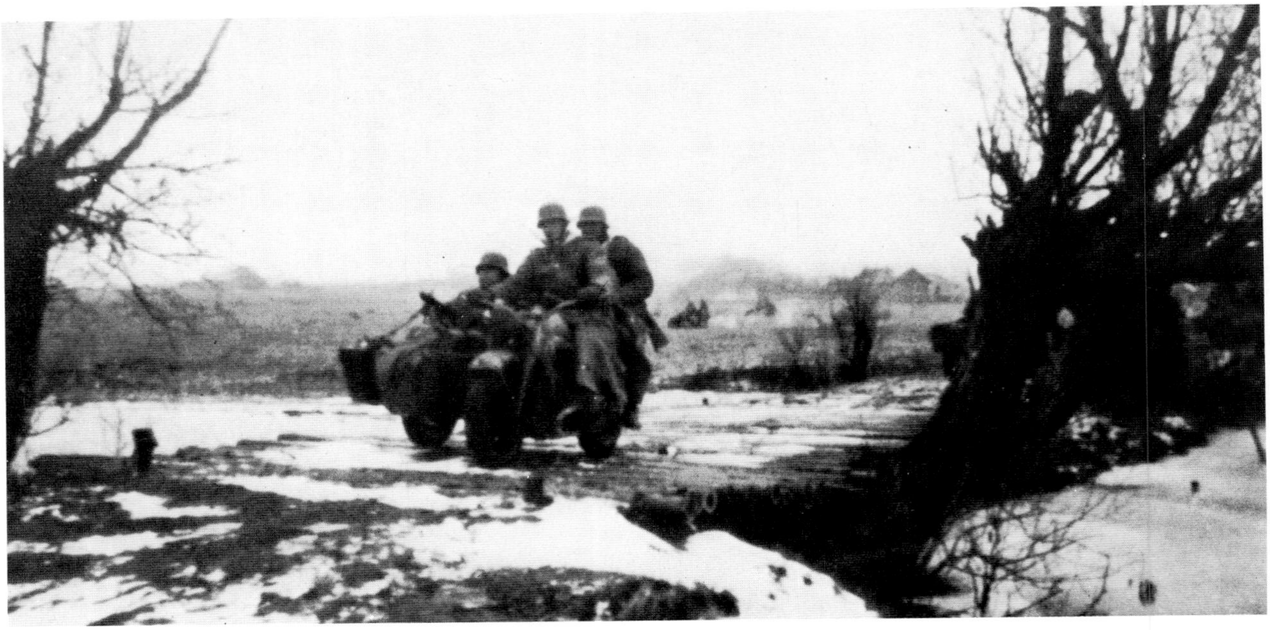

An early winter surprises the unprepared troops and insufficient winter equipment forces the men to improvise.

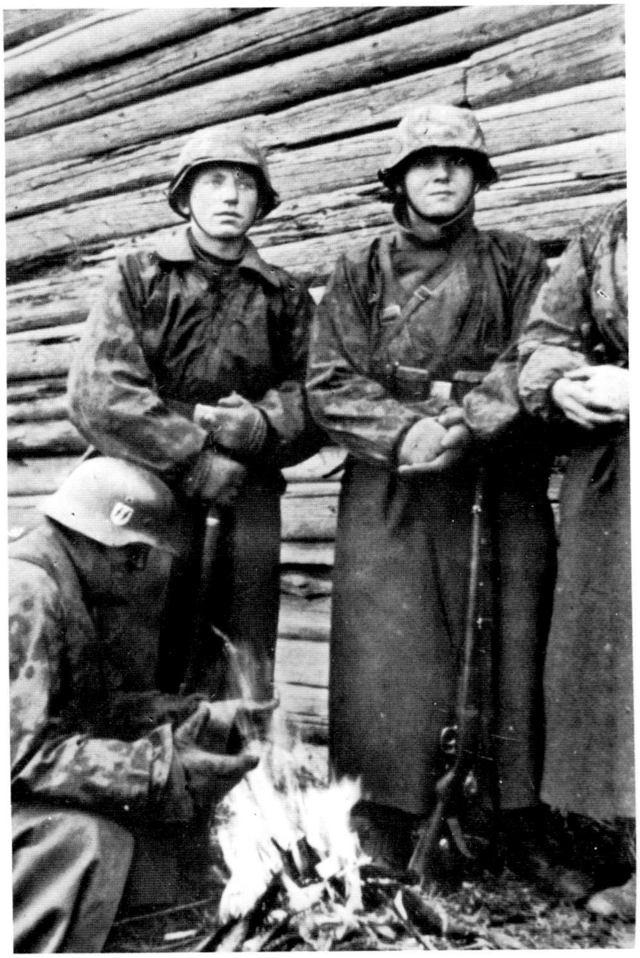

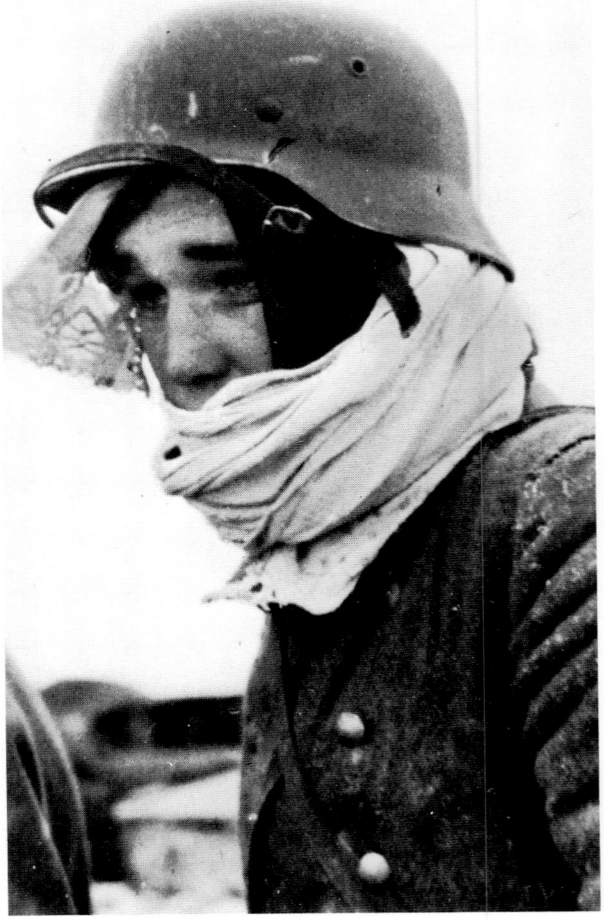

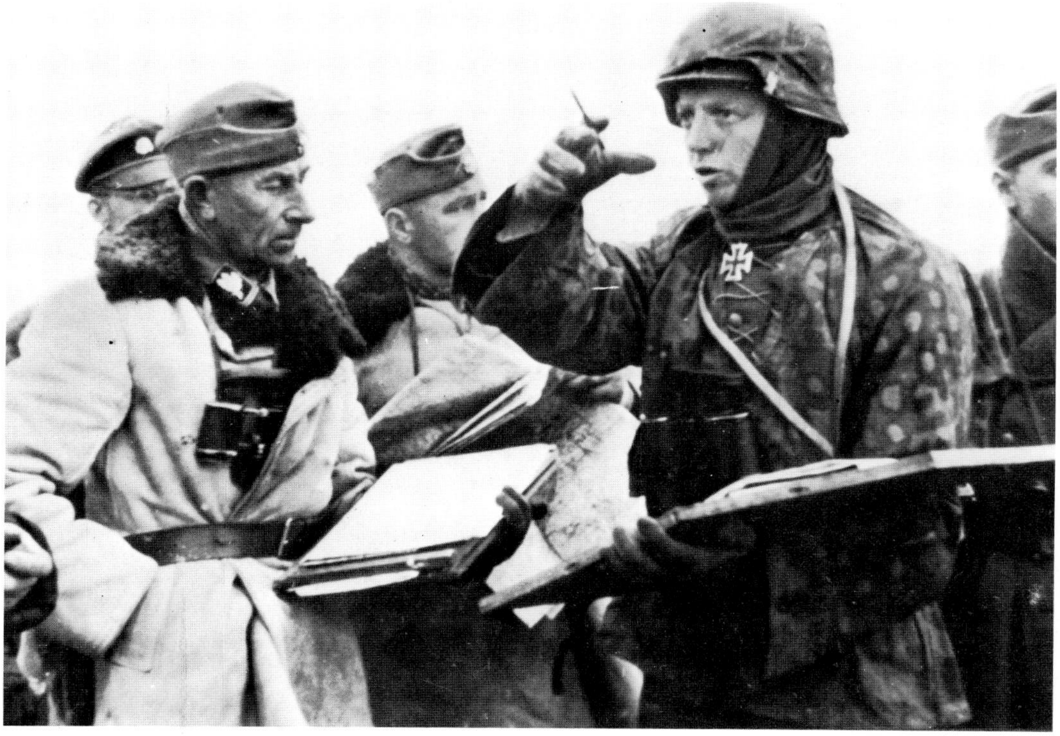

Lt. General Hausser, Lt. Colonel Ostendorff, Captain Klingenberg give orders during the attack on Moscow.

Massive Russian counterattacks on Army Group Center stop the advance. This causes the army to retreat to an unfavorable defensive position.

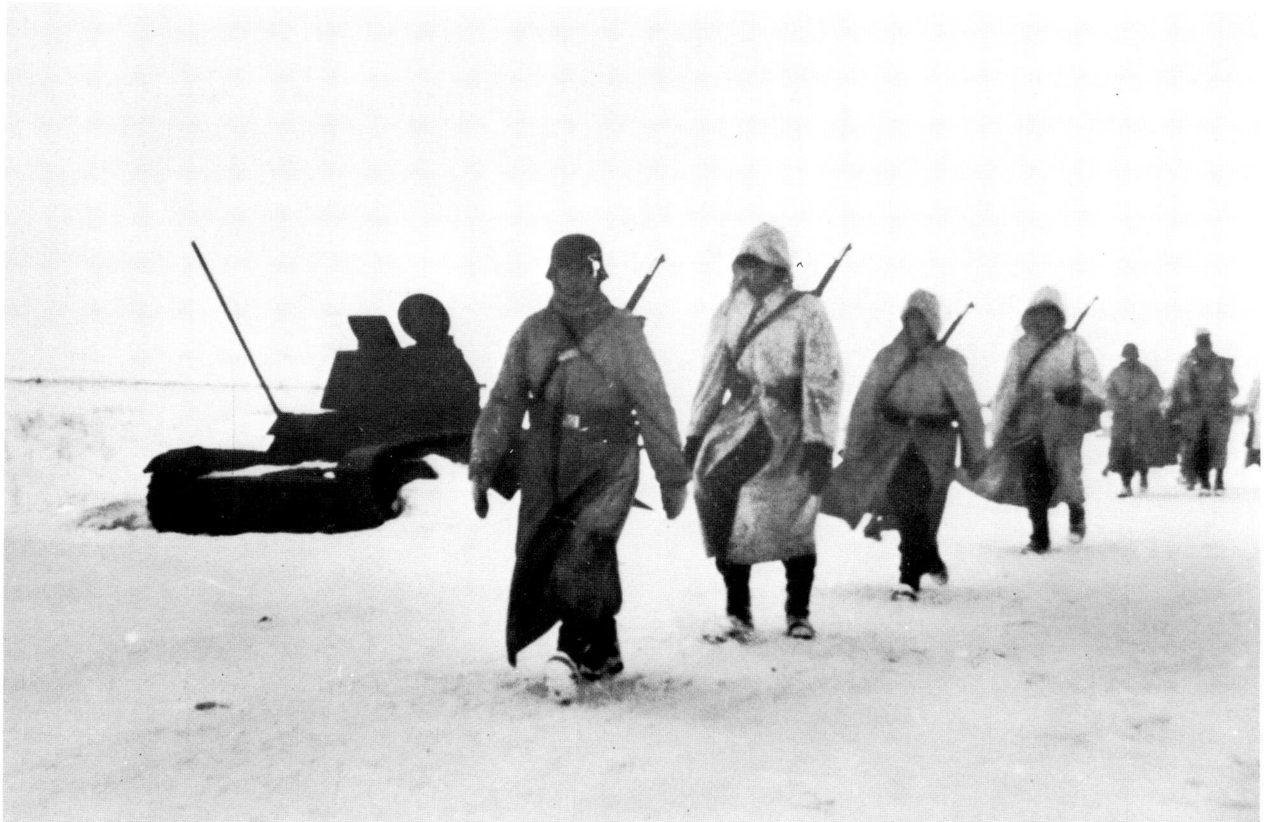

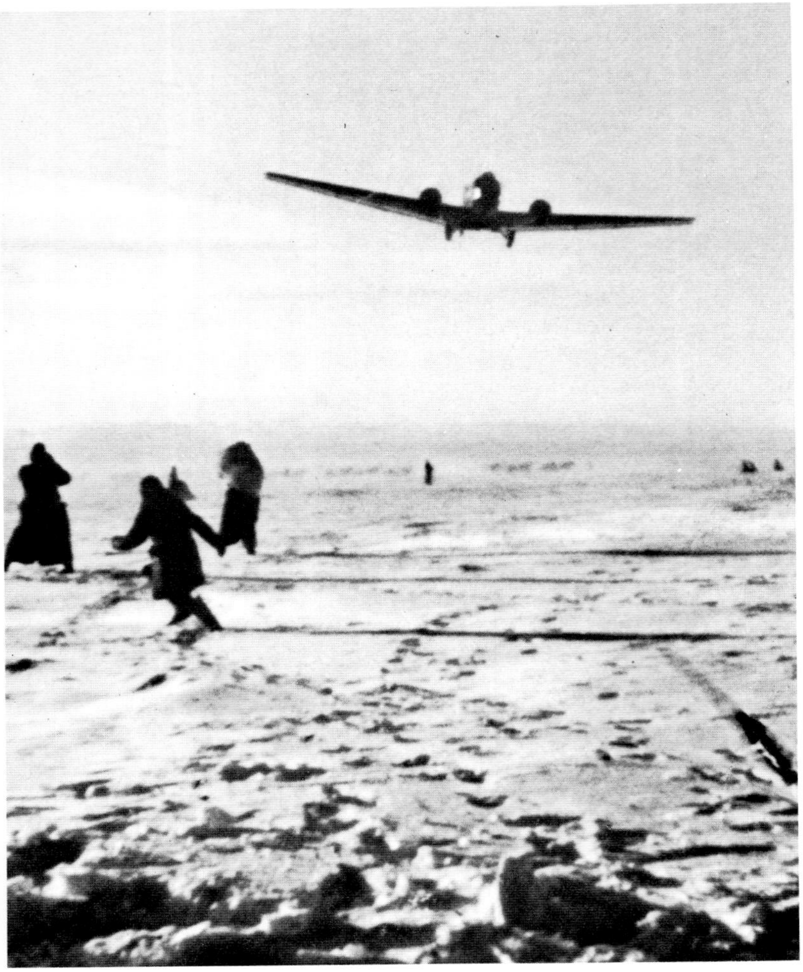

The supply problem is getting worse-as in Demjansk, encircled troops have to be supplied by air drops. The peak of the winter 1941/42: Heavy defensive battles all along the overextended and numerously penetrated front line demands the complete engagement and fighting energy of the German soldier.

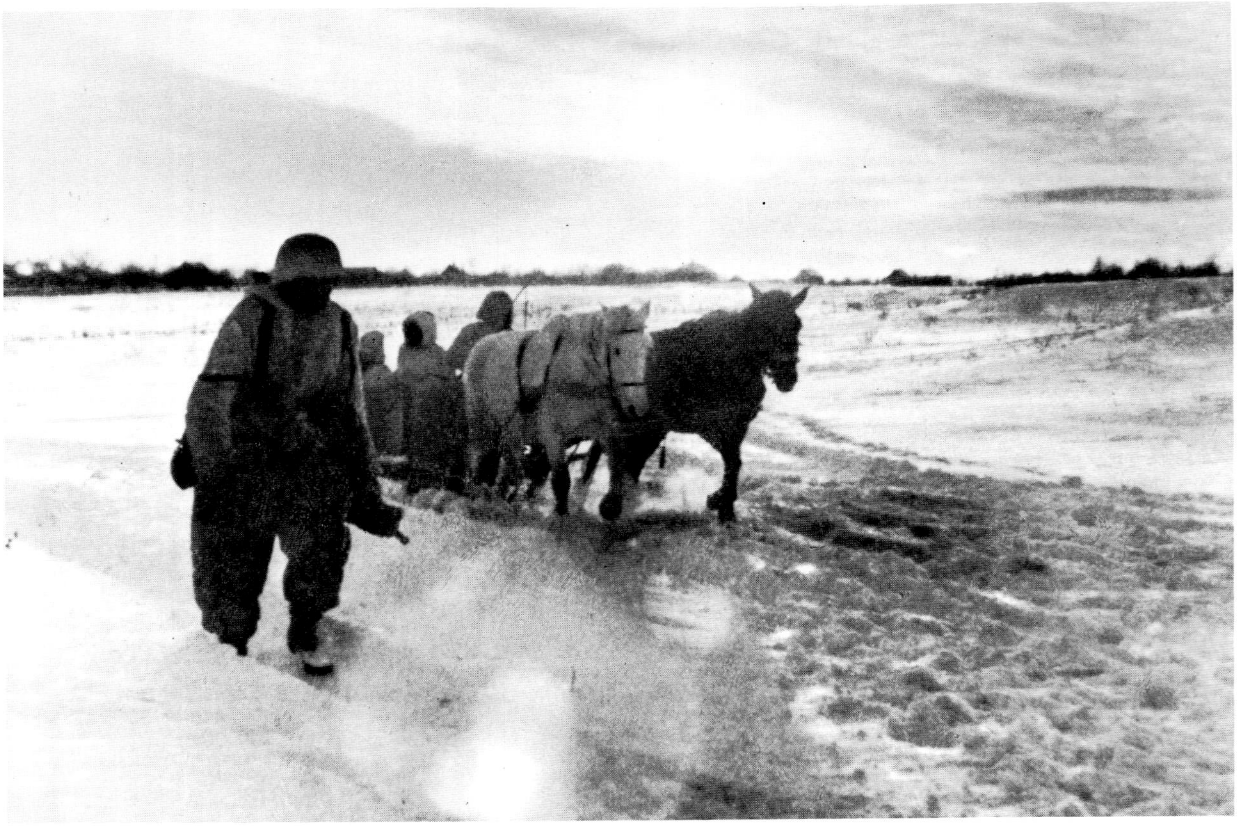

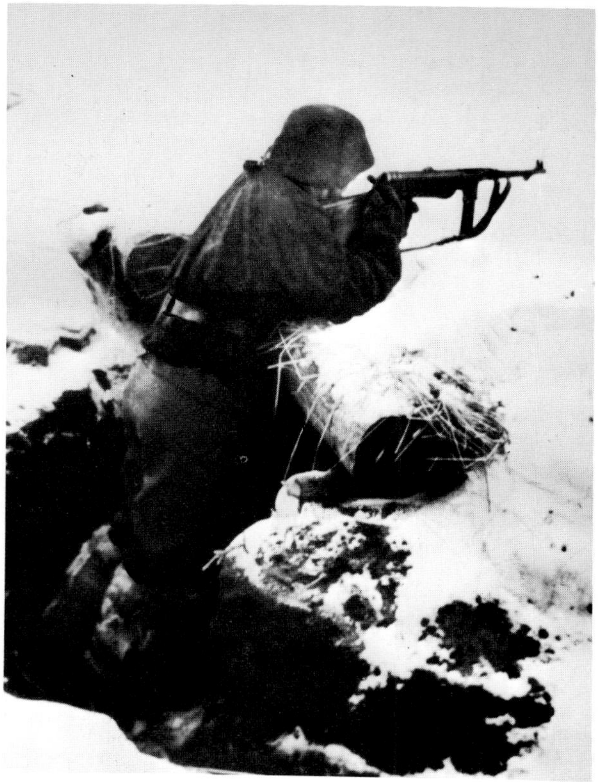

Divisions of the Red Army thrust into the bogged down German attack. The Soviet soldiers who had tried to throw back the German invaders now threaten to destroy Army Group Center.

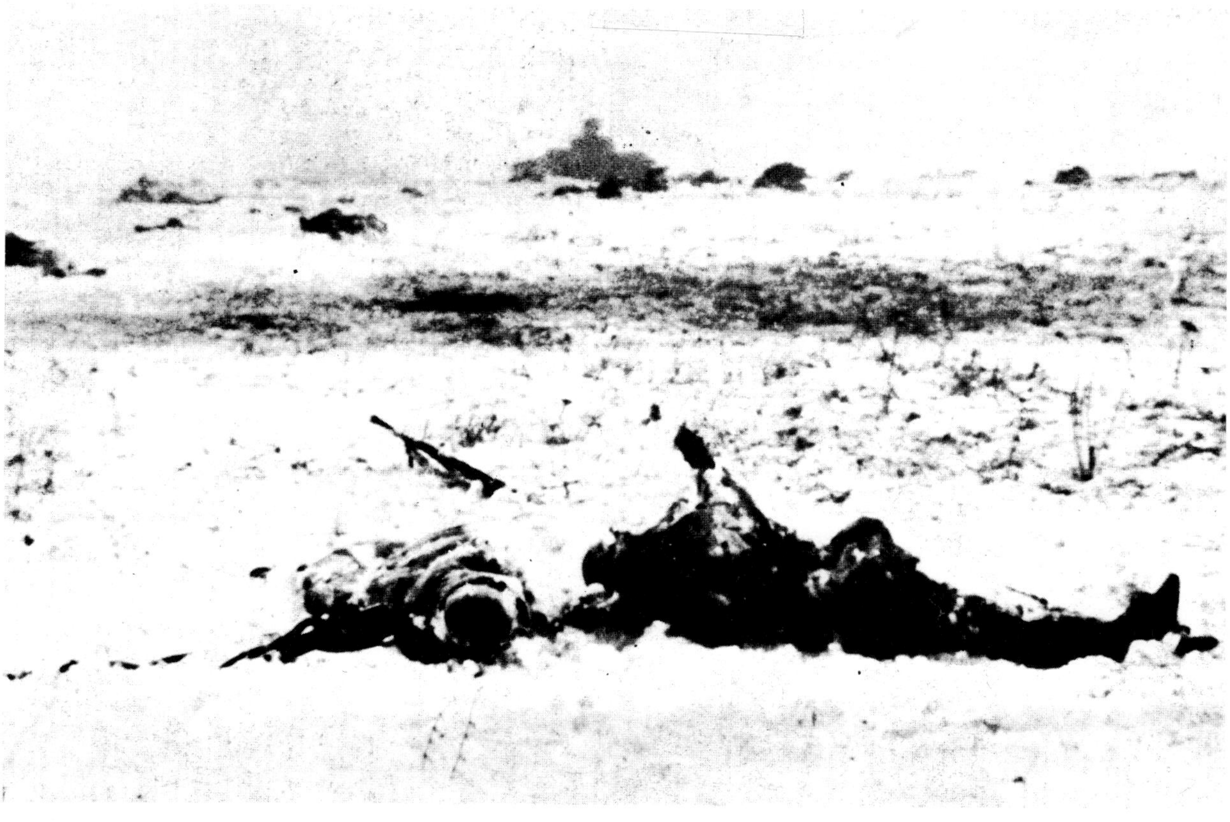

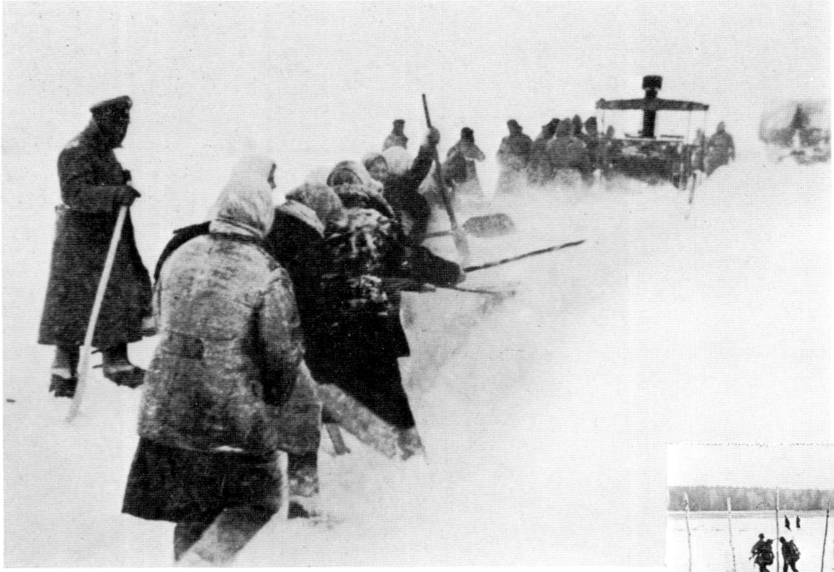

Russian civilians are employed to clear supply routes.

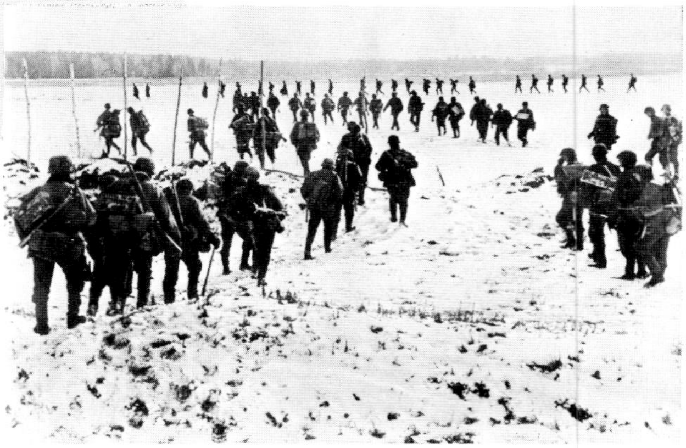

Counterattack over a frozen lake in the northern sector of the eastern front.

Improvised transport of a 37 mm anti-aircraft gun on a sleigh.

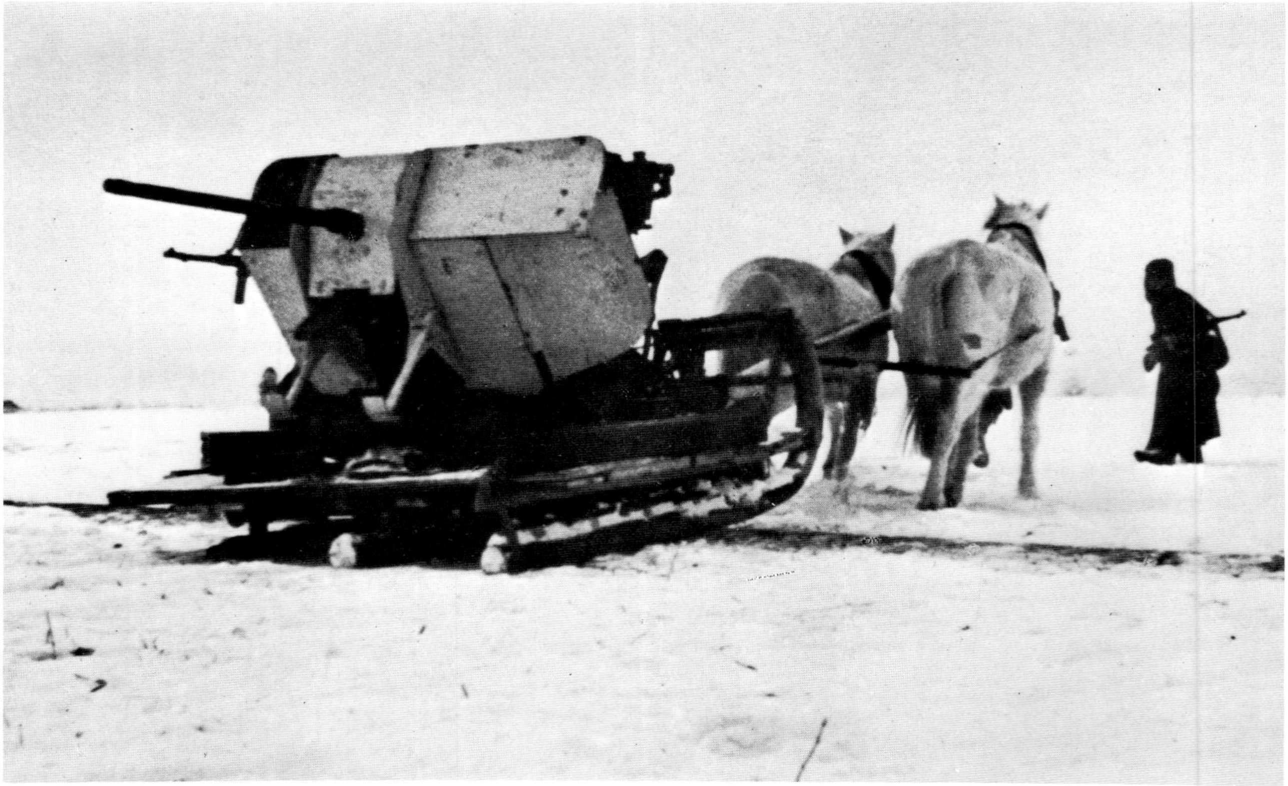

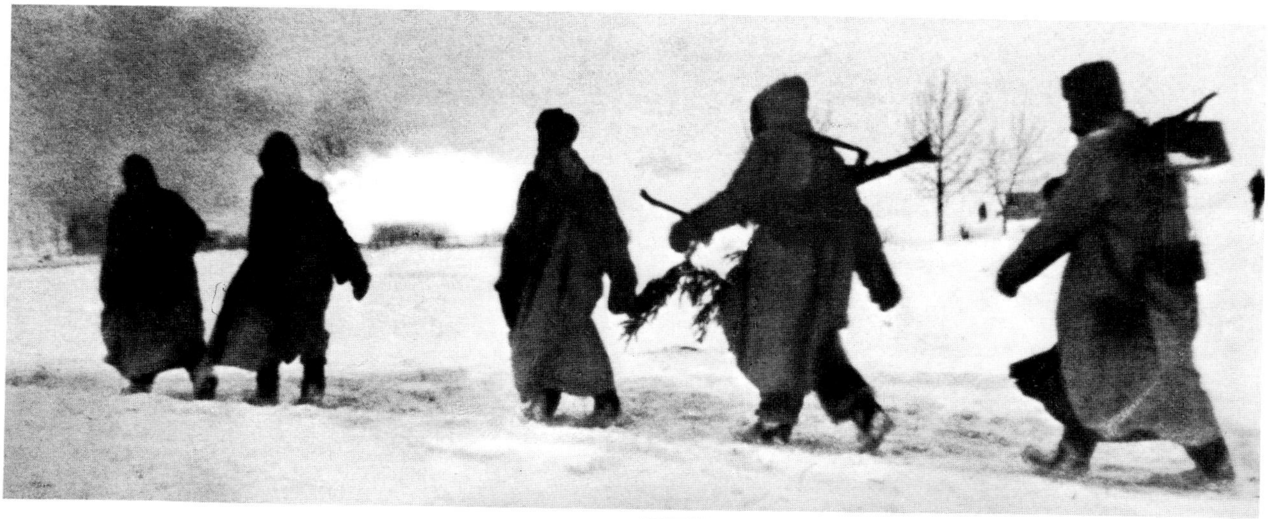

Two Russian weapons, certainly remembered by everyone who fought in Russia: Tank T-34 and 76.2 mm anti-tank gun, called "Ratsch-Bumm".

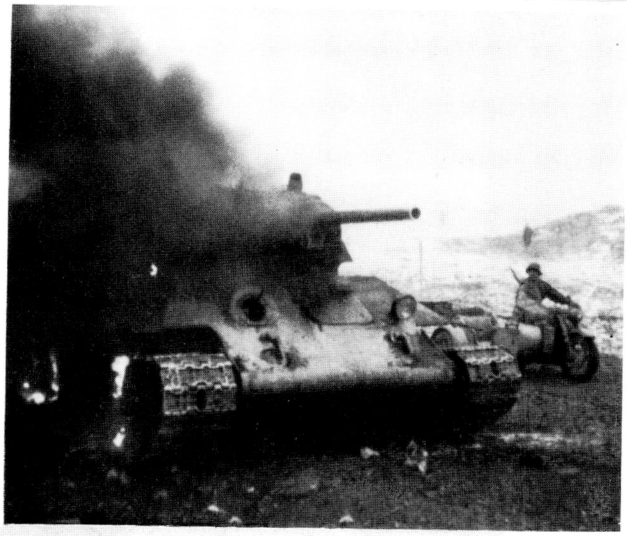

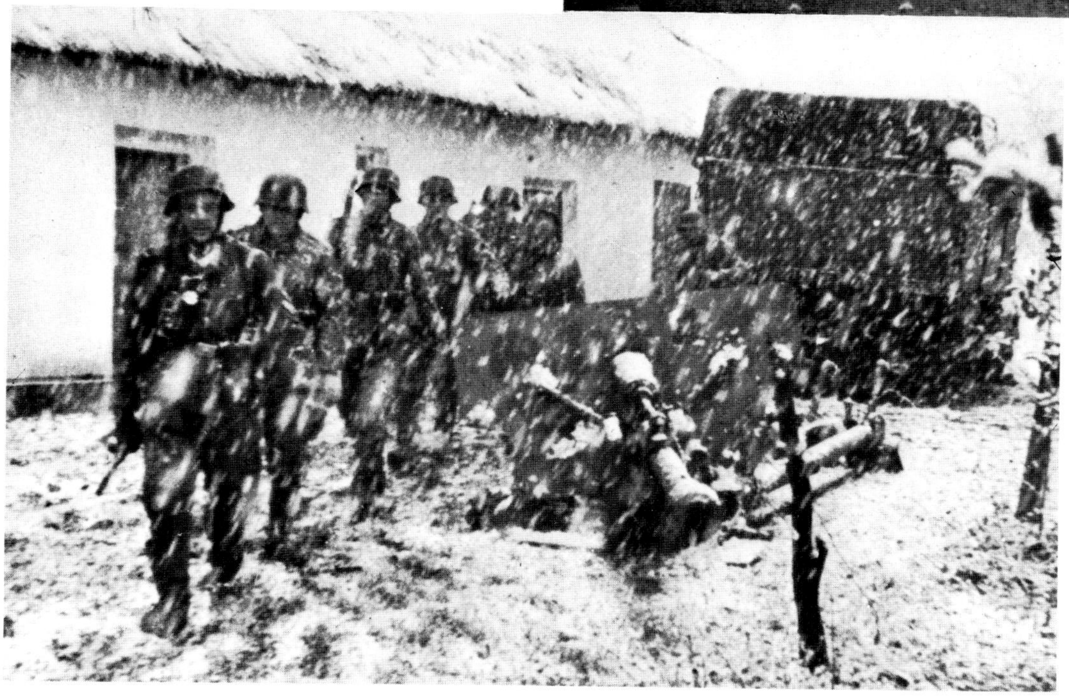

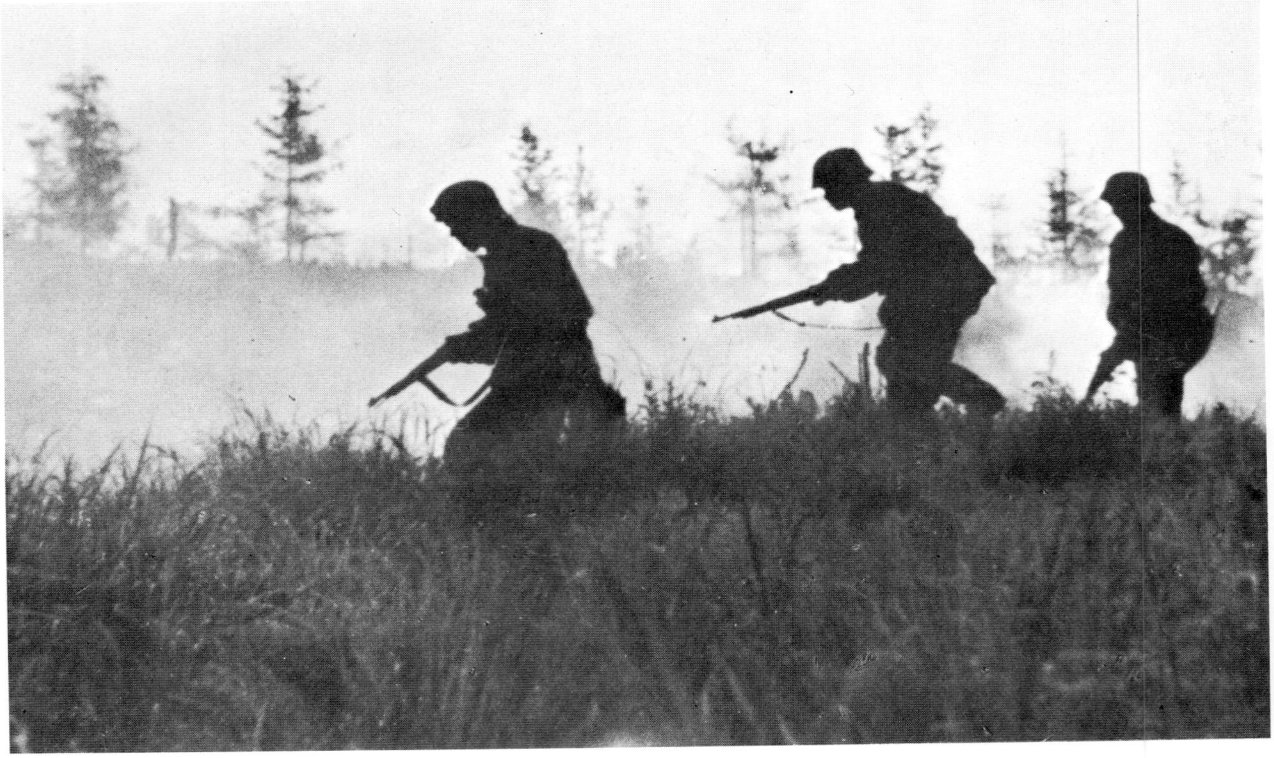

At the Wolchow River in the northern sector of the eastern front, the war has a "special face".

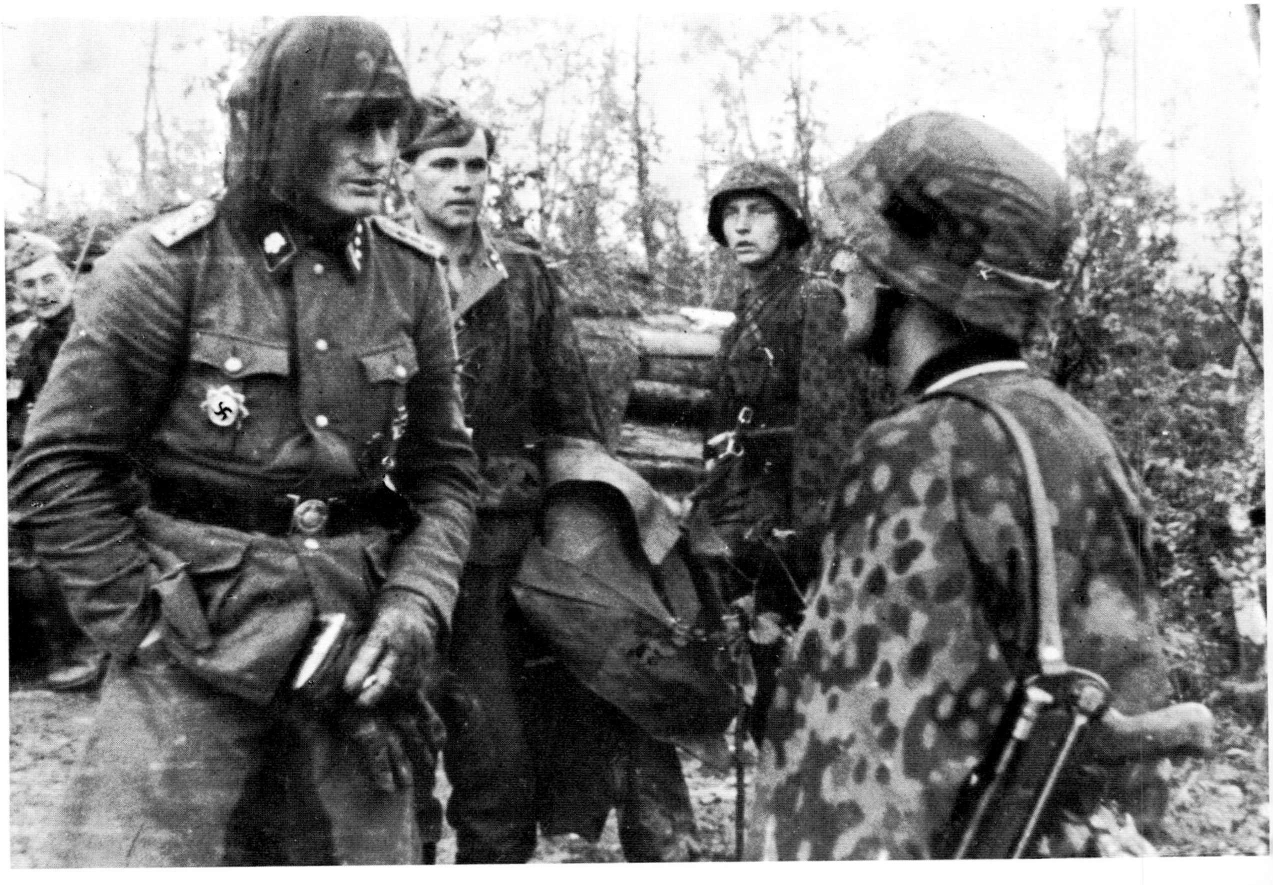

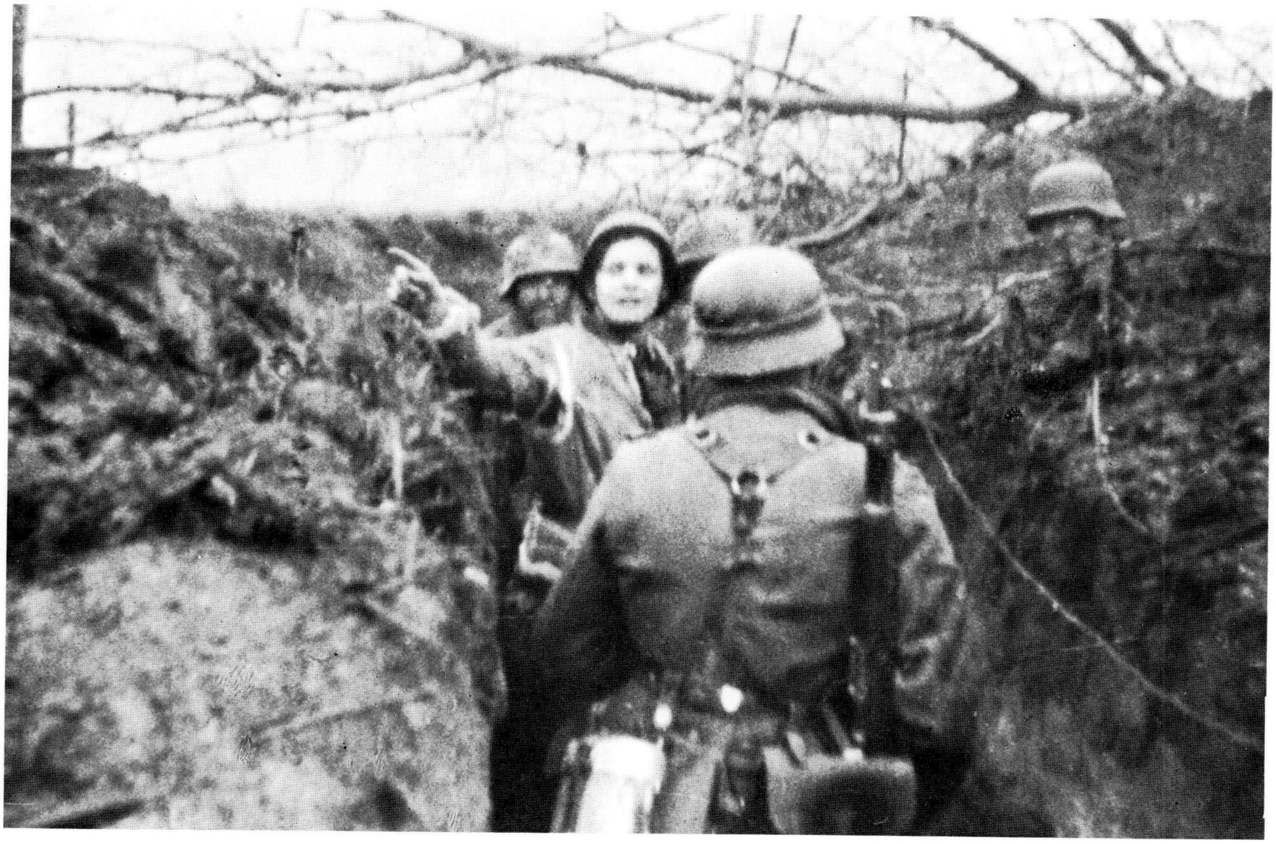

Deep trench systems, holes and log-roads in these forests and swamps are characteristic of the condition under which the defensive battles were fought.

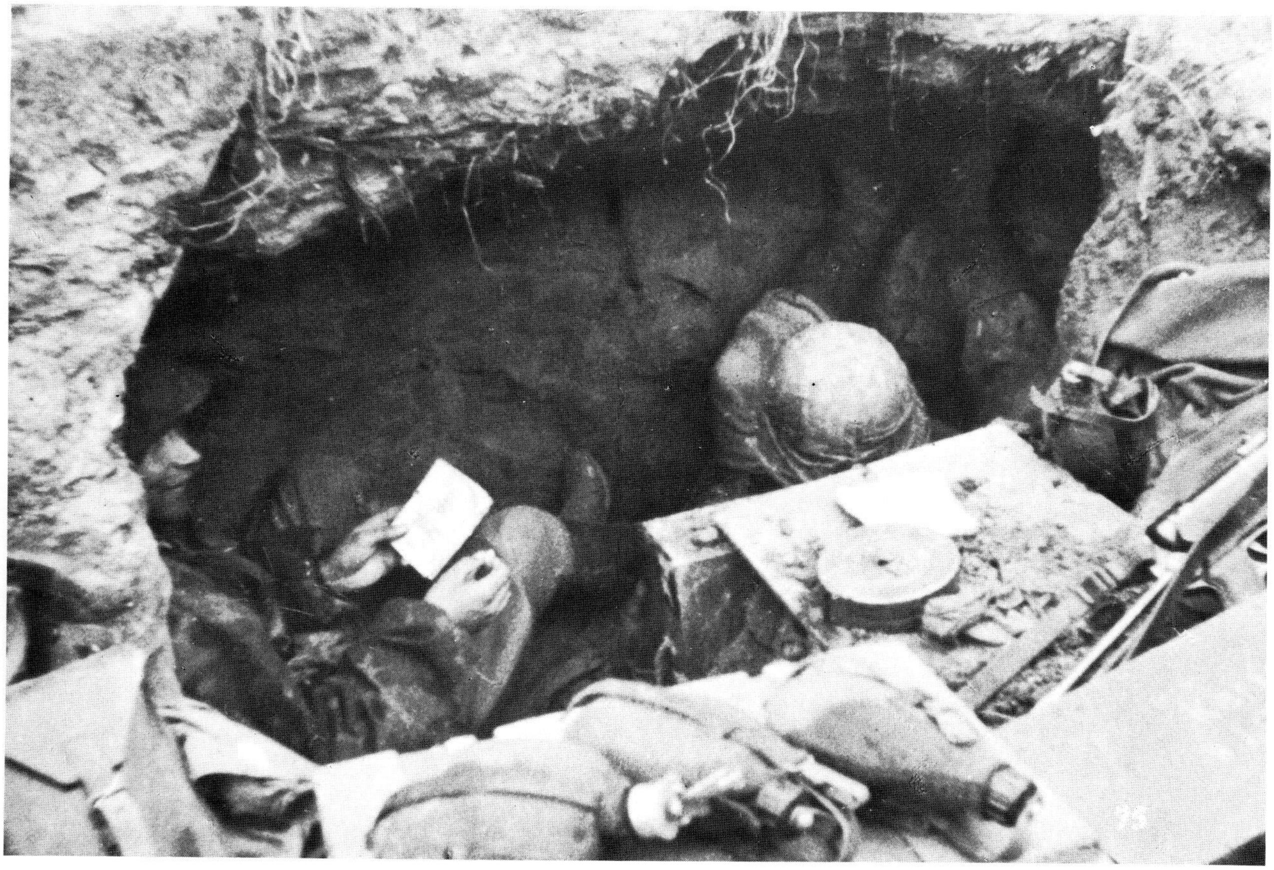

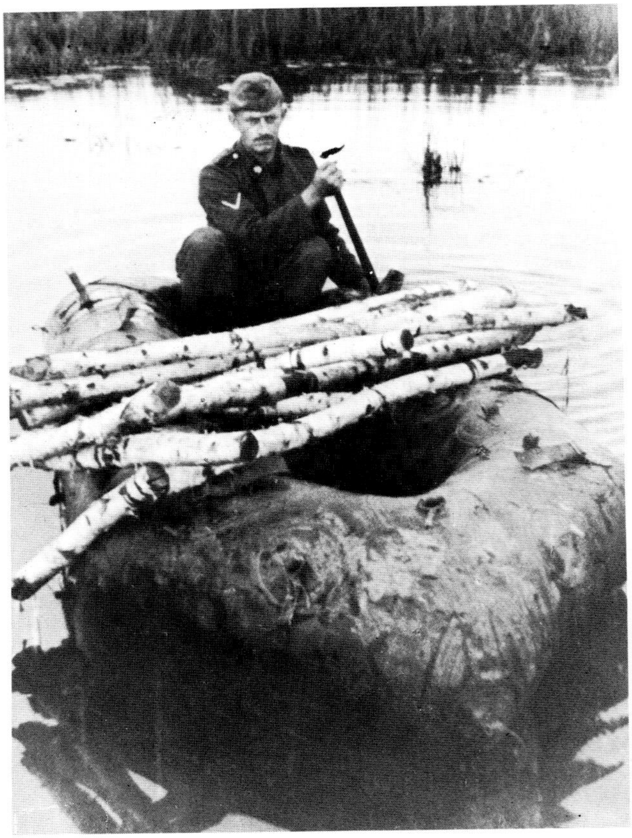

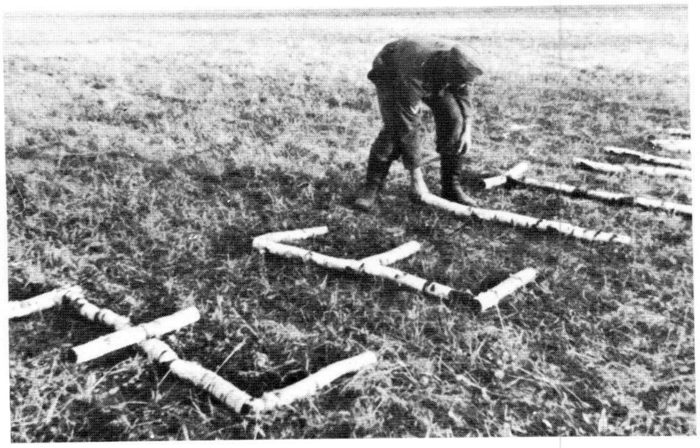

"Another supply problem": Newspapers from home are delivered by Ju 52 cargo planes.

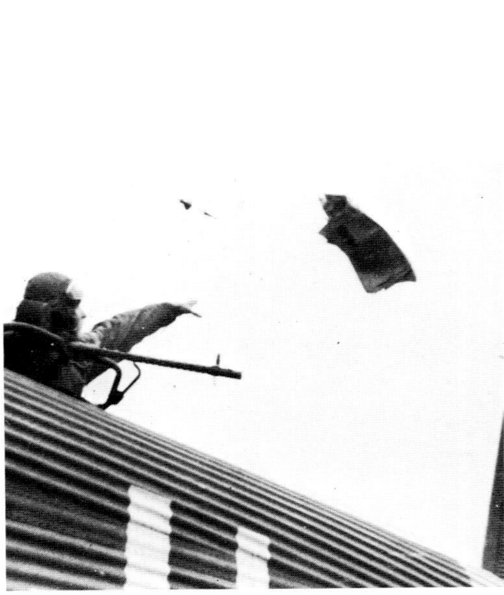

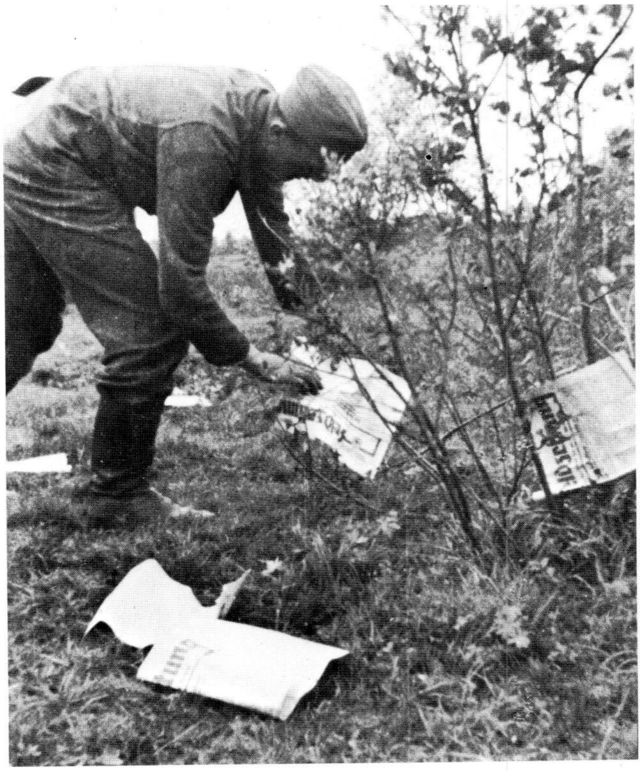

Major Otto Kron of the T-Division at a conference with army officers.

"Wire rope performance" at the Wolchow River.

# THE OFFENSIVE IN THE SOUTH, 1942

After the drastic reverses in the winter of 1941-42, the German armies were ready for a new offensive in May of 1942. A Russian counterattack, aimed at the German preparations, ended on May 28 with the beating back of four enemy armies. After the retaking of Kharkov, Hitler decided, immeasurably overestimating his military potentialities, to have the two German armored armies attack to the east and southeast—two eccentric directions. To be sure, the oil region of Maikop was gained, but further advances suffered from a lack of supplies, especially a lack of fuel. Here the German troops did not get any farther than Terek, staunchly defended by the Russians.

Army Group B had meanwhile fought its way forward in the direction of Stalingrad. The western edge of this fateful city was reached on August 25.

Here, as in the south, the offensive that had begun so spiritedly ended in bitter fighting against an enemy who had known how to escape any attempts at outflanking and surrounding during the German attacks, and who began to make determined counterattacks.

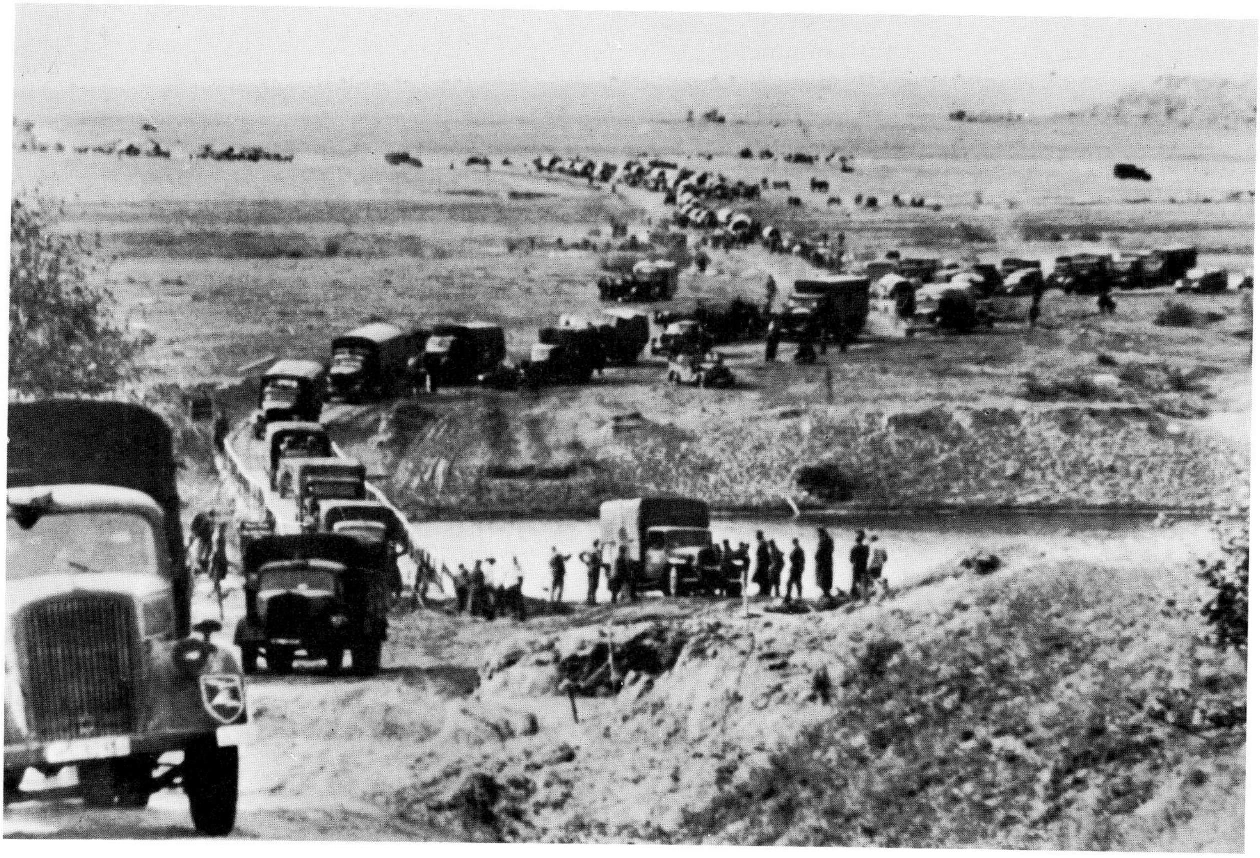

The great offensive in the south of Russia shall bring the decision.

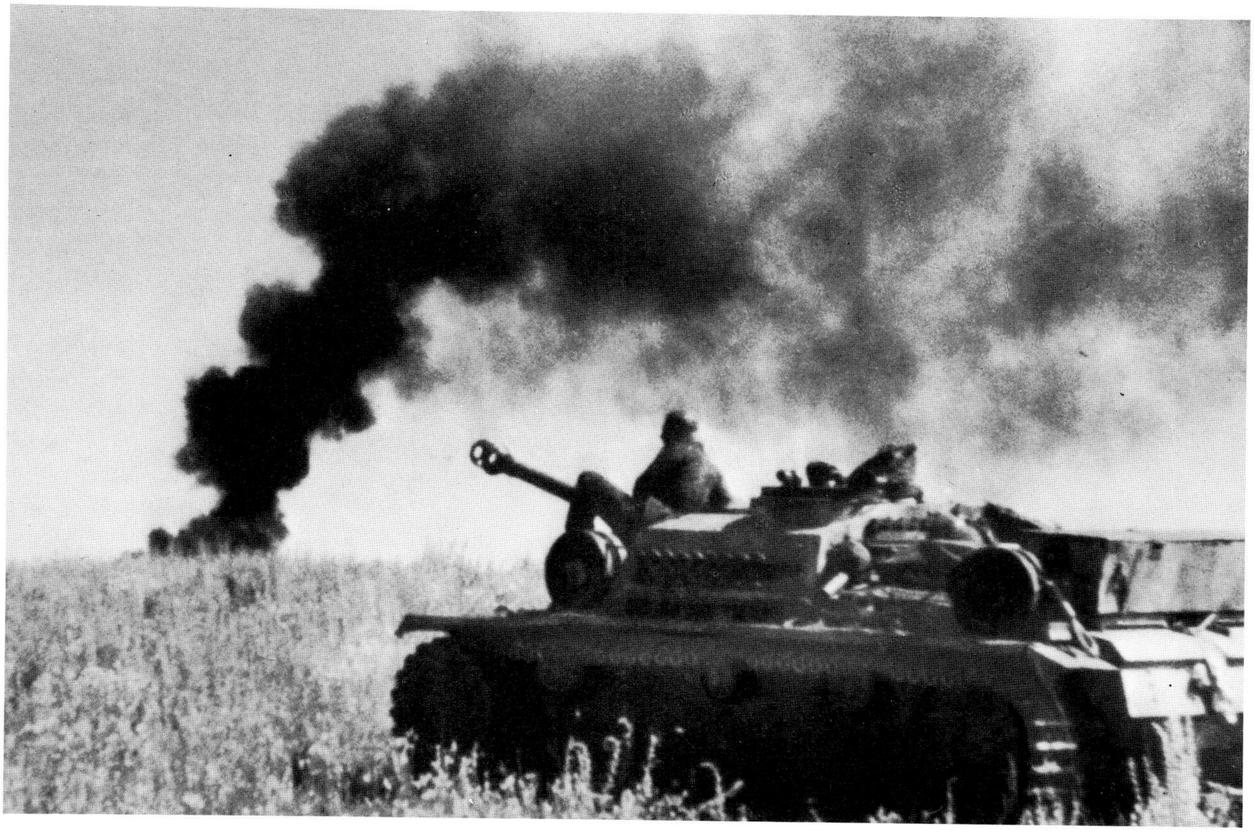

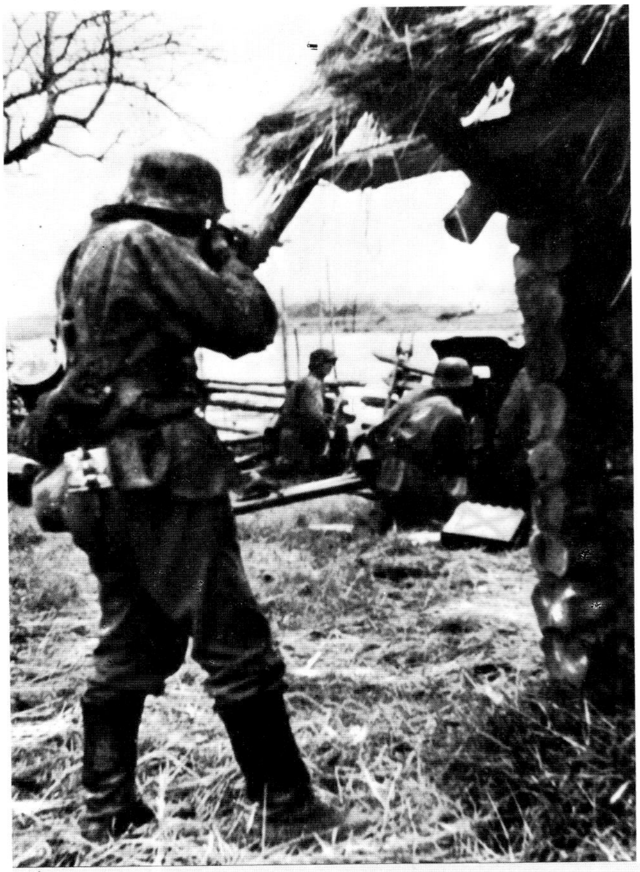

Again the advance is bogged down and must be pushed forward by infantry attacks.

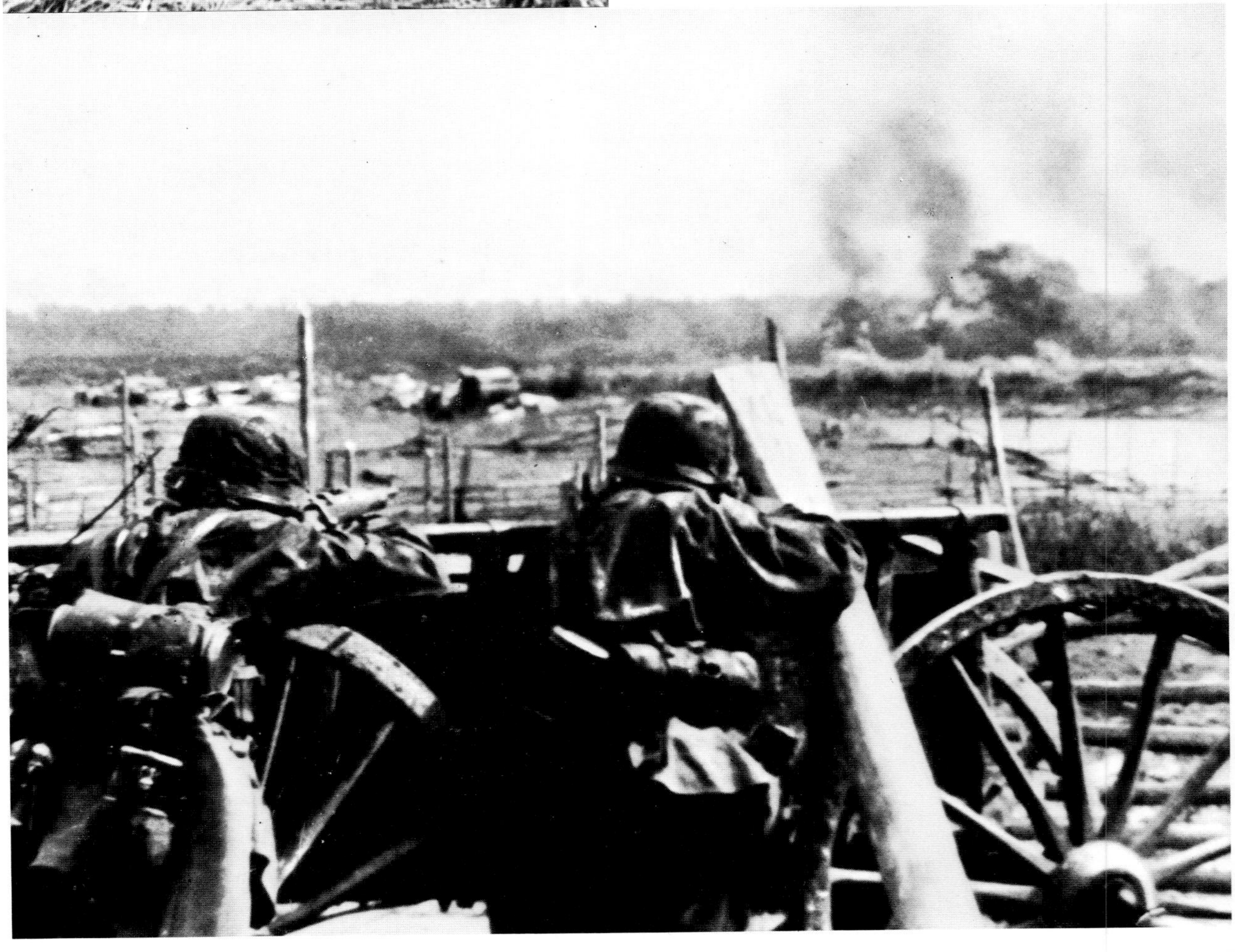

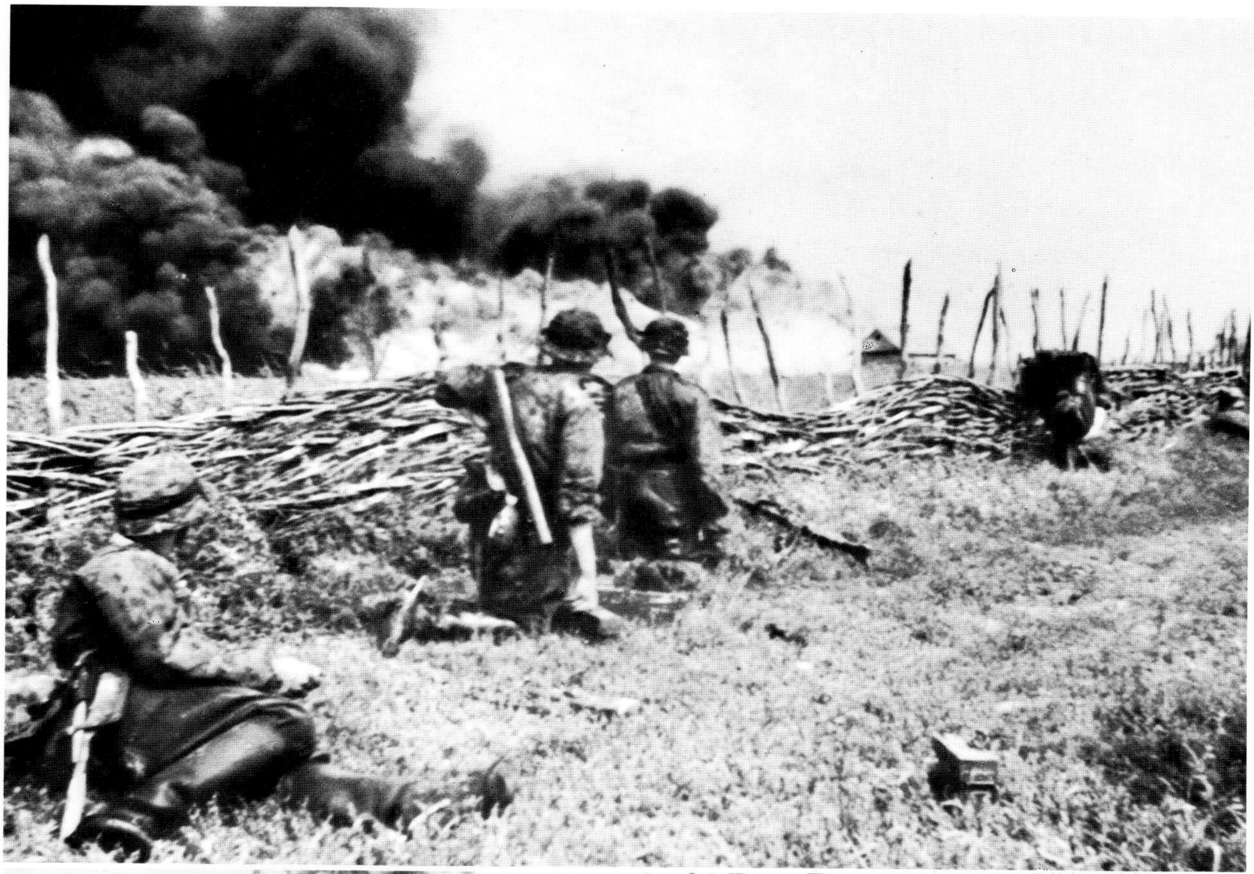

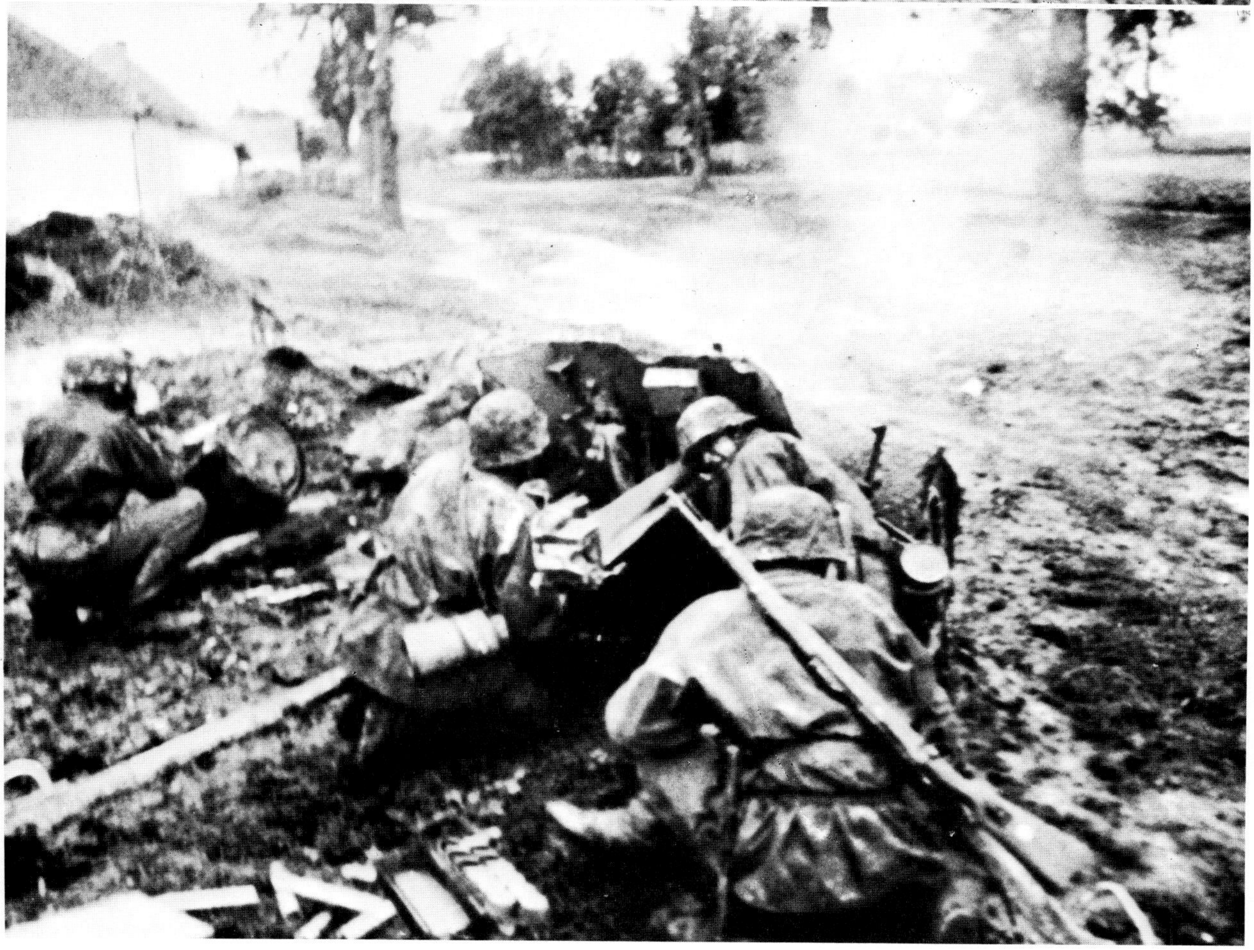

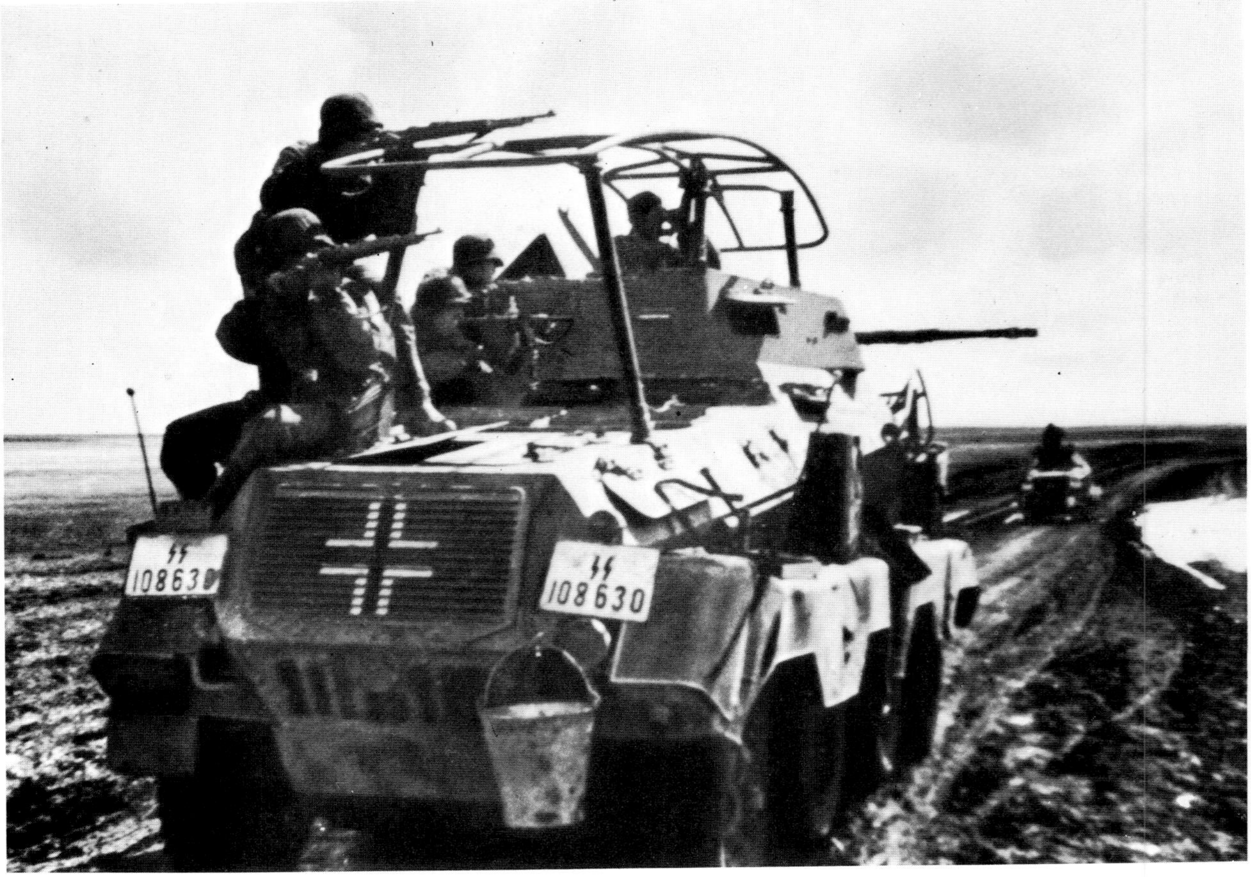
108630

Now, the motorized troops (here SS-Division "Wiking") advance, covering endless plains and rapidly seizing terrain further to the East.

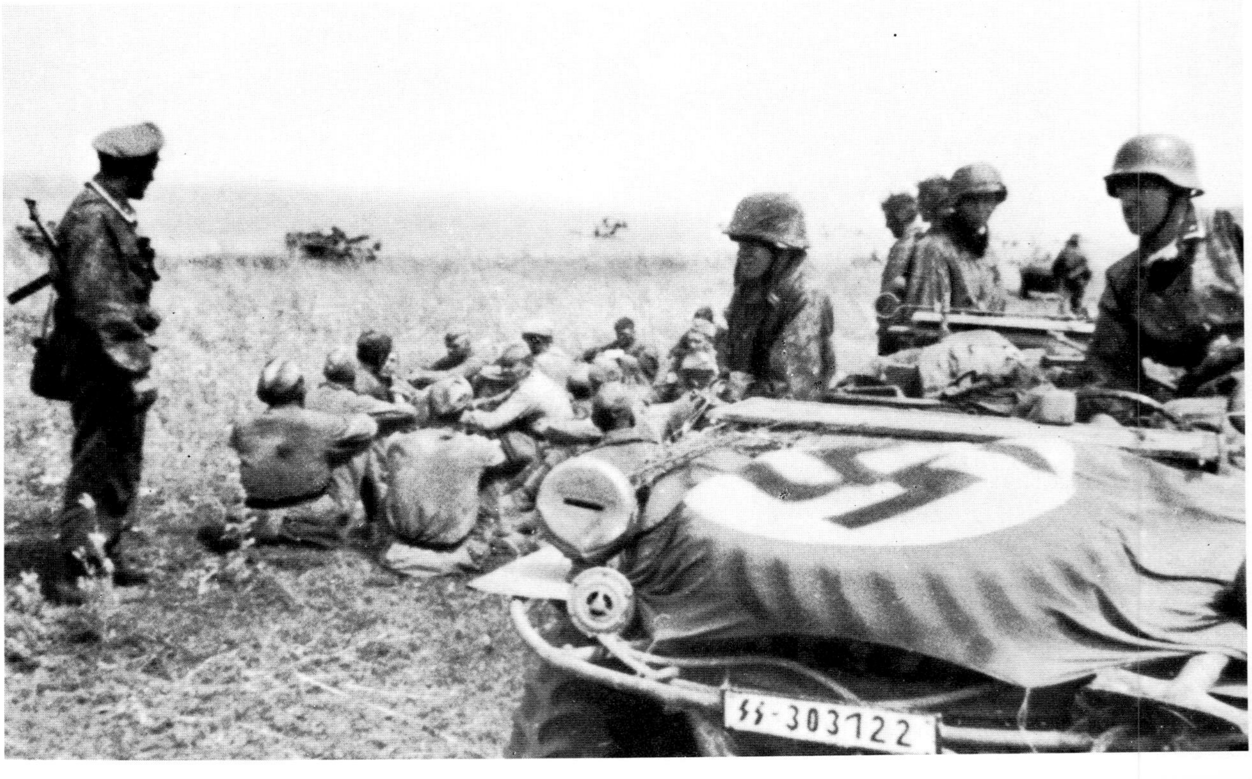
303122

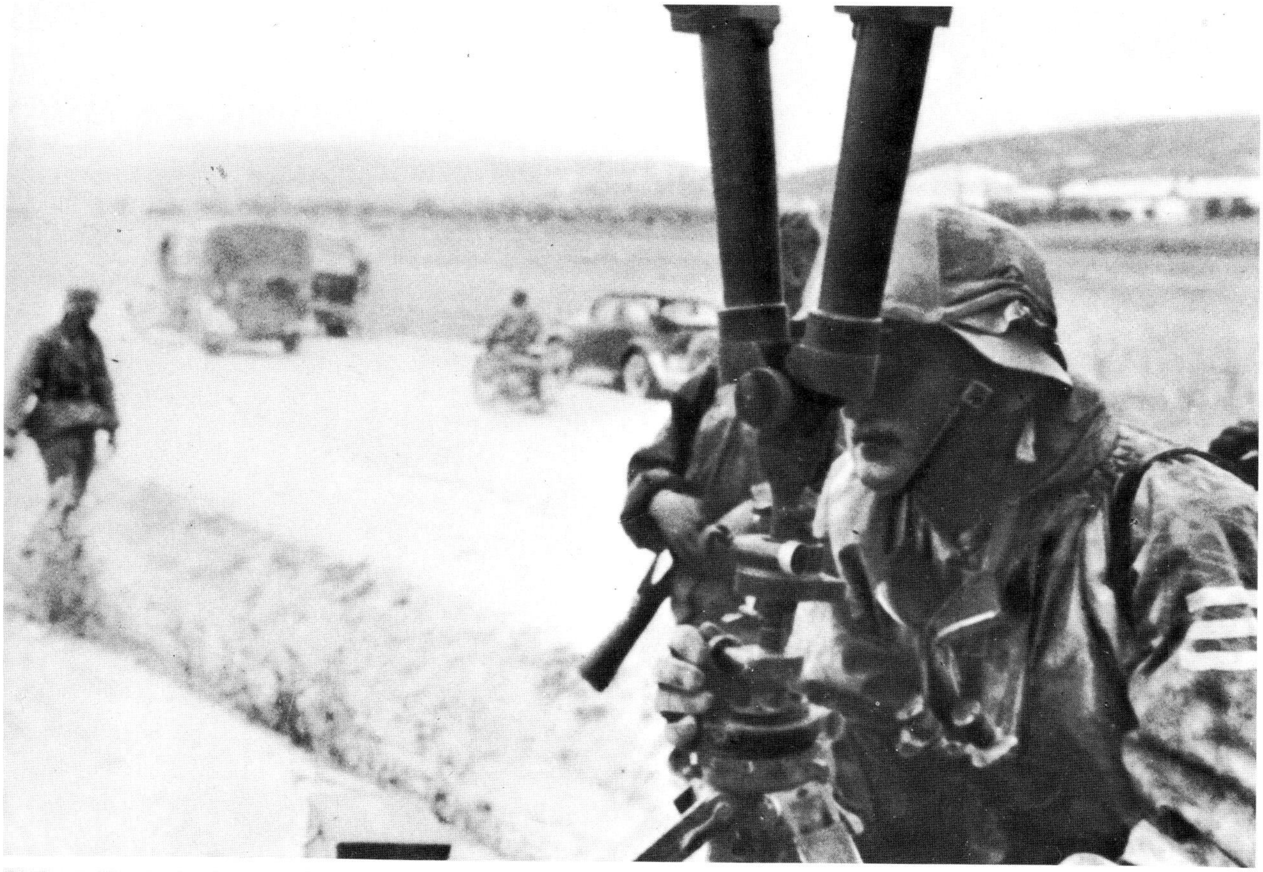

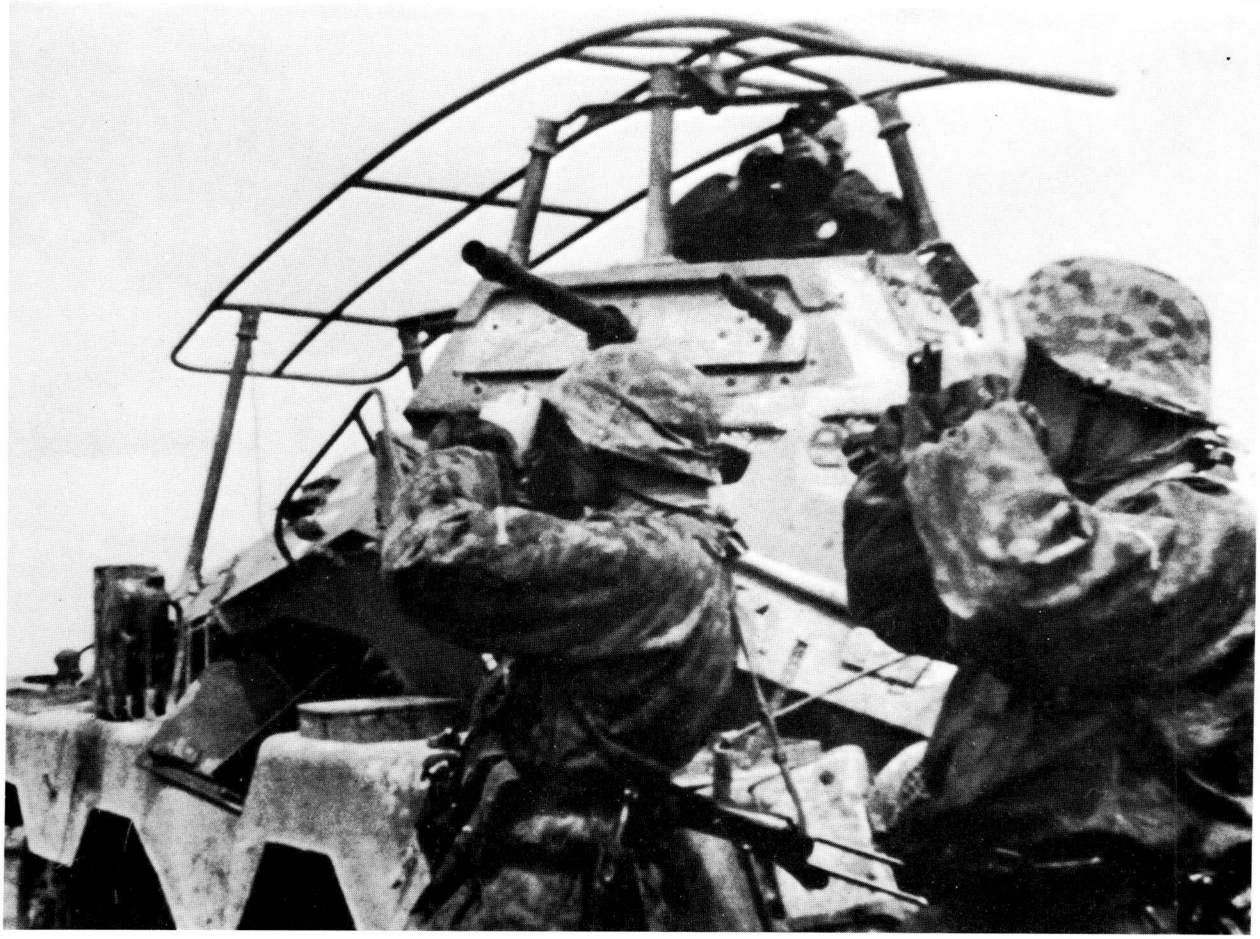

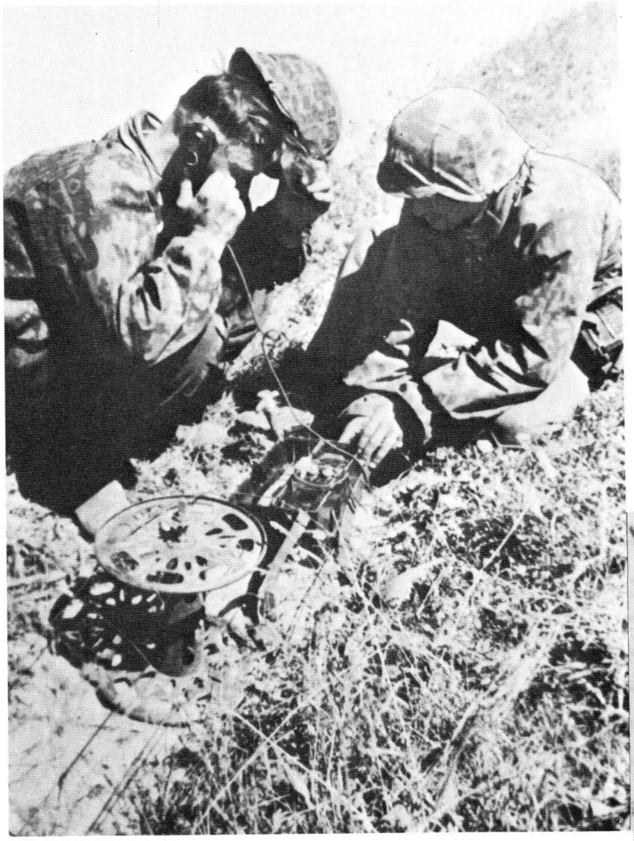

In the vastness of the Russian country, communications are extremely important.

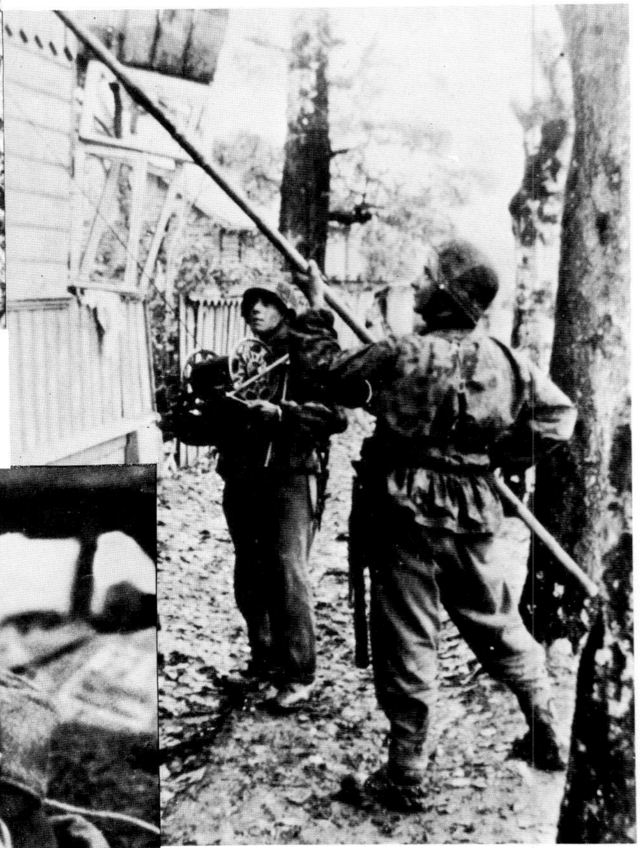

Working at the wiring system.

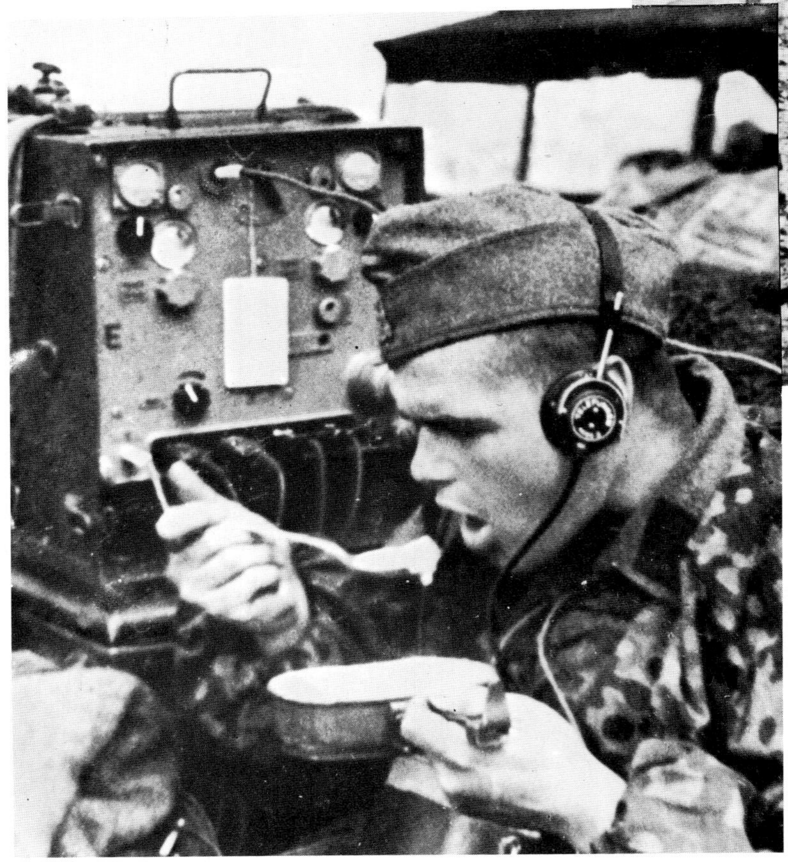

In the same way that the field telephone is indispensible for the observation post...

...the radio and the drop type switchboard are just as indispensible for the command of the troops.

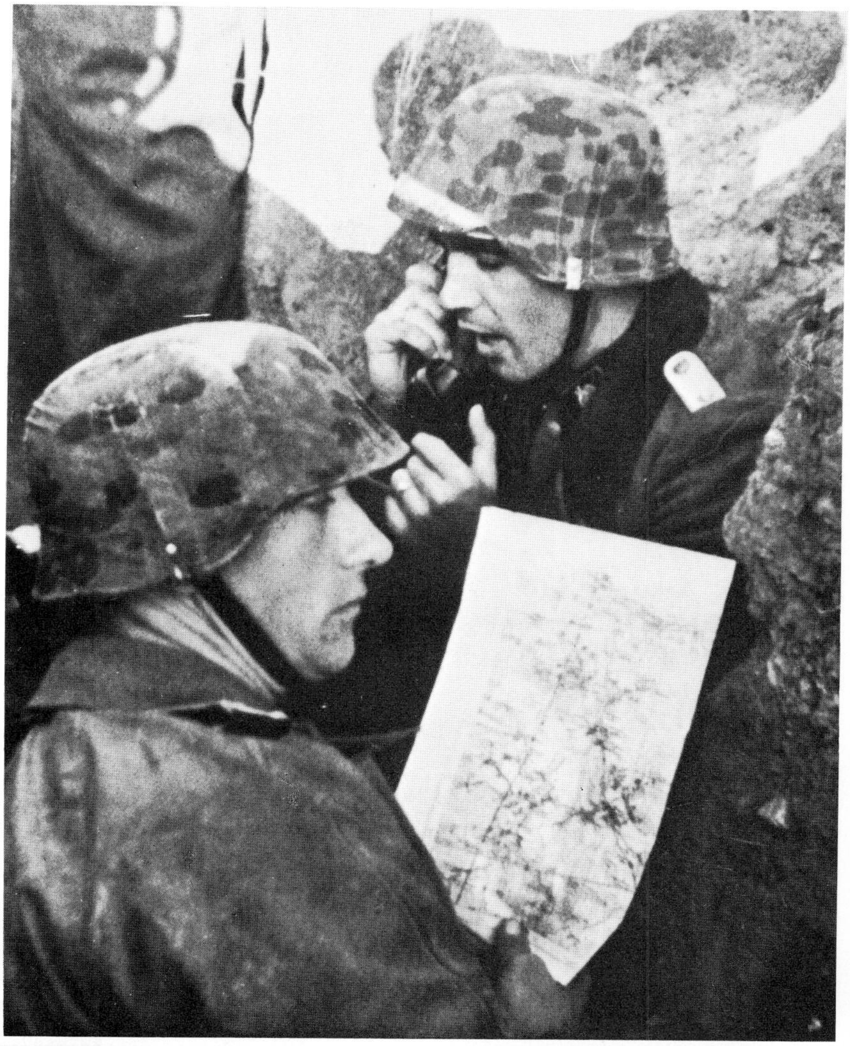

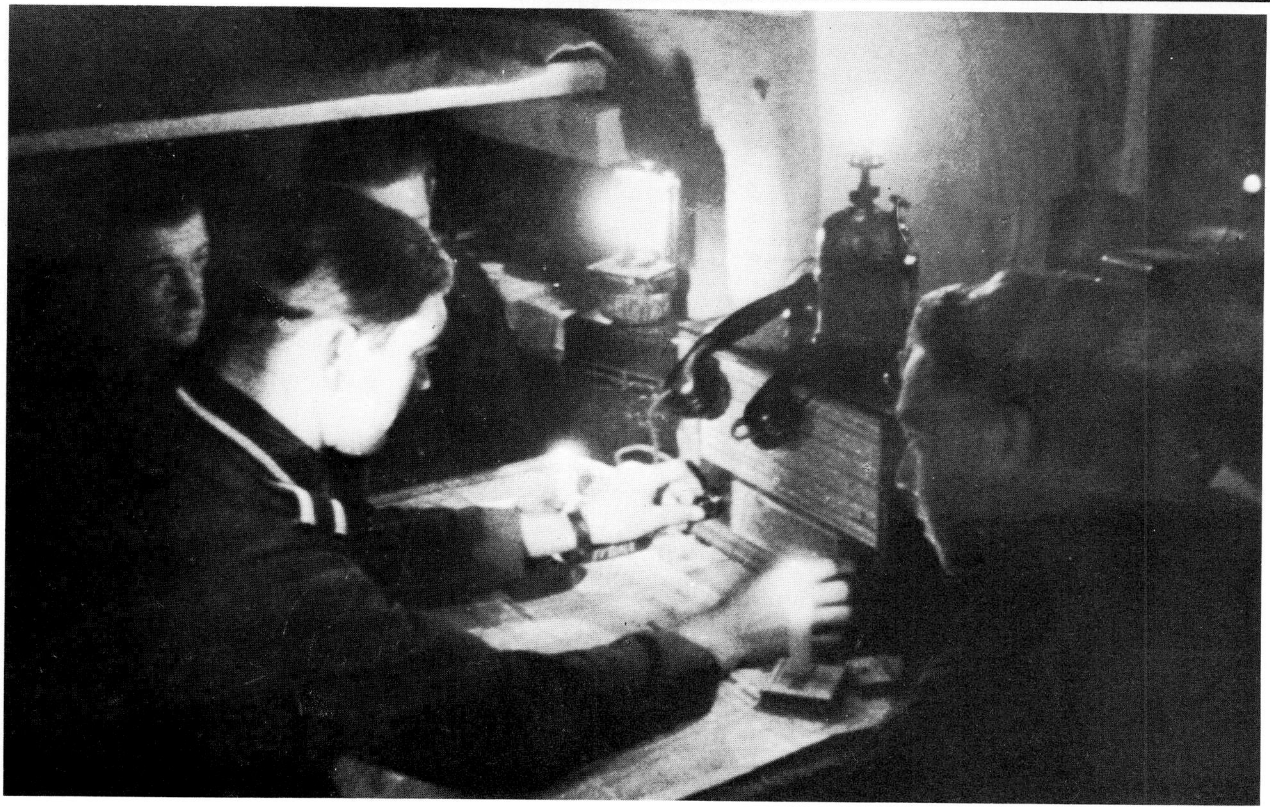

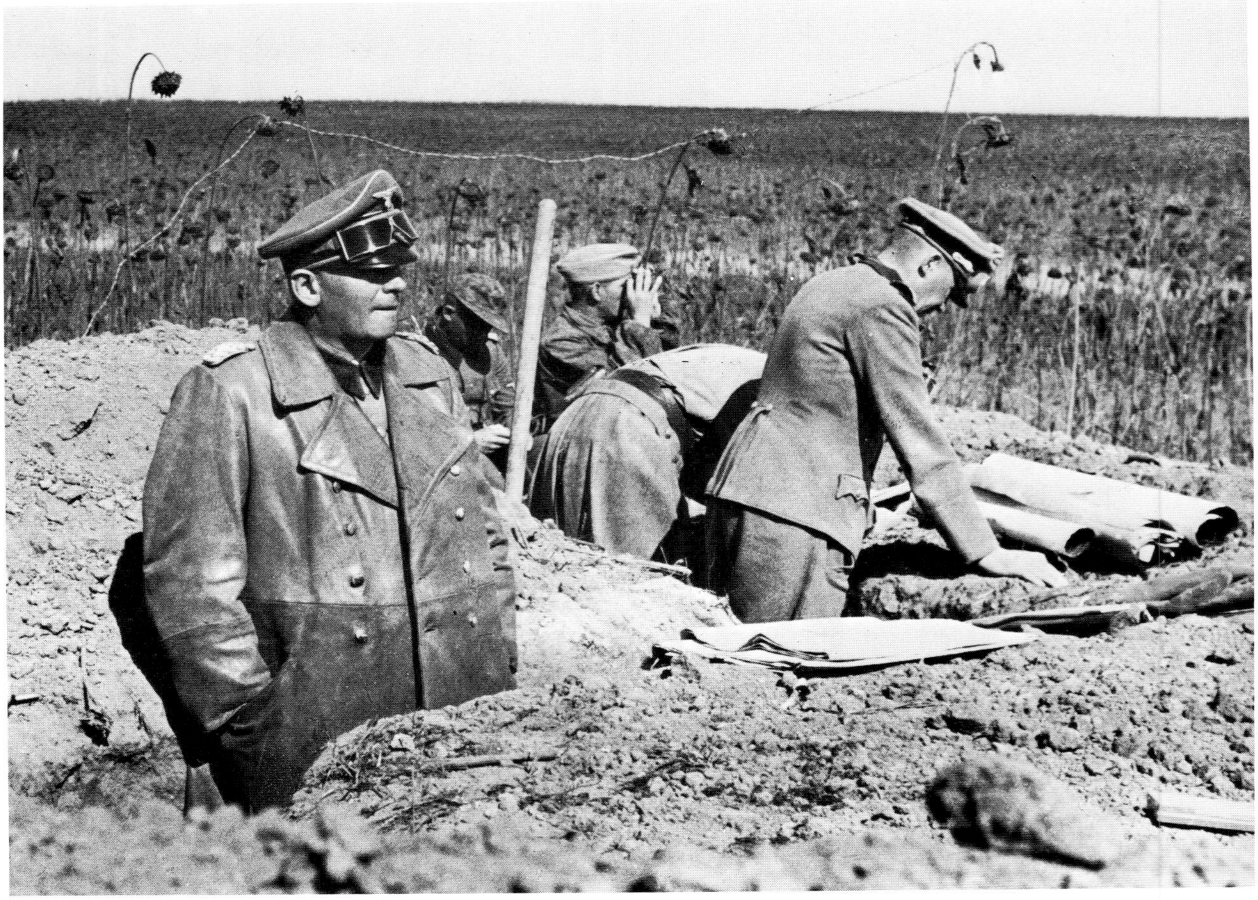

Under the command of Lt. General Felix Steiner, the division "Wiking" is advancing southward towards the Caucases in tanks and self-propelled gun vehicles.

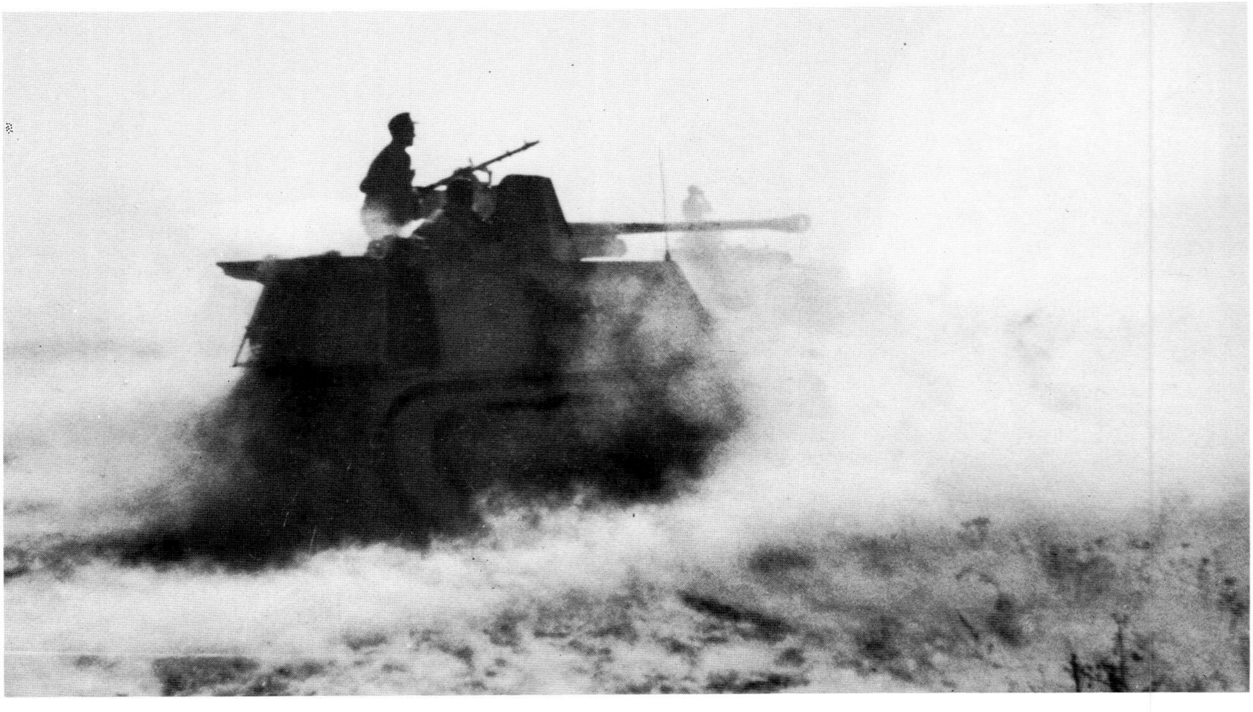

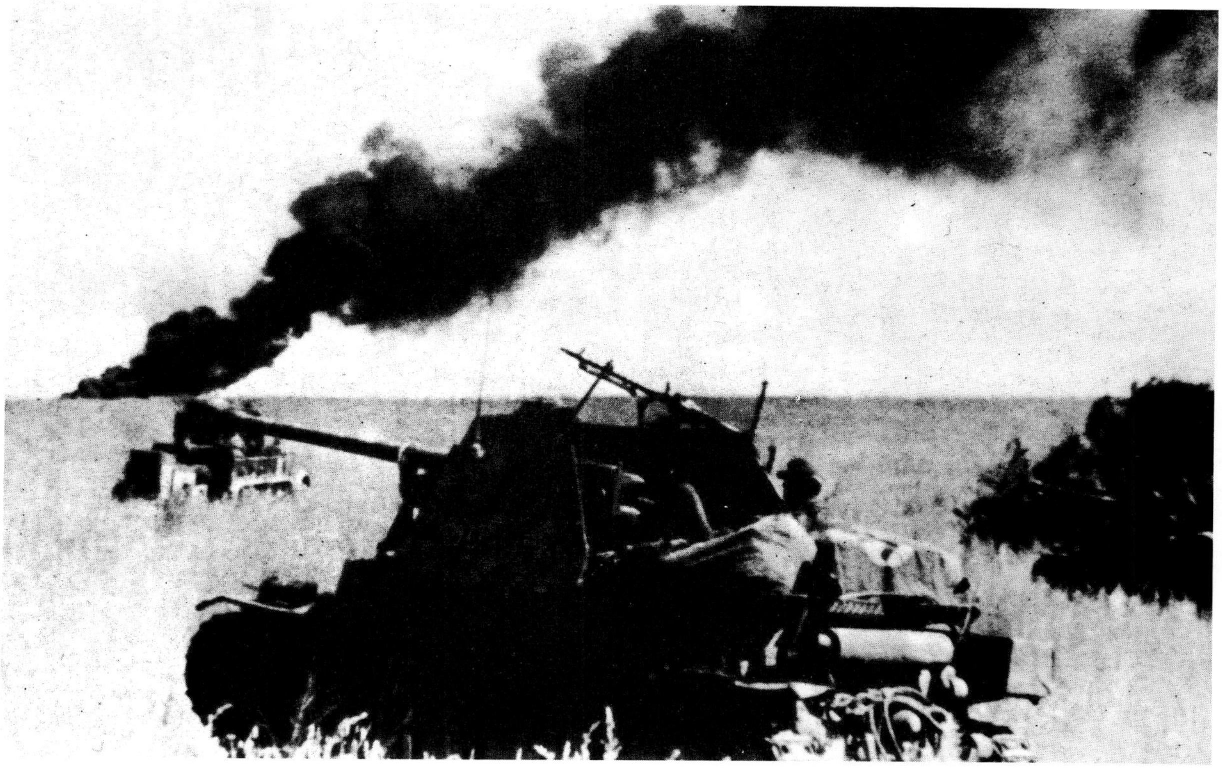

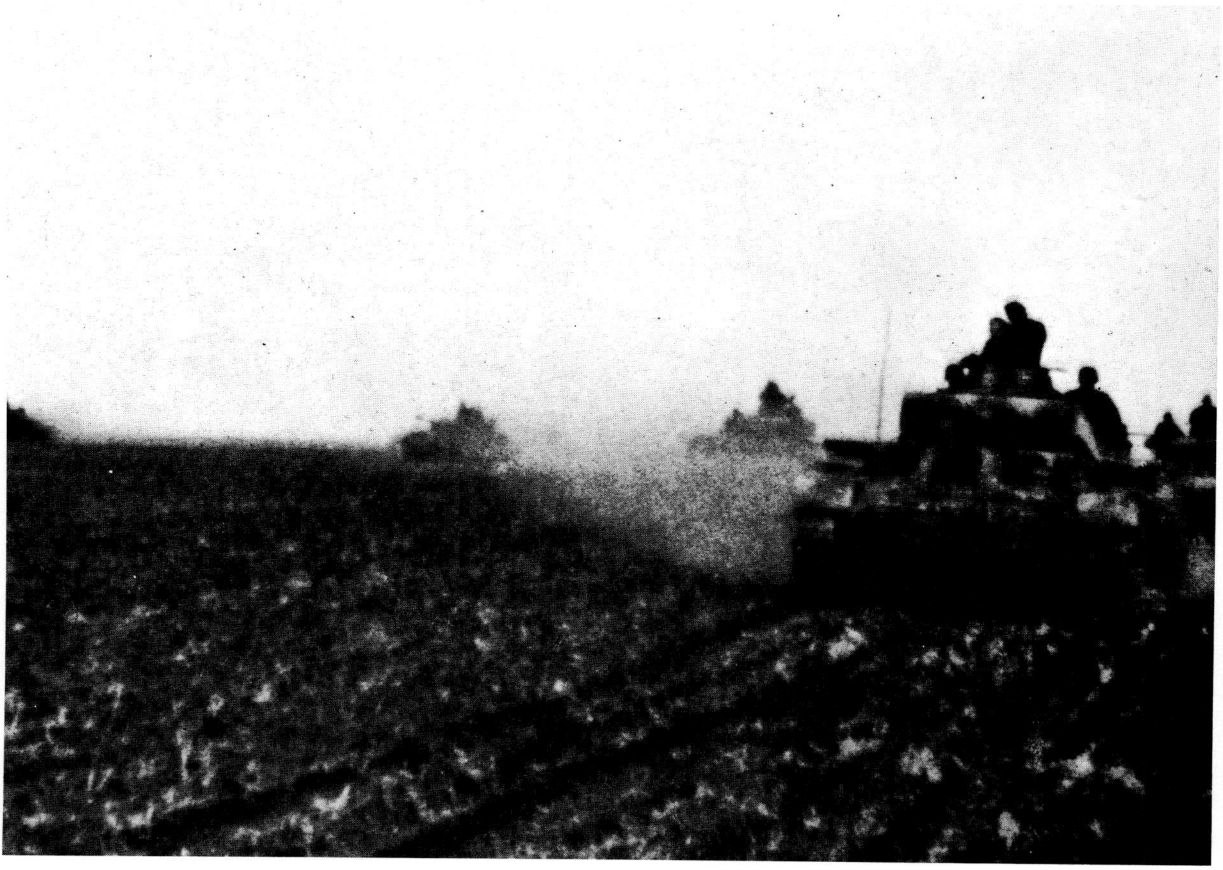

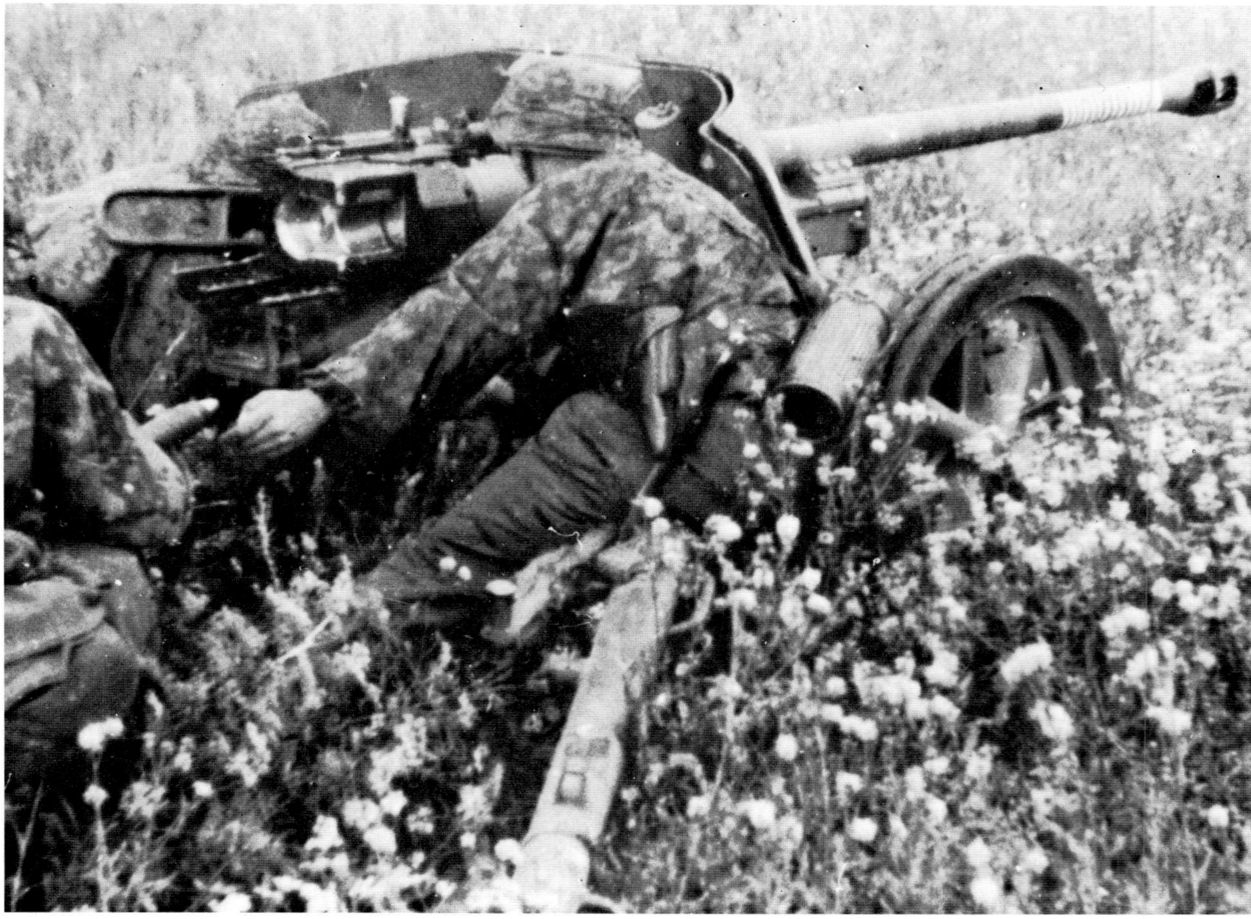

75 mm anti-tank gun in position.

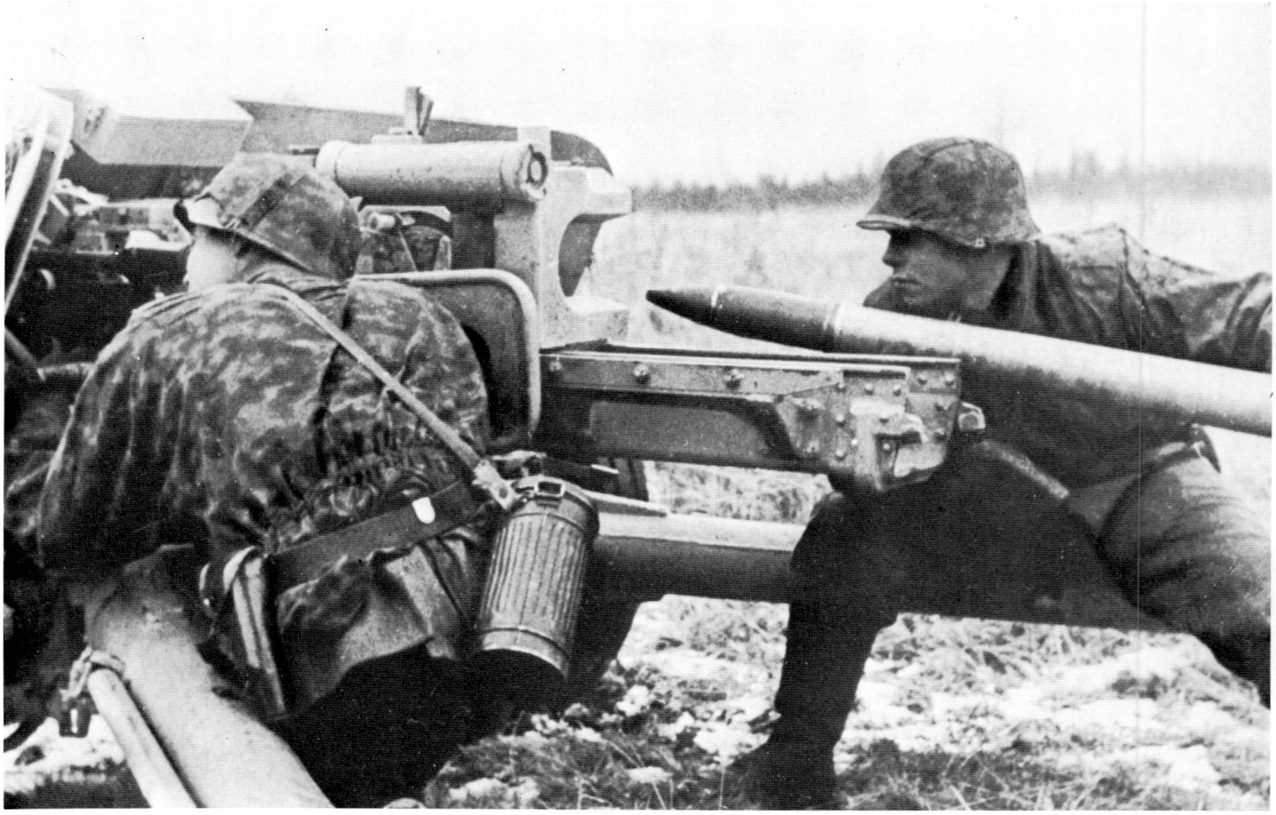

Heavy trench-mortars and light infantry guns are engaged in combat.

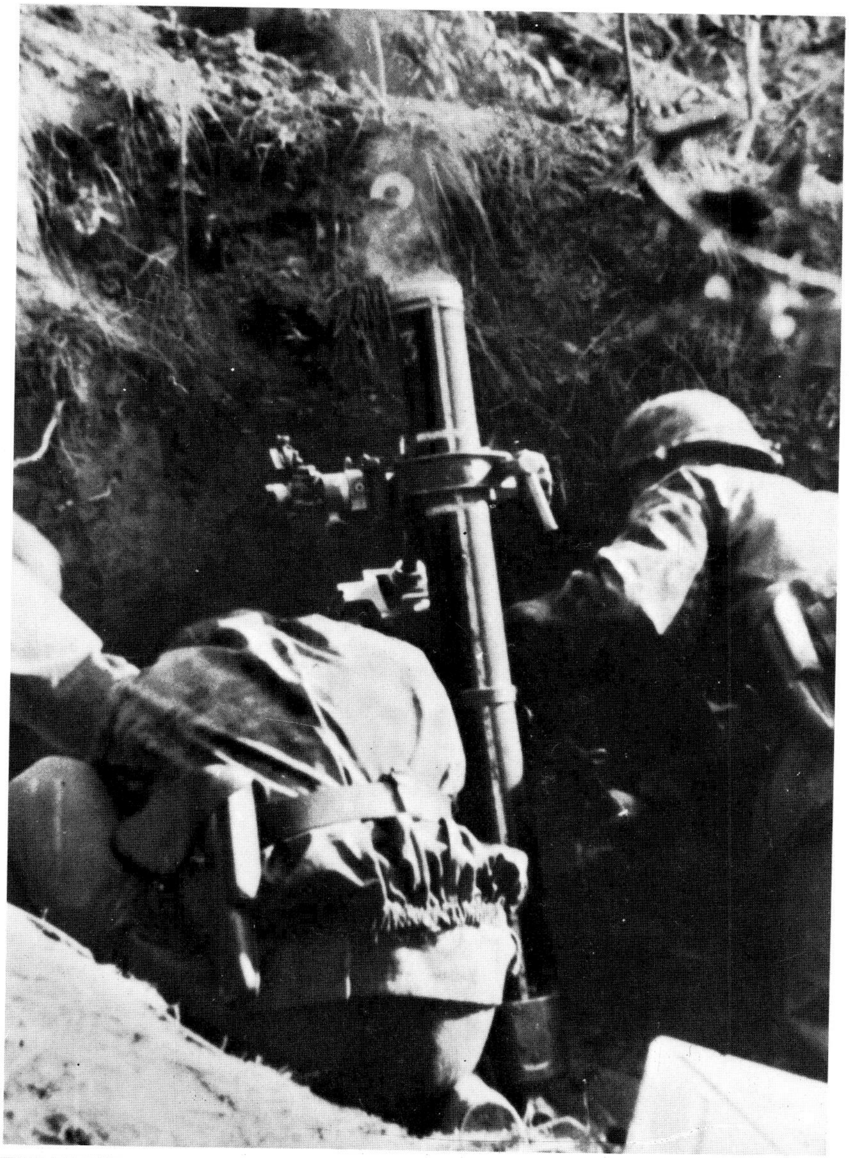

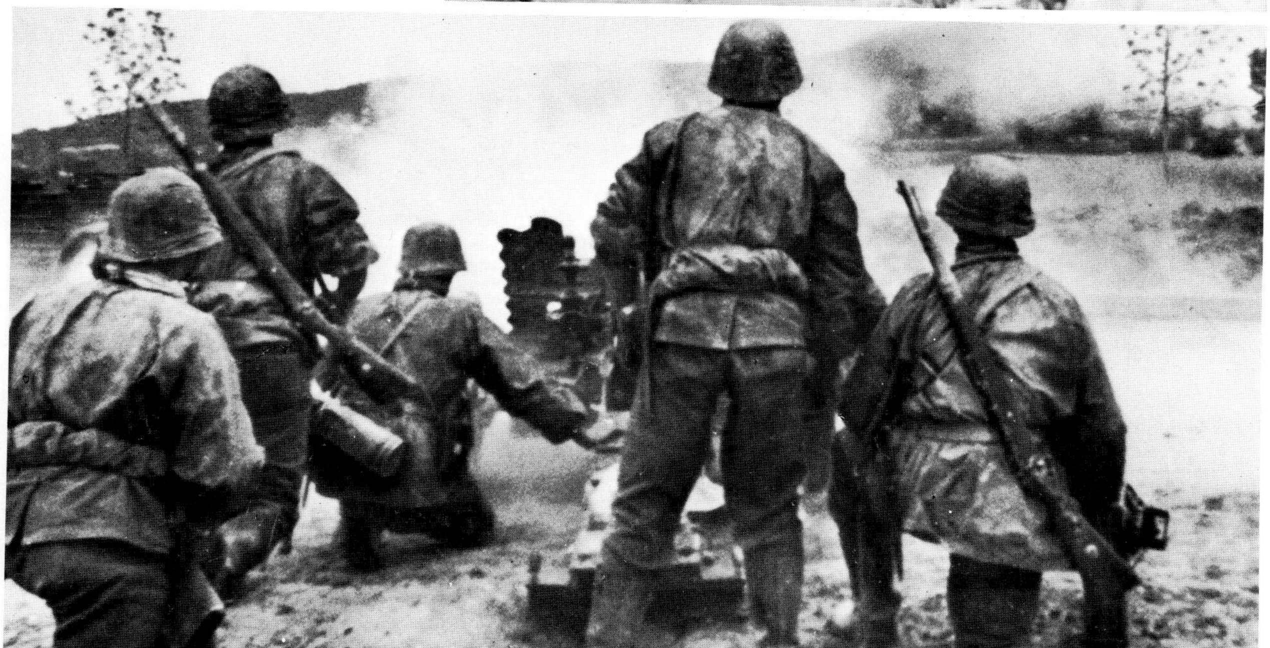

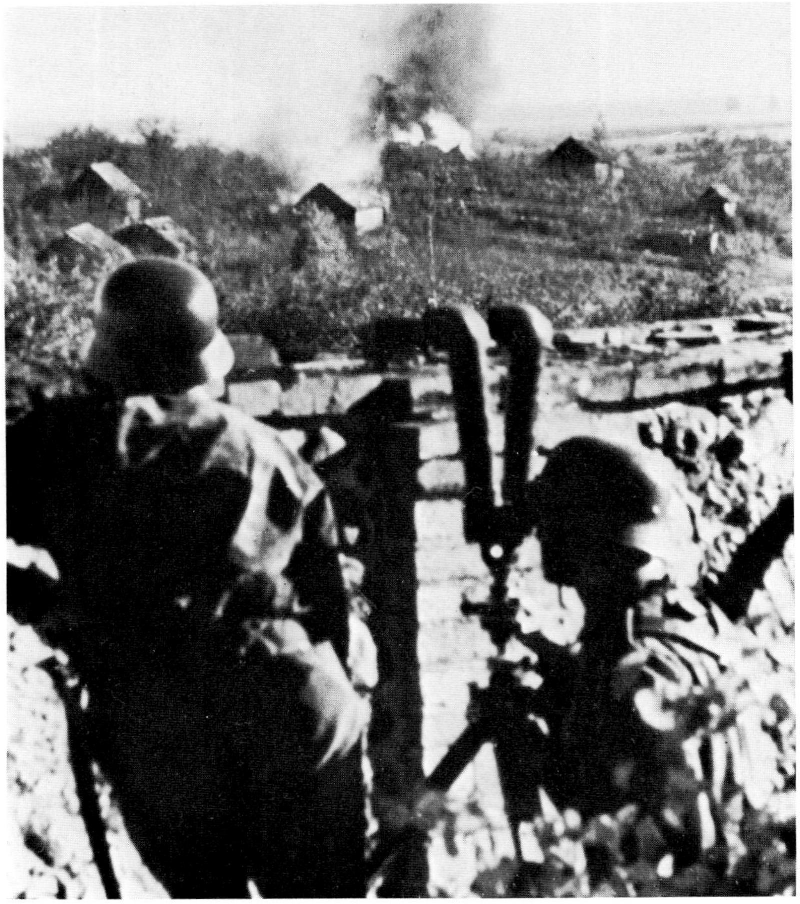

A forward observer directing the fire of heavy infantry guns.

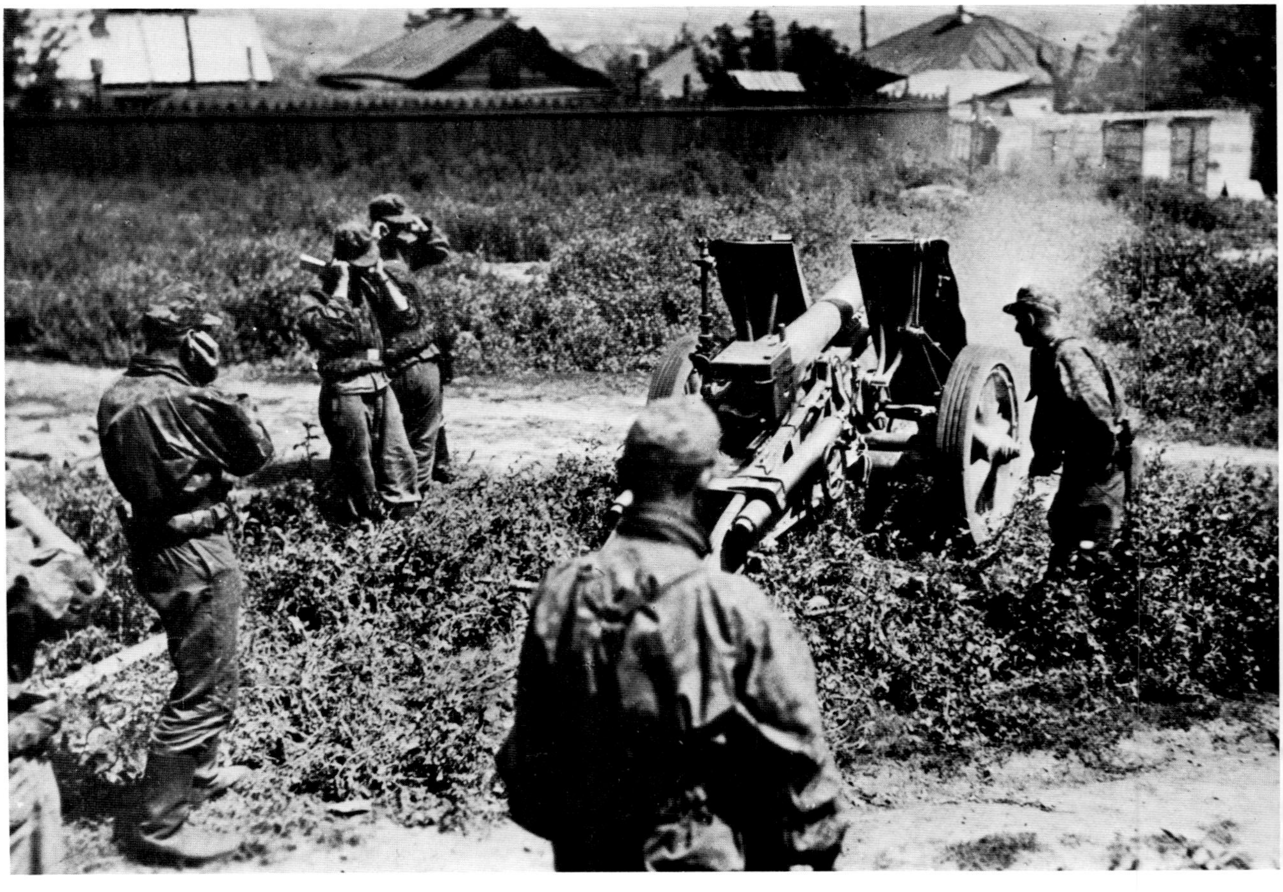

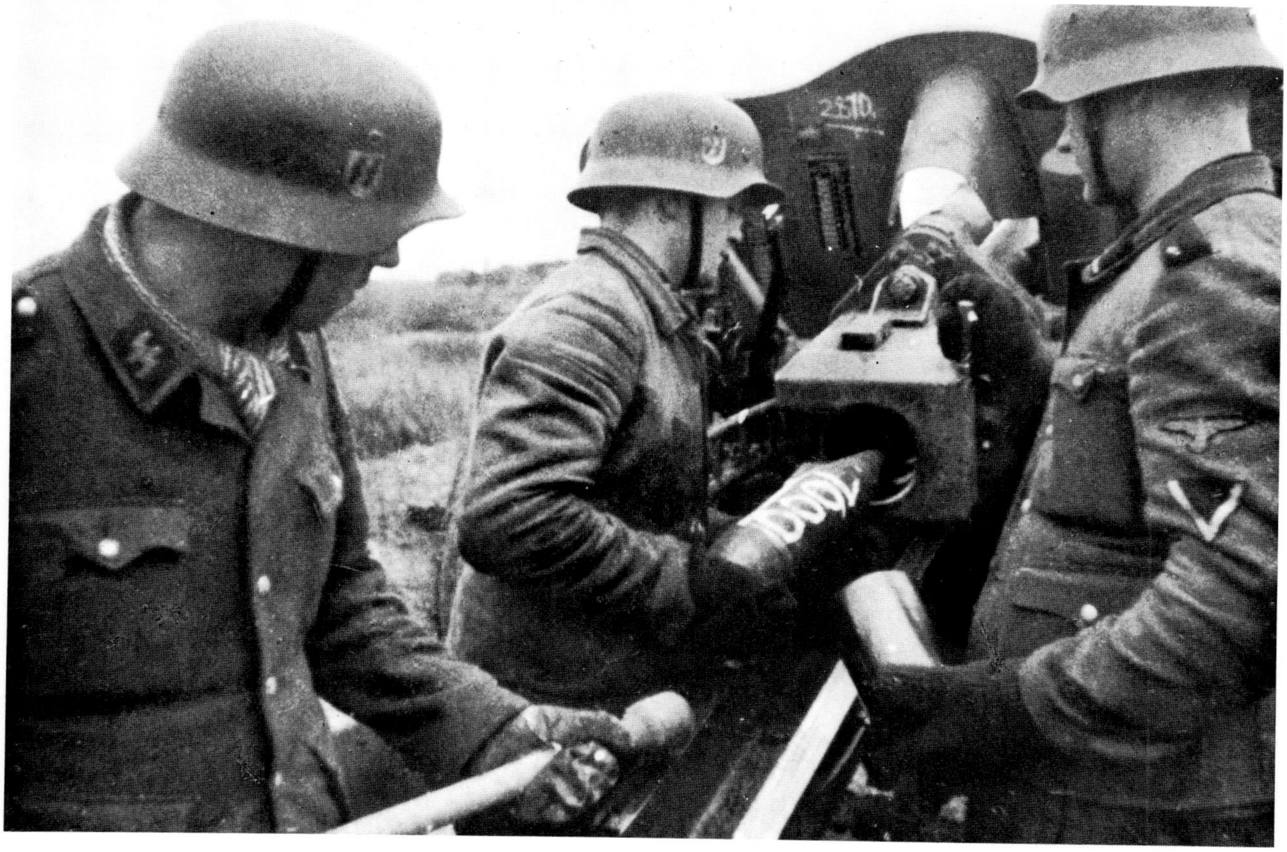

The thousandth shot of a 1FH-18 is being loaded.

Muzzel burst: Nightmare of every artillery man.

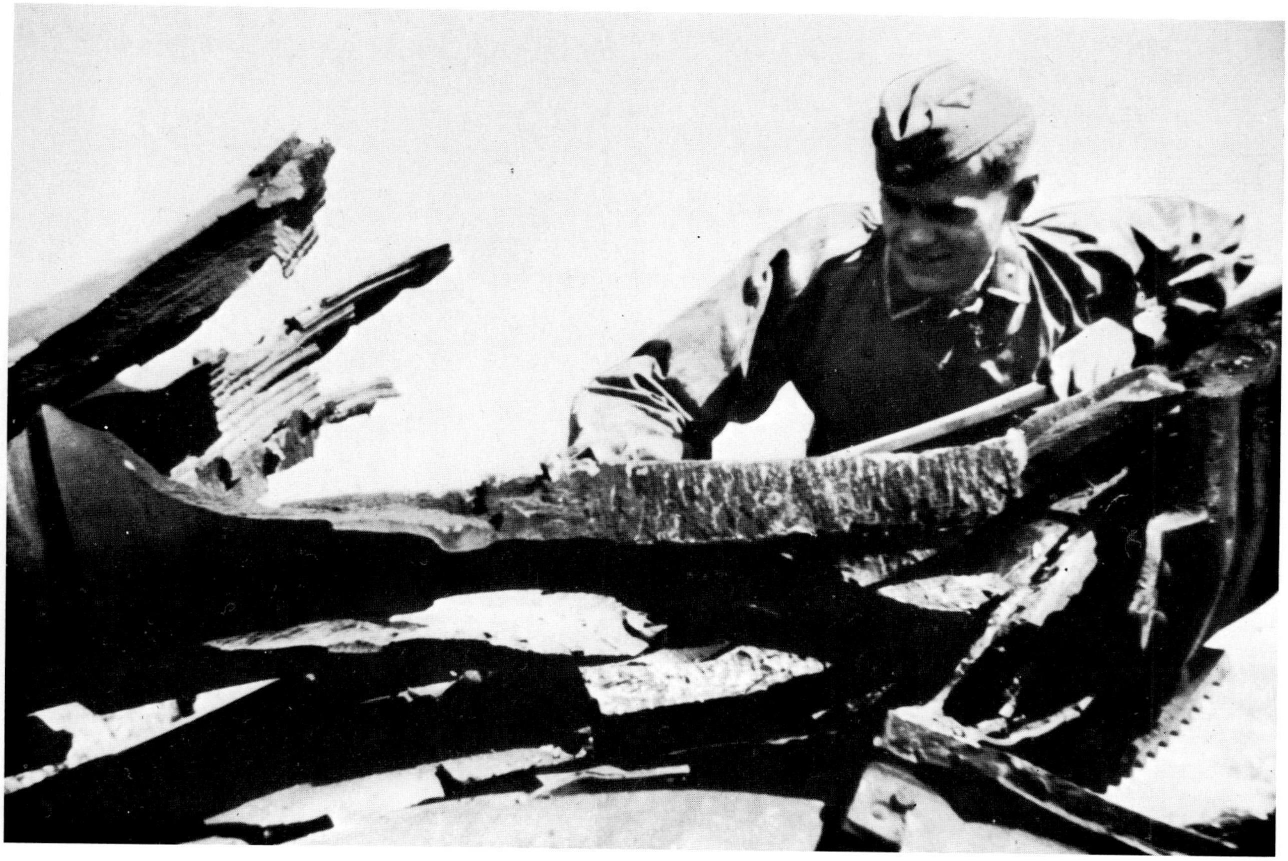

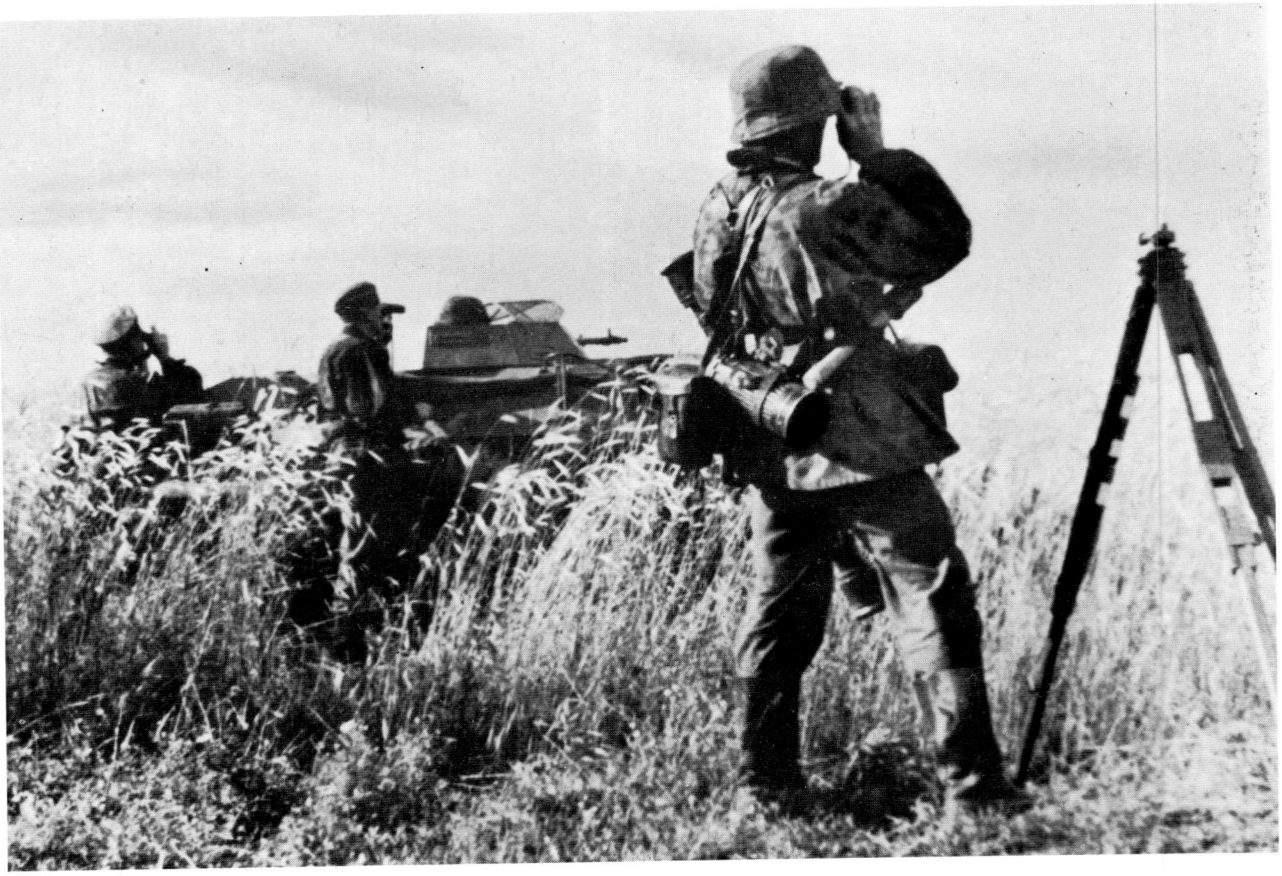

Division "Wiking" reaches the fore front of the Caucasus.

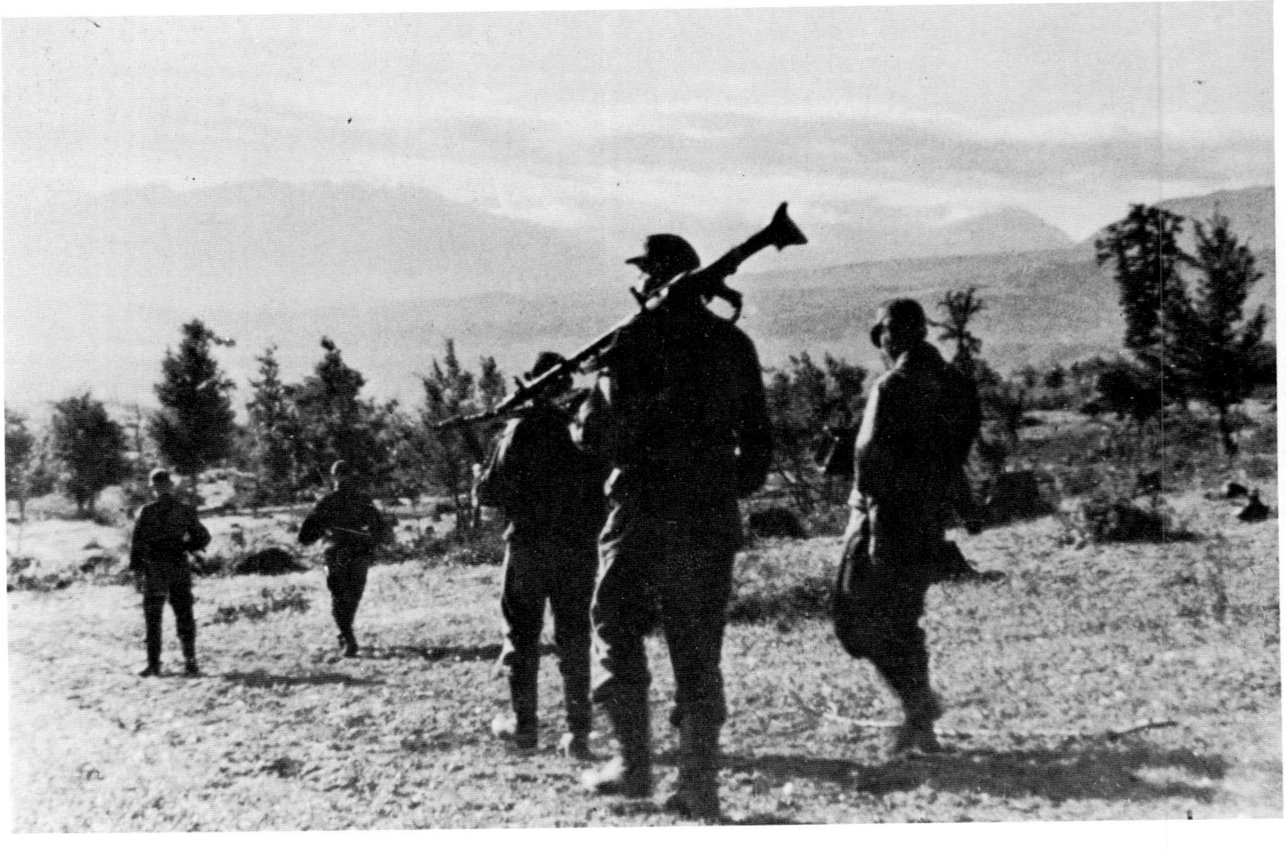

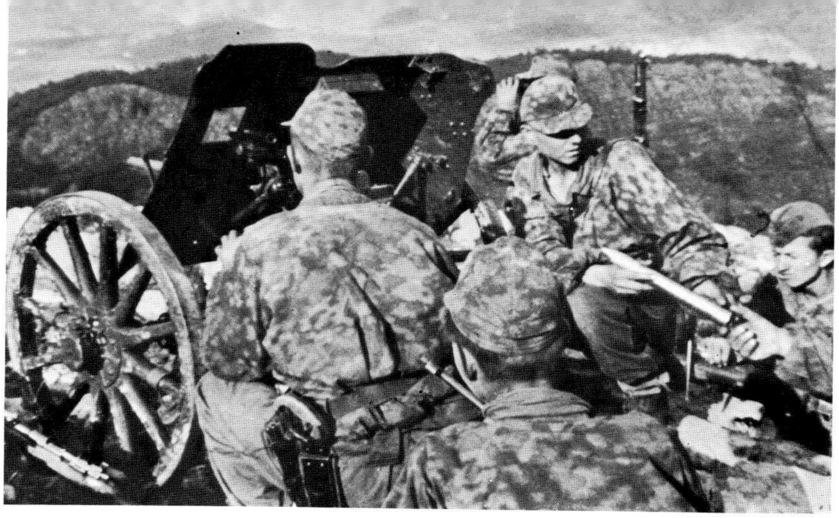

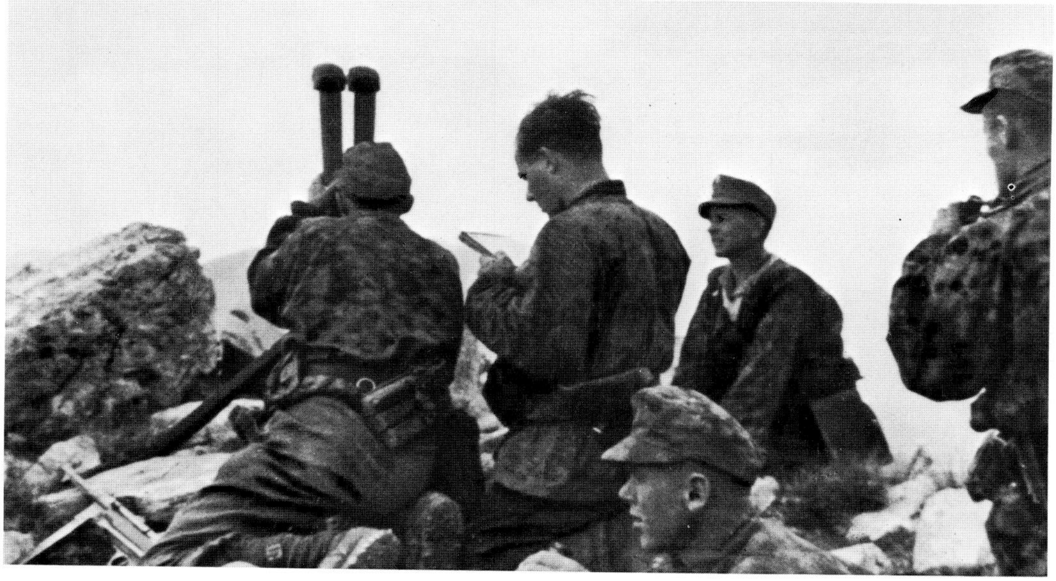

Members of the SS-Division "Wiking" place their gun in a dominating position in the Caucasus.

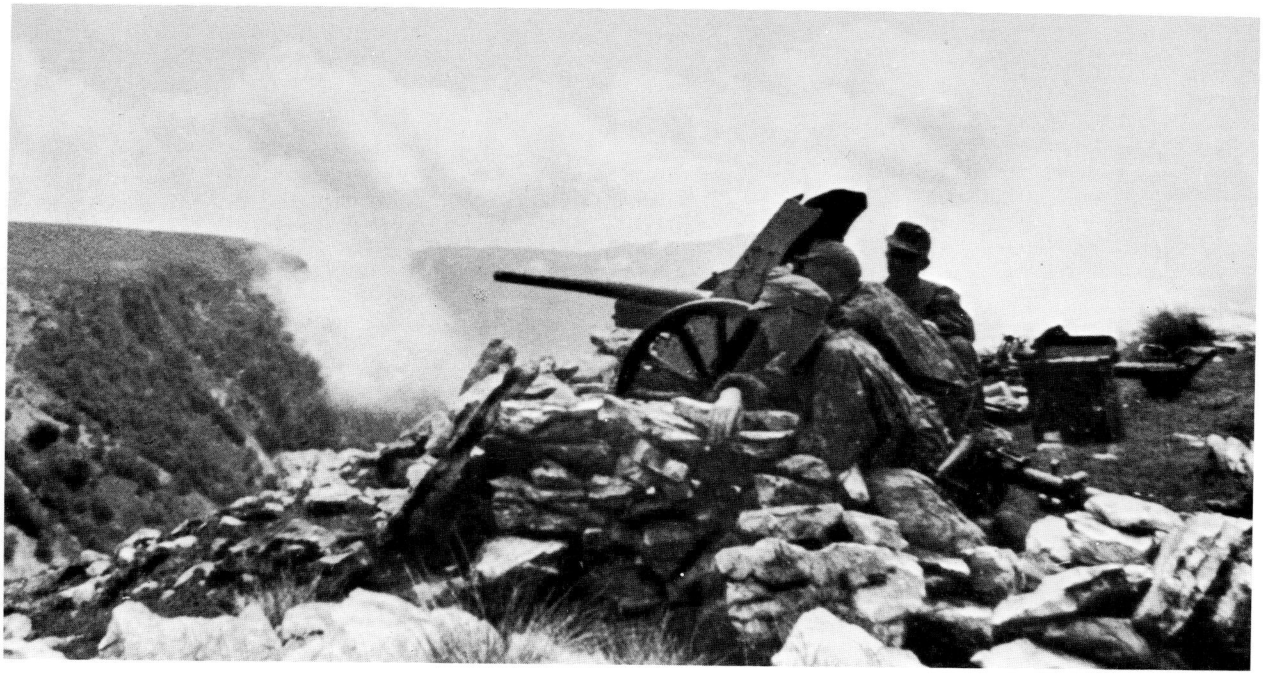

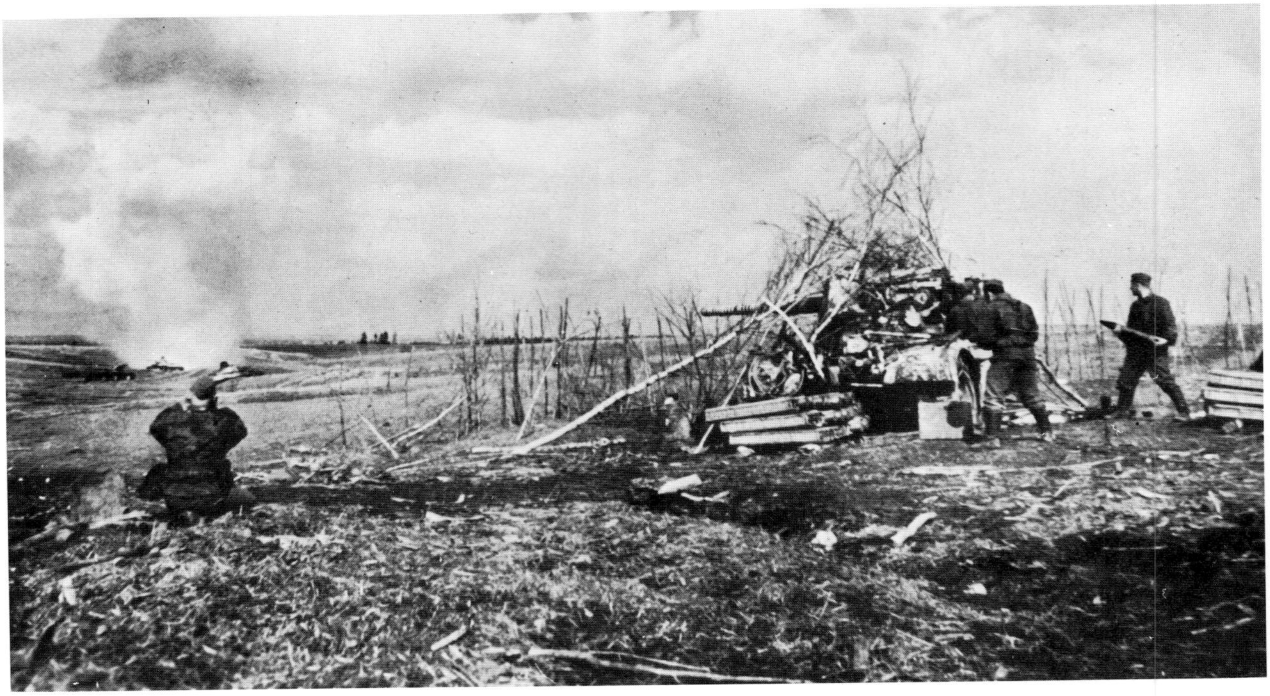

The 88 mm anti-aircraft guns and 75 mm anti-tank guns always prove effective in defending Russian tank assaults.

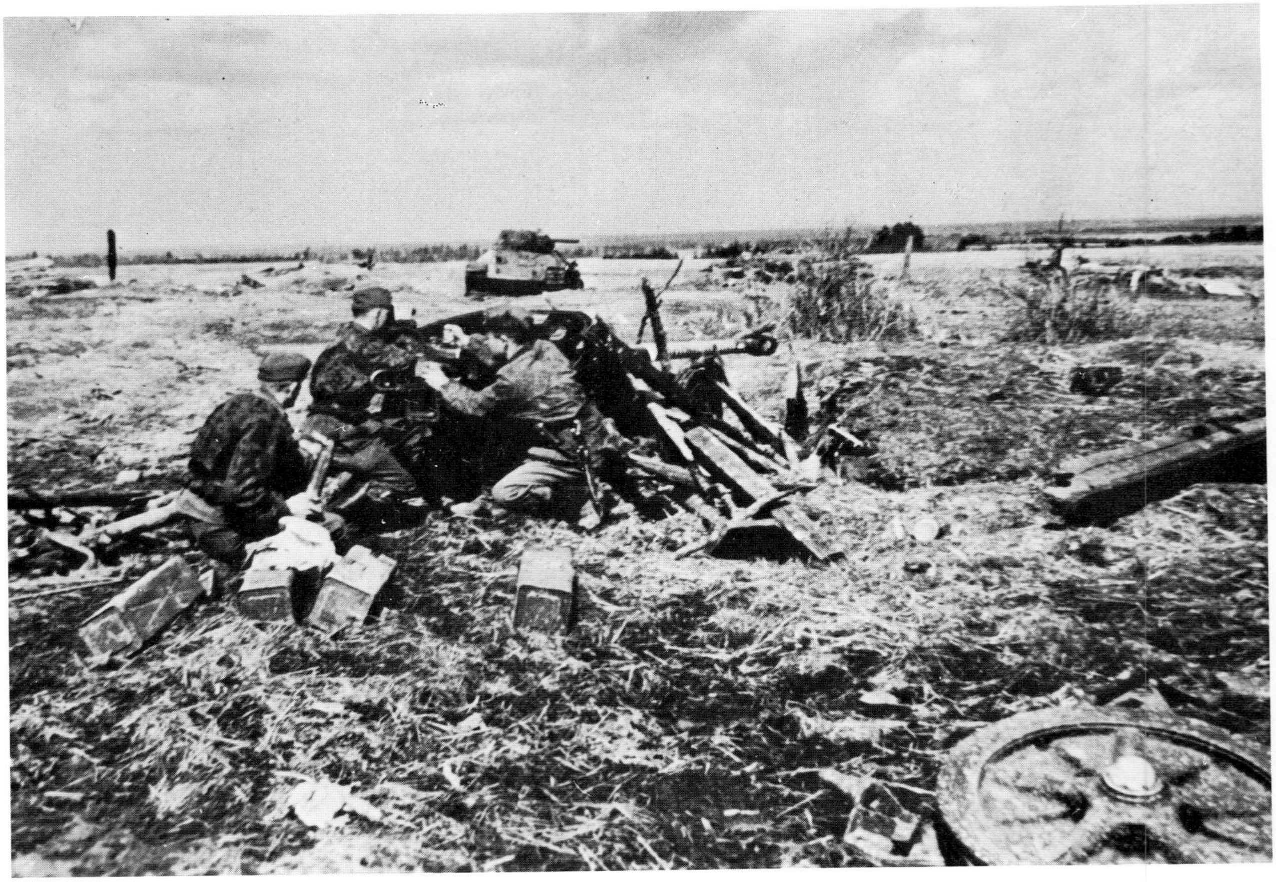

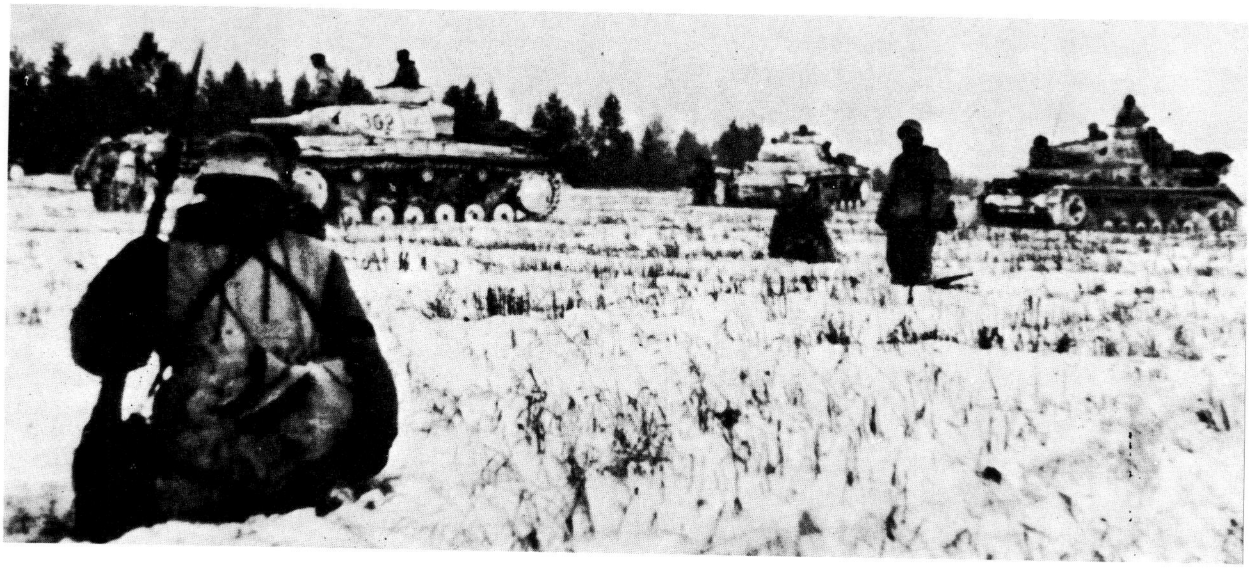

The second winter in Russia begins. All along the front, the divisions of the Waffen-SS are involved in fierce defensive battles.

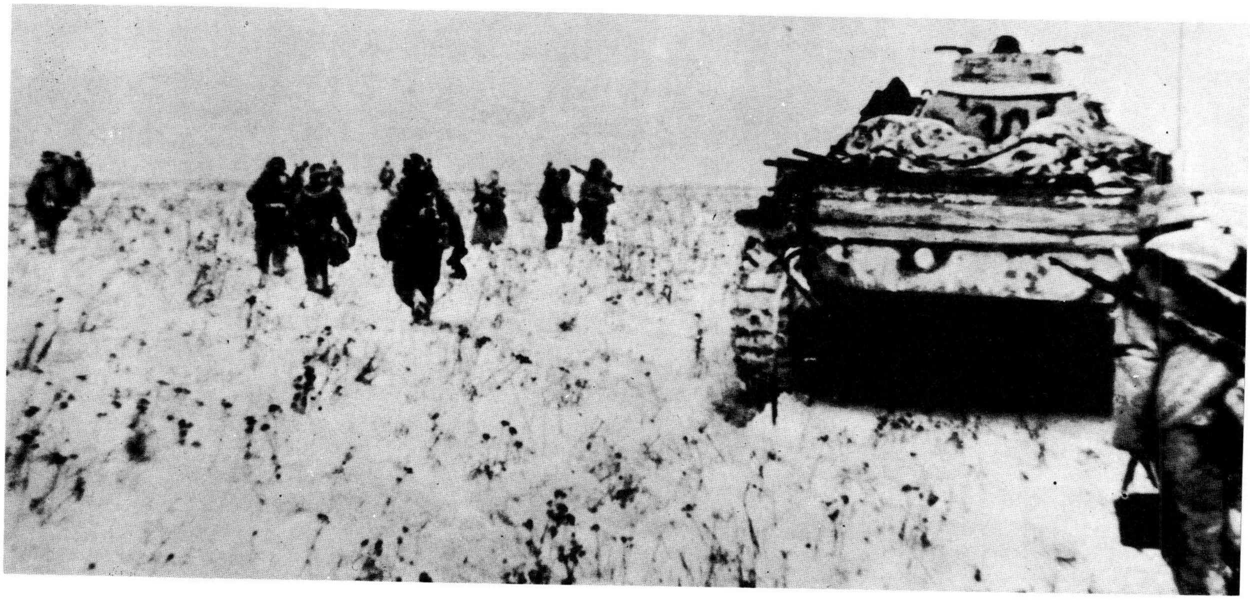

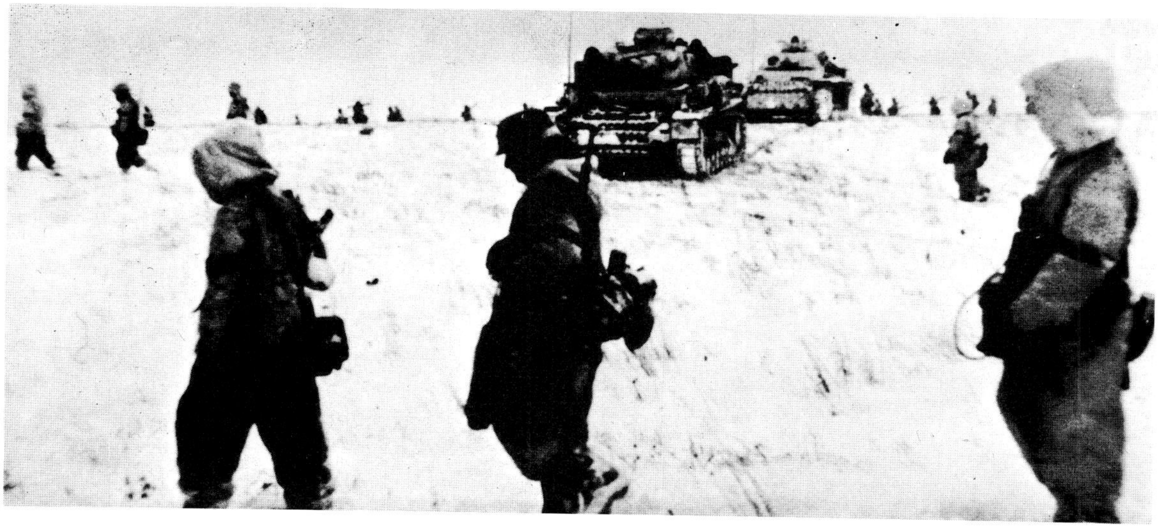

# KHARKOV, 1943

by Field Marshal von Manstein

February of 1943 was characterized by constantly stronger Russian attacks. The danger that the Army Group South would be thrown for a loss increased constantly. On February 15 the SS armored corps had evacuated Kharkov after it became obvious that the troops in the city were in danger of being surrounded. I had understood and approved this evacuation, even though I only learned of it after the fact. On February 17 Hitler walked into my headquarters and I informed him of my intention to advance from the Krasnograd area in the direction of Pavlograd and, together with the 4th Armored Army, lead a strike in the direction of Kharkov.

On March 7 our troops began the advance, which went well thanks to their striking power and readiness, including the SS divisions. Of course the enemy had now recognized the danger that threatened his Voronesh front. Here it was a matter of the "Great Rochade", which I had suggested and then carried out, the quick transfer of the focal point from the right to the left wing of the army. For that reason we had to try to prevent the enemy forces that had advanced far to the west in the direction of Achtyrka from dropping back to the east. This led to the second operation, the decisive "Strike from the other hand". Perhaps it would be possible to take Kharkov in a bold move. In any case, I wanted to avoid a battle for streets and houses. Naturally the city drew troops as if by magic during the attack, and I had to intervene energetically again and again to prevent the units from placing themselves firmly in the city. Finally, against strong opposition, the SS Armored Corps were able to move eastward around Kharkov. That was the decisive stroke. The city fell into the hands of the SS Armored Corps on March 14. All the divisions of this corps, "Leibstandarte Adolf Hitler", "Das Reich", the "Totenkopf Division" and later also the SS "Wiking" Division, played an outstanding part in the success of this operation, which the law of action again granted us for a short time. That the opportunity now available was lost, that Hitler gambled away a possible evening of the score, is another matter. Here it is only to be reported that the involved SS divisions, in good comradeship with the soldiers of the army, fought the battle for Kharkov and contributed to its success in a splendid fighting spirit.

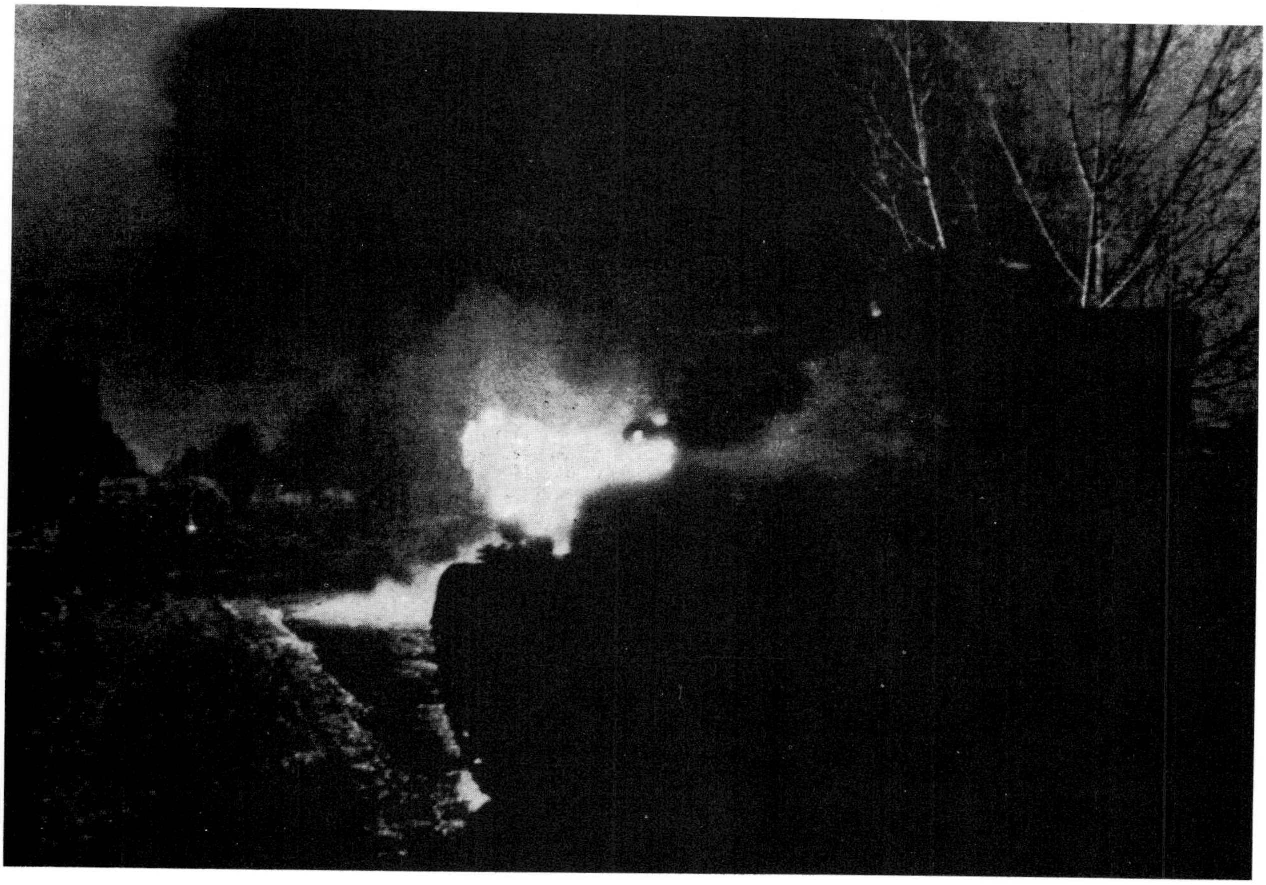

German Panzer IV tanks break through the Russian forces at night.

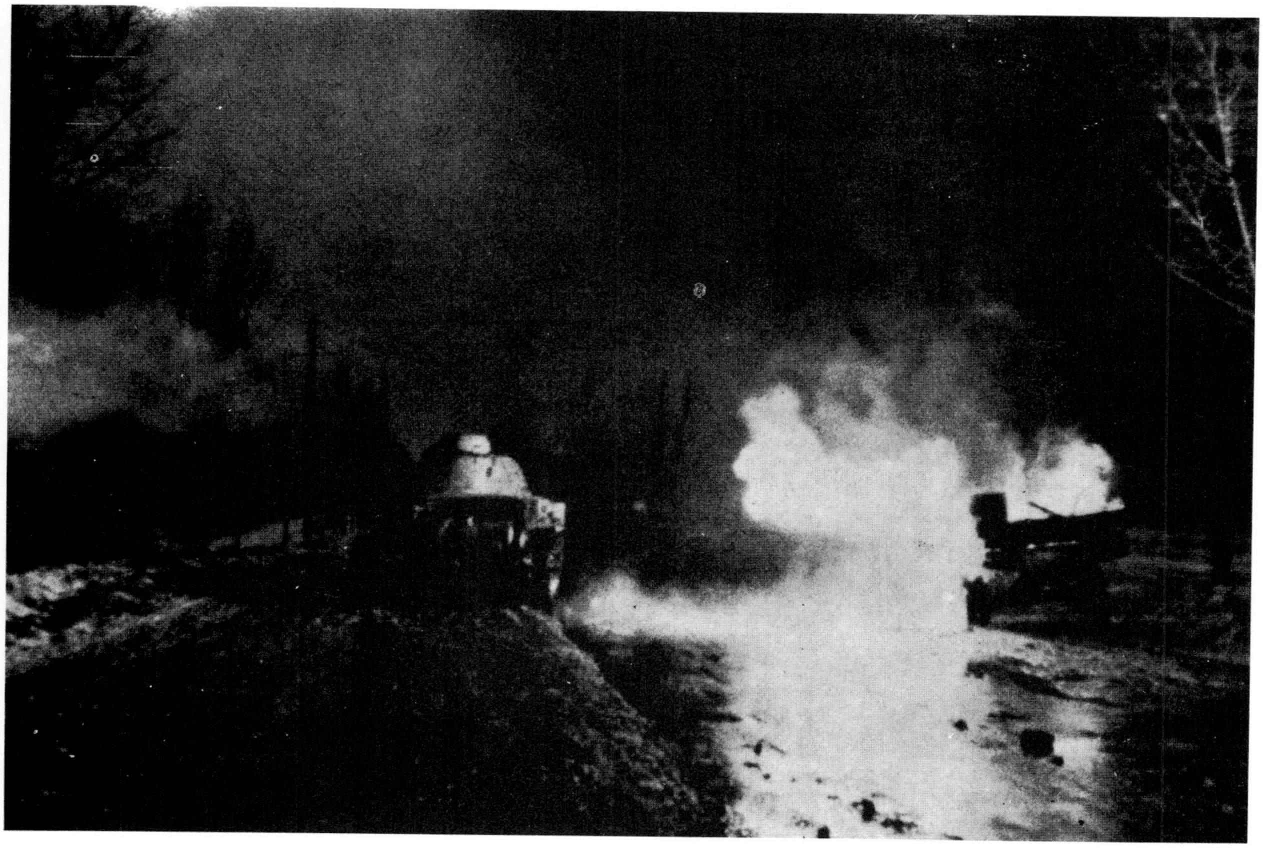

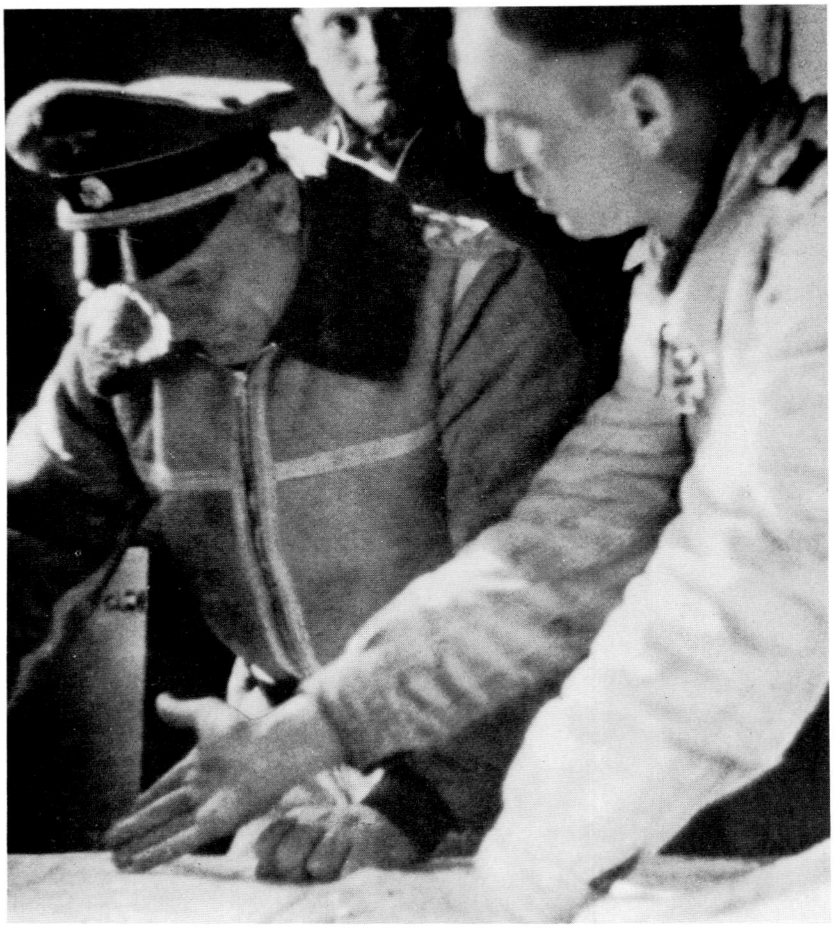

Conference to discuss the counterattack on Charkow. From the left: Sepp Dietrich, "Teddy Wisch", and Kurt Meyer, called "Panzermeyer".

Tanks of the LAH begin the counterattack.

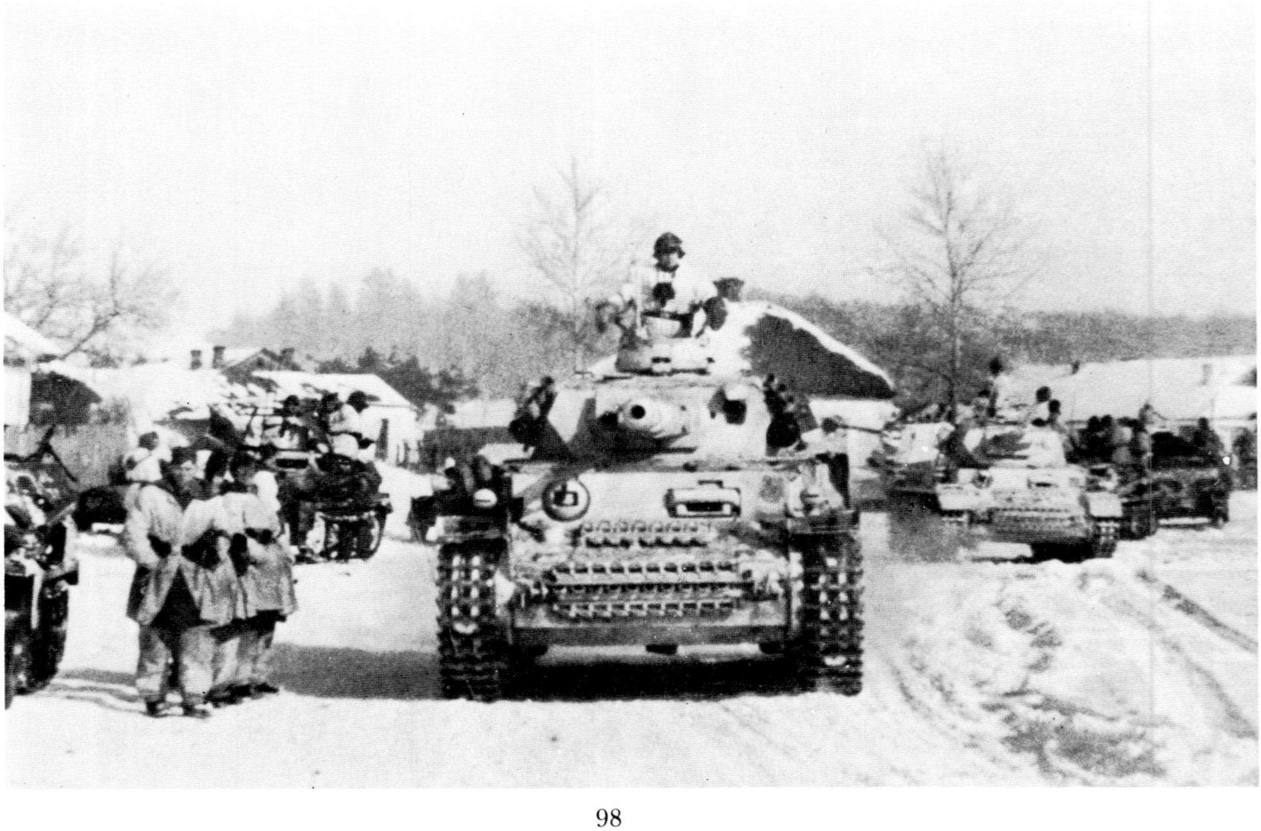

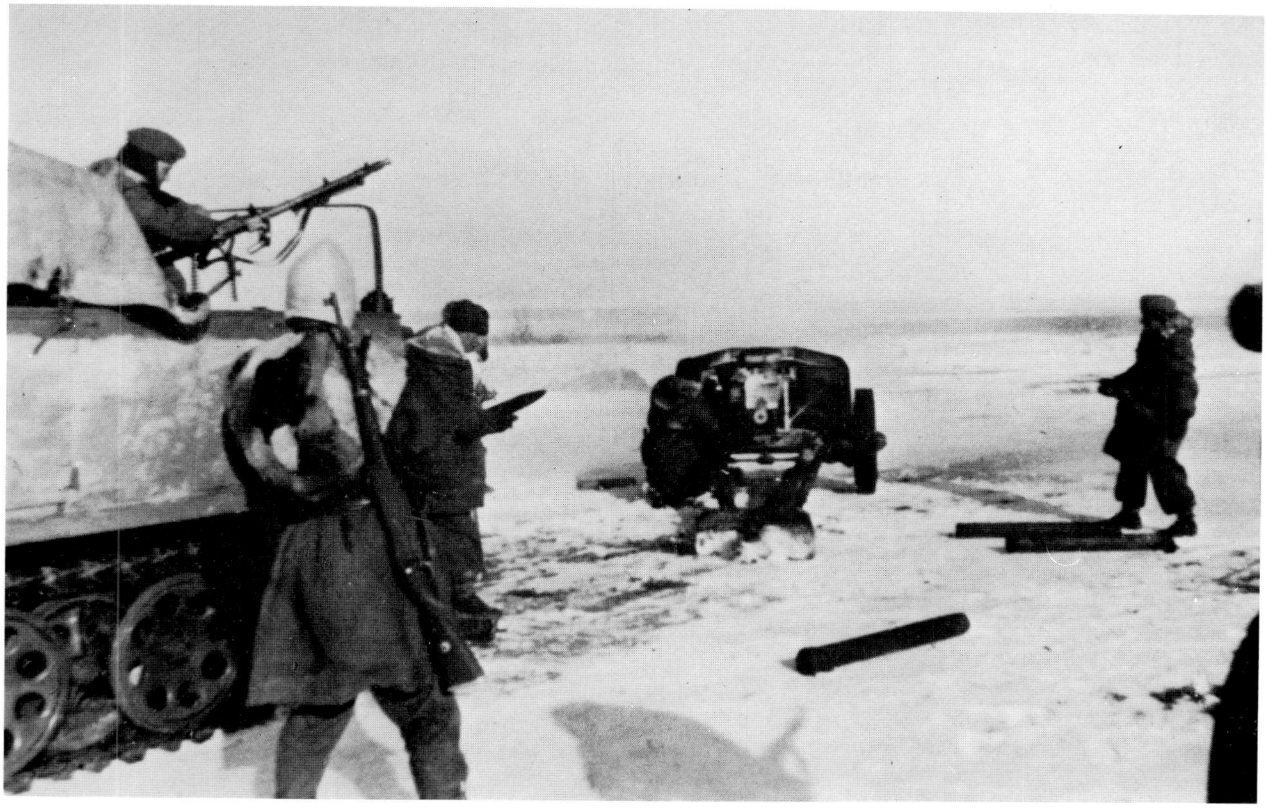

75 mm anti-tank guns support the advancing armored infantrymen of the LAH.

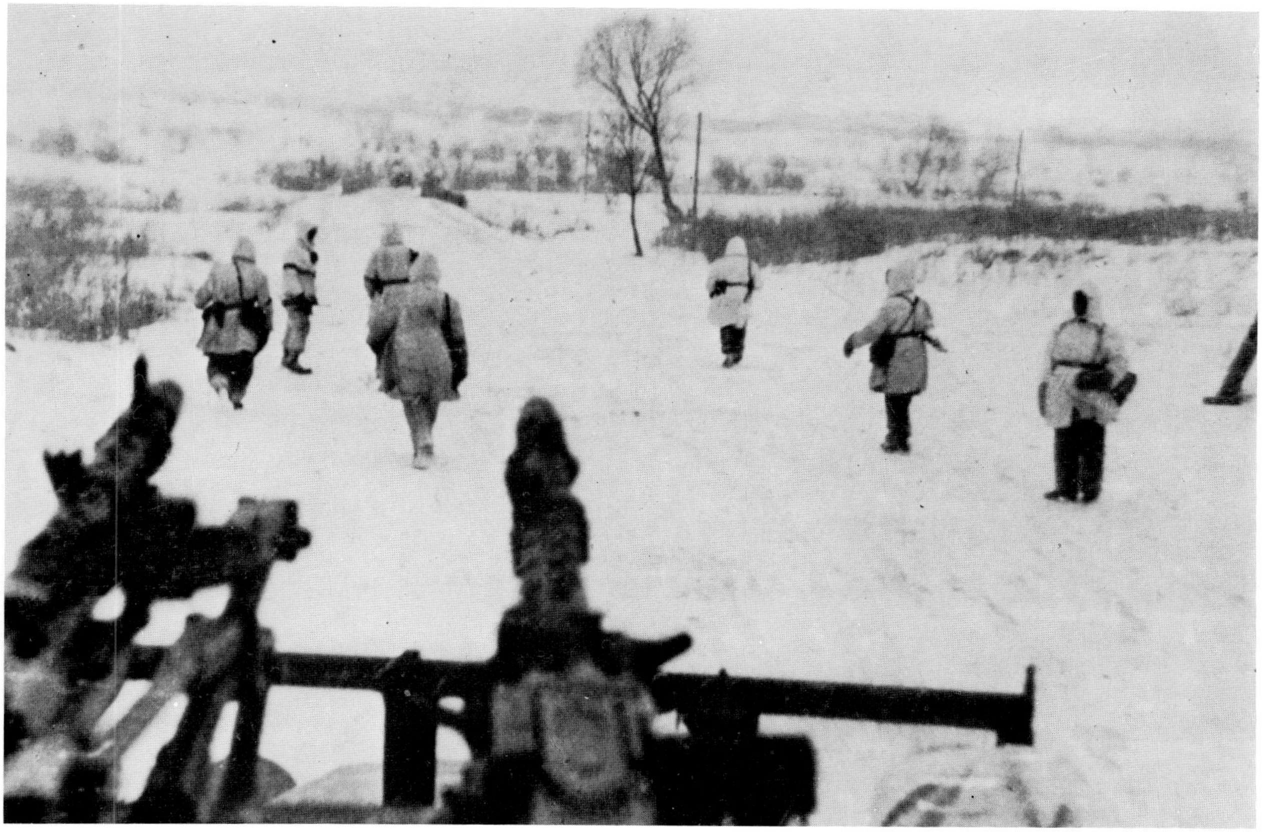

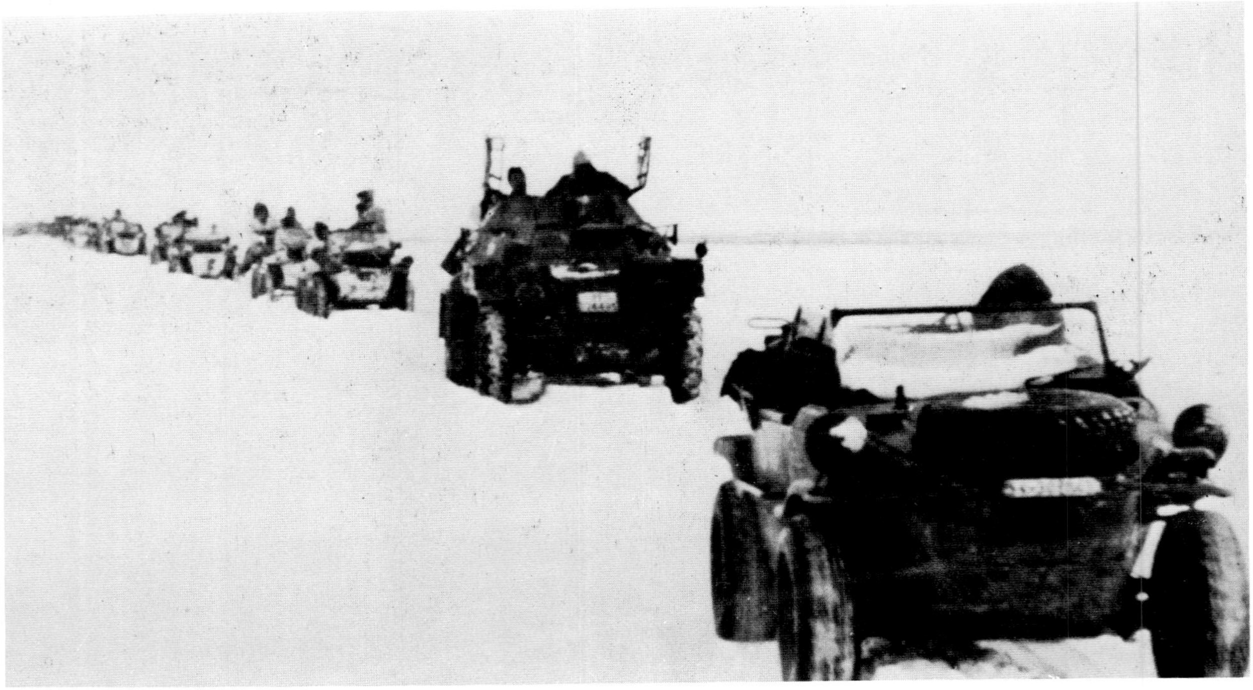

The reconnaissance unit of the LAH leads the counterattack on Charkow...

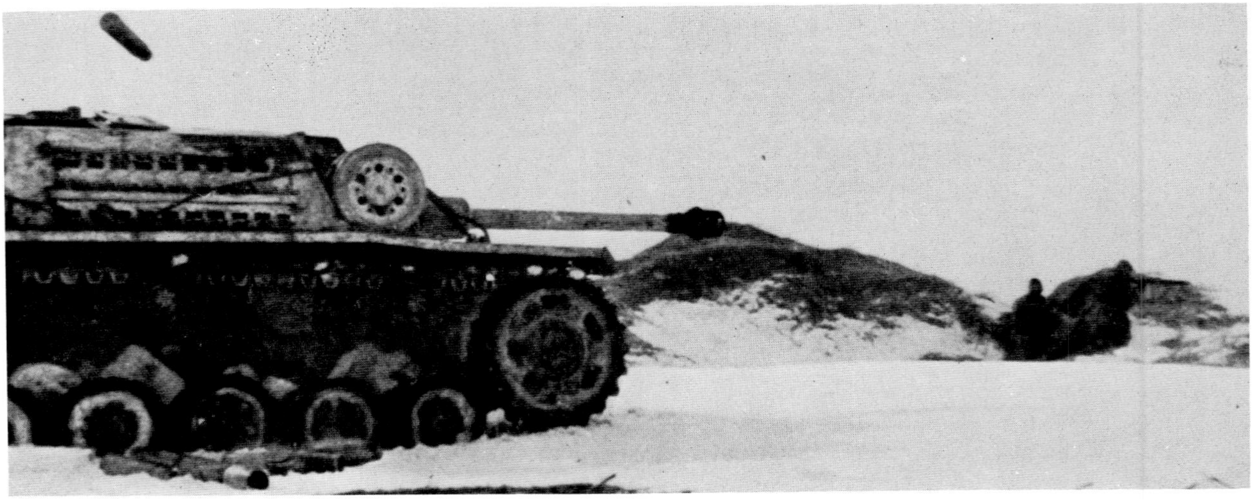

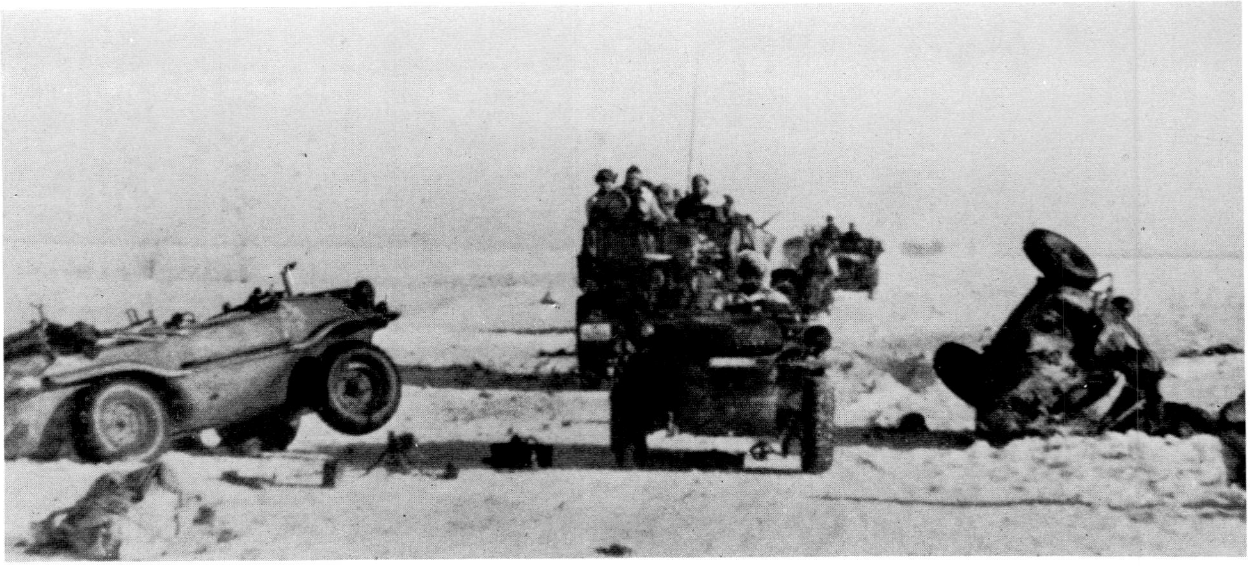

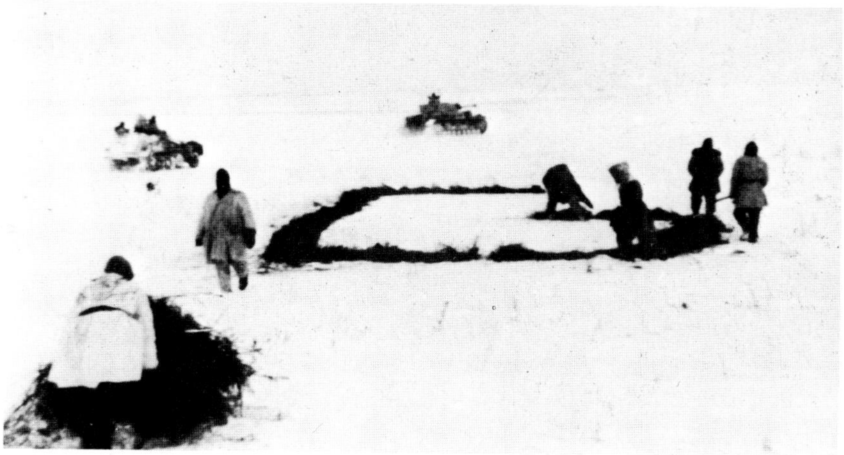

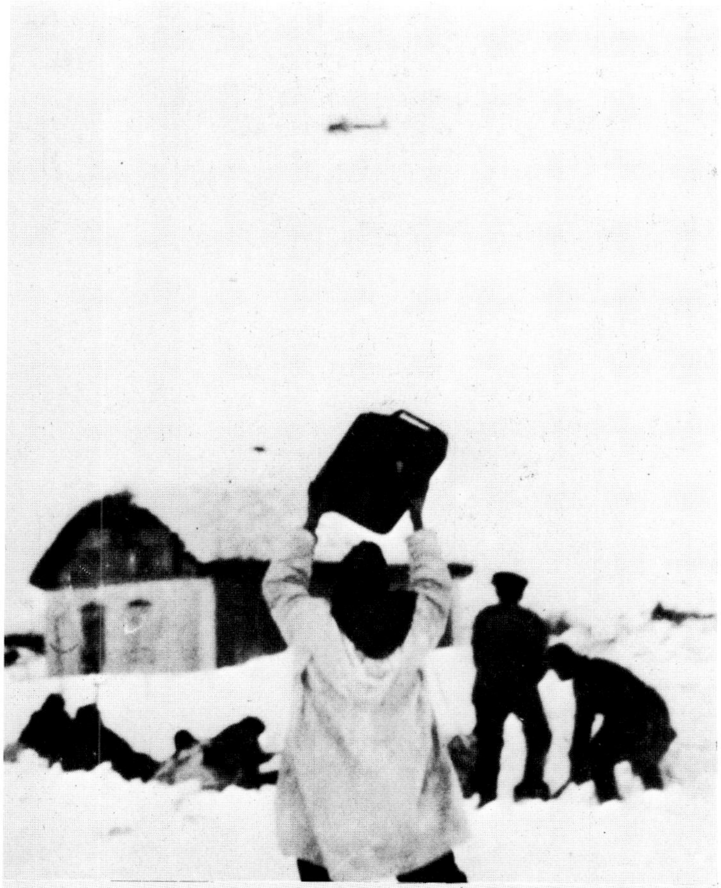

...and must stop due to a lack of gasoline. In a funny way, it is a now demanding supply through the air.

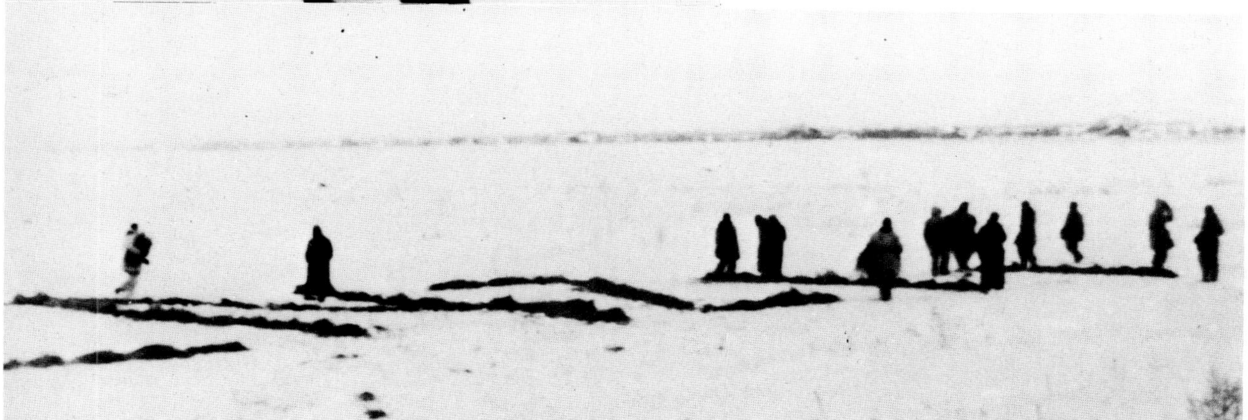

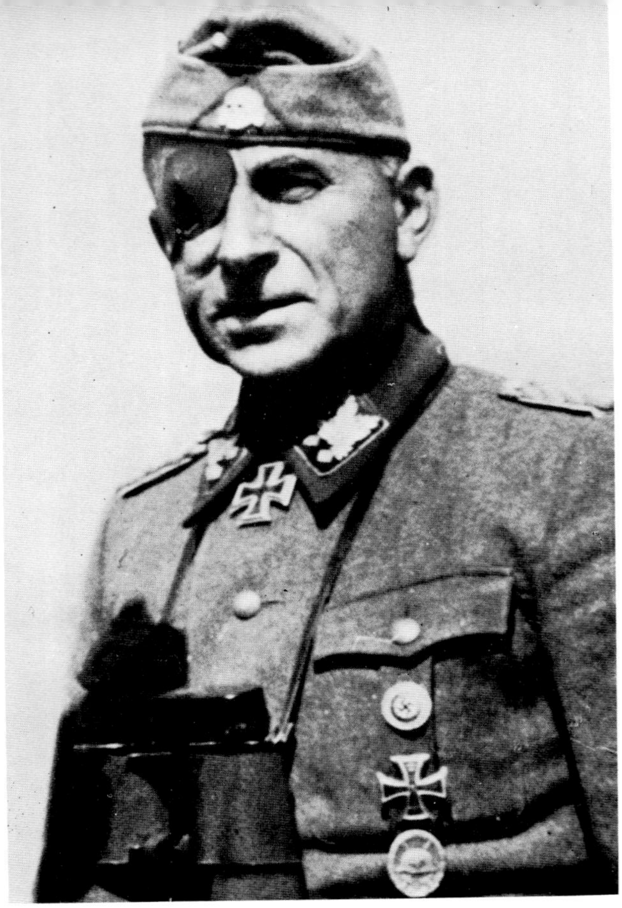

Lt. General and General of the Waffen-SS Paul Hausser makes the decision to withdraw from Charkow. He will recapture it later on.

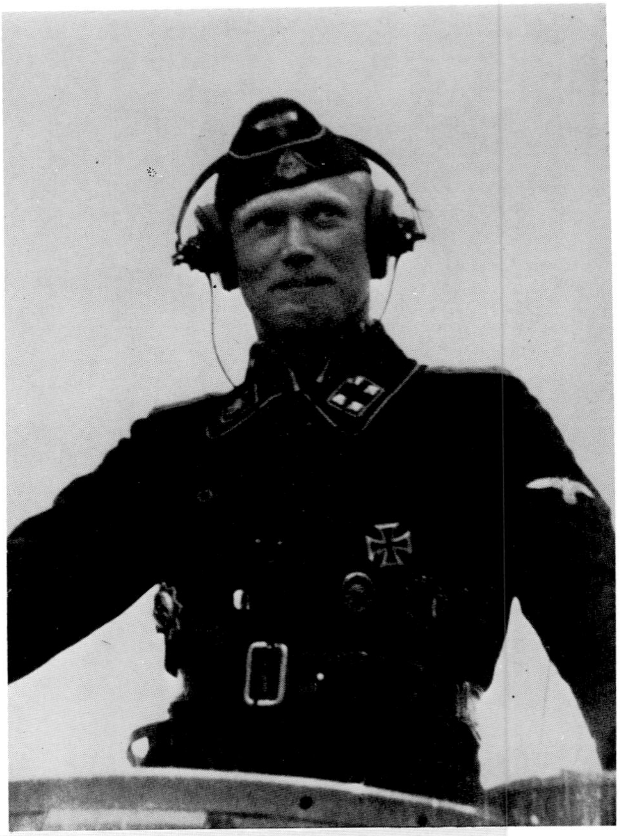

Major Christian Tychsen, "Das Reich".

Lt. Colonel Otto Kumm, "Der Führer" Division.

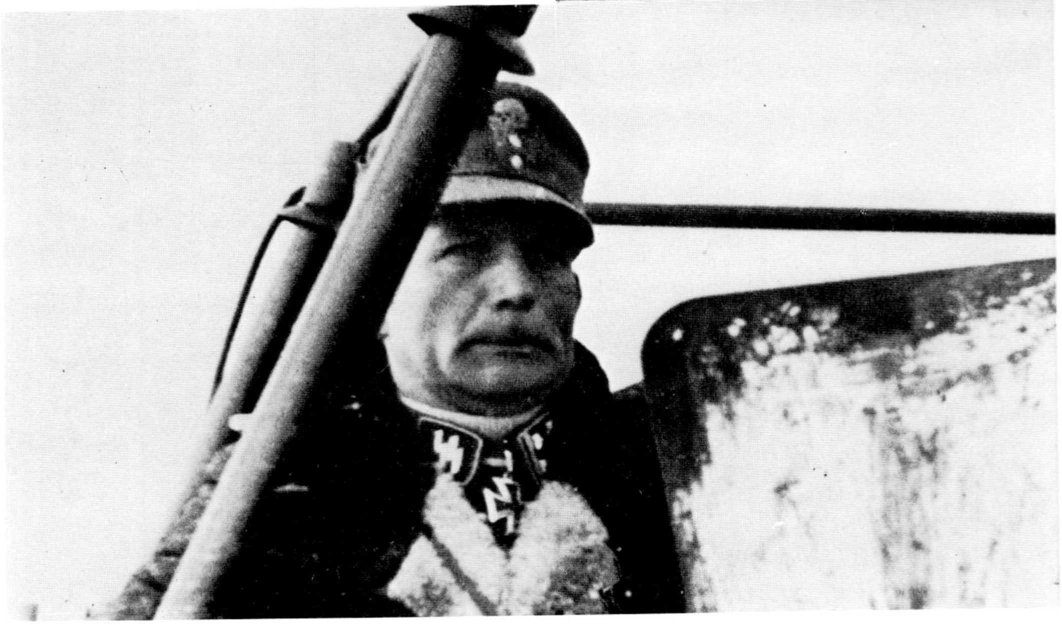

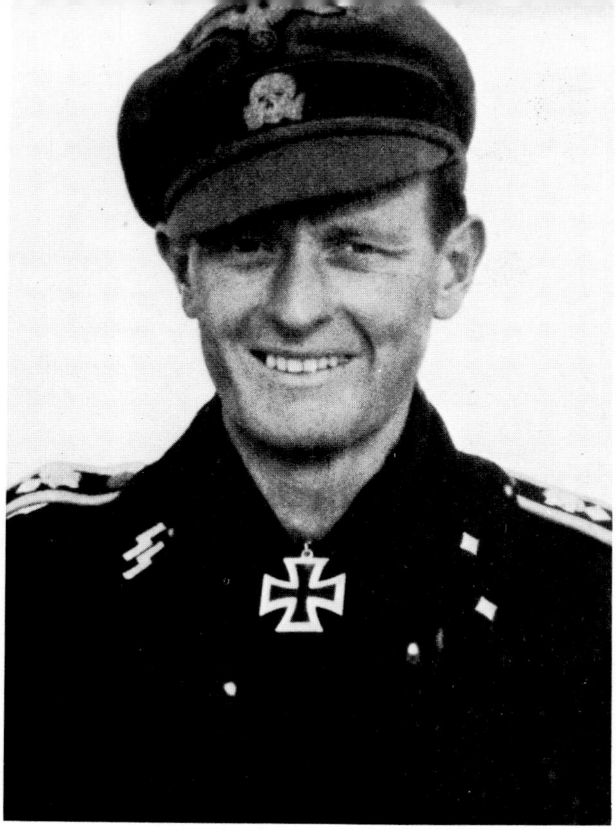

Captain Hans Reimling, 2. Pz. Rgt. LAH.

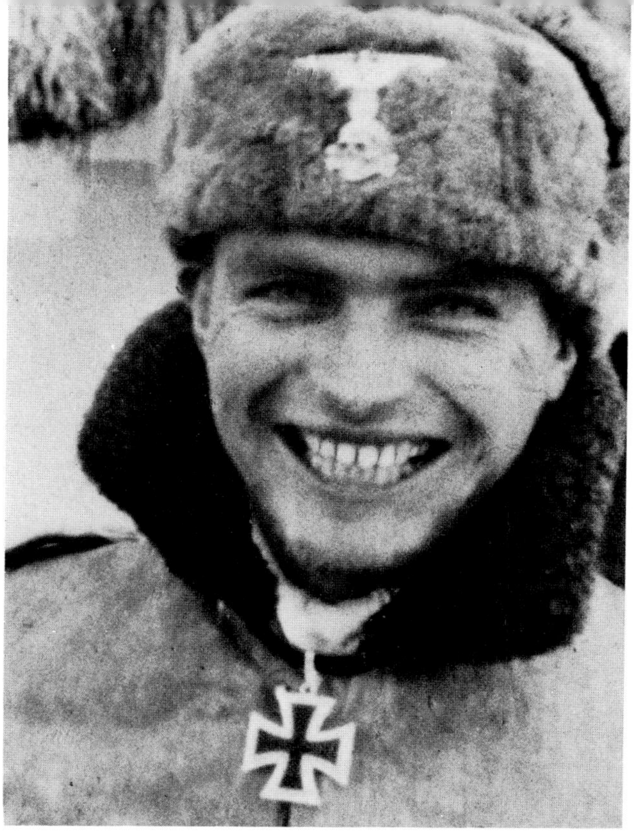

Major Max Wünsche, Cdr. I. Pz. Rgt. LAH.

Lt. Rudolf von Ribbentrop, son of the former Reichsminister for Foreign Affairs, in the turret of his Panzer IV tank during the counterattack on Charkow. von Ribbentrop was awarded the Ritterkreuz in July 1942.

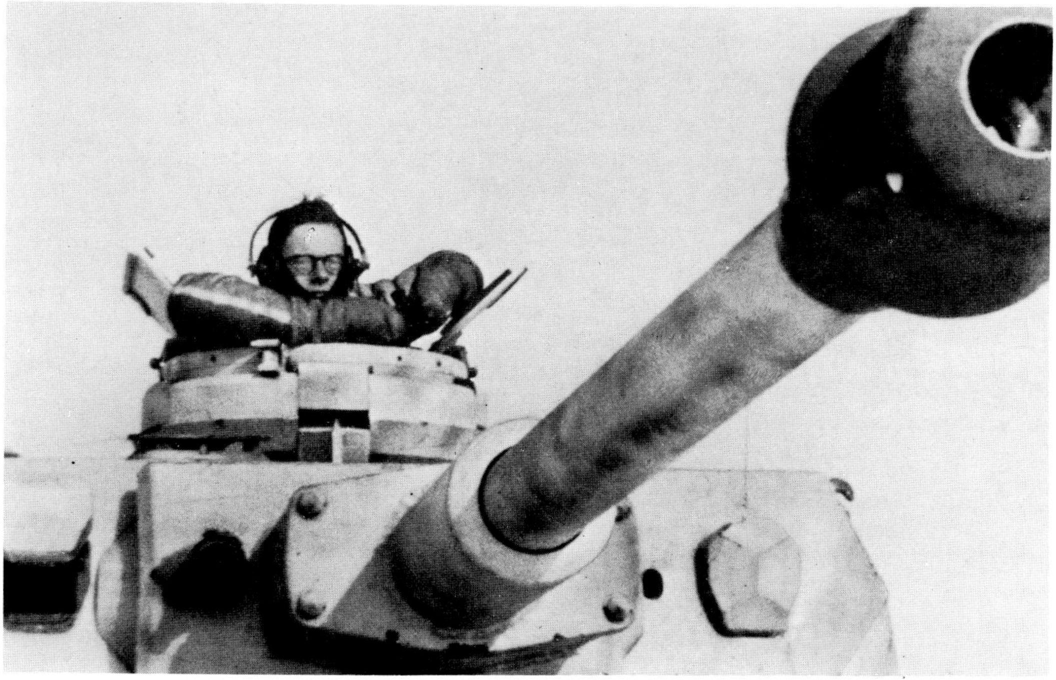

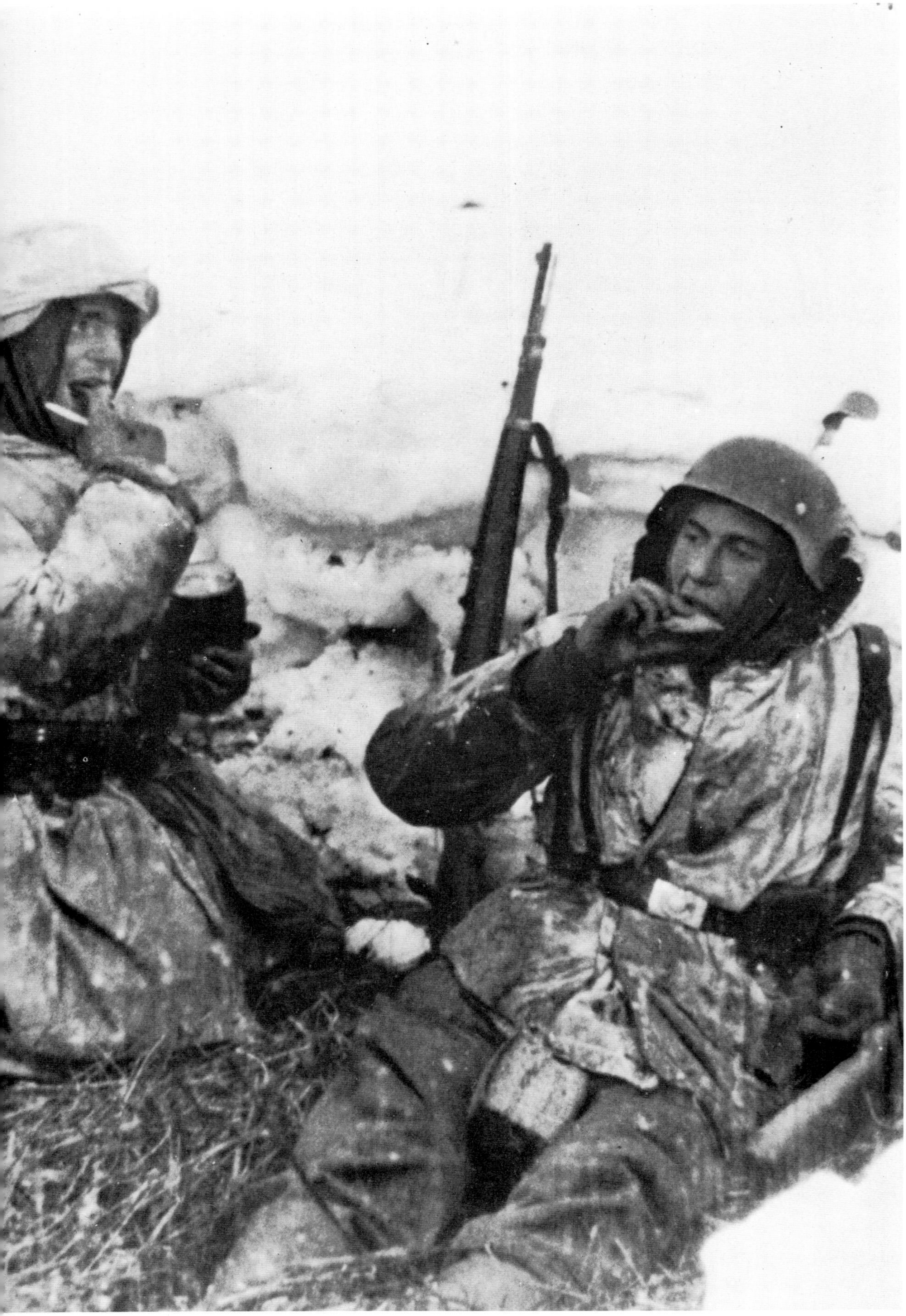

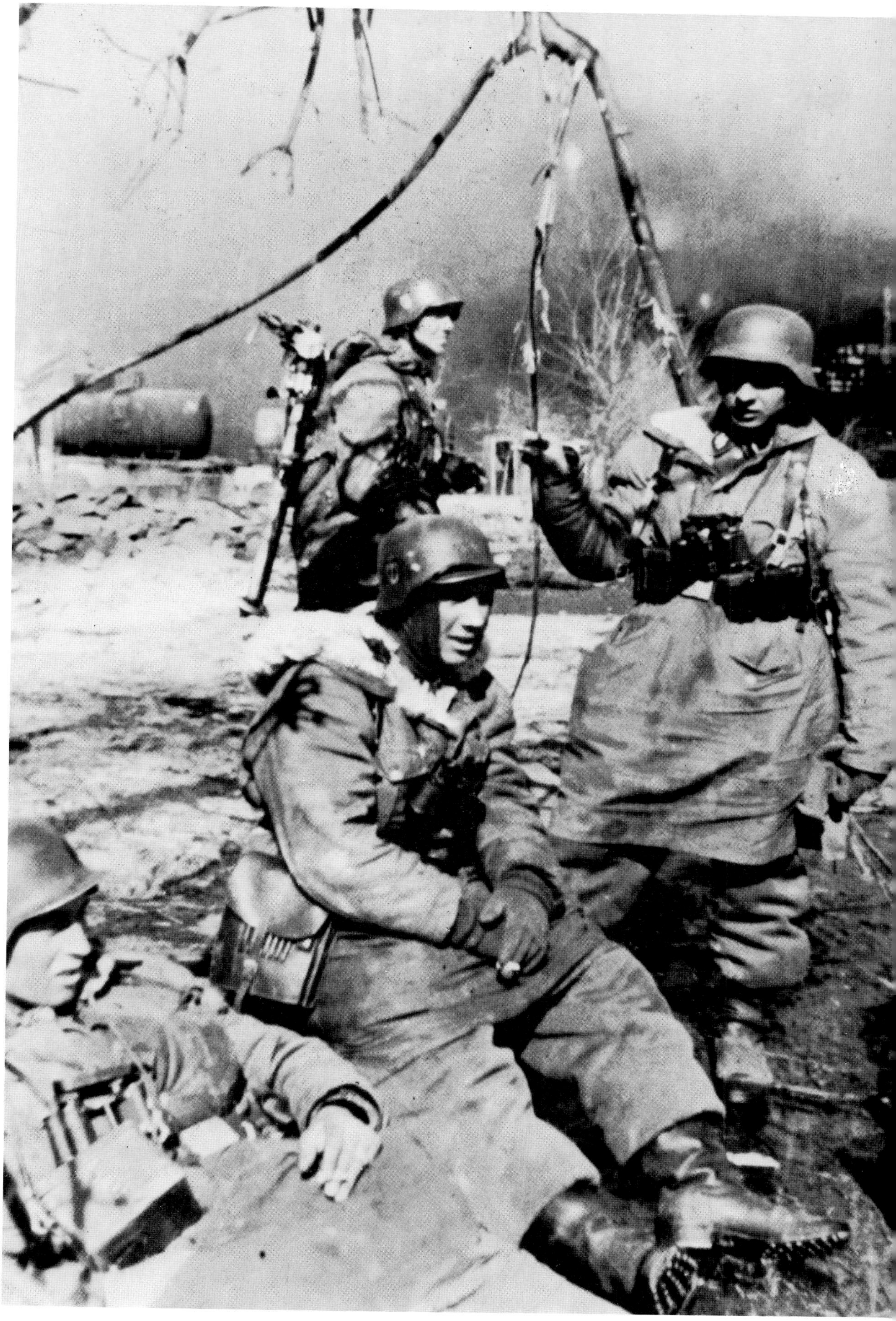

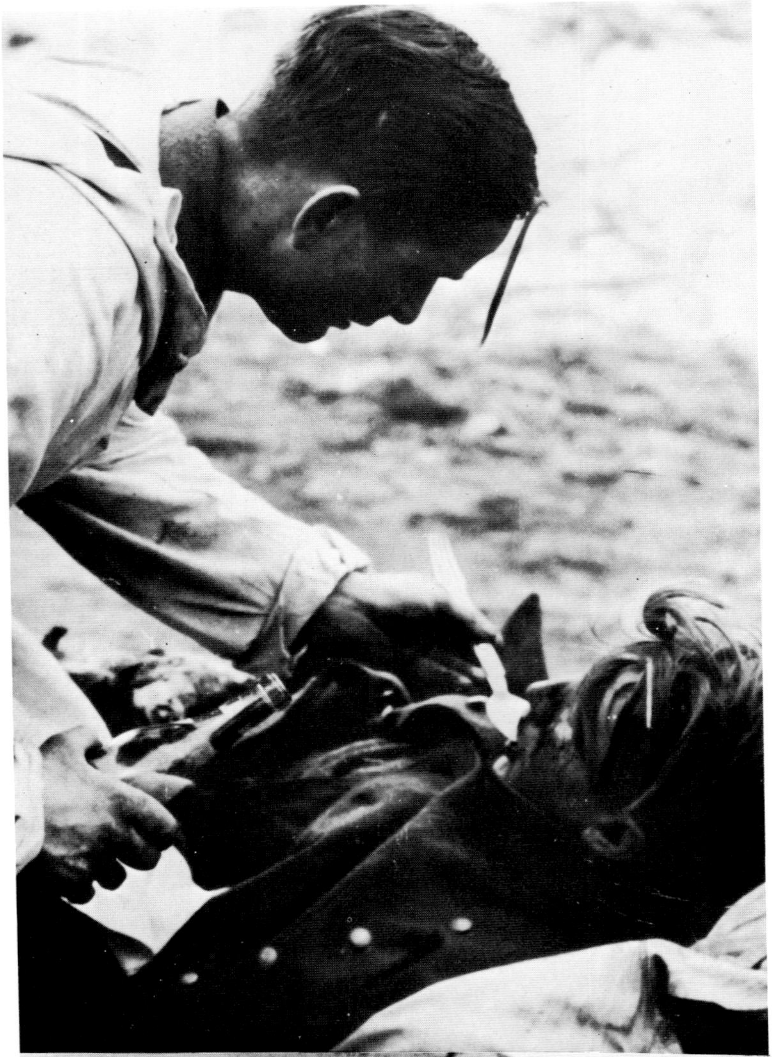

These two pictures illustrate the treatment of injured soldiers on the battlefield. They are some of the last photographs taken by the SS reporter Augustin who was killed during the Battle of Charkow.

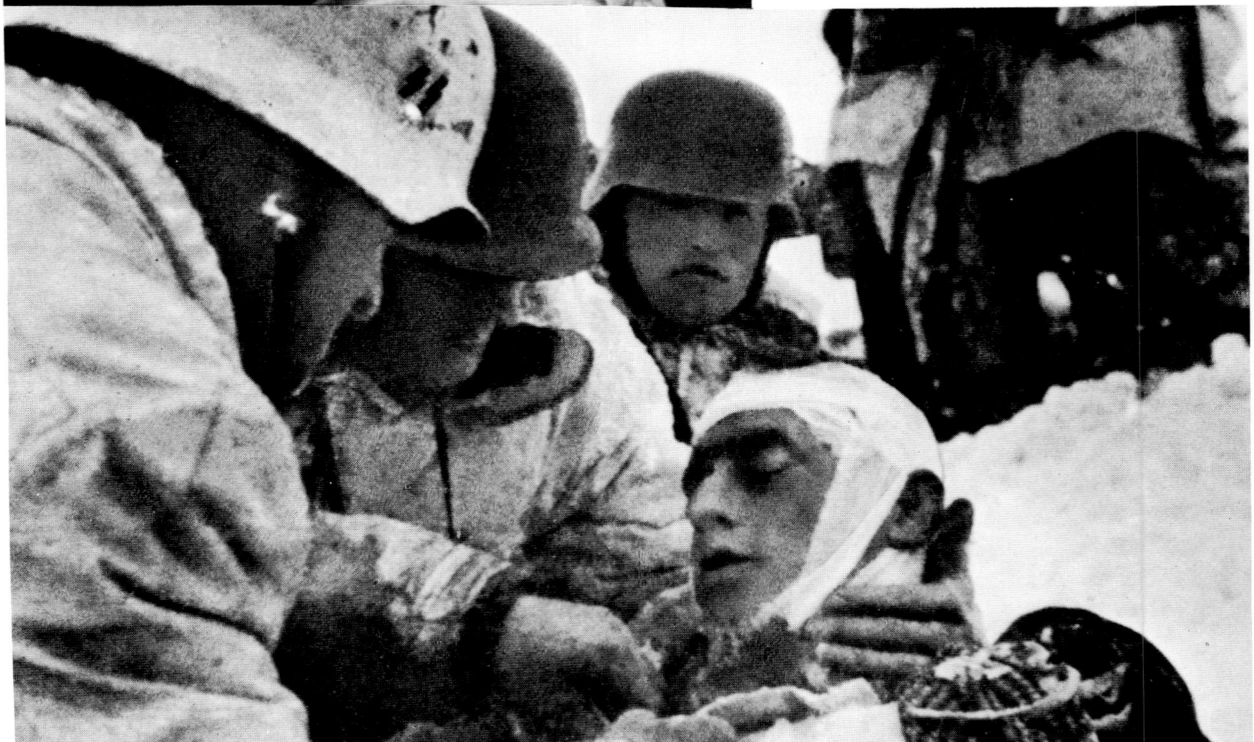

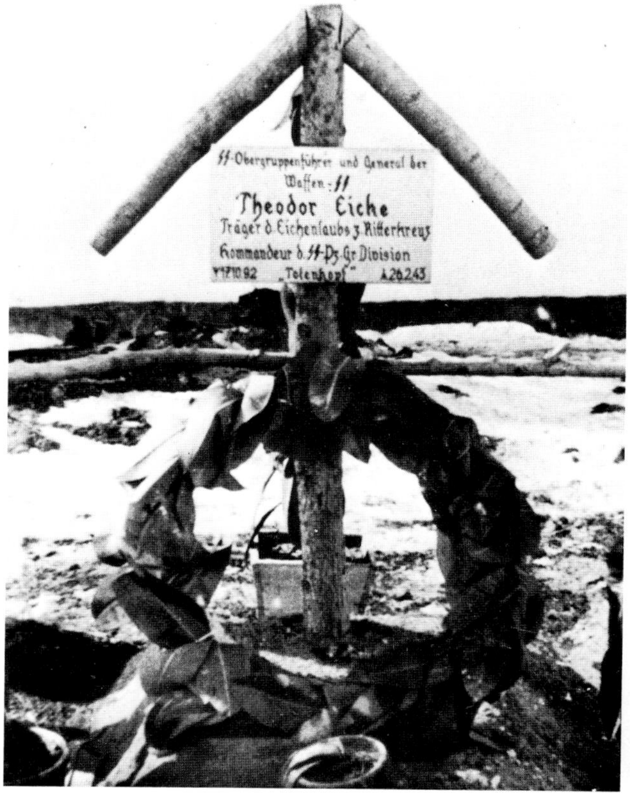
SS-Obergruppenführer und General der
Waffen-SS
Theodor Eicke
Träger d. Eichenlaubs z. Ritterkreuz
Kommandeur d. SS-Pz.Gr.Division
*17.10.92 „Totenkopf" †26.2.43

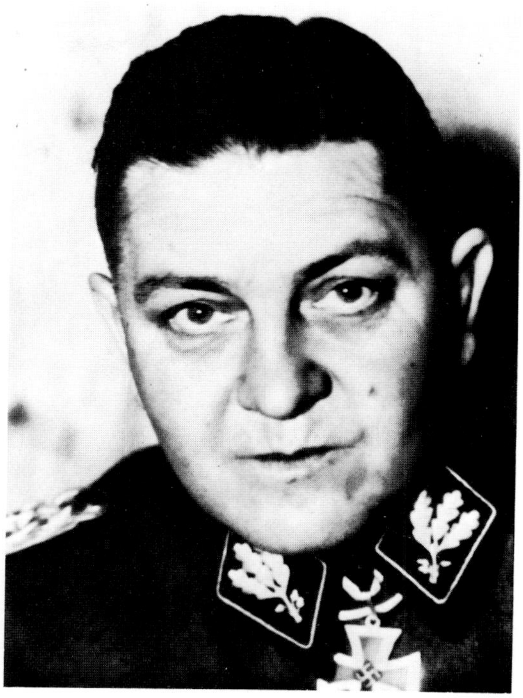

The grave of SS-Lt. General Theodor Eicke near Orelka.

Burial of an unknown SS-soldier on the Red Square of Charkow.

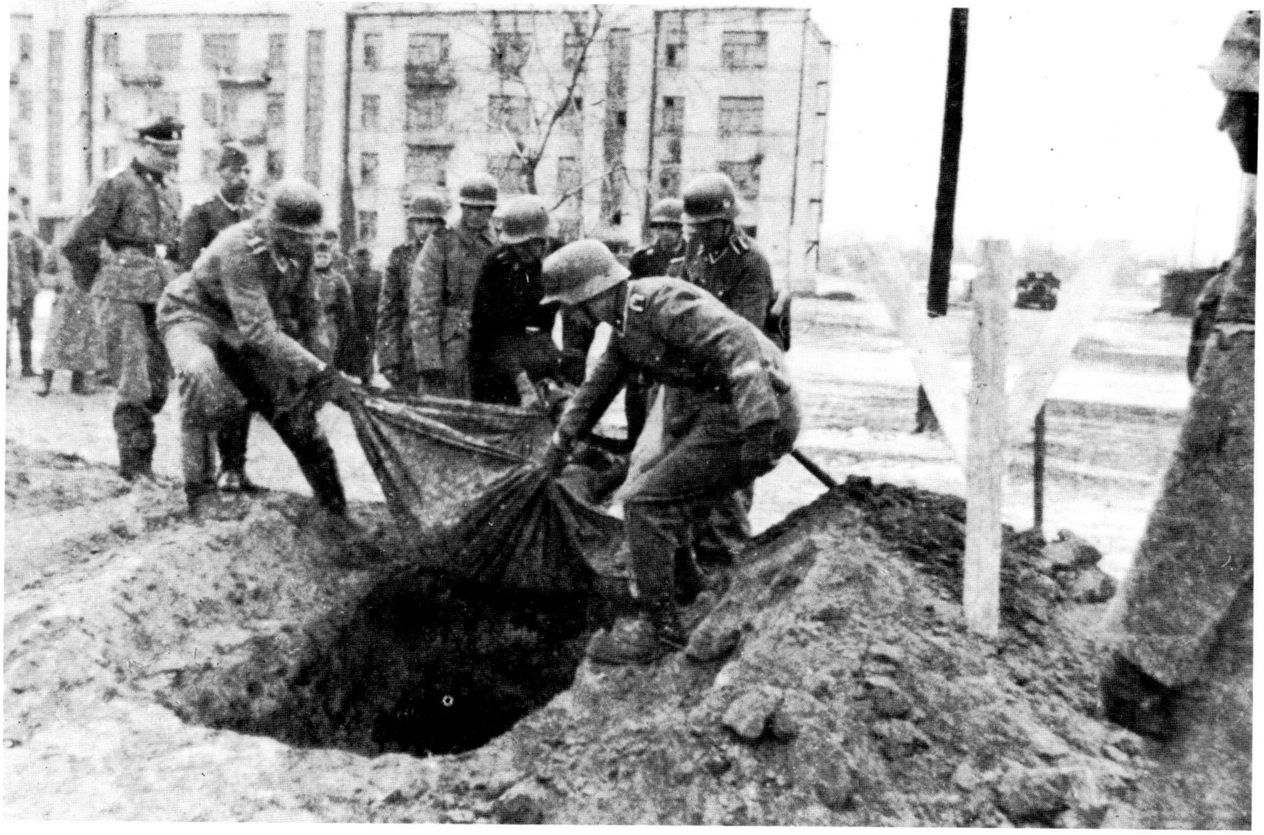

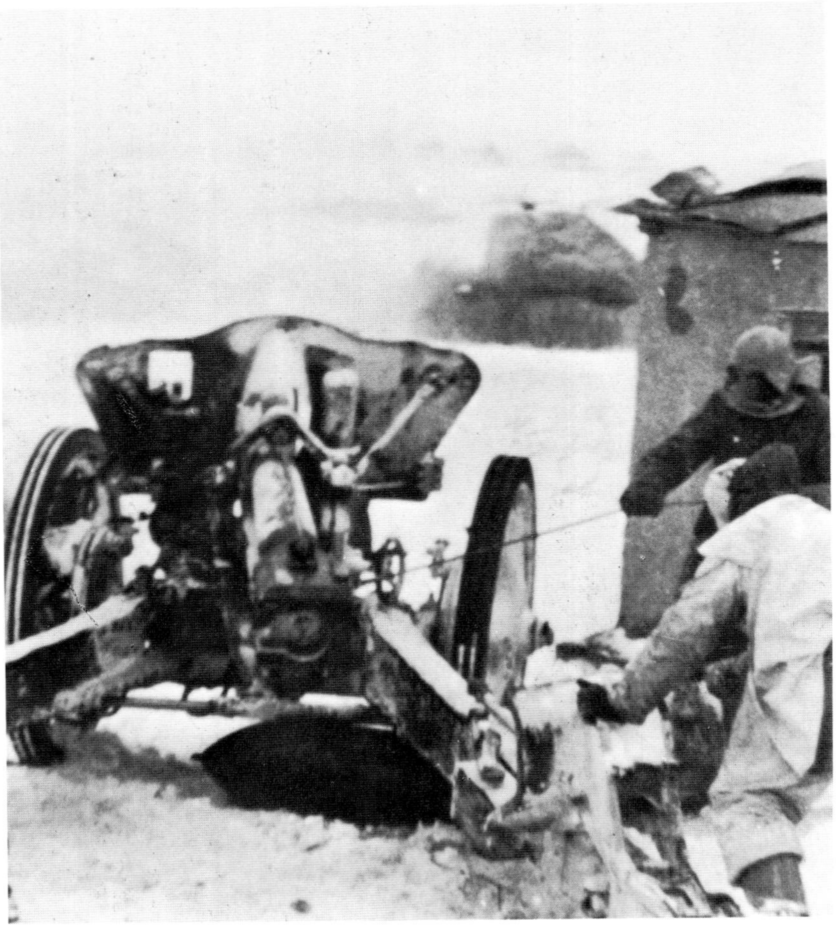

On the way to Charkow. A firing light field-howitzer.

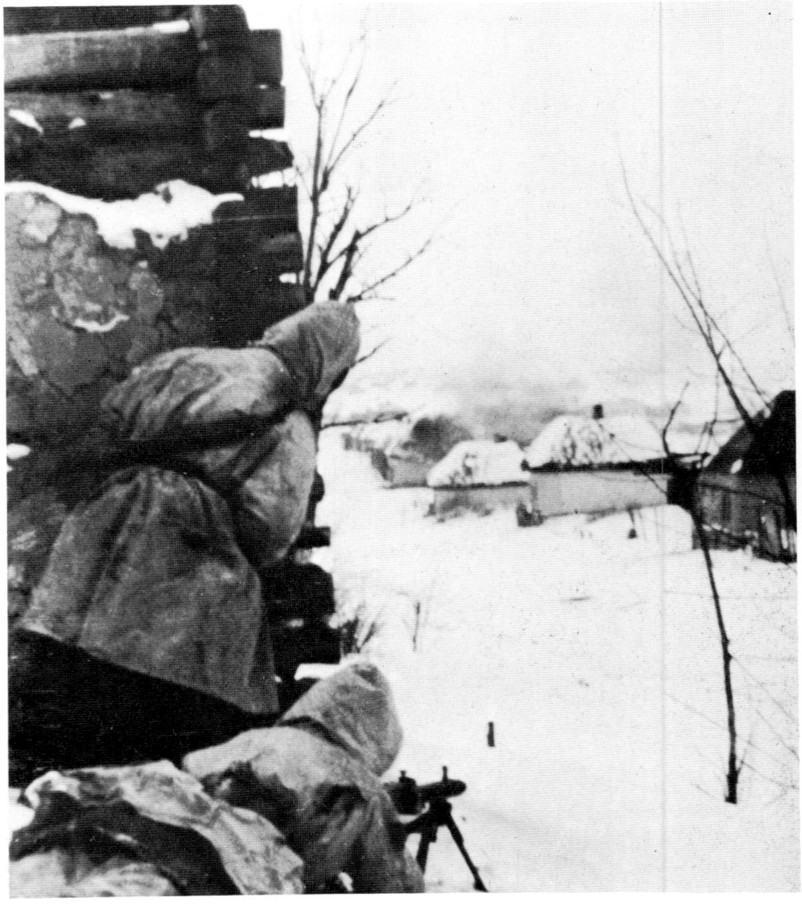

A machine gun providing cover to the advancing infantry.

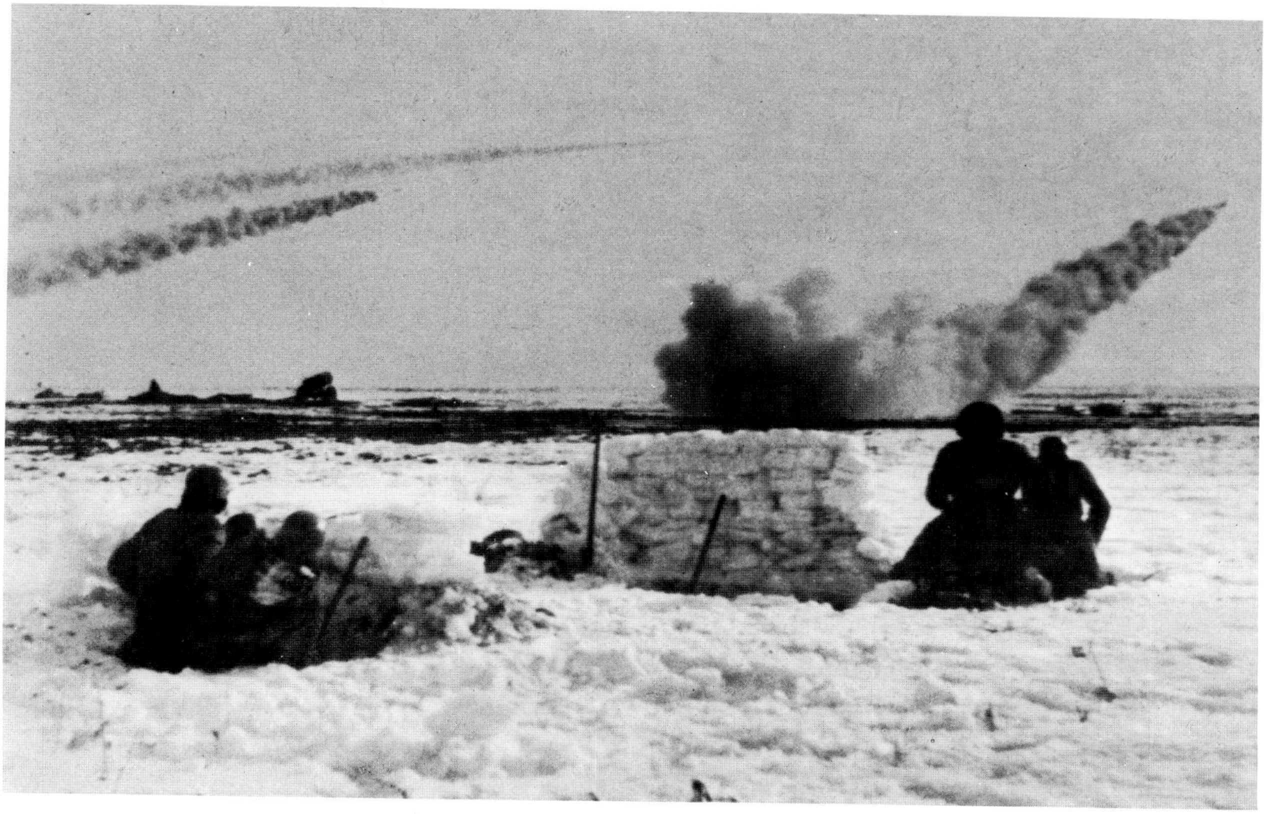

Salvo gun prepares to fire on the center of Charkow.

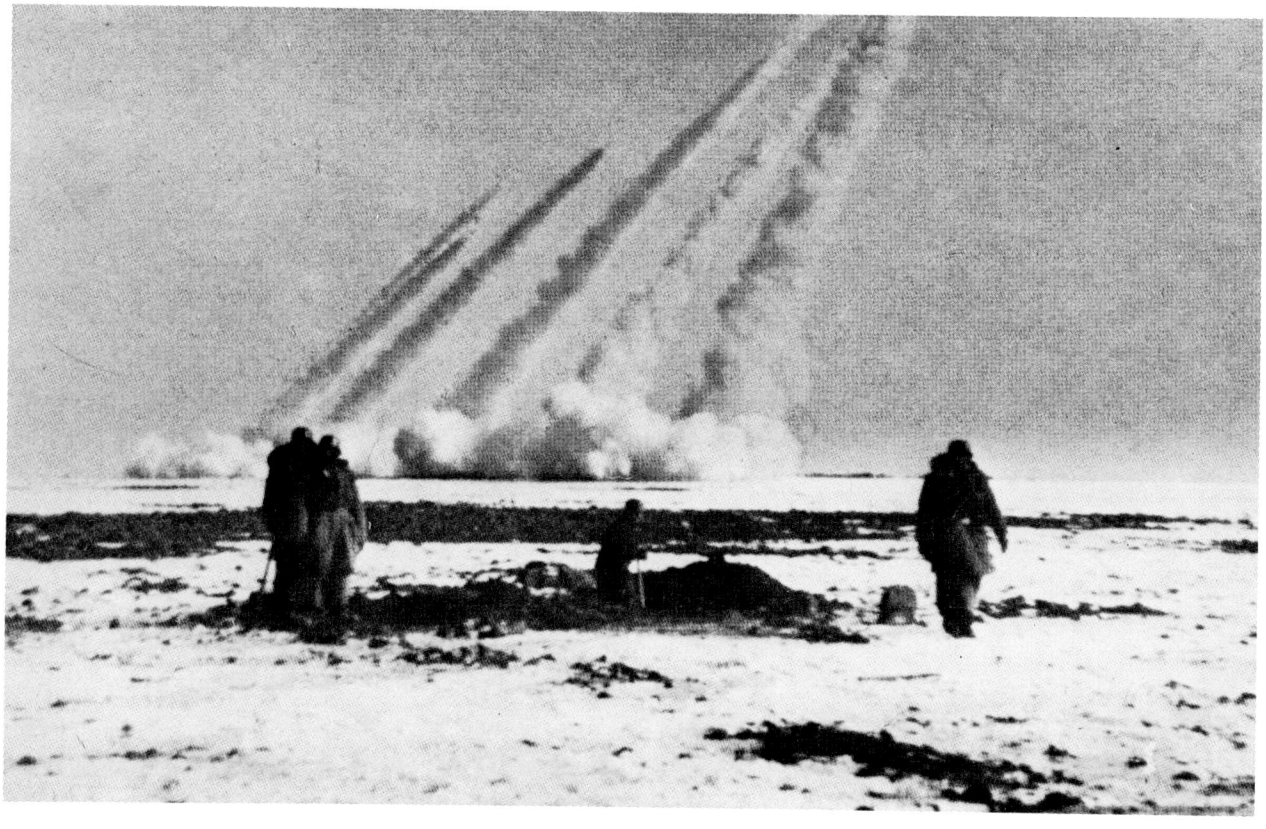

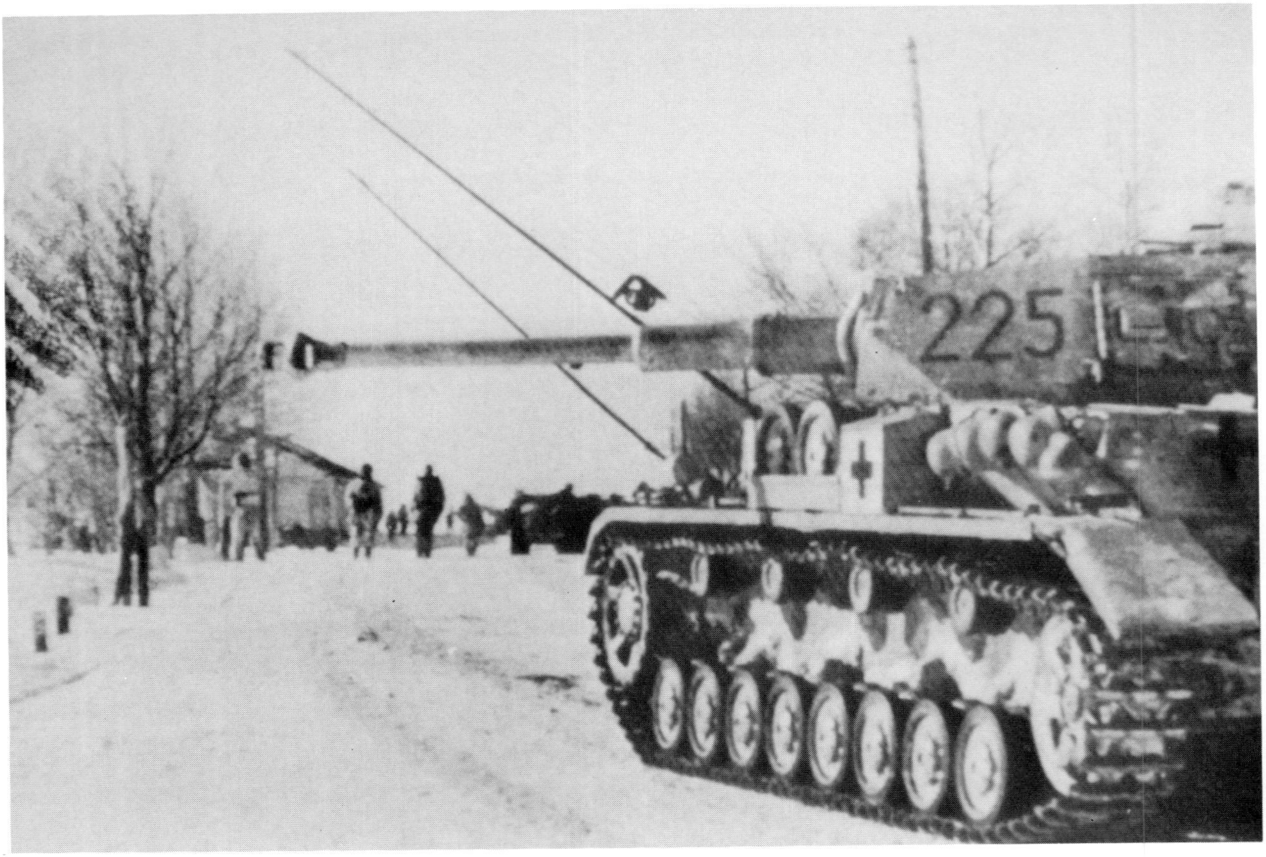
225

Units of the LAH have reached the outskirts of Charkow.

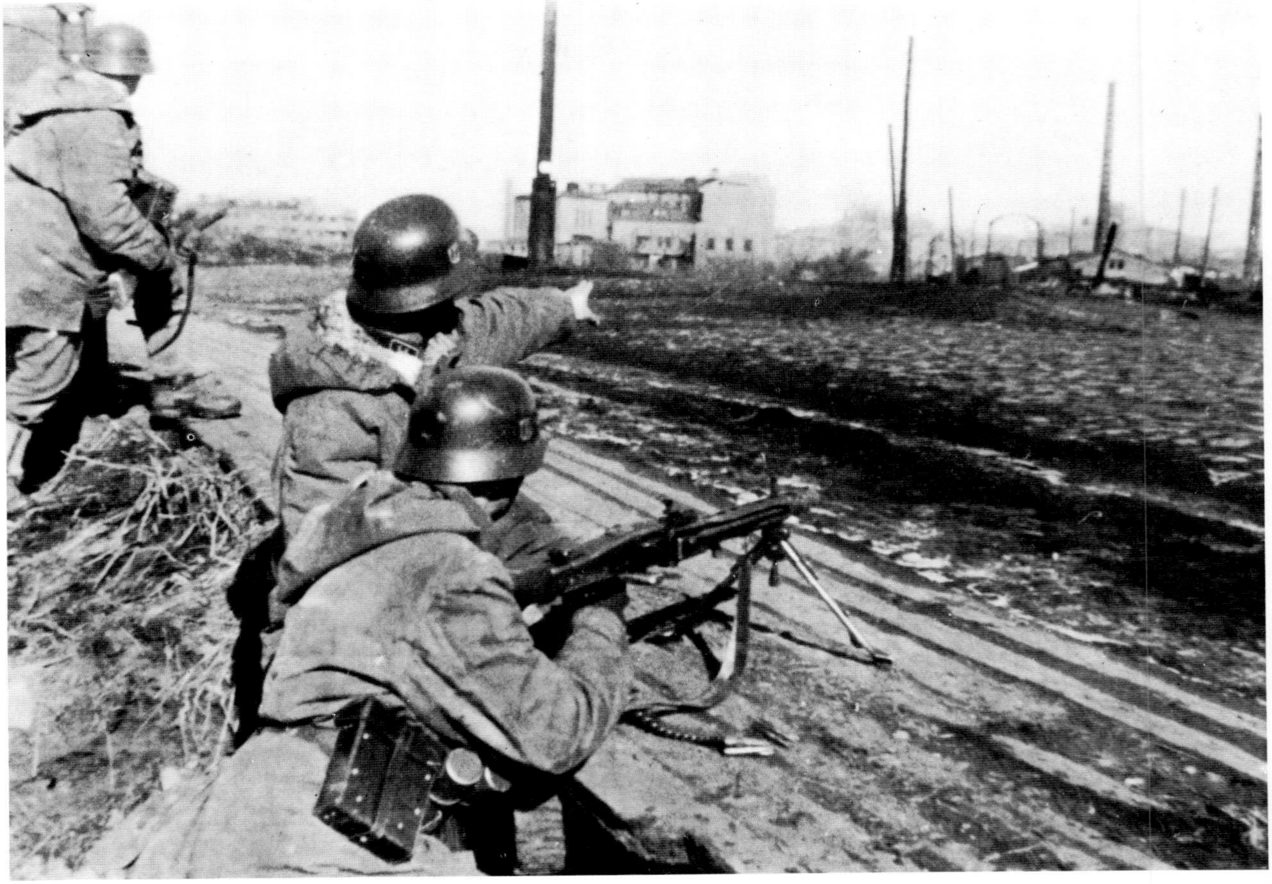

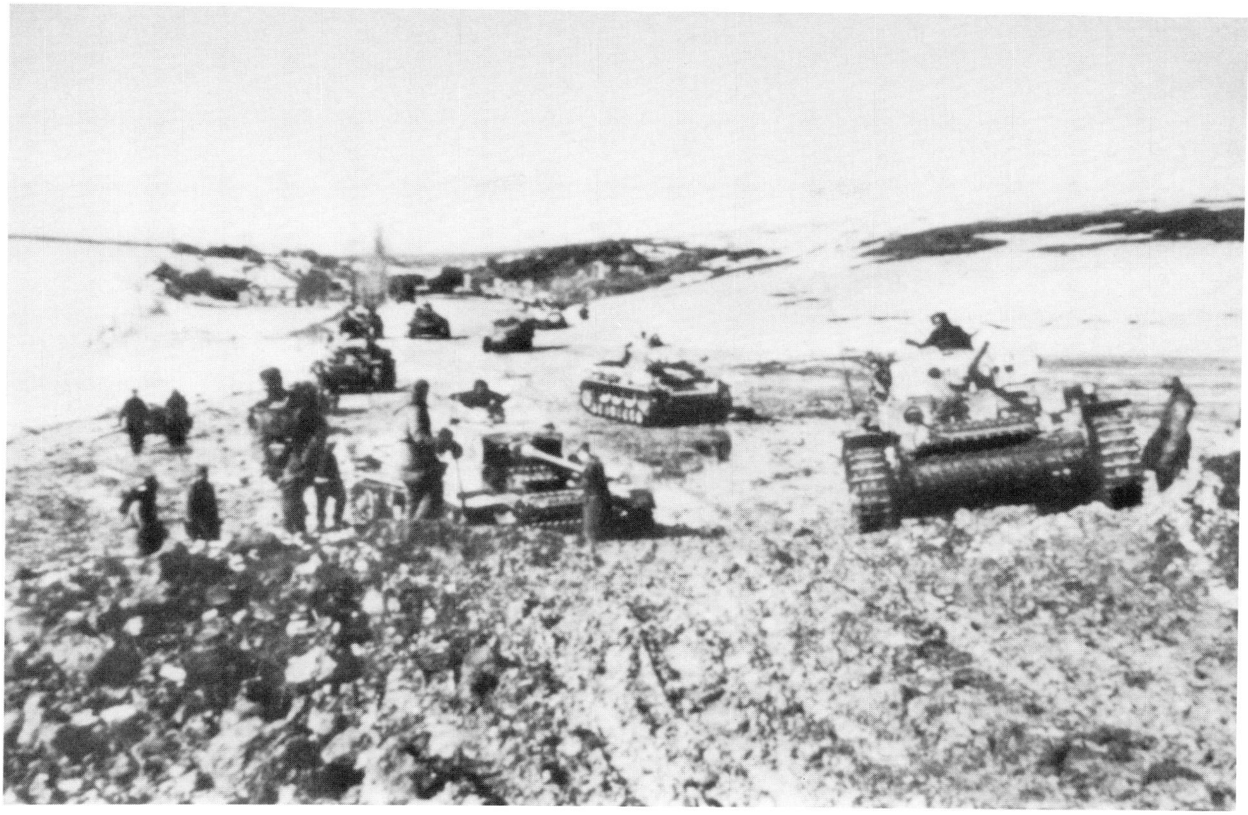

The encircling attacks of the T-Division developed successfully in spite of the difficult terrain.
Tanks of the Division "Das Reich" enter Charkow.

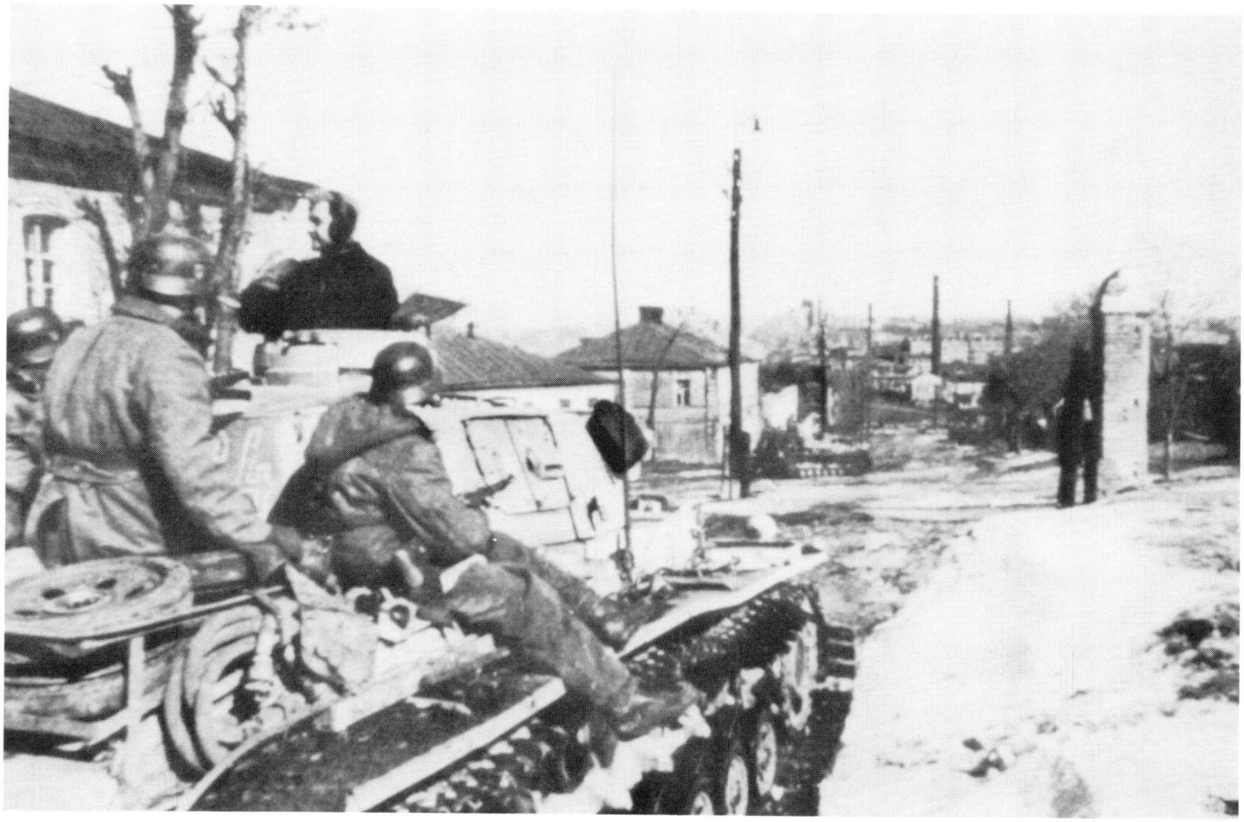

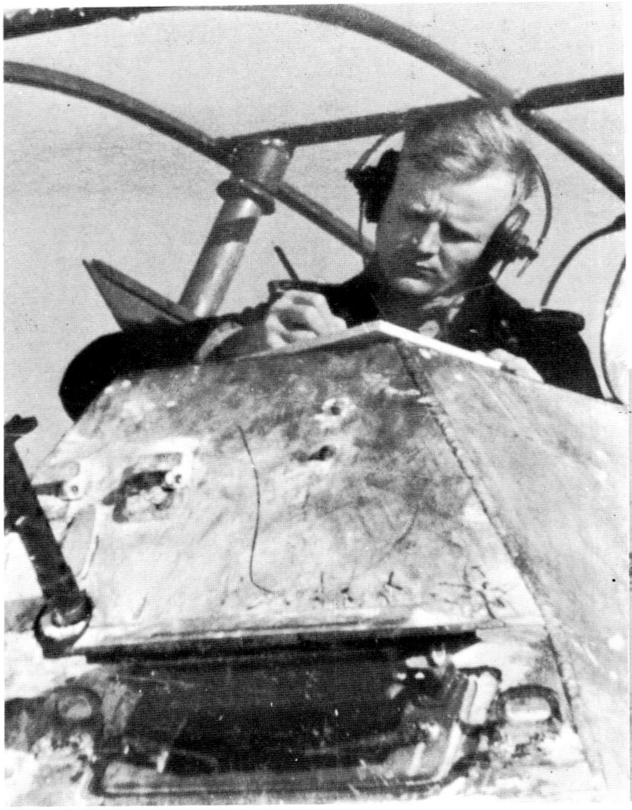

The commander of an armored car reports.

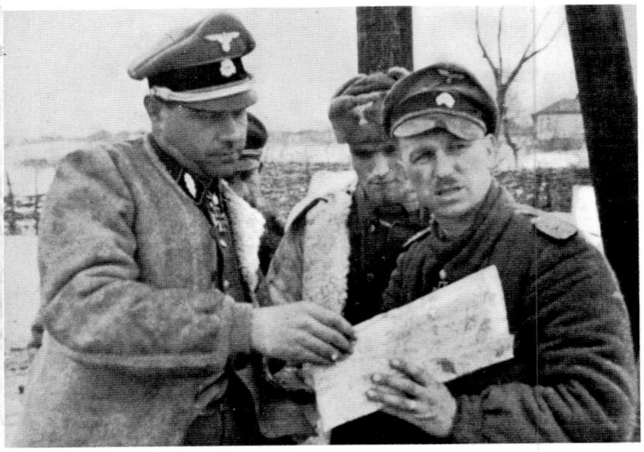

Commander of the LAH. From the left: Witt, Wünsche, "Panzermeyer".

"Panzermeyer" gives fire commands to Panzer IV tanks while his Alsatian dog obviously complains about the noise.

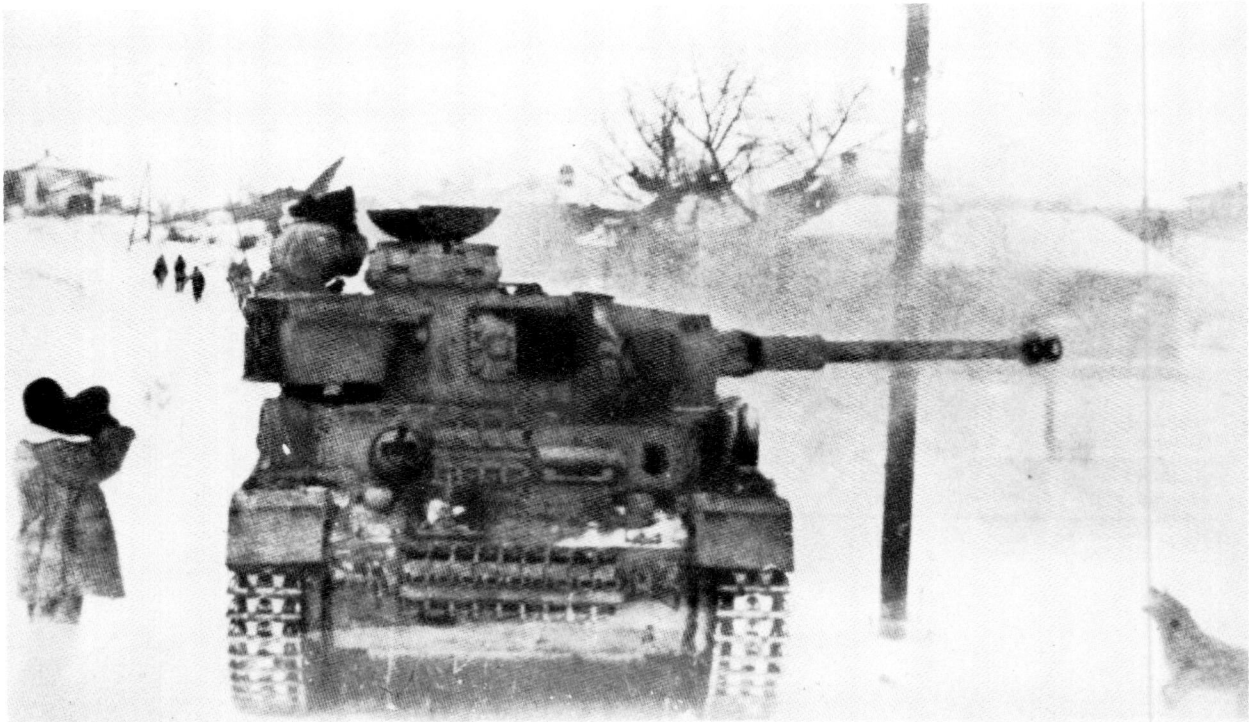

75 mm self-propelled anti-tank gun and a light machine gun are involved in street battles for the "Peiper bridge".

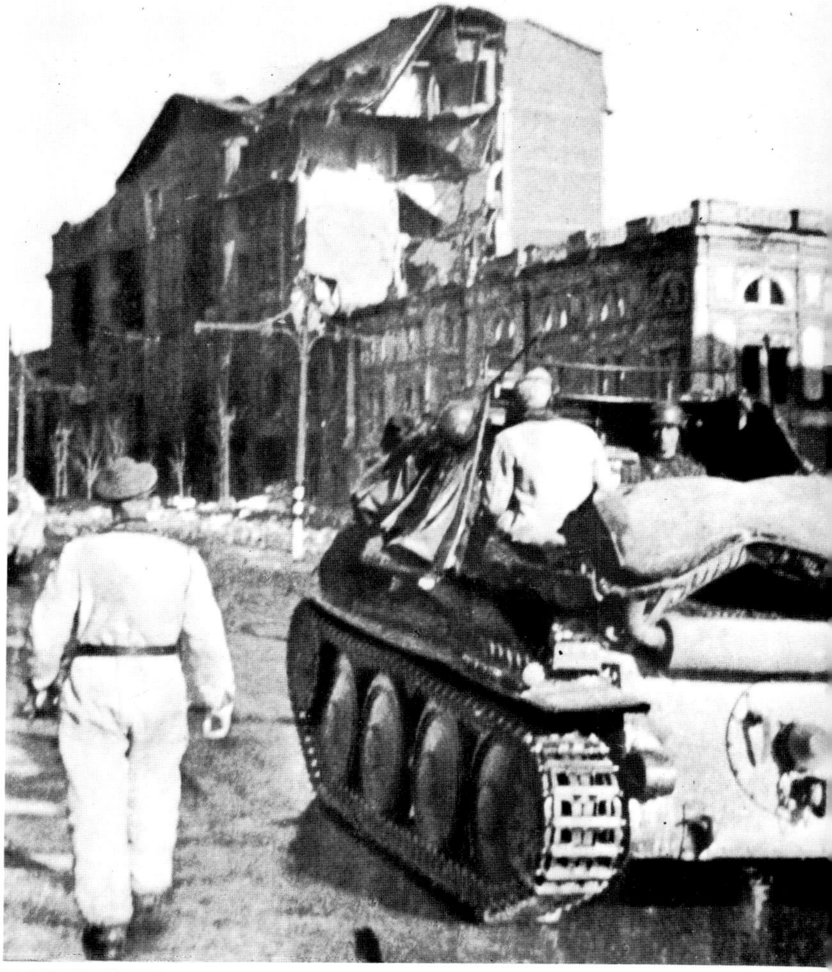

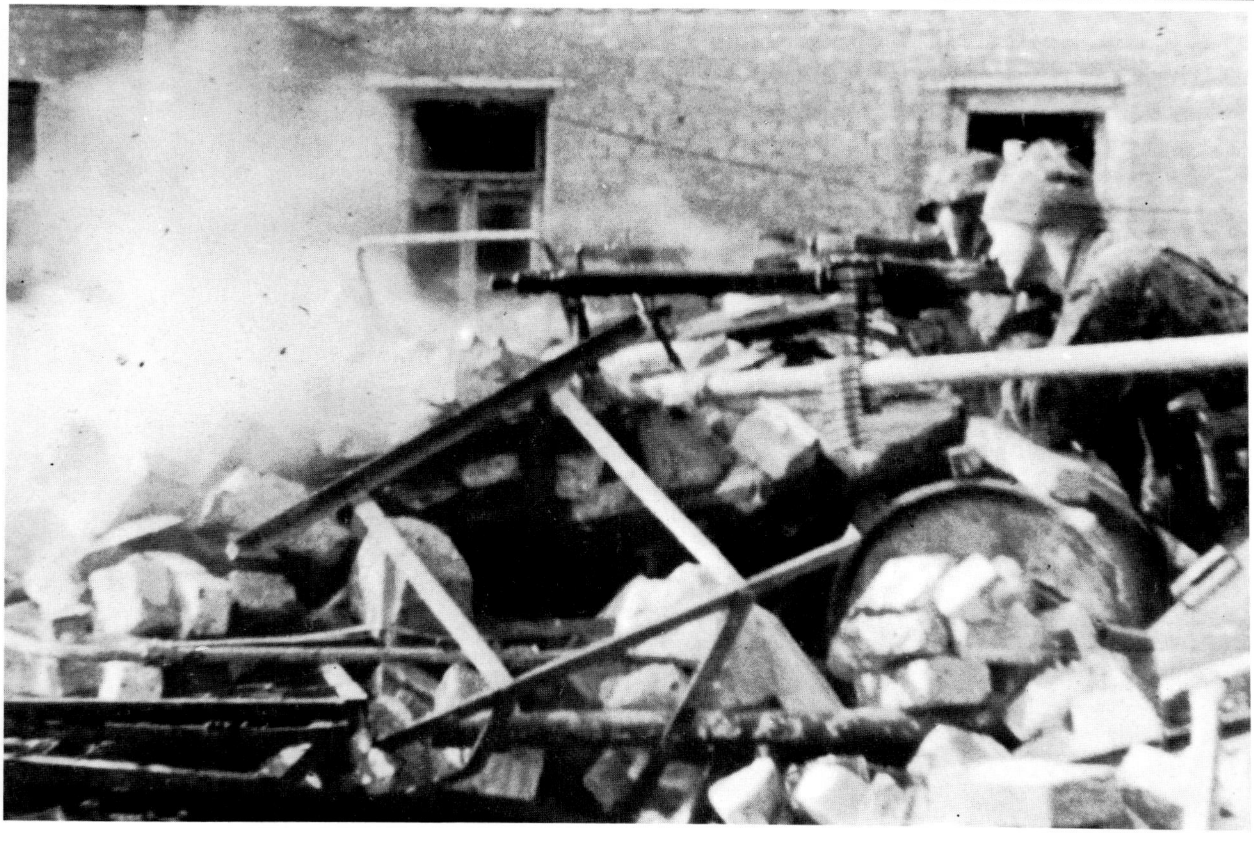

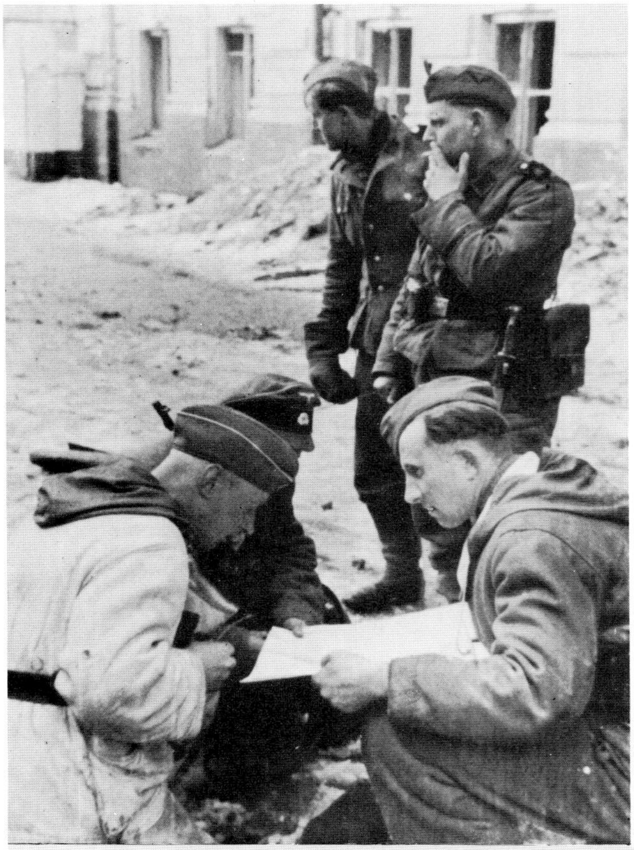

On the Red Square in Charkow. Left: Major Max Hansen, Photo below, from the left: Captain K.H. Prinz, Colonel Witt and Colonel Wisch in his SPW.

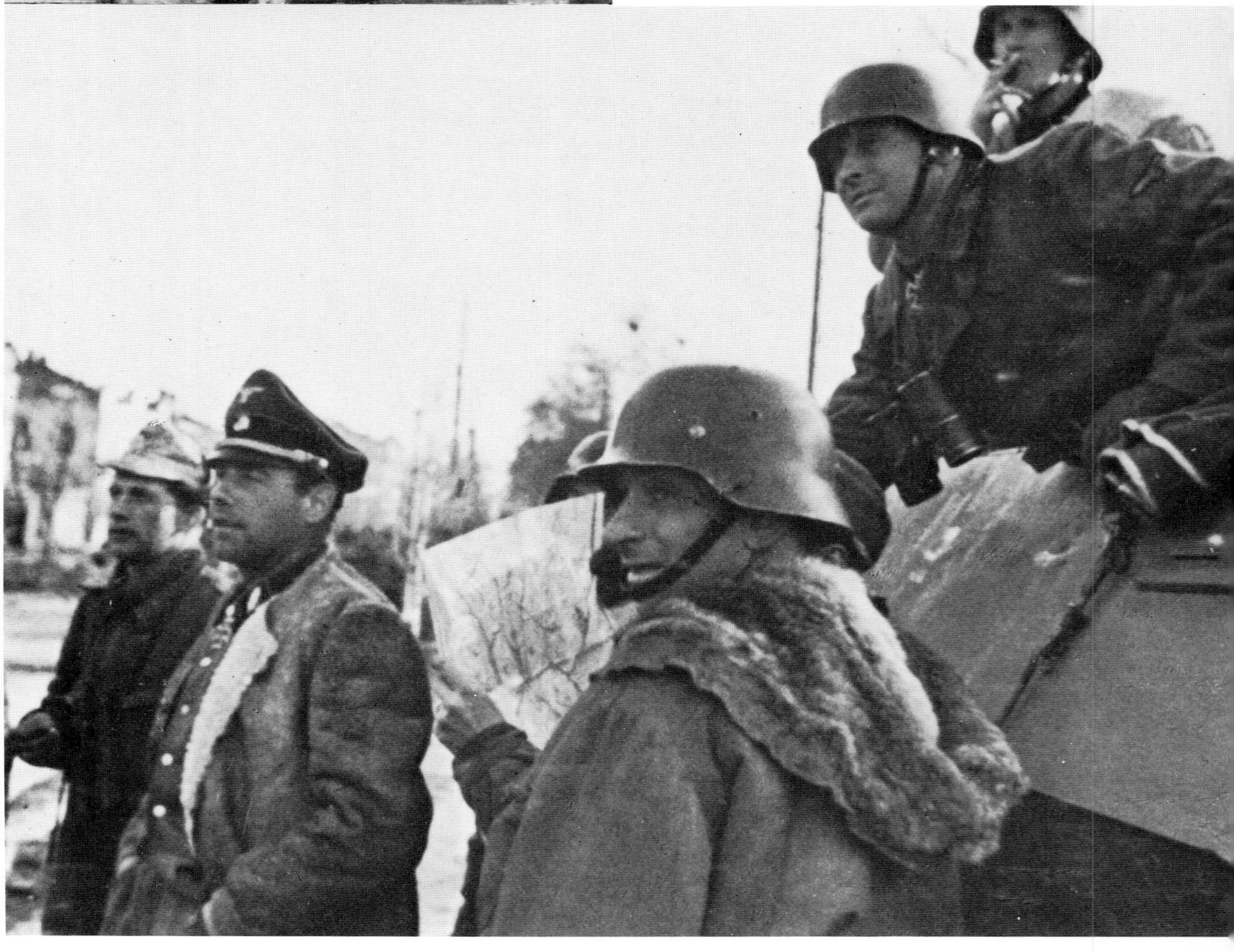

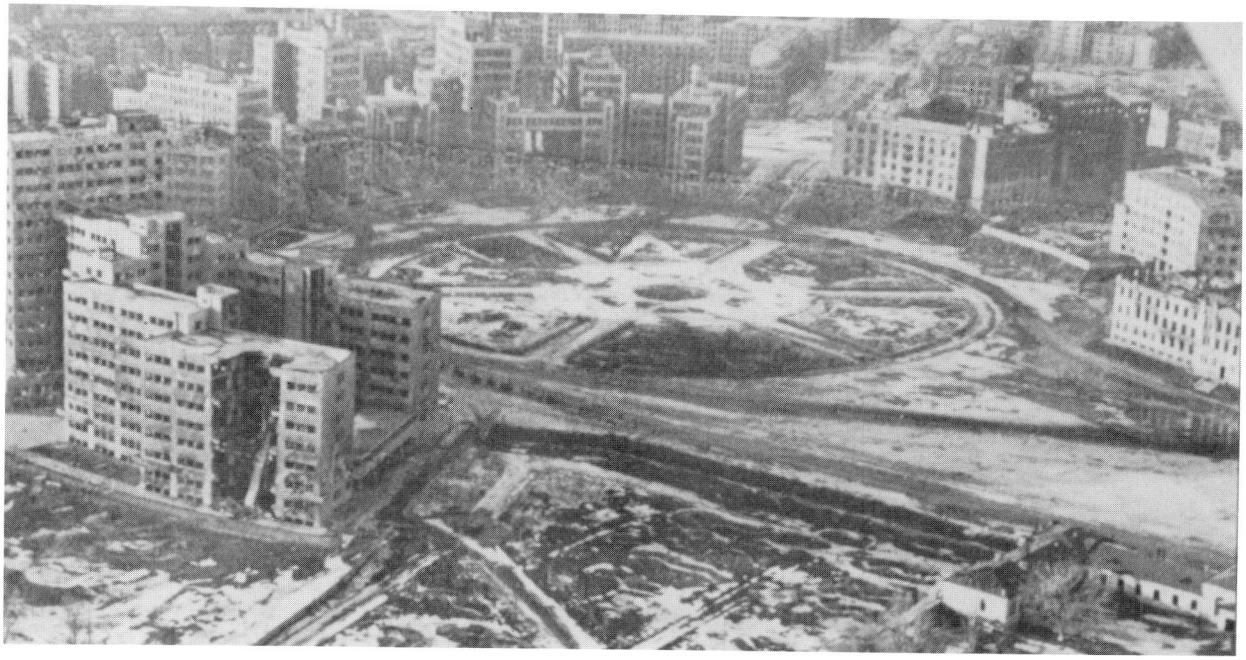

An aerial view of the Red Square in Charkow...

...which was renamed the "Square of the LAH". The indicators show the names of the three SS-divisions which were engaged in the battles of Charkow.

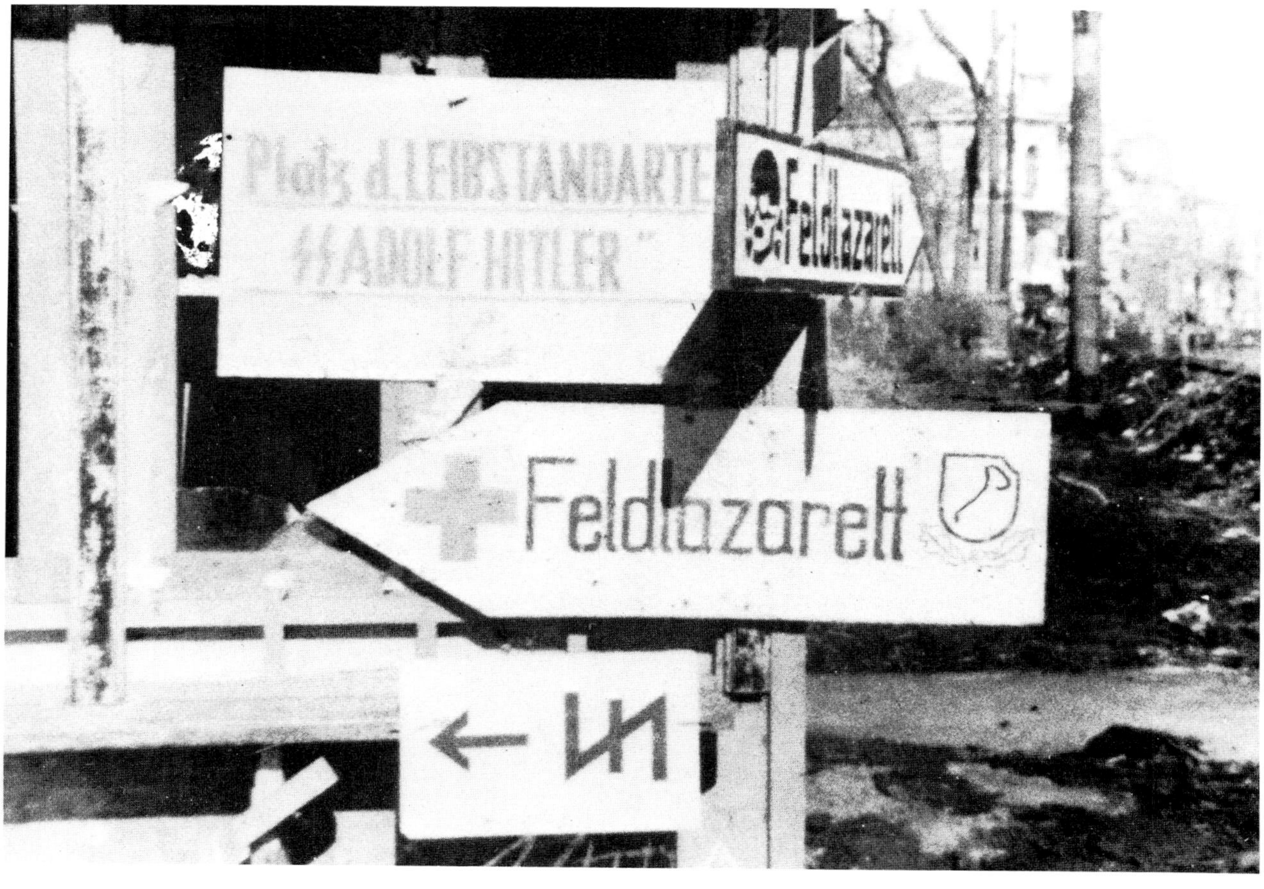
Platz d. LEIBSTANDARTE
SS ADOLF HITLER"
Feldlazarett
Feldlazarett

The captured tractor factory in Charkow continues producing T-34 tanks, however, under German control now.

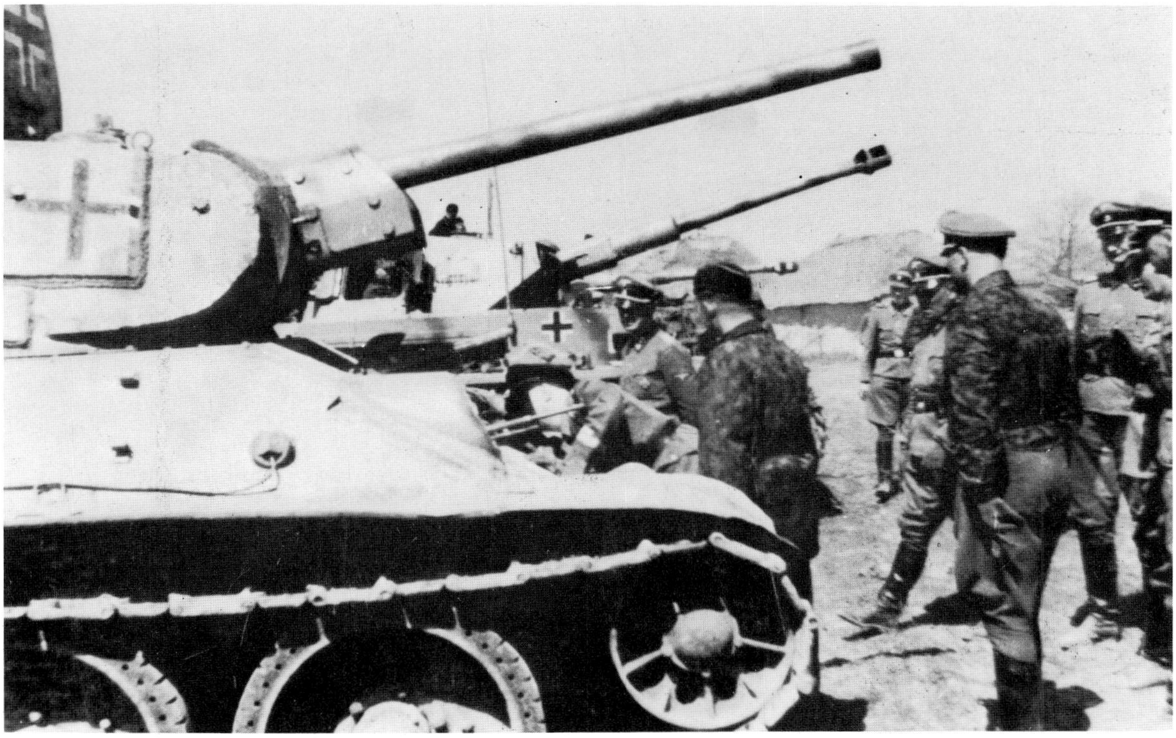

These tanks, which were later used in guerilla warfare, were of special interest to Reichsführer SS Himmler. "Reichsheini" in the turret of a tank, which he was only able to enter with assistance.

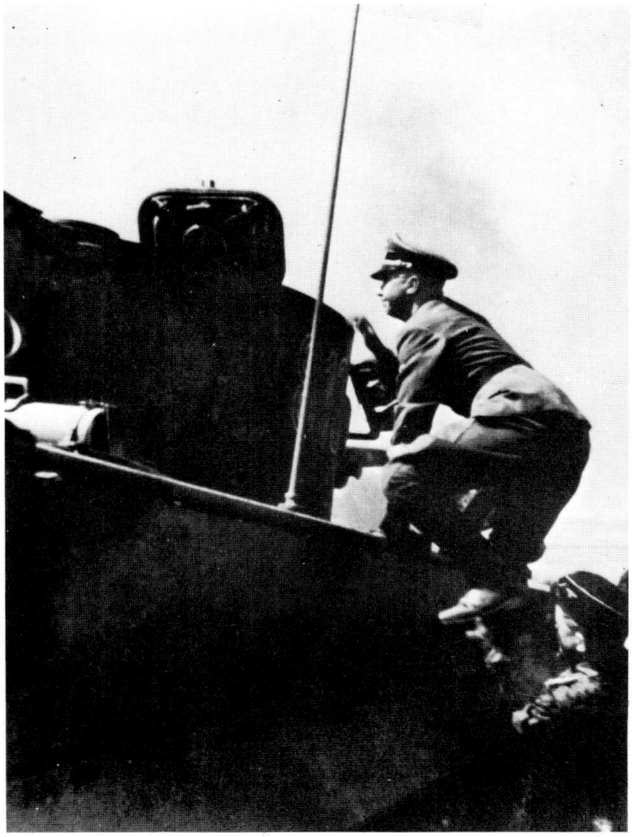

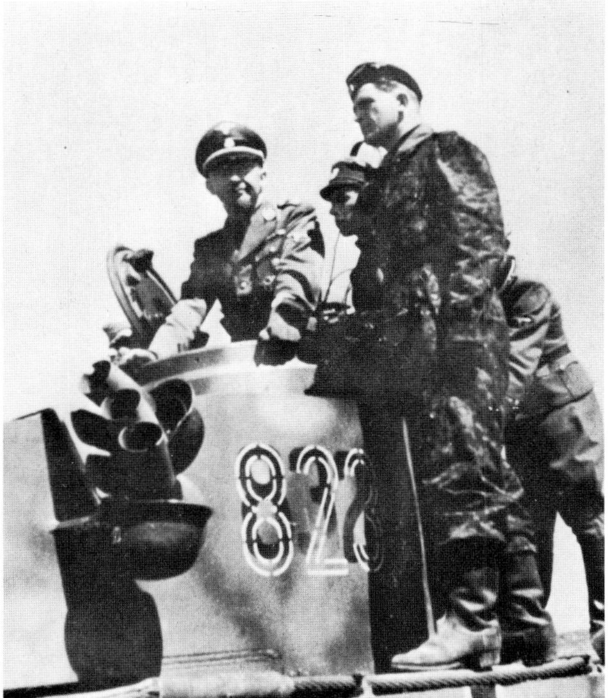

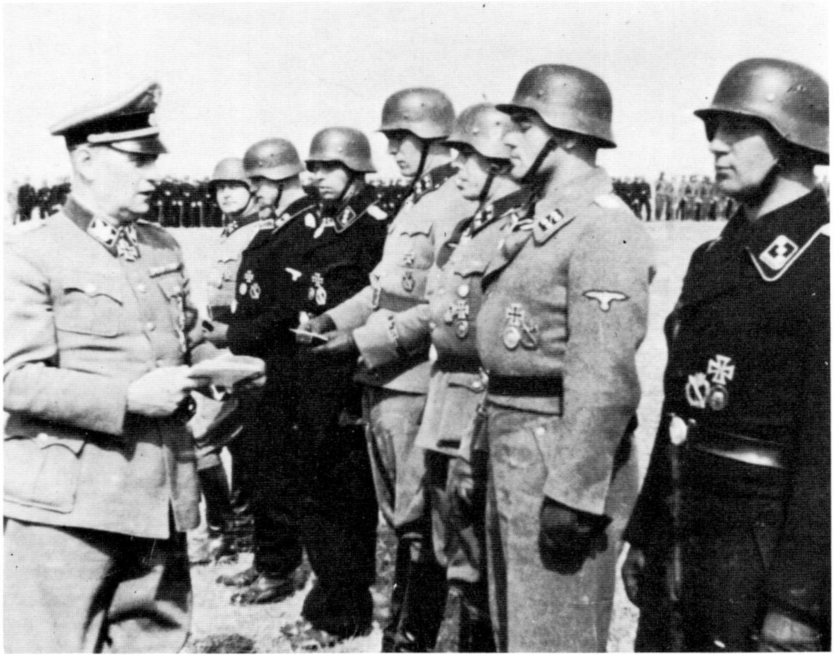

On April 20, 1943, after the battle of Charkow, Major General Krüger honors the leaders of the SSdivision "Das Reich". From left: Eichenlaub to Otto Kumm, Ritterkreuz to Ch. Tychsen, S. Stadler, V. Kaiser and Hans Weiss.

Congratulations for the receipt of the Ritterkreuz are extended to Unterscharführer Thaler, Pz.Rgt. "Das Reich".

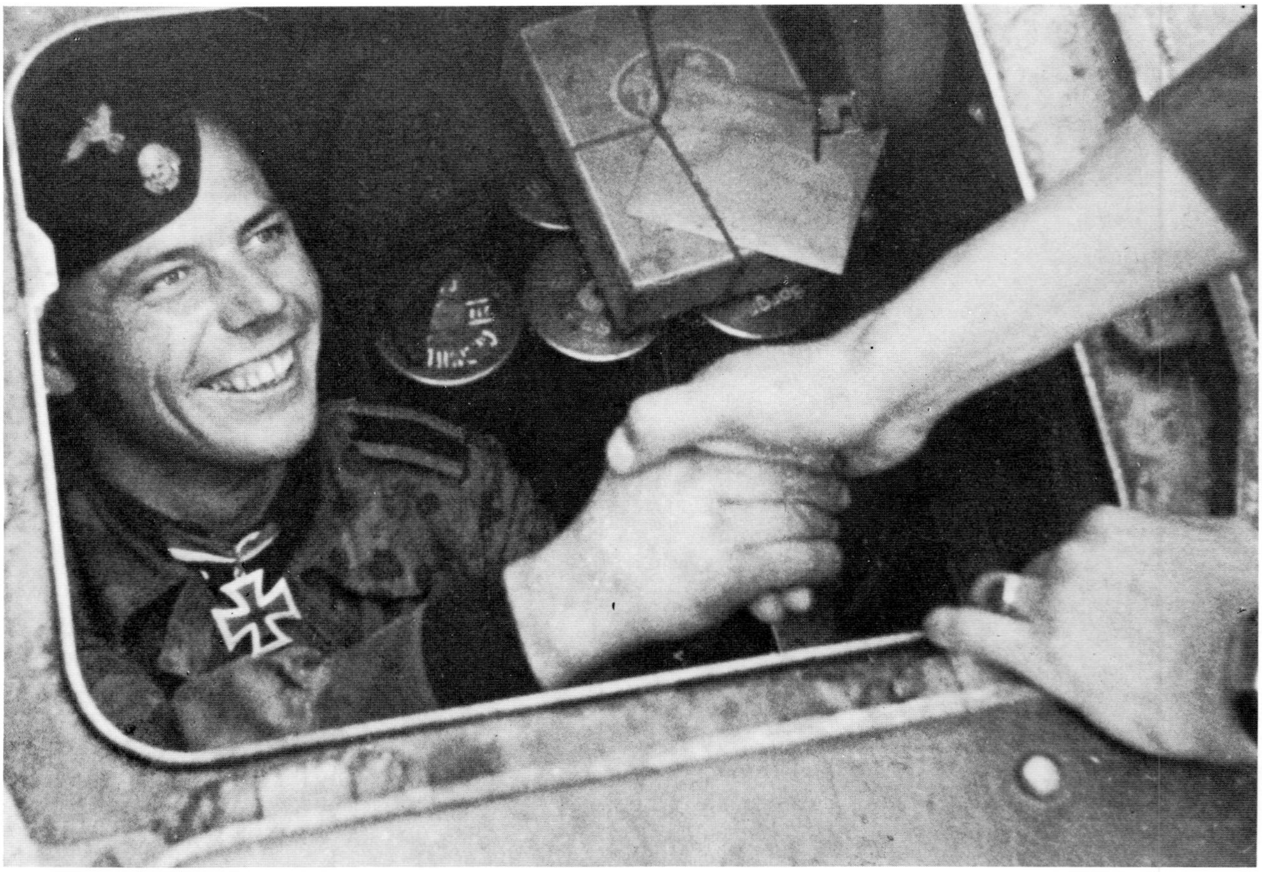

Sepp Dietrich presenting the Ritterkreuz medal to (from the left) Max Hansen, Hans Becker and Hermann Weiser.

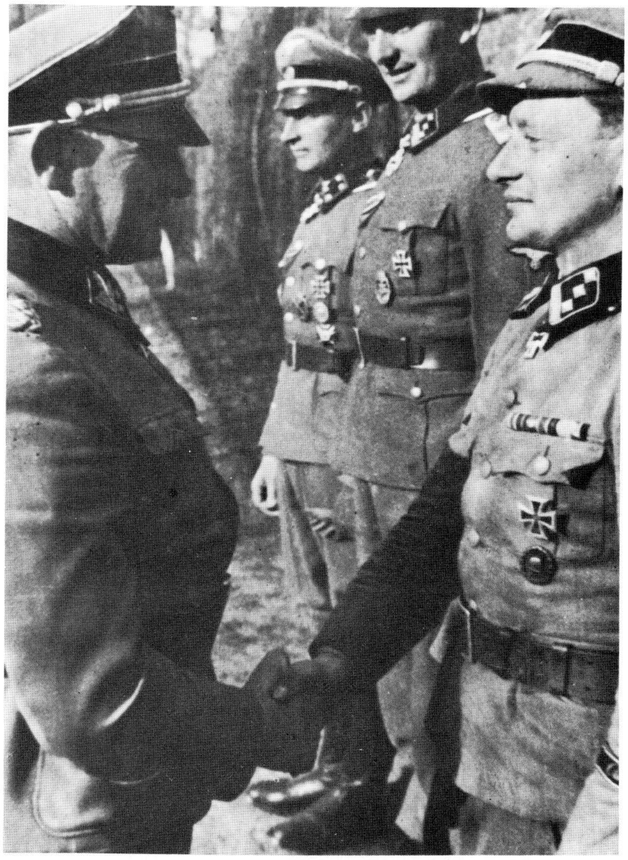

Commanders of the LAH.
1st row: Ewert, Staudinger, Besuden, "Panzermeyer", Sepp Dietrich, Weiser, Sandig, Bludau and Schönberger.
2nd and 3rd rows: Siebken, Becker, Wisch, Westernhagen, Kraas, Günther, Lehman, Frey, Hubert Meyer, Maass, Krause.

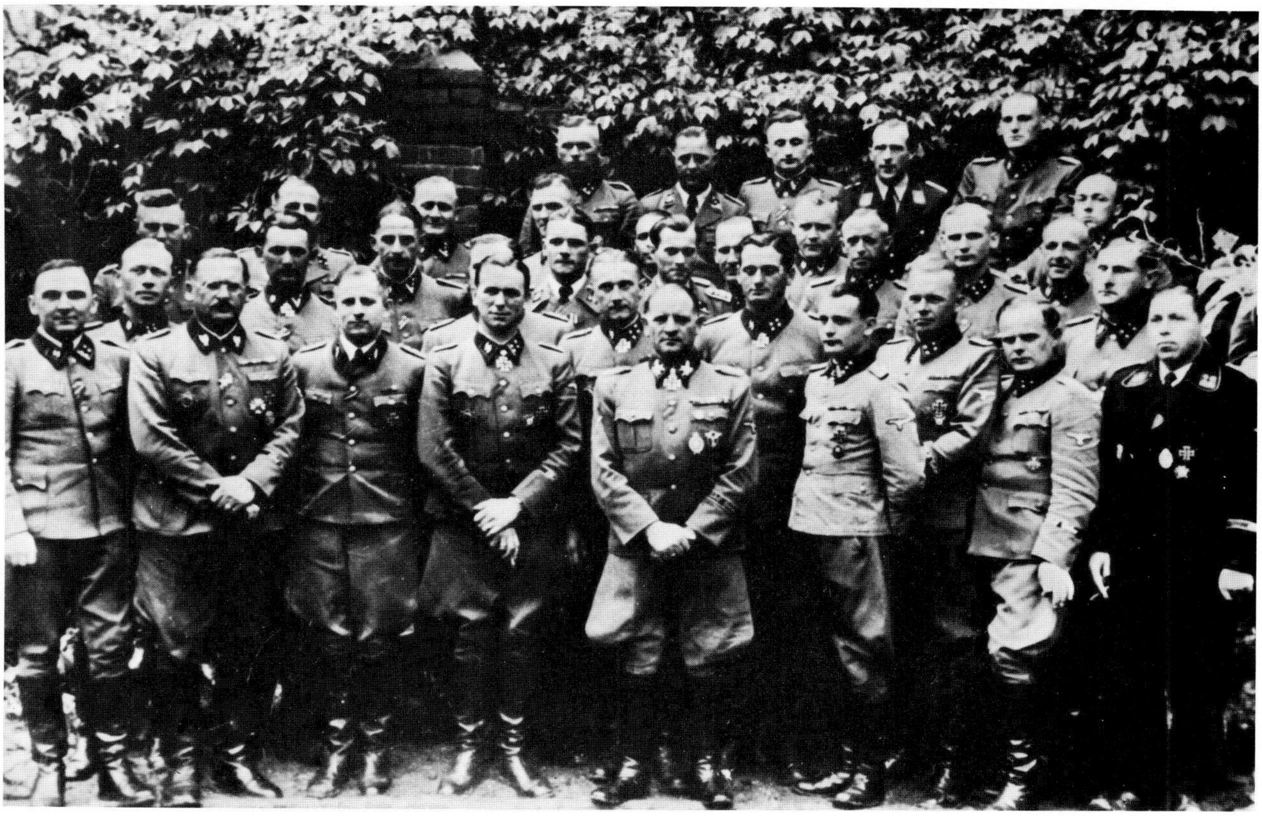

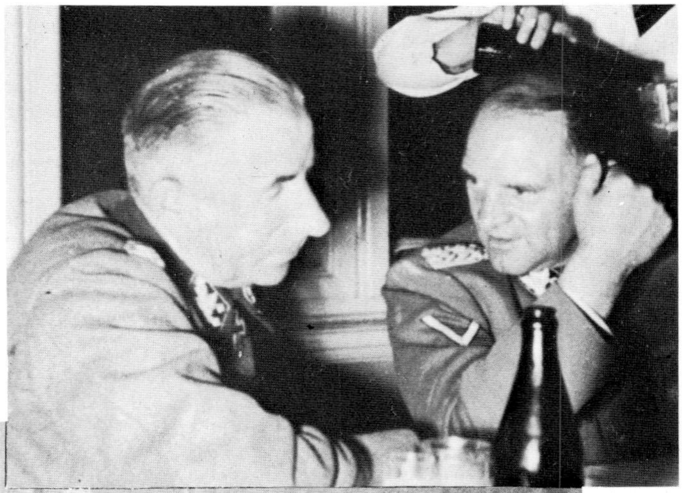

High level commanders meeting.

From the left: Hausser, Dietrich, Gille and "Panzermeyer".

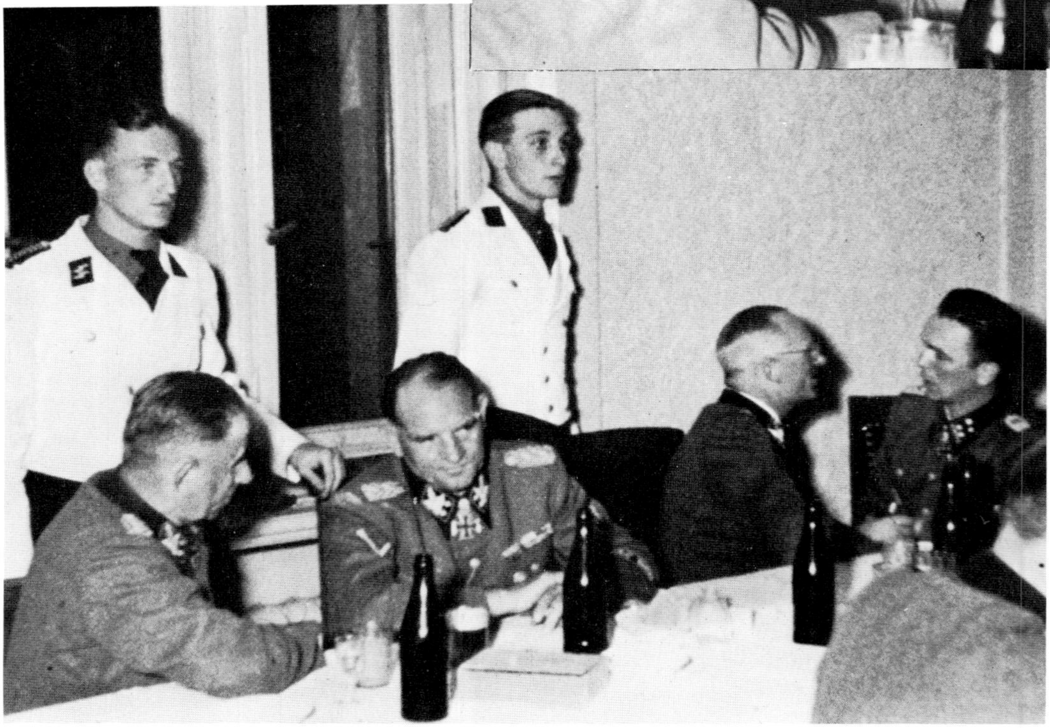

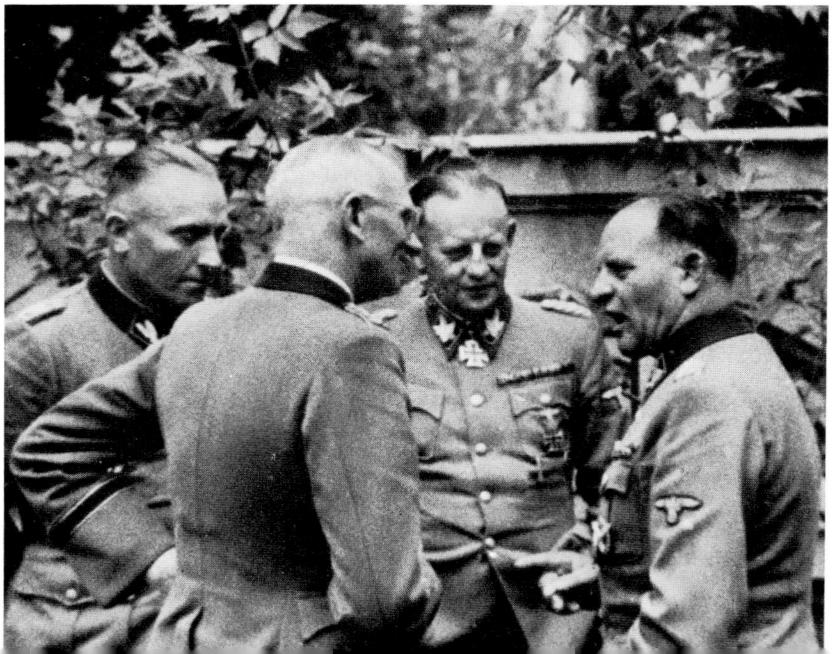

From the left: Priess, Gille, Krüger and Dietrich.

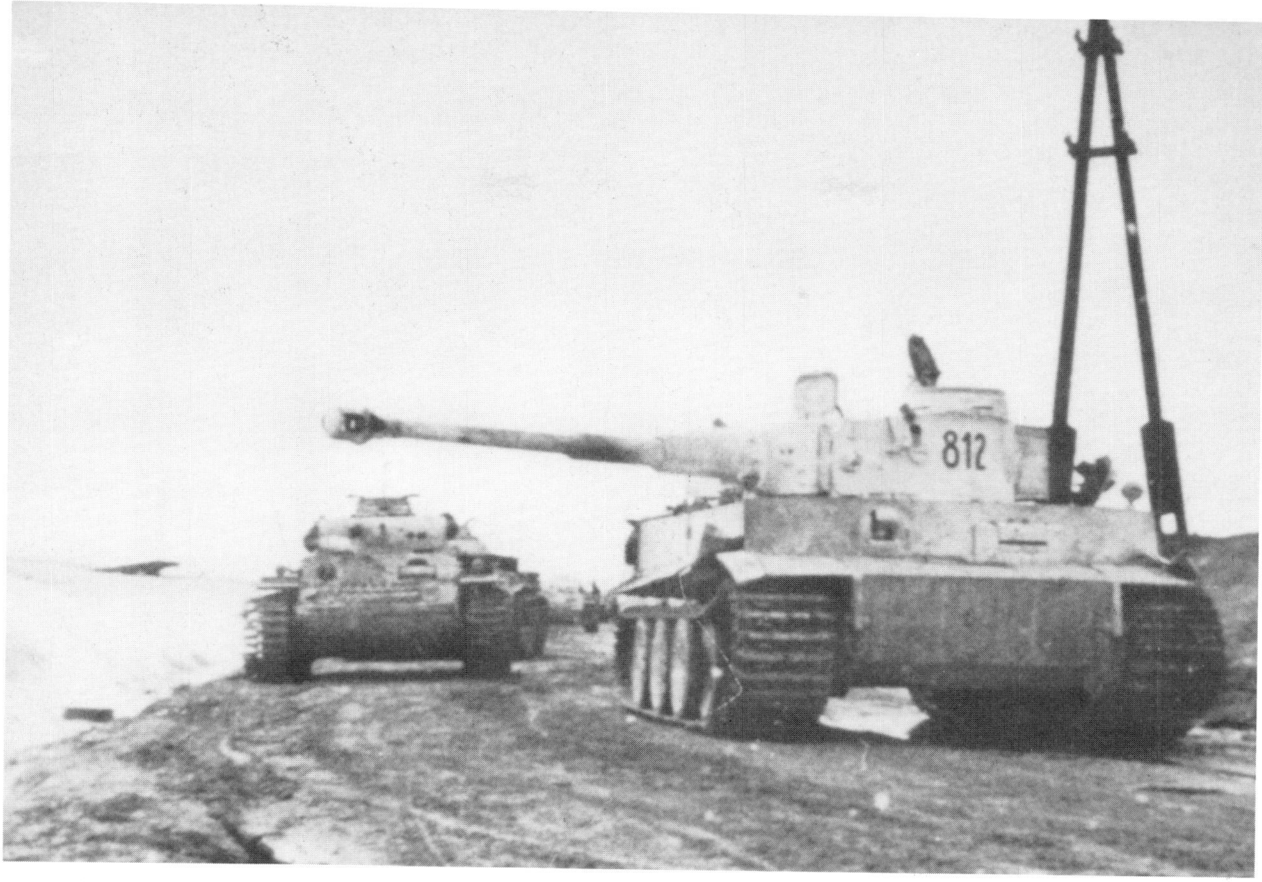
812

The Tiger tanks, already successfully used during the battles of Charkow, again prove themselves effective during the "Operation Citadel".

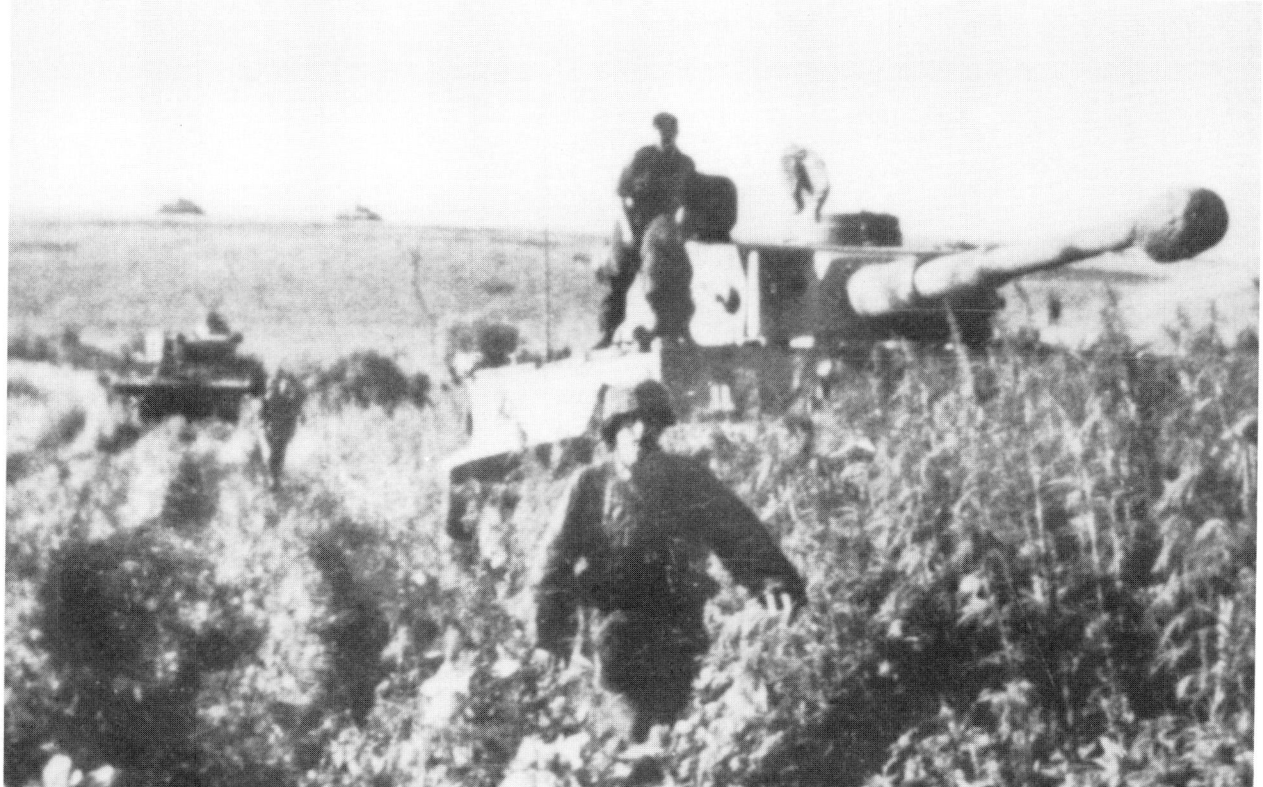

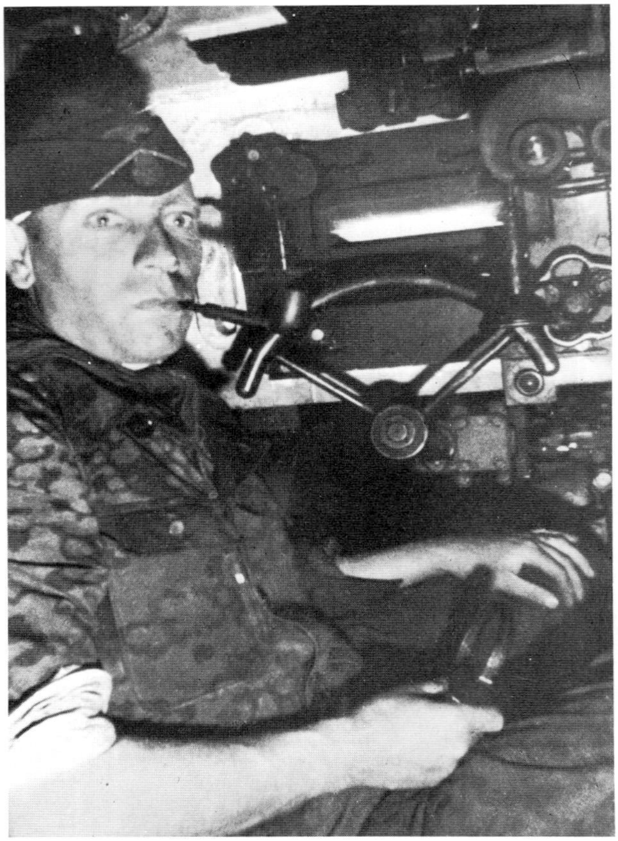

The inside of a Tiger Tank: The driver.

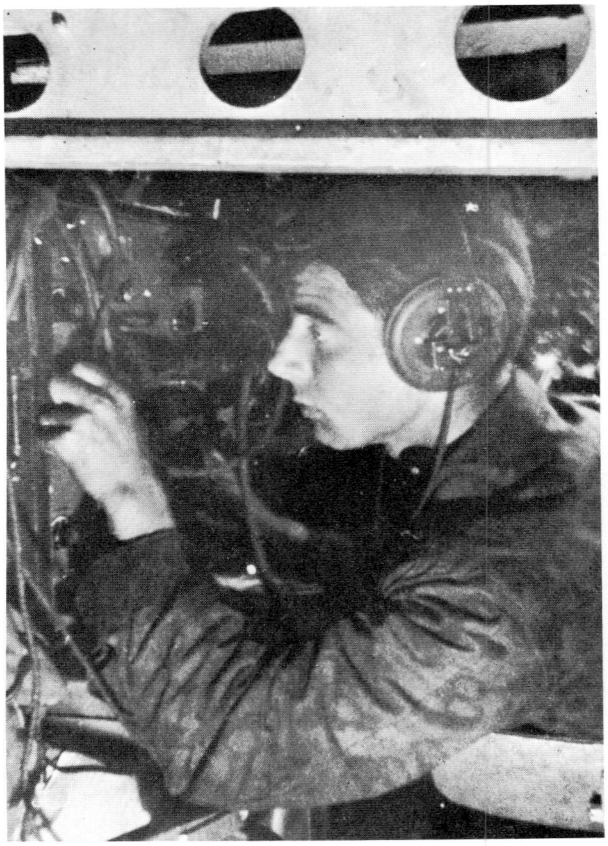

The radio operator.

The gunner.

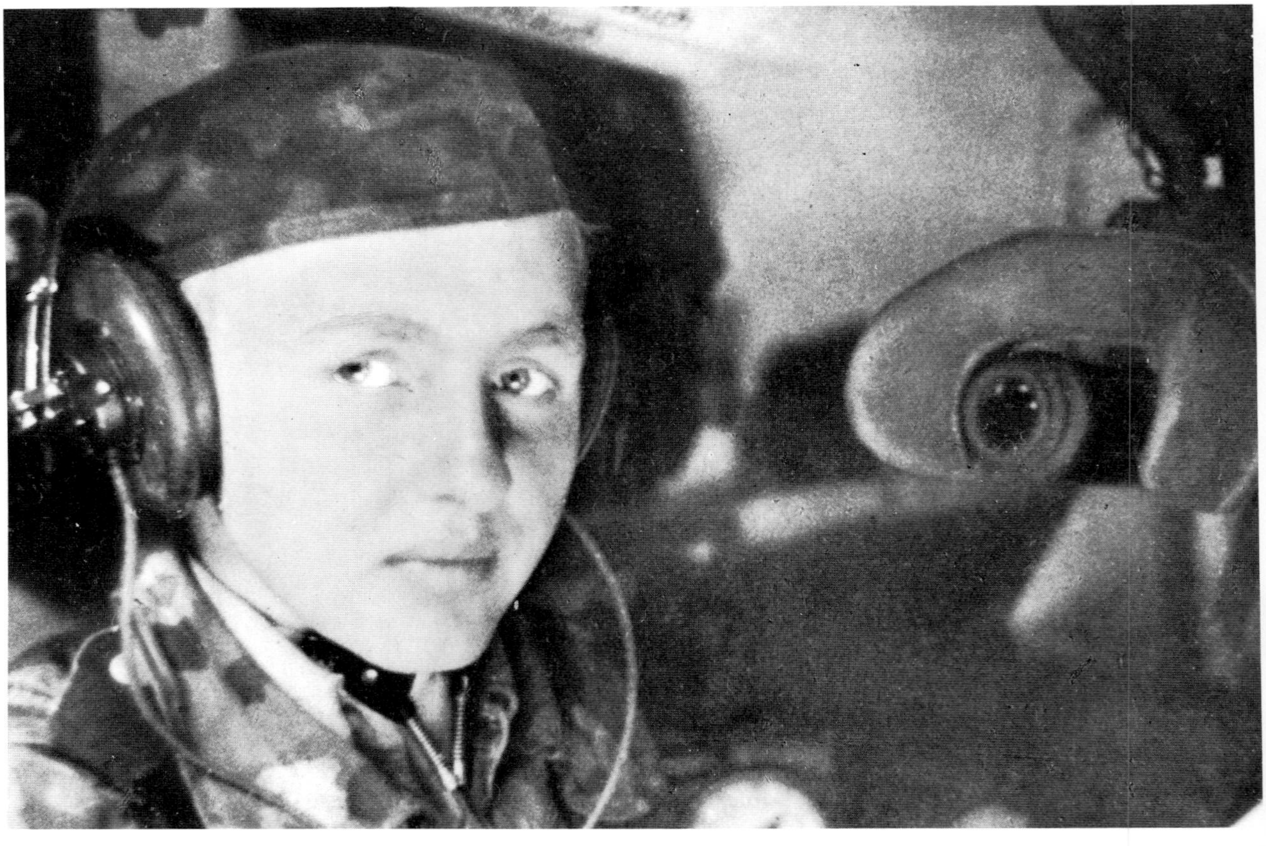

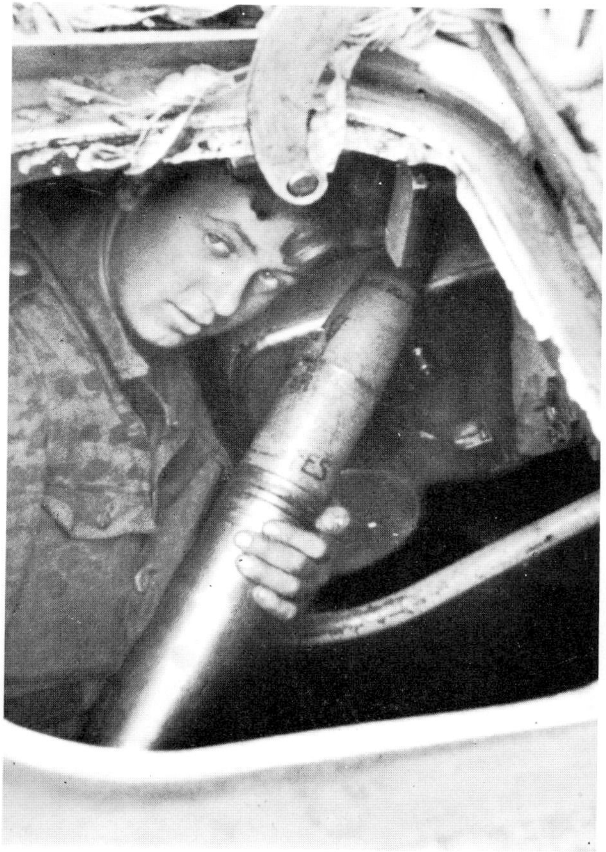

The gunner.

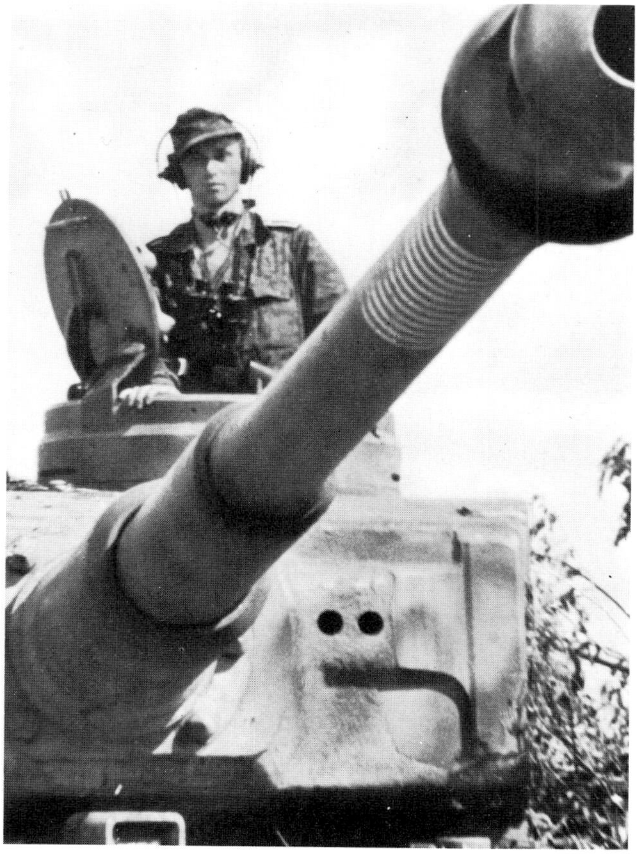

The commander.

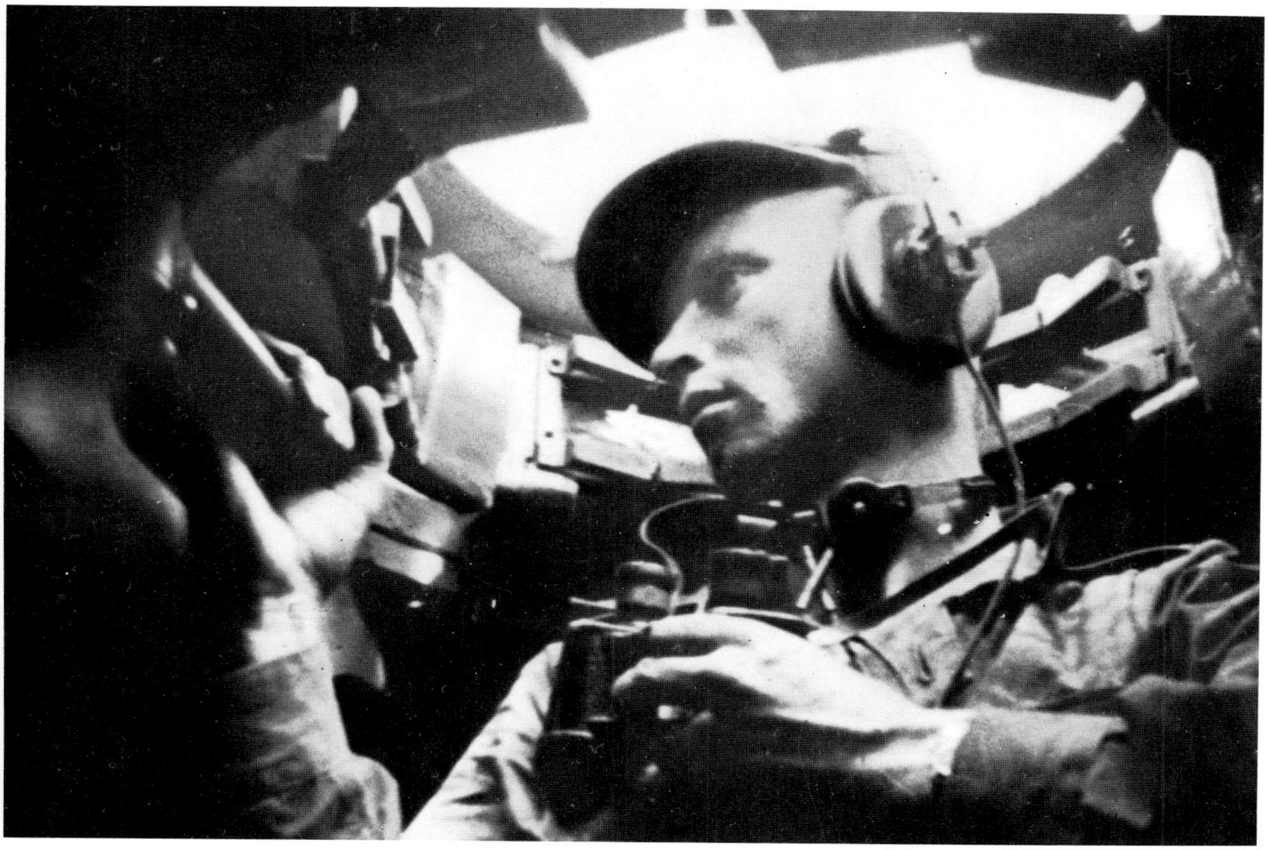

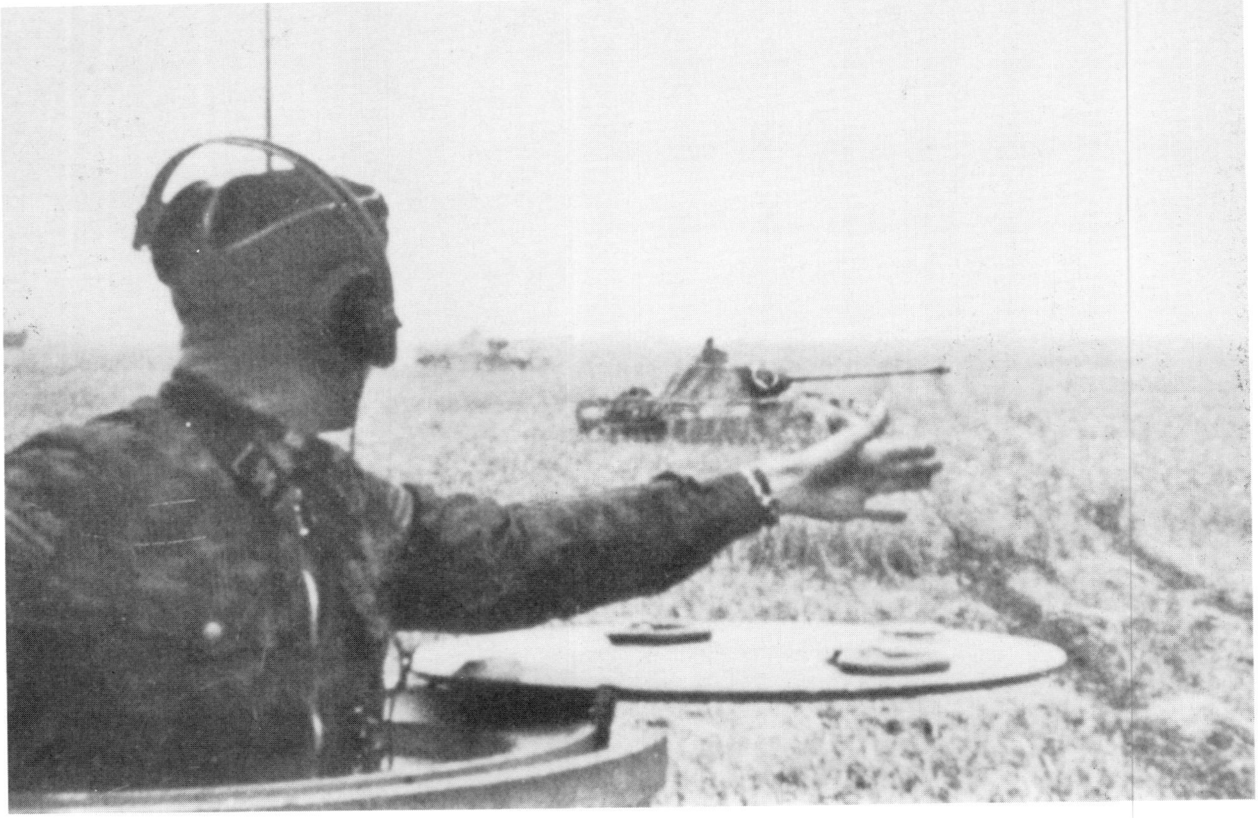

Once again all available Tank forces are amassed for a concentrated attack during "Operation citadel". Panther tanks, armored utility vehicles, and Panzer III tanks are in an assembly area.

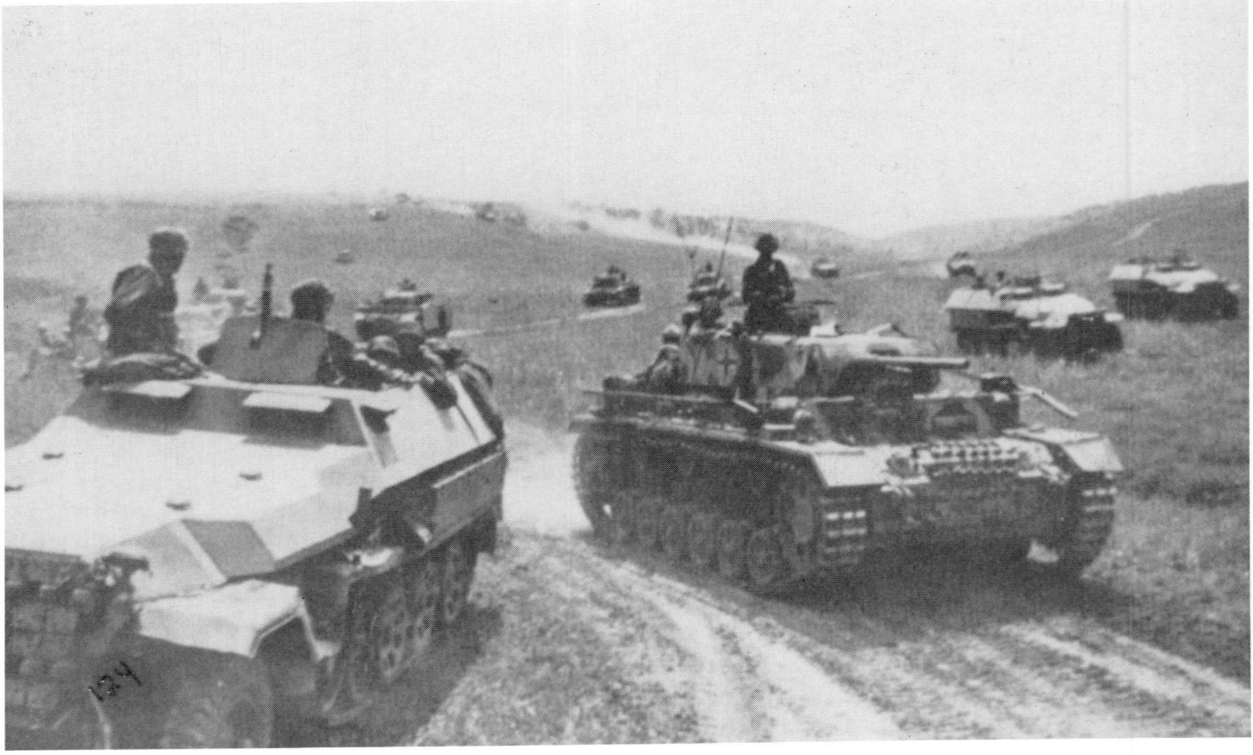

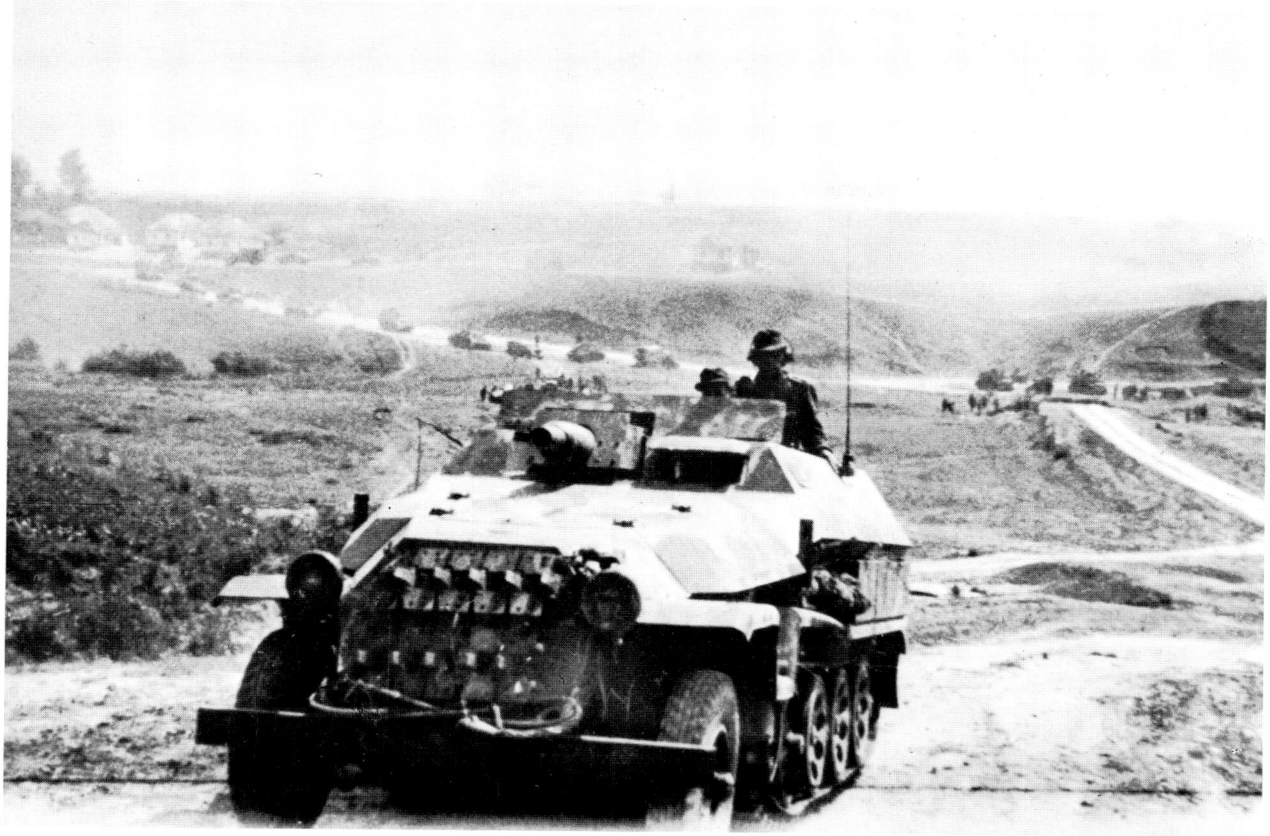

Armored utility vehicles with 75 mm tank gun.

"Tiger" tank ready for action.

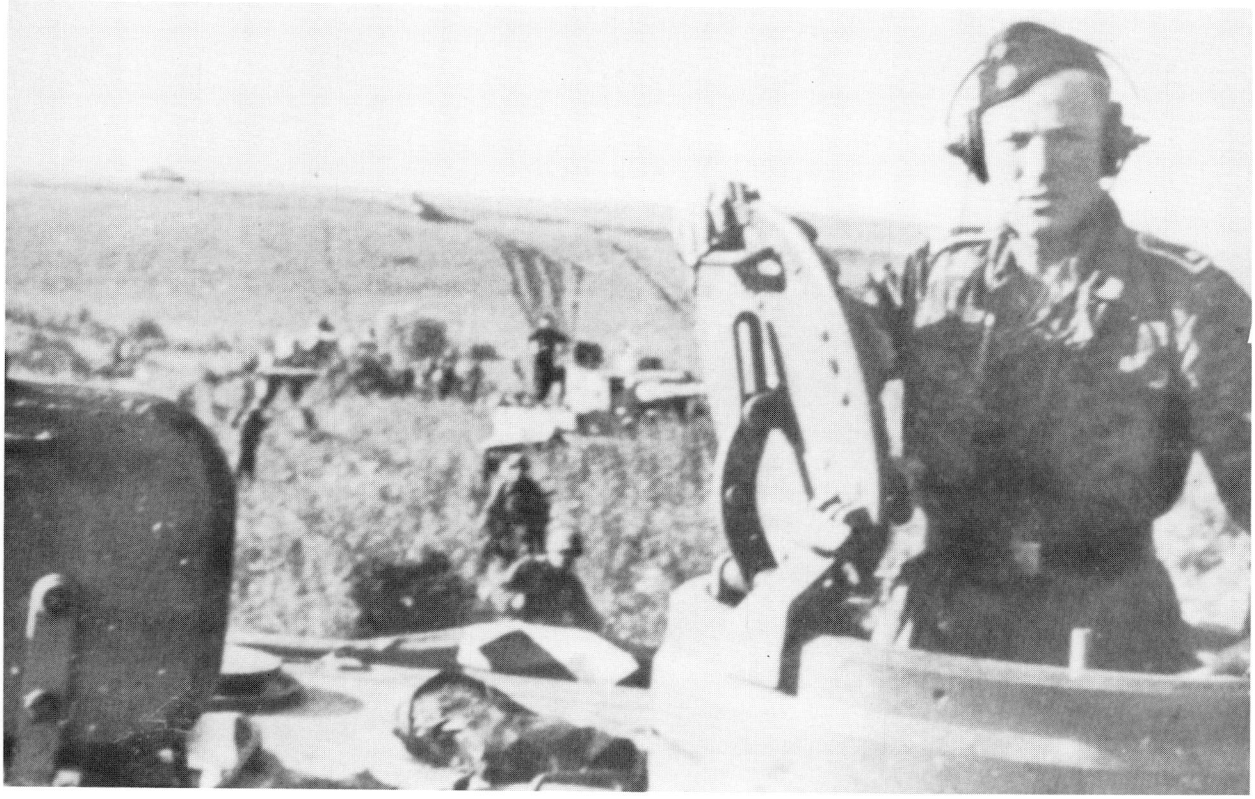

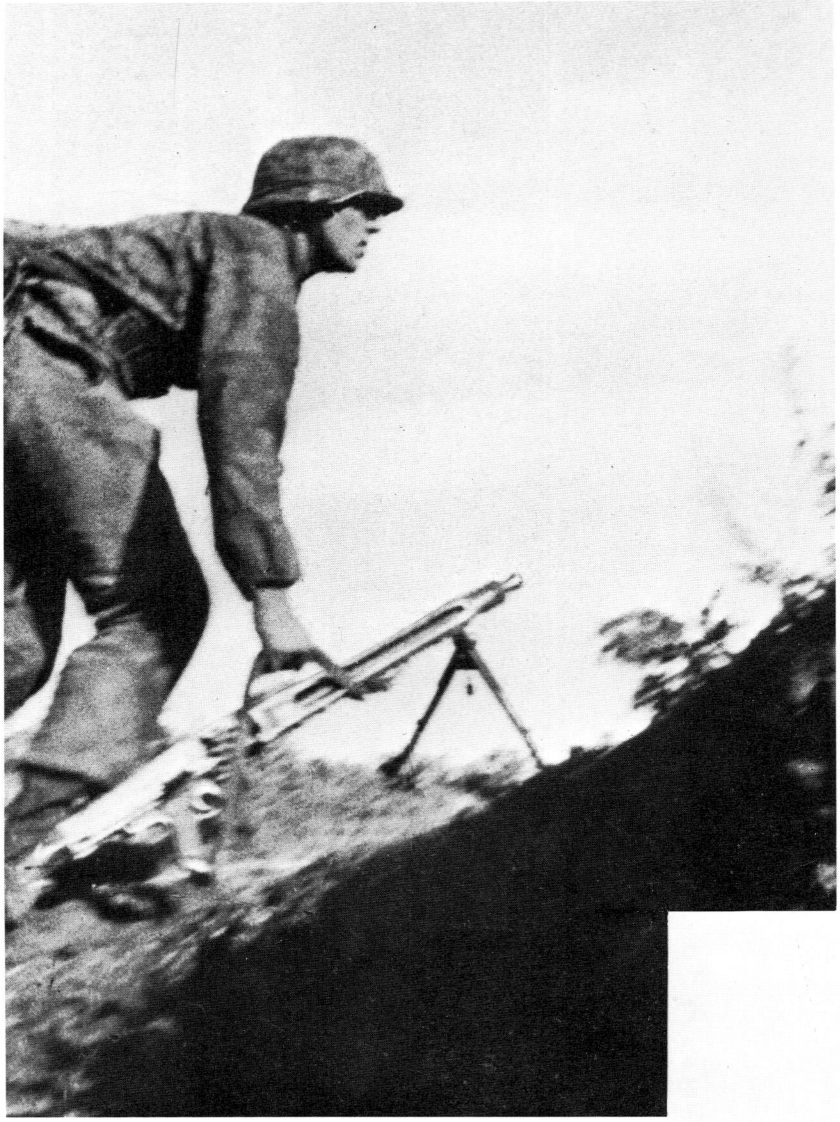

"Operation Citadel" begins. This is an attempt to cut off from the North and South the large salient of Kursk.

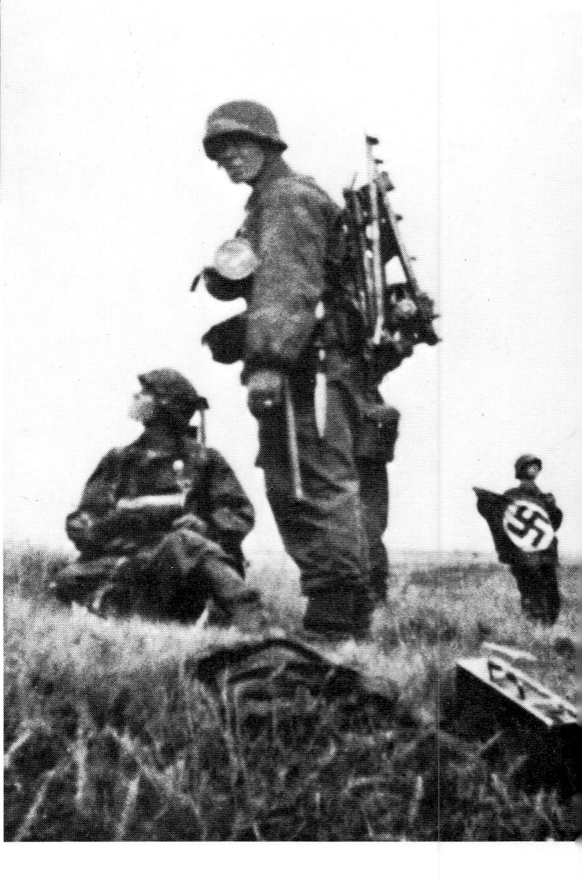

Infantrymen mark the forward edge of the battle line for the combat aircraft.

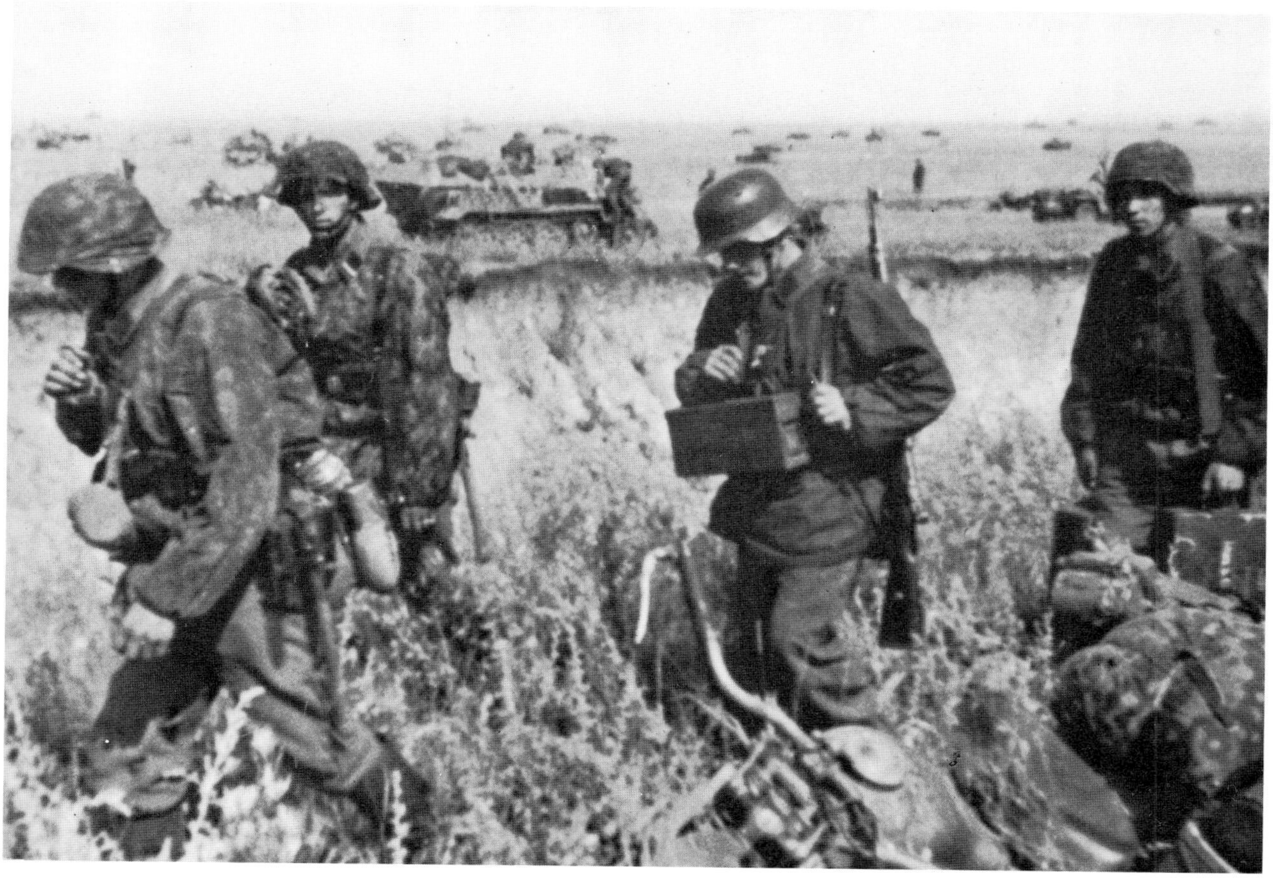

Infantrymen advancing supported by tanks.

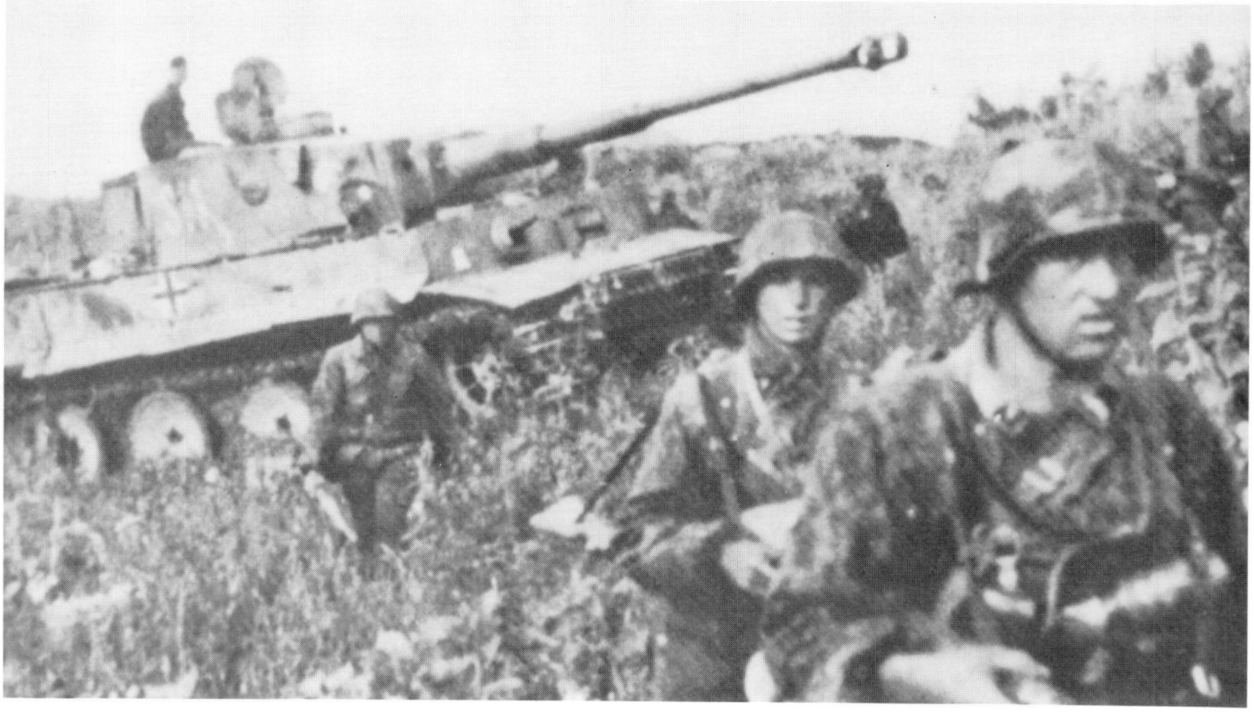

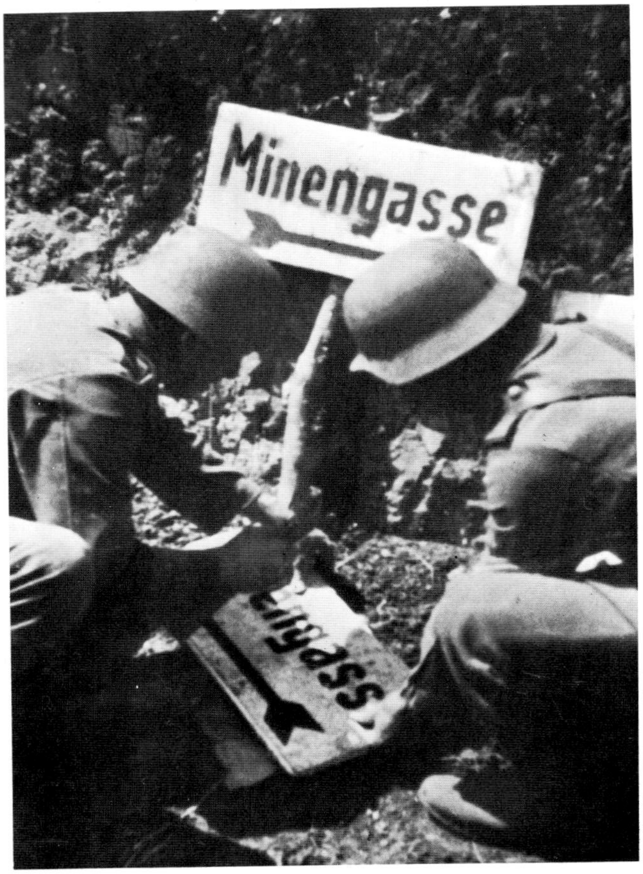
Minengasse

Engineers sweep and mark mine fields. An assault gun covers the passage shown in this picture.

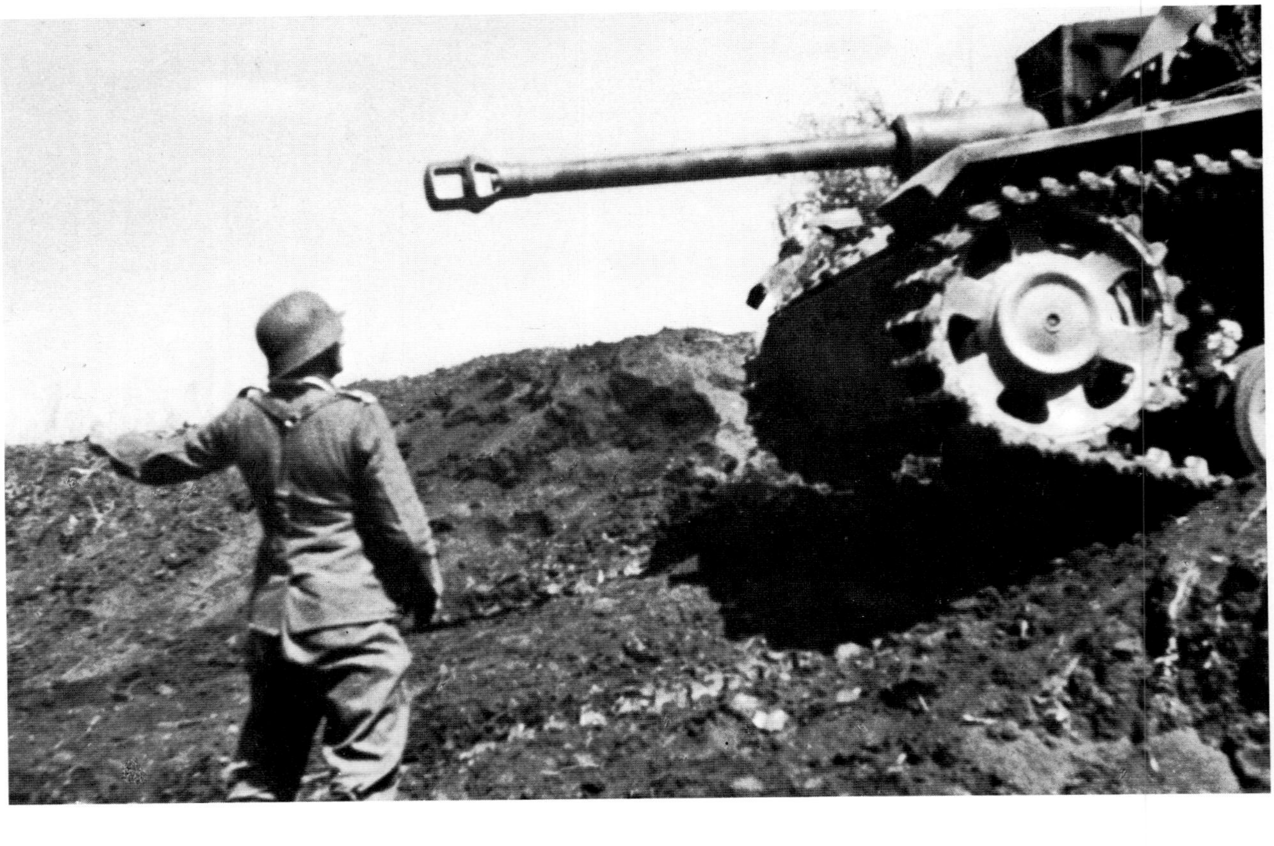

At the beginning, the Germans rapidly seize land. Prisoners are used for transporting ammunition.

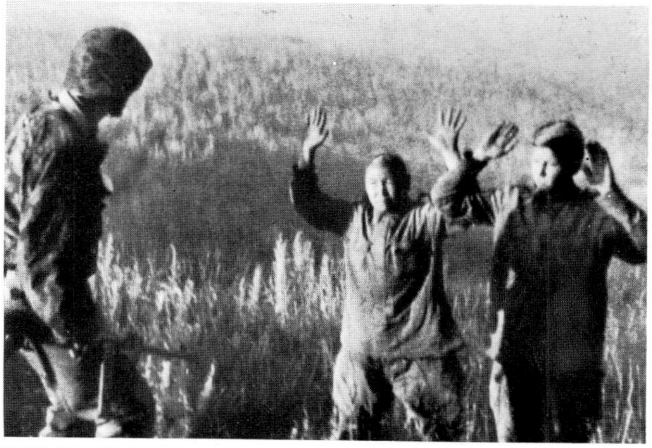

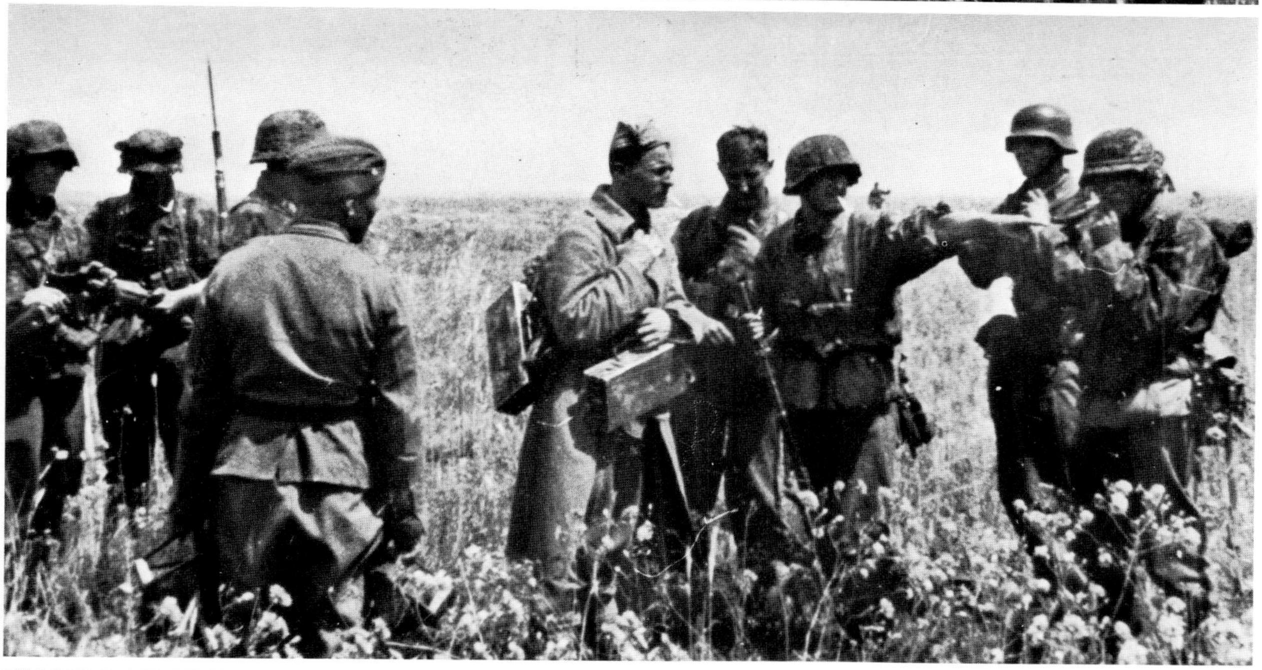

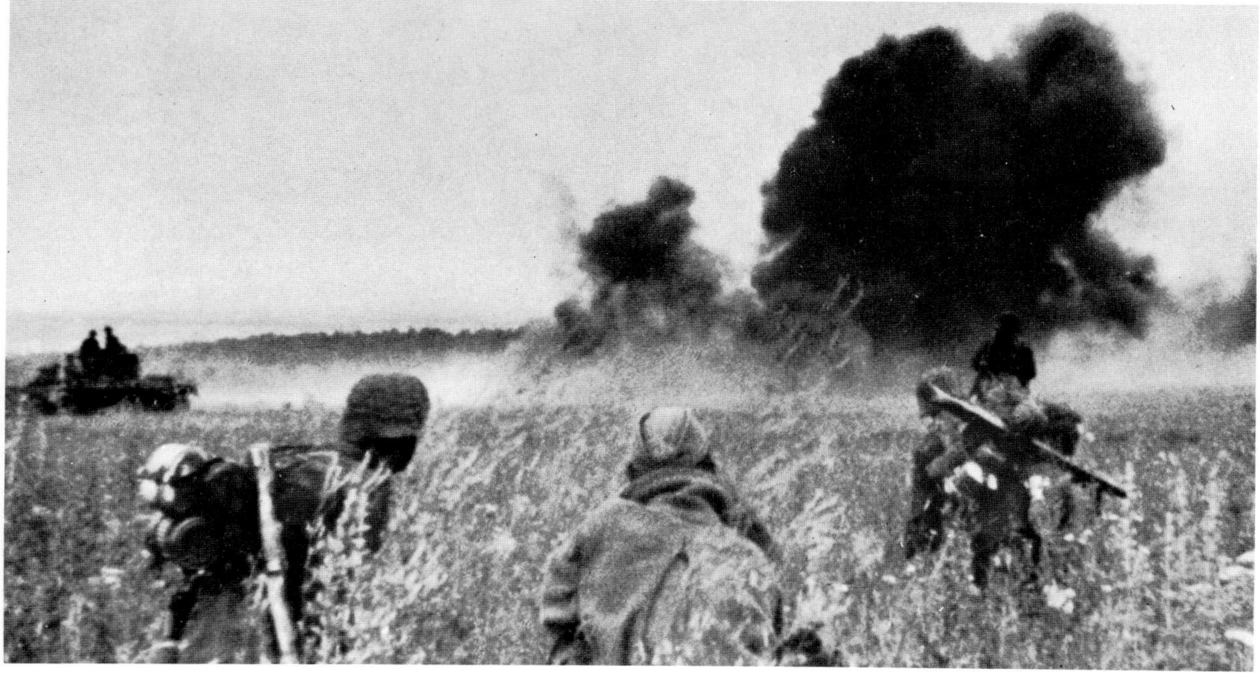

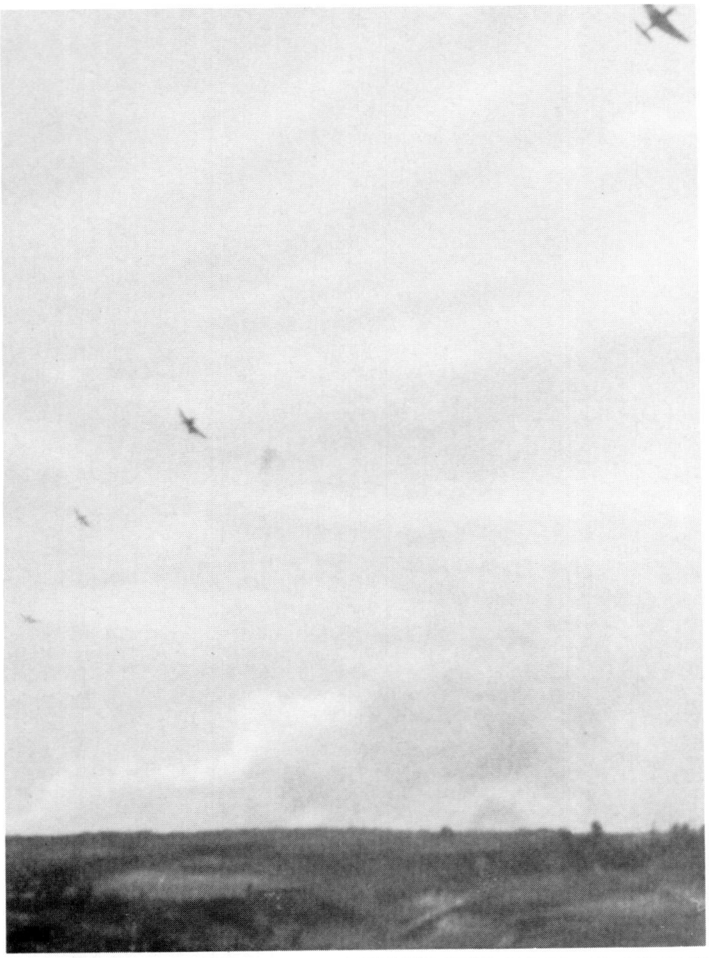

The Russian resistance stiffens. SS units are confronted with Russian elite troops. Stuka dive-bombers of the Ju 87 type open a passage through the enemy lines.

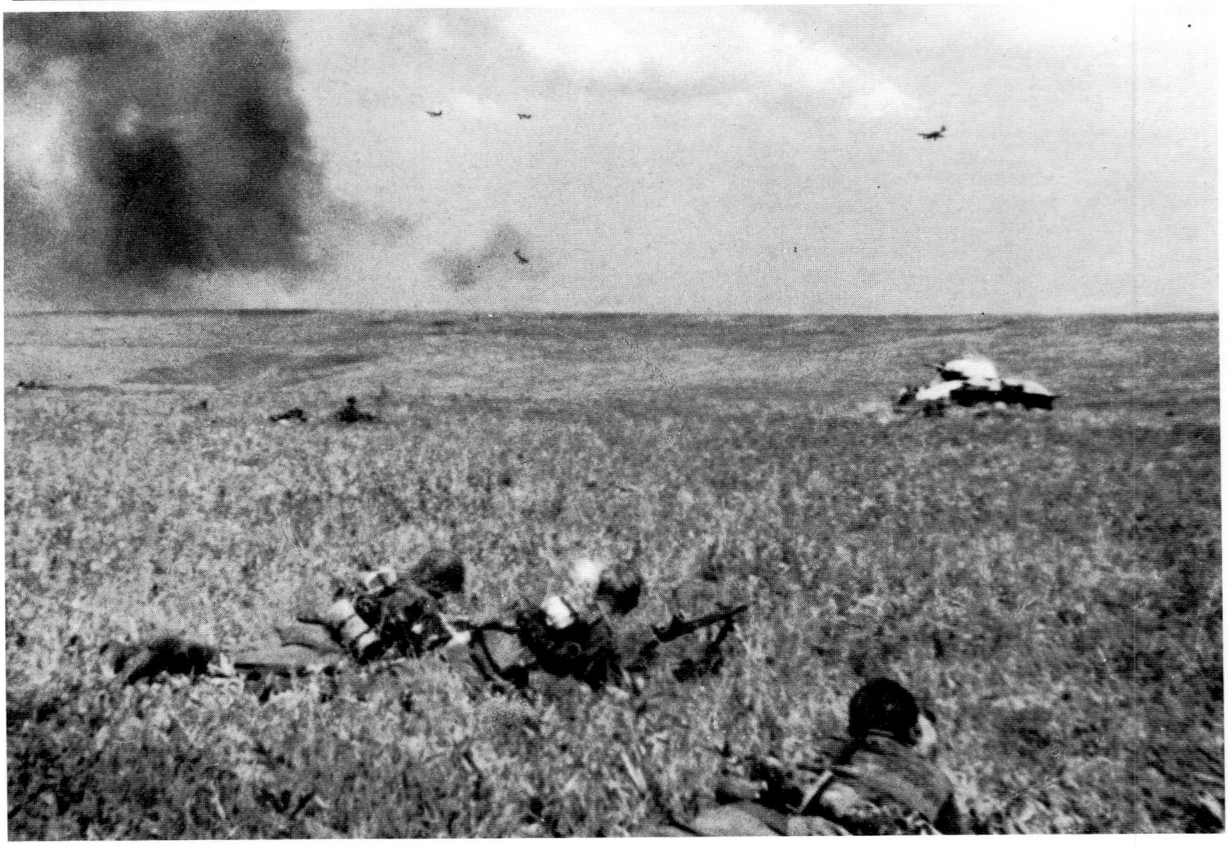

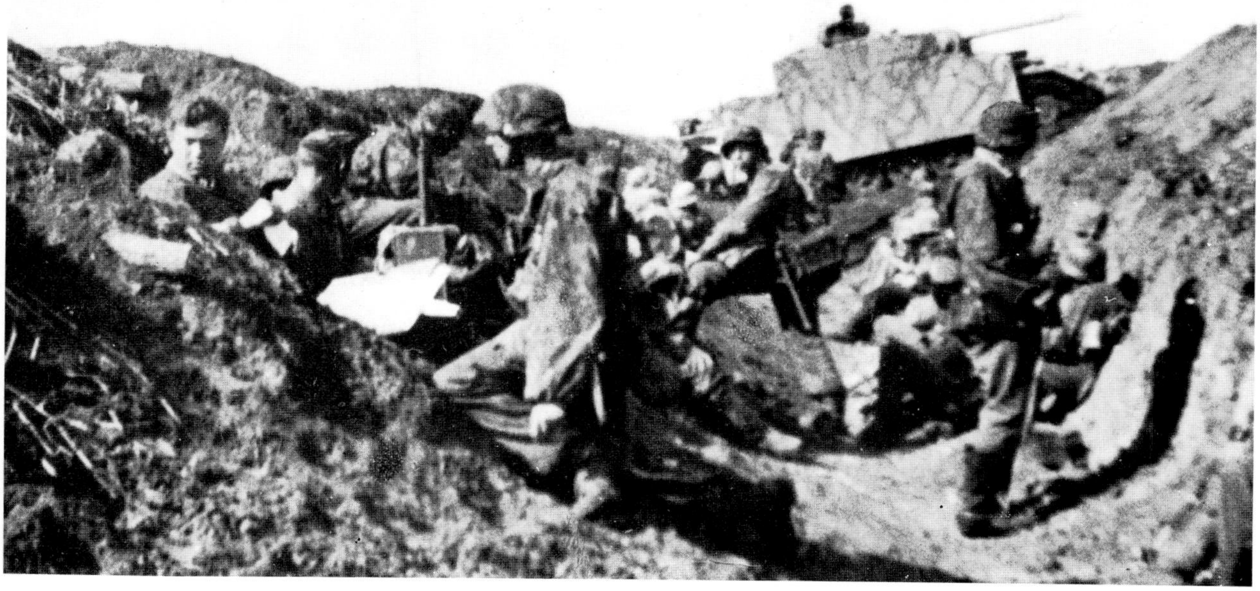

A command post in a Russian tank trench.

Major Peiper with his adjutant Lt. Wolff in the command post.

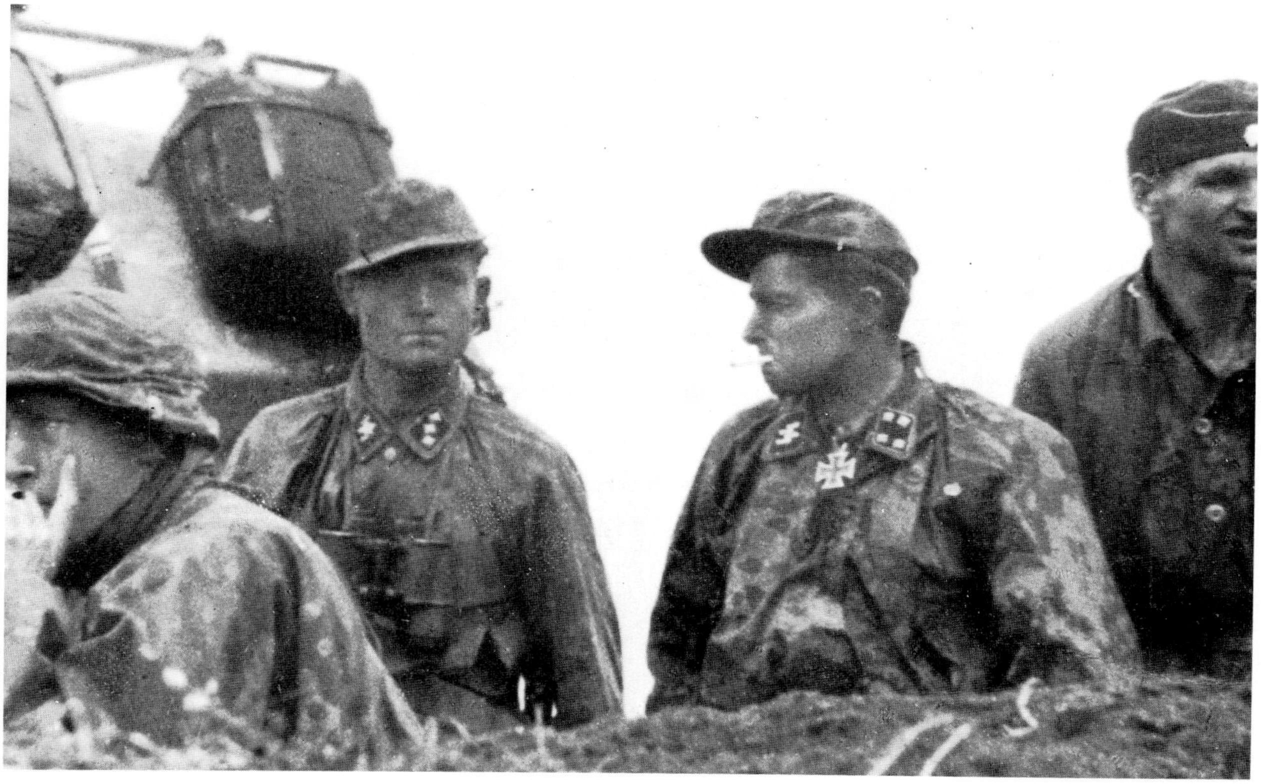

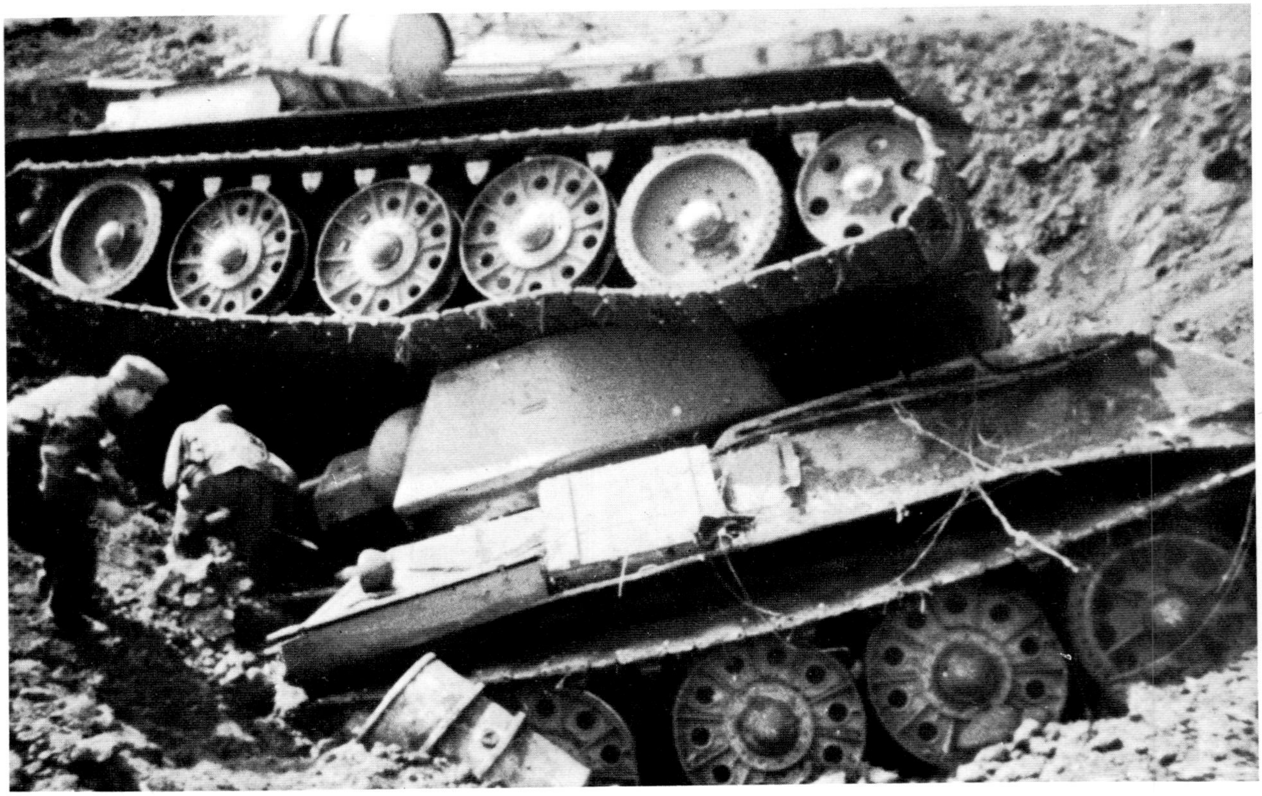

Destroyed Russian T-34 tank.

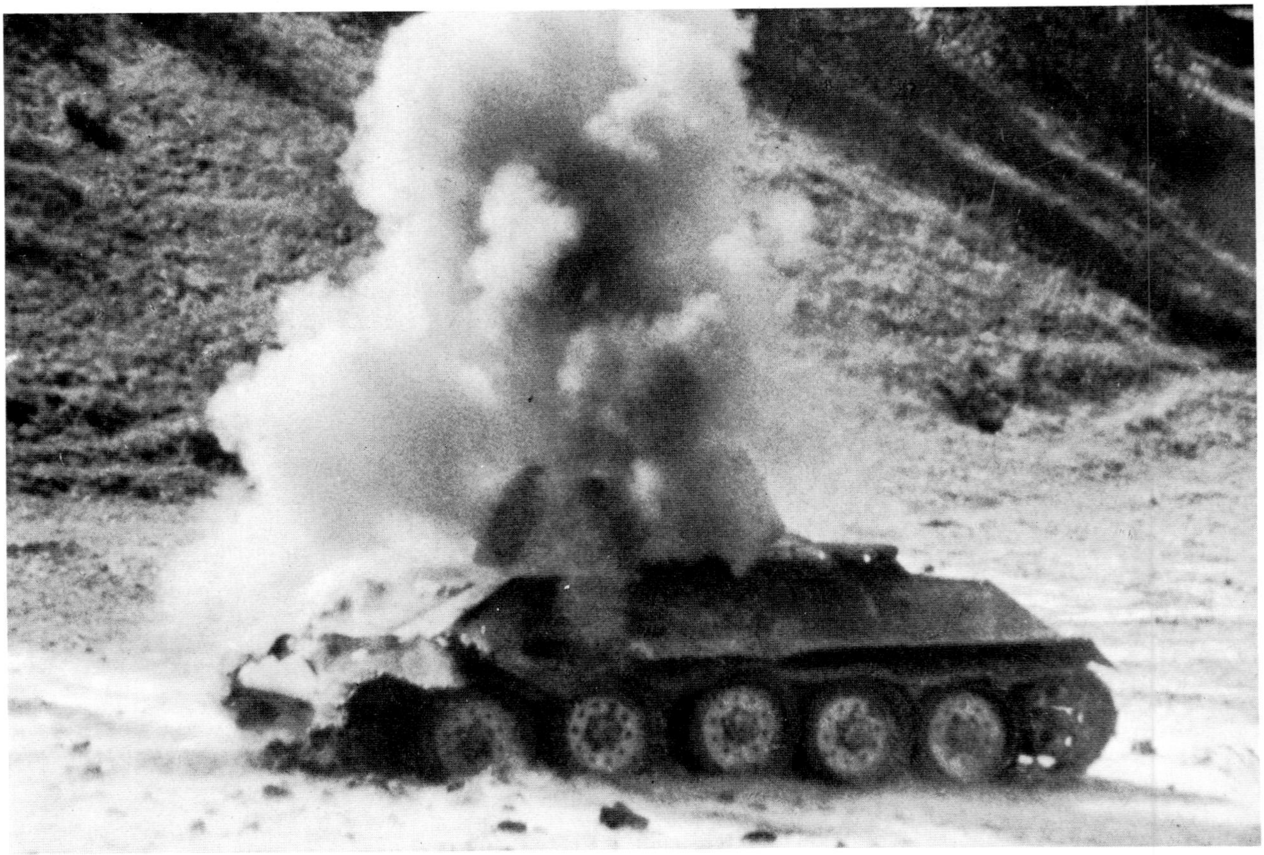

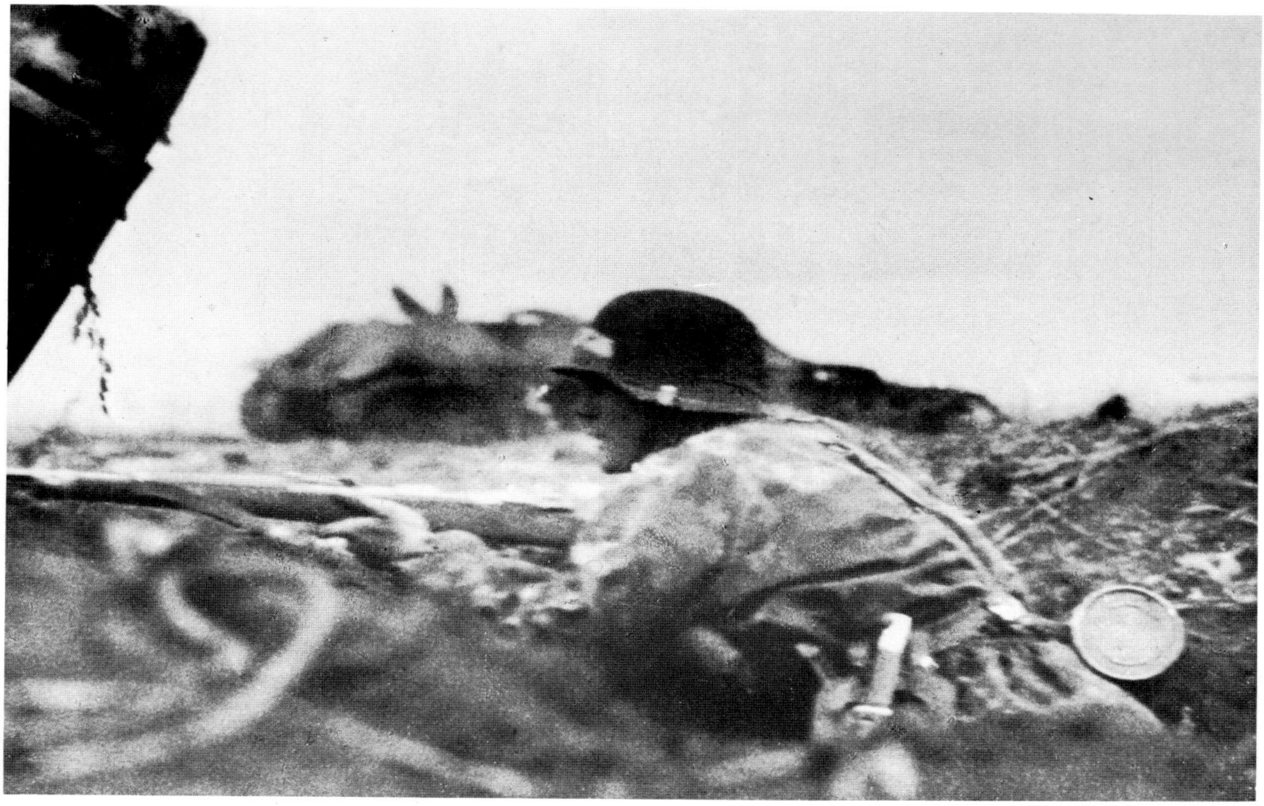

Armored infantrymen take cover behind a destroyed T-34 tank.

The armored assault is stopped by the heavy defensive fire of the Russians.

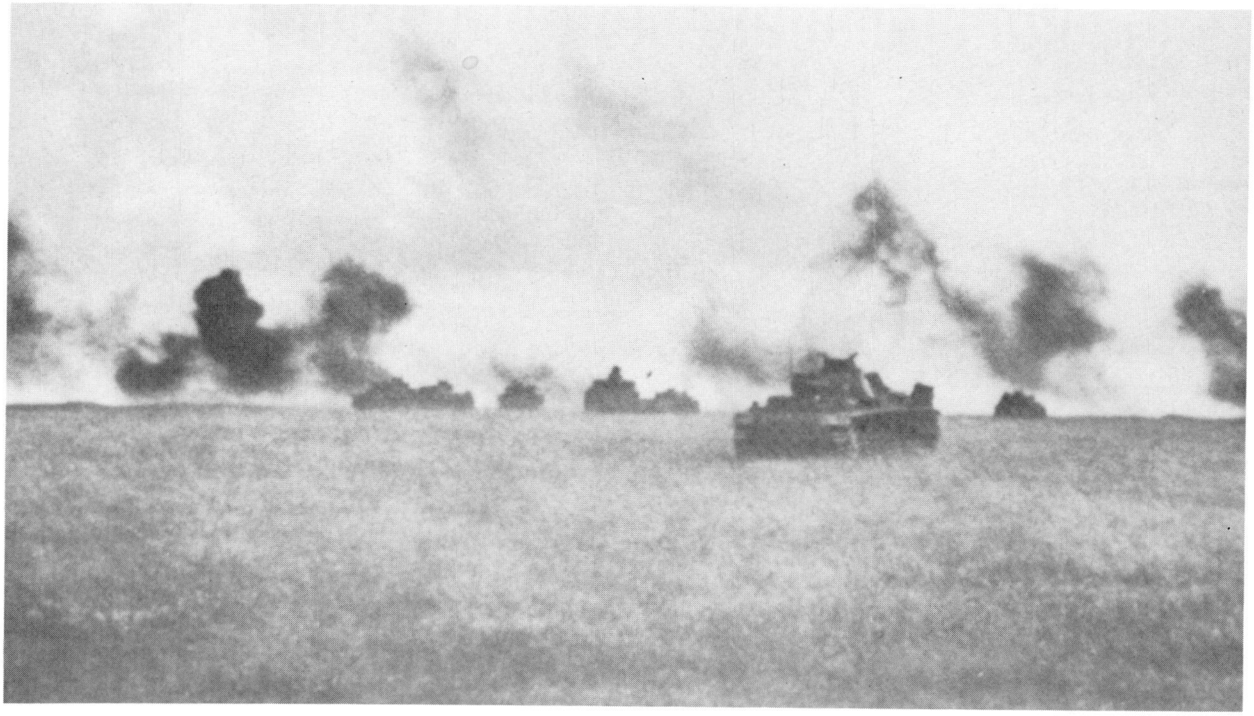

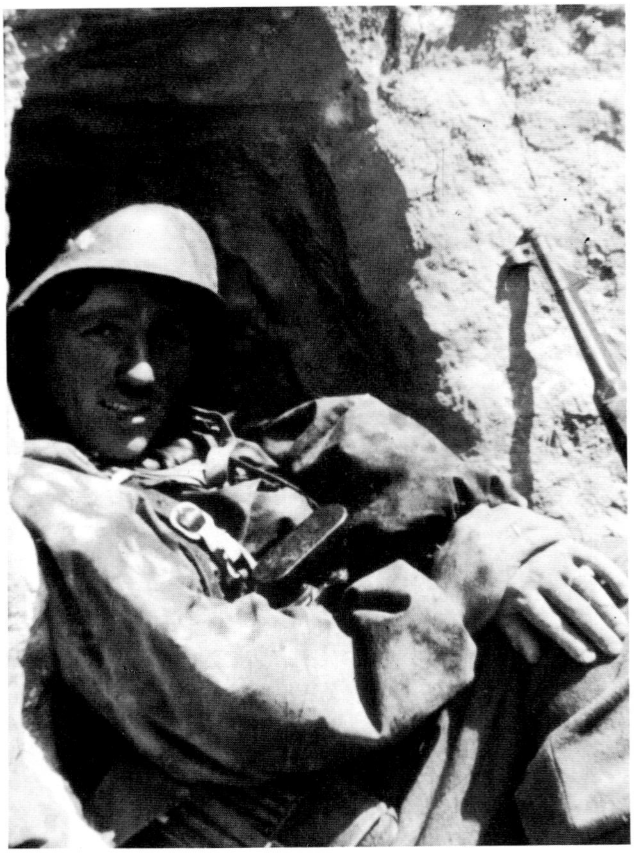

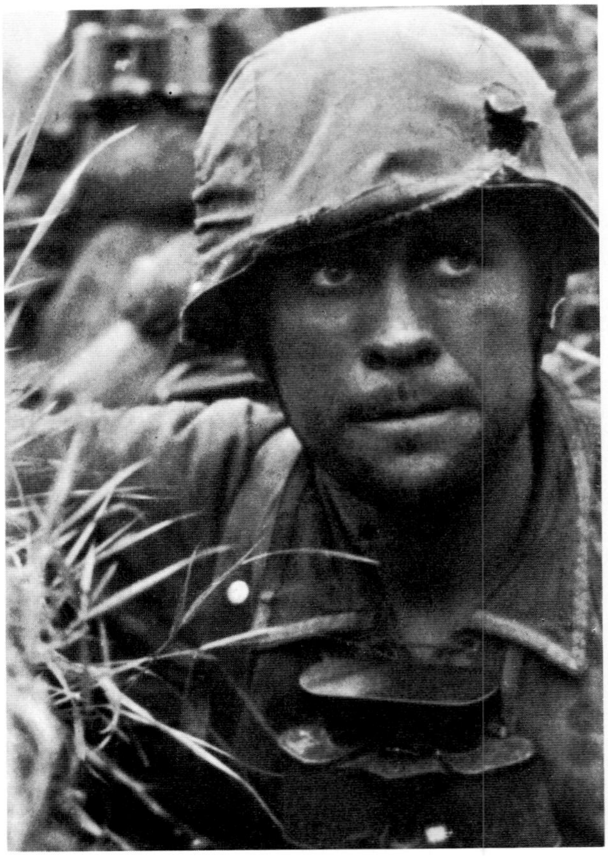

The faces of the young infantrymen show the strain of battle.

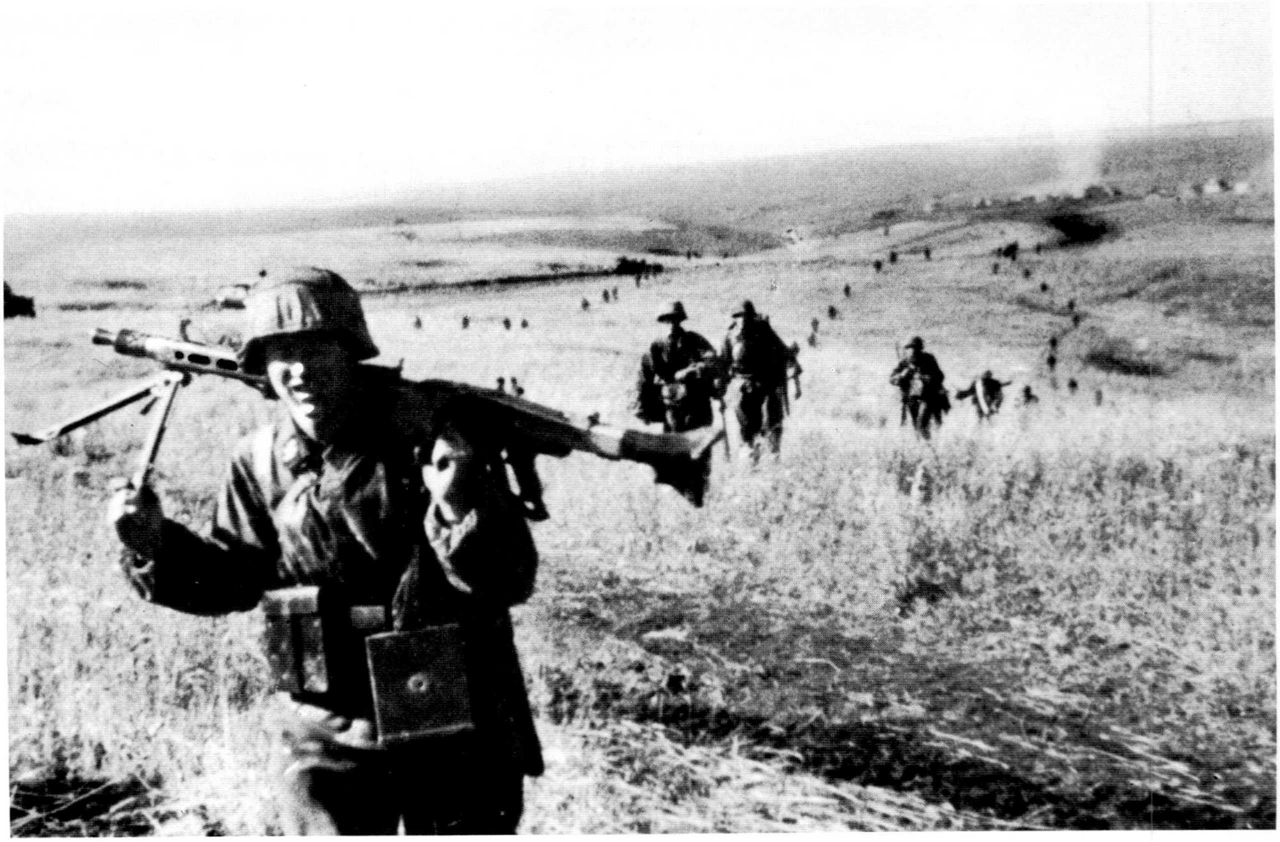

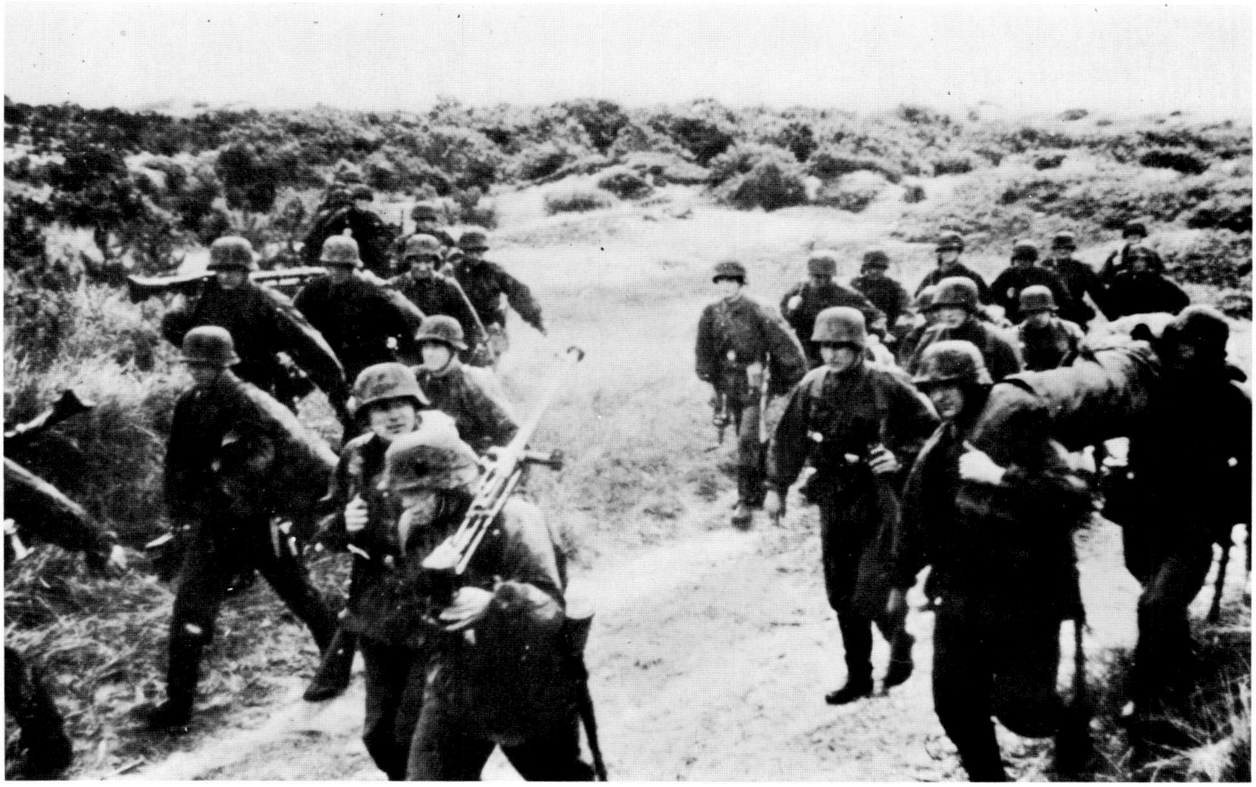

Nevertheless, the counterattack is pushed forward.

The collecting station for wounded soldiers is situated directly behind the mainline of resistance.

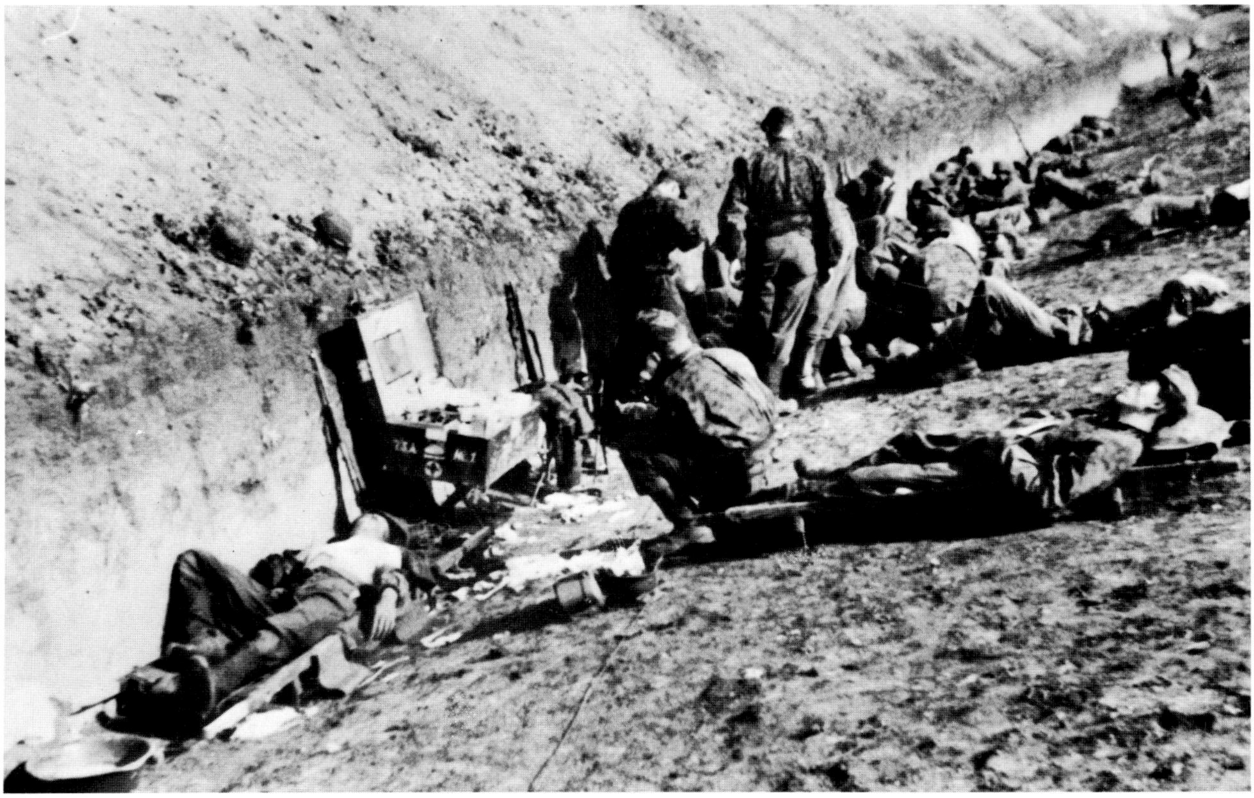

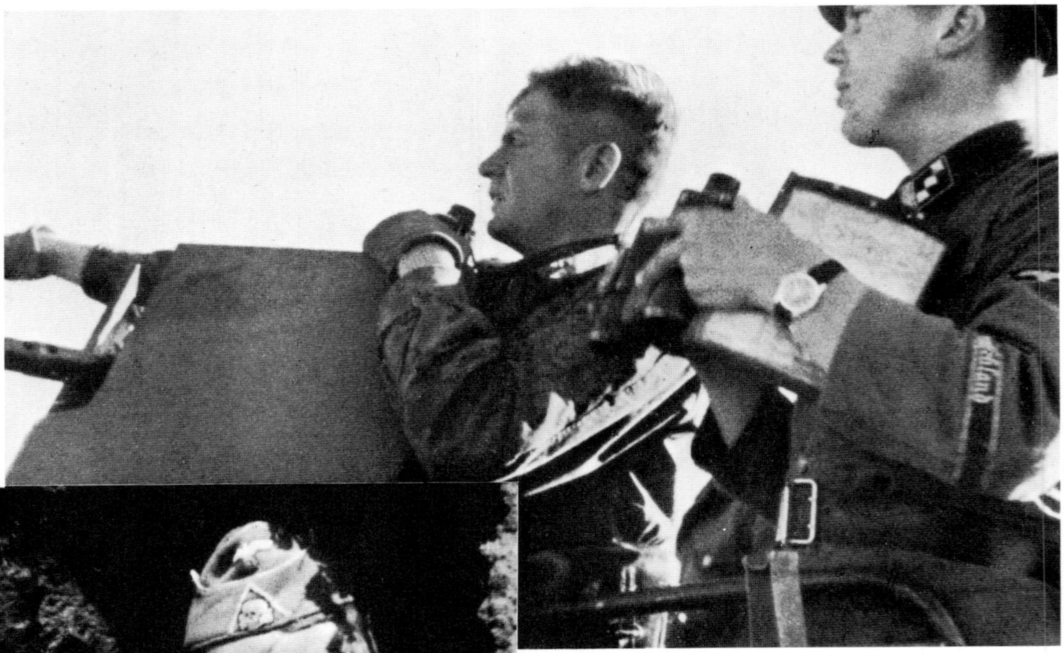

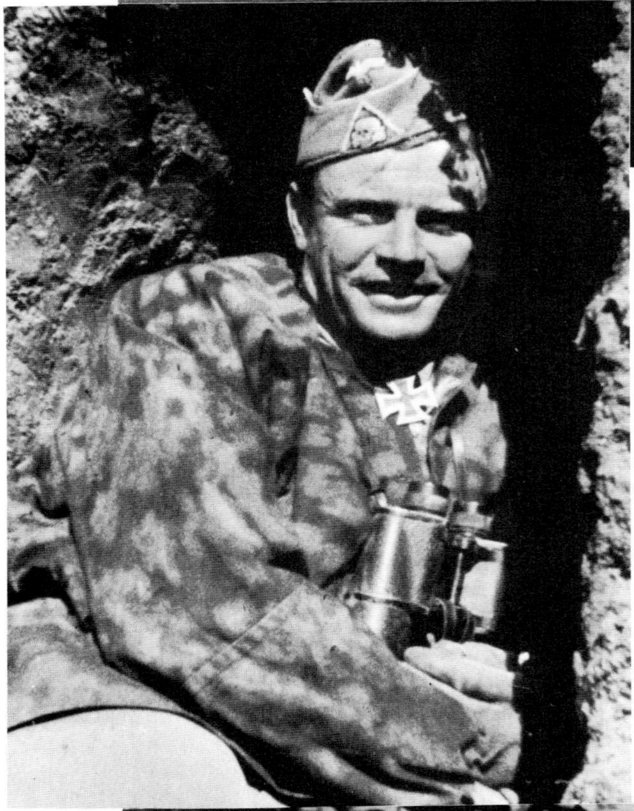

Colonel Heinz Harmel under the cover of his command tank drinks to the health of G.E. Wisliceny and Helmut Schreiber. Both men were just awarded the Ritterkreuz medal.

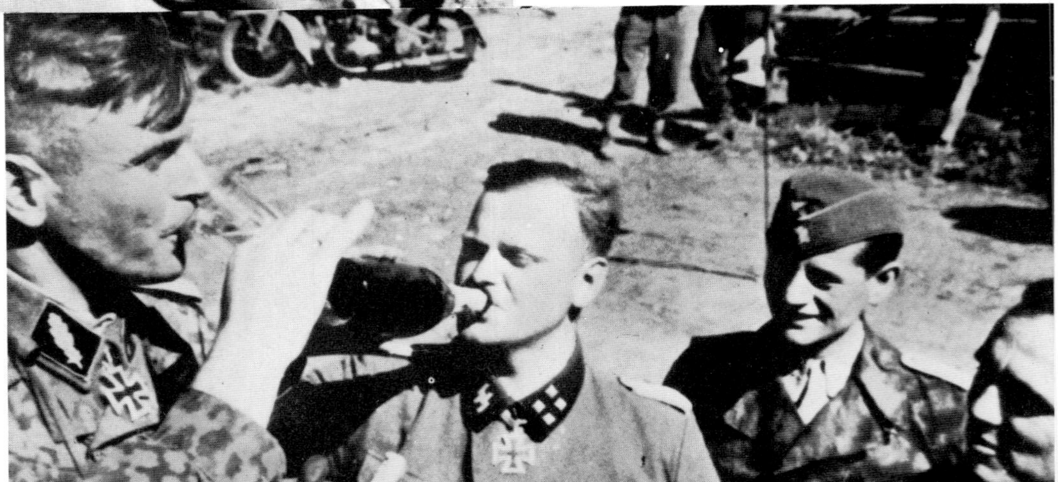

Ritterkreuz for Master Sgt. Kurt Sametreiter (3. Pz. Jäg. Abt. LAH), and Colonel Ostendorff, Ia division "Das Reich".

After the battle of Kursk is lost, a fierce retrograde action is fought in the south, the central and even in the northern sectors.

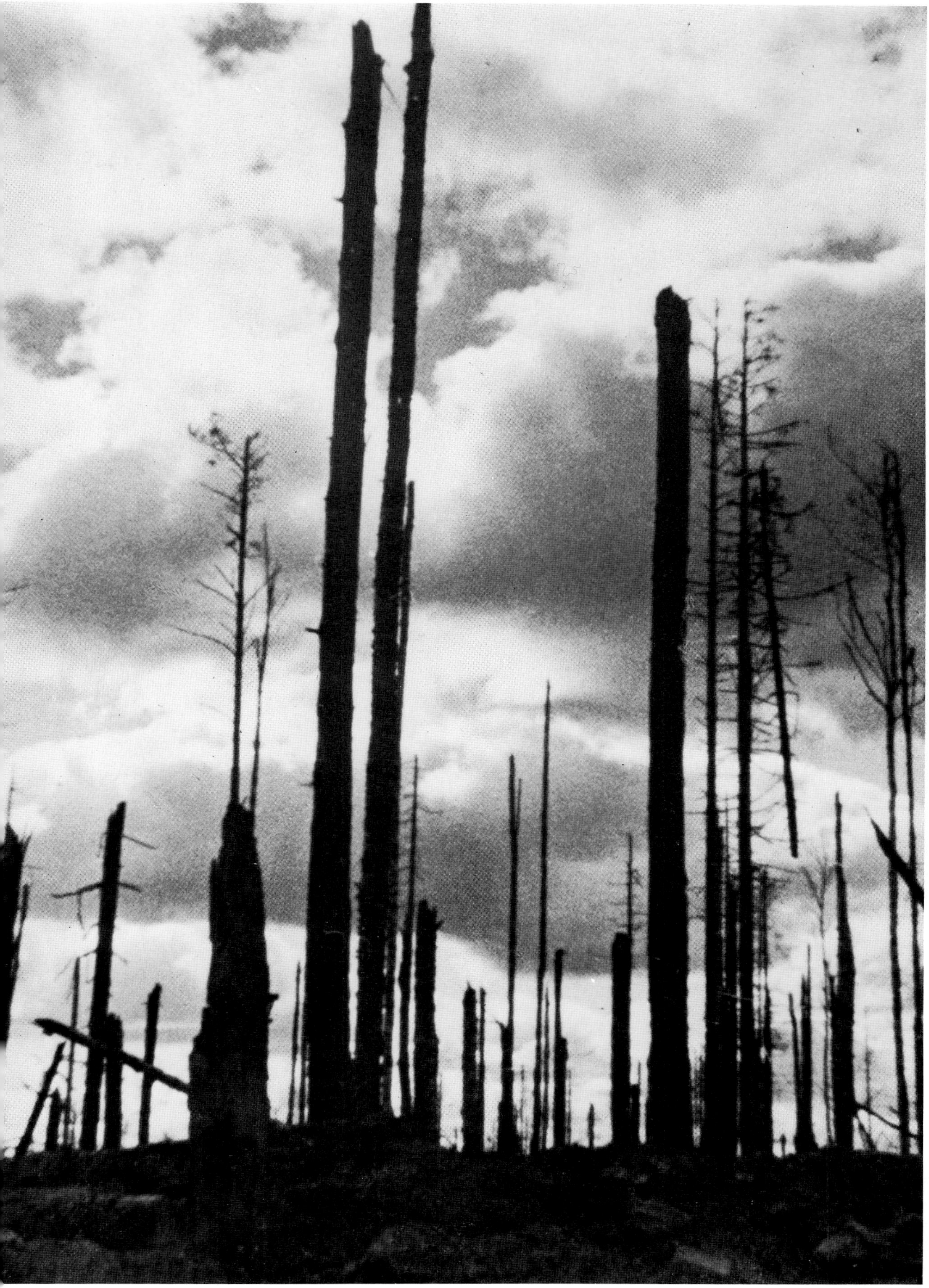

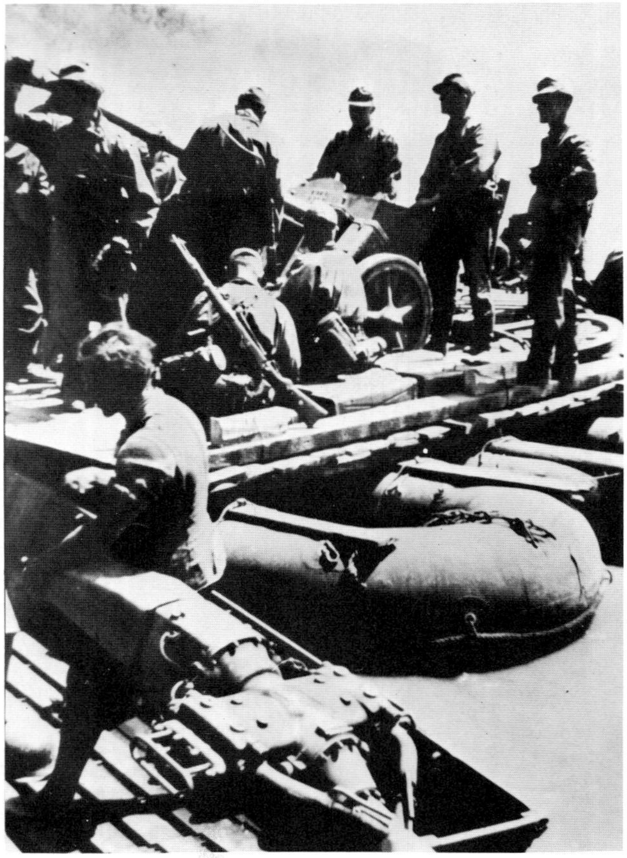

Under the pursuit of the enemy, river crossings become extremely difficult. These must be overcome by clever improvising.

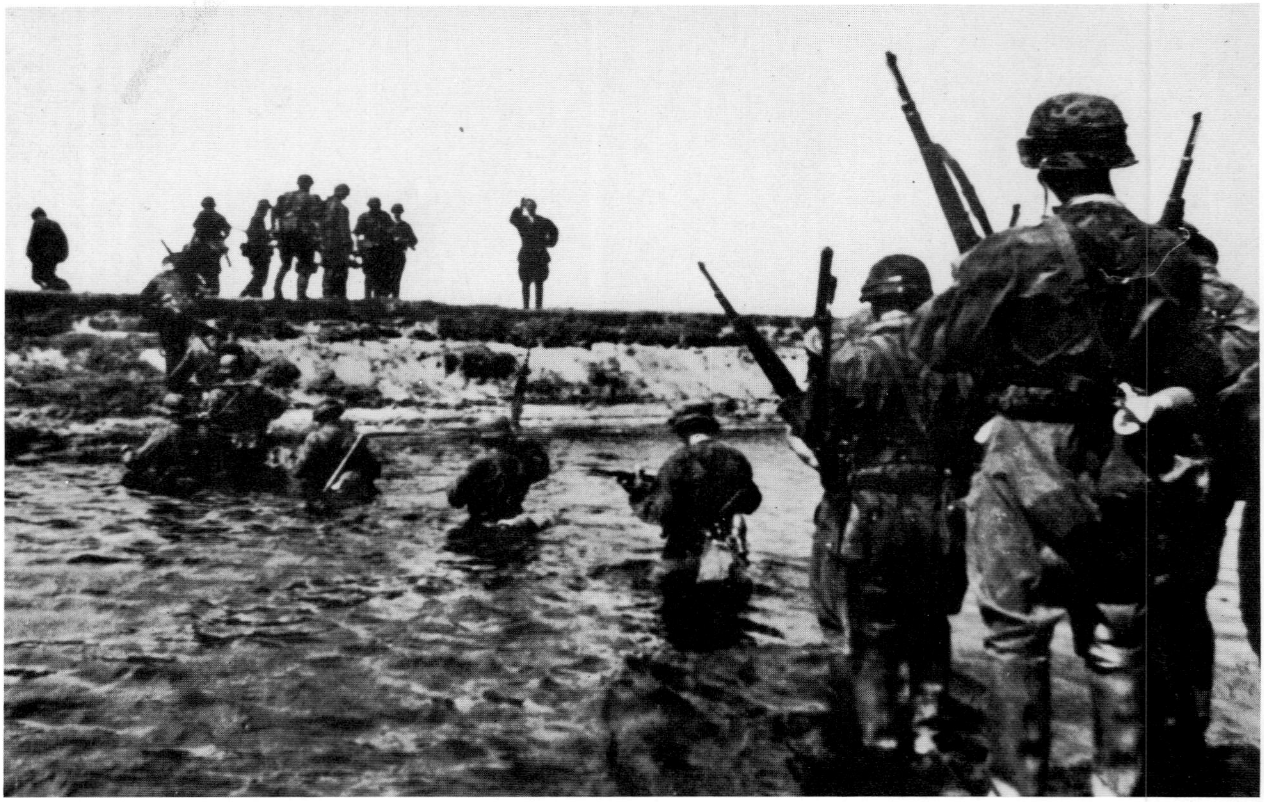

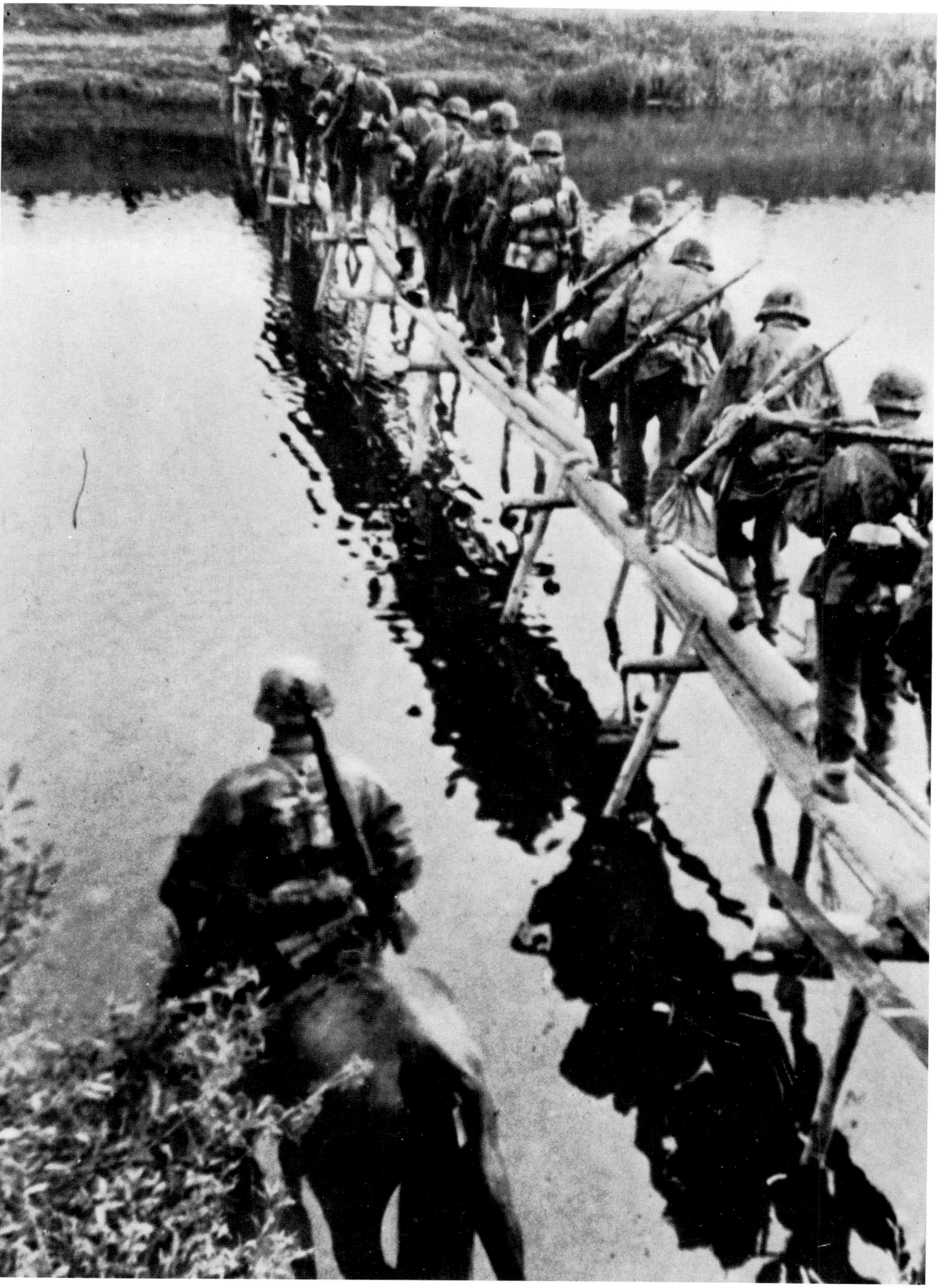

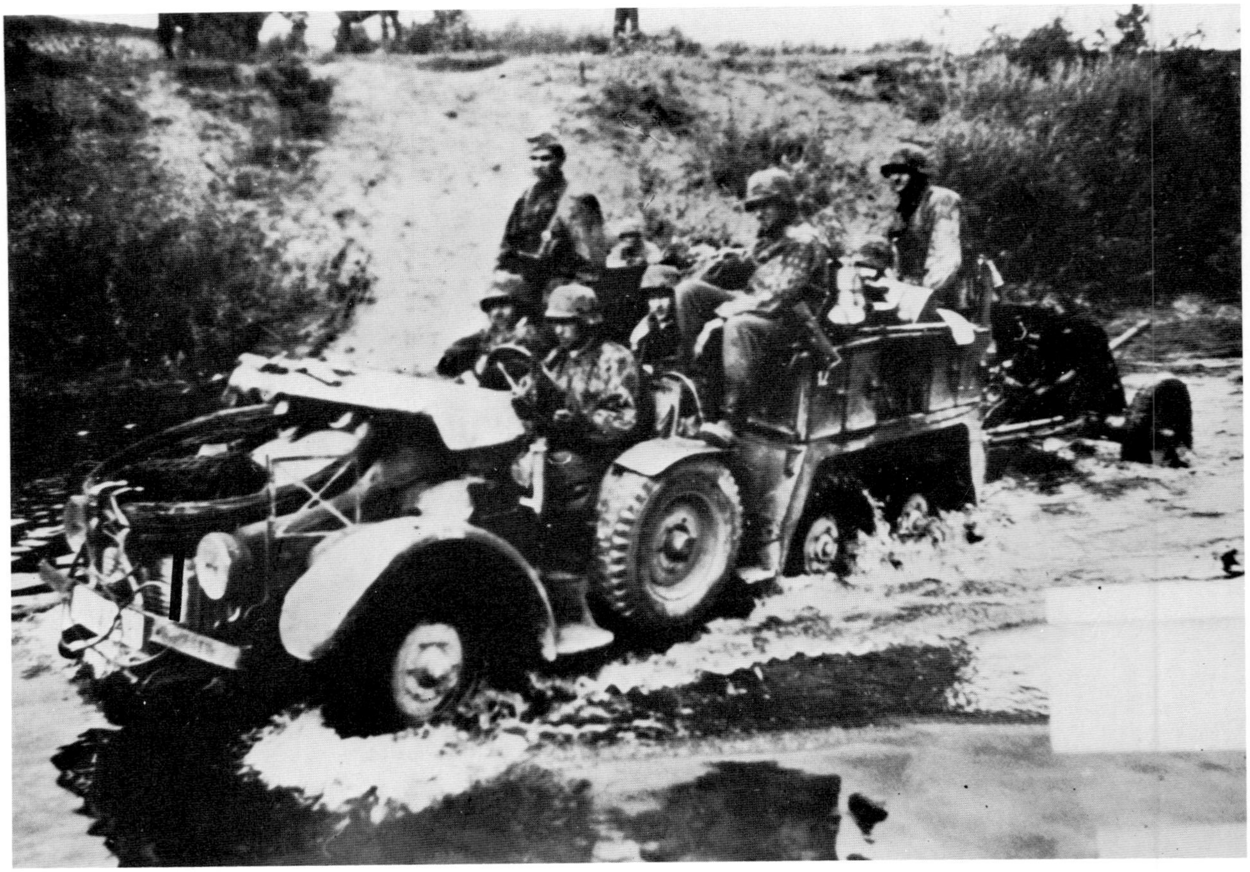

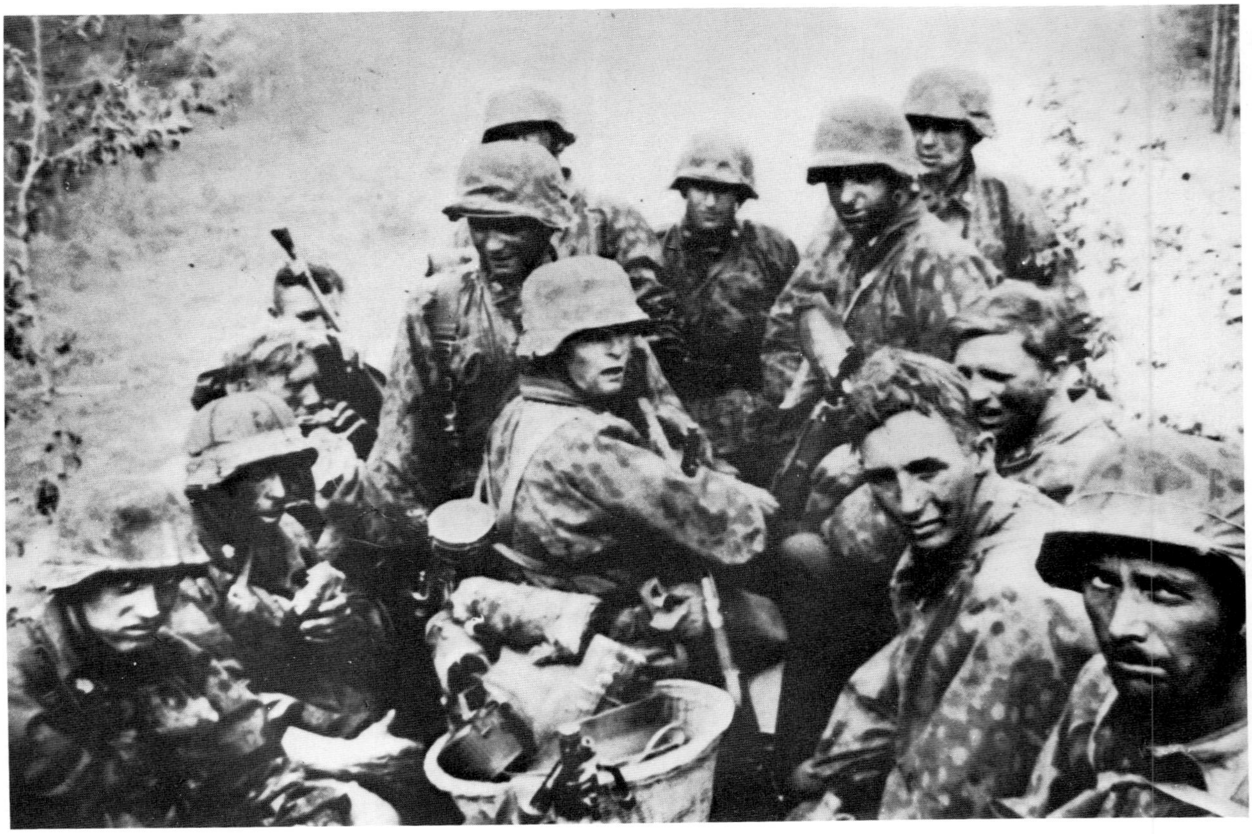

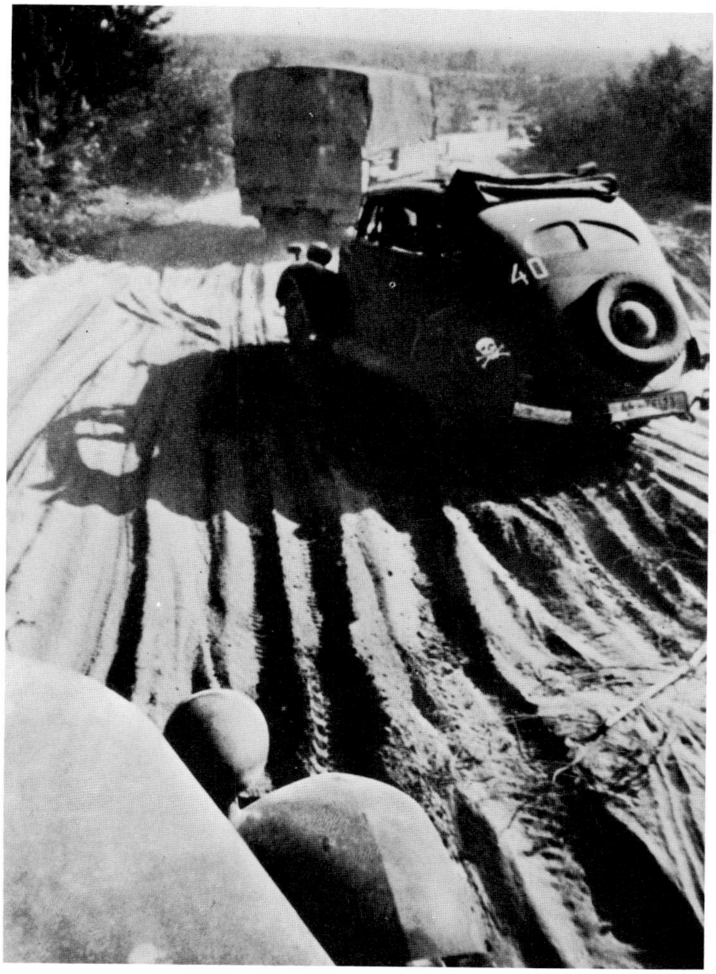
40

All troop movements are retarded by the poor condition of the Russian roads.

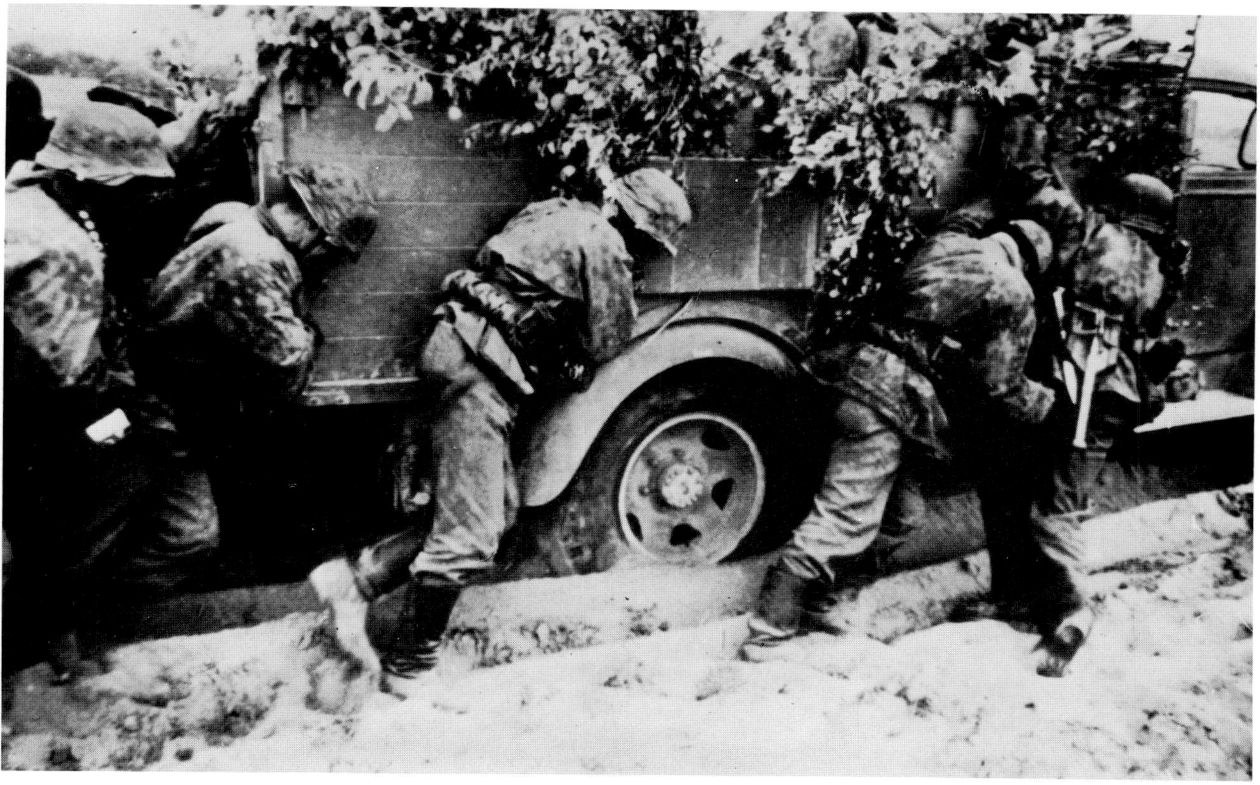

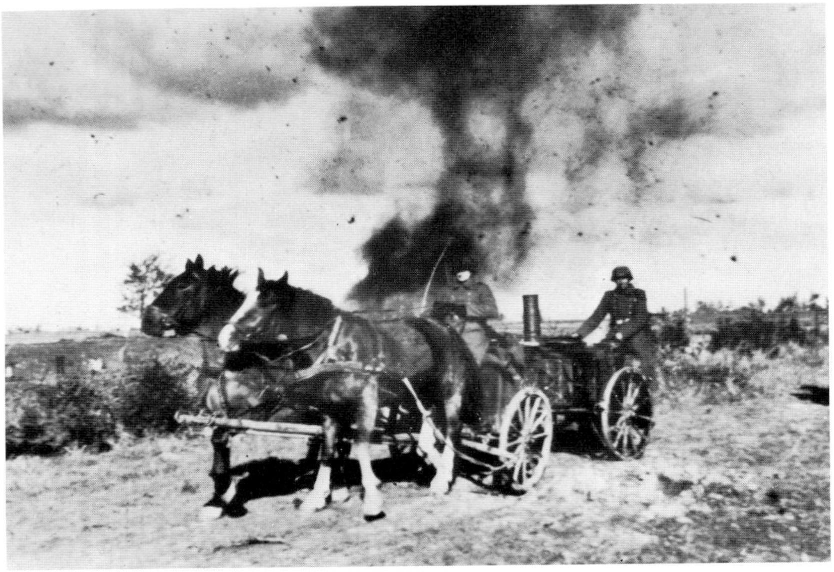

Field kitchen ahead.

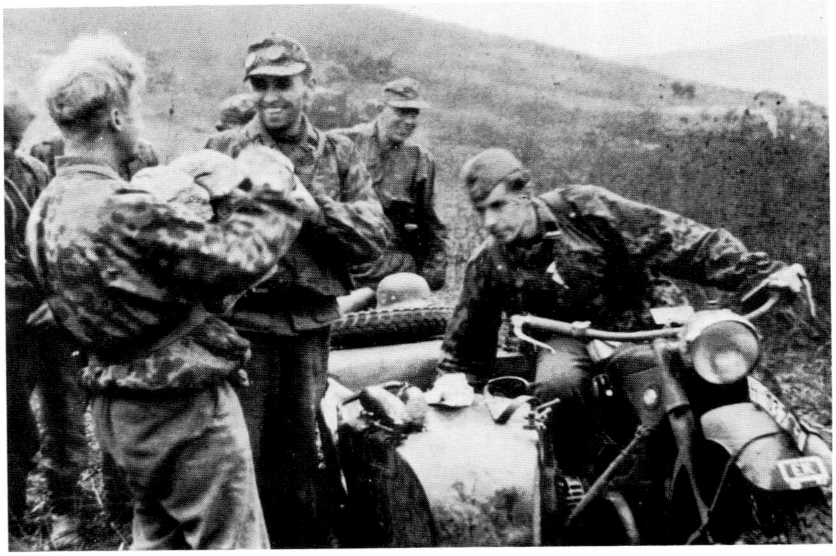

Eventually bread arrives...

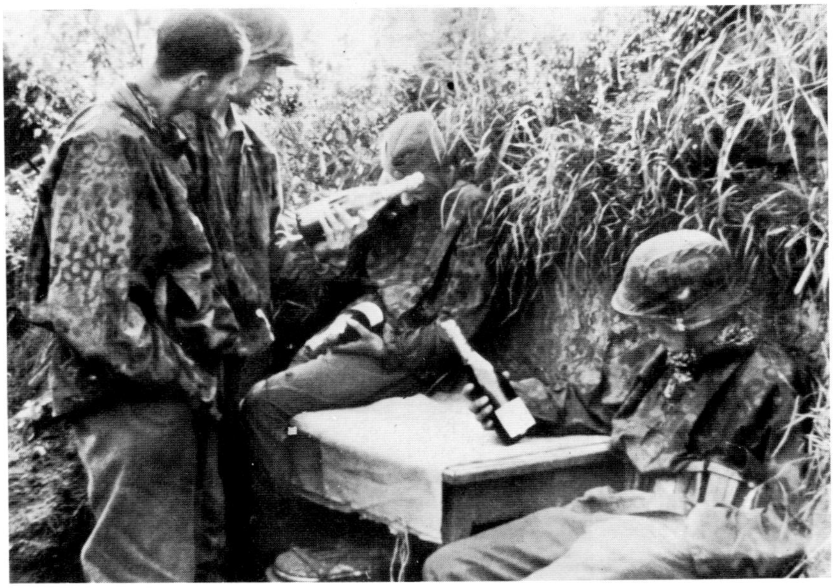

...and occasionally even champagne find its way to the front line.

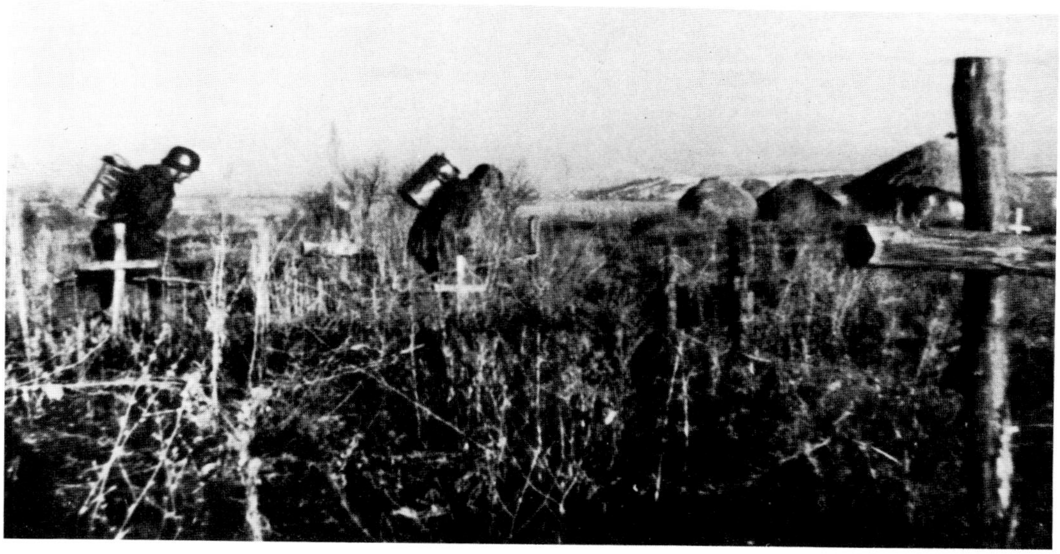

In spite of the heavy enemy fire, German mess personnel bring the warm food to the front lines, something every soldier has longed for.

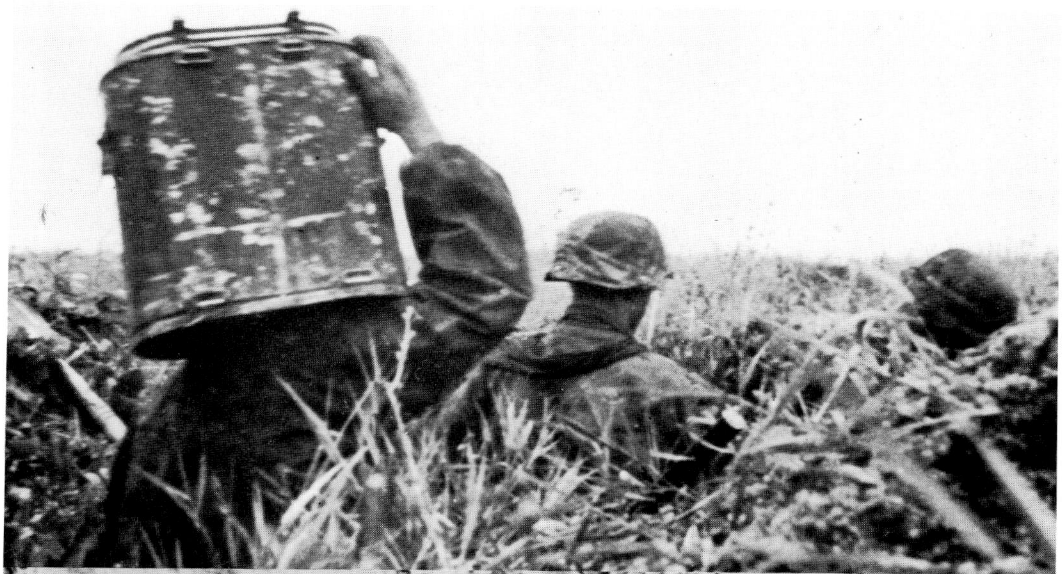

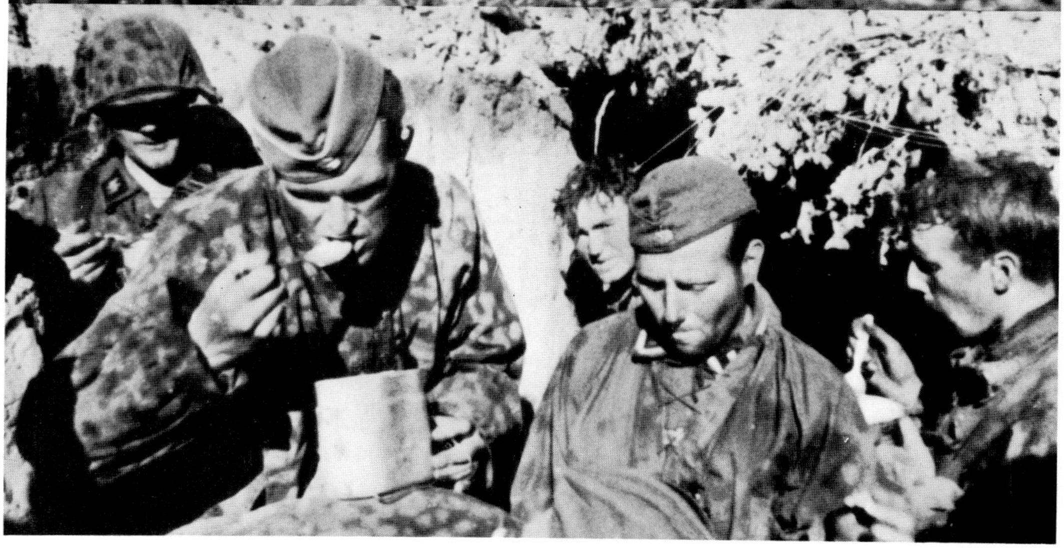

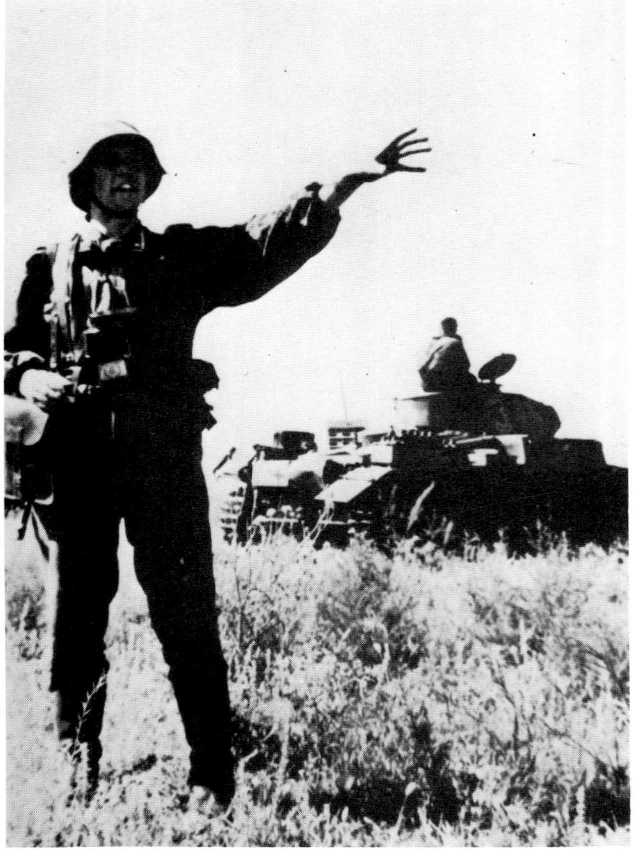

After the battle of kursk was lost, the Red Army at long last took the initiative. During the summer and autumn of 1943 the Soviets began their offensives with superior forces. The movable units of the Waffen-SS were always used where they were needed most during heavy defensive battles.

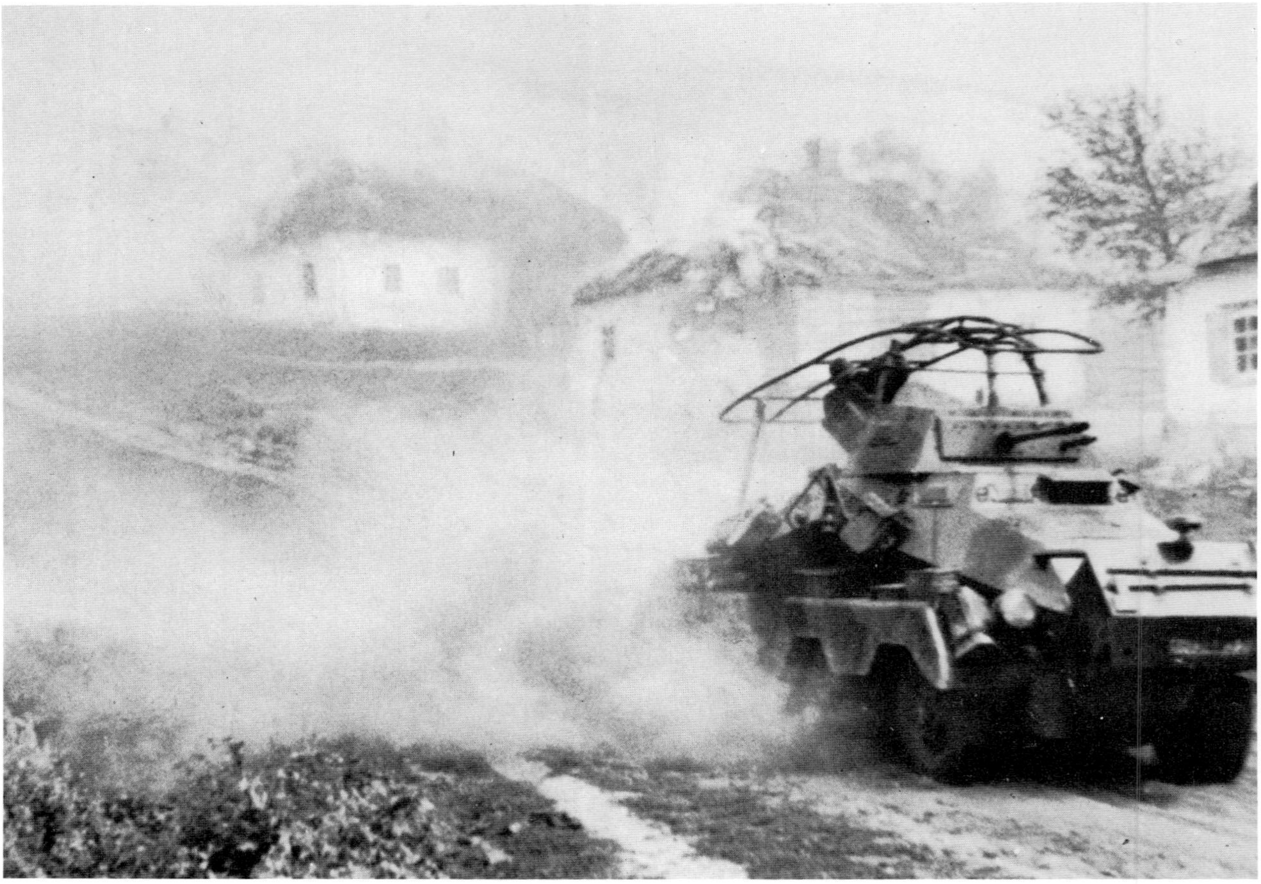

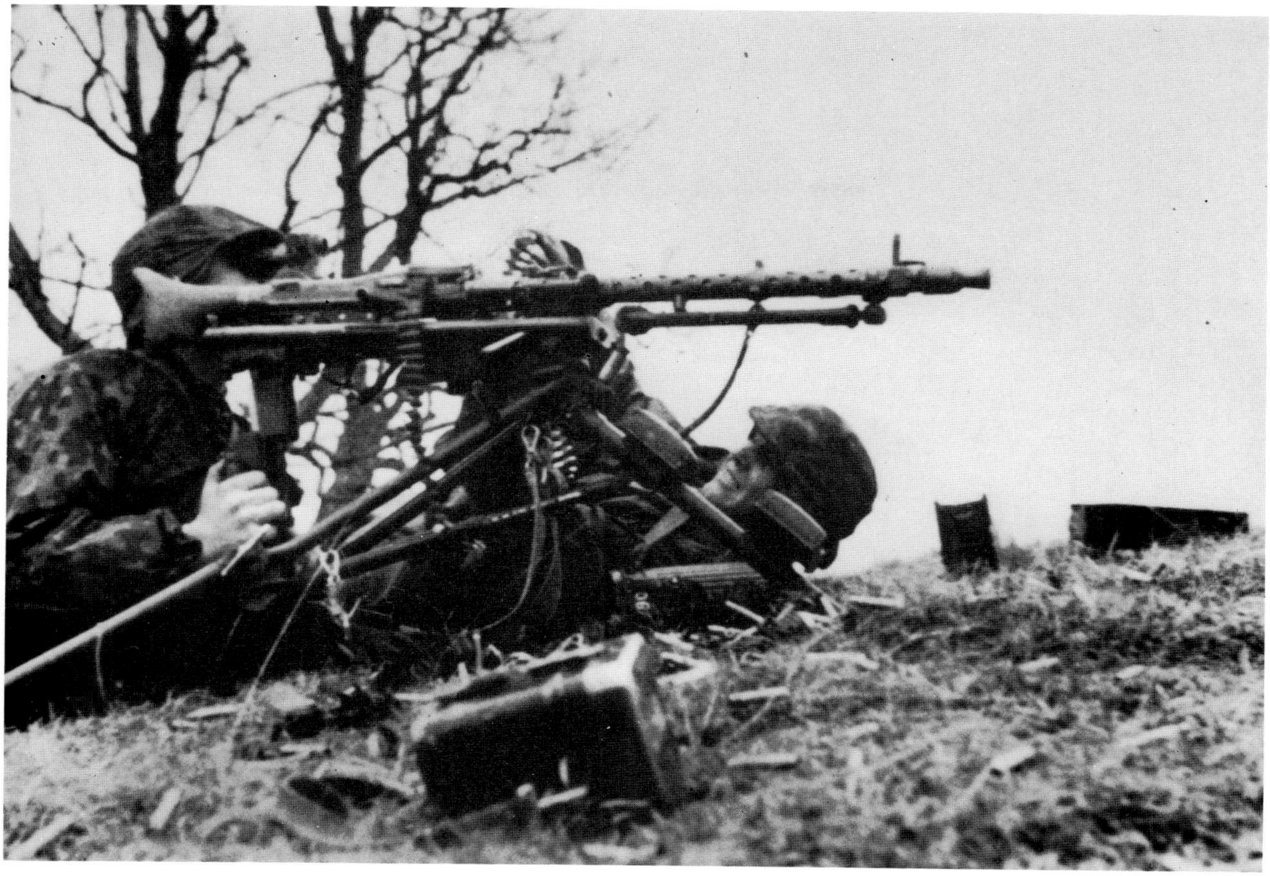

Local counterattacks brought relief for only a short time.

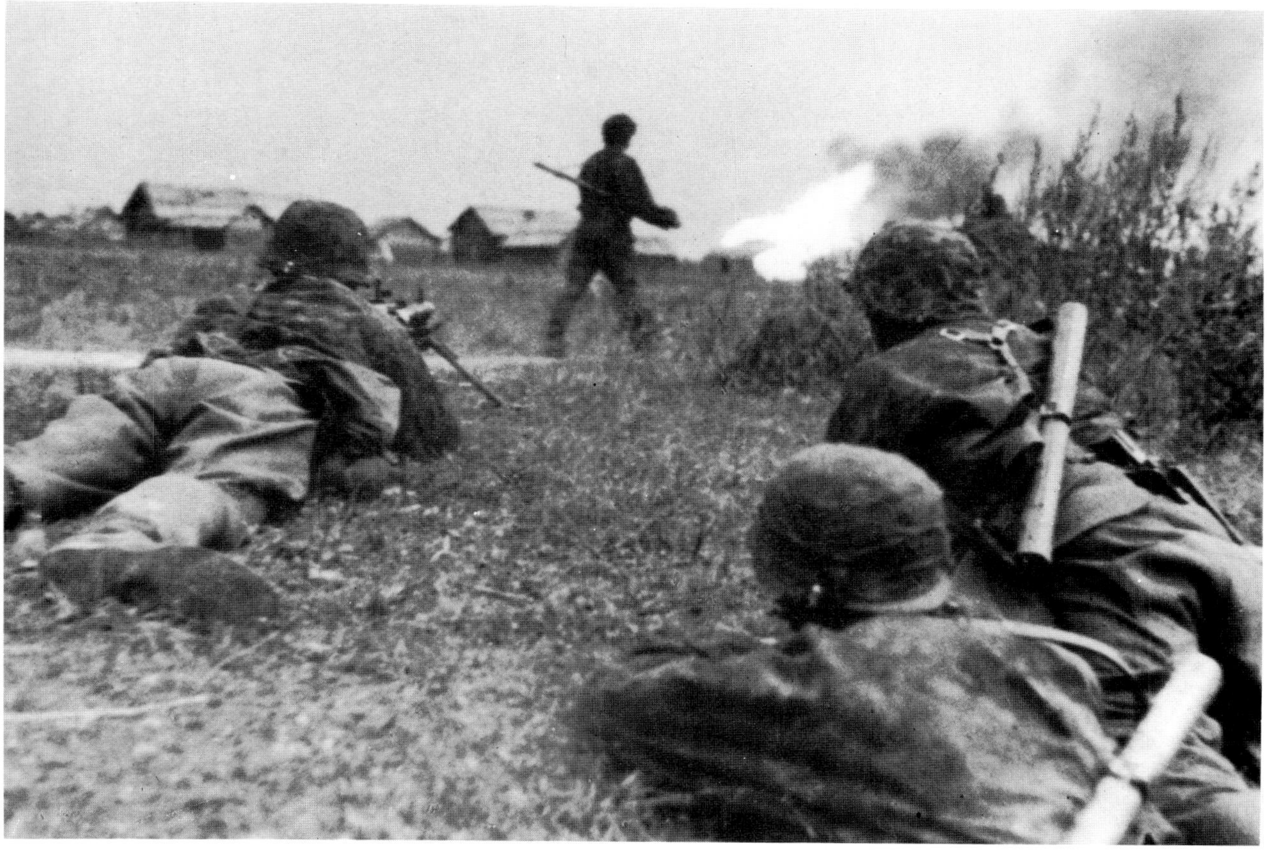

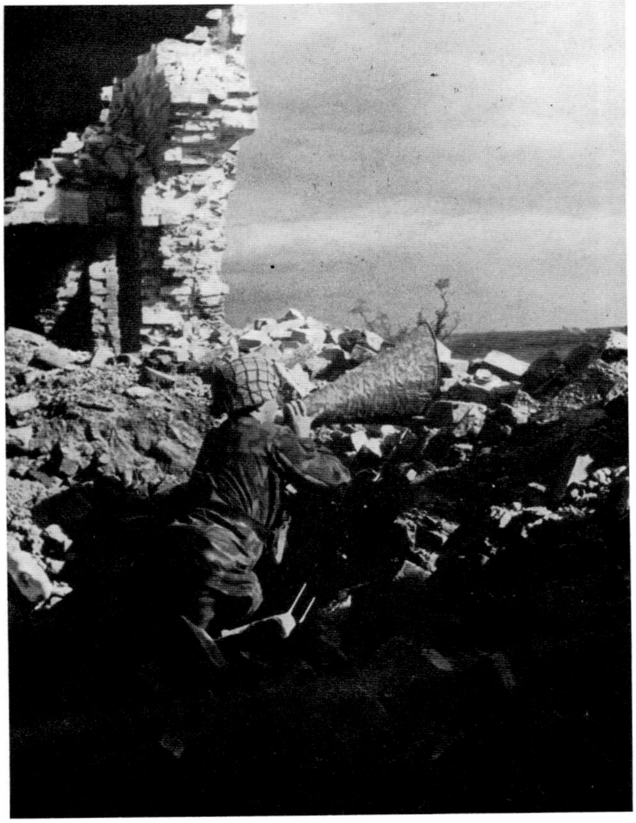

At the front before Leningrad: psychological warfare with the megaphone. The Russian positions are only forty meters away.

Observation post before Leningrad.

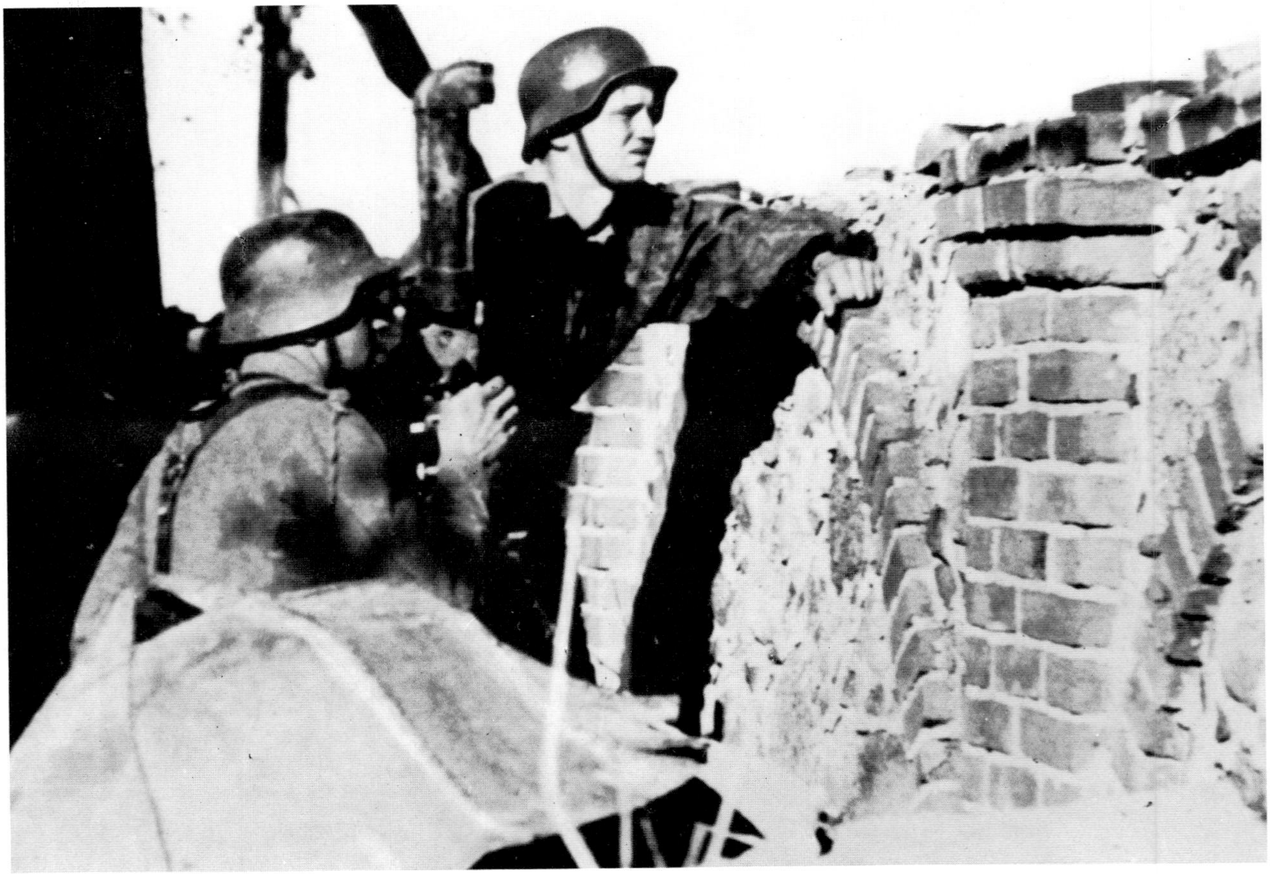

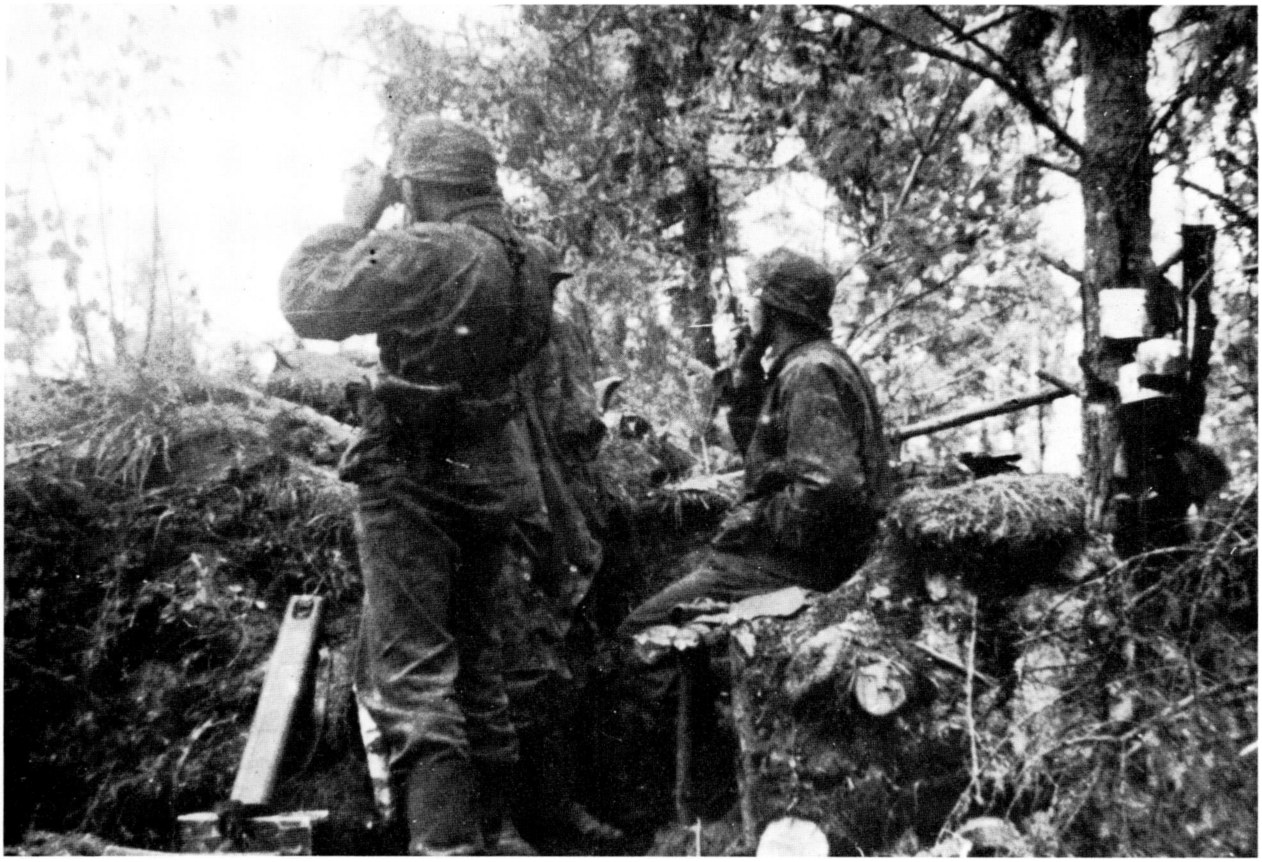

Trenches in the marshlands of the Wolchow.

Difficult ammunition supply over a corduroy road.

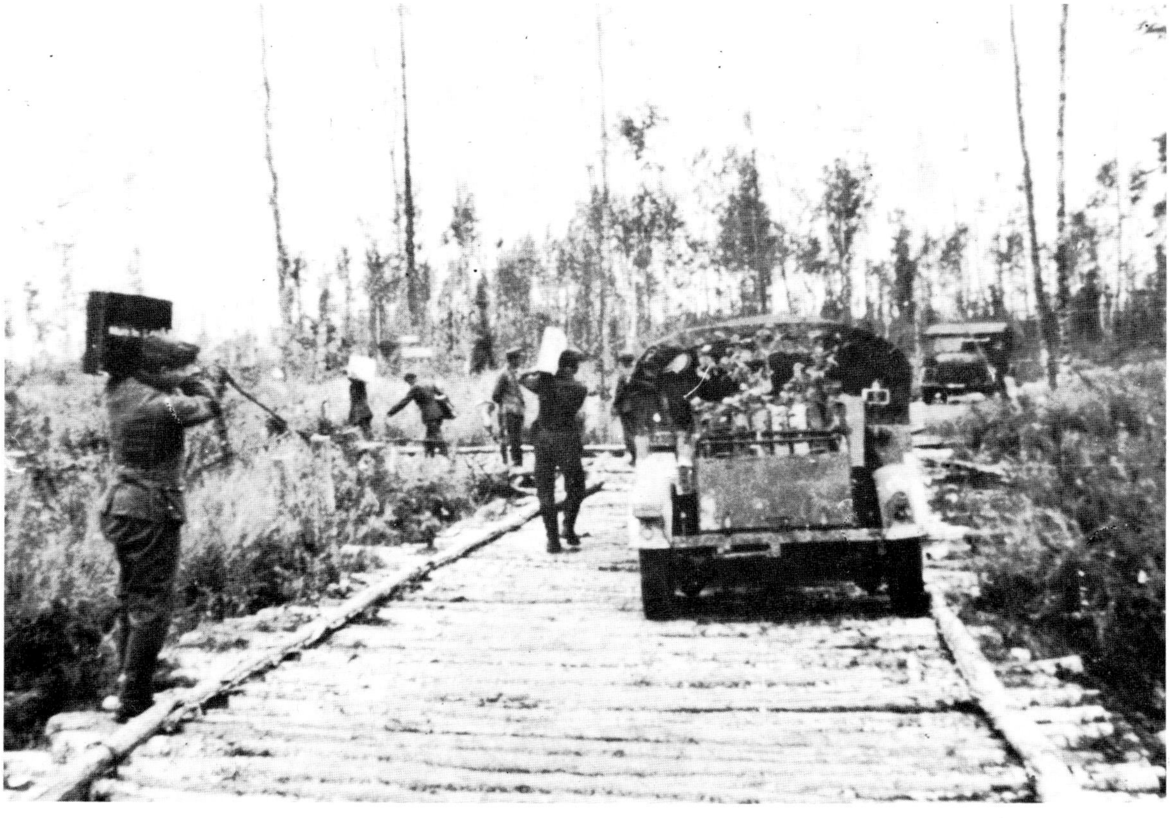

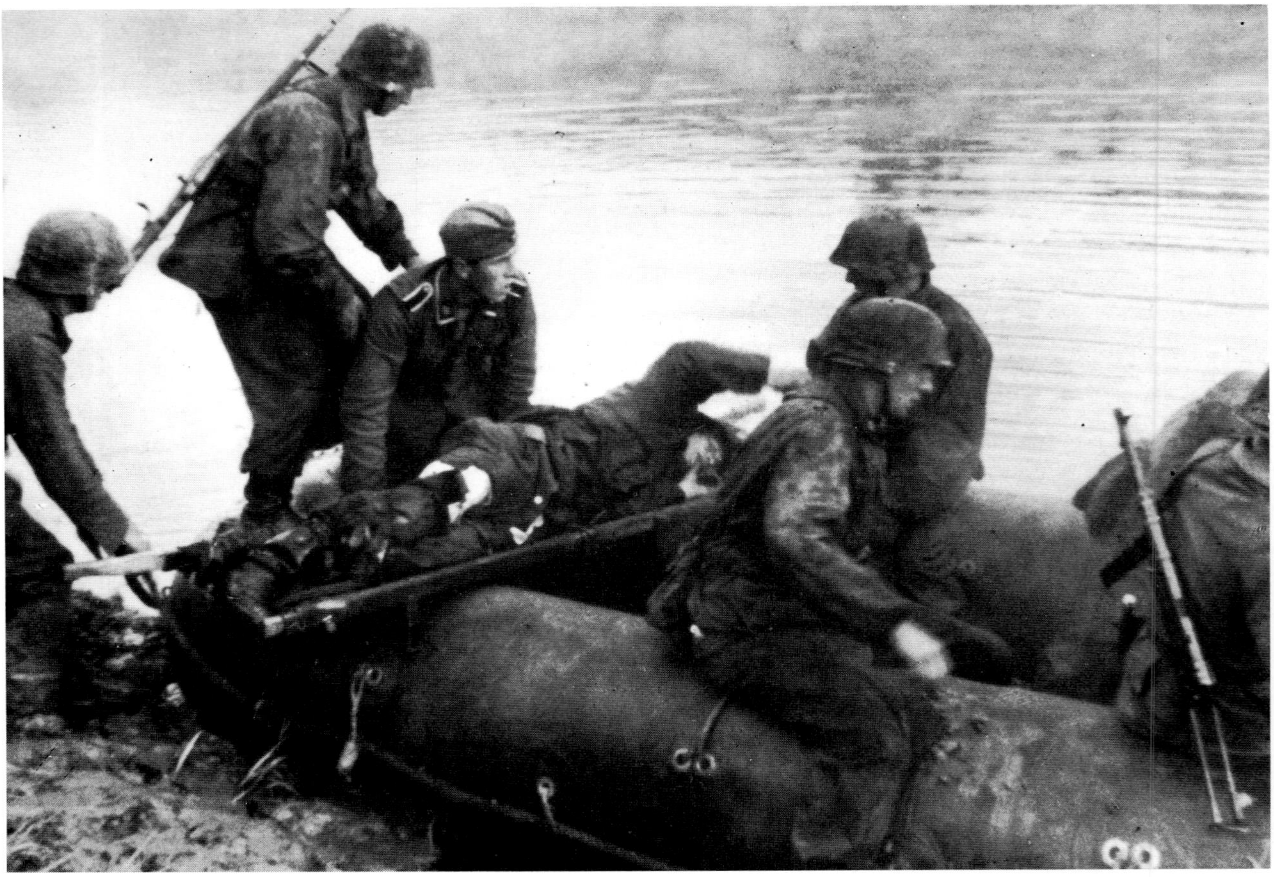

Narwa front: The main battlefield of the bridgehead of Narwa. While this photograph was taken this area was under Soviet mortar fire. The defenders of this bridgehead are mainly Germanic volunteers of the SS-units from Ethonia, Denmark, Holland, Norway and ethnic Germans from Banat and Transylvania.

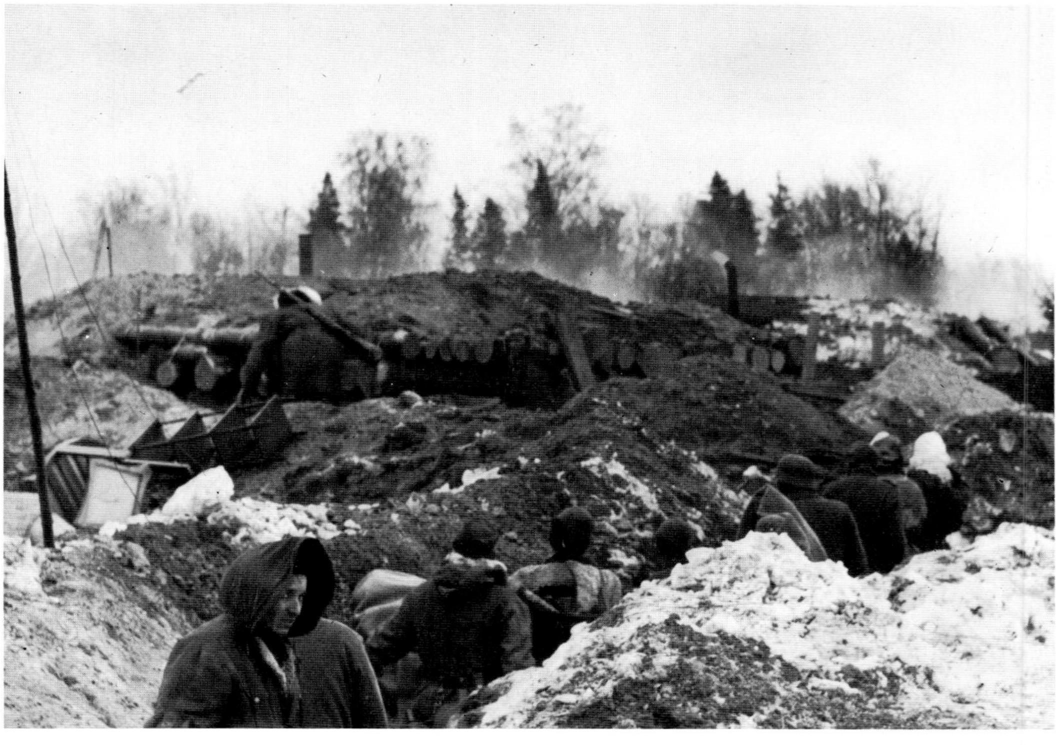

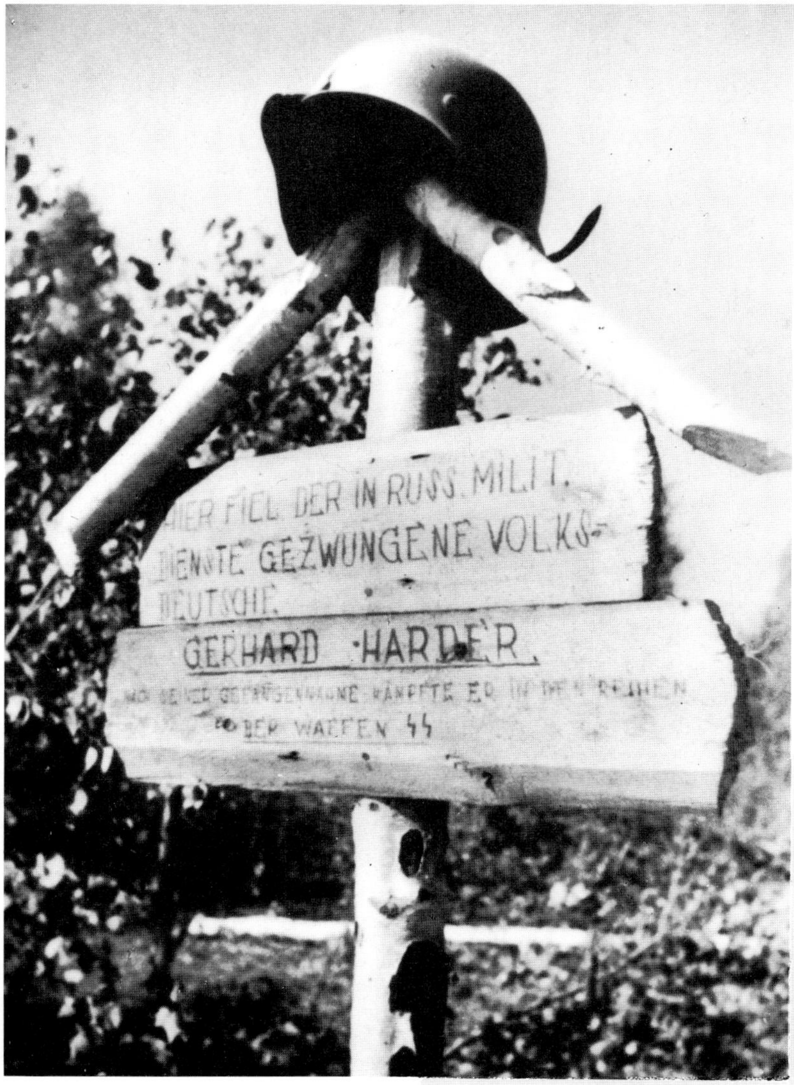
FIEL DER IN RUSS. MILIT.
GEZWUNGENE VOLKS-
GERHARD HARDER
DER WAFFEN SS

"Here the ethnic German Gerhard Harder, who was forced into Russian Military Service, was killed. After he was taken prisoner he served with the Waffen-SS".

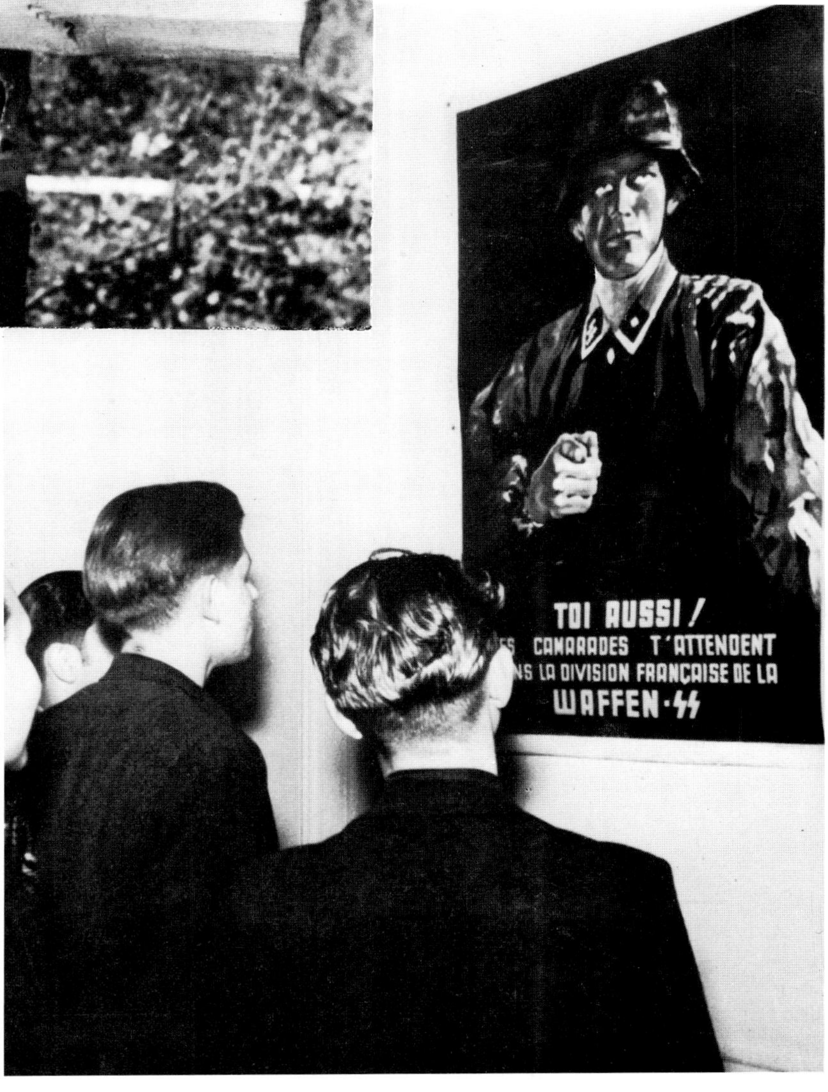
TOI AUSSI !
CAMARADES T'ATTENDENT
LA DIVISION FRANÇAISE DE LA
WAFFEN-SS

Reporting poster for French volunteers of the Waffen-SS.

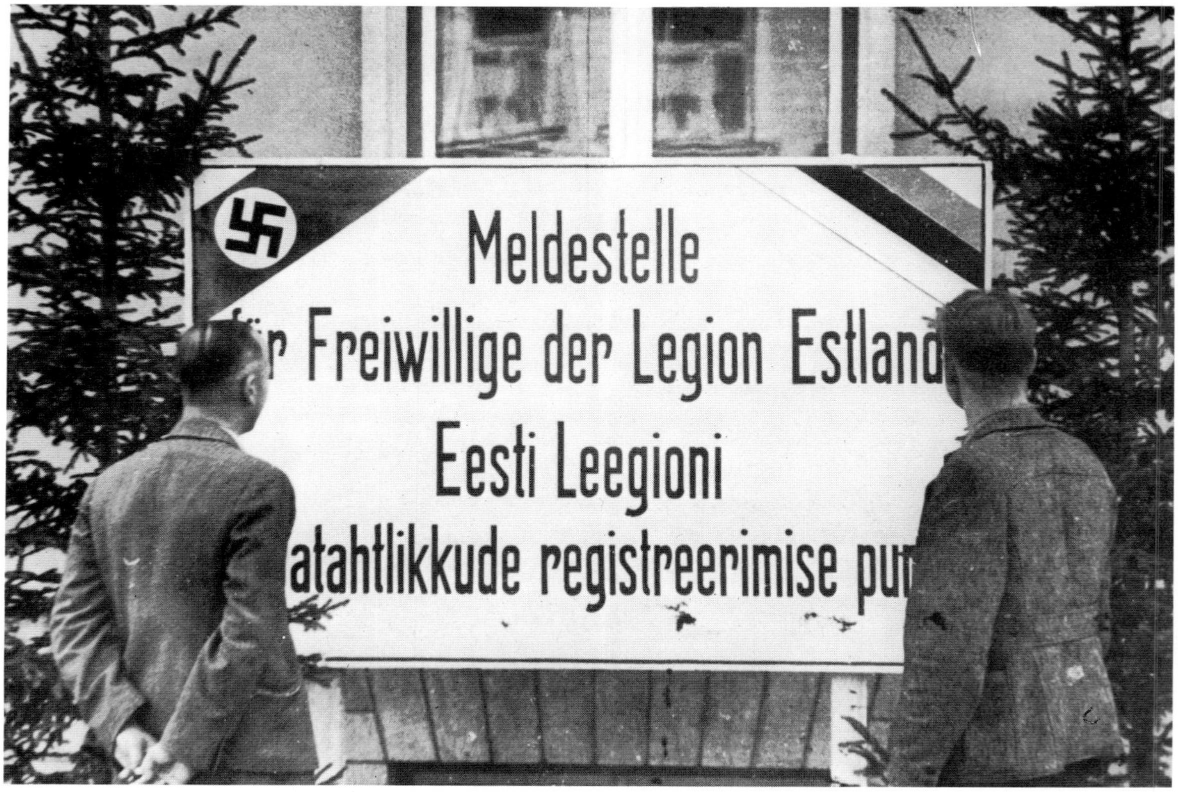
Meldestelle
ür Freiwillige der Legion Estland
Eesti Leegioni
atahtlikkude registreerimise pu

Reporting post of the legion "Estland".

Norwegian signpost a few miles from Leningrad: "A long way to get home".

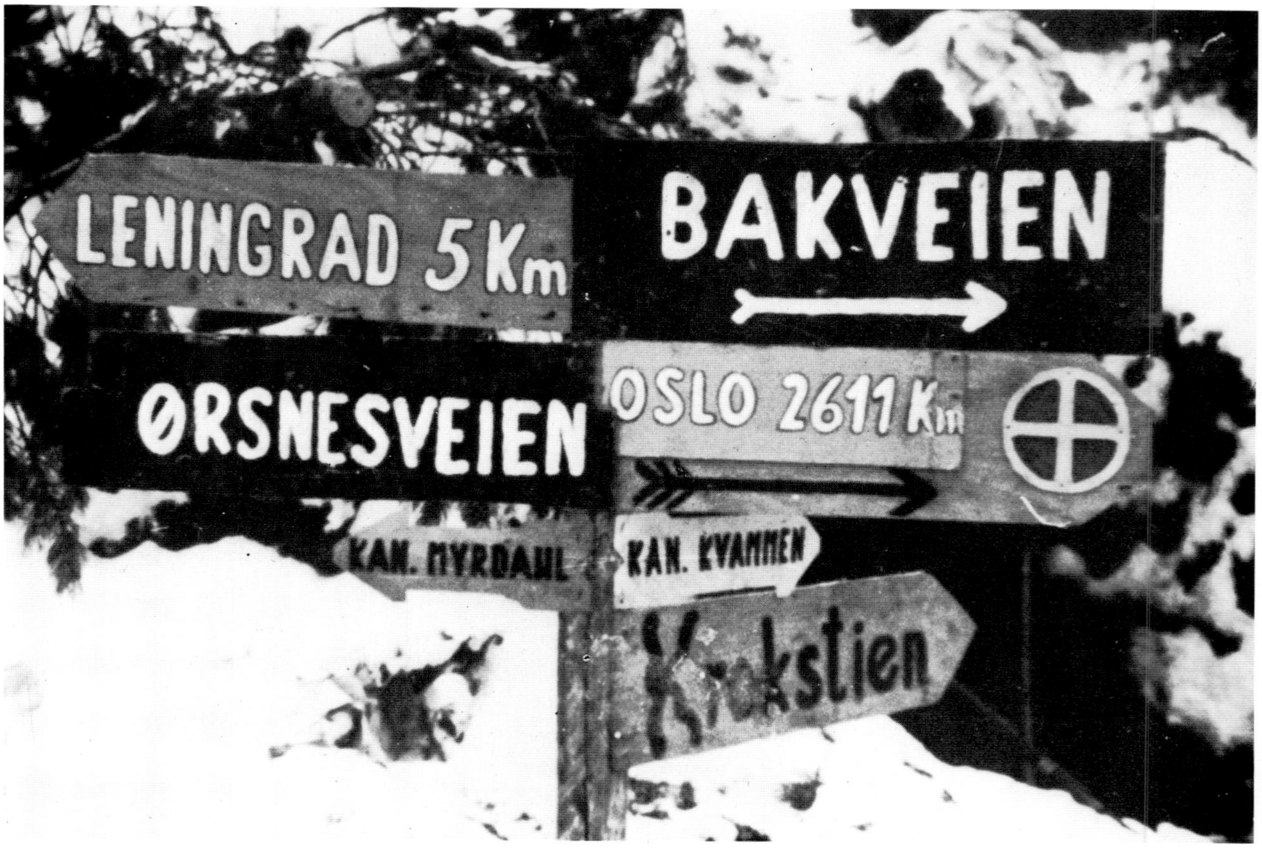
LENINGRAD 5 Km
BAKVEIEN
ØRSNESVEIEN
OSLO 2611 Km
KAN. MYRDAHL
KAN. KVAMMEN

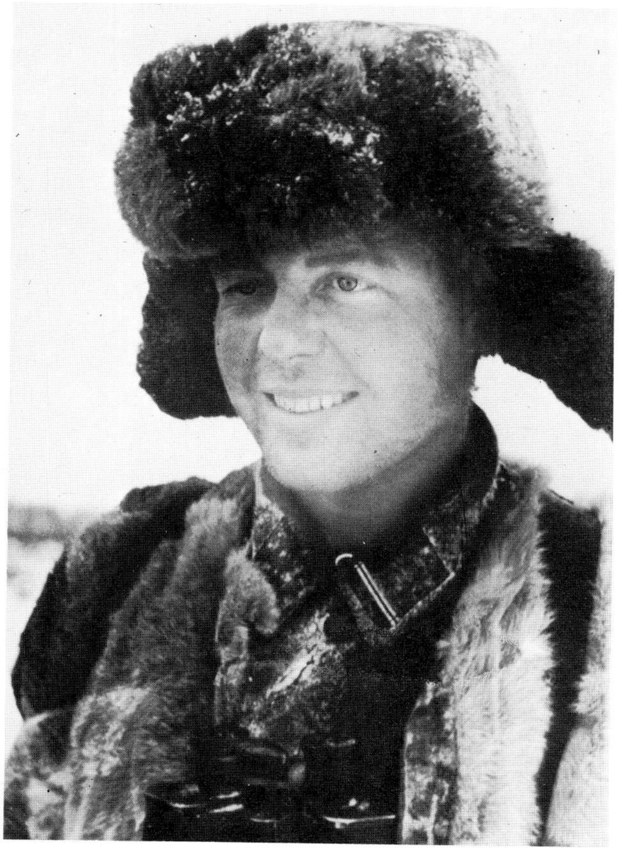

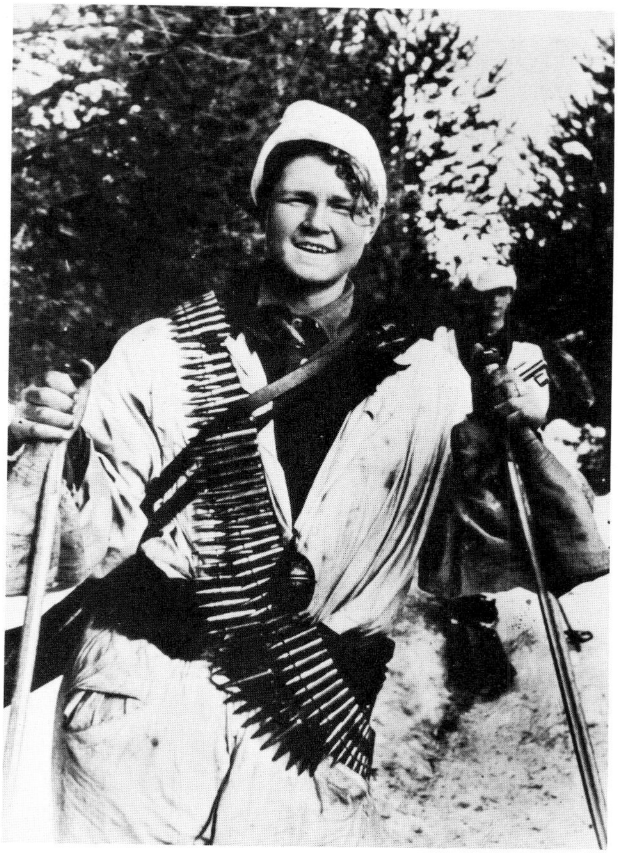

Dutch, Norwegian and Finnish "Lottas"-they are all volunteers of the Waffen-SS.

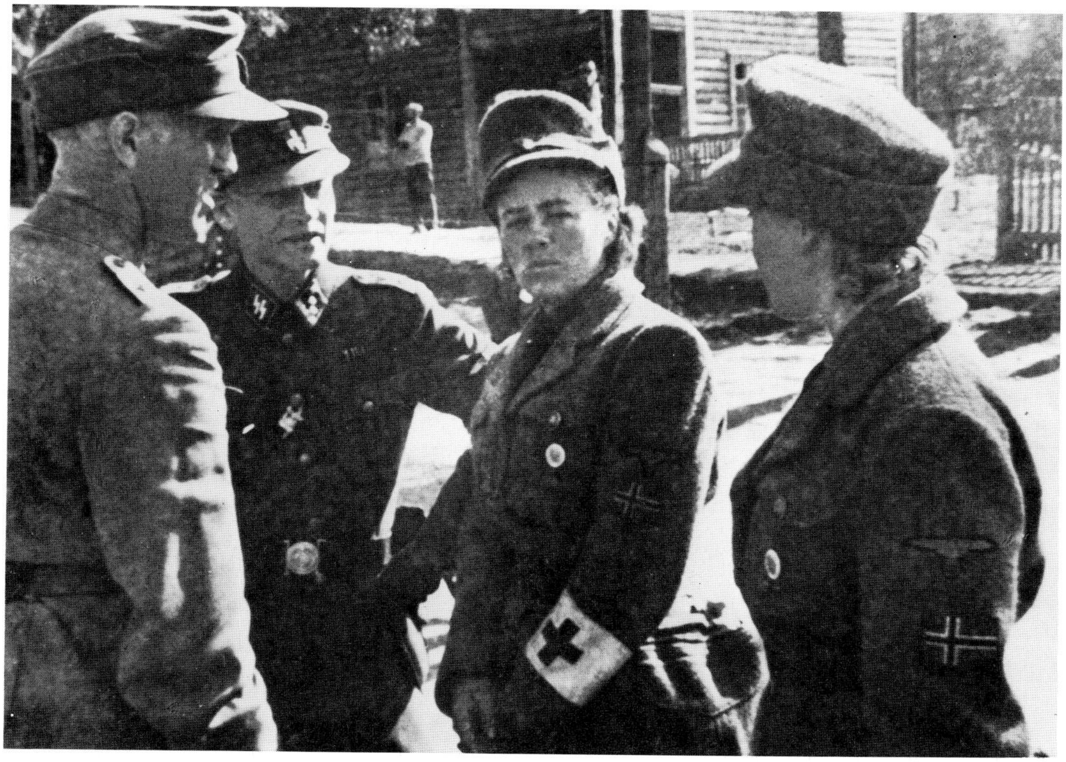

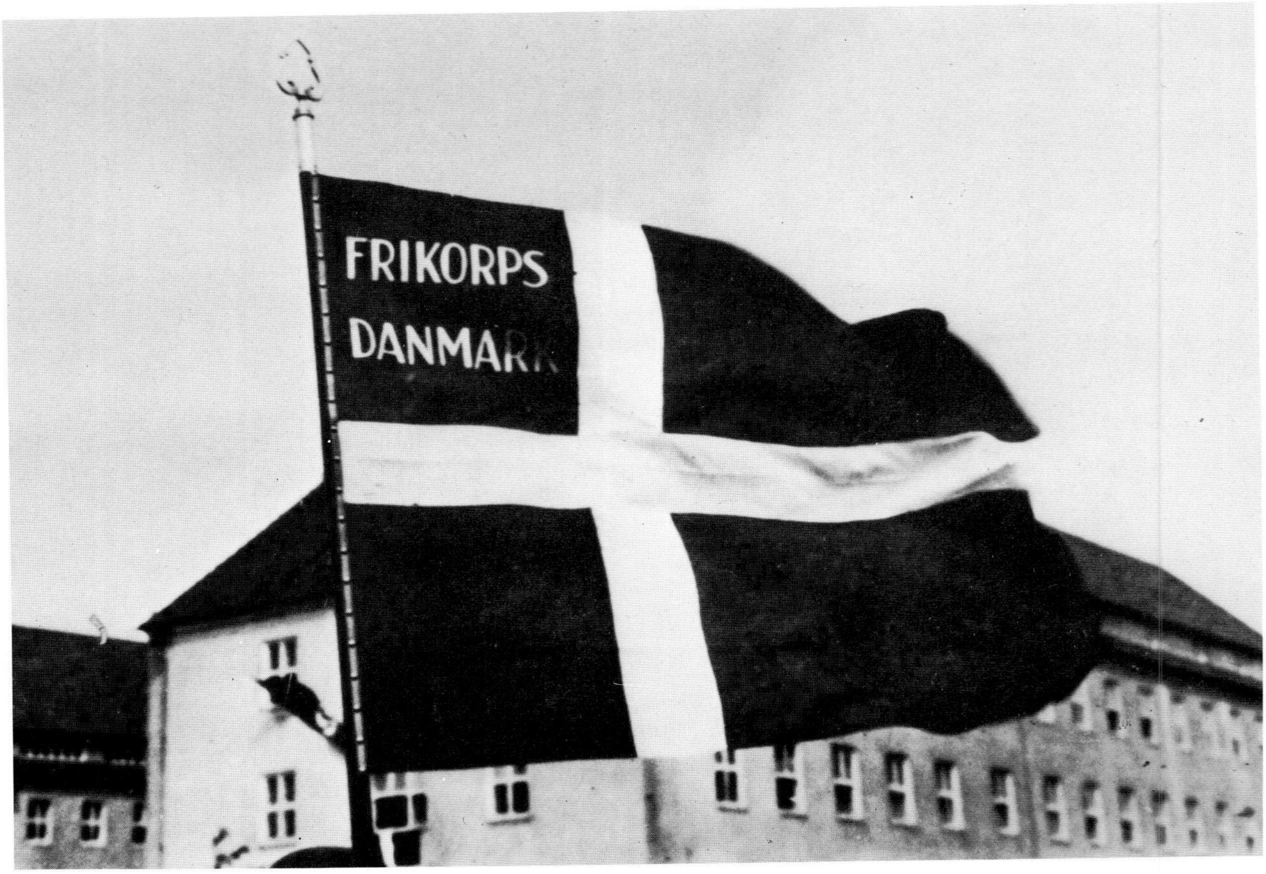
FRIKORPS
DANMARK

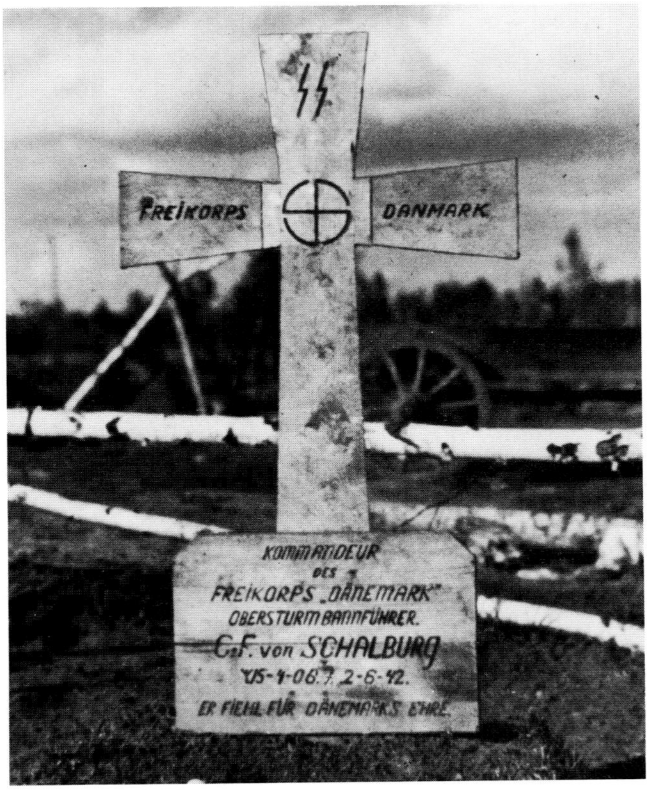
FREIKORPS
DANMARK
KOMMANDEUR
DES
FREIKORPS „DÄNEMARK"
OBERSTURMBANNFÜHRER.
C.F. von SCHALBURG
ER FIEHL FÜR DÄNEMARKS EHRE.

The flag of the volunteer corps "Danmark".

The grave of the commander of the volunteer corps "Danmark", Lt. Colonel Graf von Schalburg.

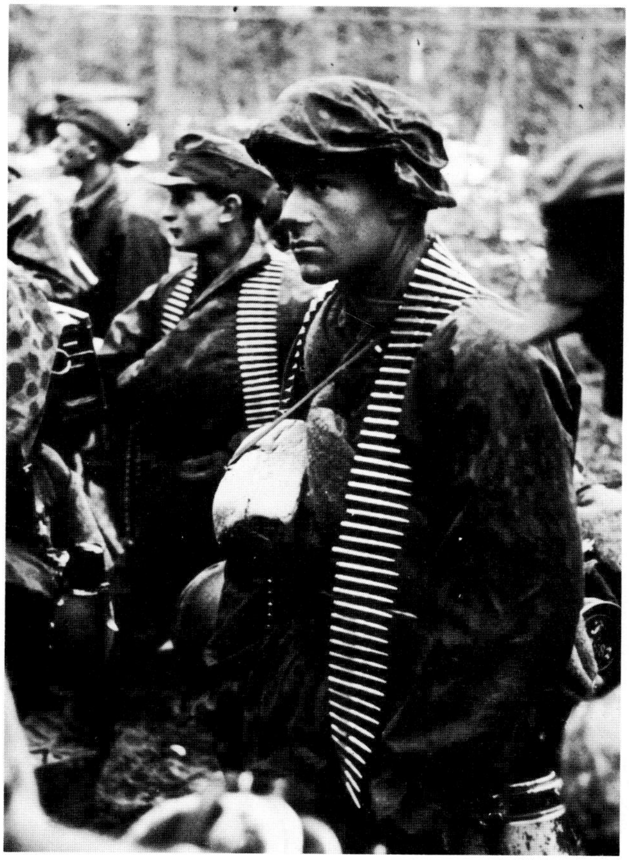 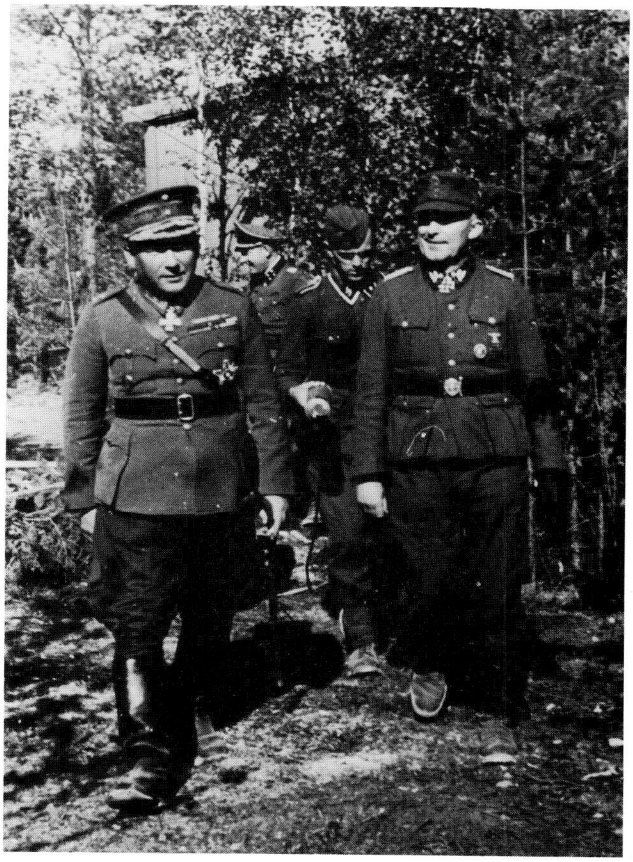

In Karelia, Finland the SS-division "Nord" is involved in heavy defensive fighting. The Finnish General Malmberg, together with the division commander Kleinheisterberg.

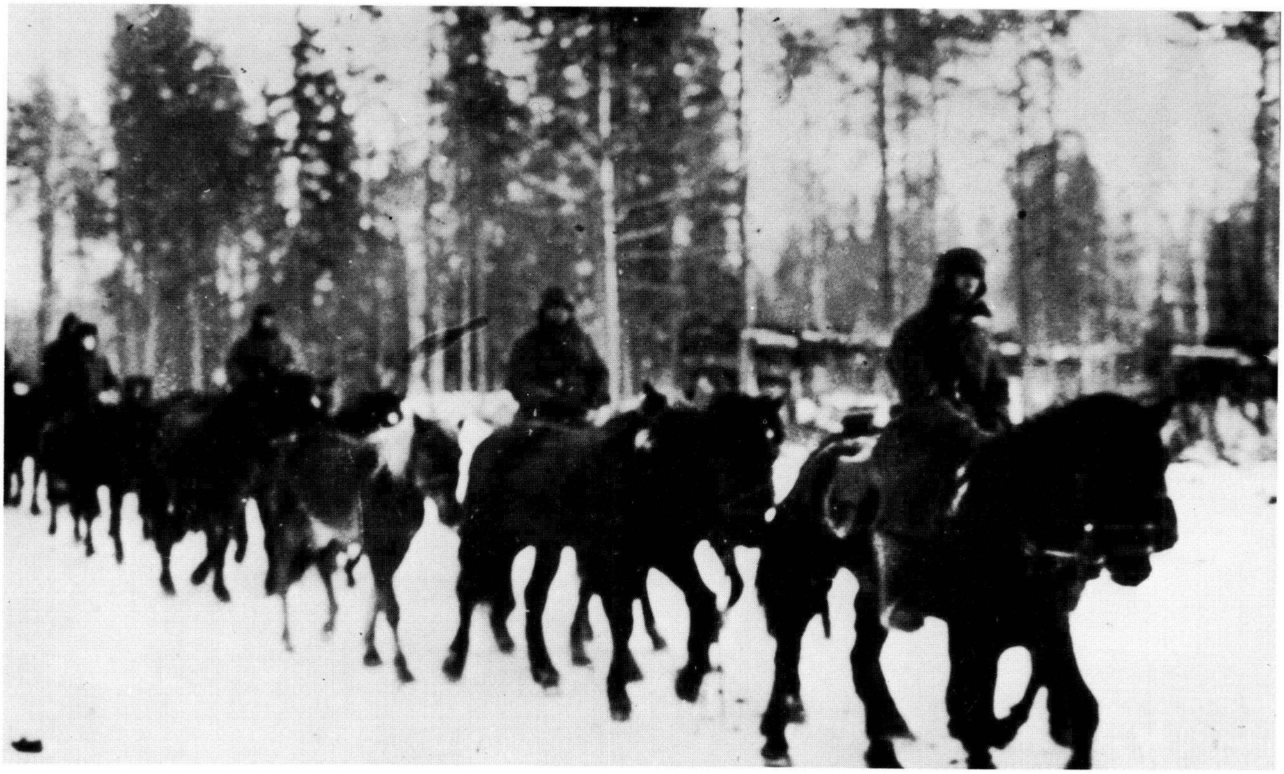

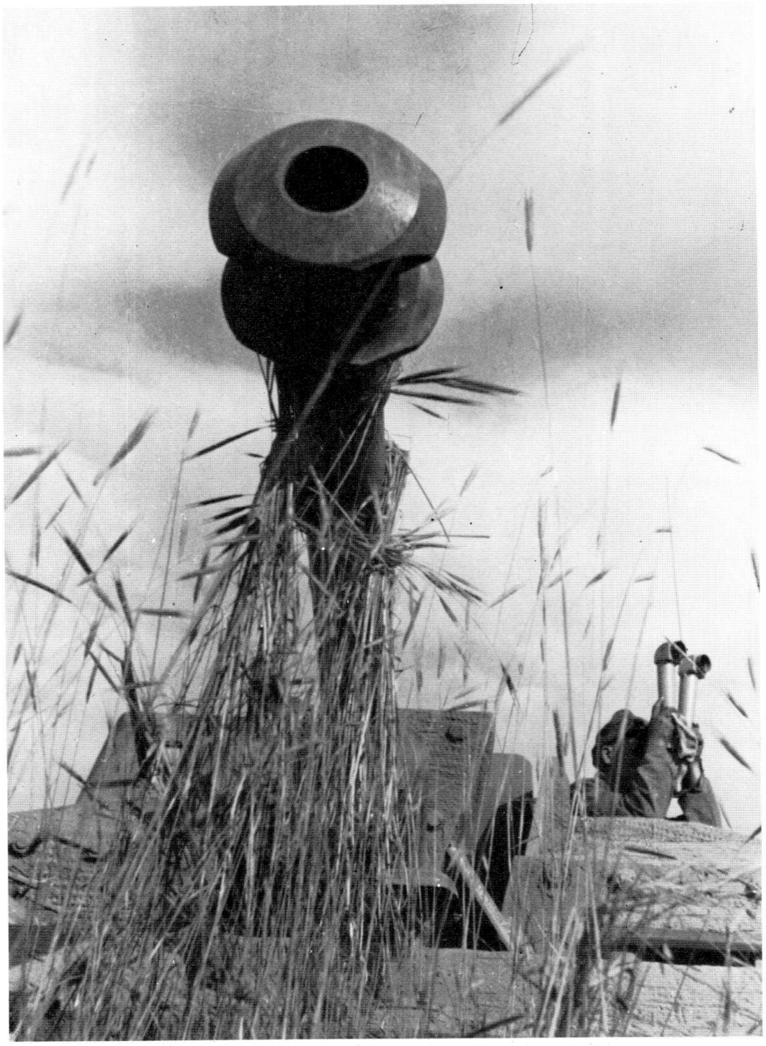

An ever increasing number of Russian tanks continues the attacks on German defensive positions. The heavy and armor-piercing weapons are becoming increasingly important. (On the left: self-propelled assault-gun, on the right: 75 mm anti-tank gun)

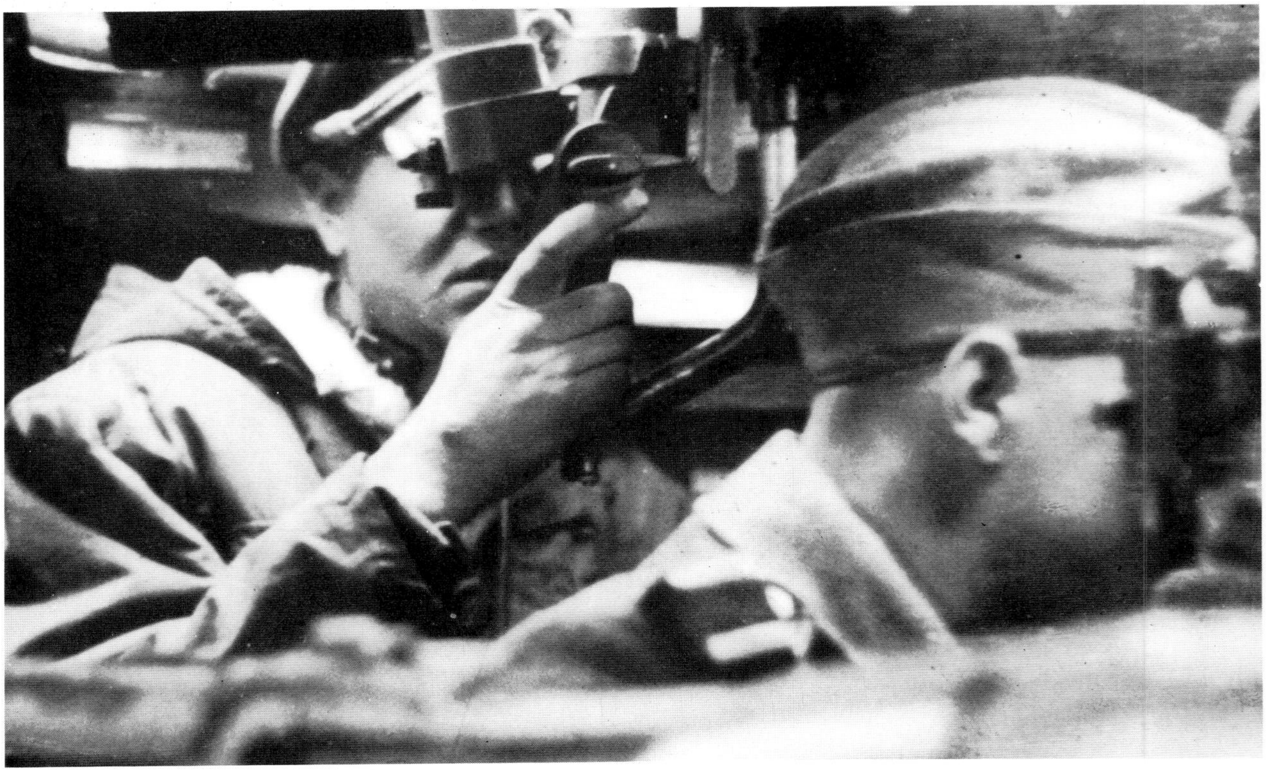

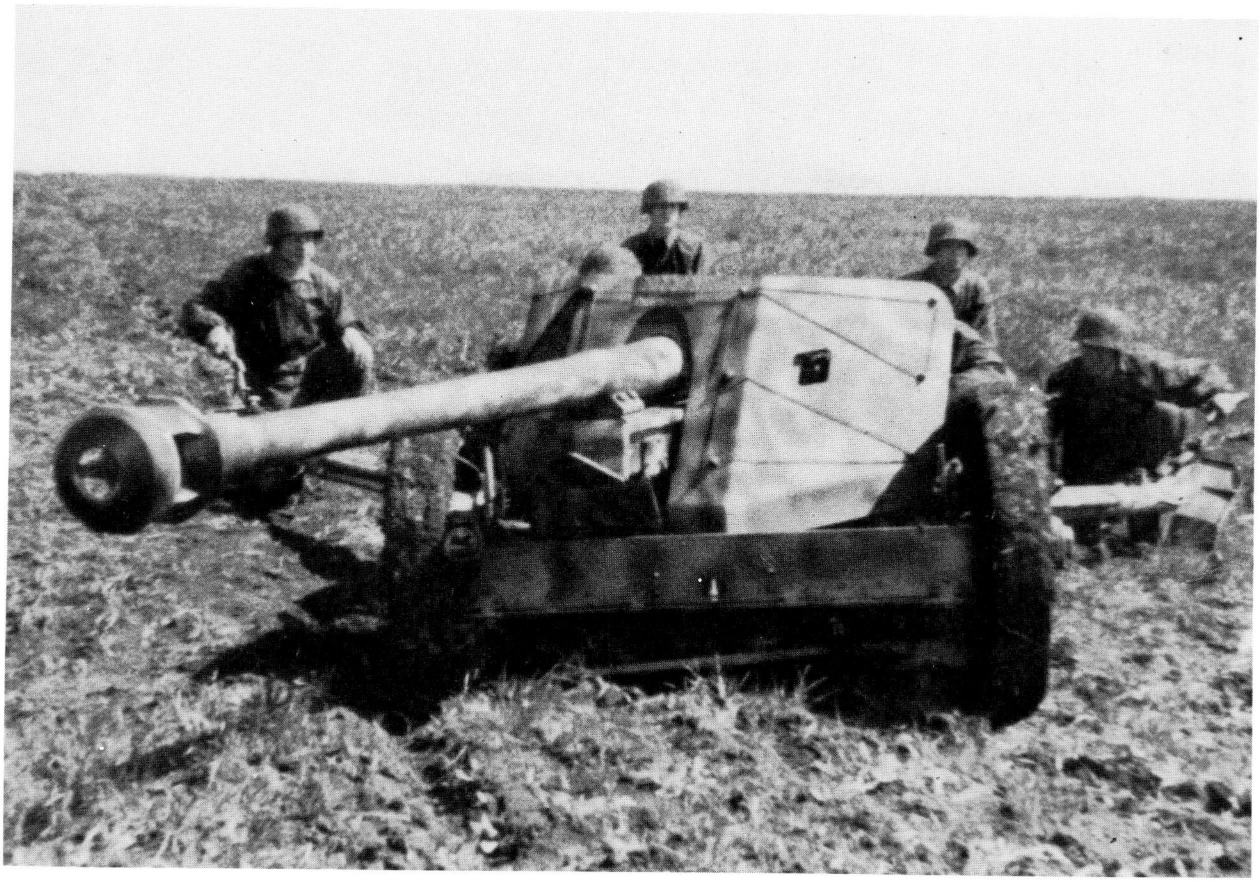
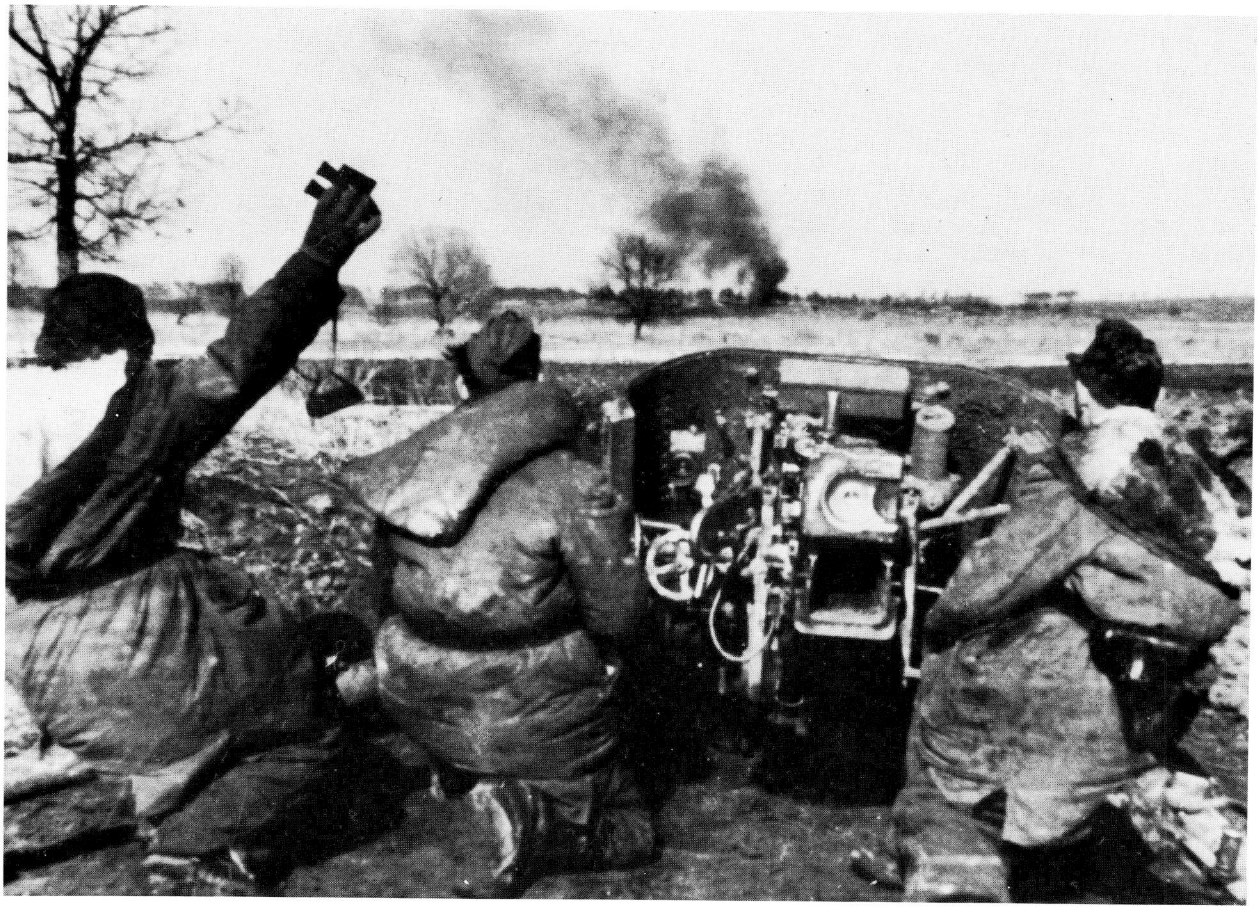

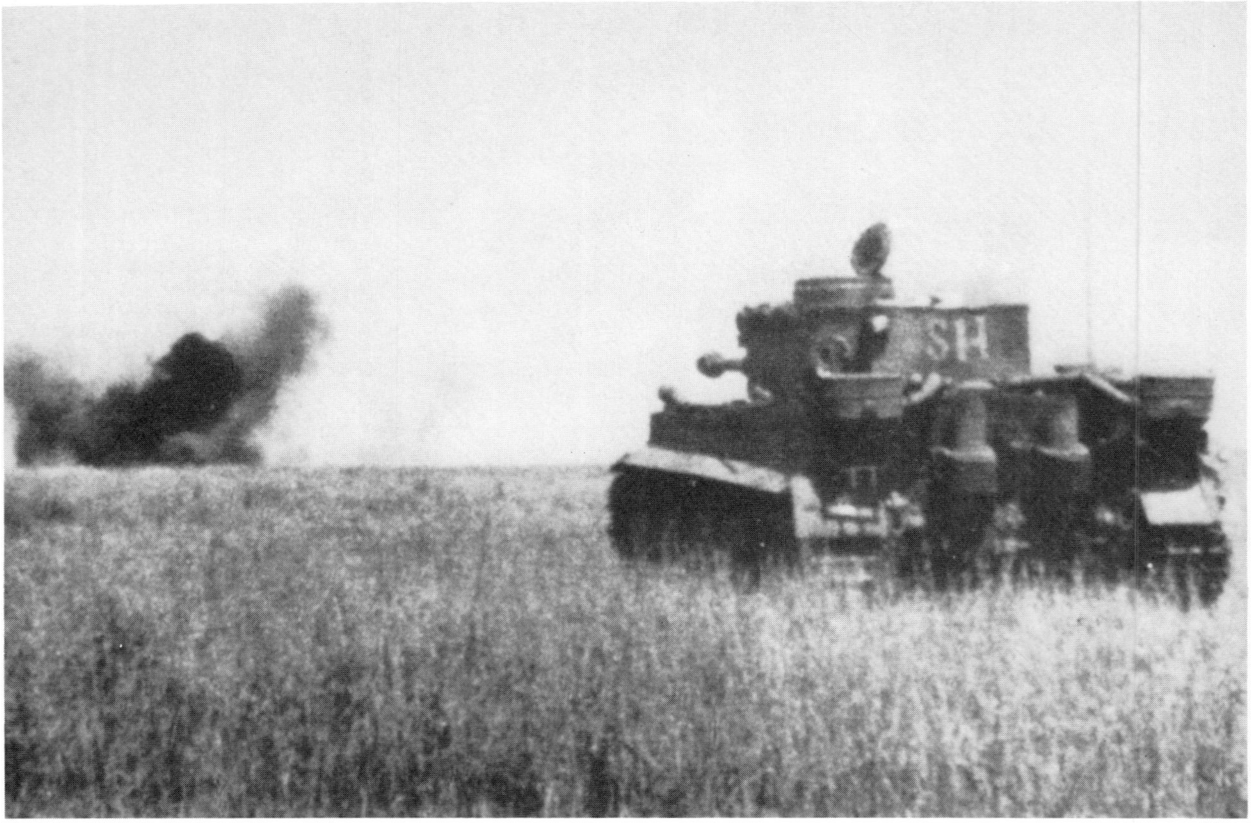
SH

Wherever "Tiger" tanks can be used, they bring temporary relief. Because of its armor-plating and its armament it is superior to all Russian armored vehicles.

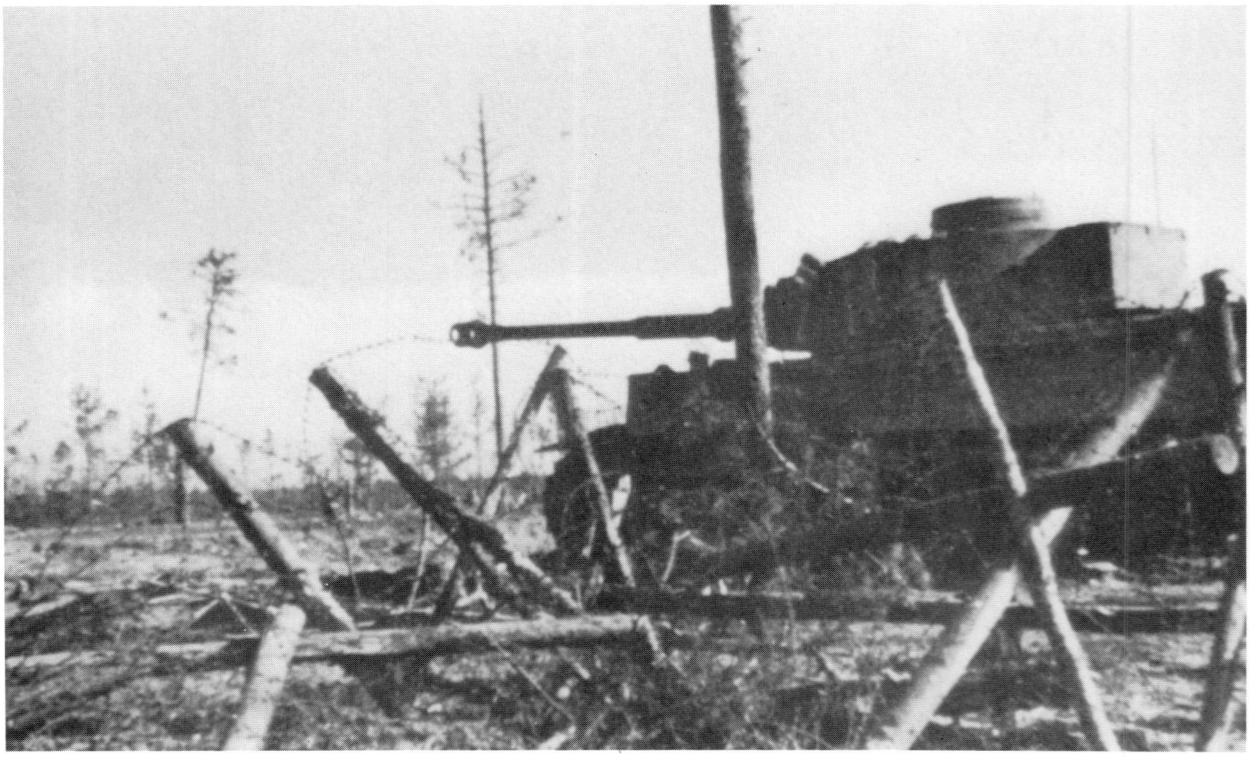

# THE WINTER OF 1943-44 IN THE EAST

Even before the third Russian winter began, the initiative in the East had long passed to the Red Army. The German armored troops could not recover from the heavy losses after the failure of "Operation Citadel". The Russian autumn offensives had resulted in defensive actions, but vast areas had to be given up. The front between the Donetz and Dniepr collapsed, the line between Army Groups Center and South was torn apart. The front in the "Panther Position" could be held only with difficulty. There was a lack of reserves, equipment and ammunition. The Waffen-SS divisions were involved in desperate defensive fighting everywhere in the East during the whole winter. On January 3 the Soviets reached the Polish border, the fighting in the Cherkassian Basin and the break out of it caused the involved Waffen-SS units particularly heavy losses, as did the defense against Russian attacks west of Kirovgrad and the retreat fighting to the Bug. In the northern area of the Eastern front too, the divisions had to withdraw to behind Pleskau at the beginning of 1944, after 900 days of heavy fighting. At Kamenez-Podolsk, at the end of this difficult winter, the First Armored Army was able to break out of the basin against far superior enemy forces.

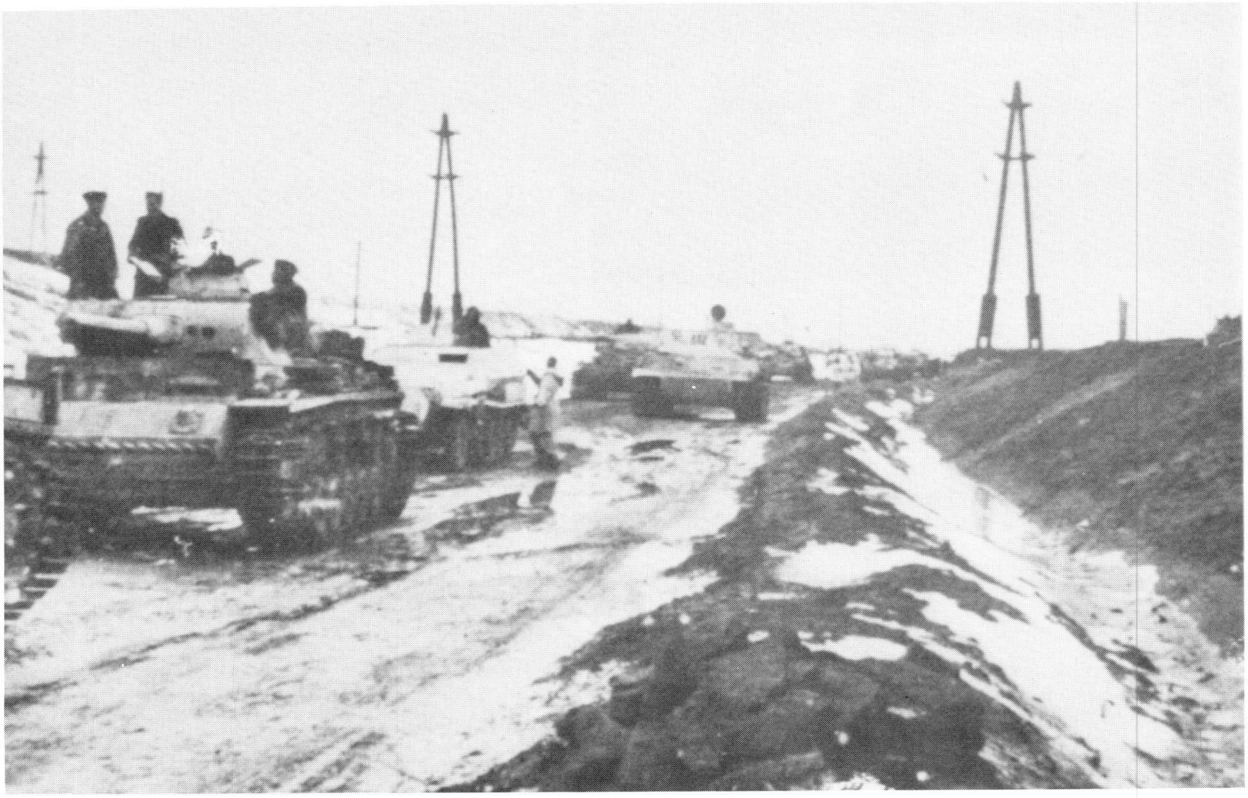

During this third winter in Russia, all of the SS-divisions fighting in the east are involved in heavy defensive battles. Time and again the frontline has to retreat-often against Hitler's orders.

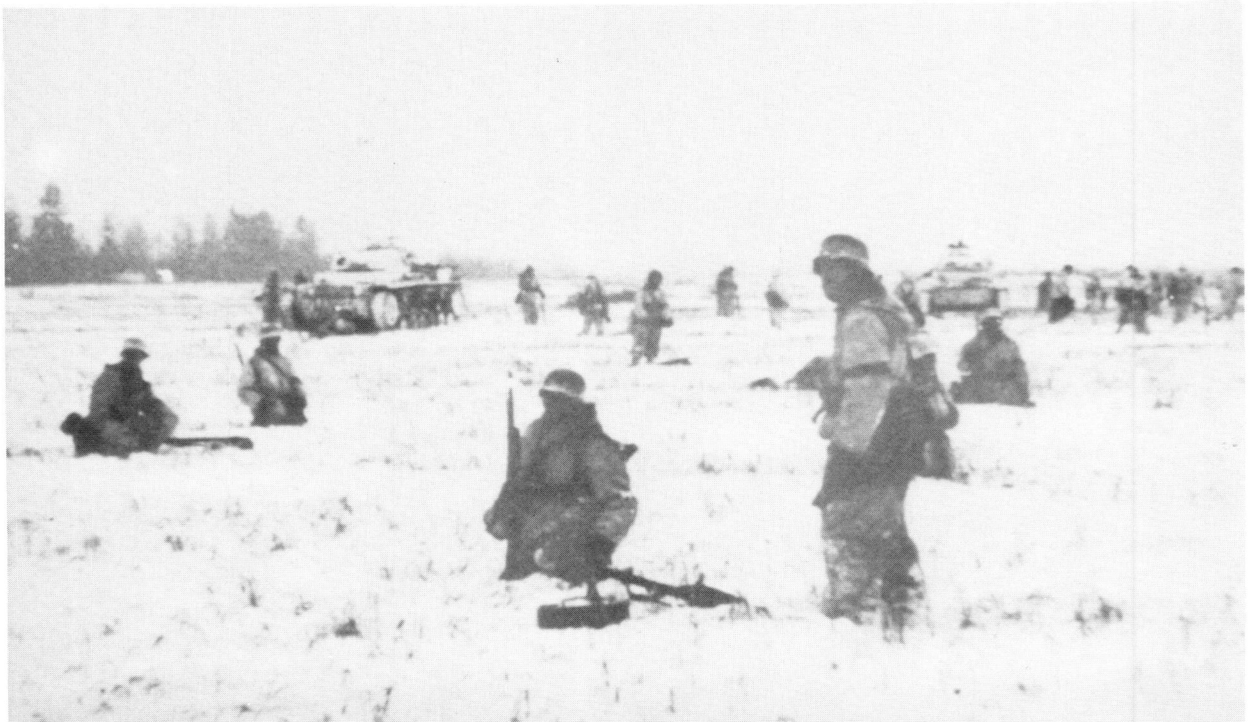

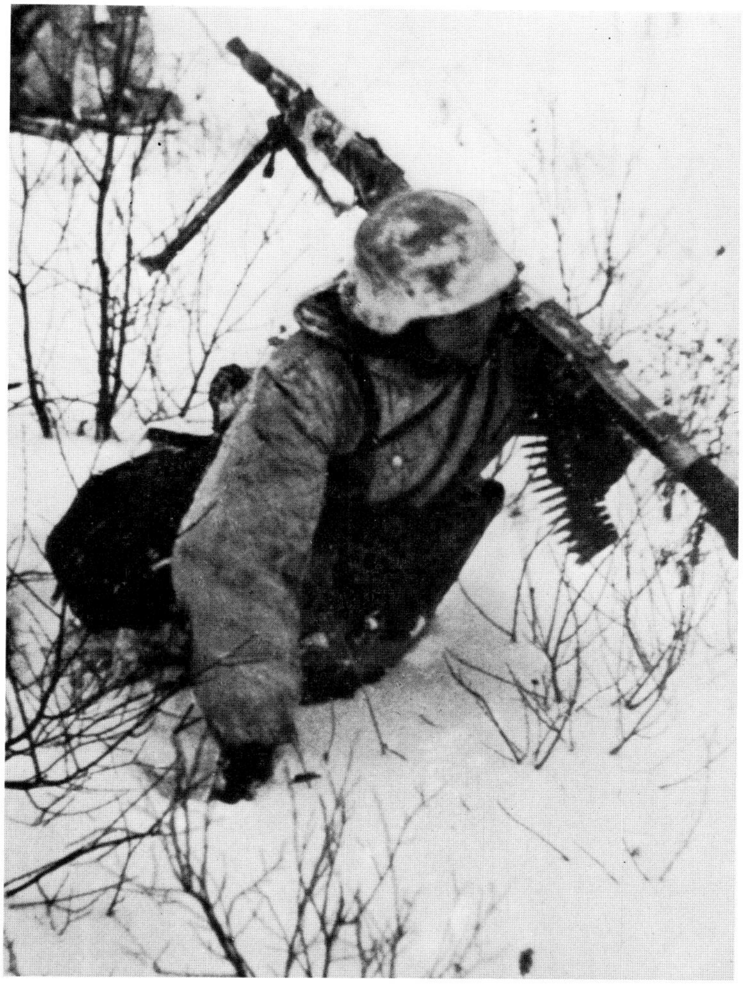

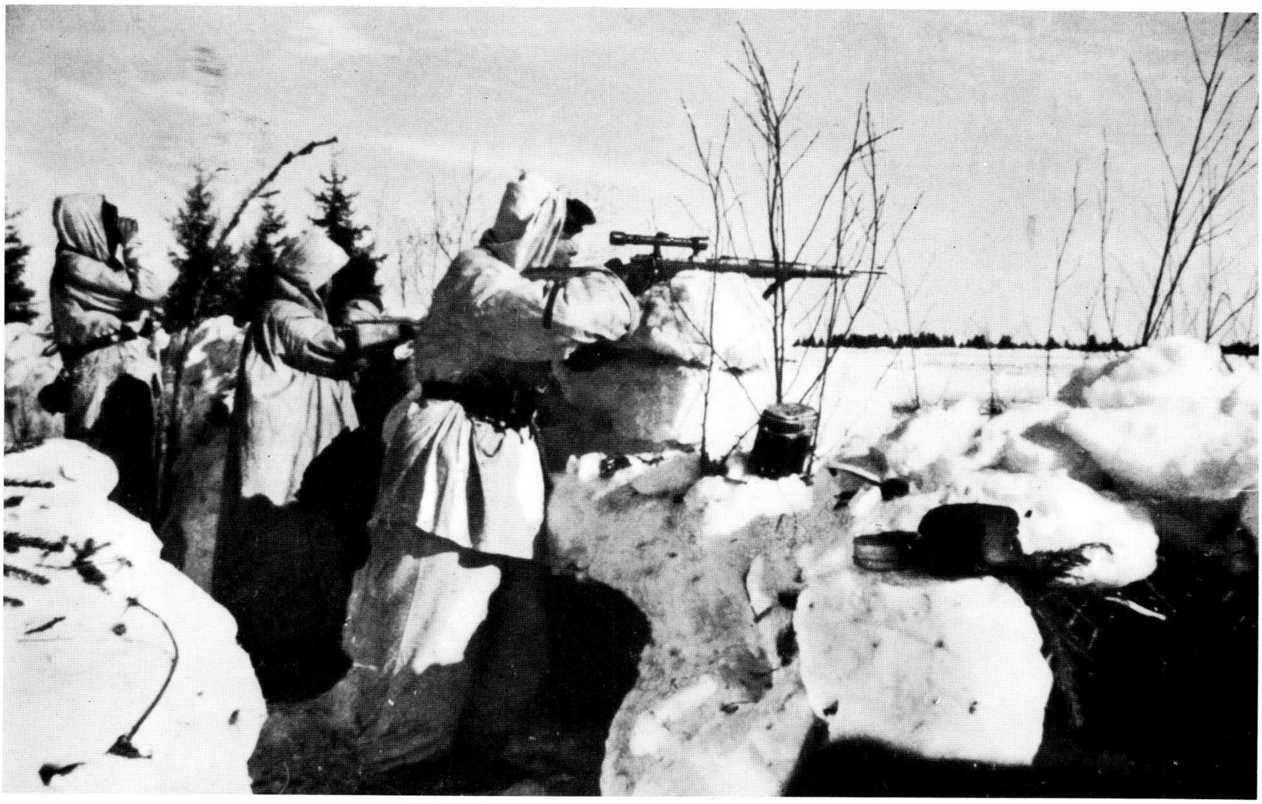

Two centers of the defensive battle: Kowel and Tscherkassy. In both places the "Wiking"-division under the command of Herbert O. Gille, takes an important part.

The Kowel pocket was broken by tanks of the SS-division "Wiking" from the outside. The Tscherkassy battle of encirclement, involving heavy losses, was won through their engagement from the inside.

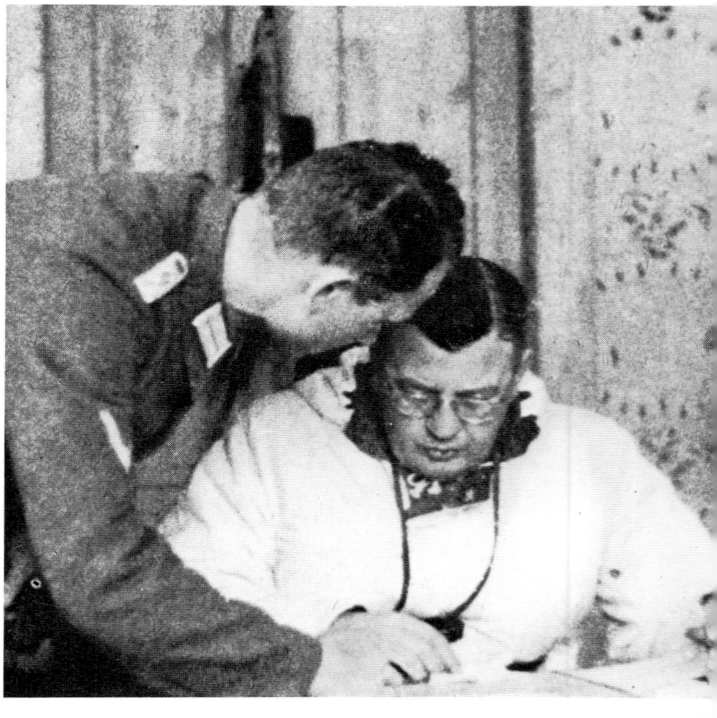

SS-Major General von dem Bach, who for a time led the encircled units in Kowel.

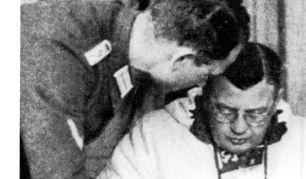

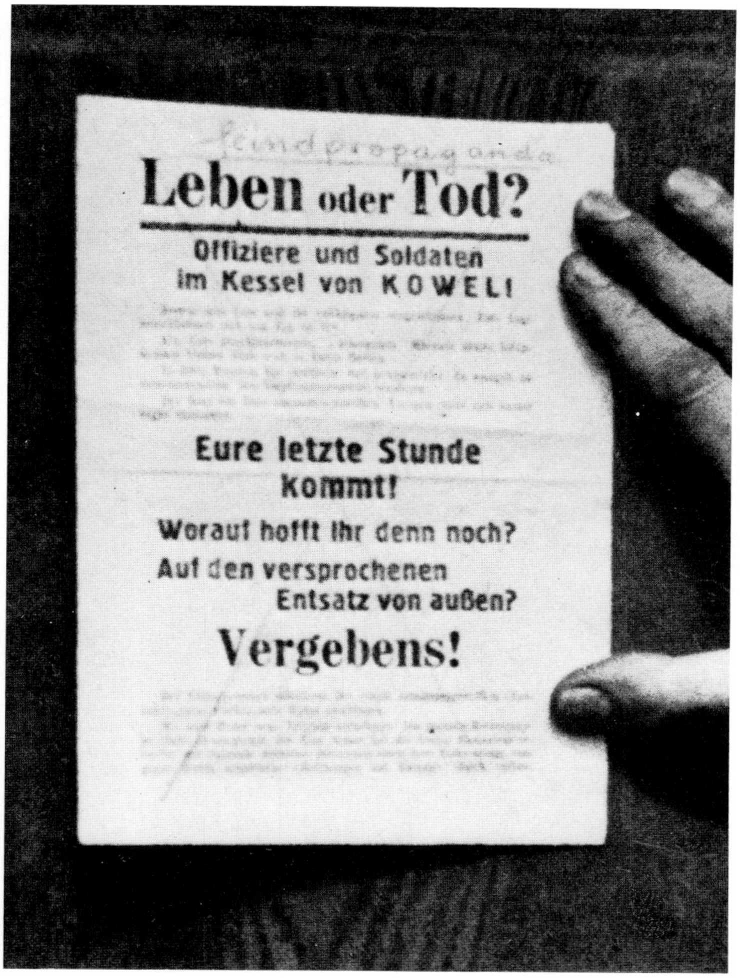
Feindpropaganda
Leben oder Tod?
Offiziere und Soldaten
im Kessel von KOWEL!
Eure letzte Stunde
kommt!
Worauf hofft ihr denn noch?
Auf den versprochenen
Entsatz von außen?
Vergebens!

Russian fliers demanding surrender.

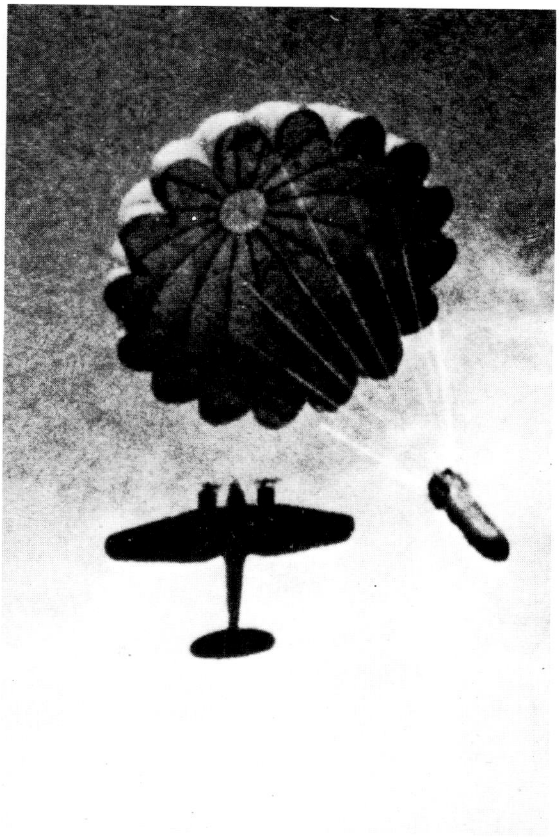

Supply to the encircled troops by air.

SS-Major General Herbert O. Gille, flown into the pocket on March 16, became the initiator of the resistance. He was the first soldier of the Waffen-SS to be awarded the Ritterkreuz with diamond.

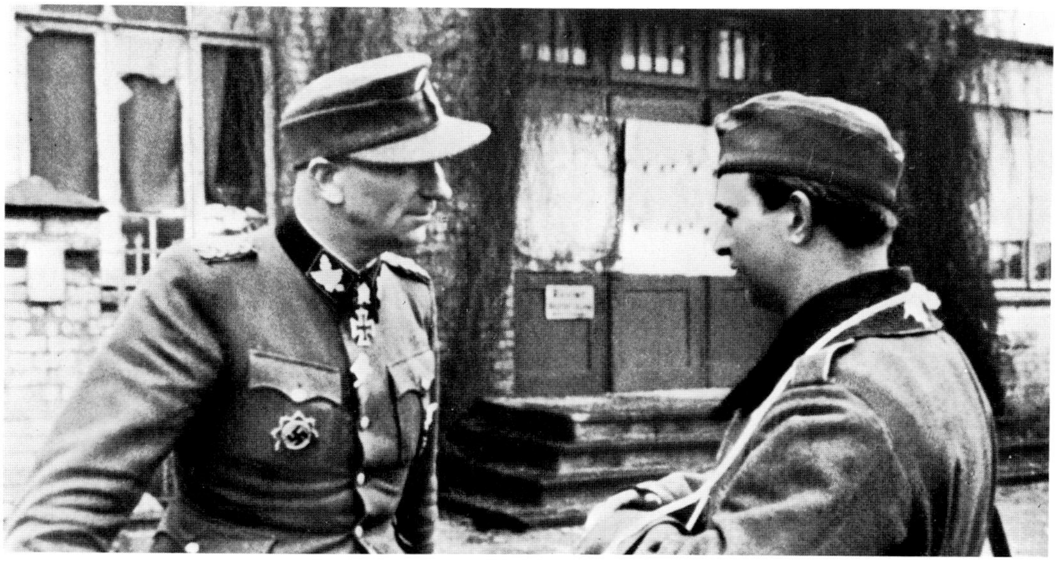

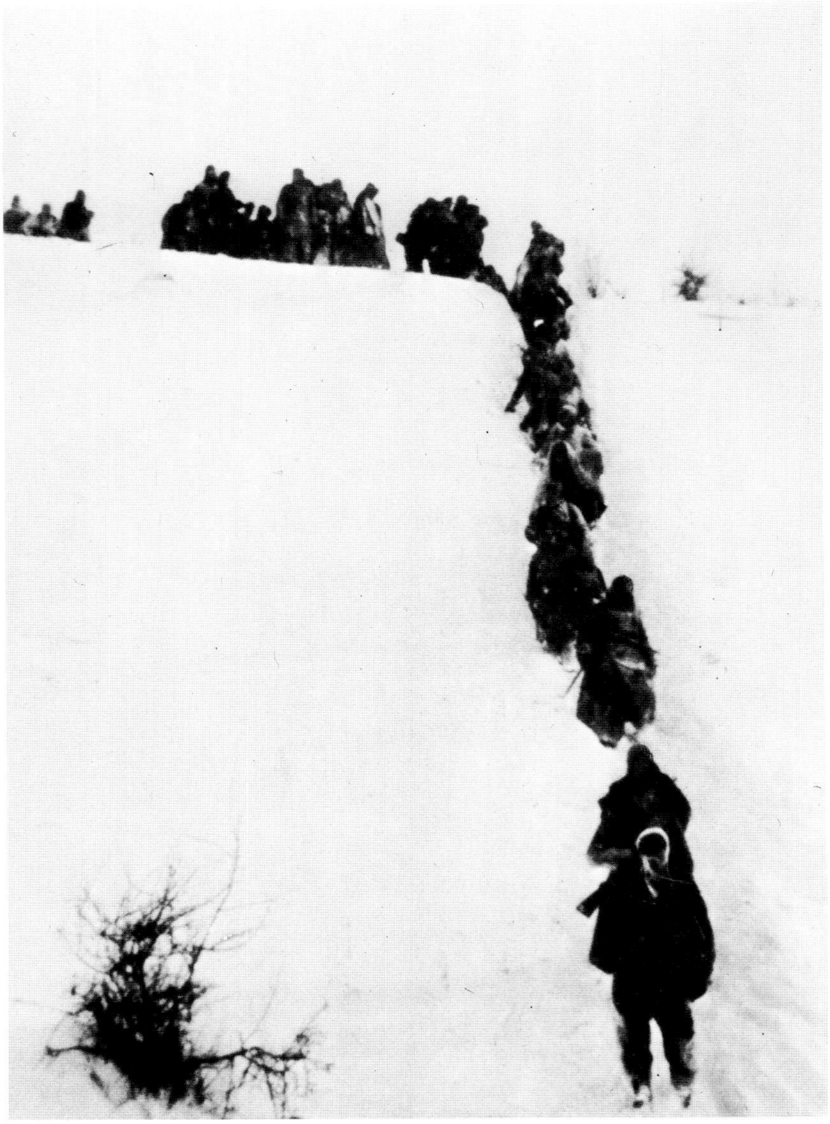

The break-outs from the Kowel and Tscherkassy pockets were among the hardest engagements of the SS-division "Wiking".

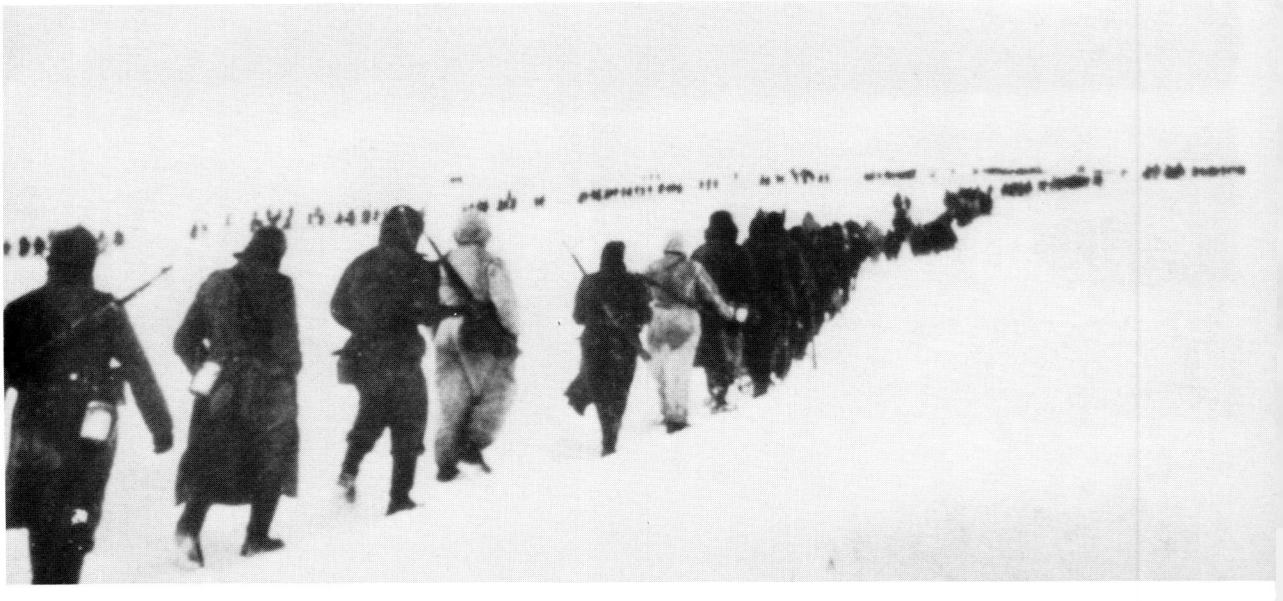

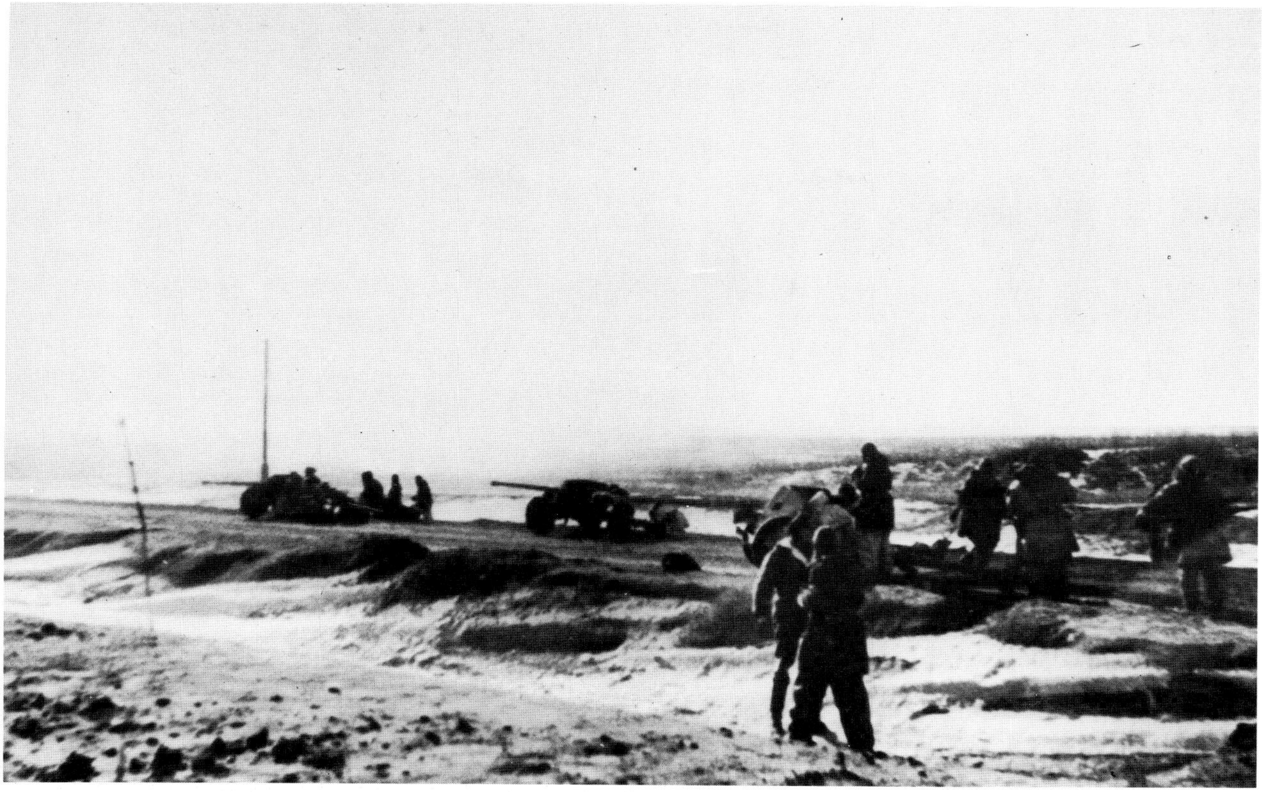

Anti-tank guns and self-propelled field artillery protect the flanks during the breakout.

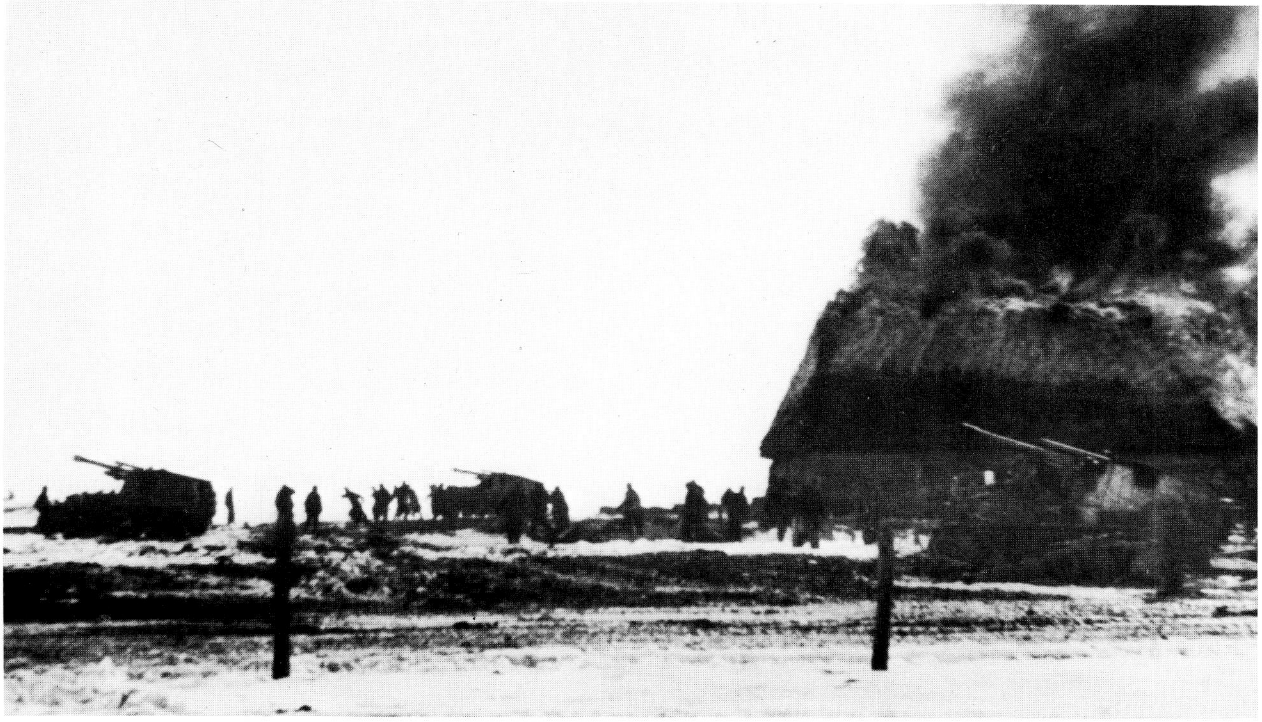

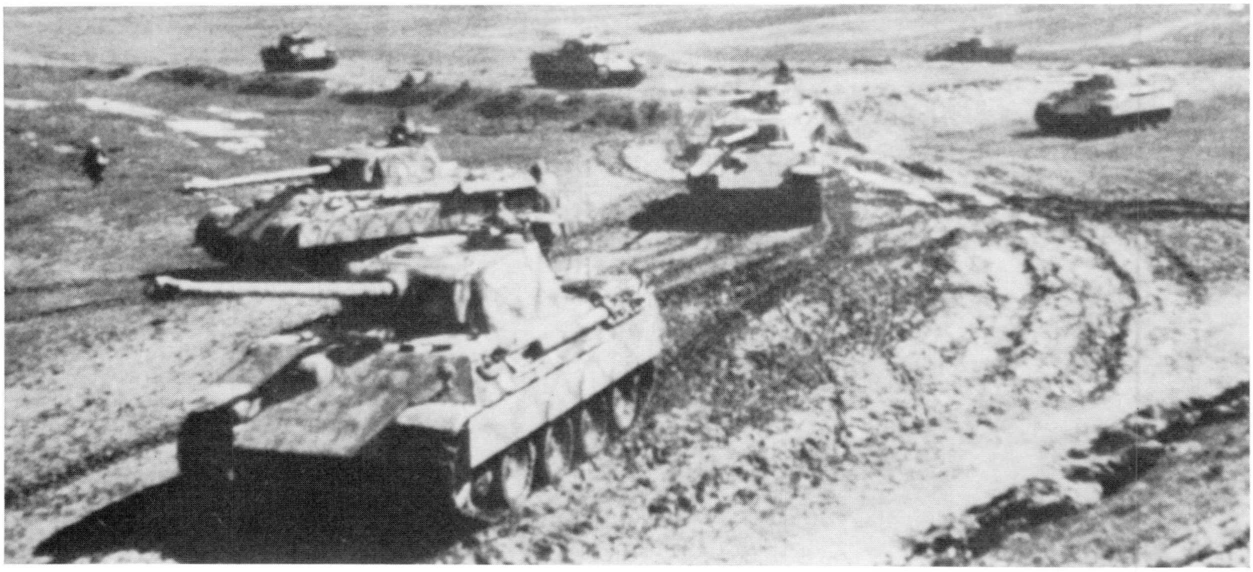

"Panther" tanks of the "Wiking" tank regiment take a decisive part in the successful defensive actions of the division.

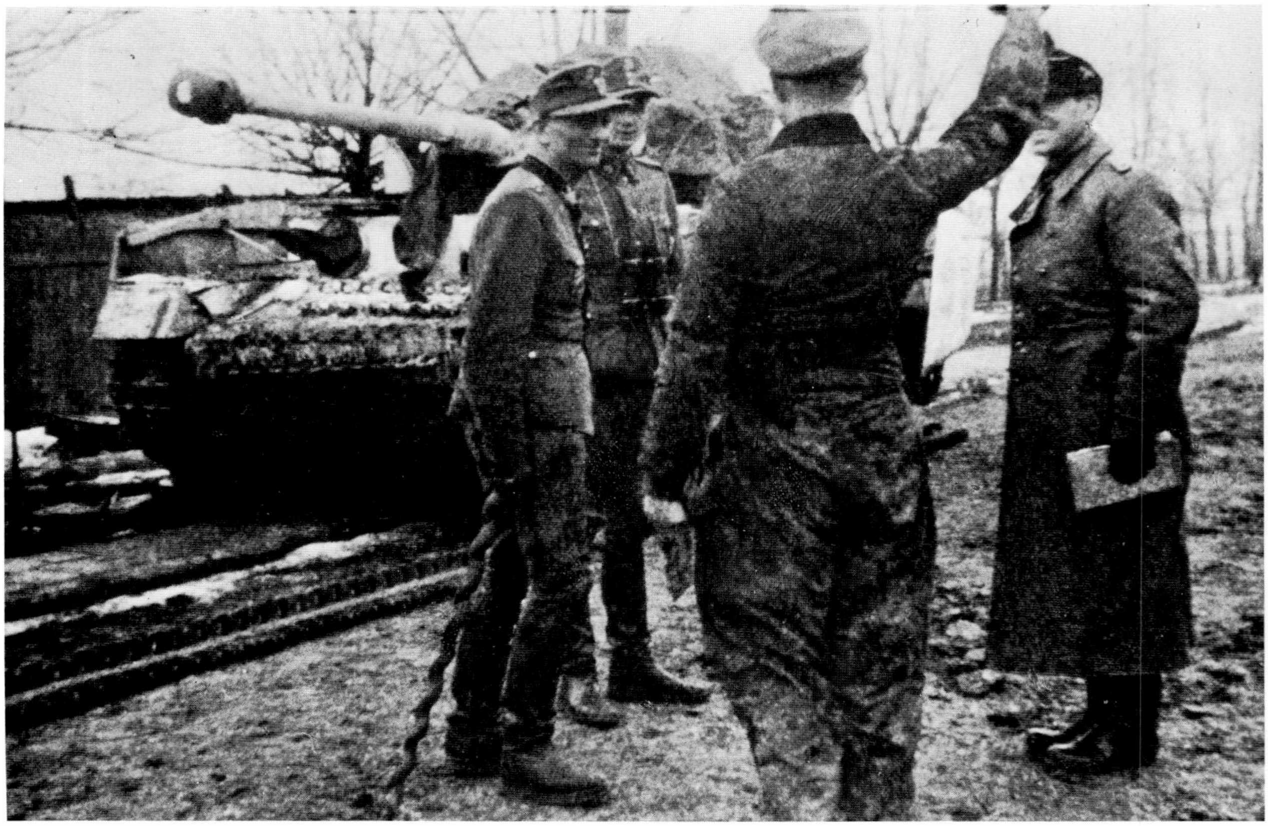

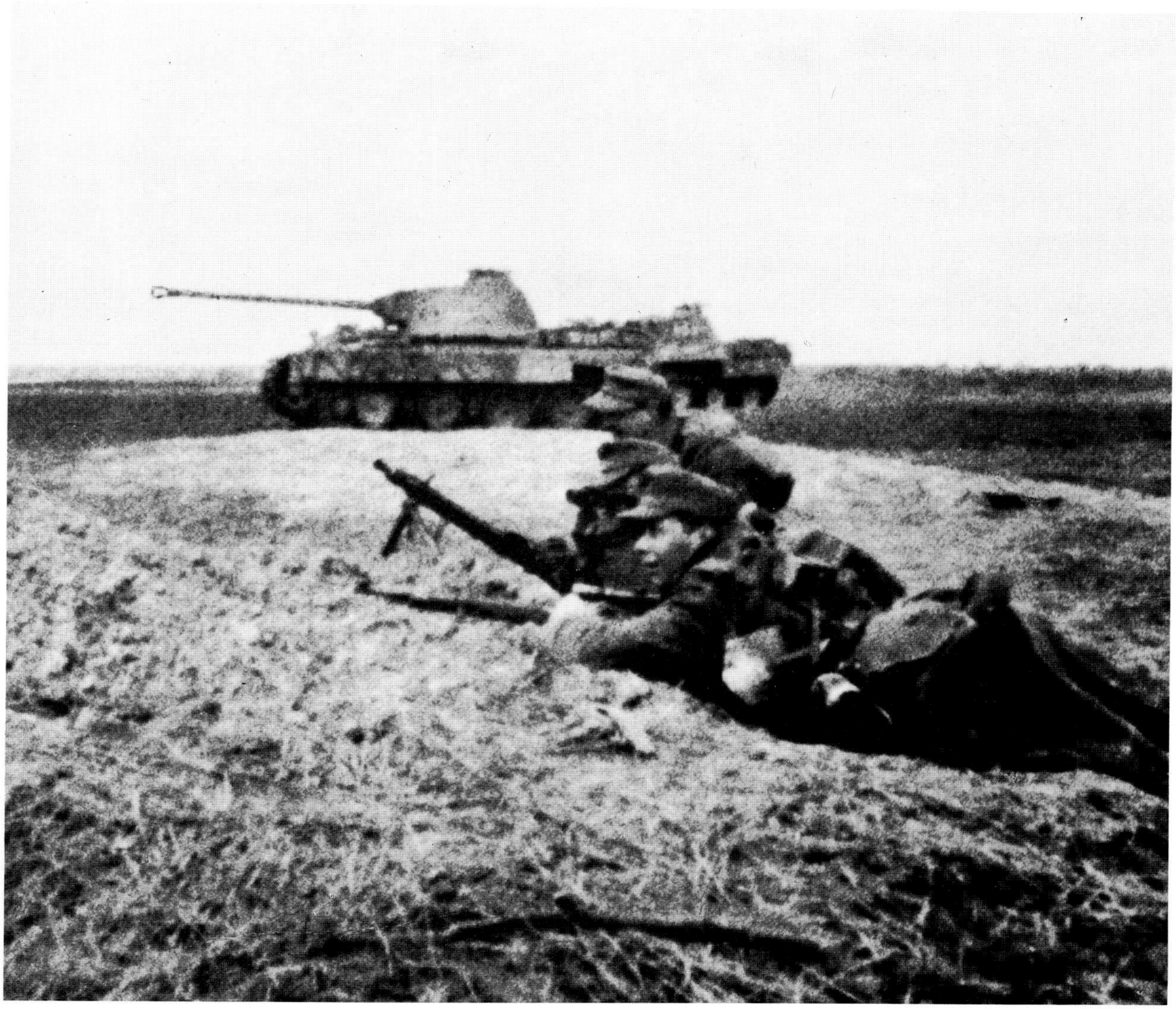

"Panther" tanks of the SS-division "Wiking" fighting east of Warsaw.

A break between the operations. On the left: The commander of a "Panther"-tank unit reports to Major General Gille. On the right: The commander of a tank regiment: H. Mühlenkamp.

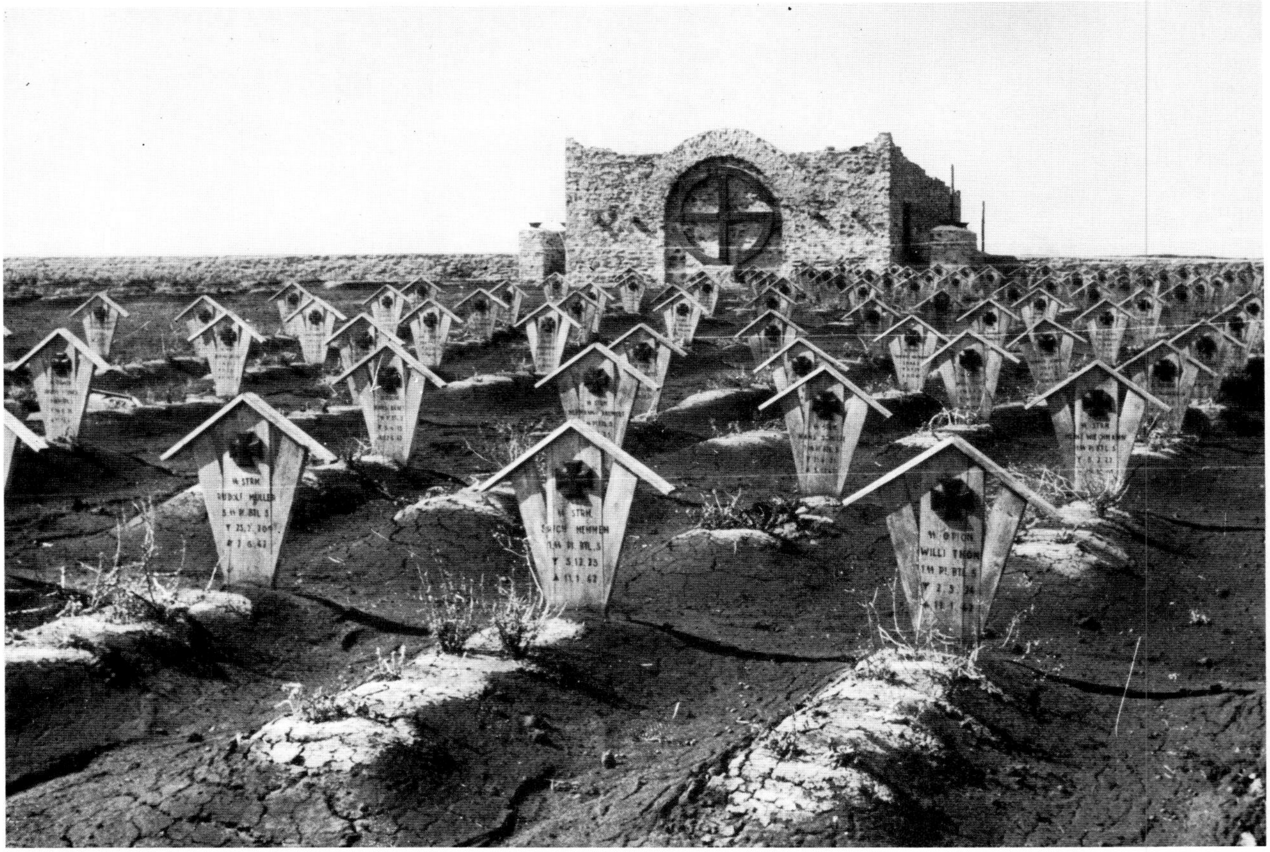

The cemetery of the SS-division "Wiking" in Uspenskaja. Before this battlefield is cleared, all grave plaques are removed.

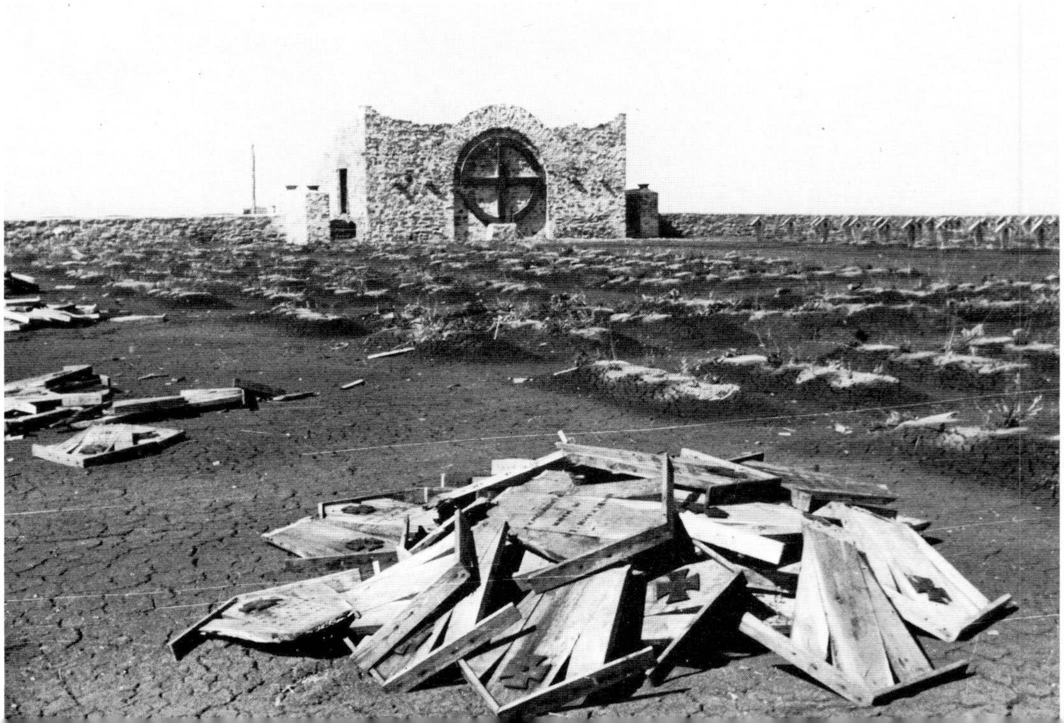

Heavy withdrawal battles in the Summer and Autumn of 1944.

The overwhelming Russian superiority of men and materiel always demands new withdrawals often into unprepared positions.

Again the burden of the fighting is carried by the infantrymen.

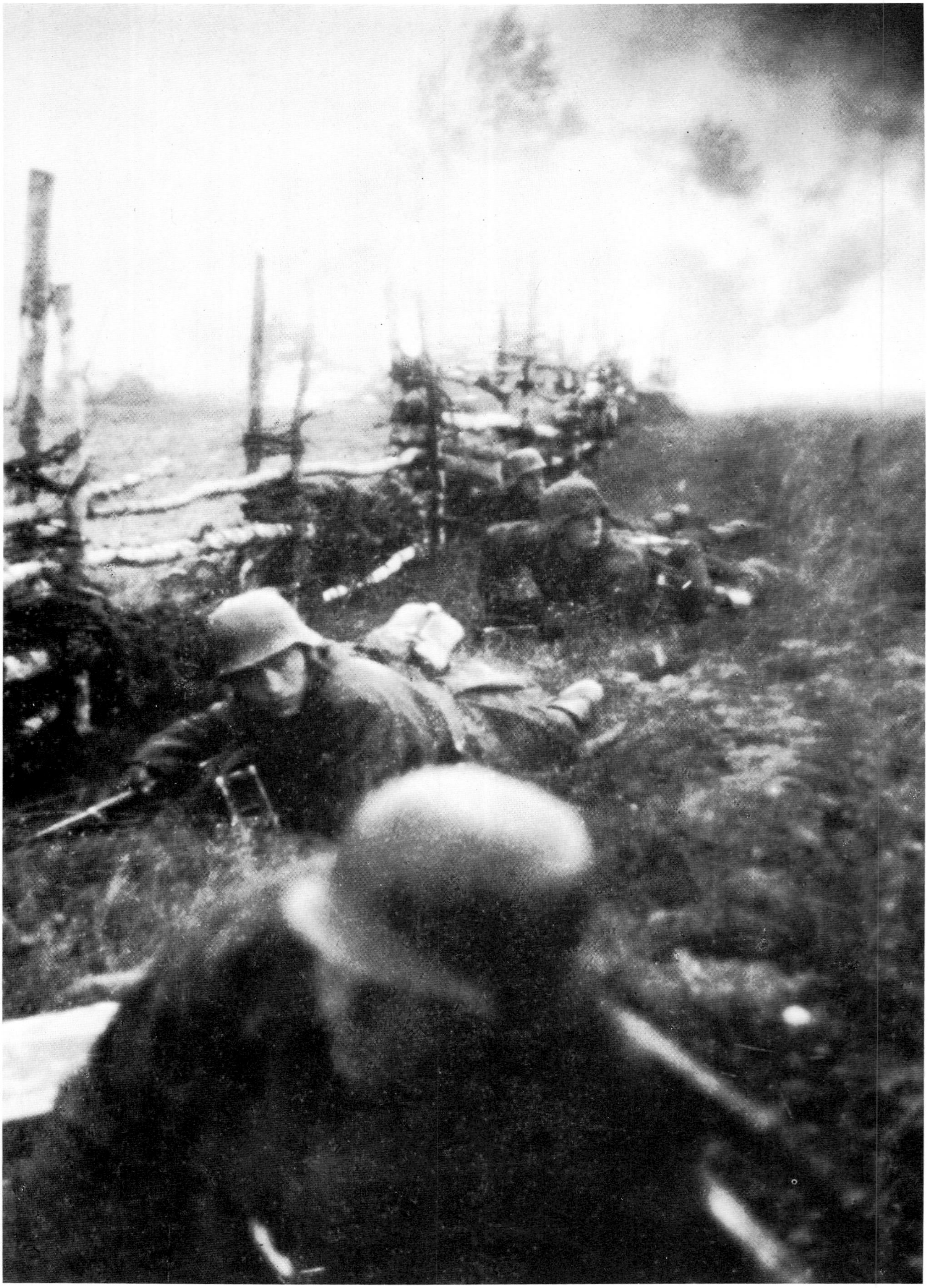

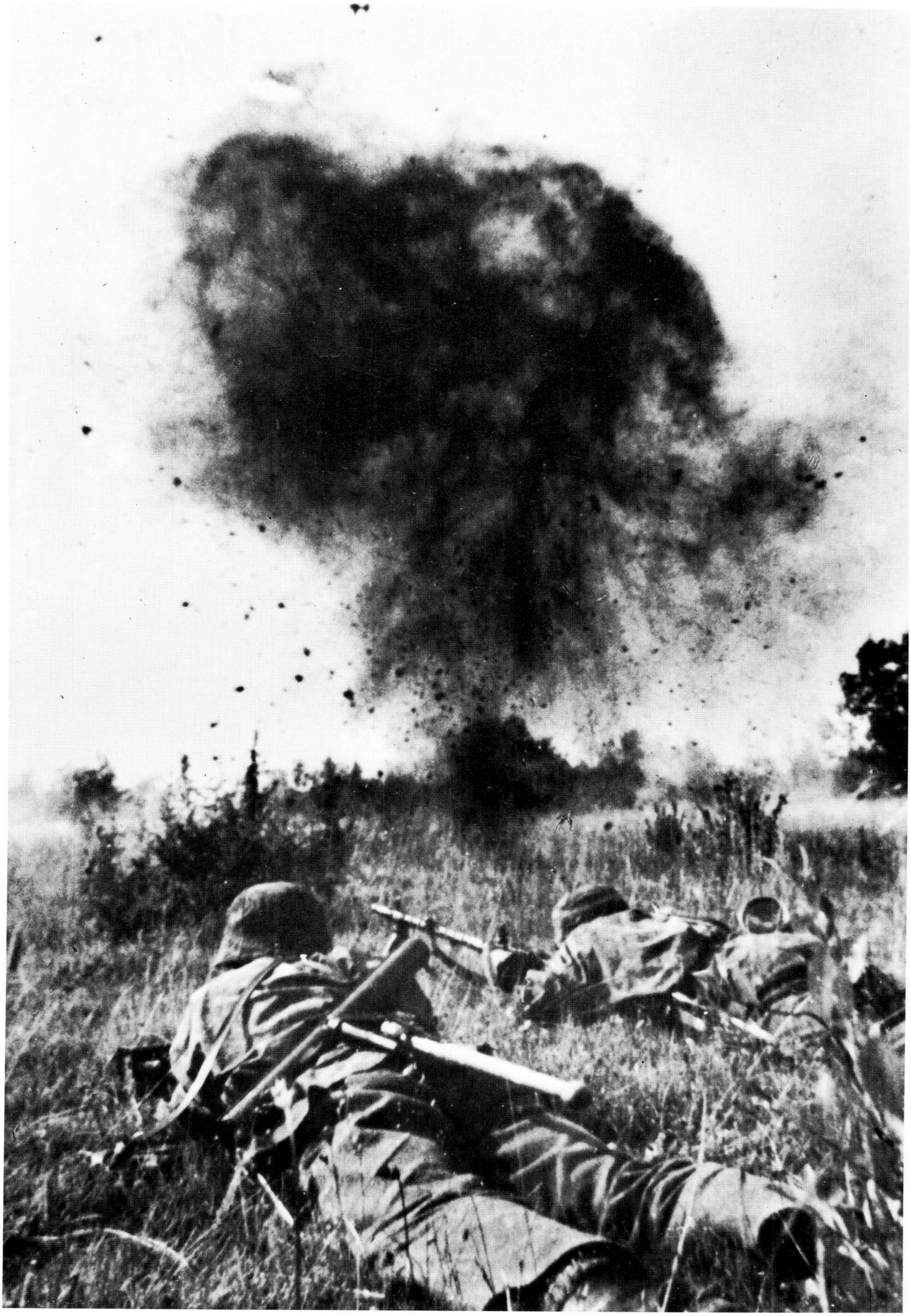

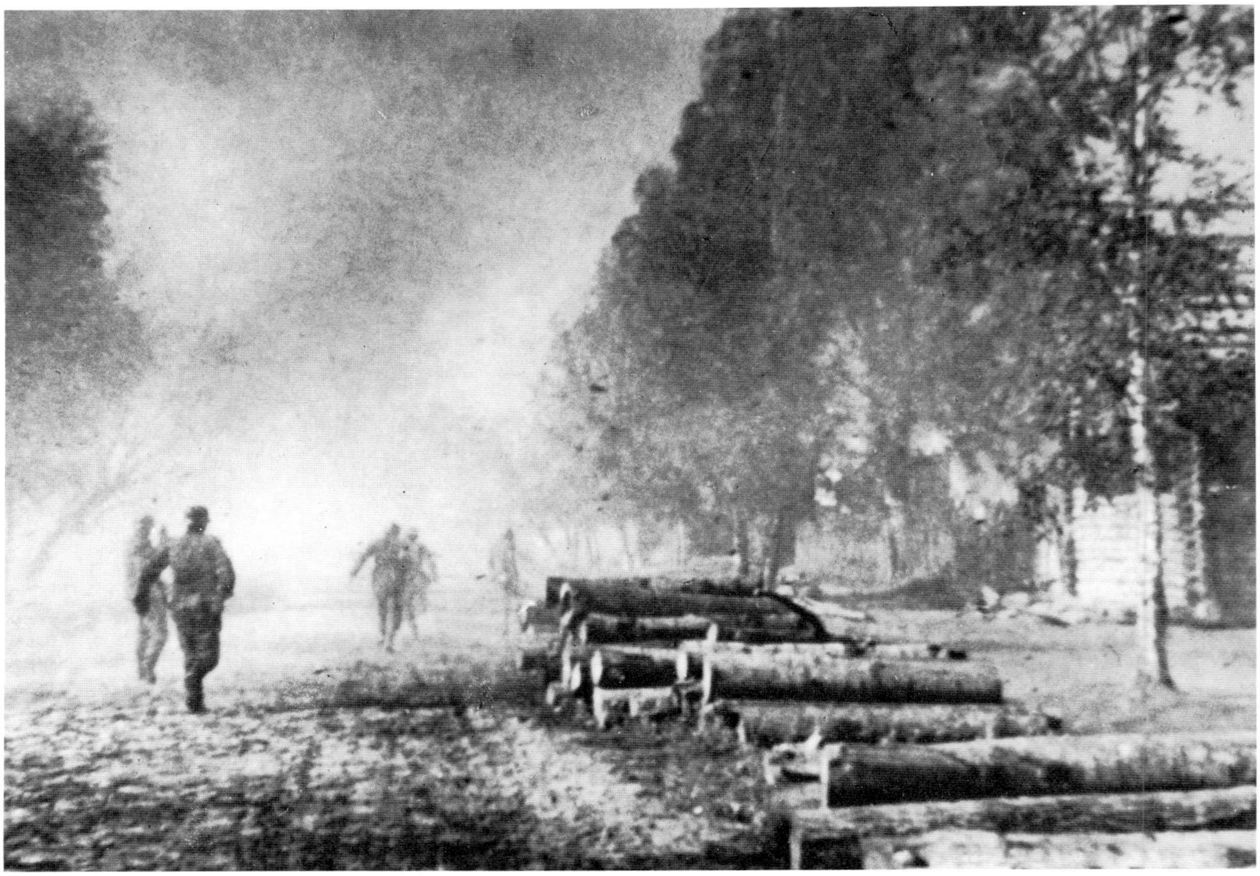

Russians have entered a village. The infantry of the Waffen-SS launch the counterthrust.

Heavy Russian defensive fire literally keeps the infantrymen stuck to the spot.

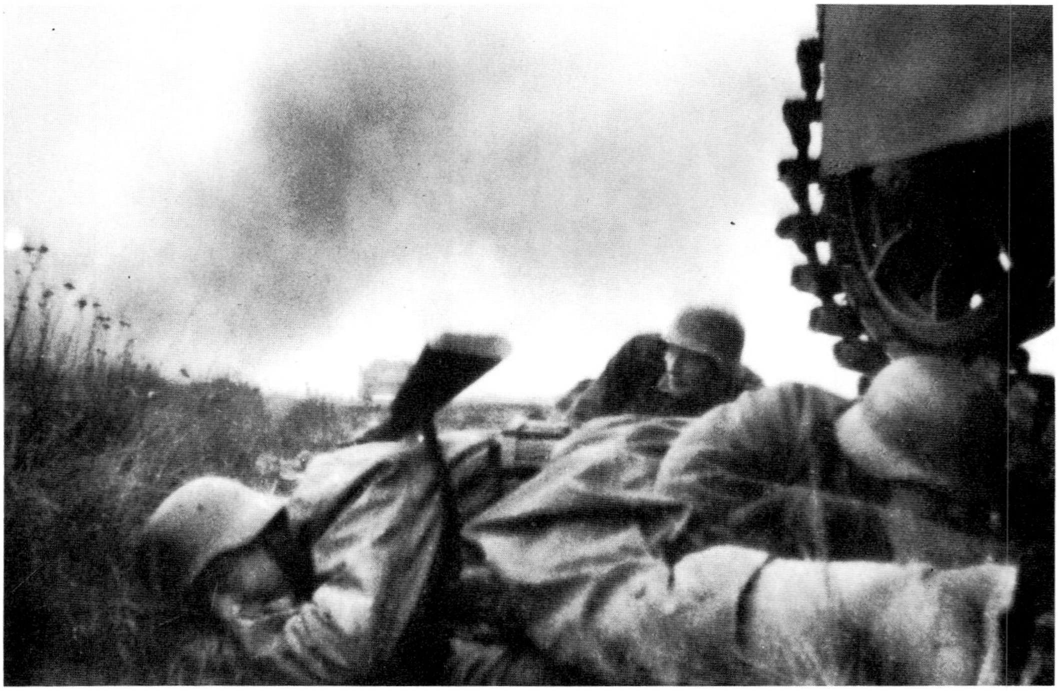

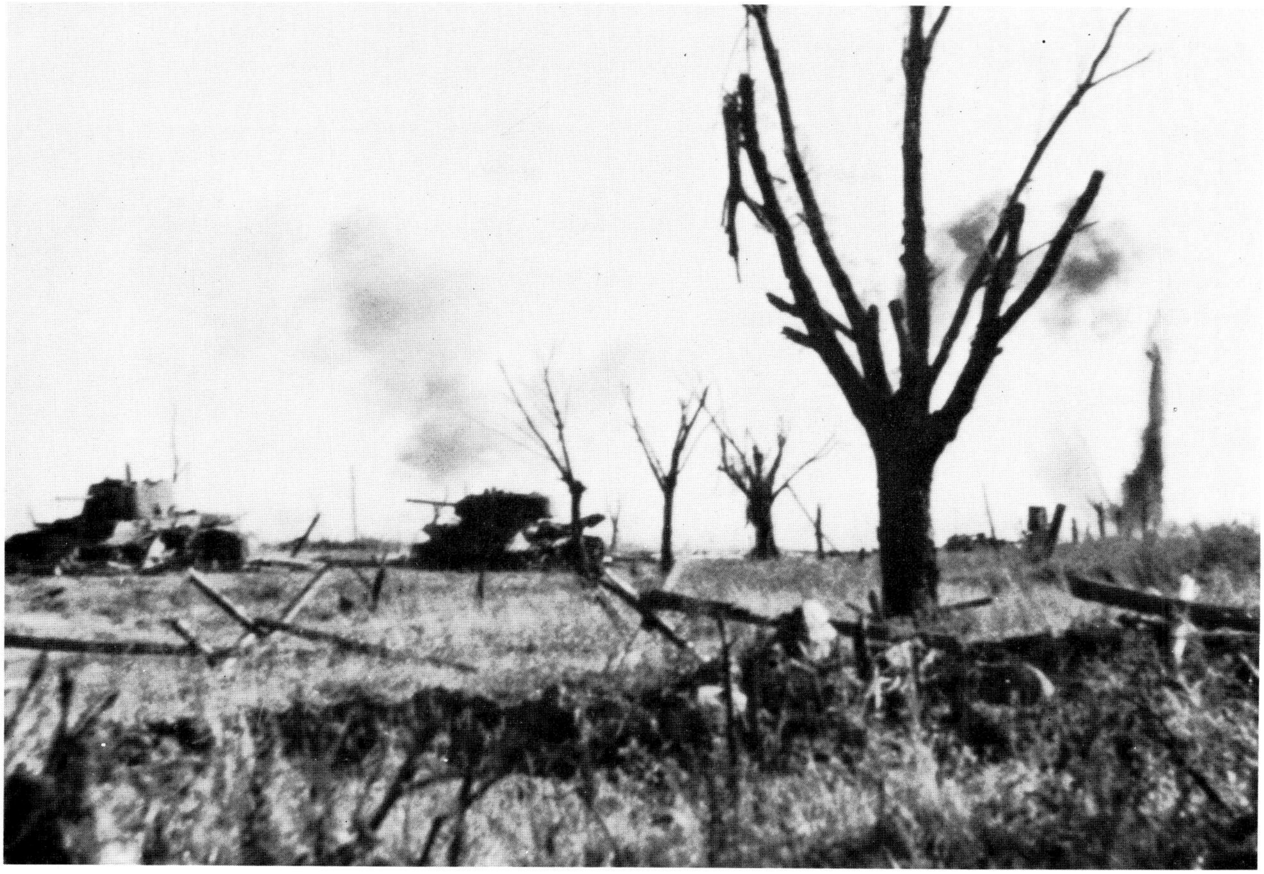

Destroyed Russian tanks immediately before the forward line of attack illustrate the harshness of the defensive fighting.

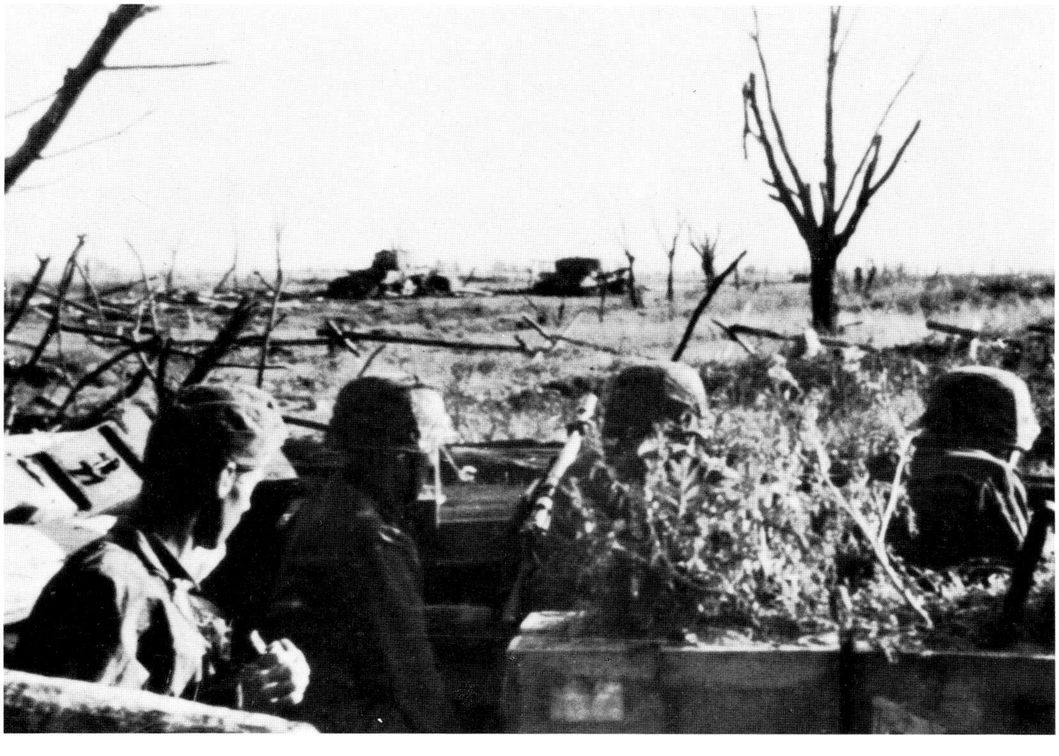

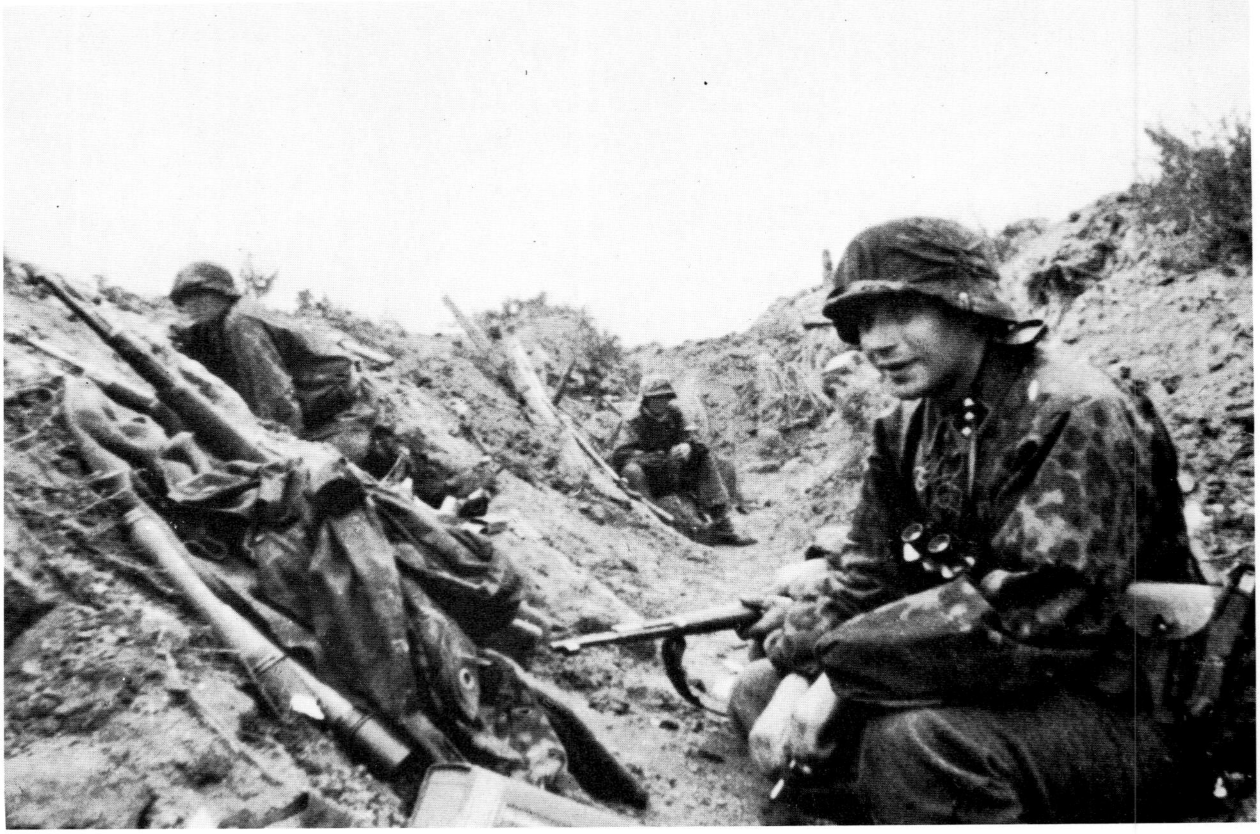

A trench position, just taken up.

A sharp-shooter with his telescopic sight rifle.

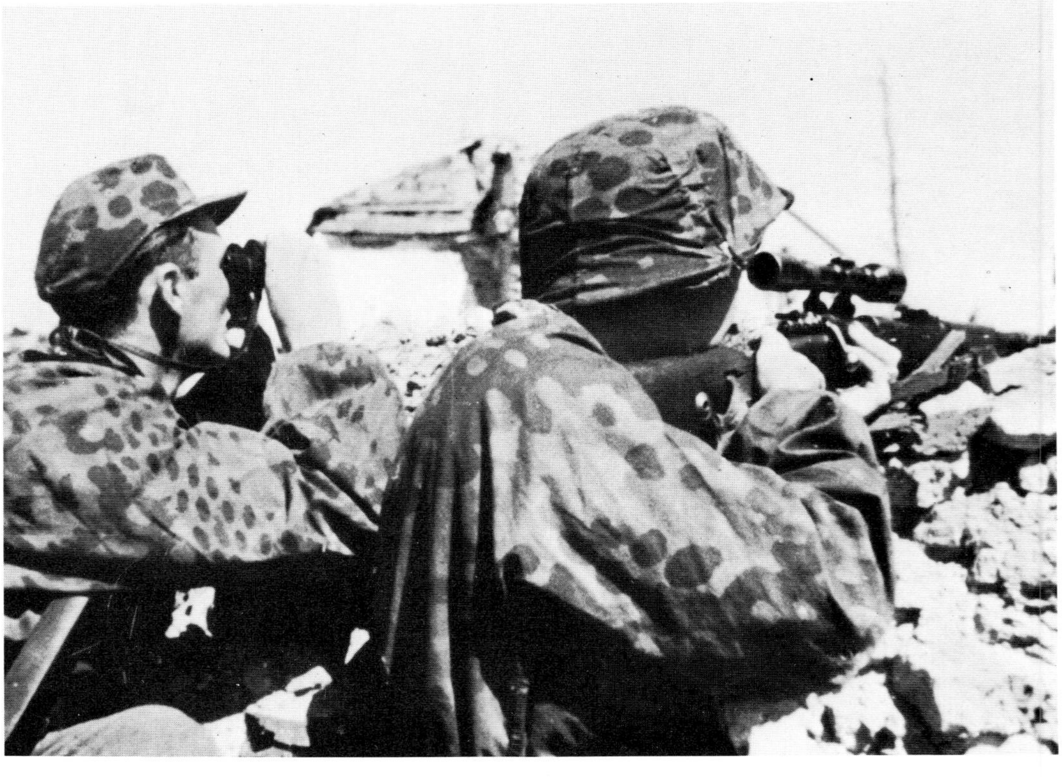

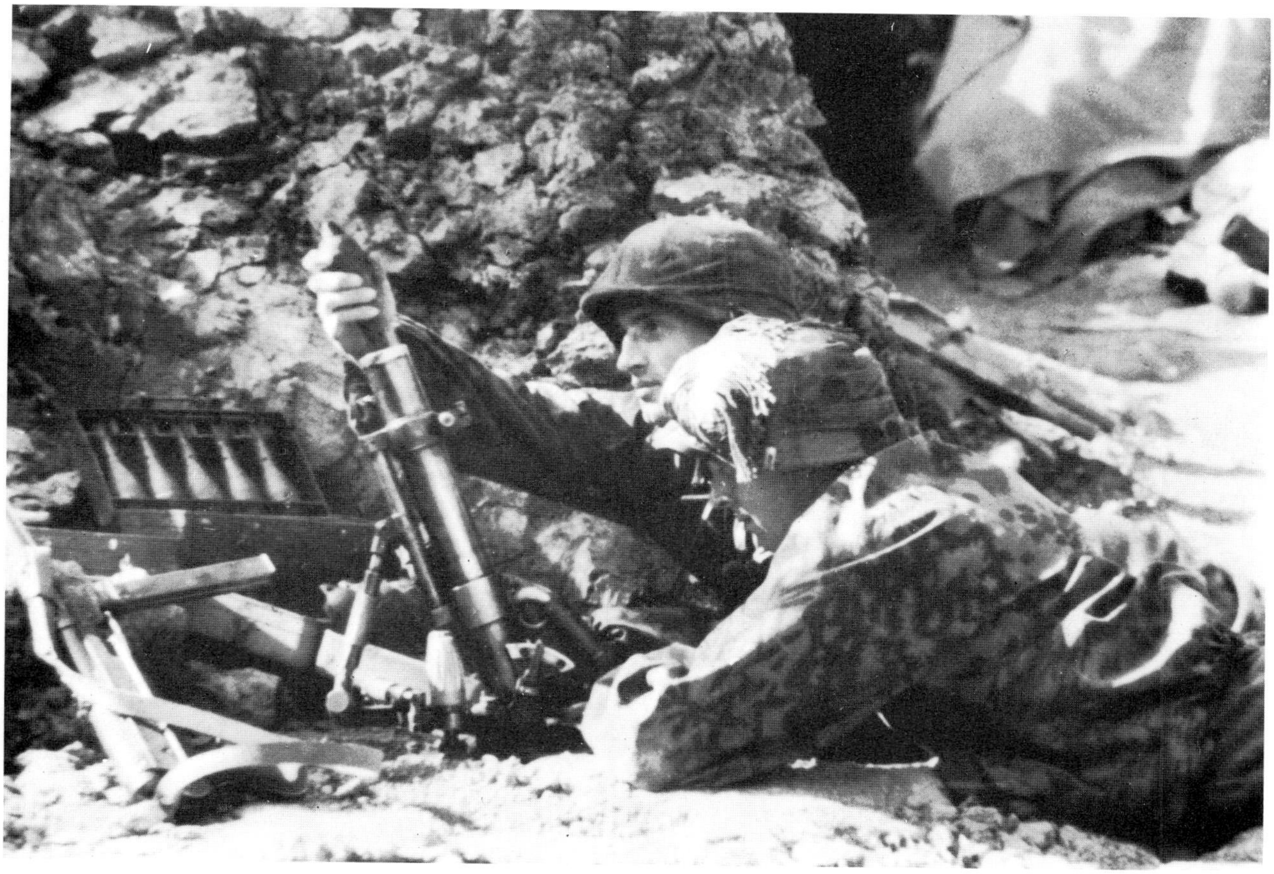

Radio station in a command post.

Firing light trench mortar.

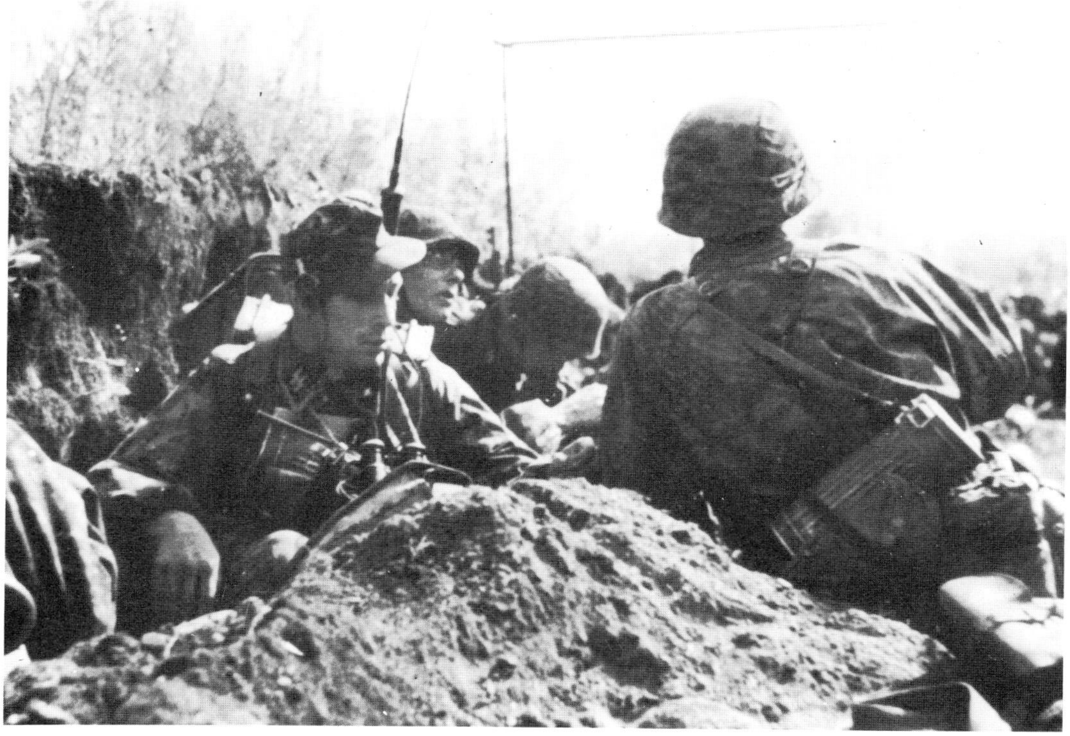

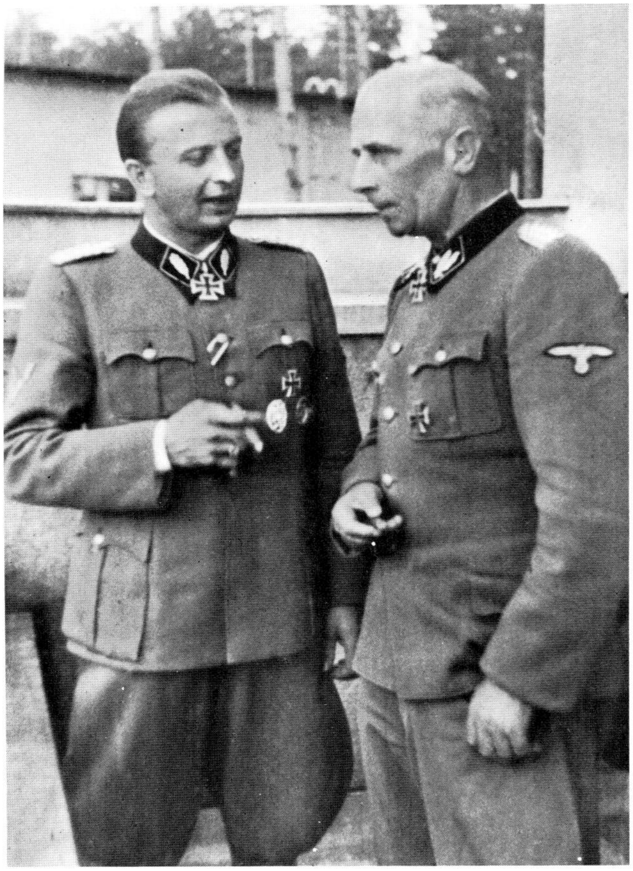

Colonel Hermann Fegelein-later Hitler's brother-in-law and executed on April 29, 1945-the commander of the SS-cavalry brigade seen here talking to Brigadier General Wilhelm Bittrich.

Bicycle squadron of the SS-cavalry brigade.

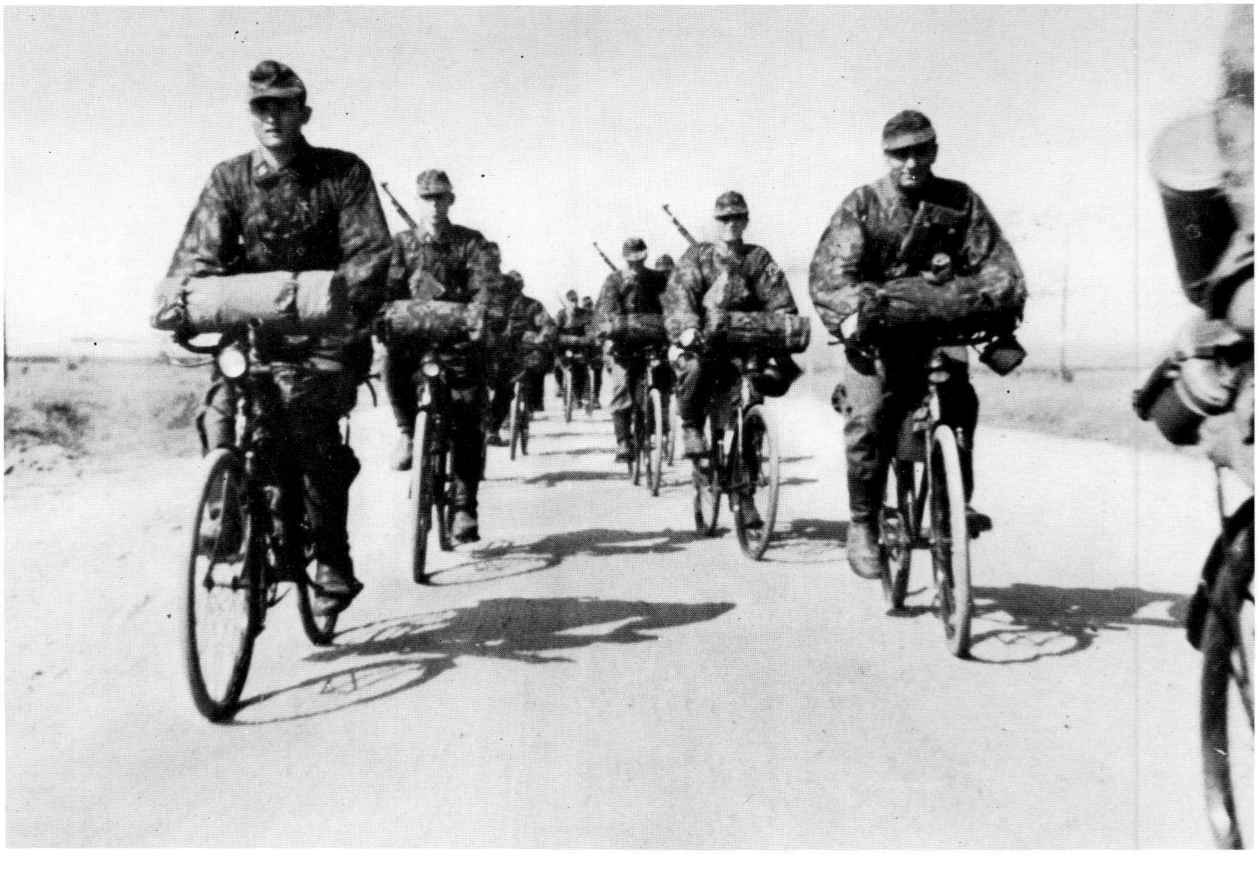

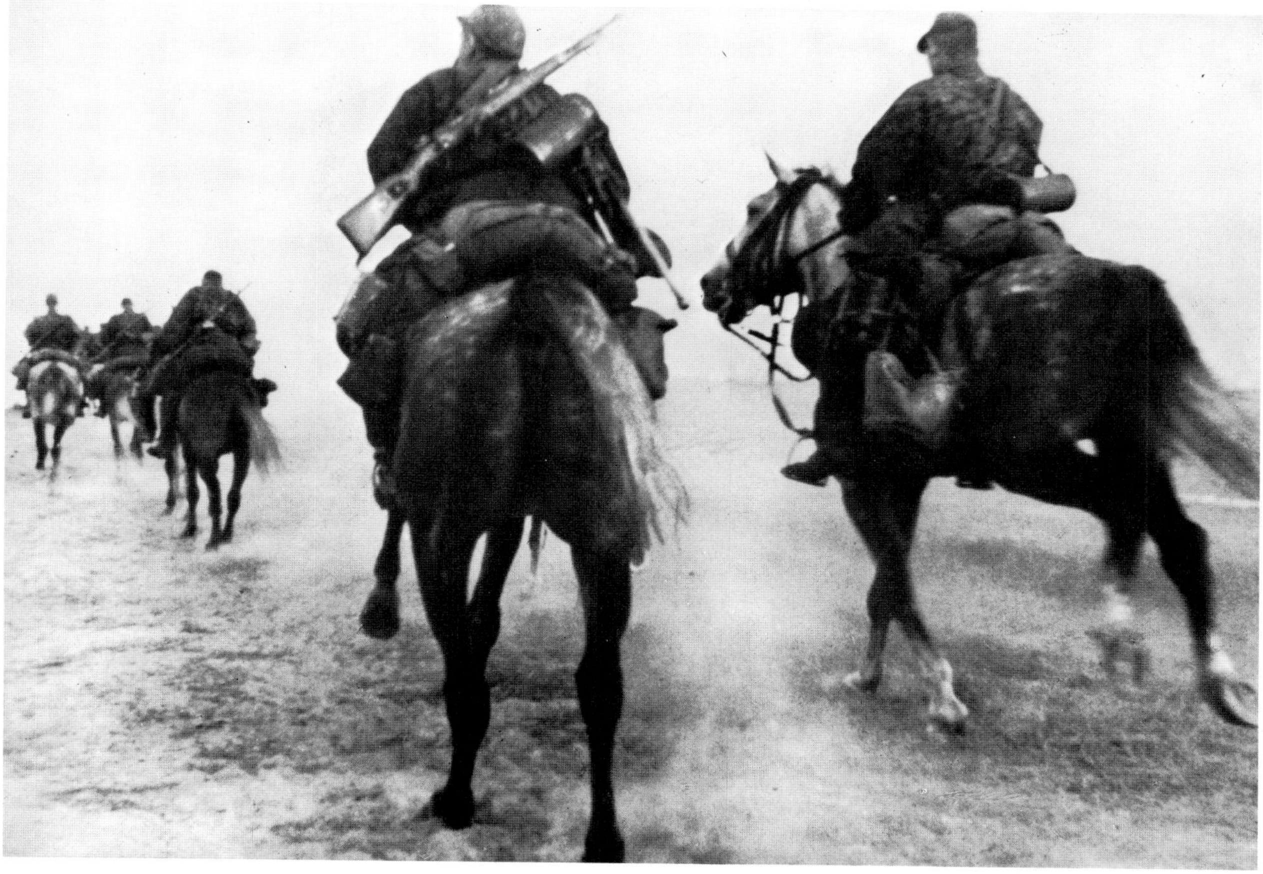

SS-cavalry in action.

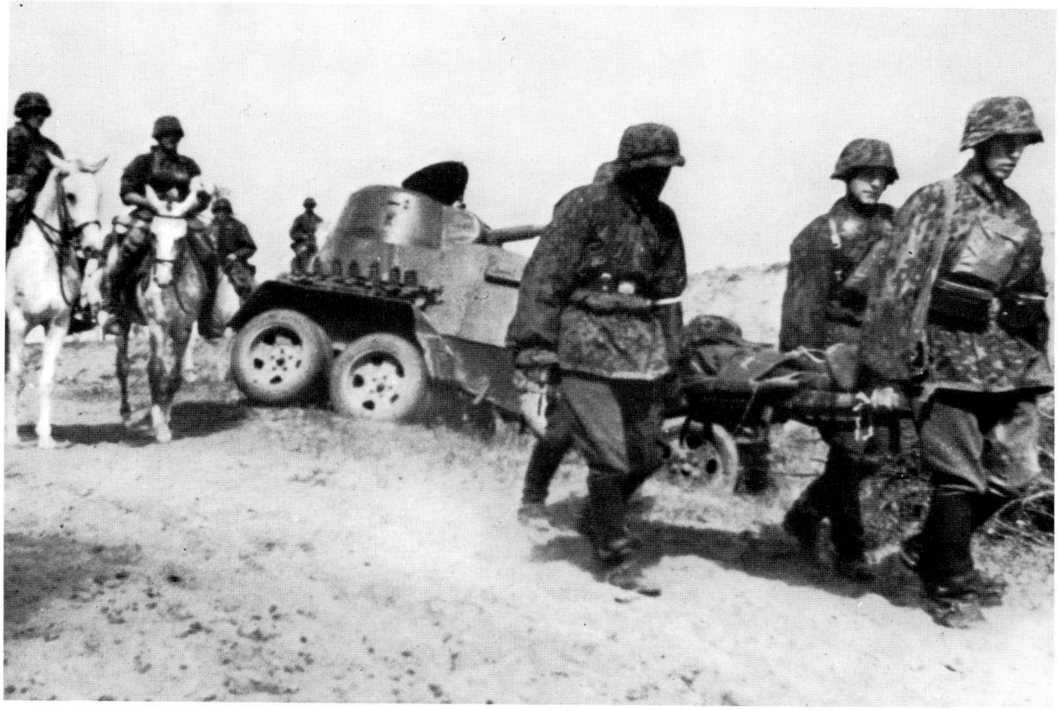

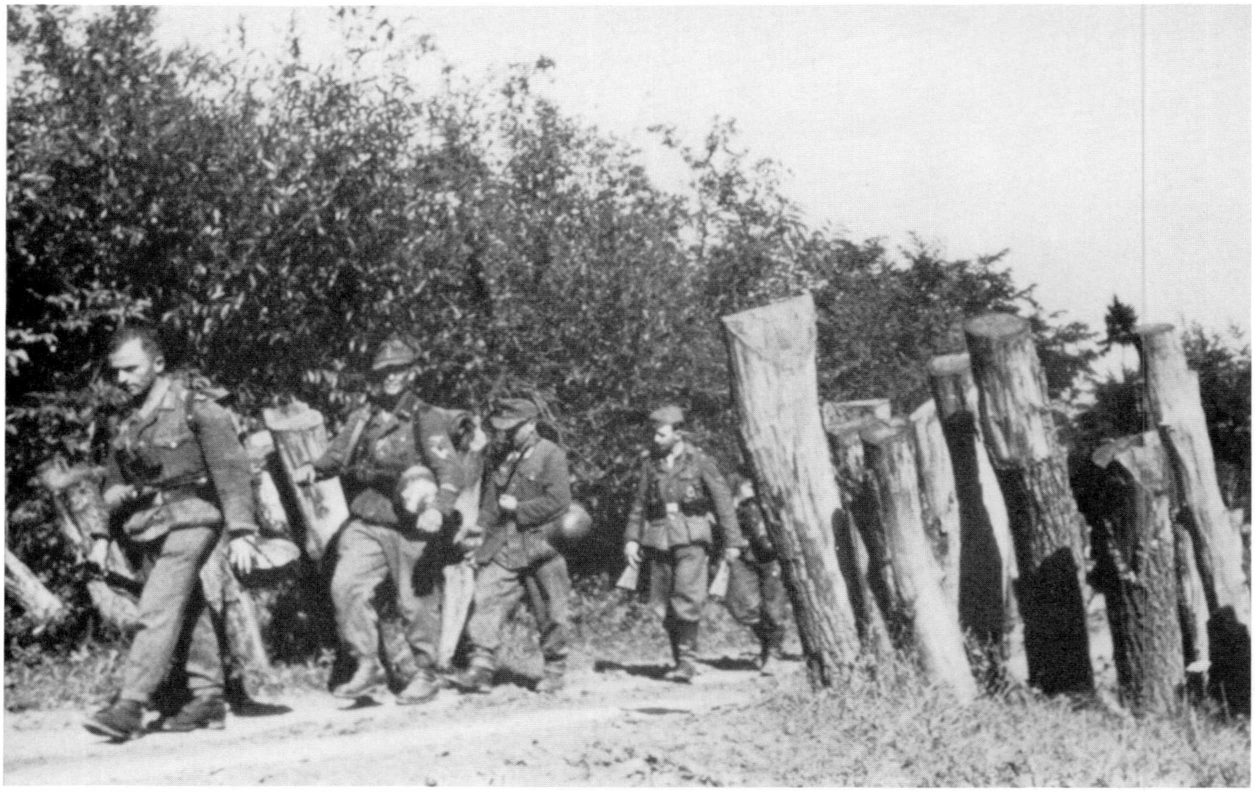

On the southern eastern front, German units, among them parts of the depleted SS-division "Totenkopf" and "Frundsberg", are driven back into Romania.

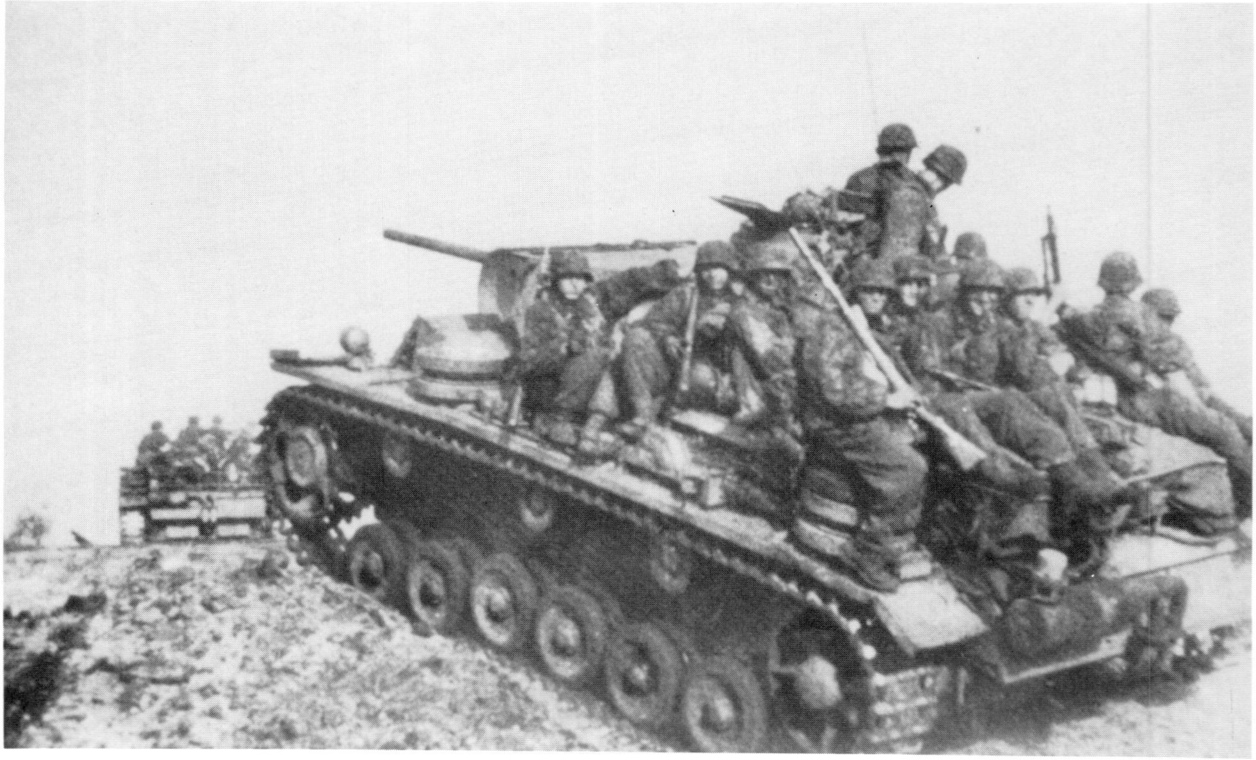

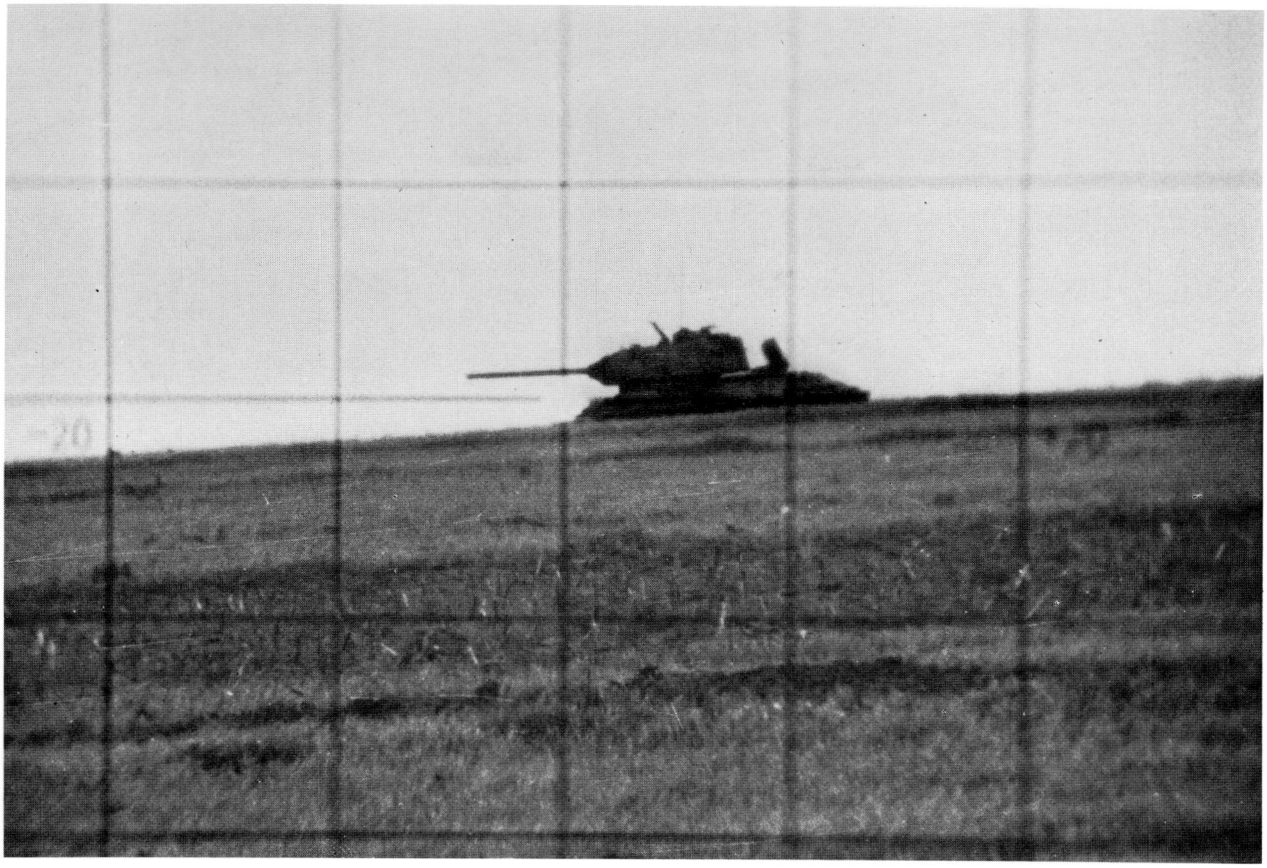

New Russian weapons appear: Here the much improved T-34 tank with a long barrel.

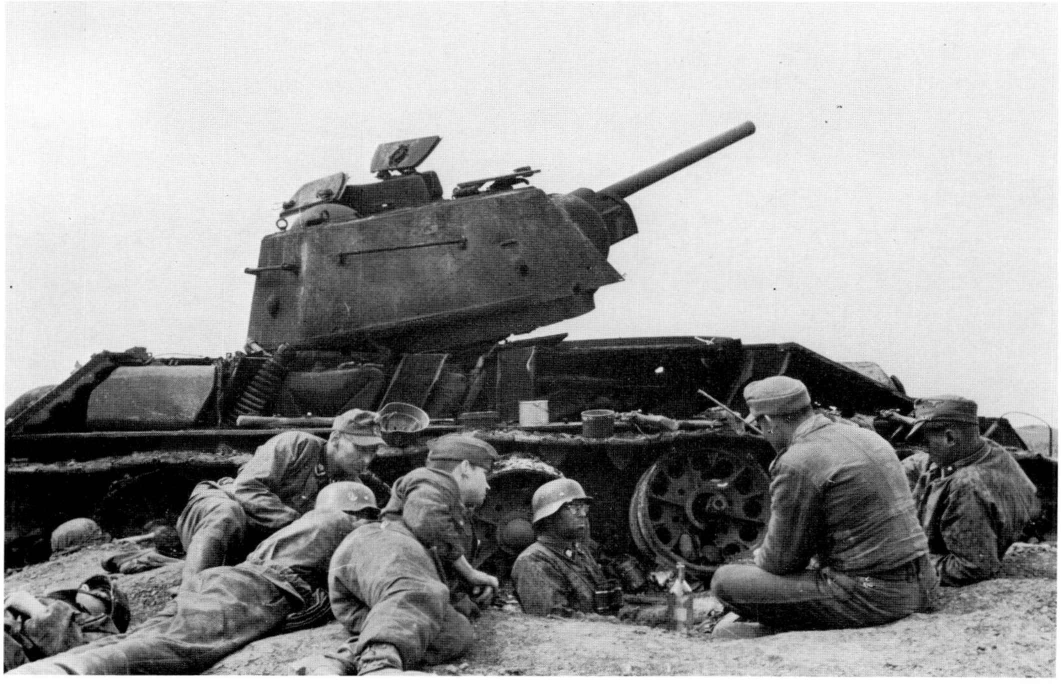

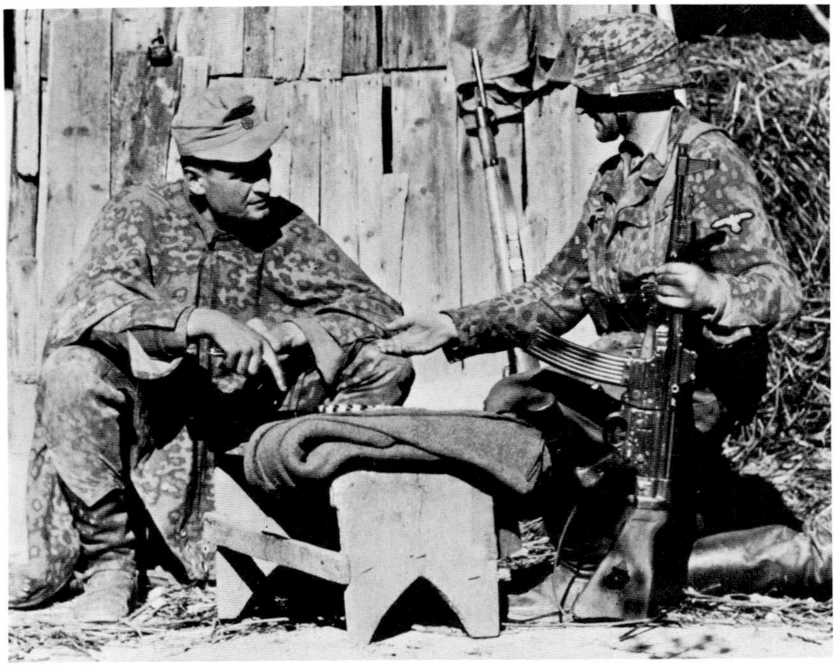

The Germans too use new weapons. Infantrymen with 44. assault carbine.

An insufficient number of the new fast anti-tank "Hetzer" (division "Florian Geyer"), especially feared by the Russians, was delivered to the front too late.

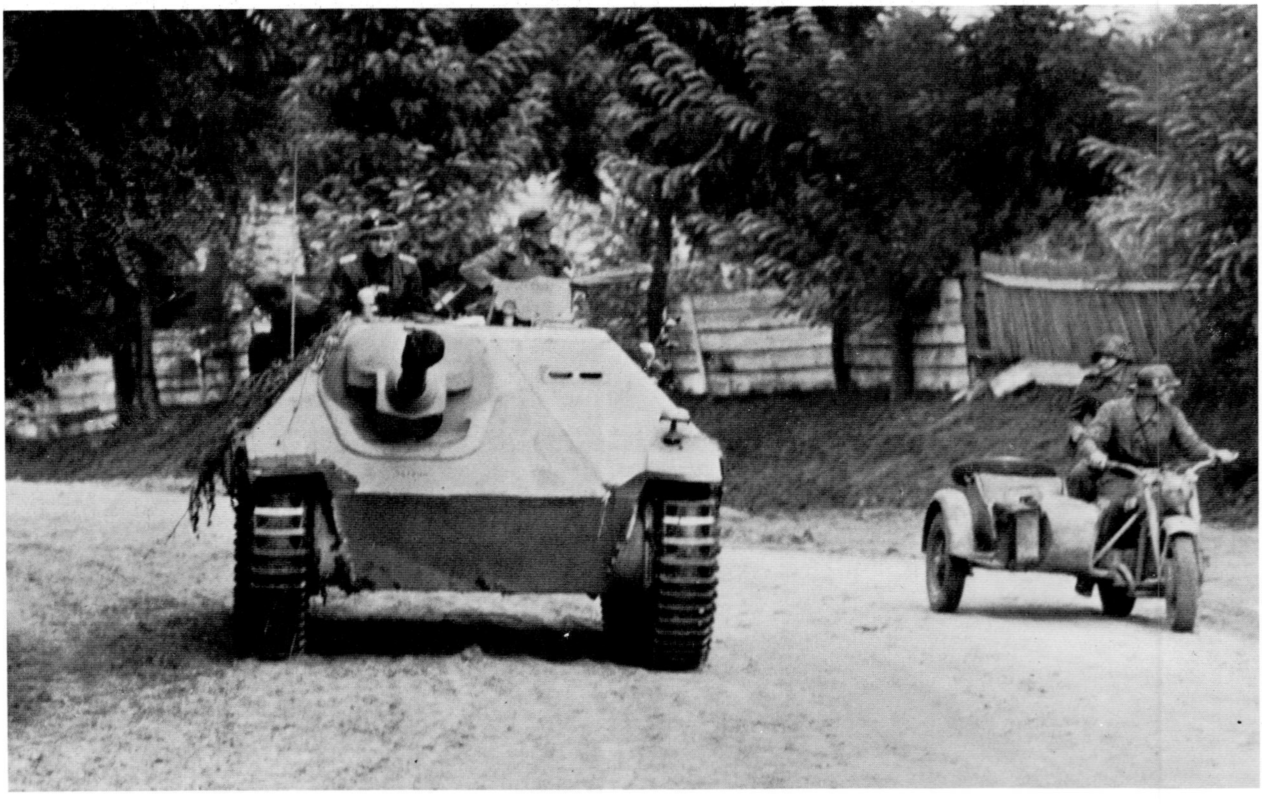

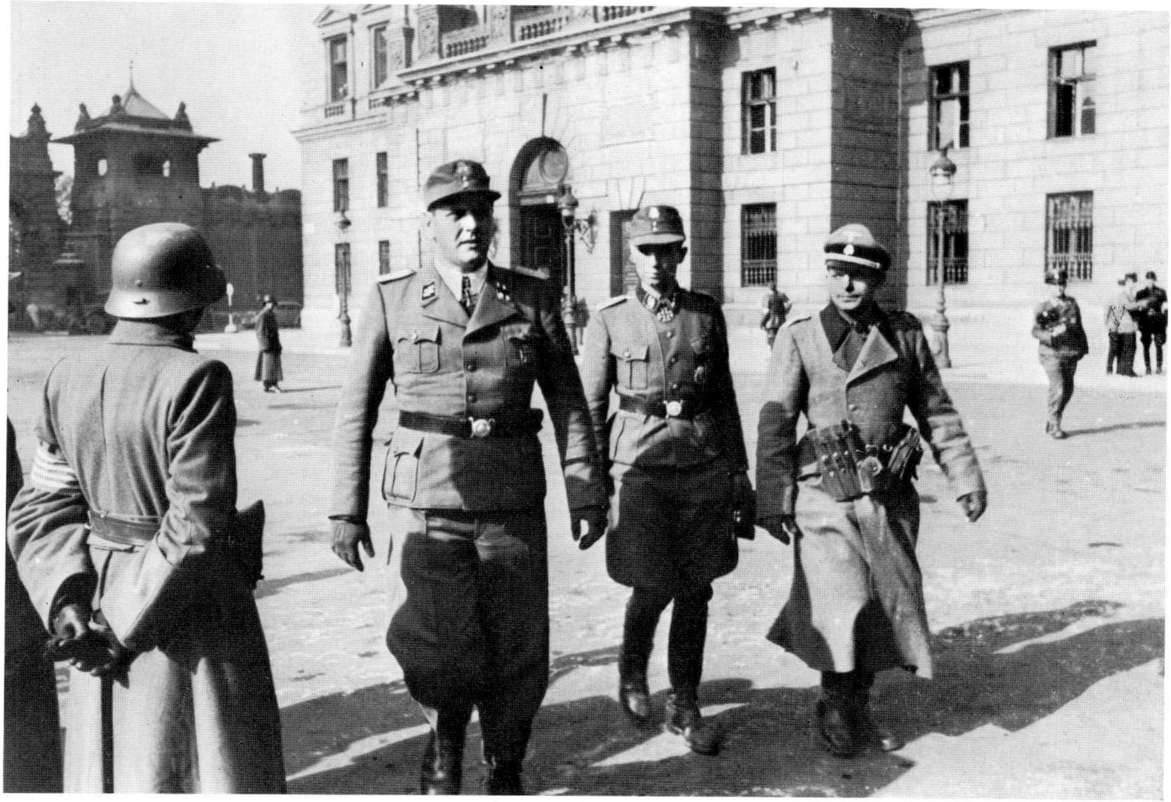

Major Otto Skorzeny, who became well known when he liberated Mussolini, occupies the castle of Budapest in a surprise raid, so delaying Hungary's secession from the Axis.

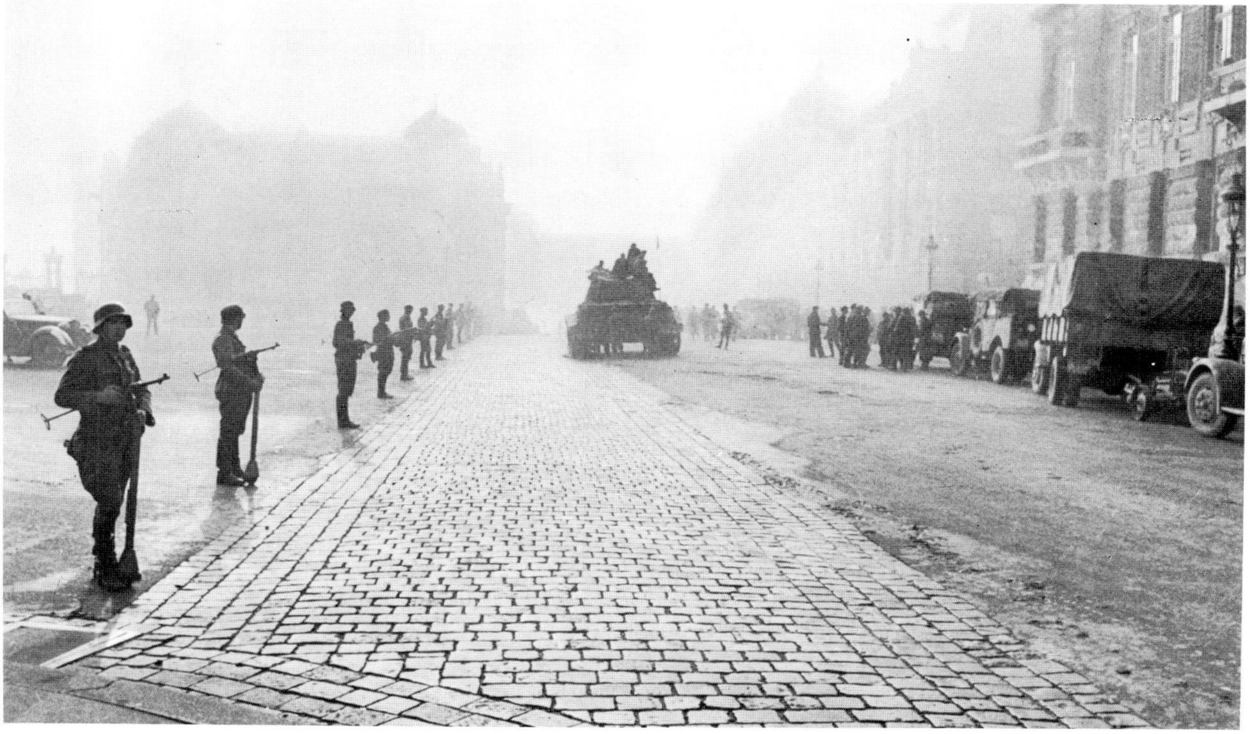

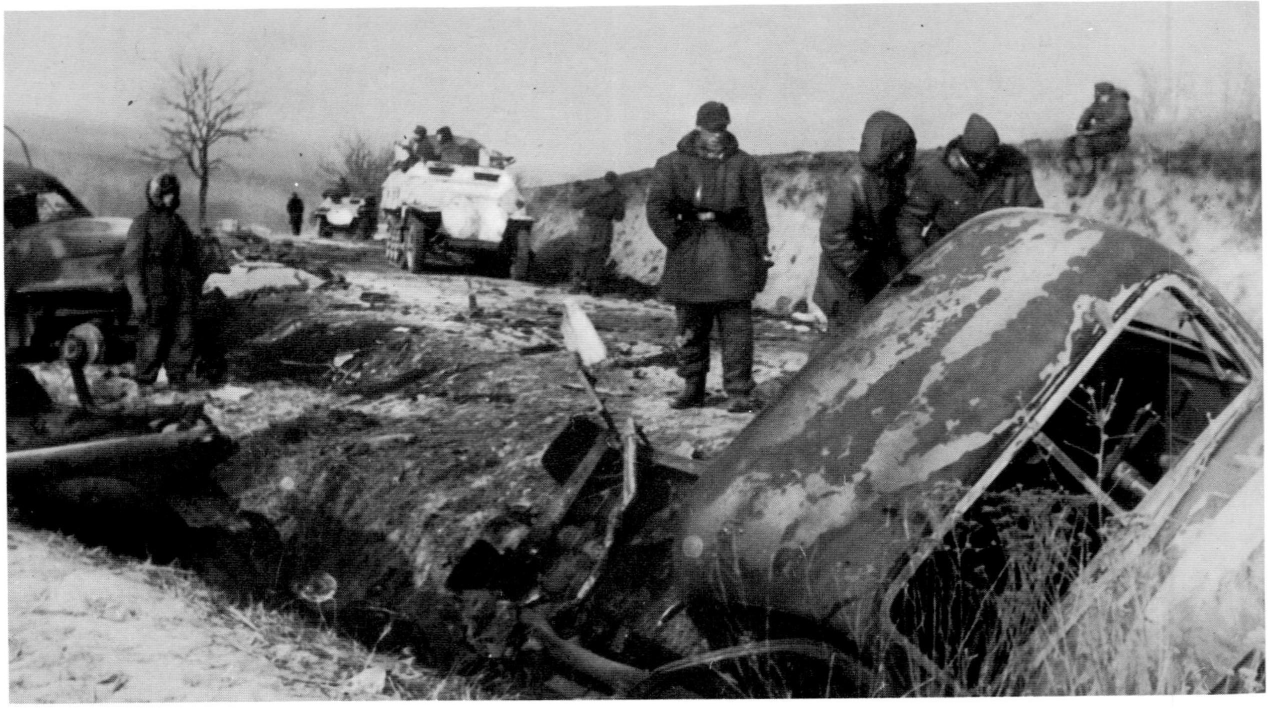

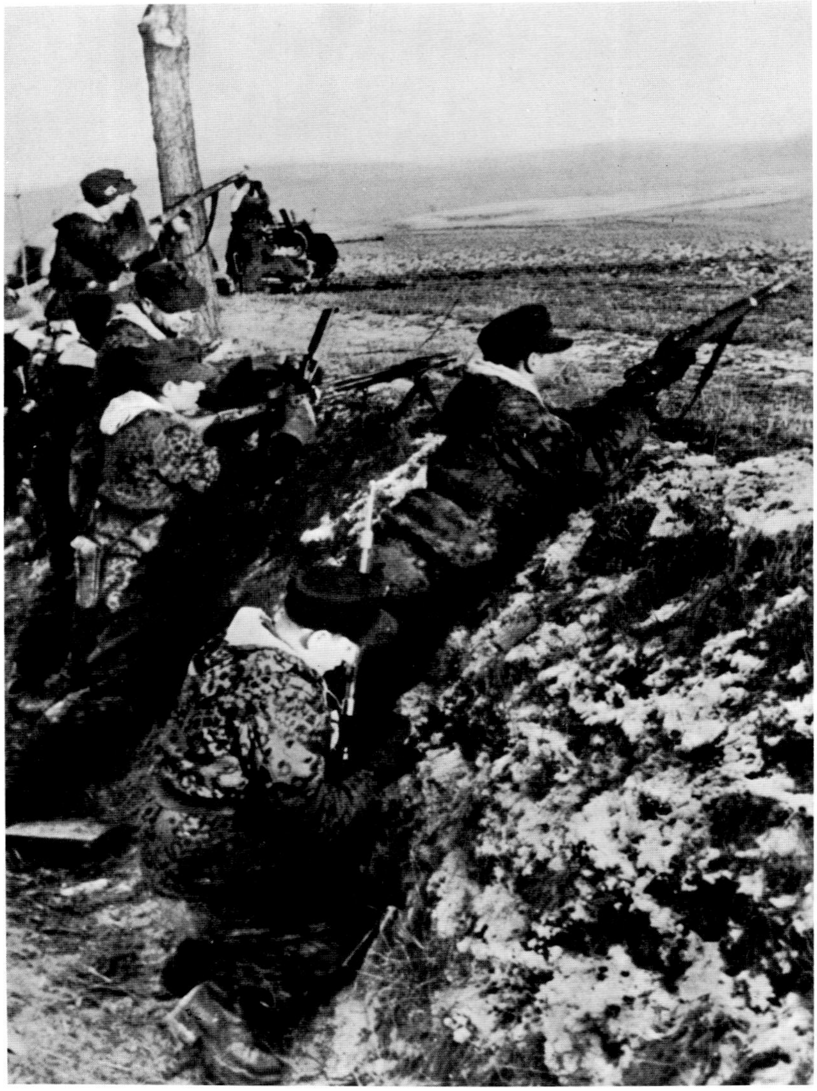

Heavy defensive battles in Hungary, in which elements of the Waffen-SS were greatly involved, continue until the spring of 1945.

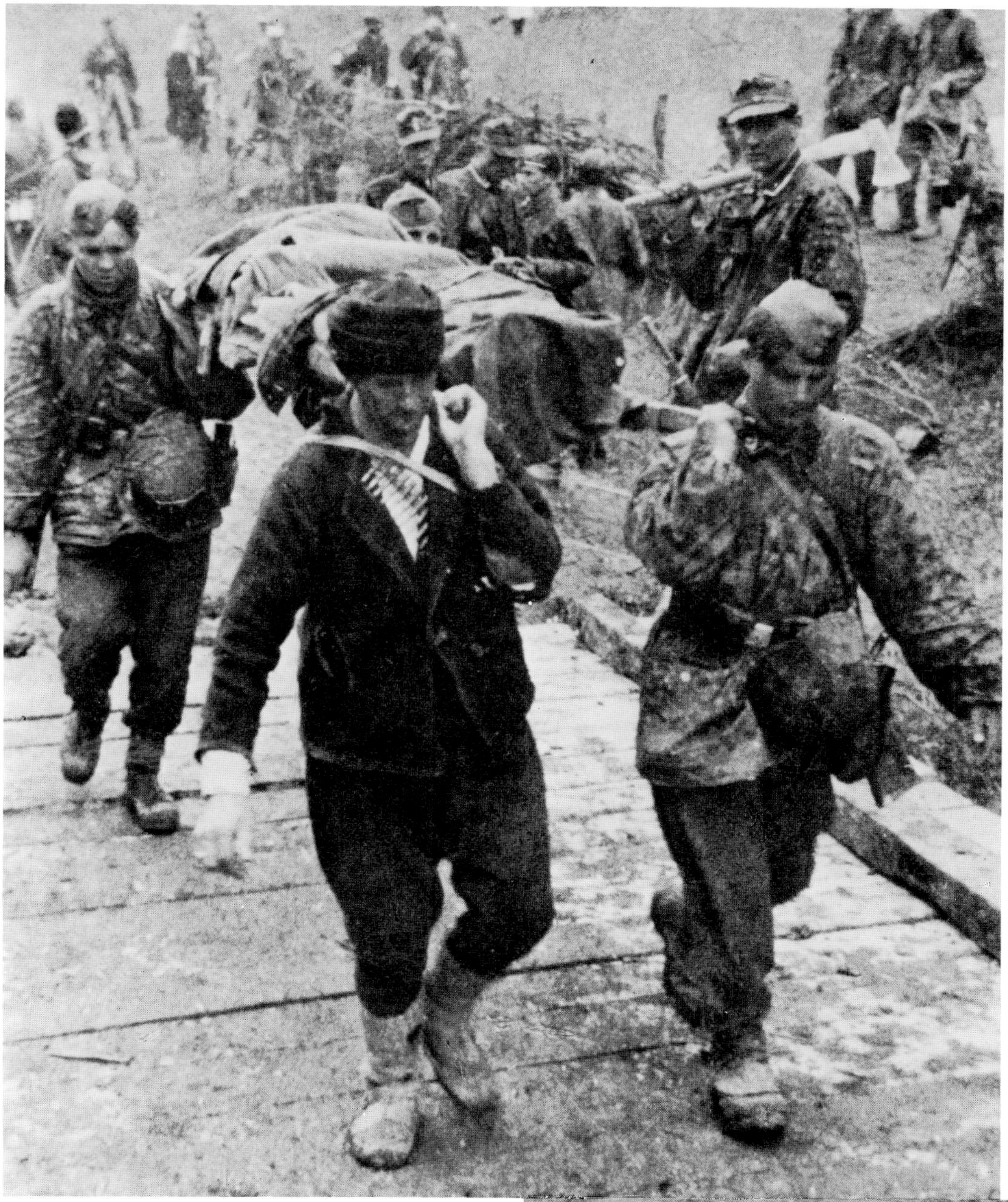

In the hilly country of Yugoslavia, units of the SS-mountain division "Prinz Eugen" supported by Yugoslav and Croat units fought heavy battles, involving many losses against Tito's partisans.

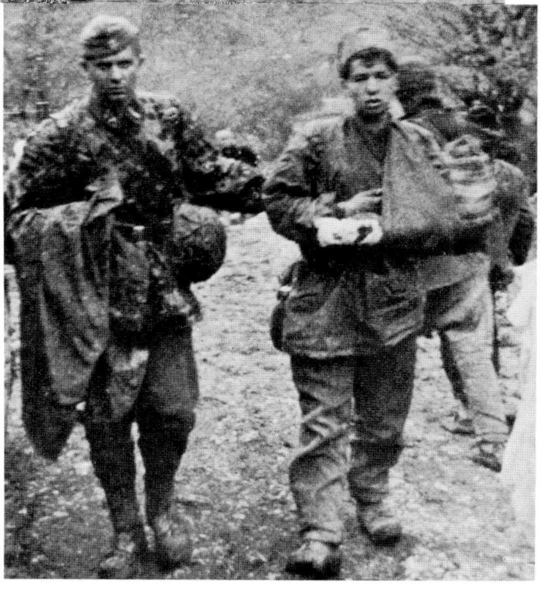

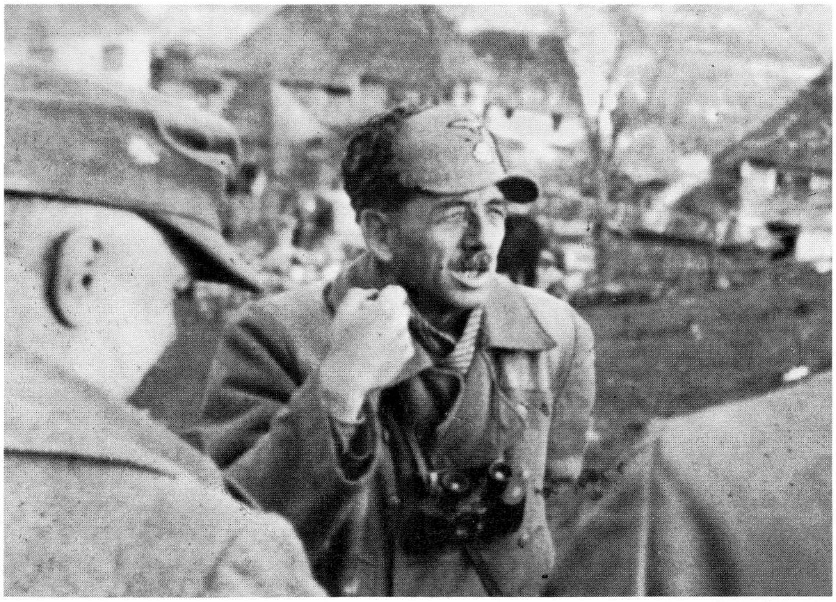

For many weeks, all of them have been fighting: Lt. General Artur Phelps, who was killed on Sept. 21, 1944 in Transylvania, as the commanding general of the V. SS-Mountain Corps.

An unknown motorcycle messenger of the "Prinz Eugen" division.

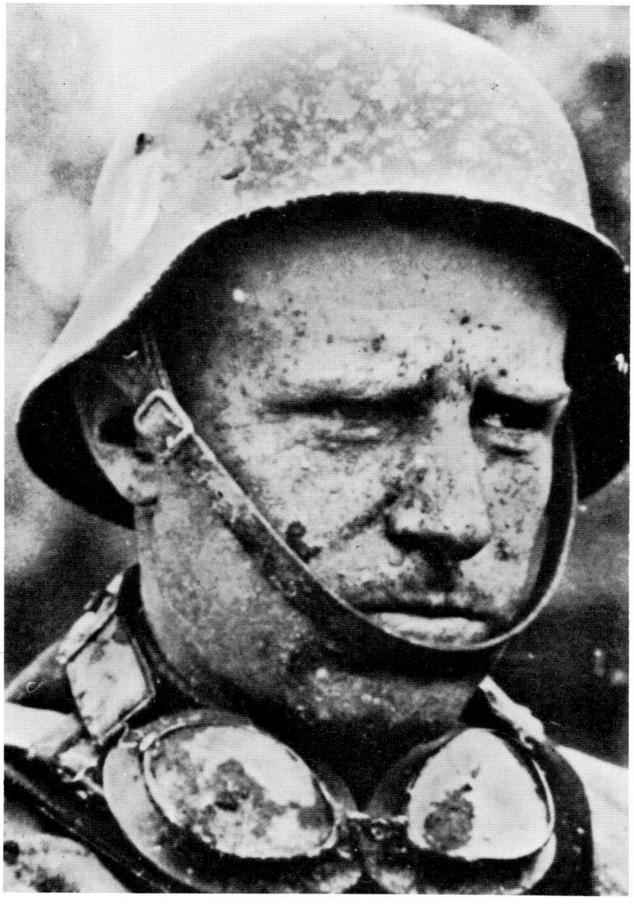

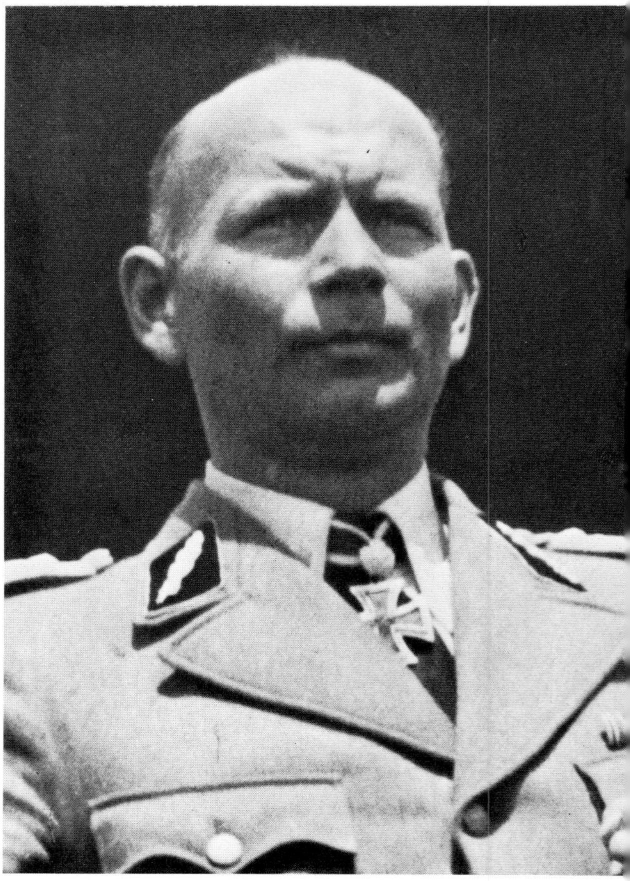

Colonel Otto Krumm, commander of the 7th SS-division "Prinz Eugen".

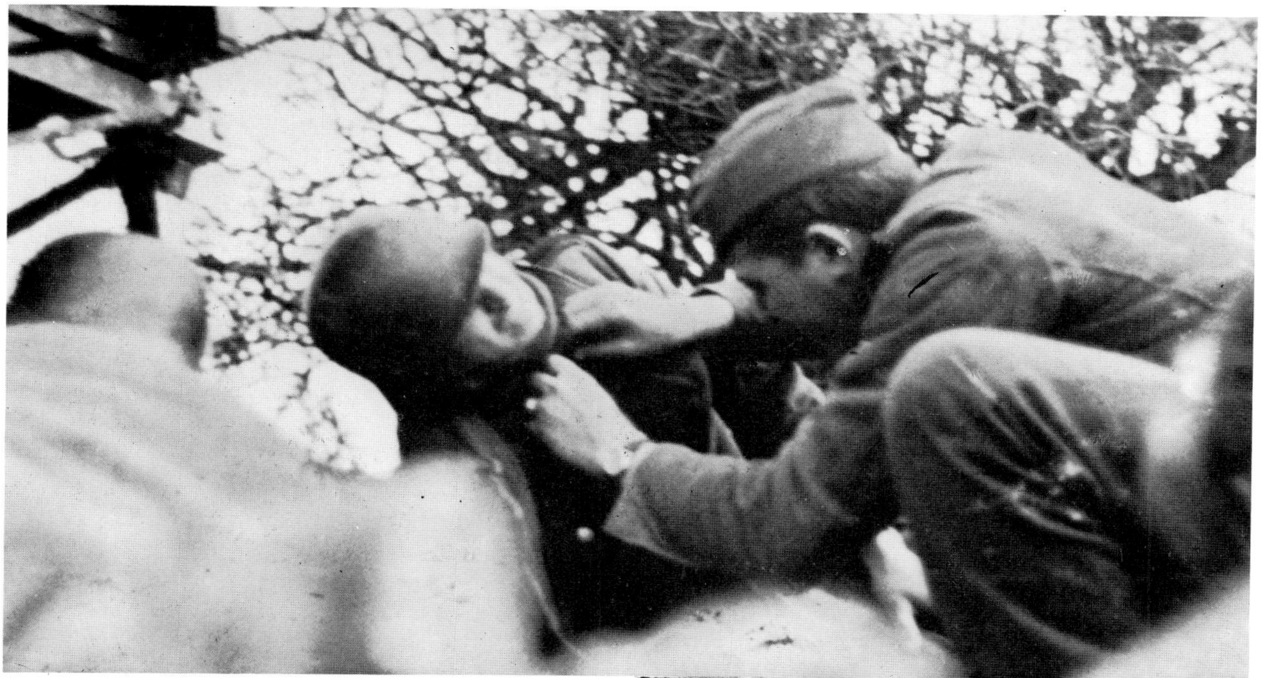

The rescue of an injured soldier under enemy fire.

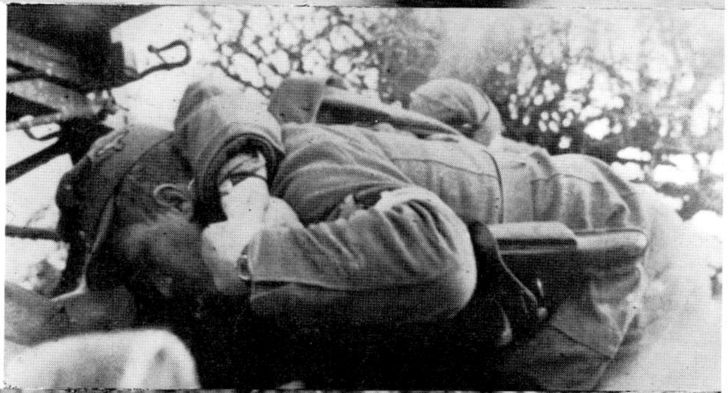

Defensive position in the mountains.

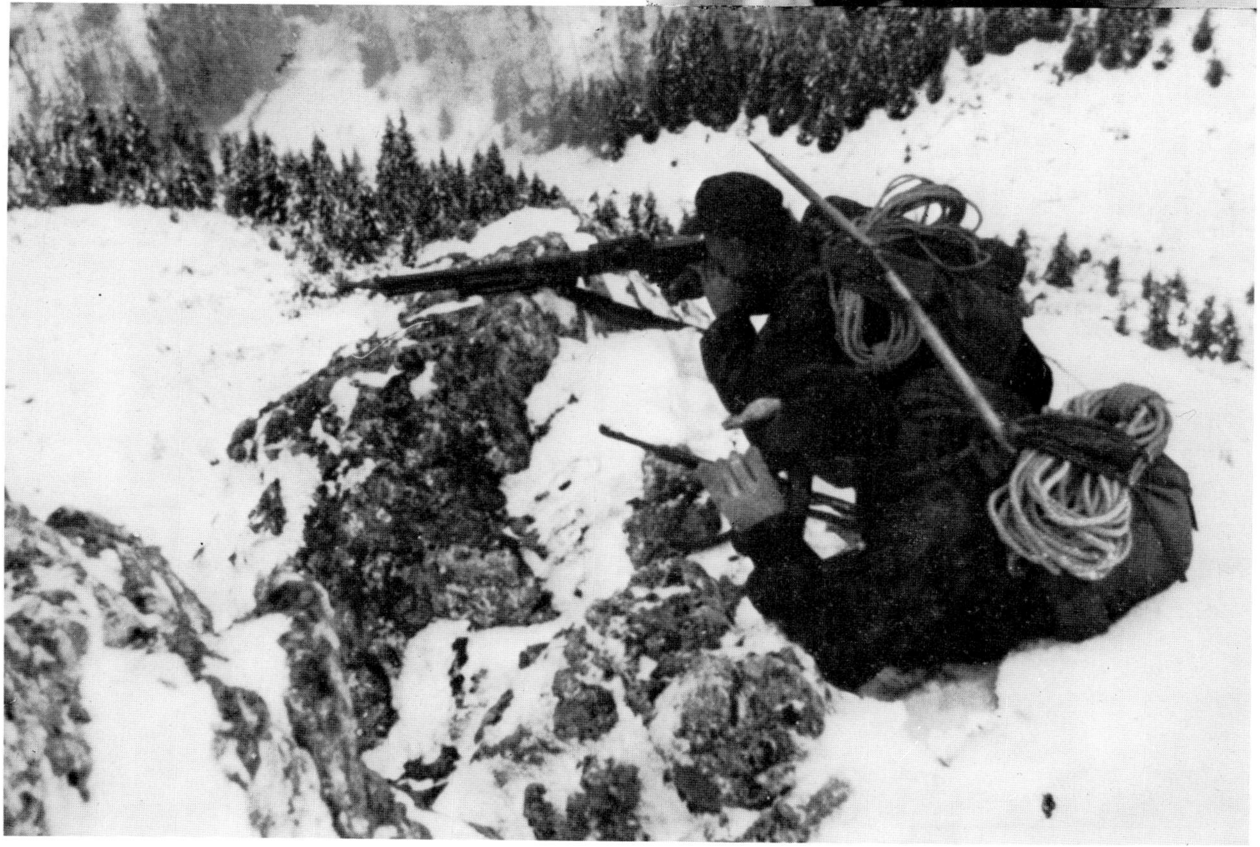

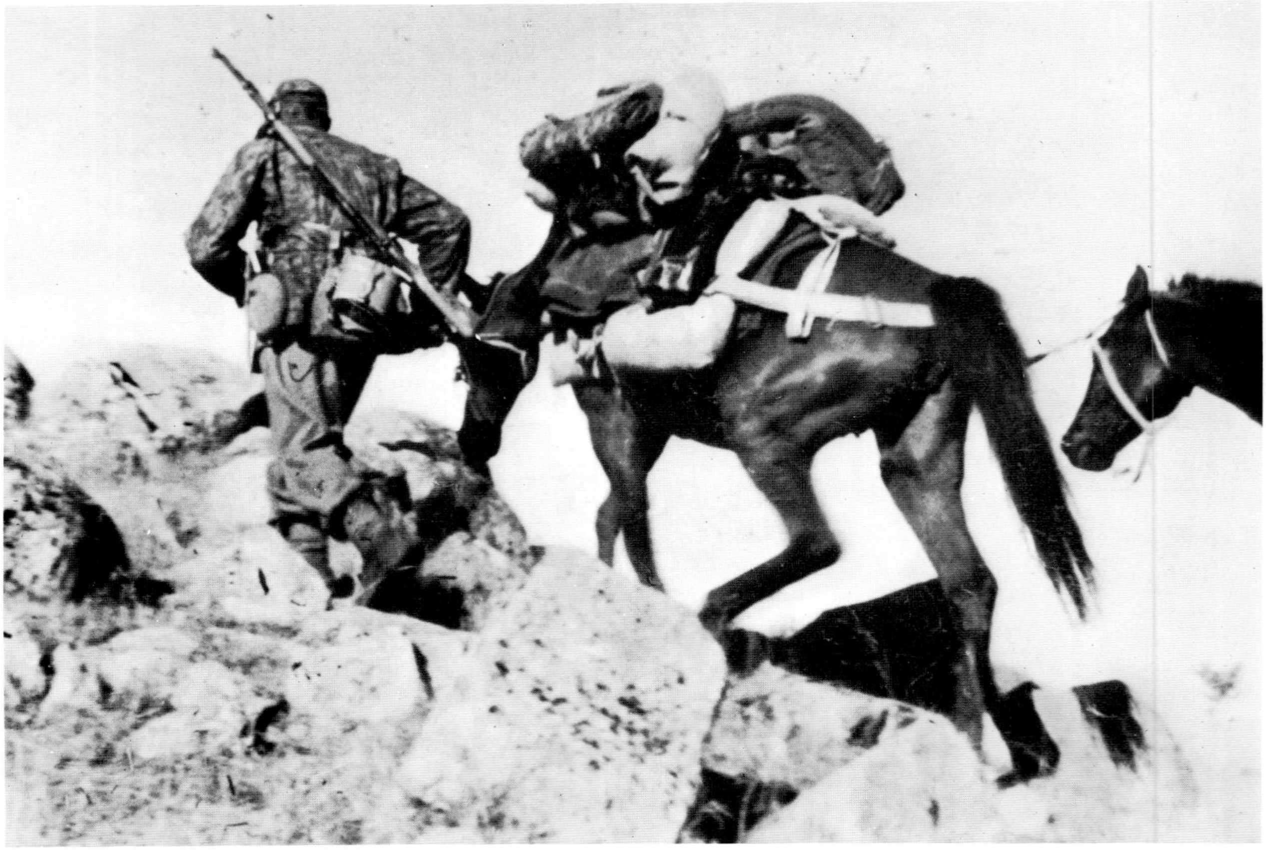

In the high mountains: with horses and captured French tanks against Tito's partisans.

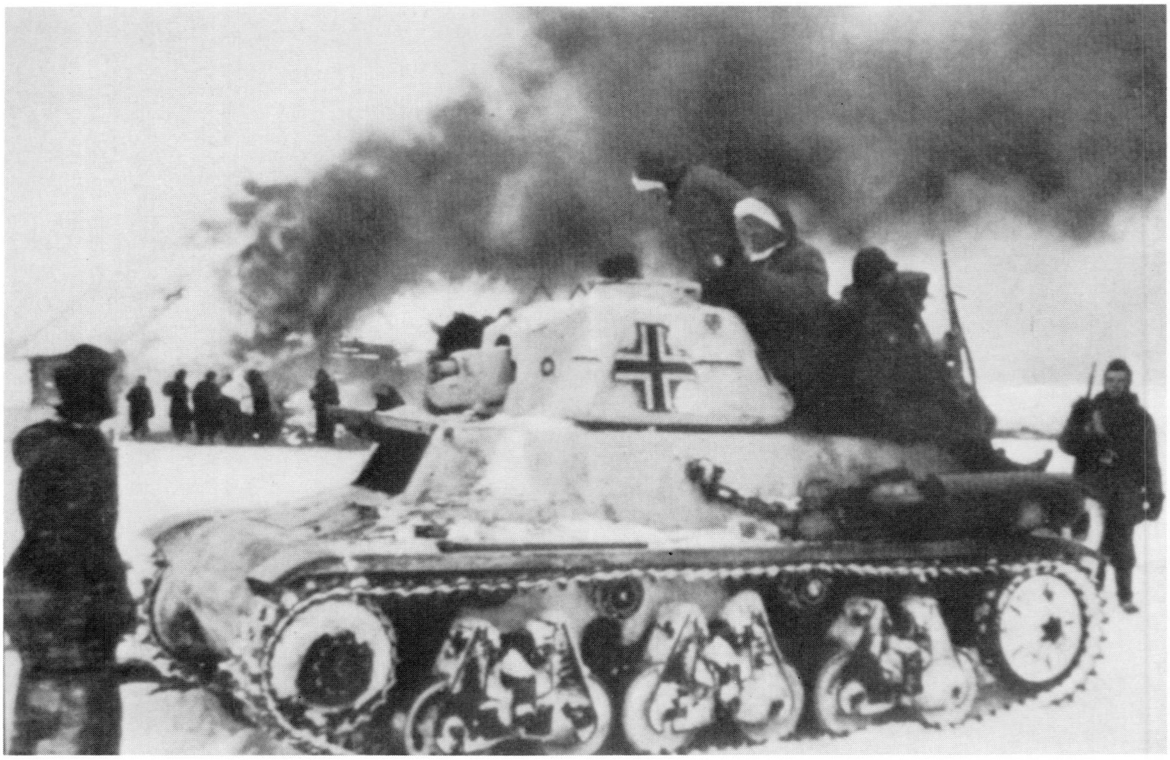

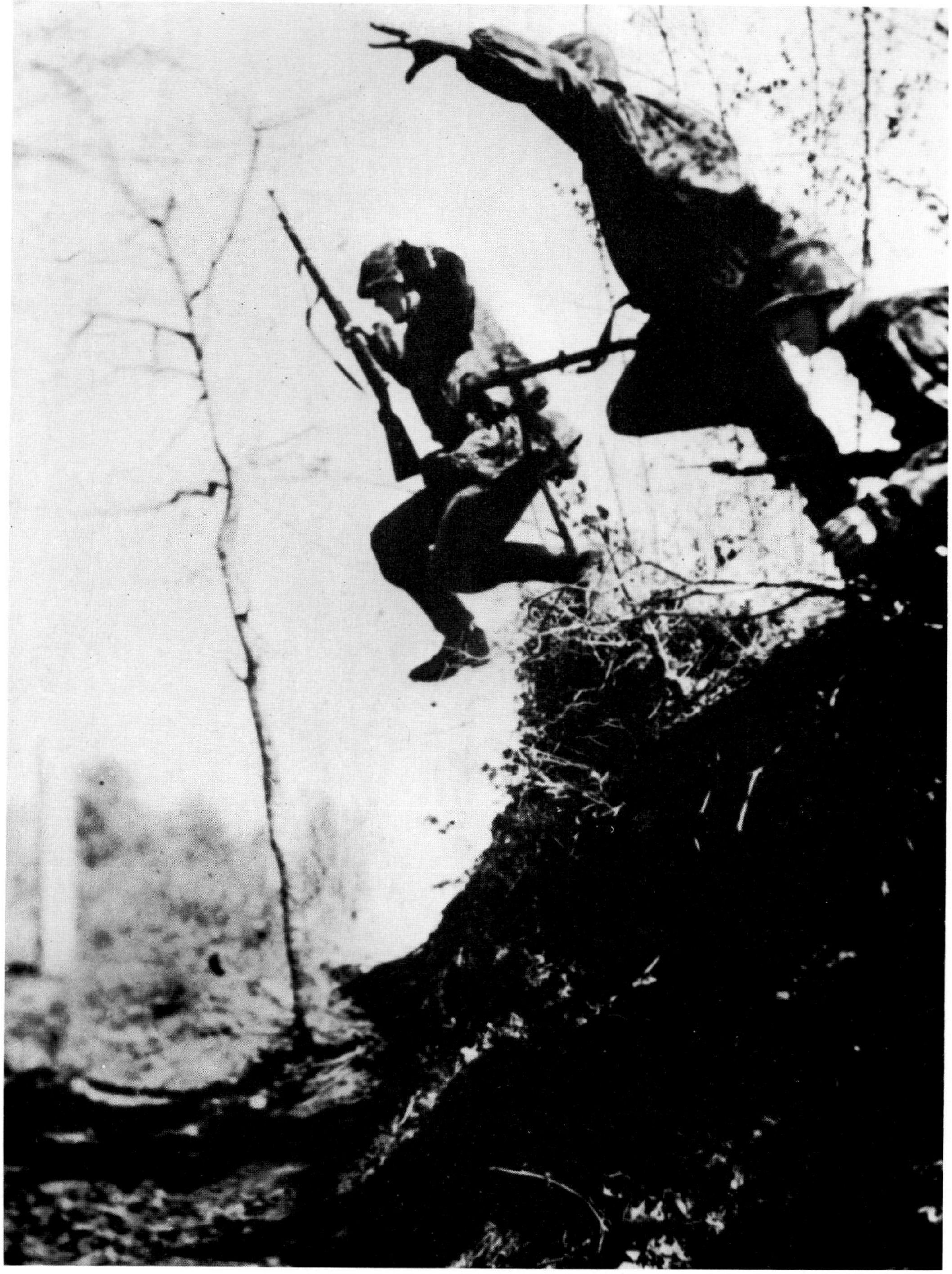

While battles involving heavy losses continued on all fronts, young volunteers of all reserve battalions of the Waffen-SS were drilled in a hard basic military training course.

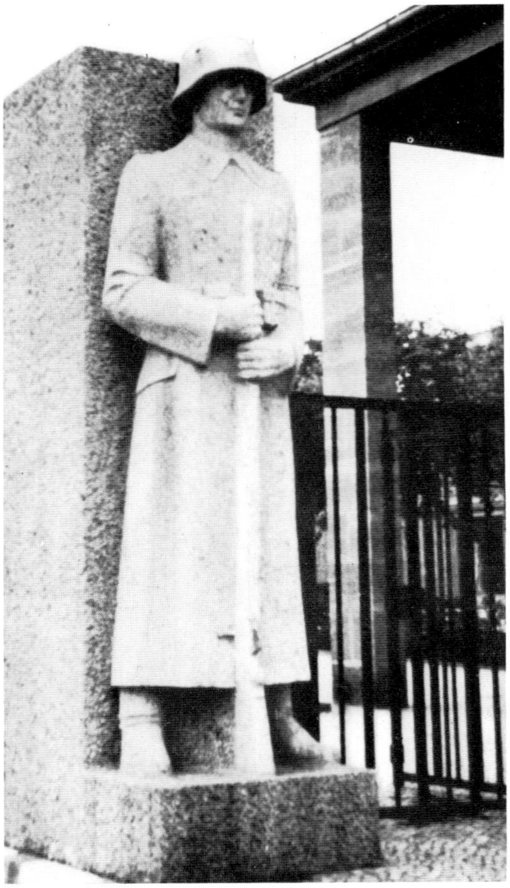

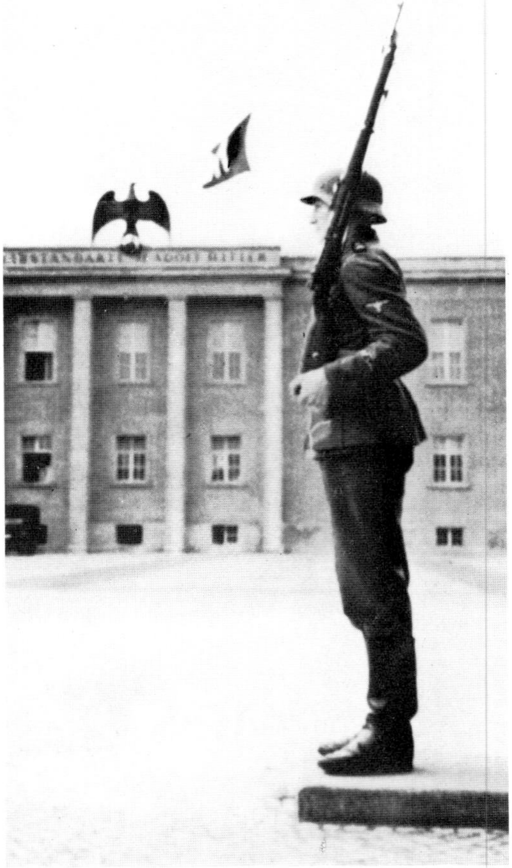

Sentries in front of the barracks of the "LAH" in Berlin-Lichterfelde.

Guard of honor of the LAH in the courtyard of the chancellory.

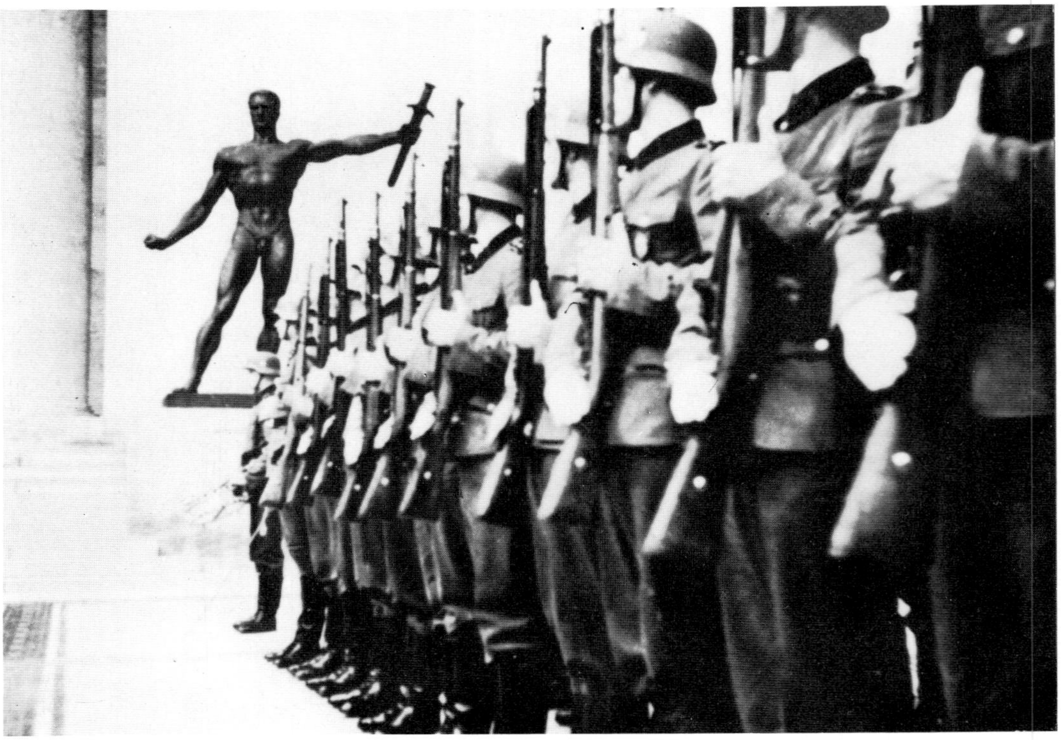

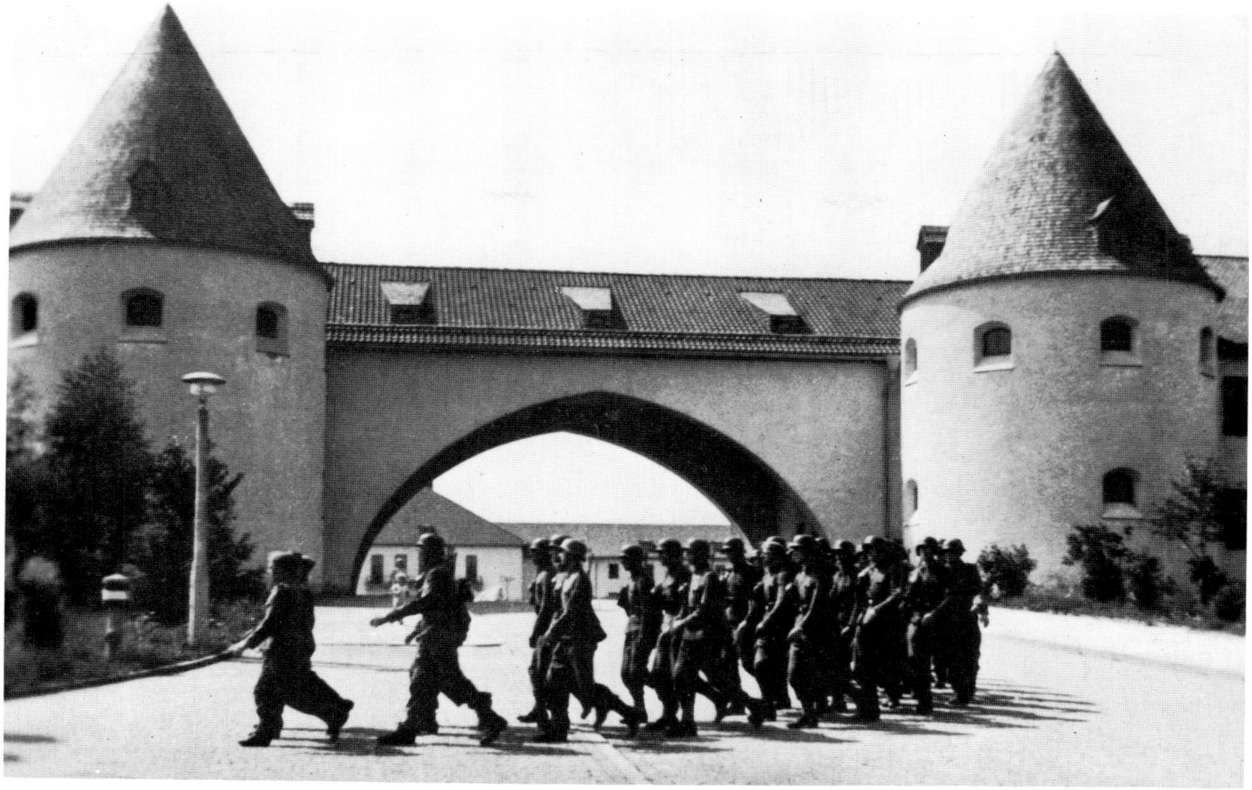

At the SS-cadet academies in Bad Tölz (photo) and Brunswick, the training of the rising officer generation continues.

German volunteers at the sand pit.

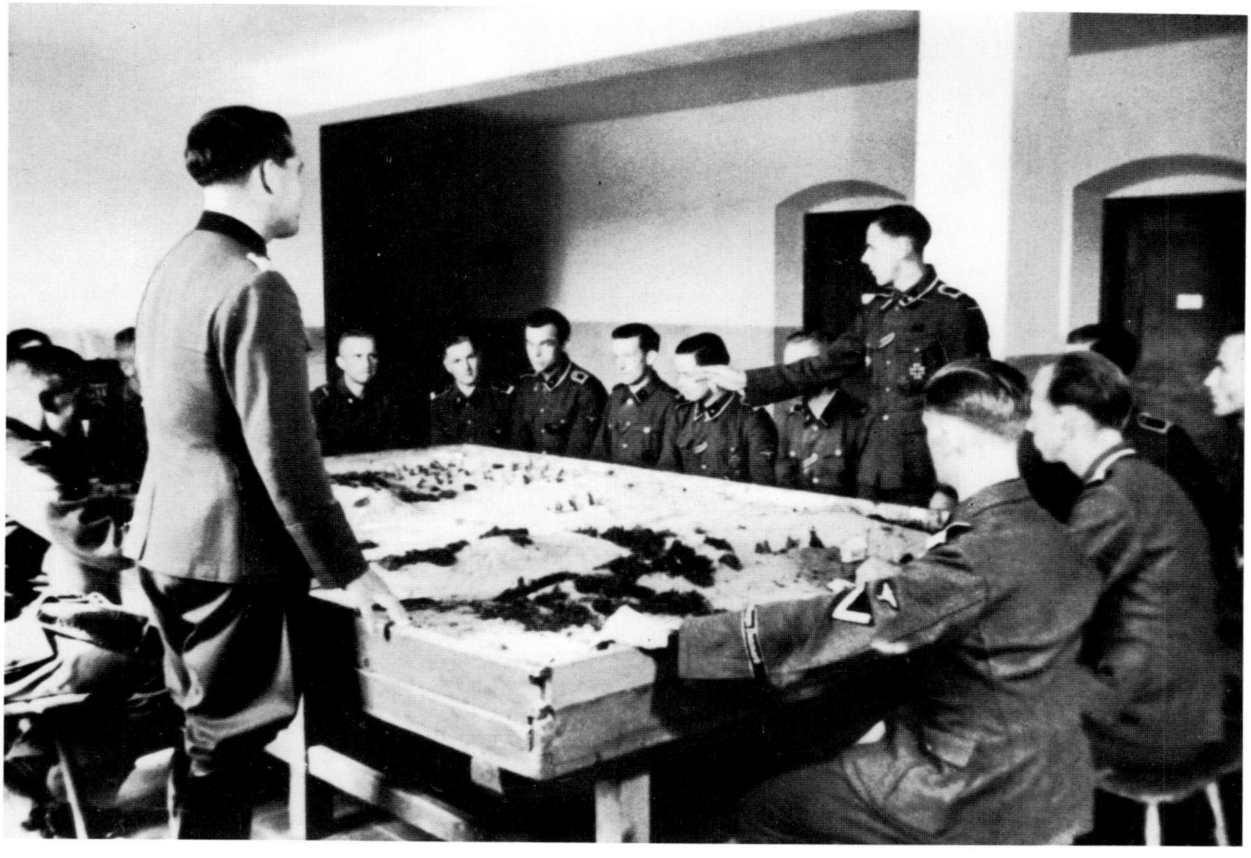

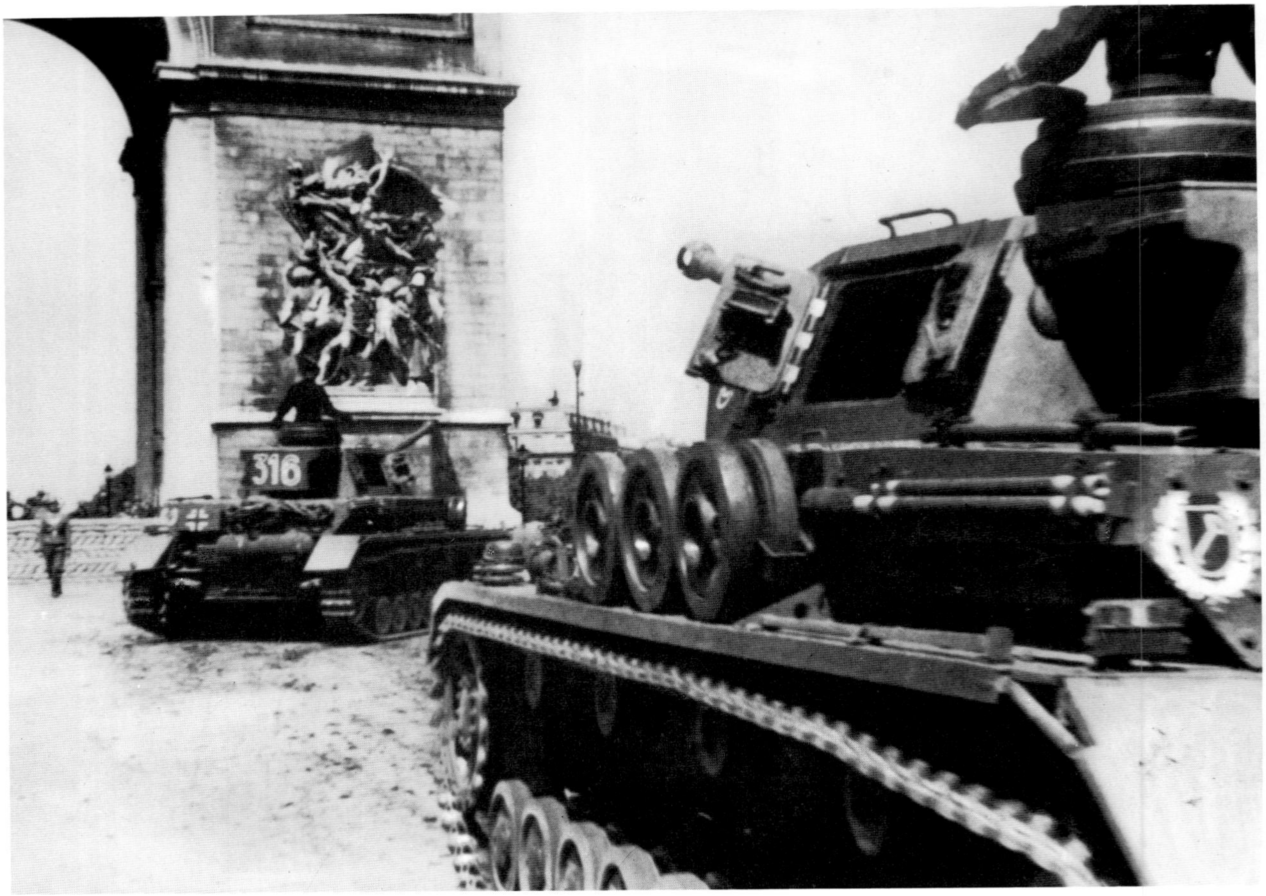
316

In August 1942, the division "LAH" was withdrawn from Russia and transferred to the Atlantic wall as a reserve troop.

A spectacular parade on the Champs Elysees.

Photo below, from the left: Sepp Dietrich, GFM von Rundstedt, Lt. General Hausser.

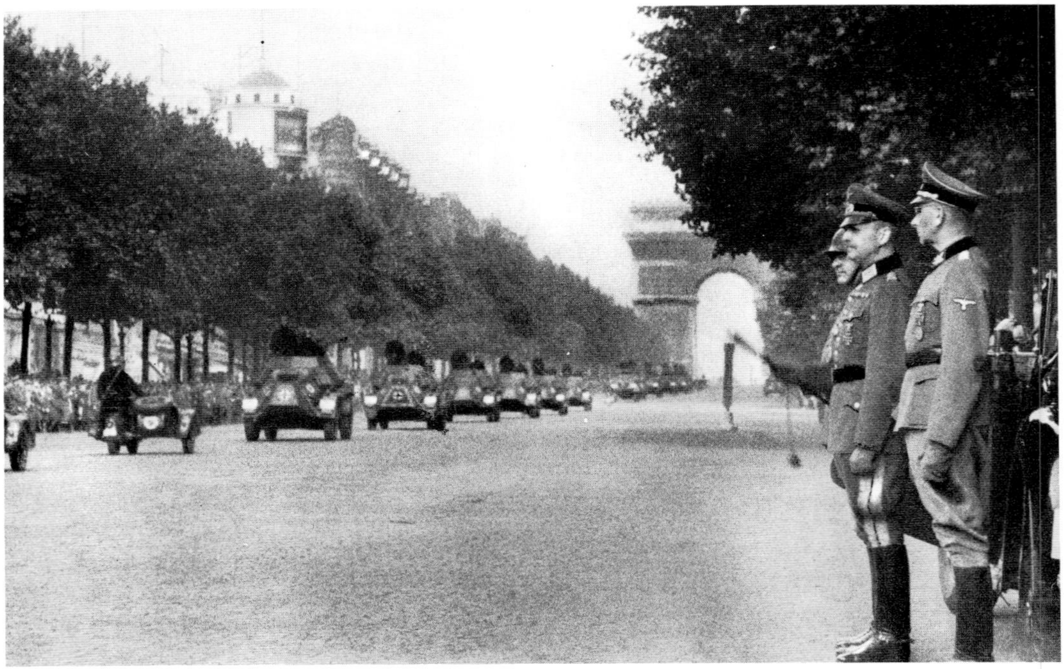

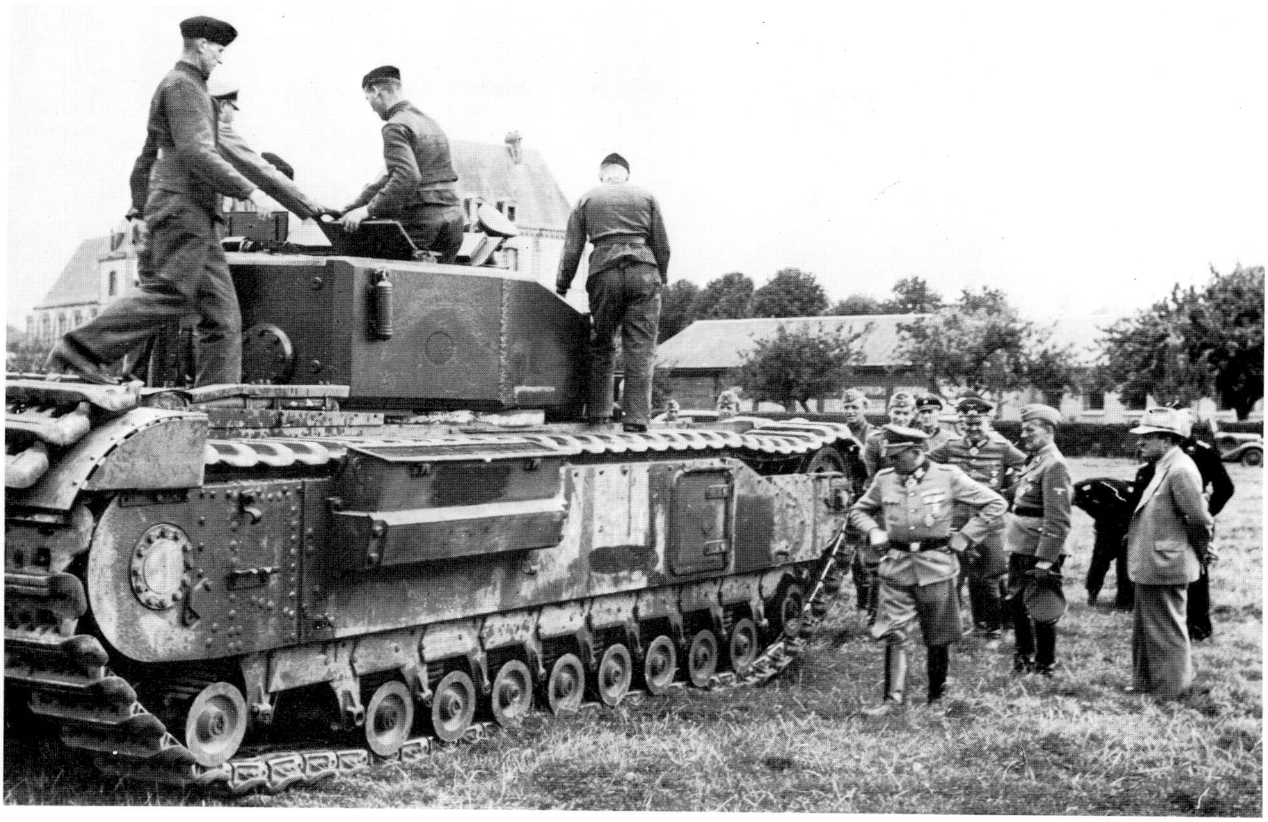

When English troops tried to land near Dieppe, the LAH was not used. Sepp Dietrich as a tank expert was asked to give his opinion on captured Cromwell tanks.

Photo below, from the left: Minister Speer, General d. Pz. Tr. Kuntzen, Major R. Lehmann, Sepp Dietrich.

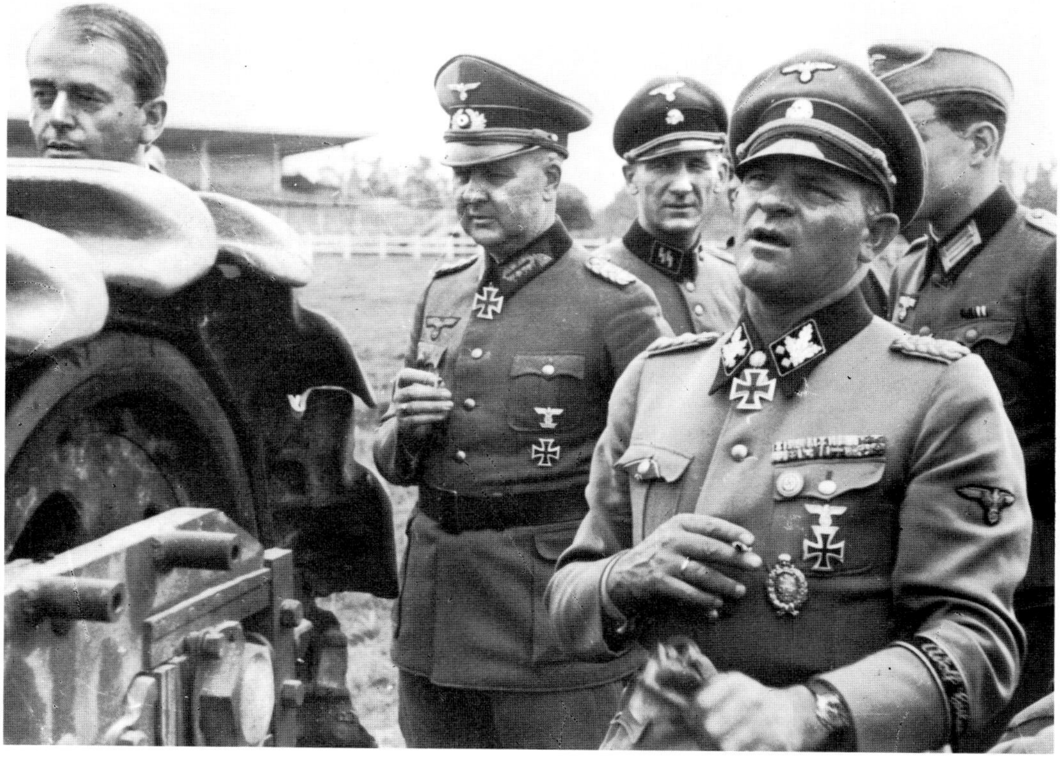

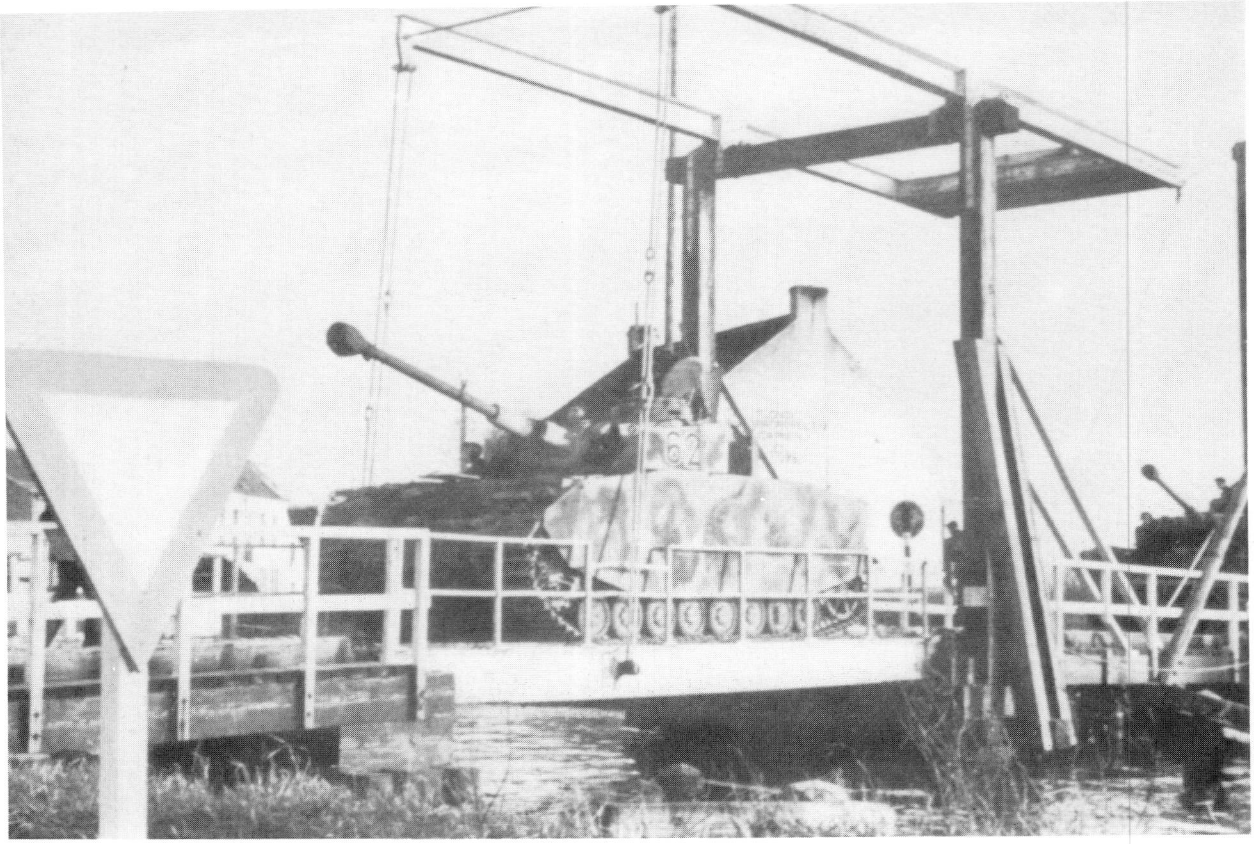

In the spring of 1943, the 12th SS-armored division "Hitler Jugend" was newly formed in the west.

Photo above: tanks IV, II. SS-Pz. Rgt. 12 in Holland. Photo below: flame-thrower-Scout car.

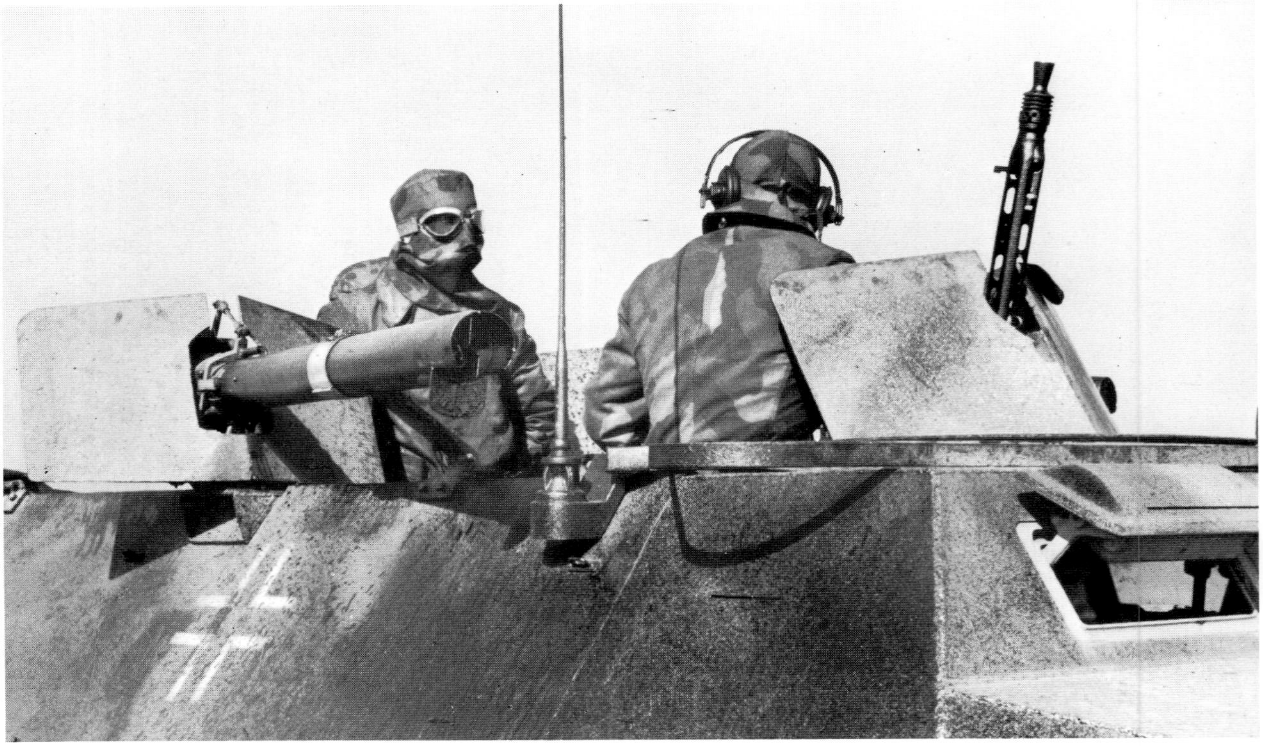

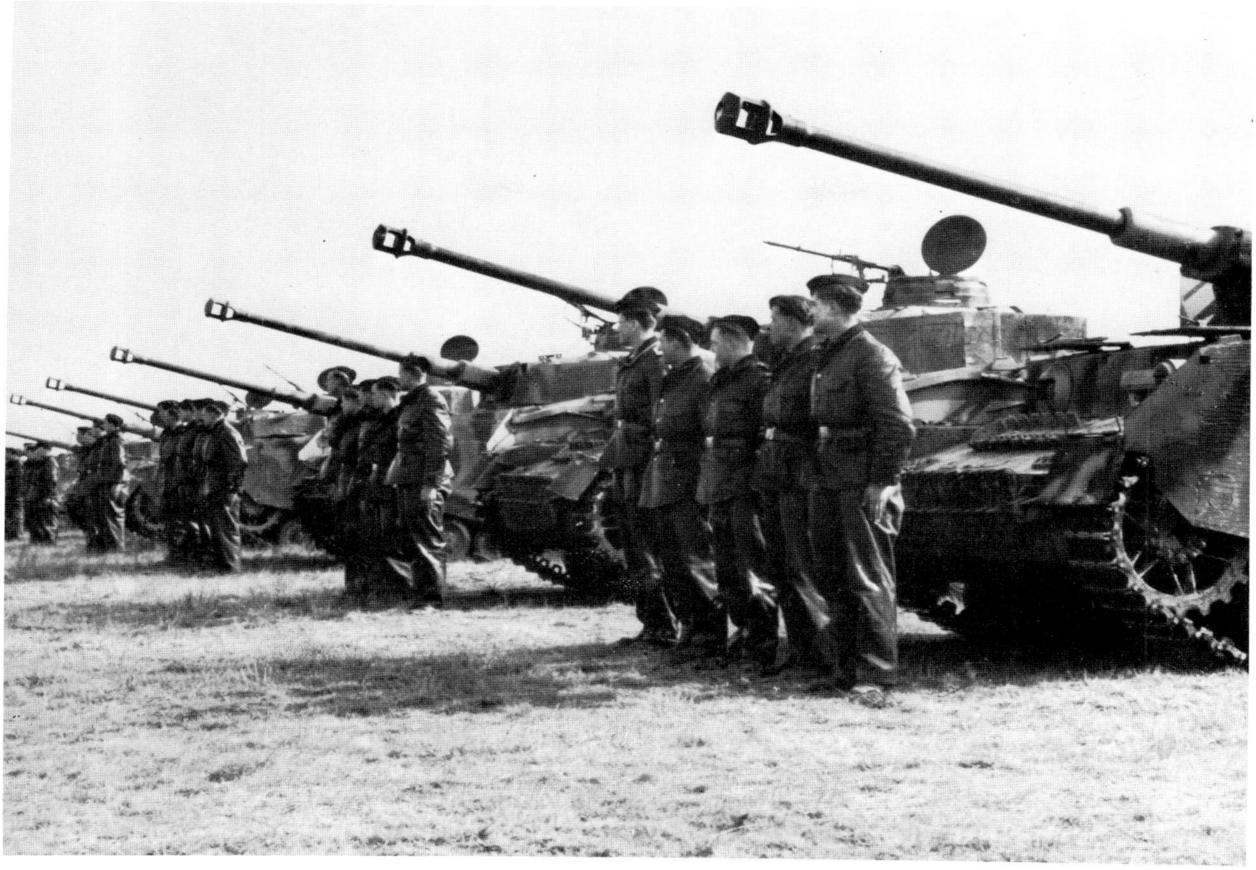

GRM von Rundstedt sees for himself the high standard of training of the young infantrymen of the "HJ" division. (The average age of all ranks was 21 years.)

From the left: Witt, Dietrich, "Panzermeyer", Rundstedt.

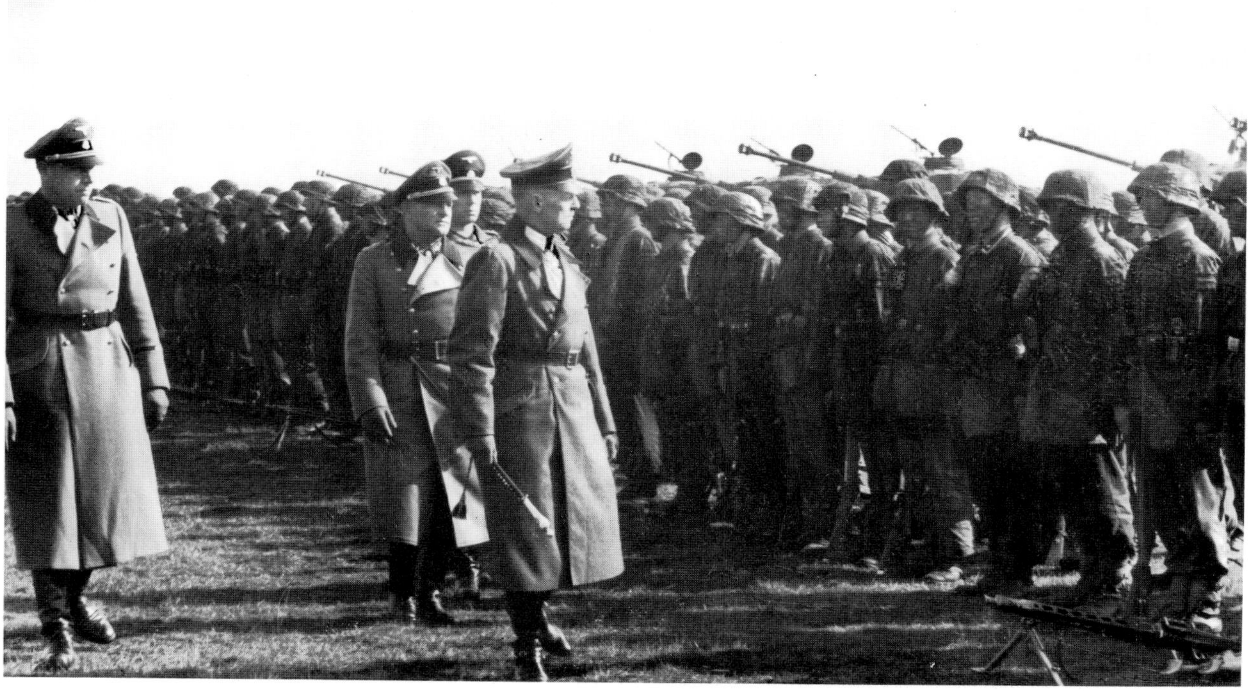

# THE INVASION, 1944

When the Anglo-American forces, in the protection of a powerful armada and under the shelter of superior air forces, initiated the greatest landing operation in the history of warfare on June 6, 1944, the SS "Hitler Jugend" Division was already at the focal point of the fighting, joined shortly thereafter by the LAH (Corps) withdrawn from Russia, parts of "Das Reich", plus "Götz von Berlichingen", "Frundsberg" and "Hohenstauffen". The enemy, once he had succeeded in extending his beachheads, had to deploy his entire air superiority to prevent precisely these divisions from unleashing their fighting power. Constant heavy bombardment, ceaseless fighter-bomber attacks, and the land forces that were strengthened daily from across the sea, held the defenders of the imaginary Atlantic Wall but could not prevent the SS divisions from constantly leading hard strikes against the units that had landed. Themselves hard hit, suffering heavy losses of men and materiel, the "Hitler Jugend", LAH and "Das Reich" fought "admirably", as English and American authorities later reported. But even the Waffen-SS divisions, taken into the German defensive units as "corset stays", could not prevent the breakthrough of the Allies from the Caen area into the breadth of France. The false conception of the German defense and the overwhelming superiority of the enemy left the Waffen-SS divisions no option but to meet the overpowering opponents over and over again with all their strength and determination. That this was done in brave soldierly operations gained the respect and recognition that the enemies of those days have not denied the men of the Waffen-SS. This is not changed by the tragic events and errors that later suffered an equally tragic judgment in the Malmedy Trials.

The Ardennes Offensive failed in December of 1944 because from an operational standpoint it was compelled to. The final battle on German soil began.

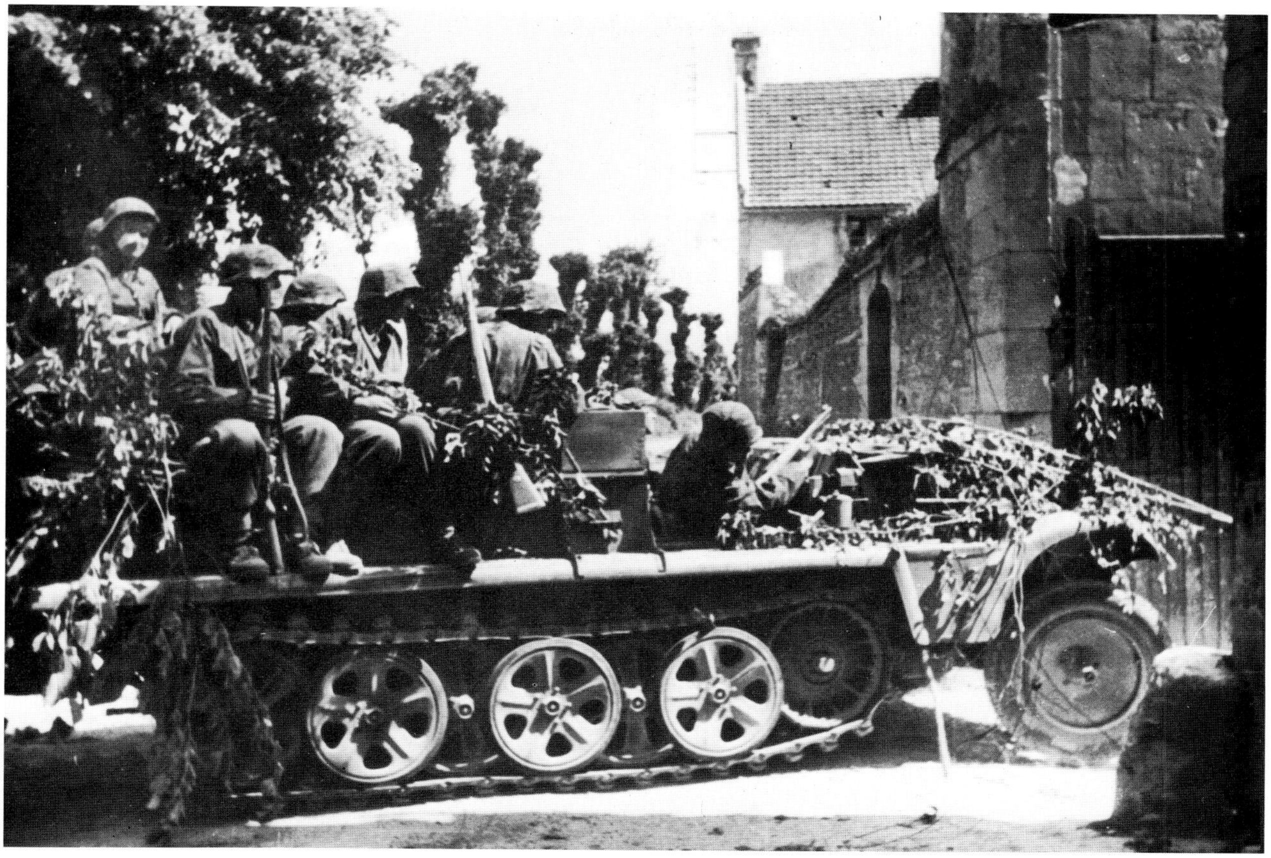

Units of the "HJ" division deployed for a counterattack near Caen.

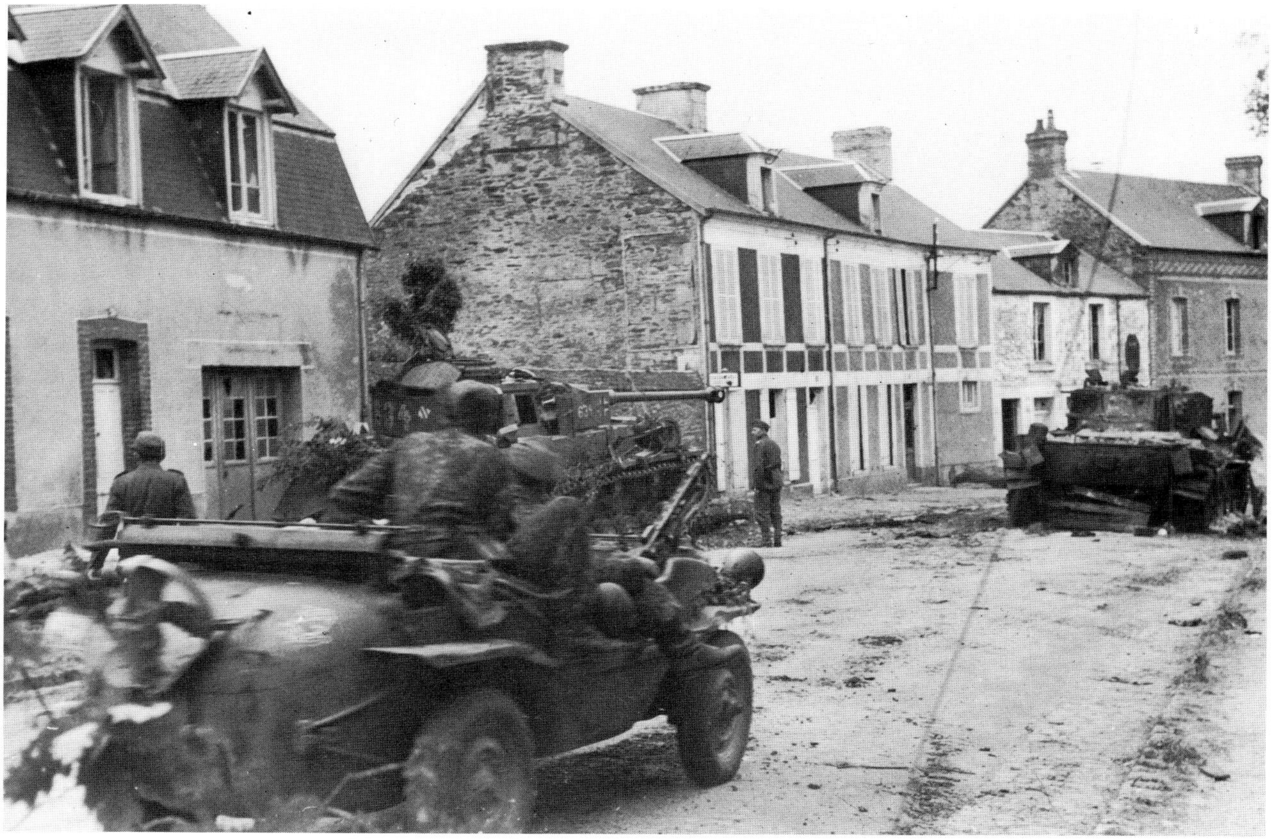

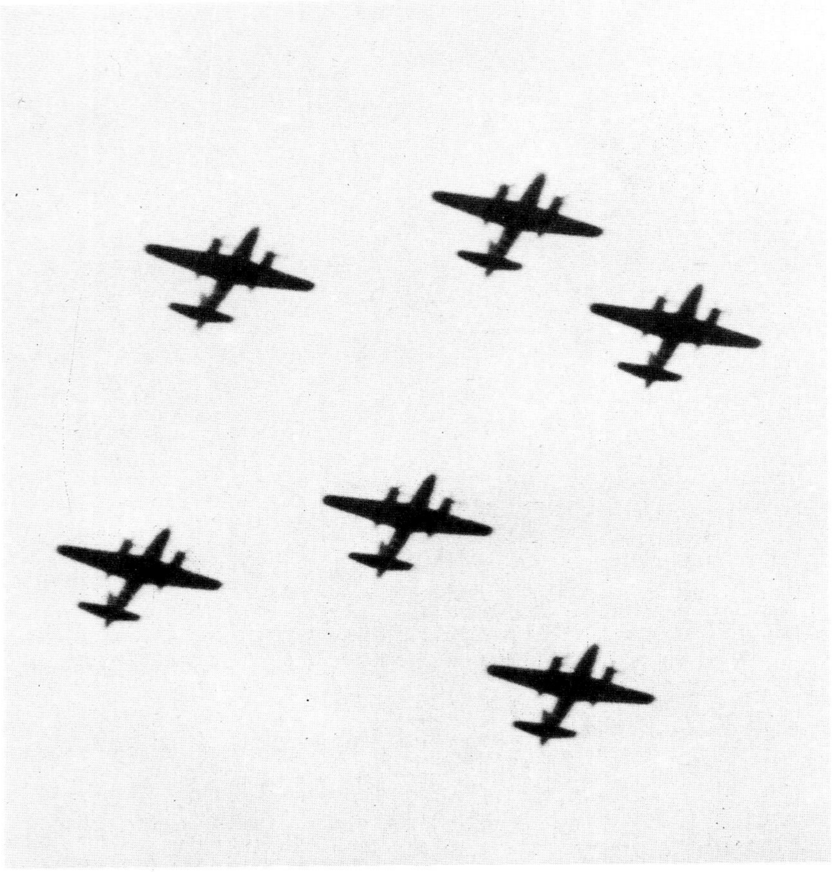

After extremely heavy bombardment and attacks by the enemy, the young infantrymen of the "HJ" division were thrown out of their positions, which they had doggedly and bravely kept for weeks.

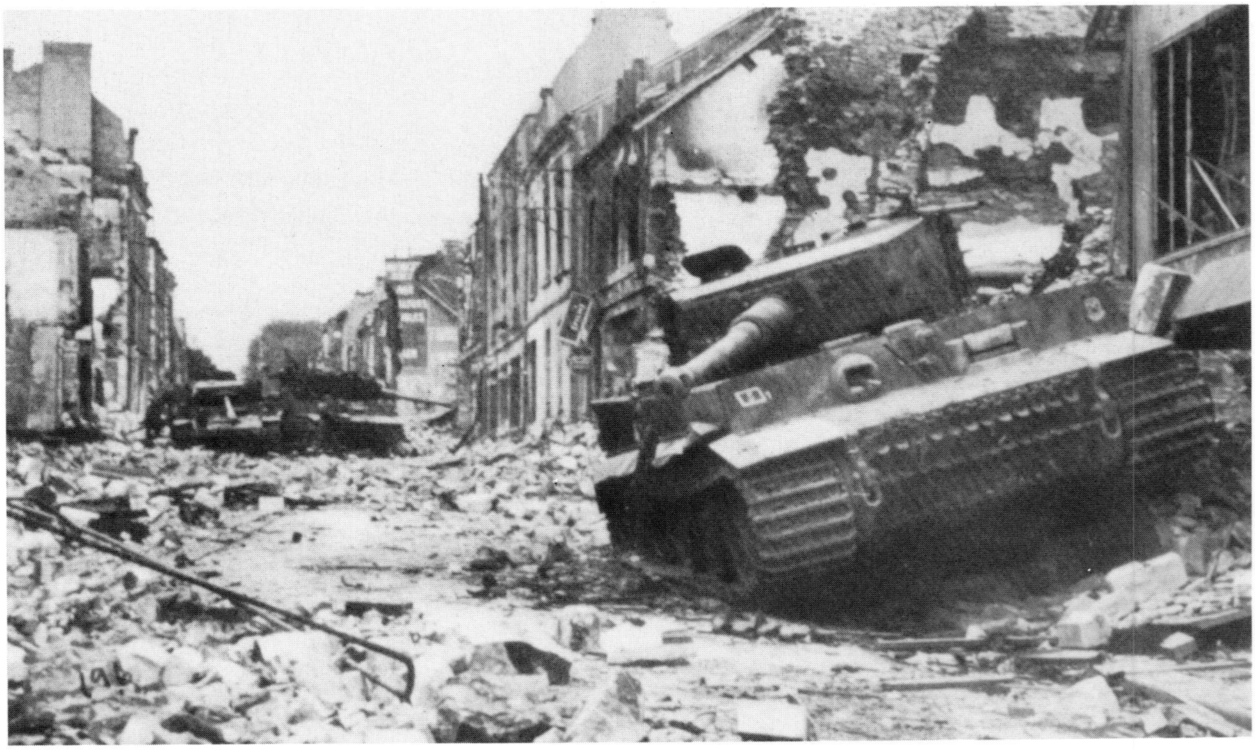

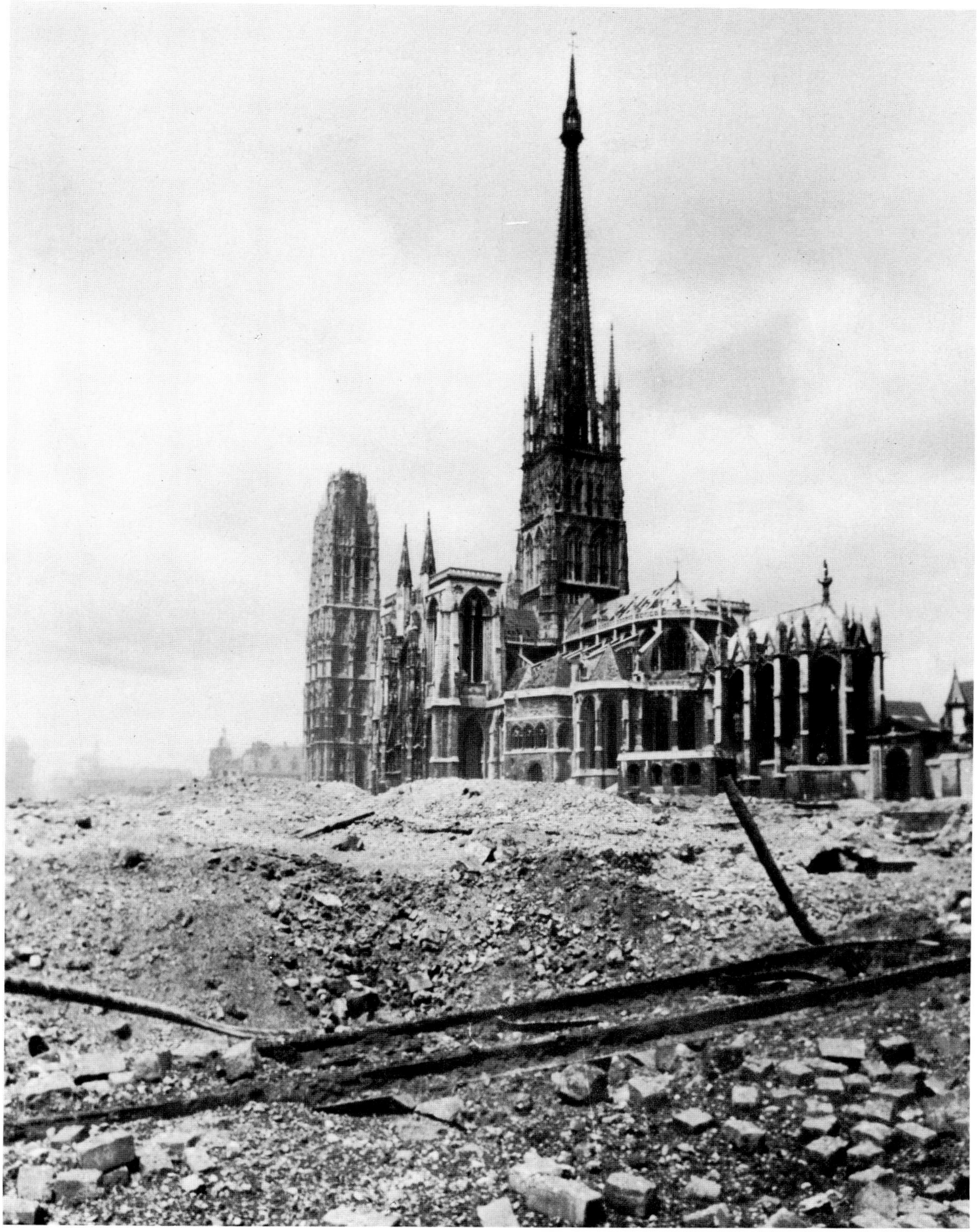
The flattened streets around the cathedral of Rouen, proved the severity of the Anglo-American air raids.

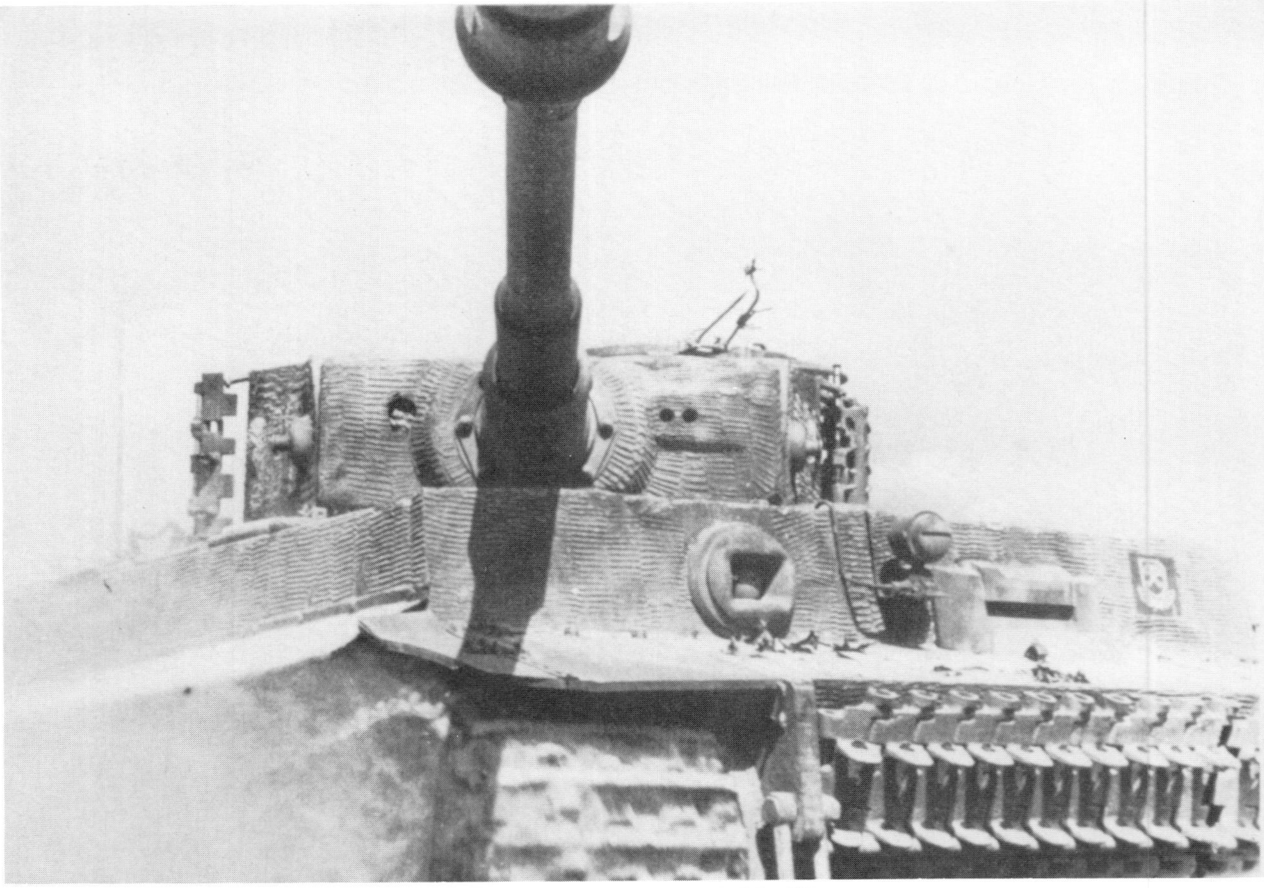

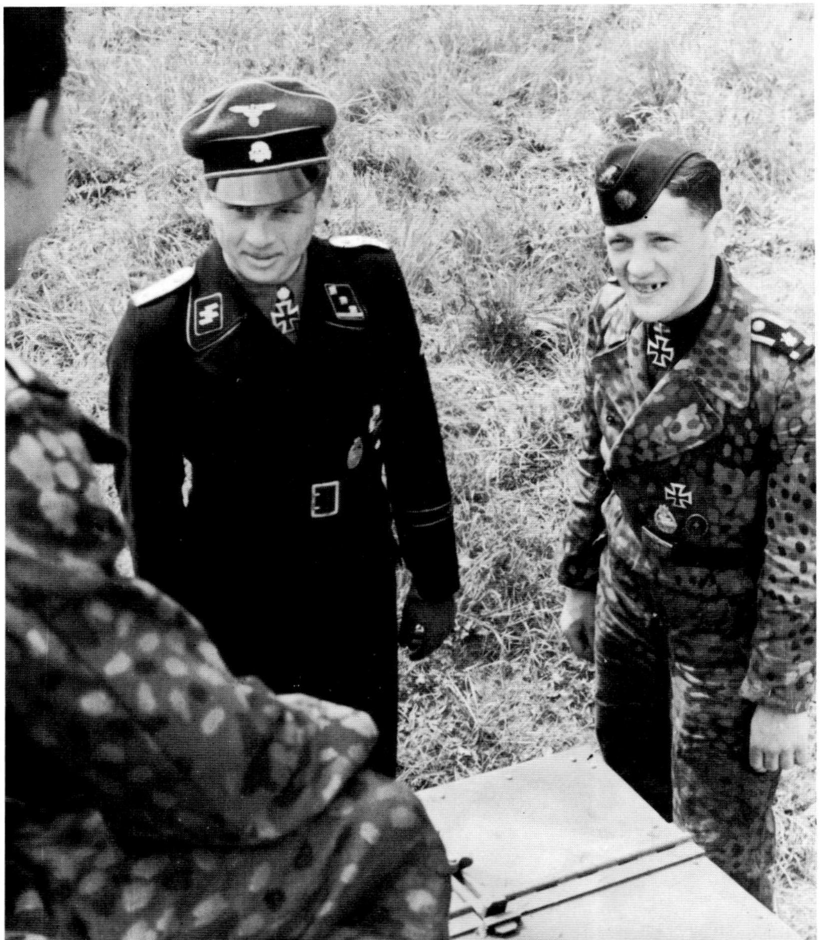

The Corps-Tiger-Abt. of the LAH in the center of the defensive battles south of Caen. Here the most successful tank commander of the Second World War, who was killed on August 8, 1944, Captain Michel Wittmann, here with his gunner Balthasar Woll, killed 138 tanks and 132 anti-tank guns.

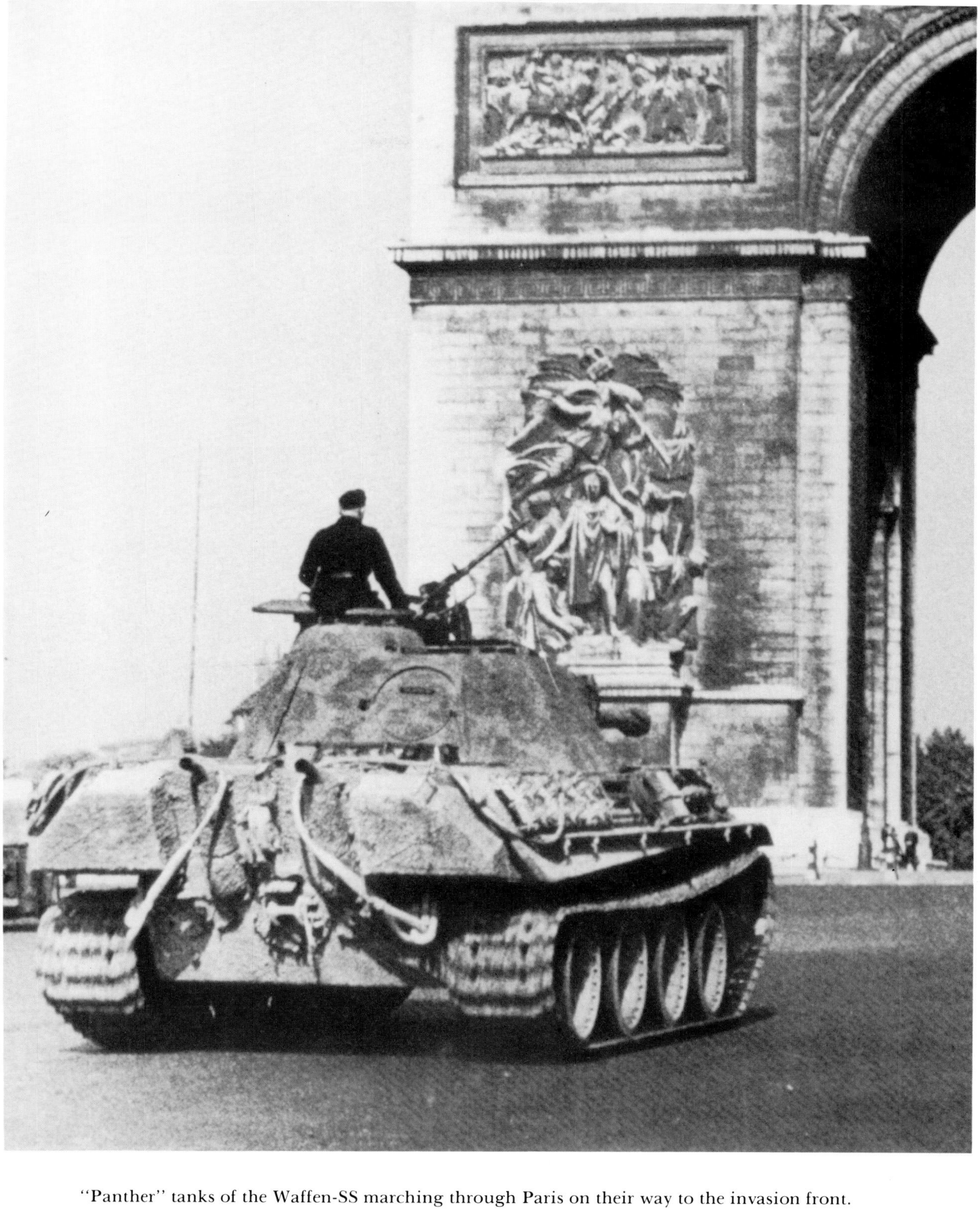

"Panther" tanks of the Waffen-SS marching through Paris on their way to the invasion front.

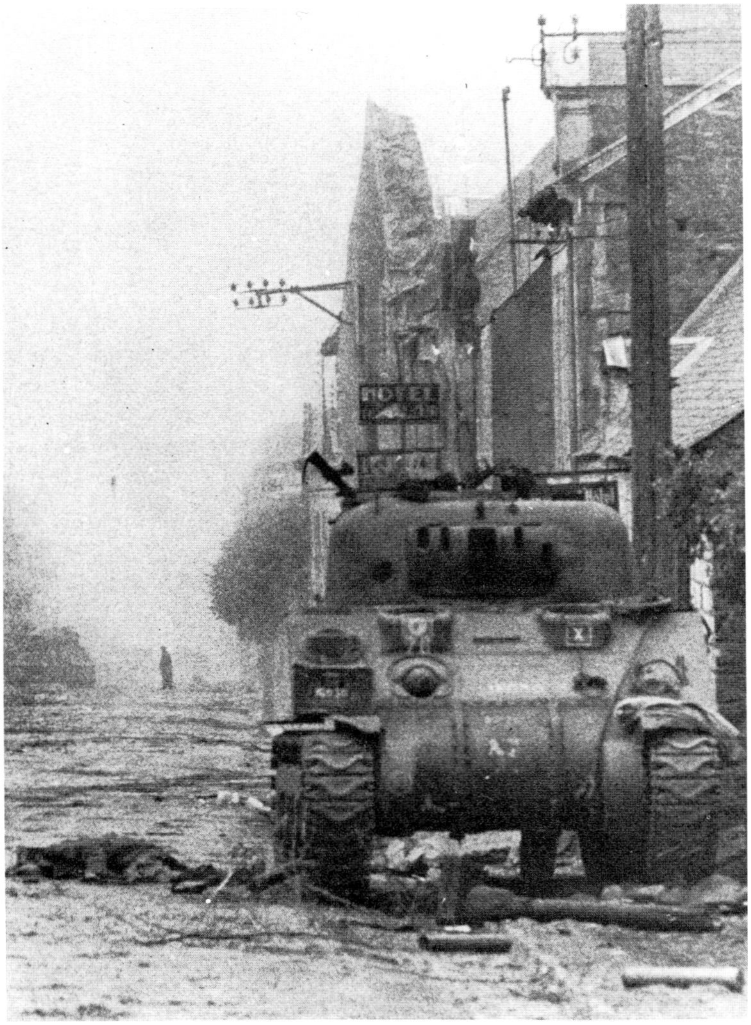

Destroyed Sherman tanks in the streets of Falaise.

Cover and camouflage against combat planes are trumps.

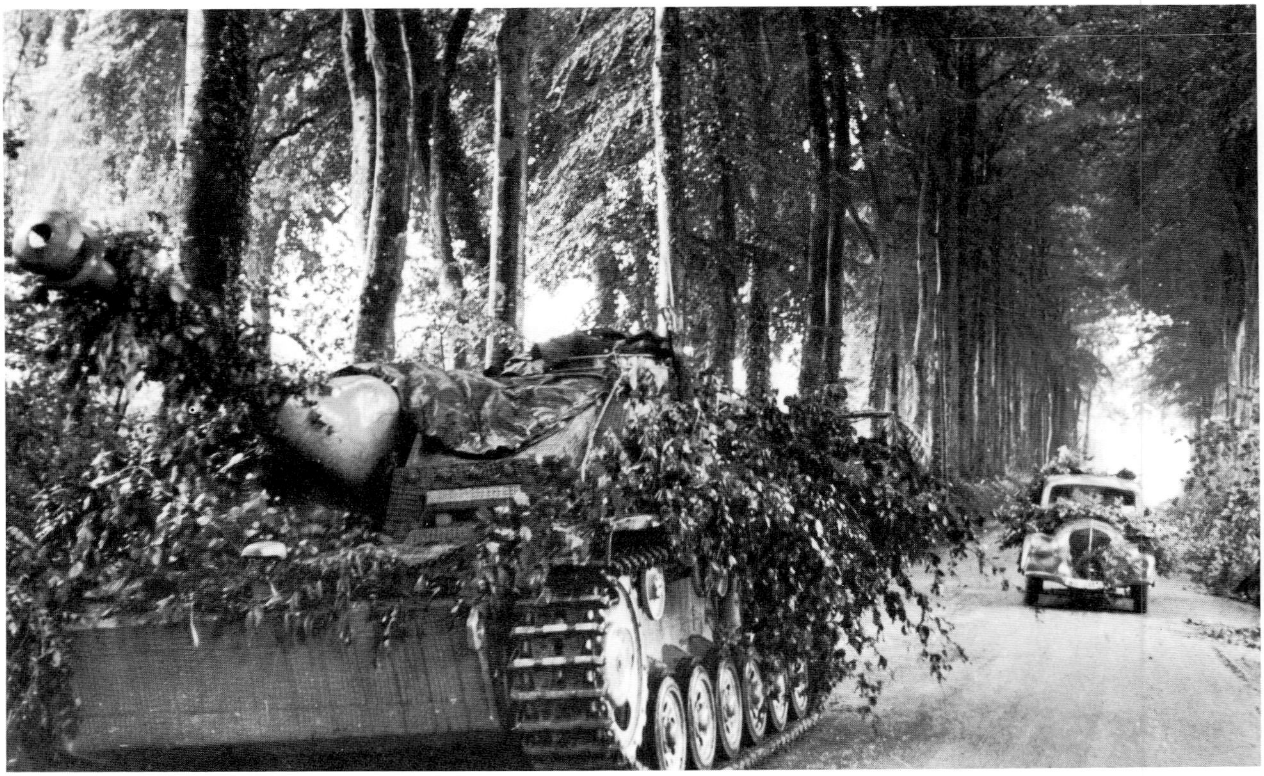

Once again combat planes have set a supply column on fire.

Geheime Kommandosache

Chefsache

Nur durch Offizier

6 Ausf.

6. Ausf.

1.7.44
18.35

Heeresgruppe B — KR-Blitz

nachr.: Lfl.Kdo. 3 — KR

" O.Qu.West — KR

Im Stabe:
IaF
Ic
V.O.Pz.
KTB
Ia (Entw.)

Bezug: 1) Ob.West röm.1a Nr. 504/44 g.Kdos.Ch. vom 1.7.44
2) An H.Gru.B u. Lfl.3 mit Ob.West röm.1a Nr.505/44 g.K.Ch. vom 1.7.44
3) OKW/WFSt/Op.(H)/West (gez.Jodl.)Nr.772243/44 g.K.Ch.v.1.7.44

" Der Führer hat entschieden :

Die augenblicklichen Stellungen sind zu halten. Durch zähe Verteidigung oder durch örtliche Gegenangriffe ist jeder weitere feindliche Durchbruch zu verhindern. Der Aufmarsch ist fortzusetzen, weitere schnelle Verbände durch herankommende Inf.Divn. freizumachen. Näherer Befehl folgt. "

Zusatz Ob.West :

Absetzbewegungen sind nicht durchzuführen.

Der Oberbefehlshaber West

Generalfeldmarschall

röm.1a Nr. 509/44 g.Kdos.Ch.

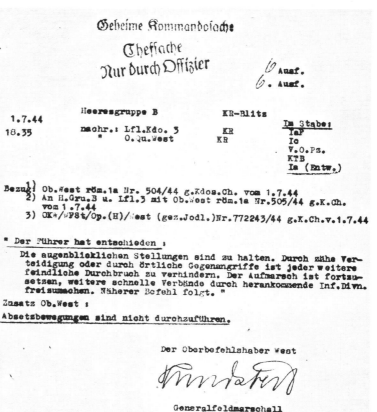

A "Führer's order", which tells its own tale: "Hold out at all costs".

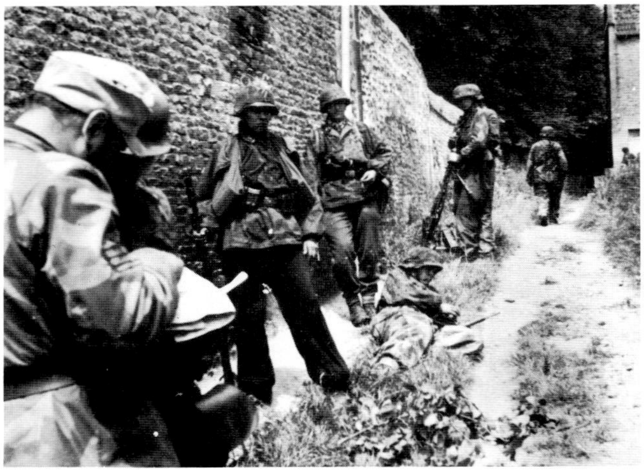

Combat group commander Major K.H. Prinz preparing a counterthrust near Caen.

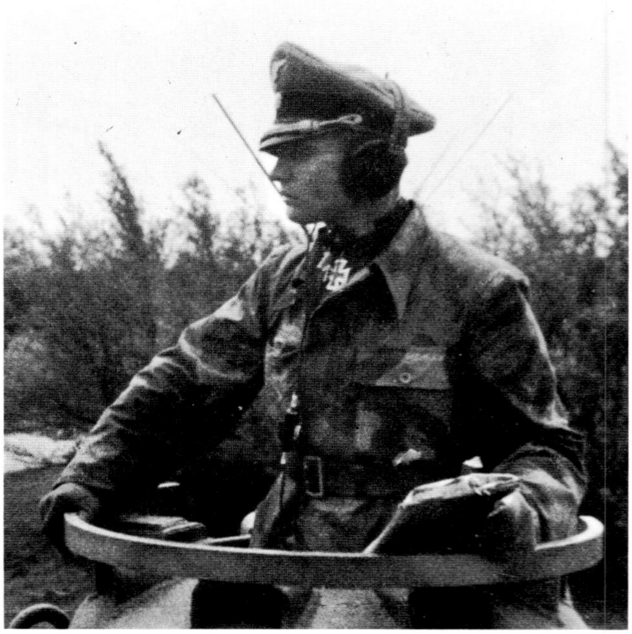

Lt. Colonel Max Wünsche, Cdr. SS-tank regiment 12 "HJ" in his command tank.

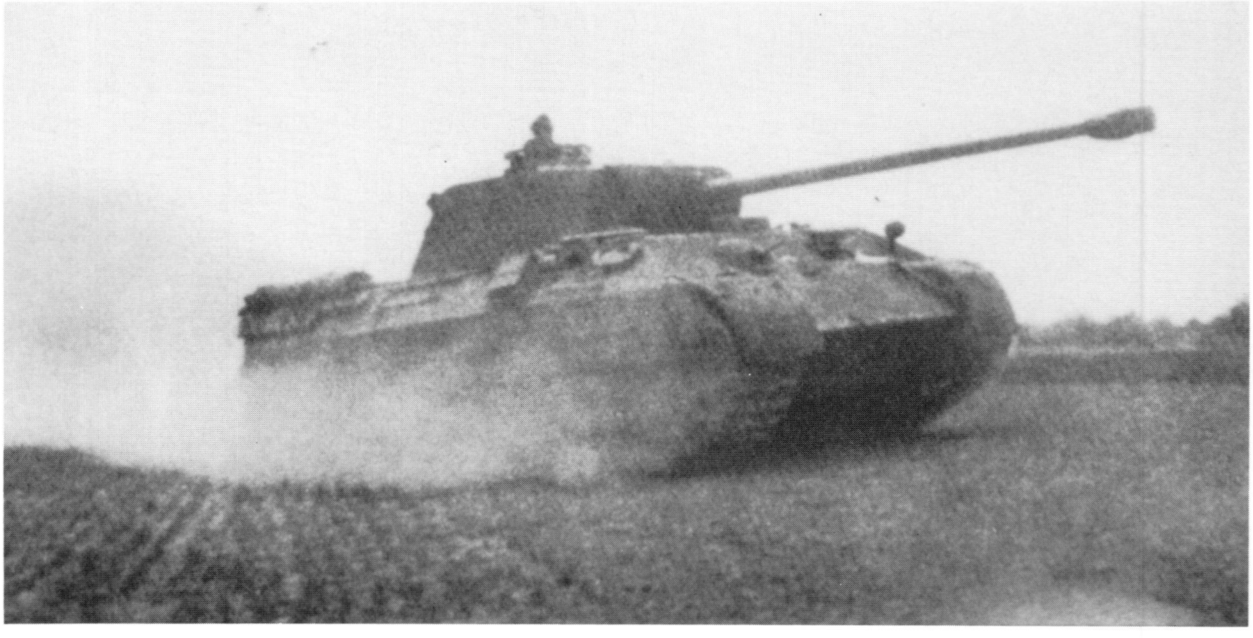

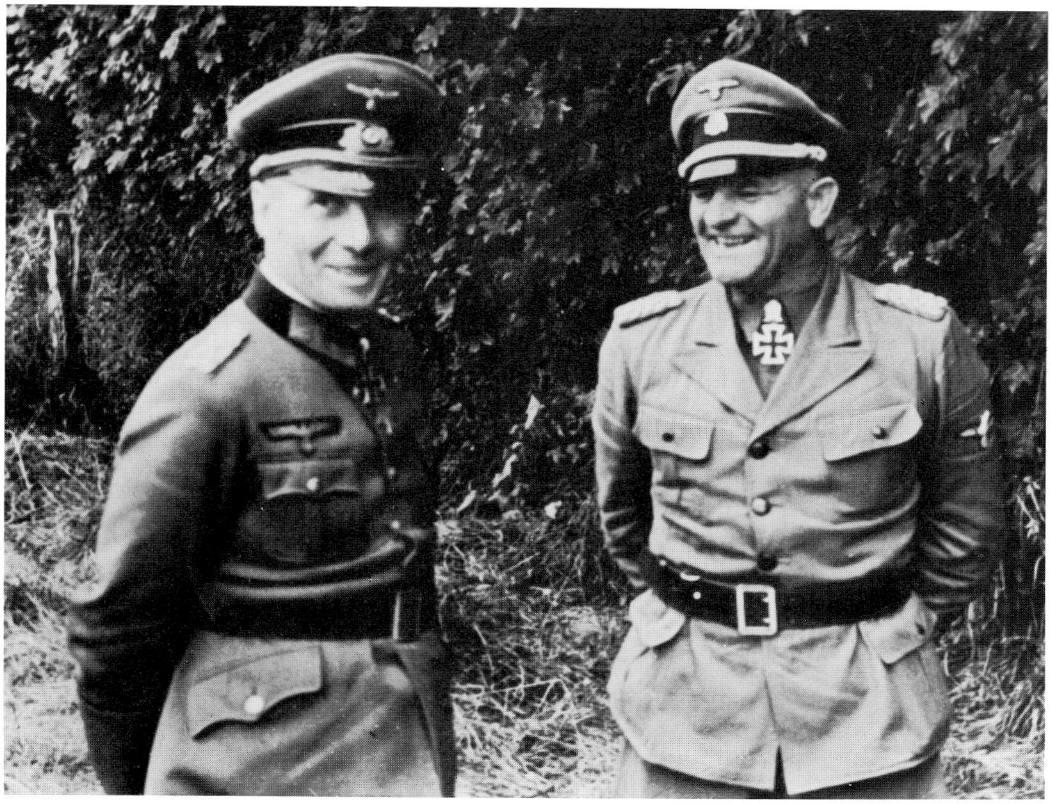

SS Lt. General Sepp Dietrich at his last meeting with GFM Rommel, who was wounded soon after.

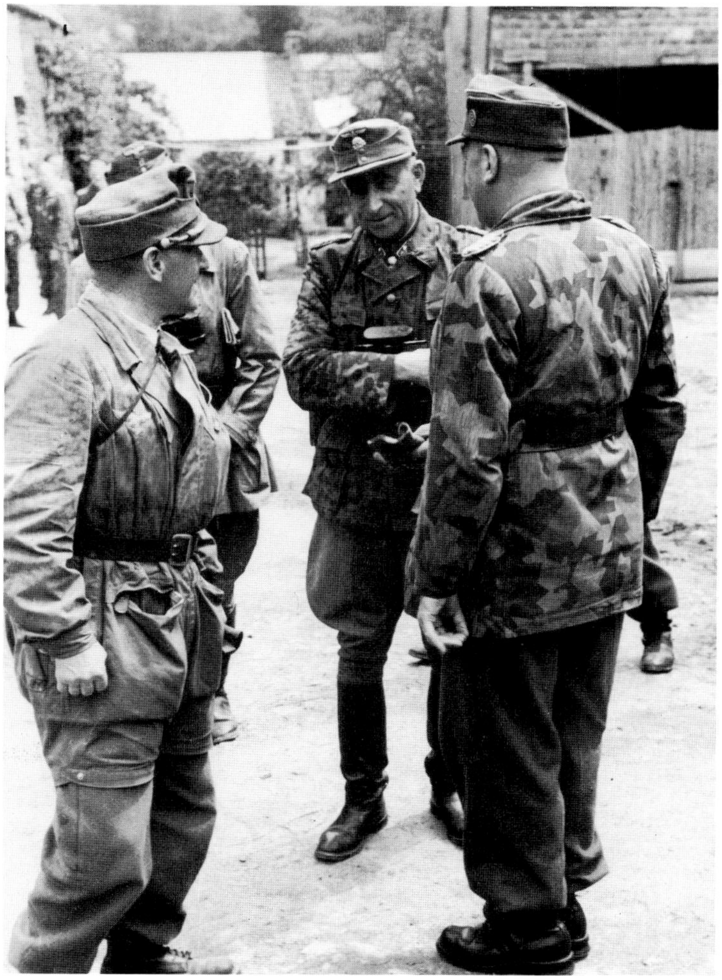

SS Lt. General Paul Hausser in a conference with paratrooper general Meindl (on the left).

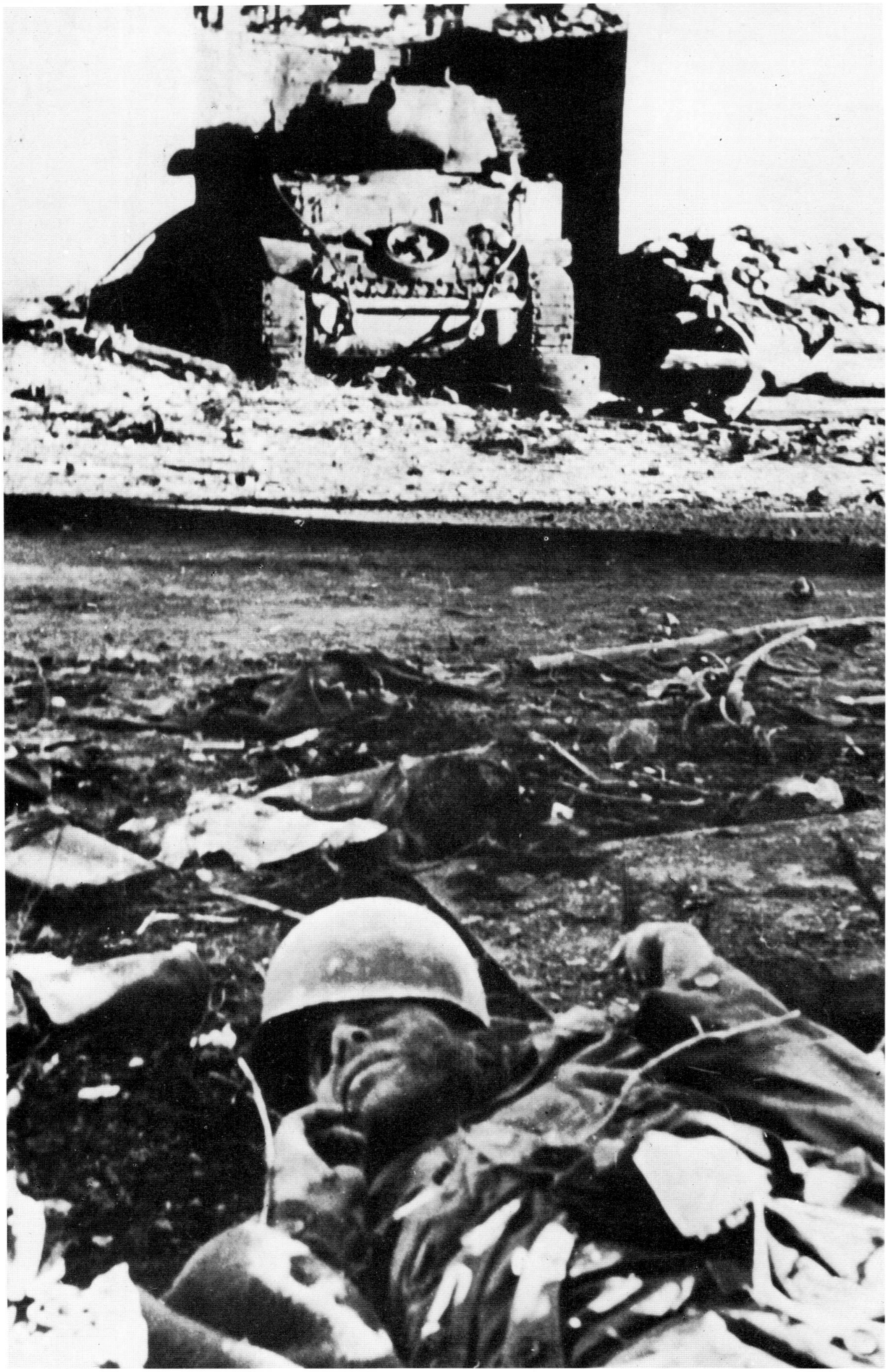

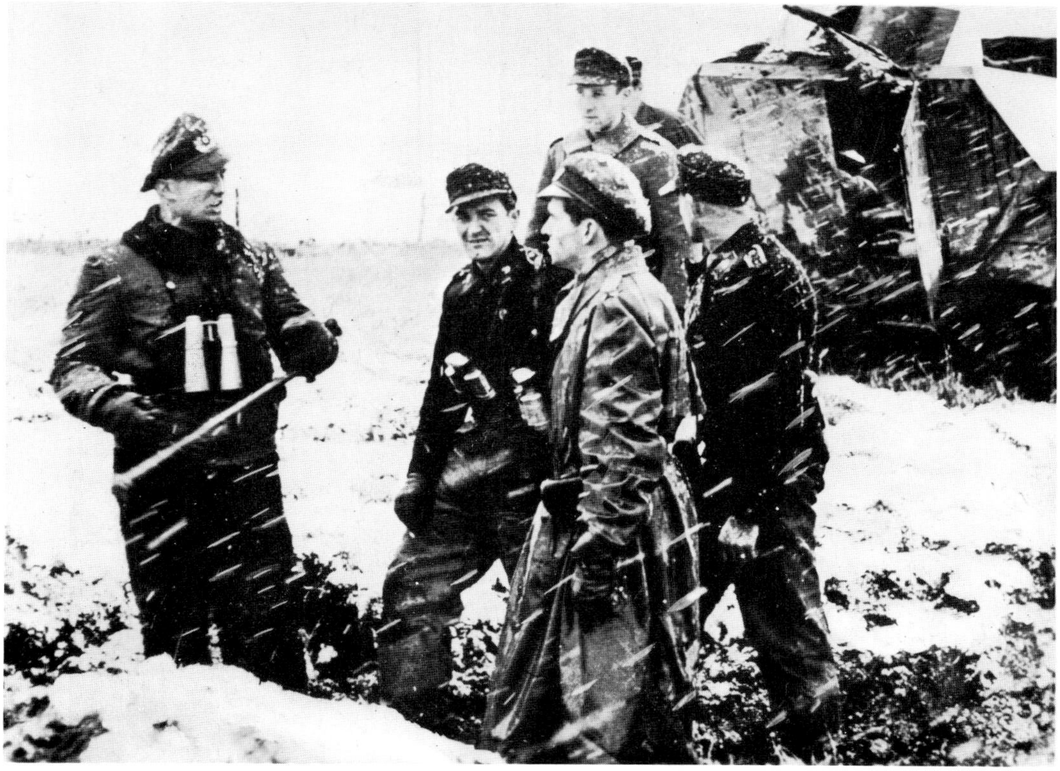

December 1944: The offensive in the Ardennes: It is the last attempt to take the initiative once again in the west.

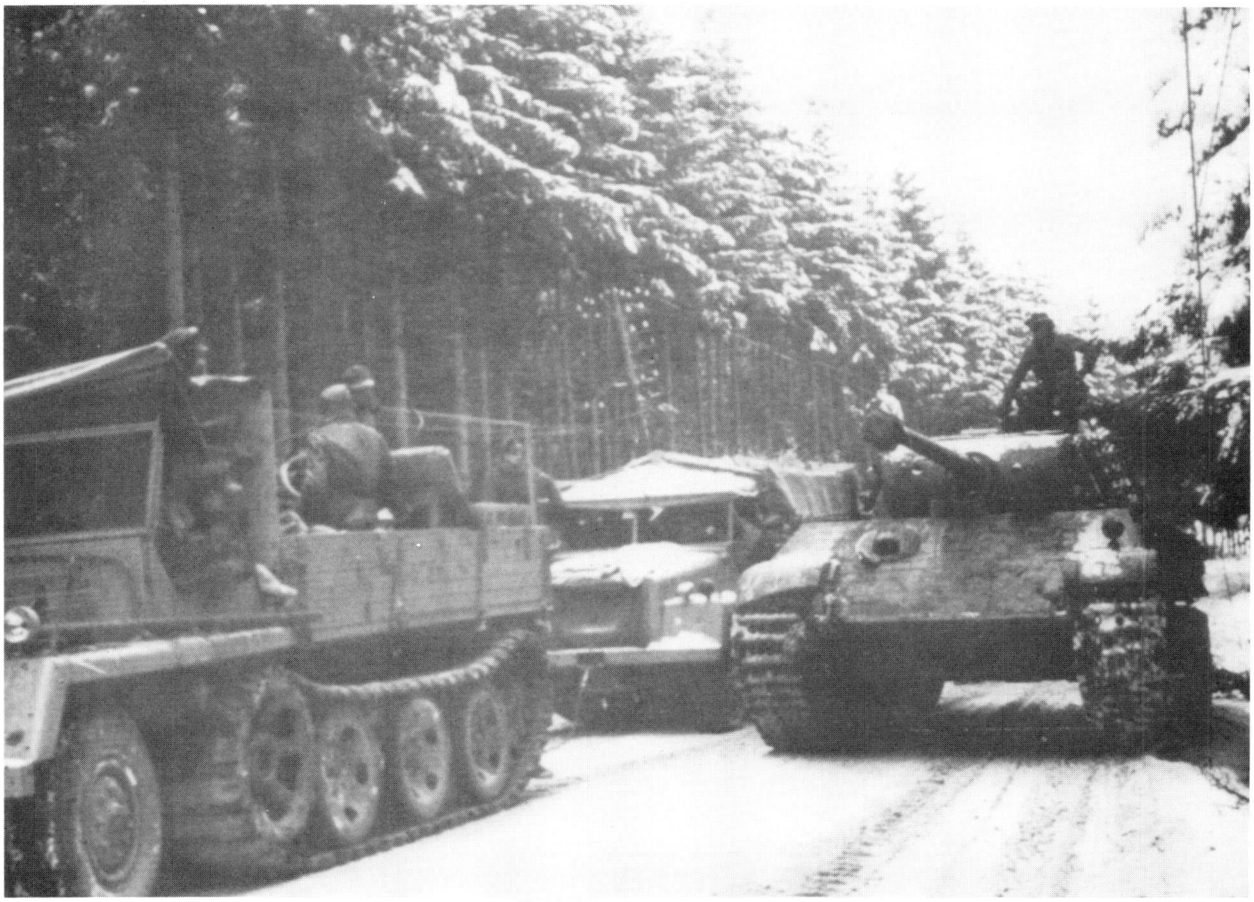

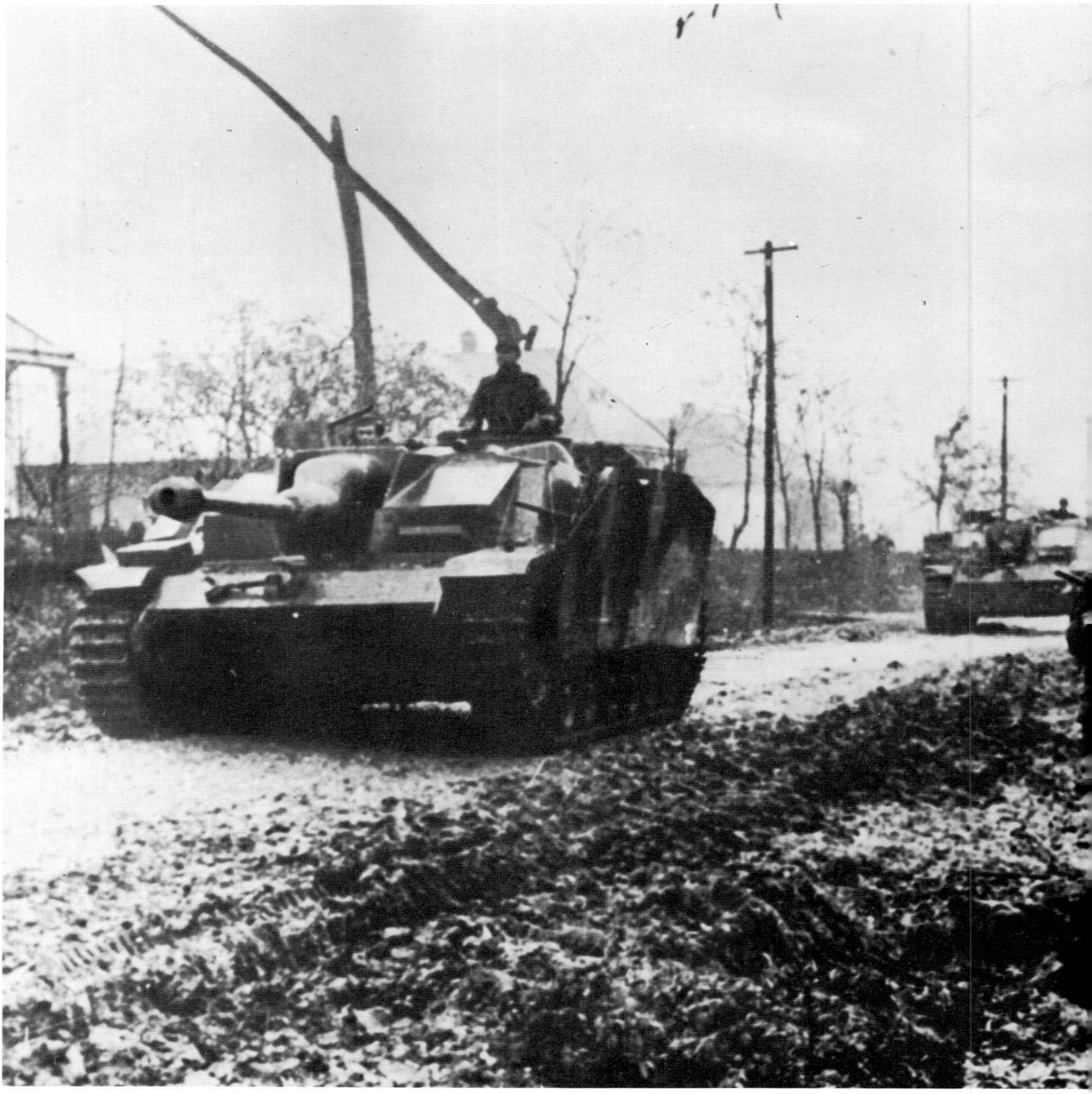

The Ardennes offensive: Self-propelled assault guns advance. The operation failed to be a success a few days later.

# THE WINTER OF 1944-45

The last winter of the war had come. As early as late autumn, the war moved into East Prussia, and if the situation seemed to stabilize somewhat in December of 1944, no one was deluded; they knew the Red Army had just stopped to catch its breath. Hitler refused to reduce the fronts; he wanted to know that every square meter of ground was being defended. This applied to the whole overextended German front in the East, which stretched from the Straits of Courland through Poland to the Carpathians over a length of 1200 kilometers. On January 12, 1945 the Soviet offensive began. At 1:30 A.M., 32,000 Russian guns of all calibers fired on the positions of the German divisions at the Baranov bridgehead. The 34 Russian rifle and 8 armored divisions rolled over the thin German front and stormed toward the Oder and northward in the direction of Graudenz and Danzig.

On January 19 the Soviets crossed the border of Silesia. The path to Germany lay open for the Red Army, no matter how hard the Waffen-SS units fought beside the army units to try and stem the flow.

In the West the Allied forces had succeeded in crossing the Rhine after the failed Ardennes Offensive and were moving eastward. The death agony of the Reich began.

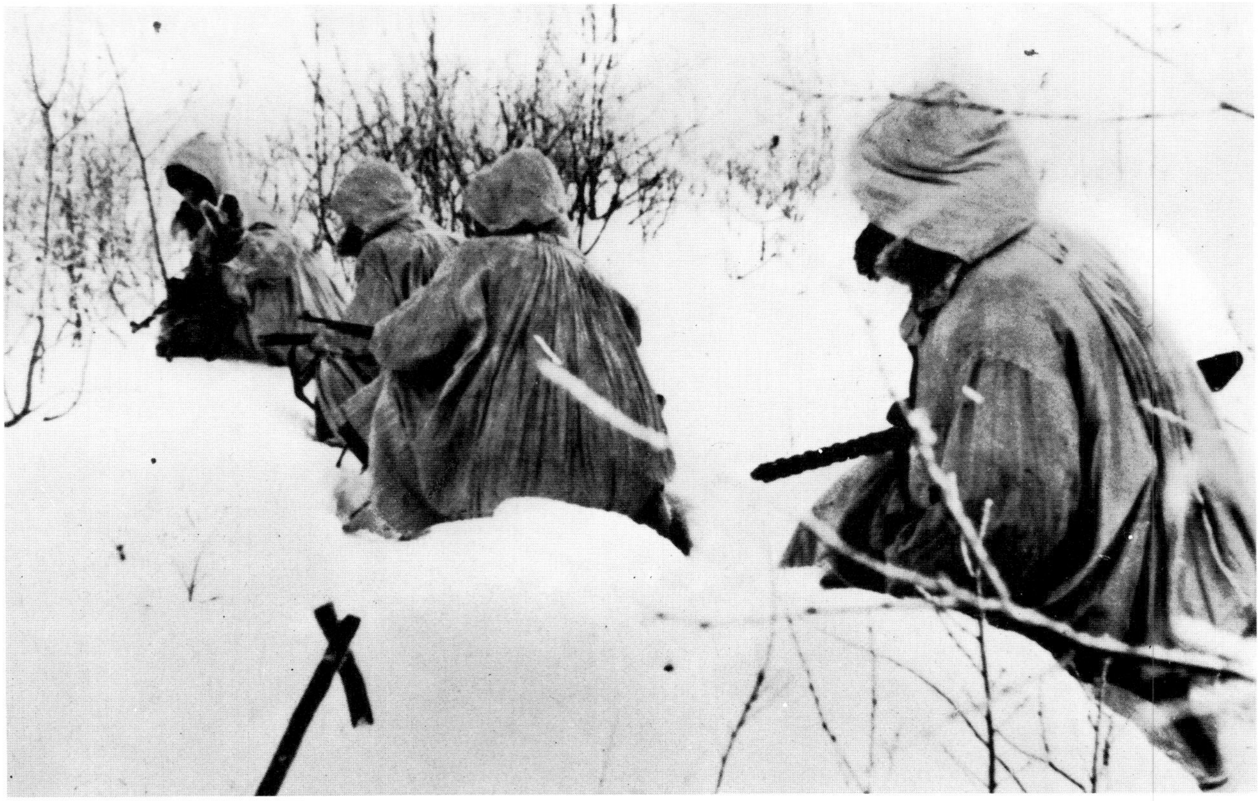

In the northern sector of the eastern front. A reconnaissance troop gropes its way to the Russian positions.

The harshness of the battles and exhaustion is written on everyone's face. On the right: Lt. Colonel Hans Dorr, Cdr. SS-Pz. Grenadier Rgt.9 "Germania" in the 5th SS-Pz. division "Wiking". Dorr was killed in Austria in April 1945.

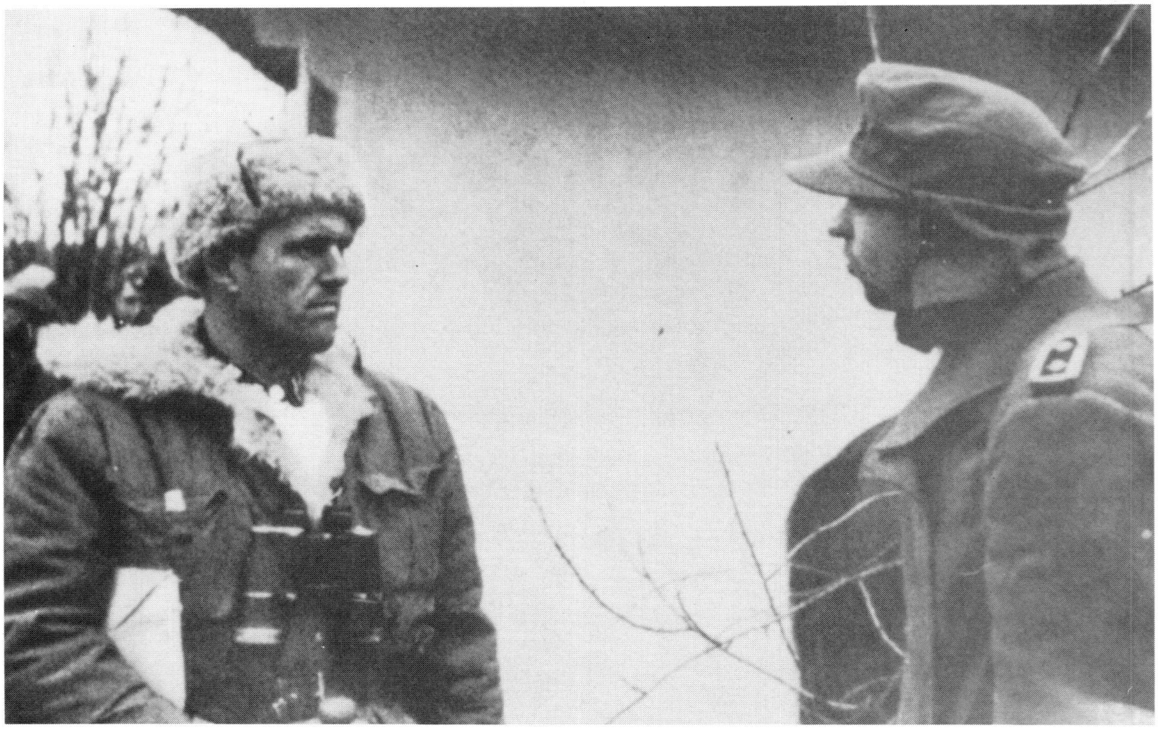

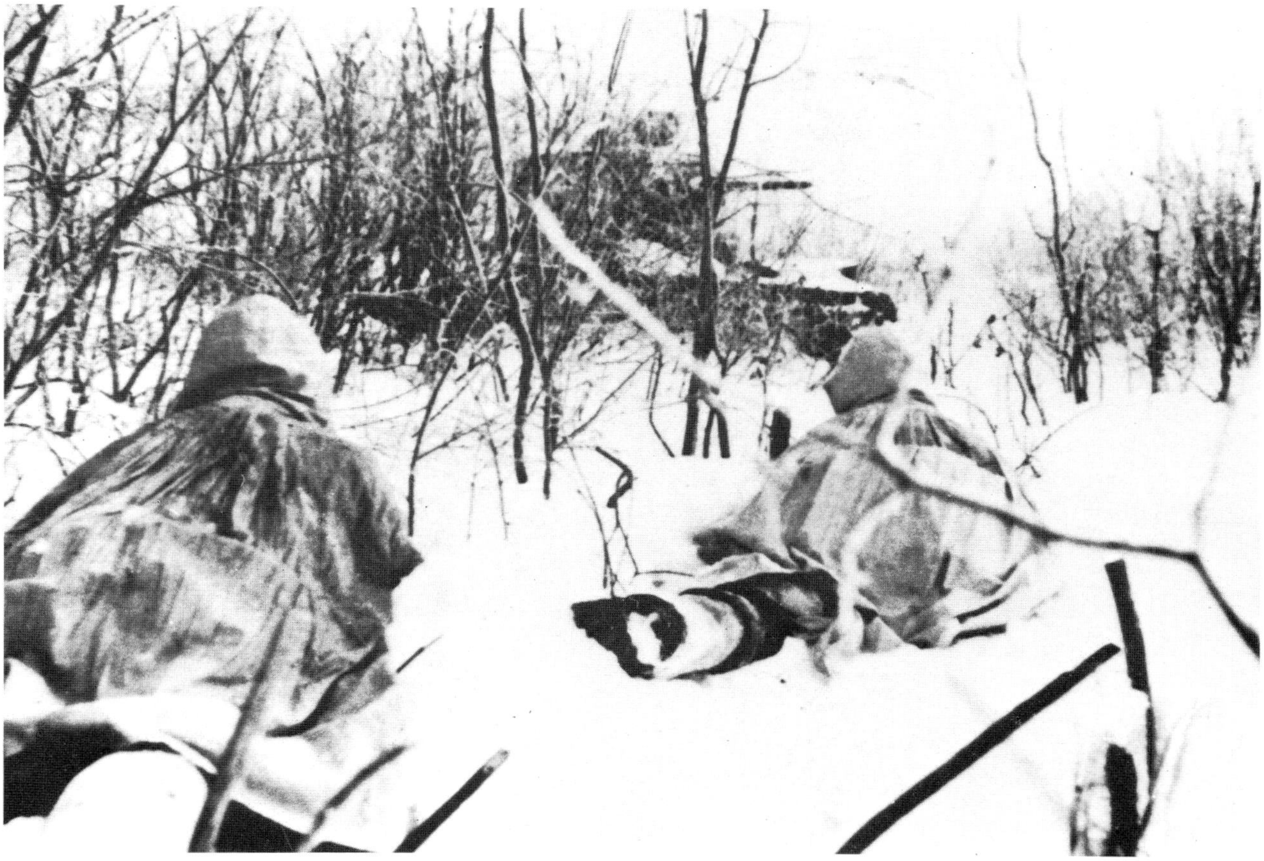

SS-infantrymen have to let the attacking Russian tanks through their own defensive lines, because their armor-piercing weapons often are not available. But where anti-tank and anti-aircraft guns are used, the Soviets suffer heavy losses.

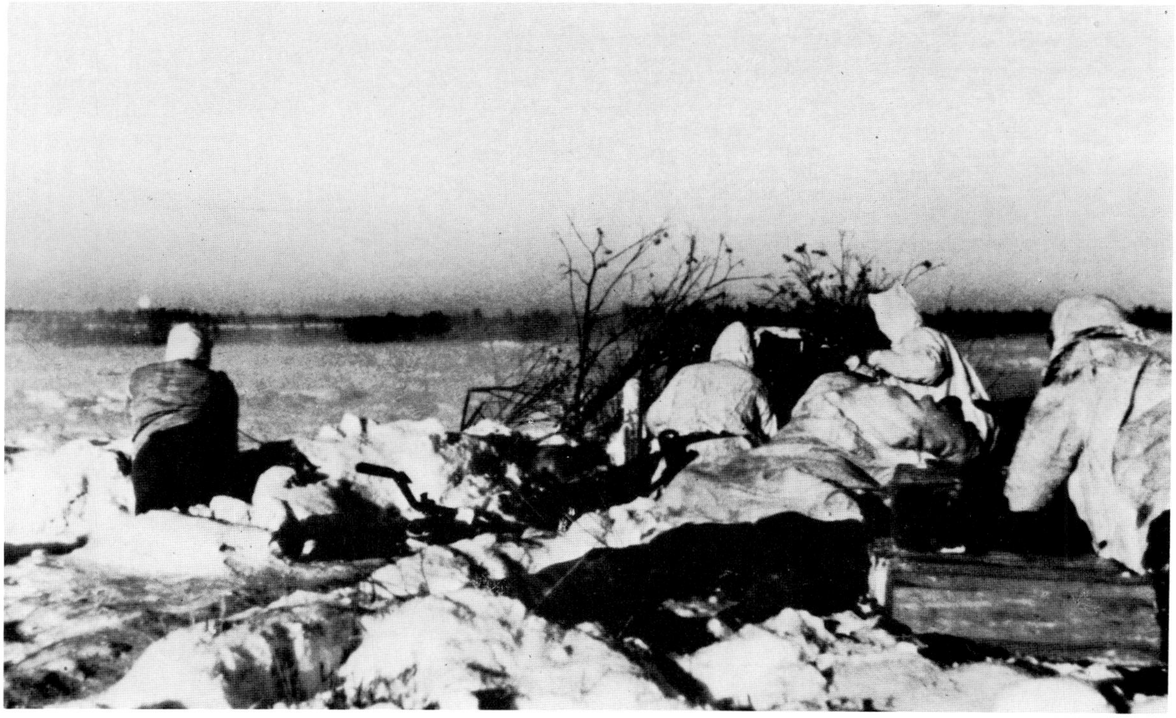

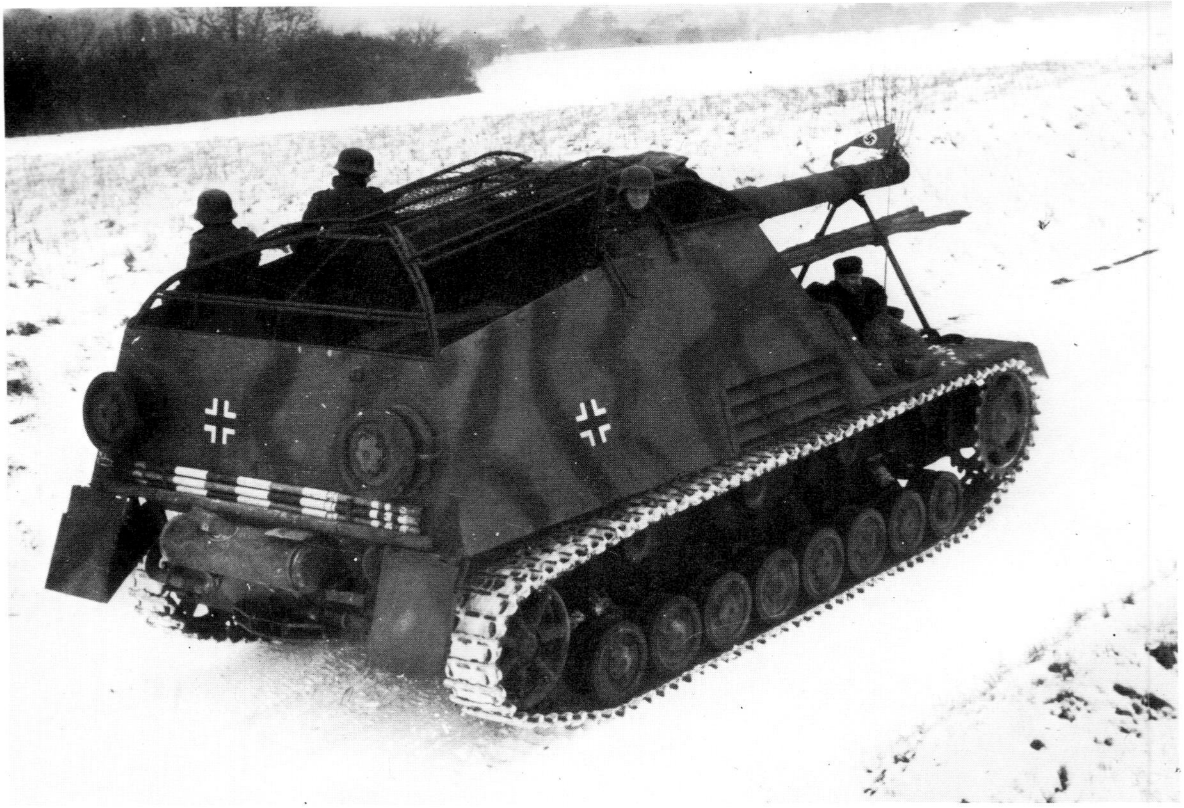

"Hummeln" ("Bumble Bees") tanks have arrived at the front and quickly bring relief to threatened front sectors.

Concentration for a counterthrust in the middle sector of the east front.

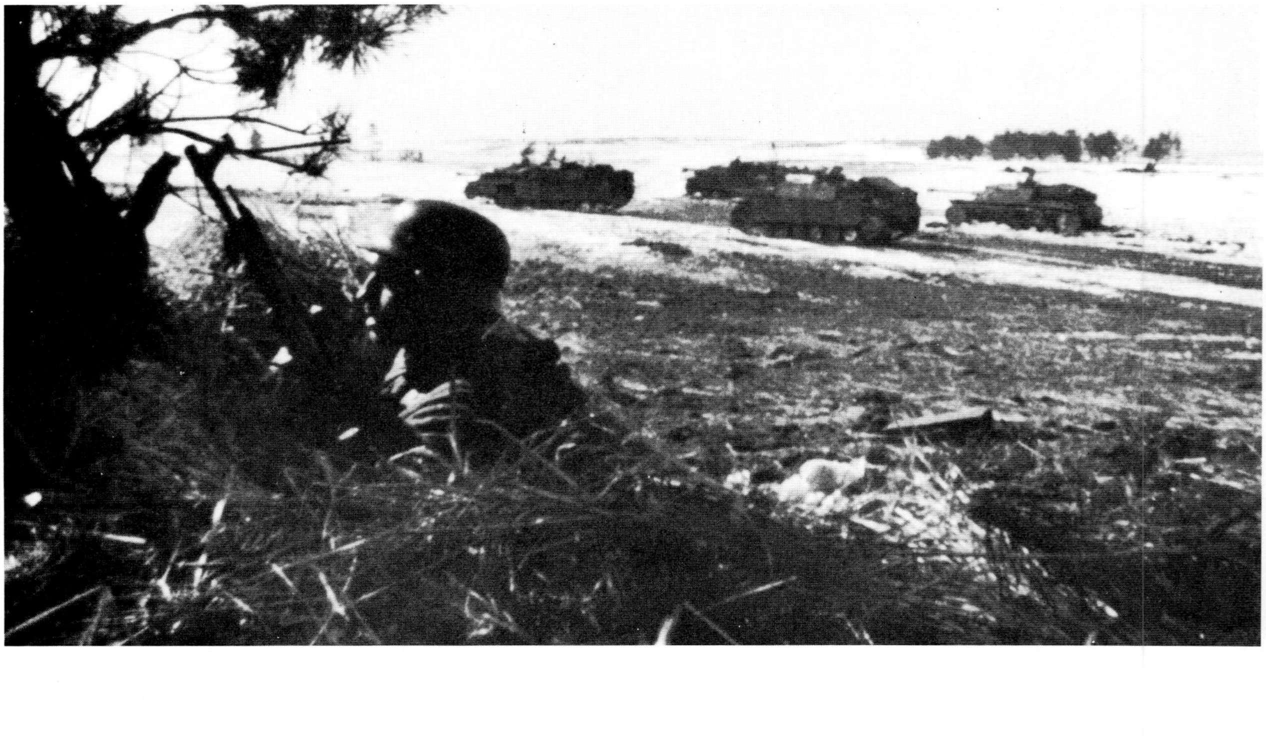

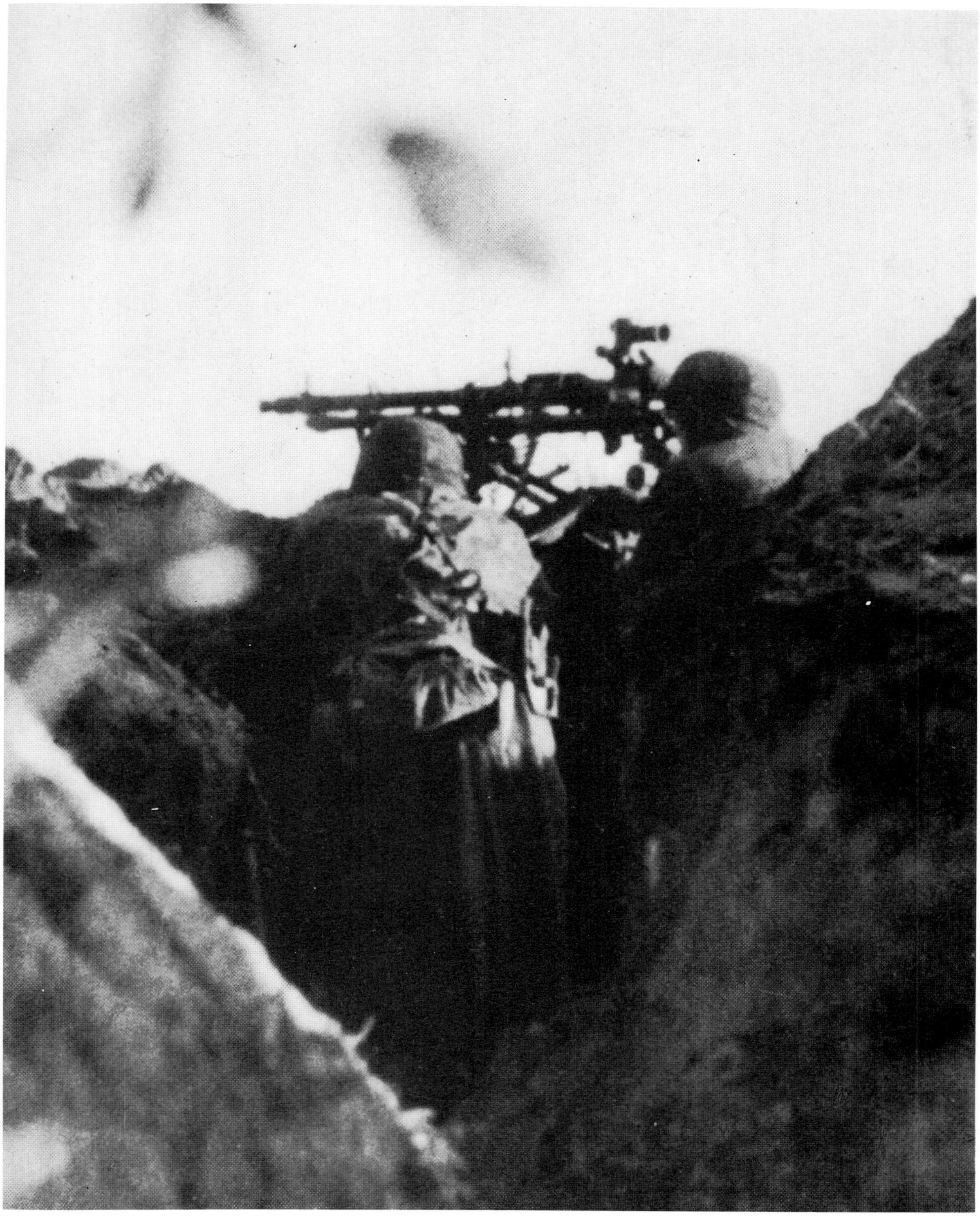

The infantrymen are continuously in action against Russian tanks which attack incessantly. No break for them.

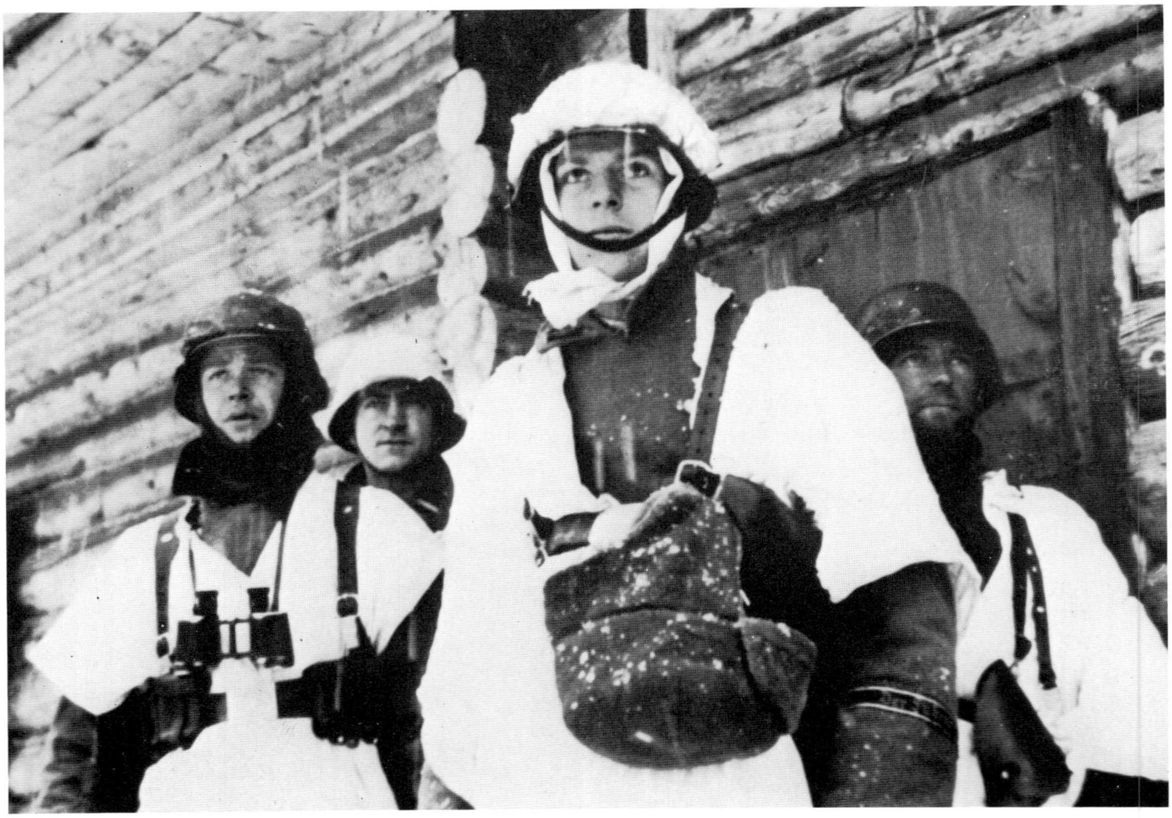

Infantrymen of the regiment "Der Führer" have broken free of the enemy and await the pursuing Soviets.

During these weeks of retreat hastily thrown up snow walls are often the only fortifications.

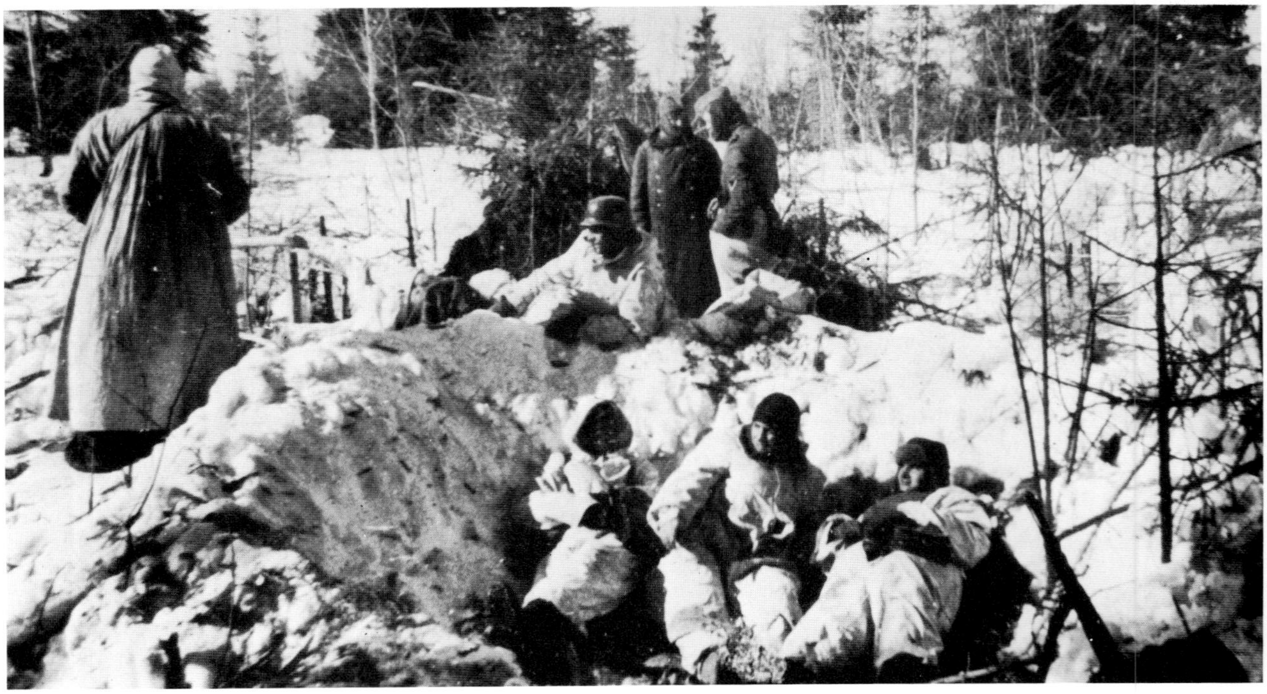

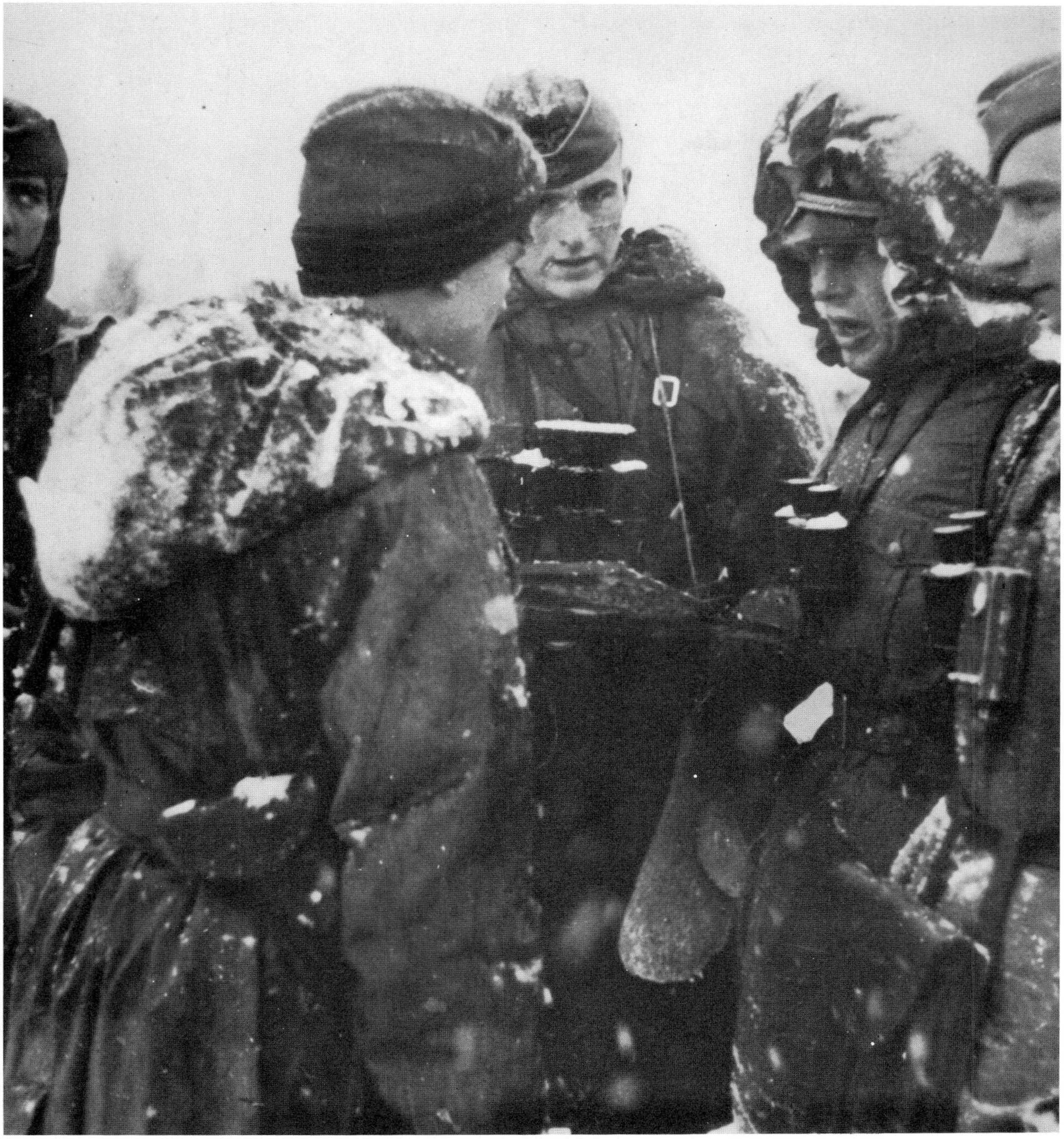

A SS-cavalry division discusses a counterthrust, which is supposed to bring relief at least for some days to the front which is retreating all the time.

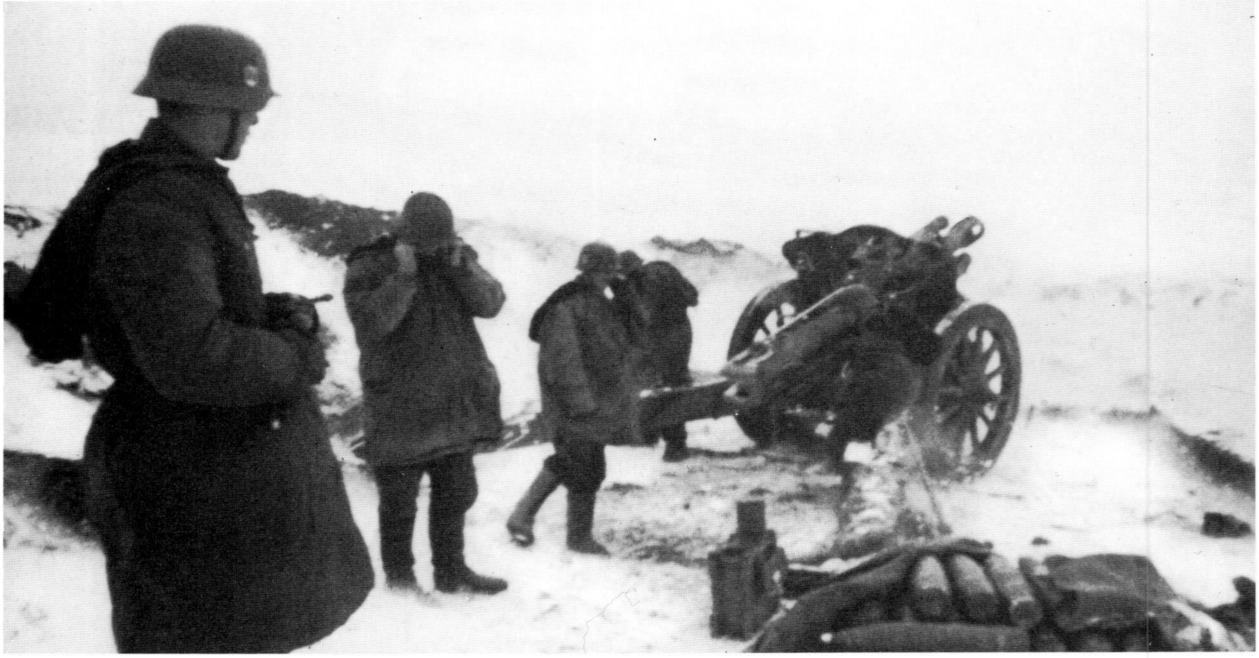

Ammunition has been rationed long since. Shooting is only allowed in states of extreme emergency, or on explicit orders.

A sniper fighting against infiltrating Russian reconnaissance troops in the northern sector of the front.

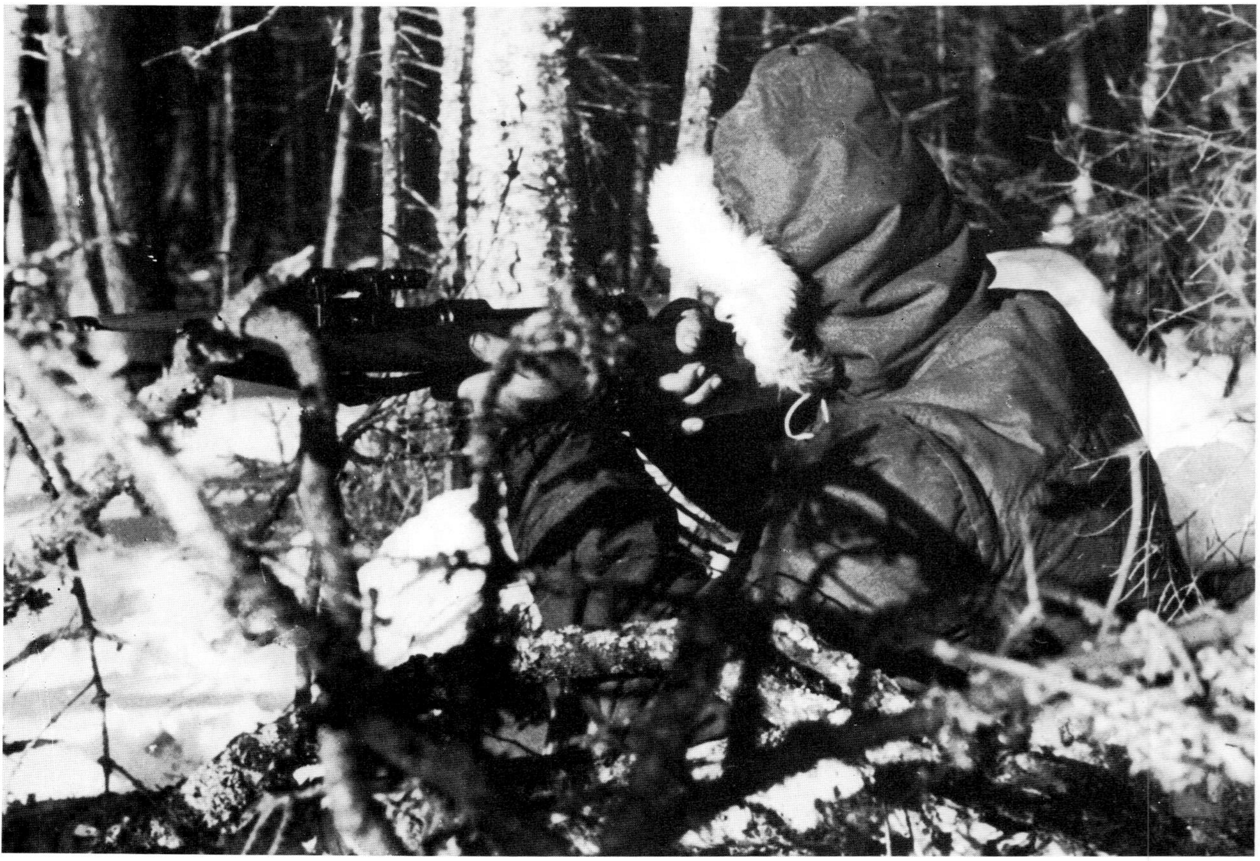

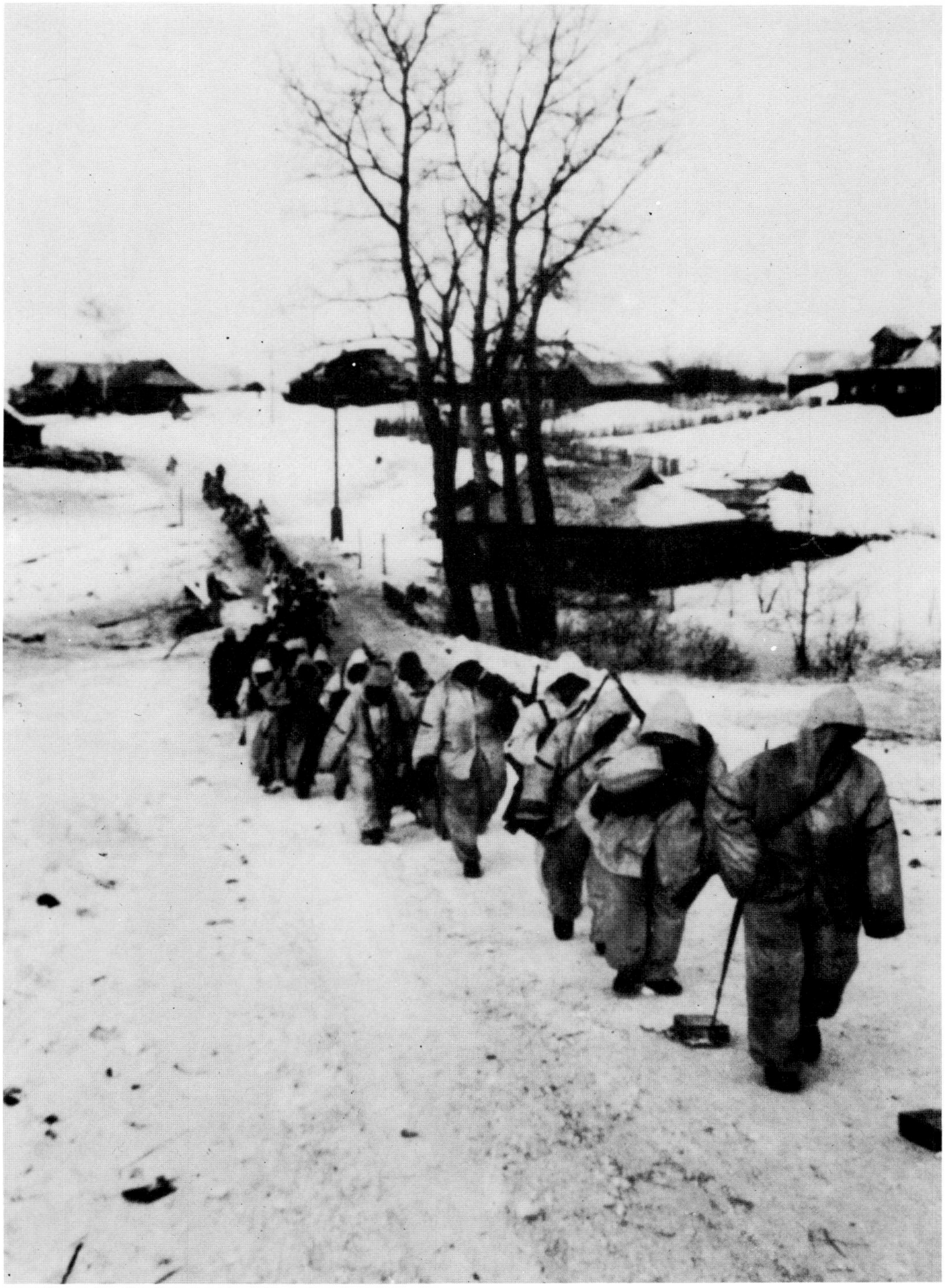

And then the order is again: Retreat. The battalions have shrunk. Long since the infantrymen have lost their illusions.

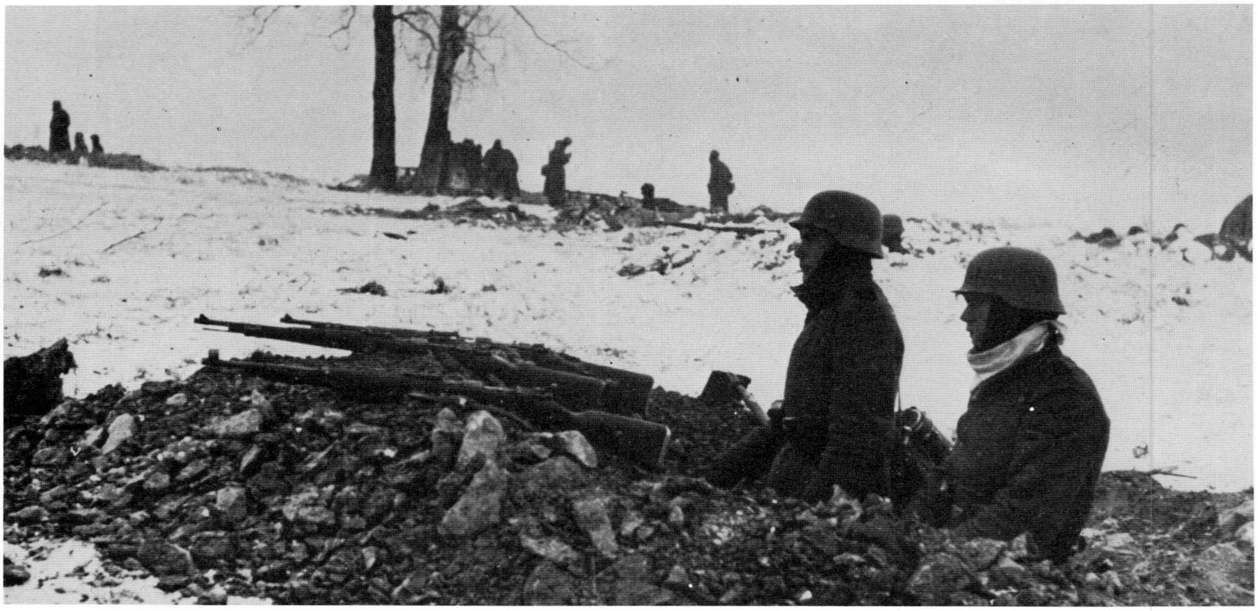

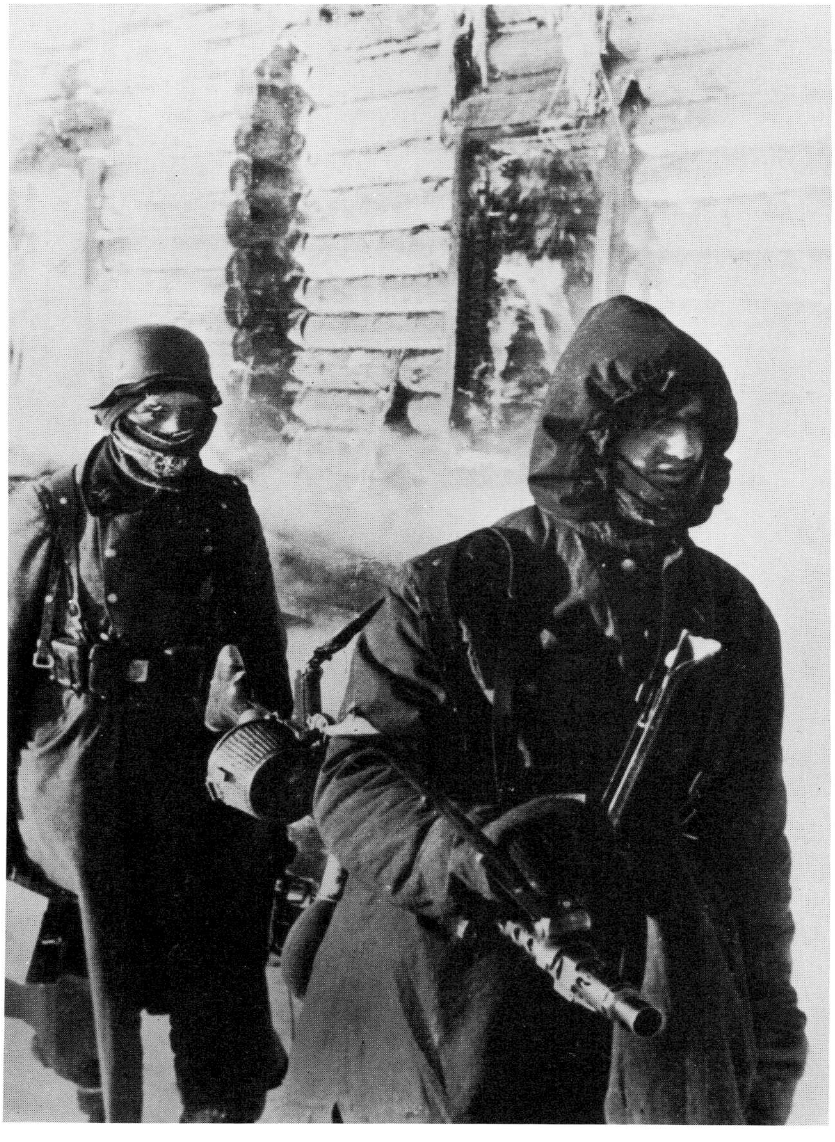

Somewhere in the middle sector on Polish ground. Shallow holes were dug in the hard frozen earth. The infantrymen are on the look-out. Soon the first soldiers of the Red Army will appear...

...and then fighting again and retreating from an overwhelming superior force.

# THE FINAL BATTLE IN THE REICH

On January 12, 1945 the Red Army opened its last, decisive attack on German territory. From the great bend of the Vistula, the Russian Army moved against the weakened and exhausted German units; they shattered the thin main battle lines on the very first day and pushed far into the hinterlands. The Waffen-SS units defended themselves, as did the army units, against the superior Russian forces with their last will to fight. Steadily attacked, torn apart and smashed, battle groups united again and again to put up a determined resistance in places. Constant retreat fighting, high losses, the danger of being surrounded, lacking ammunition and support and knowing they were hopelessly inferior to an enemy who had become overwhelmingly strong, these factors characterized the last weeks and months of the war. Only few pictures from those times are available. In this hell of the final battle, who thought about taking pictures? In Hungary as well as the Yugoslavian area, during the last efforts of the Ardennes Offensive in the West, in the fighting in East Prussia, Pomerania and Brandenburg, as in the bitter fight for Silesia, and not least in Berlin and Vienna: the soldiers of the Waffen-SS stood their ground with their divisions or battle groups to the end. Many a refugee from the East owes it to the Waffen-SS that he was able to flee from the Red Army. Along with the soldiers of the army, bound by their oath, damned to wage a hopeless battle to the bitter end, the SS men experienced the apocalypse of the last battle. Many of them fell during the last battles, many were shot after being taken prisoner. For the others, the survivors, the hardest, most severe punishment of the victors waited. Unaware of the reality of it all, they believed they could judge fairly. For the victors, there was no difference between the special units, the Security Service (SD), and the fighting soldiers of the Waffen-SS. Only many years later were they ready to grant to the men of the Waffen-SS the respect to which any soldier, fighting bravely and without disgrace, has a right.

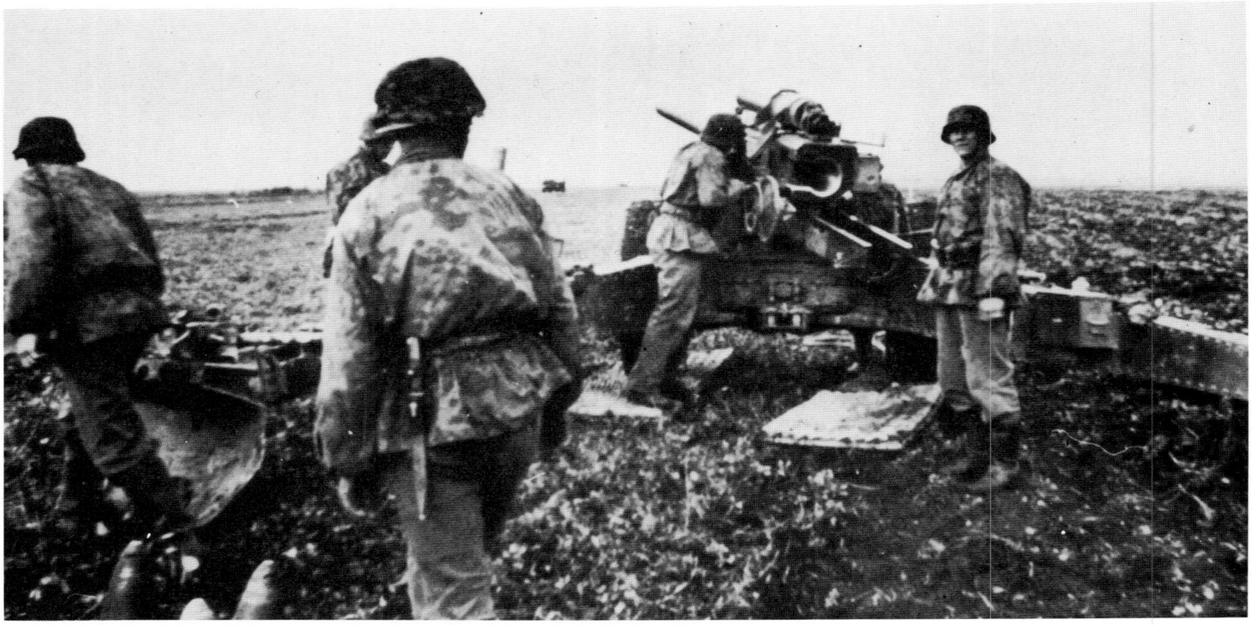

After the Russian armored attack was pushed back, the men at the 88 mm anti-aircraft artillery gun expect new Soviet advances.

Retreat through Poland. The Red Army is pursuing eagerly. The last armored car leaving the village, which will soon be taken over by the Russians, passes a tank, which has skidded from the bridge.

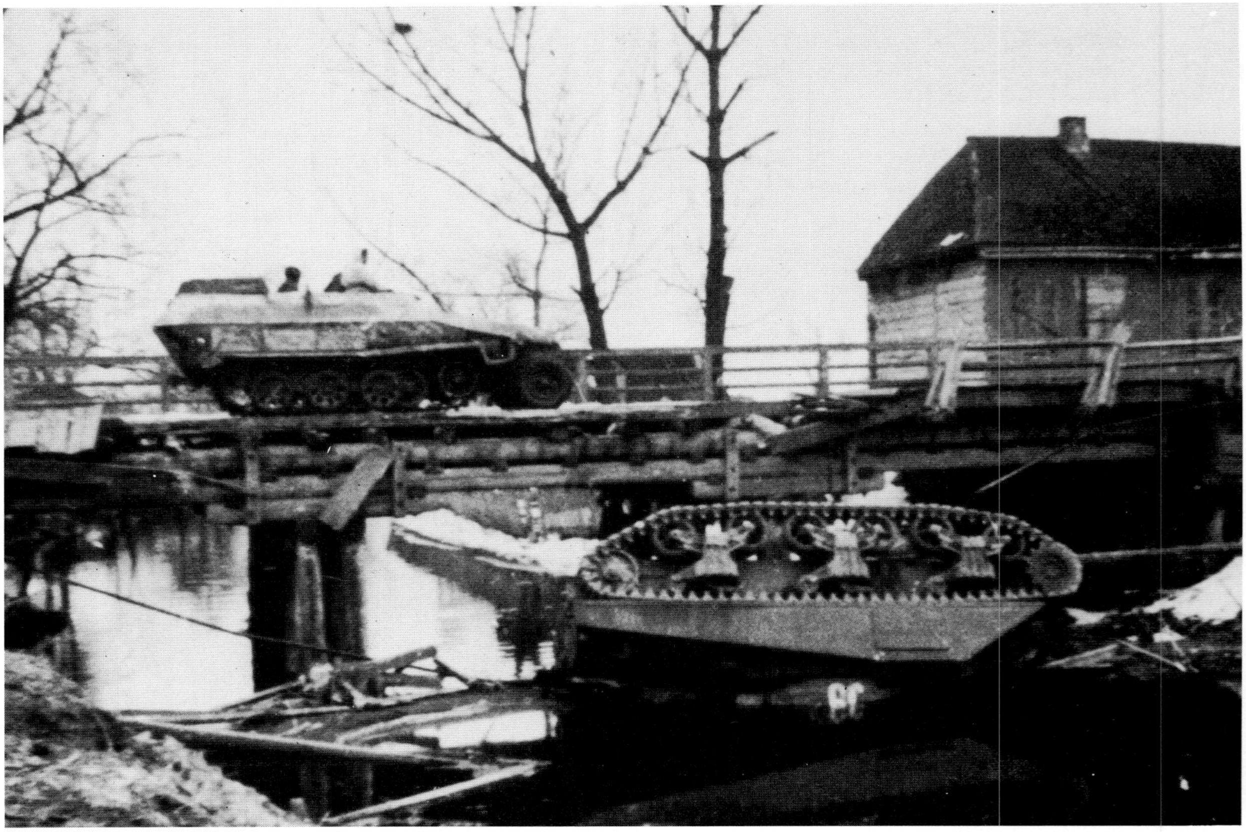

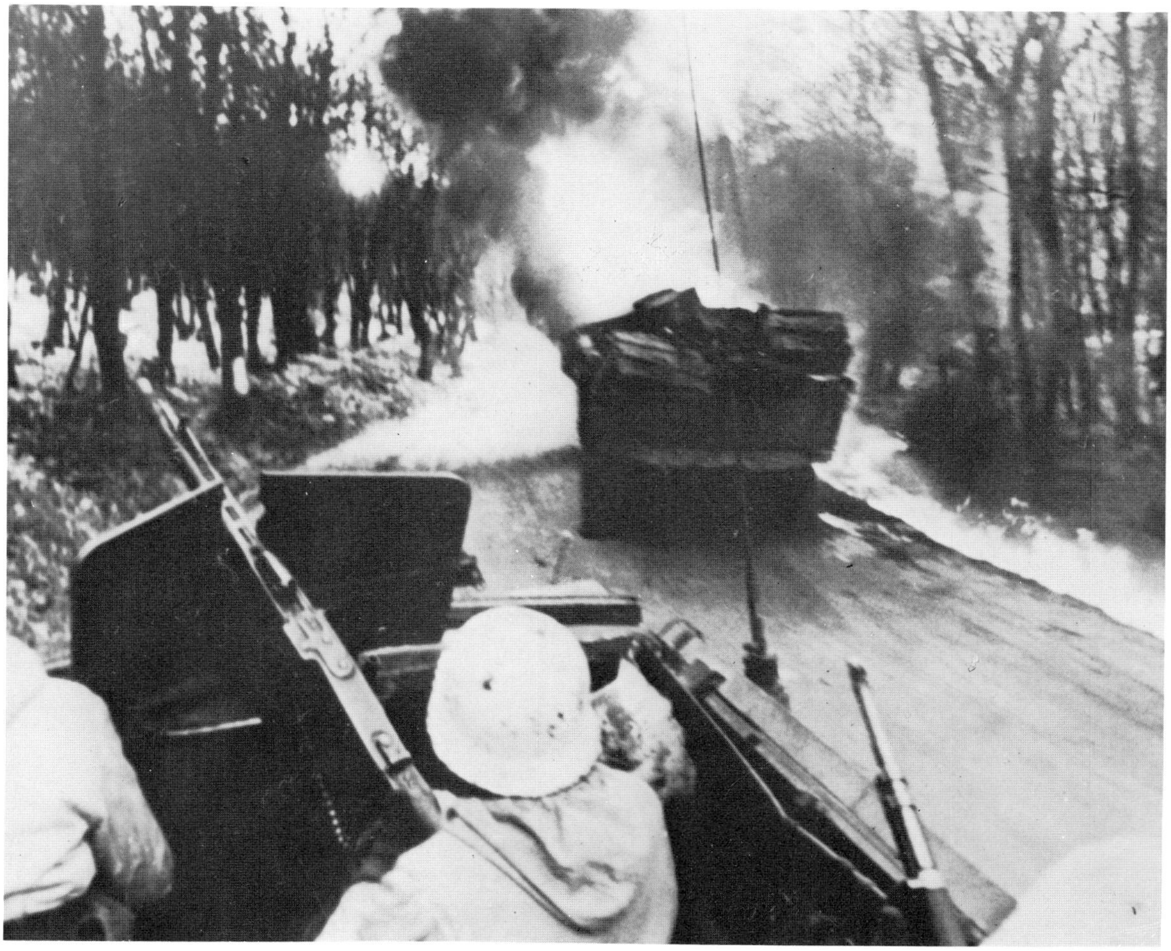

In Hungary: An exchange of fire against attacking Soviet tanks. Units of the Waffen-SS are involved in heavy battles, especially near the Plattensee and Budapest. By counterattacking they manage partly to push the Soviets back for a short time.

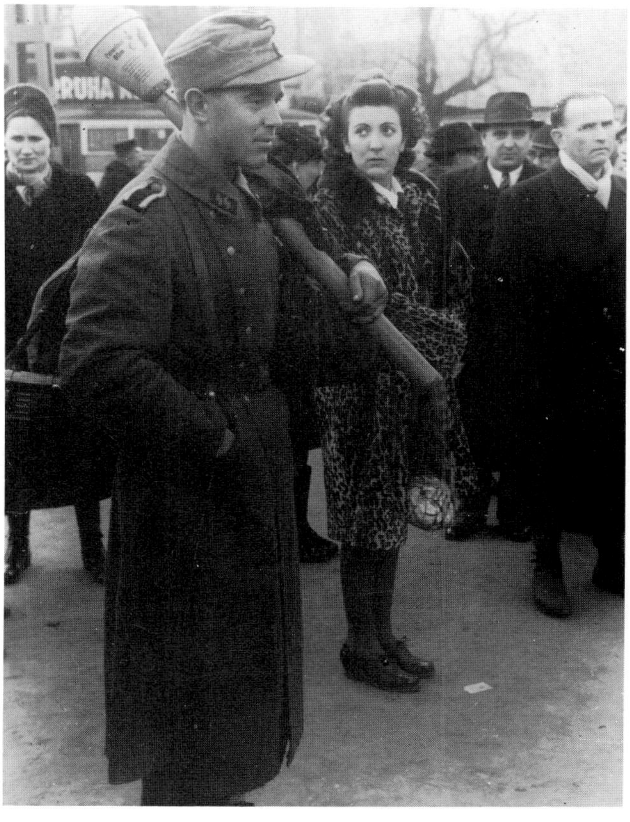

By tram to the front. The Red Army is in the outskirts of Budapest. The infantrymen can take the tram to the front.

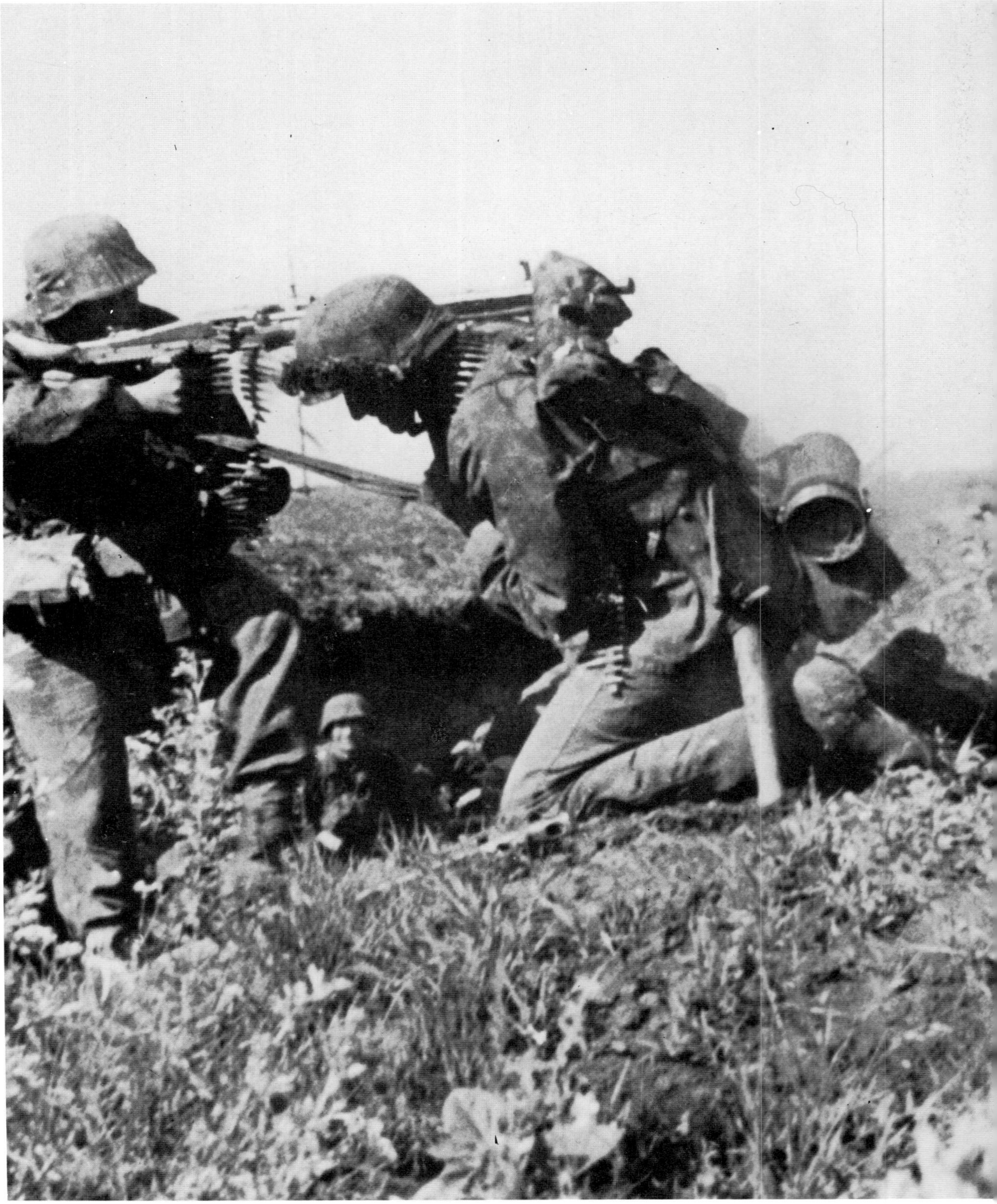

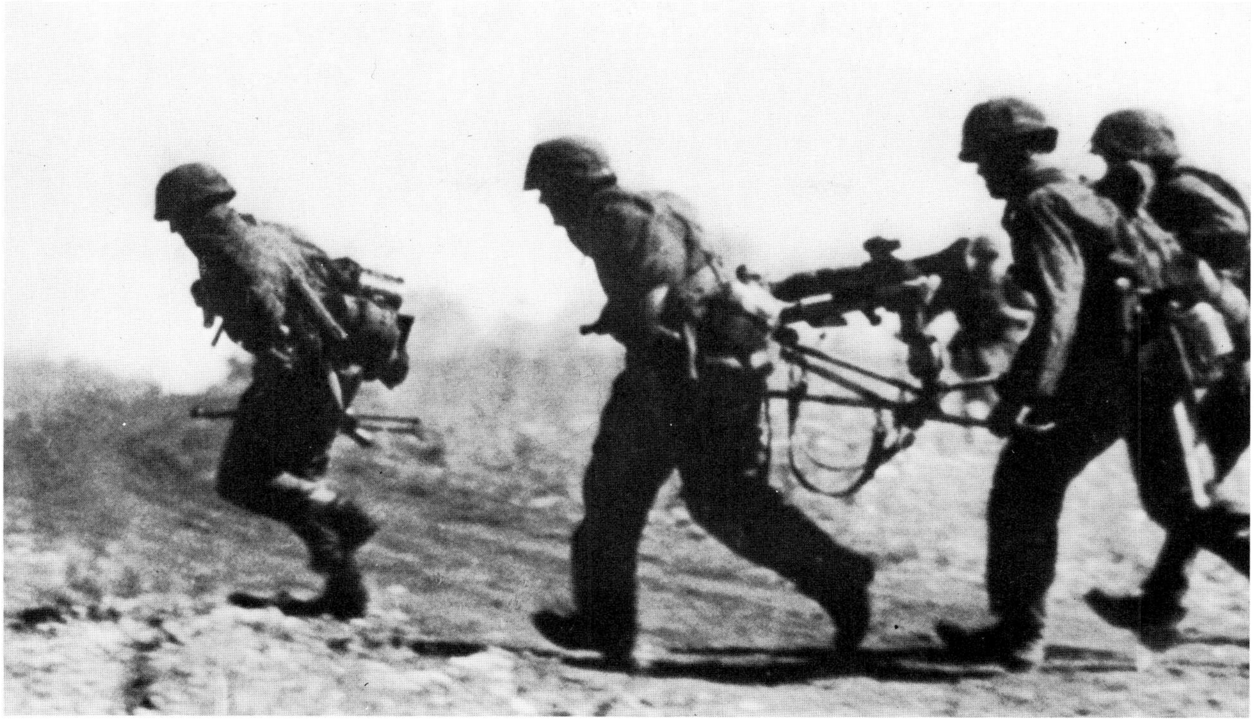

Desperate resistance on all fronts. Time and again the infantry undertake counterthrusts to bring relief, until they have to withdraw to new rearward positions—encircled or yielding to the superior forces.

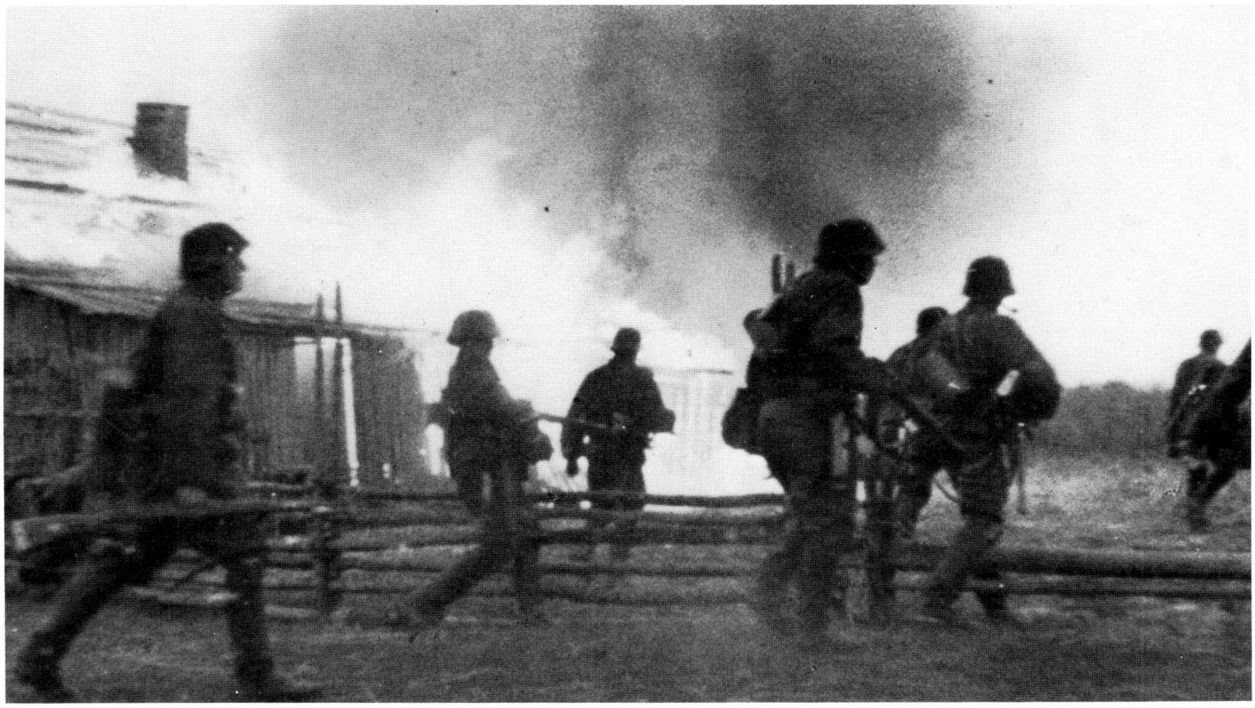

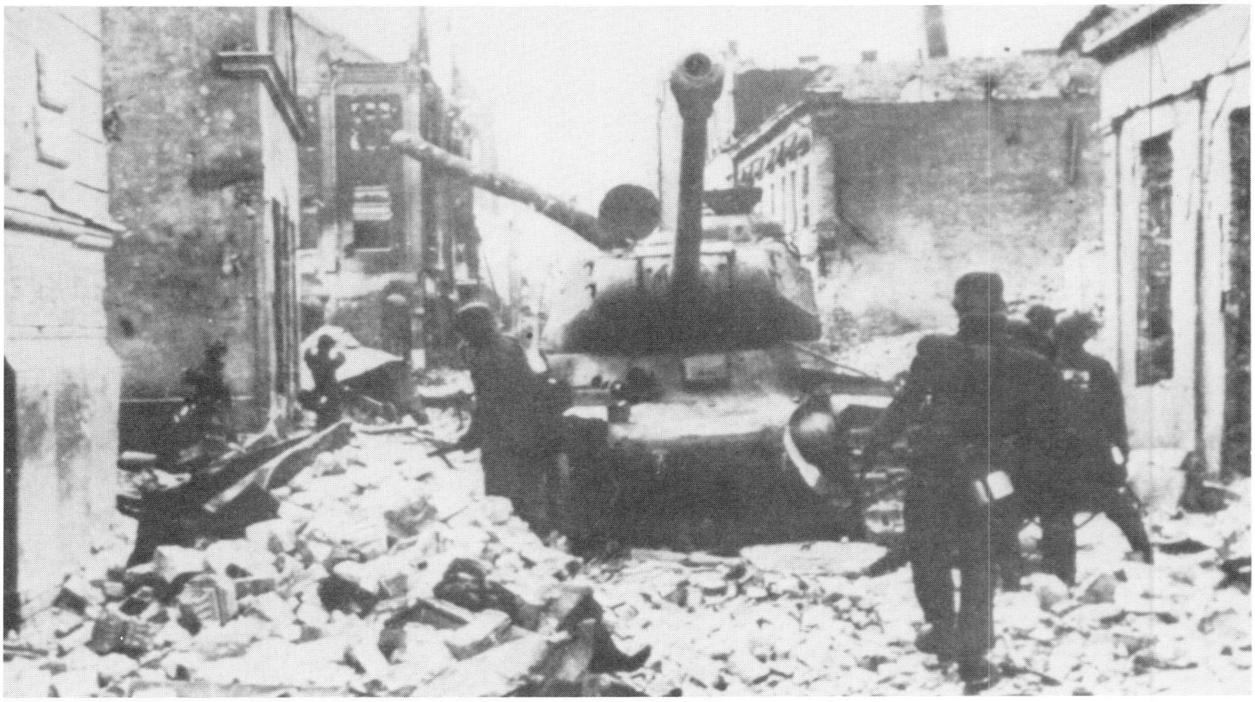

In the Baltic battle area. After heavy air raids, Russian tanks have thrust forward to attack. a T-34 tank destroyed during street fighting and infantrymen who form to counterattack.

Lt. Colonel Degrelle during the retreat of his division to the border of the Reich.

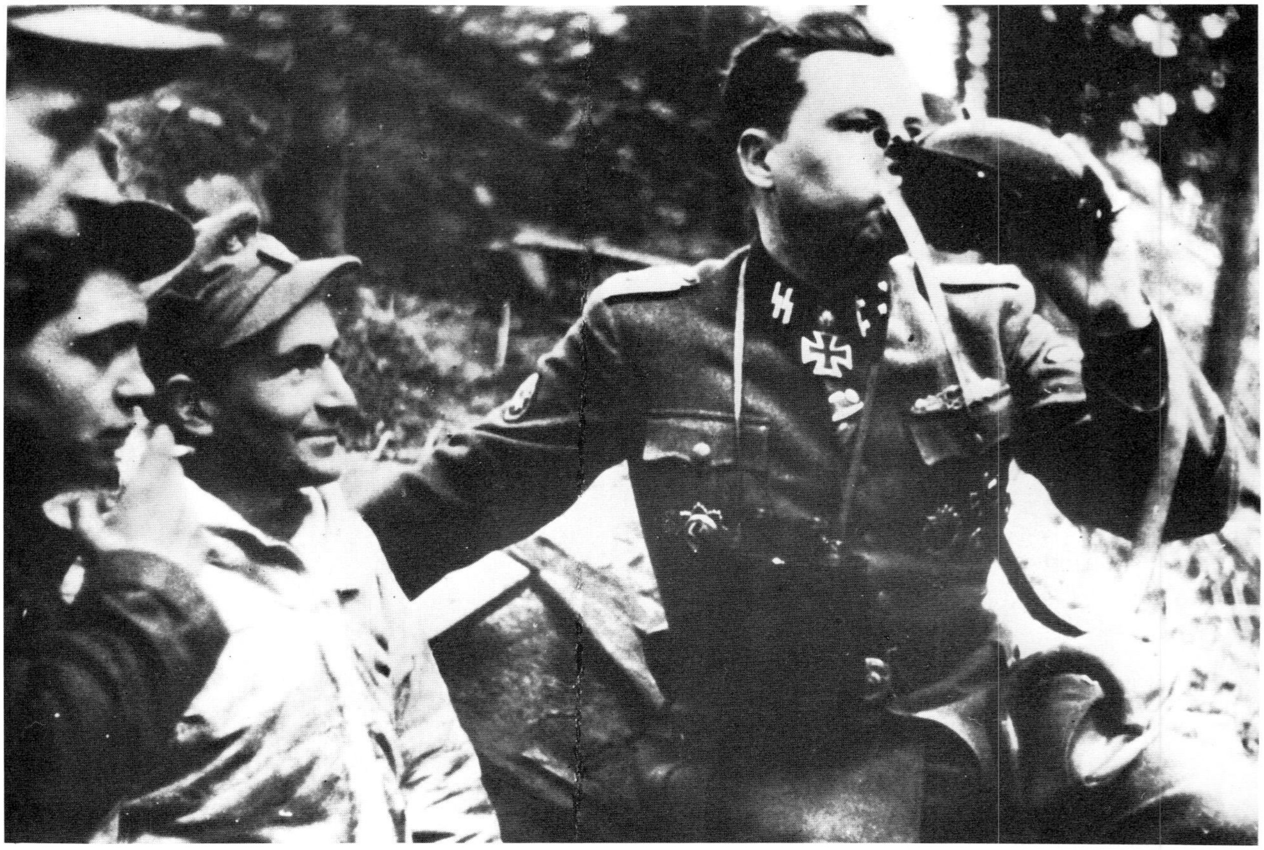

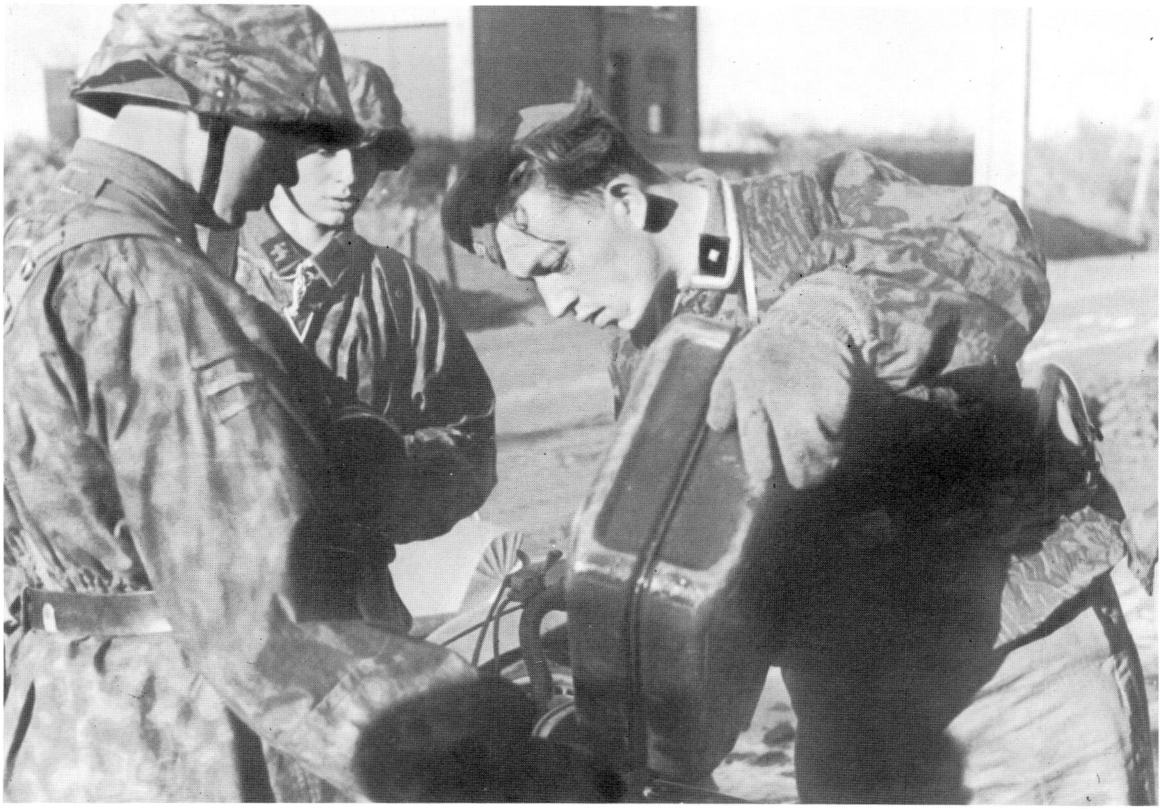

Every drop of petrol is needed to keep the vehicles going. fuel, ammunition and provisions-everything has run short.

In the east the Red Army has crossed the border of the Reich. Quickly dug defensive positions on the outskirts of a town in Lower-Silesia.

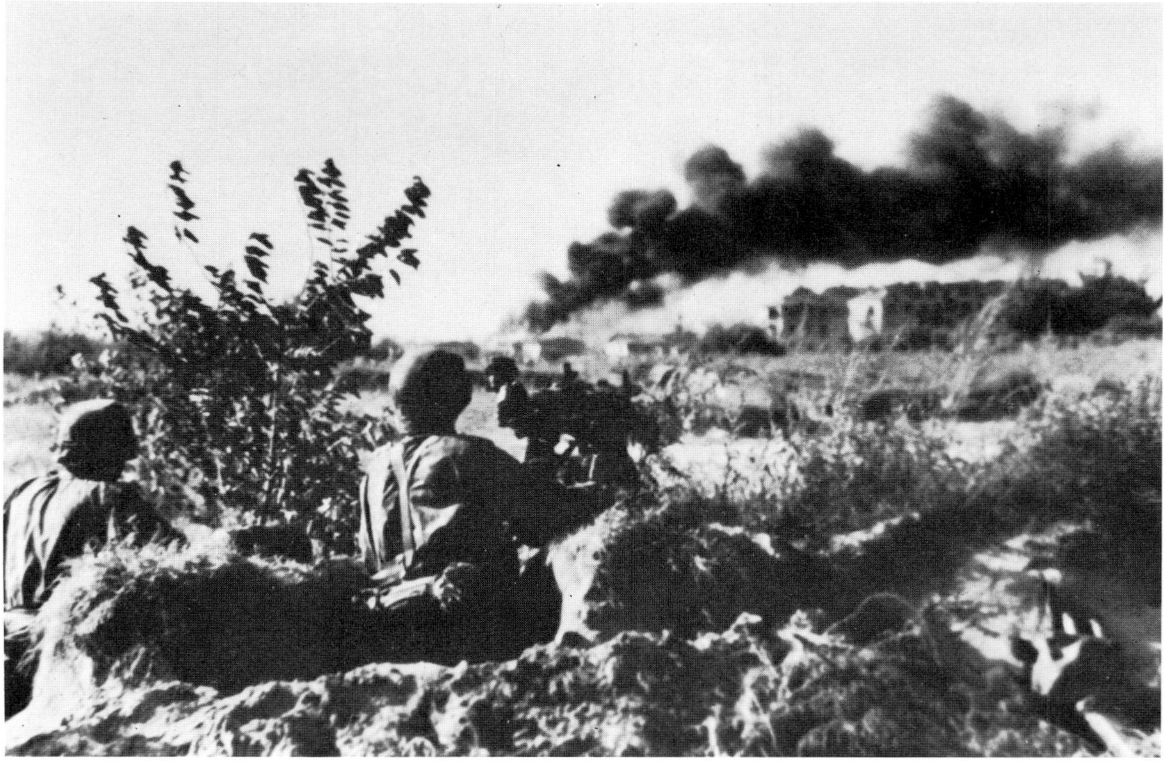

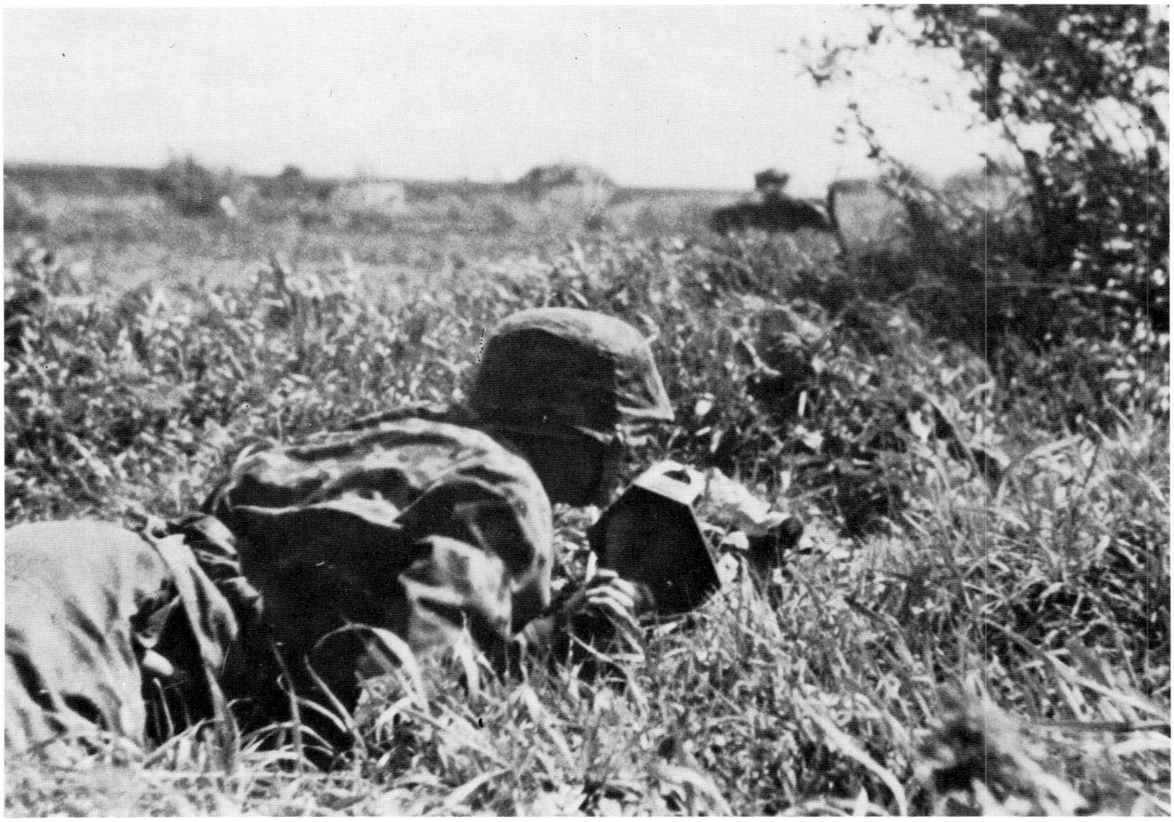

As heavy weapons are lacking, the infantrymen are fighting with "Haftladungen" against Russian armored cars.

Soldiers who are lightly wounded stay at the front with their units. Every man is needed.

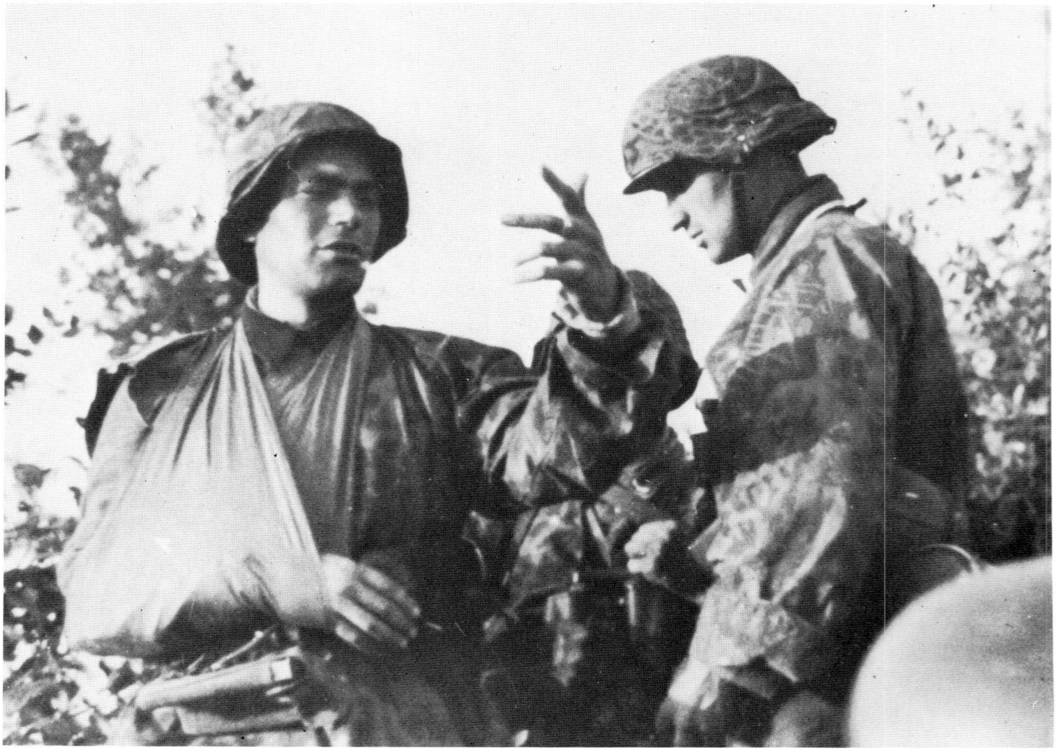

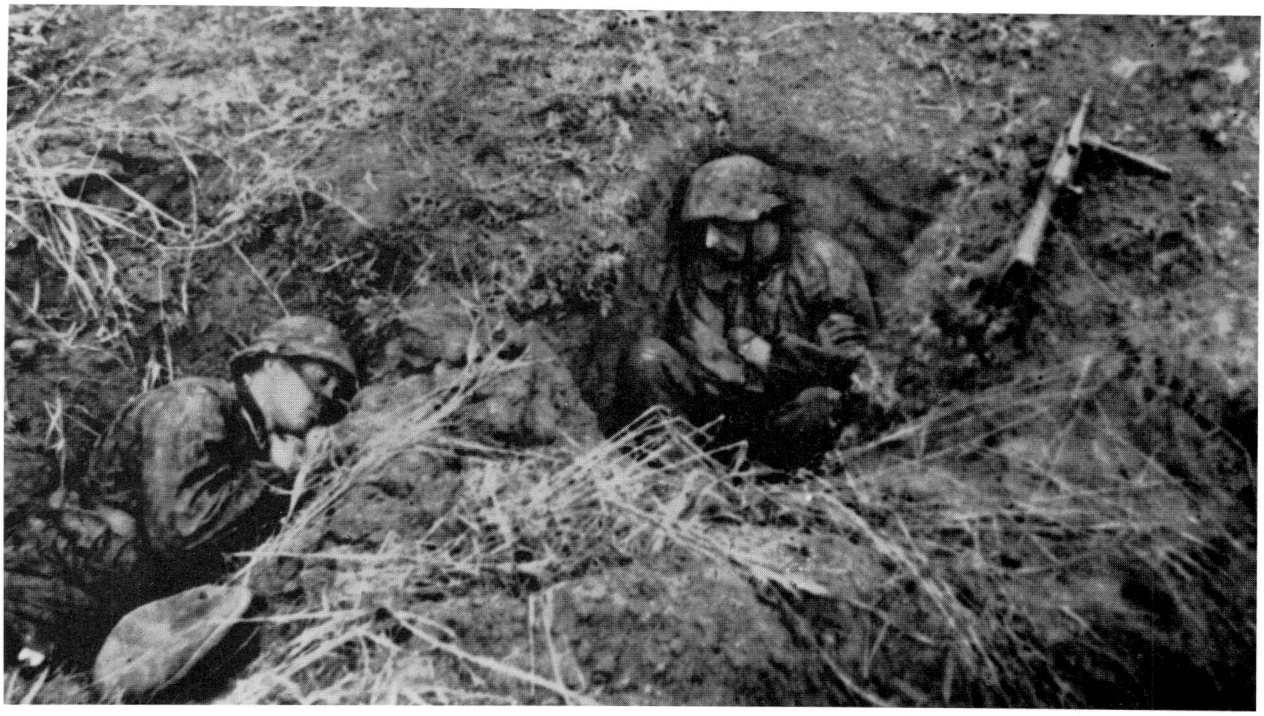

Heavy defensive battles lasting for months now, have exhausted the infantry to the limit. Every break between the battles is used to get some sleep in all possible positions.

Messengers aren't any better off. All the time Russian combat planes are in the air.

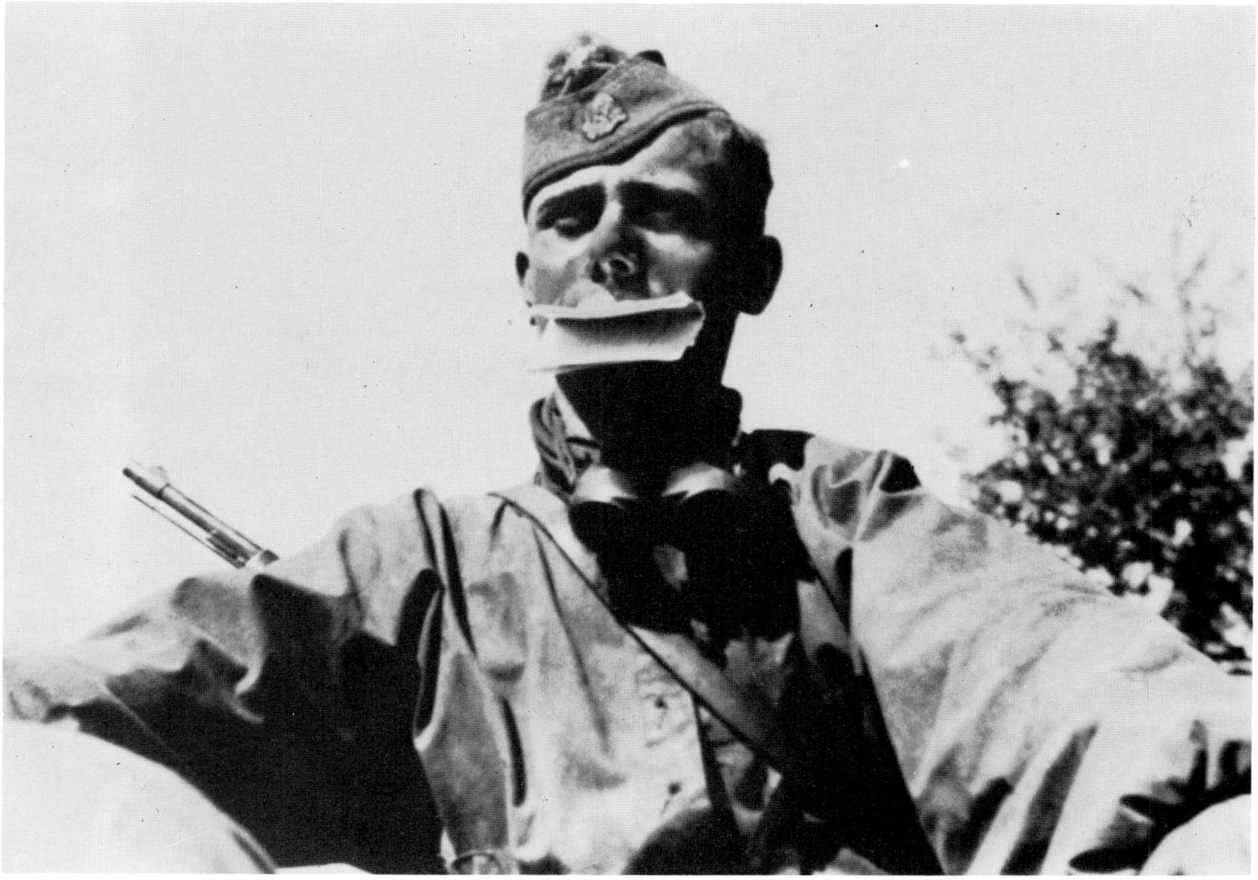

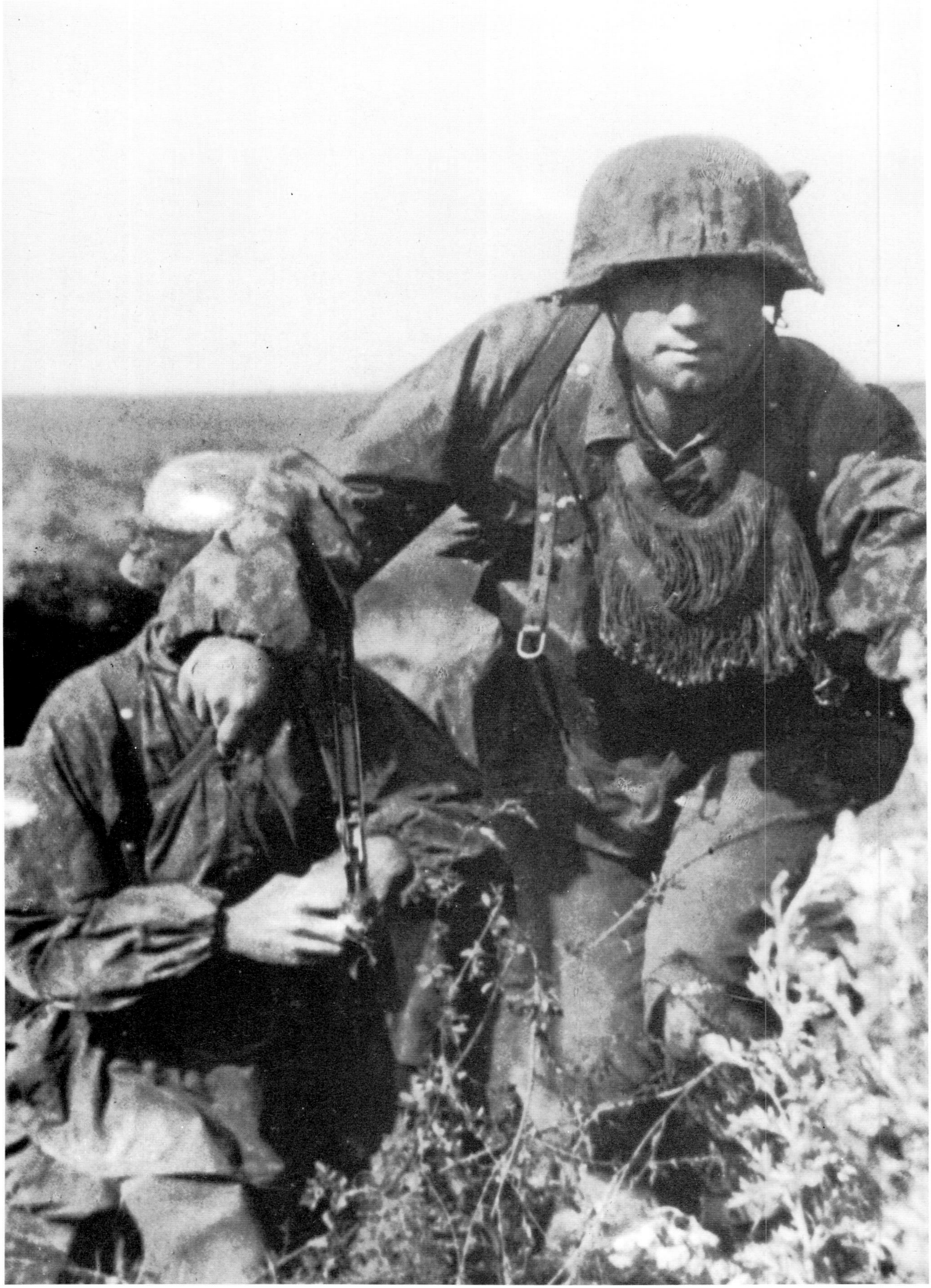

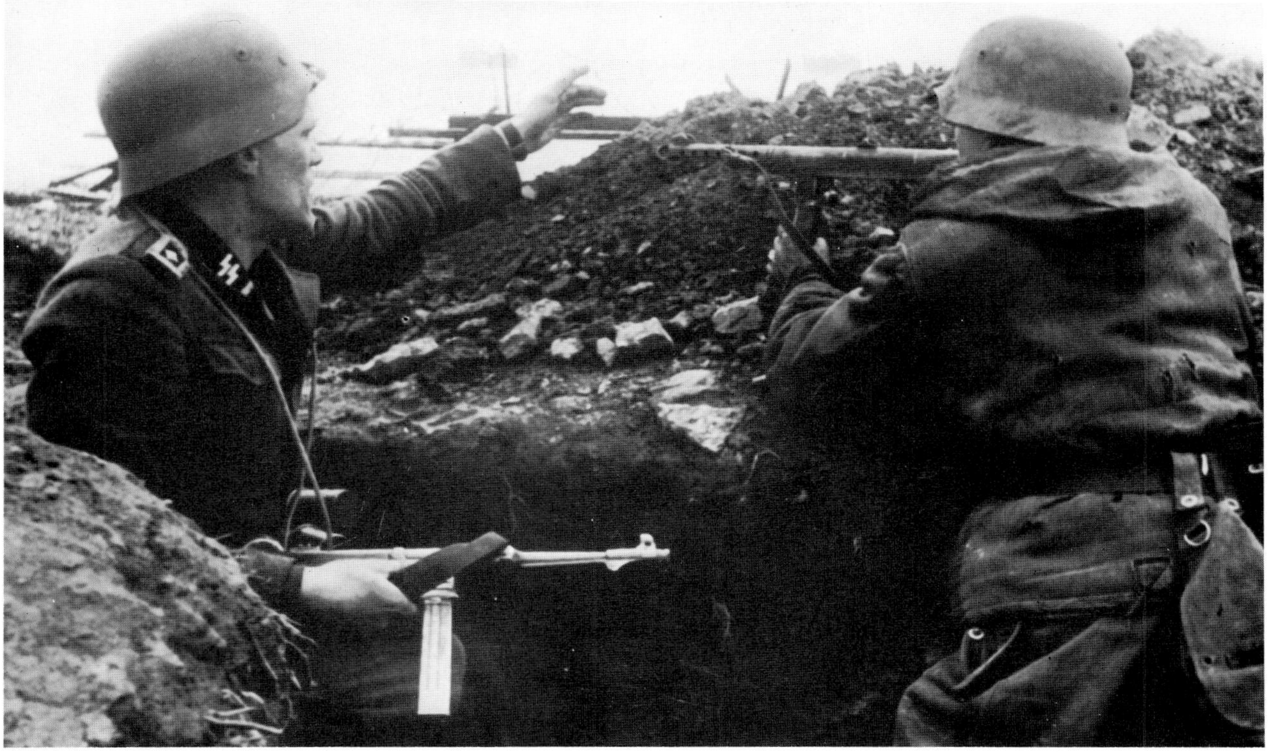

Counterattacks and defense in provisional positions, often in close combat and hardly any rest. so it goes on day to day, week by week.

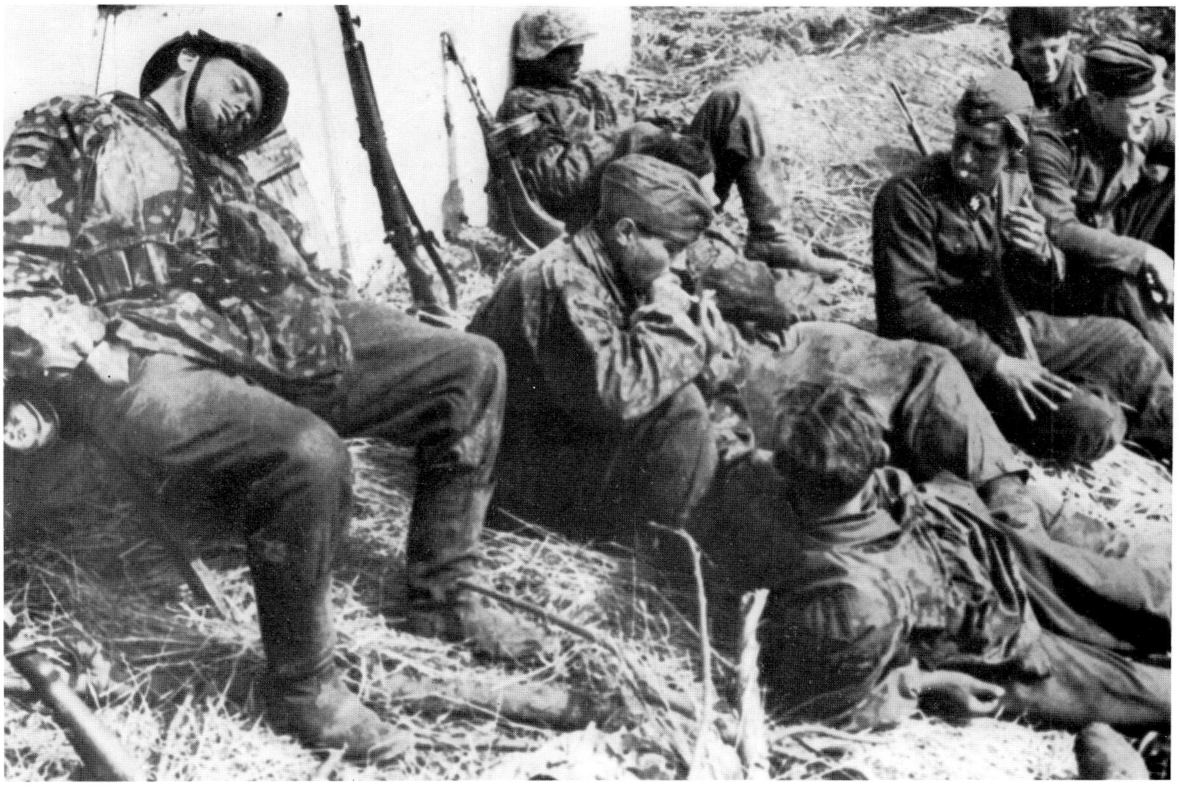

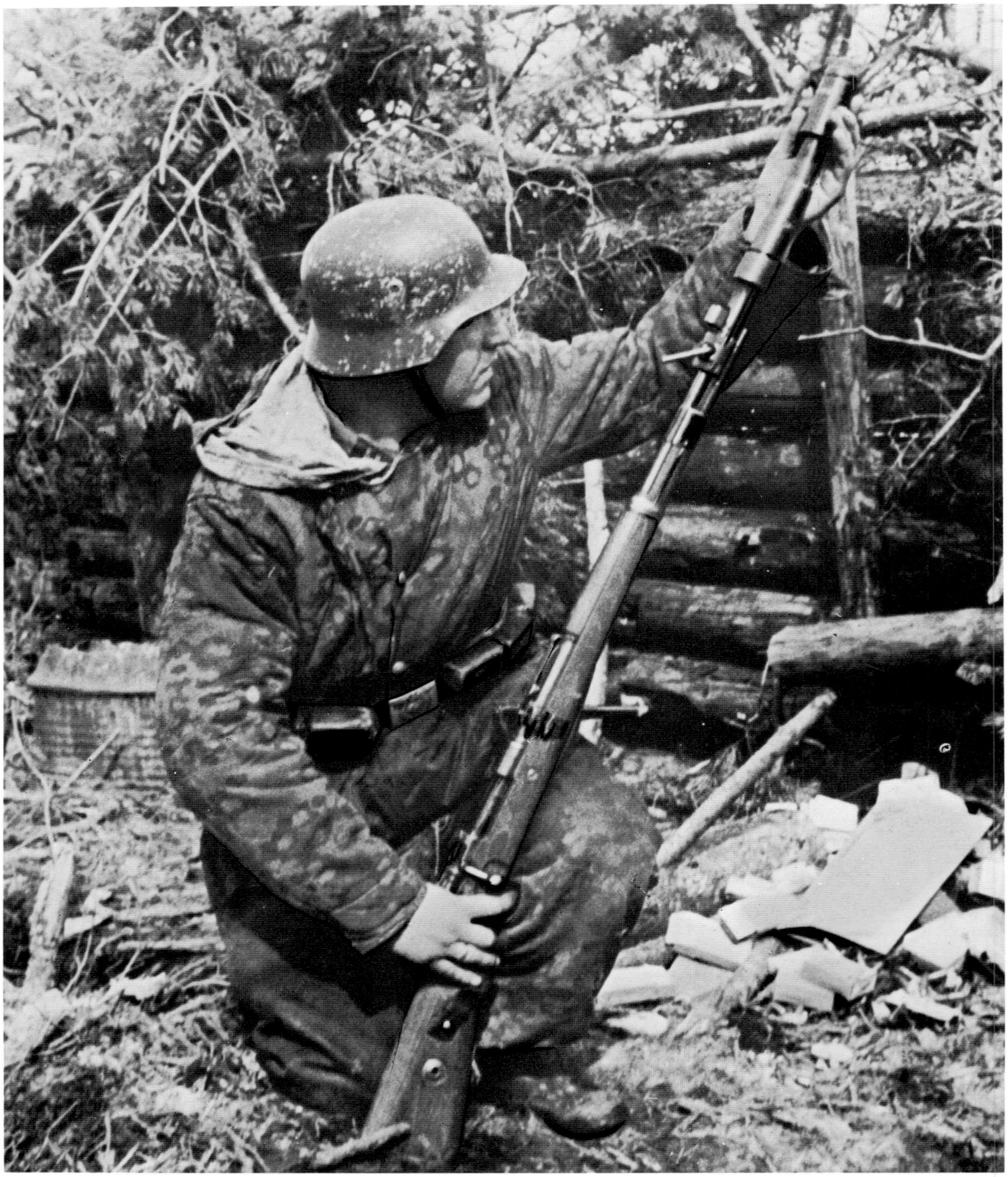

The Red Army is only 100 meters away and is being attacked with gun grenades at this distance.

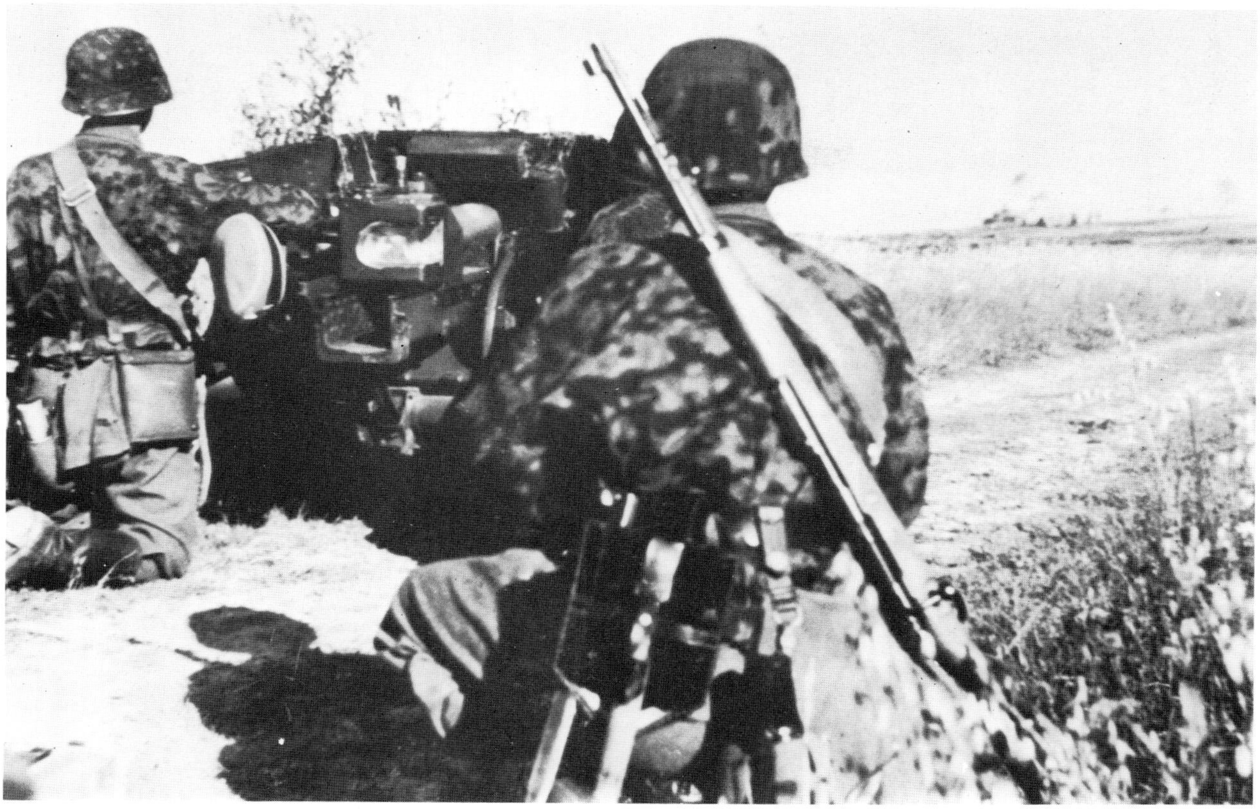

The Soviets assail with new tank platoons. Anti-tank guns are involved in the shooting.

The soviet troops at the forward line of attack can again be pushed back. The infantry attacks with hand grenades and automatic rifles.

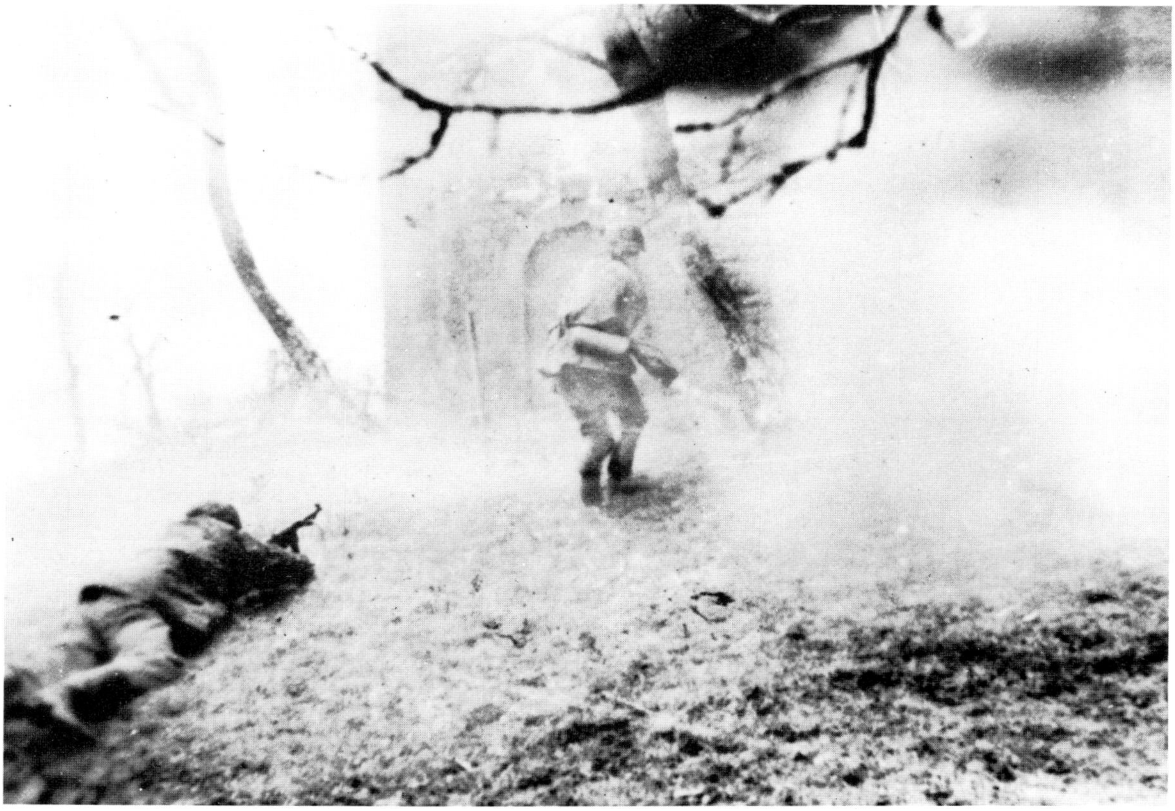

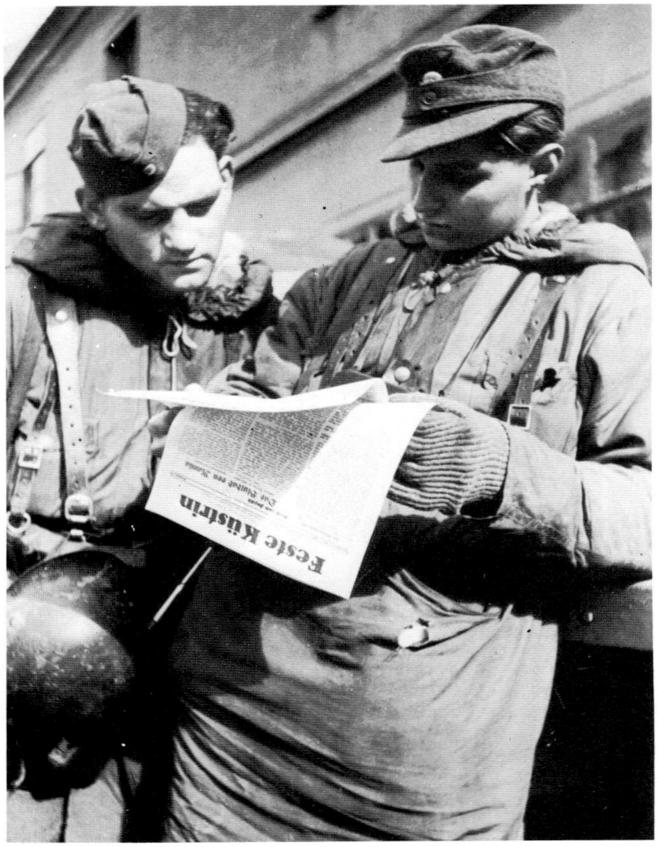
Feste Küstrin

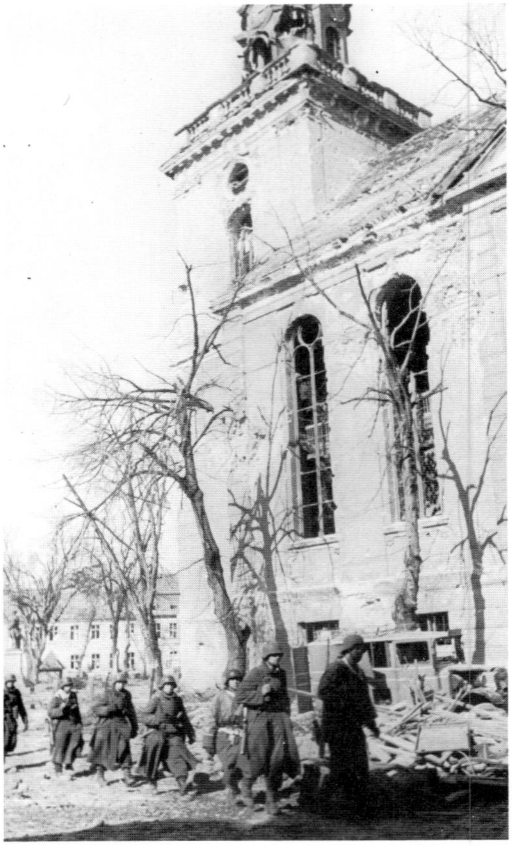

The fortress of Küstrin. Units of the Waffen—SS defended this badly destroyed town for weeks against the far superior opponent. Who still hopes the "Küstrin miracle of 1813" could be repeated?

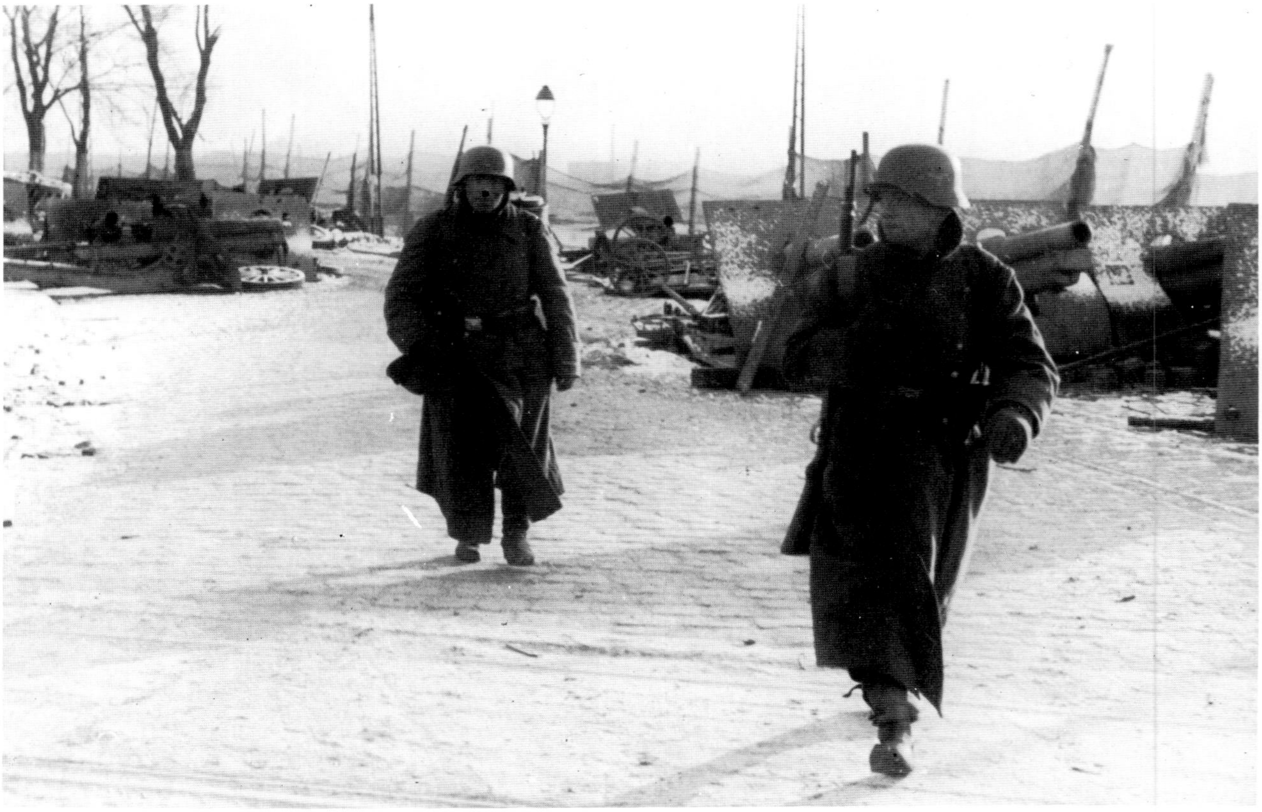

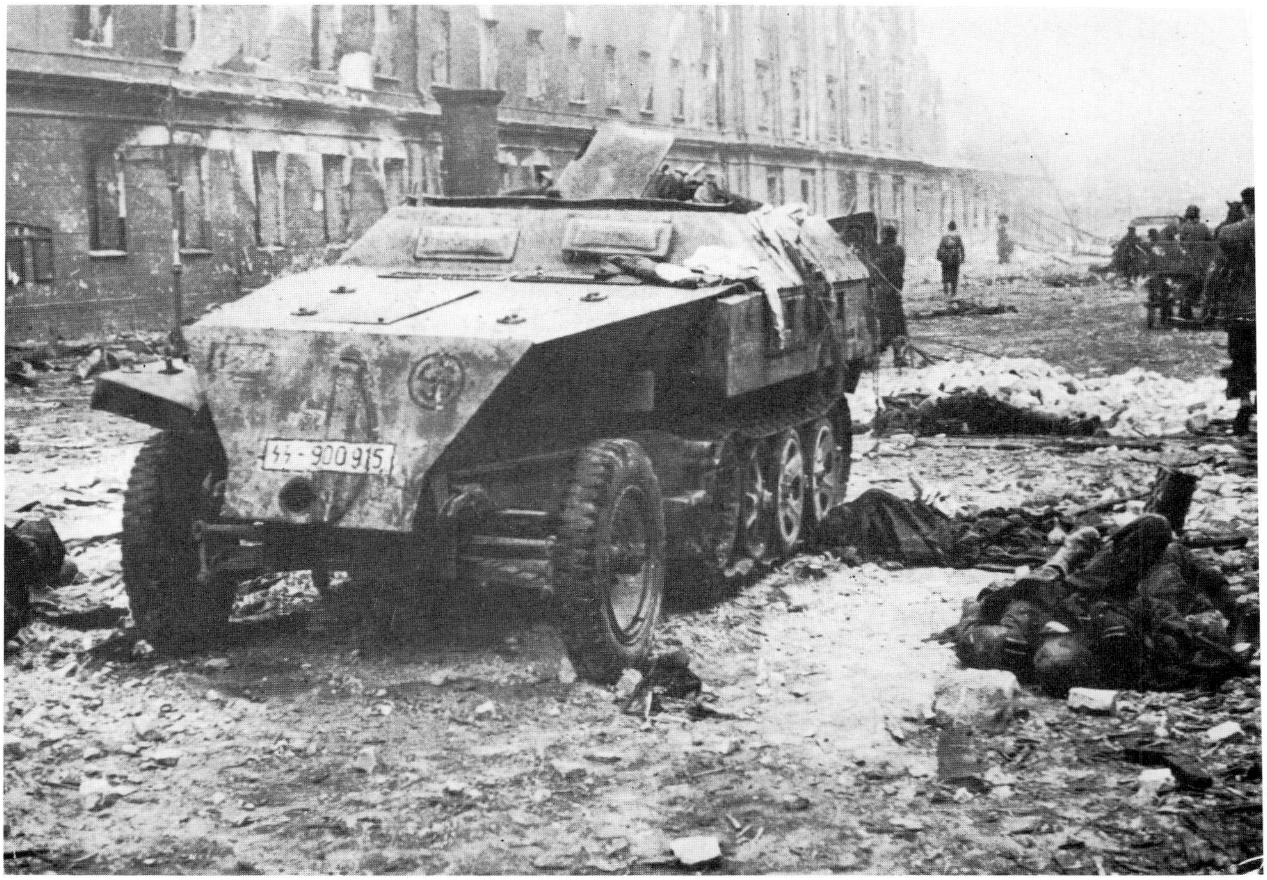
SS-900915

The fronts fall apart. While the fighting in Italy and other places has already come to an end, every single street in Berlin is bitterly fought for-a senseless battle, still claiming its countless victims on both sides.

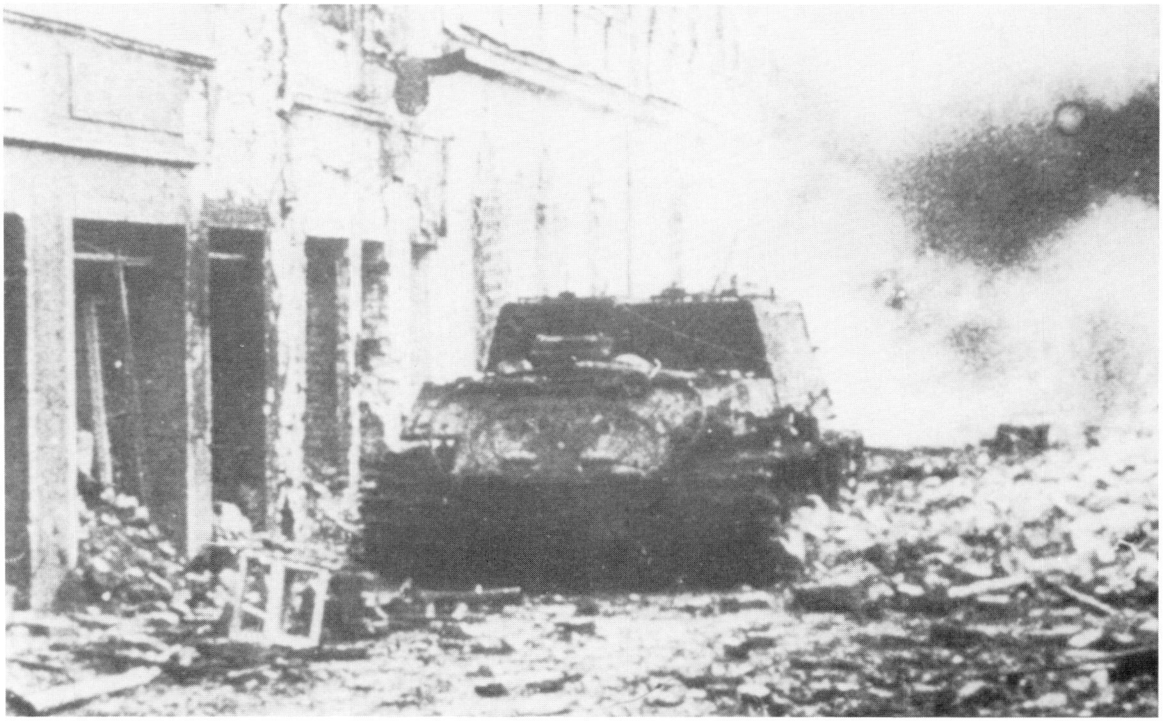

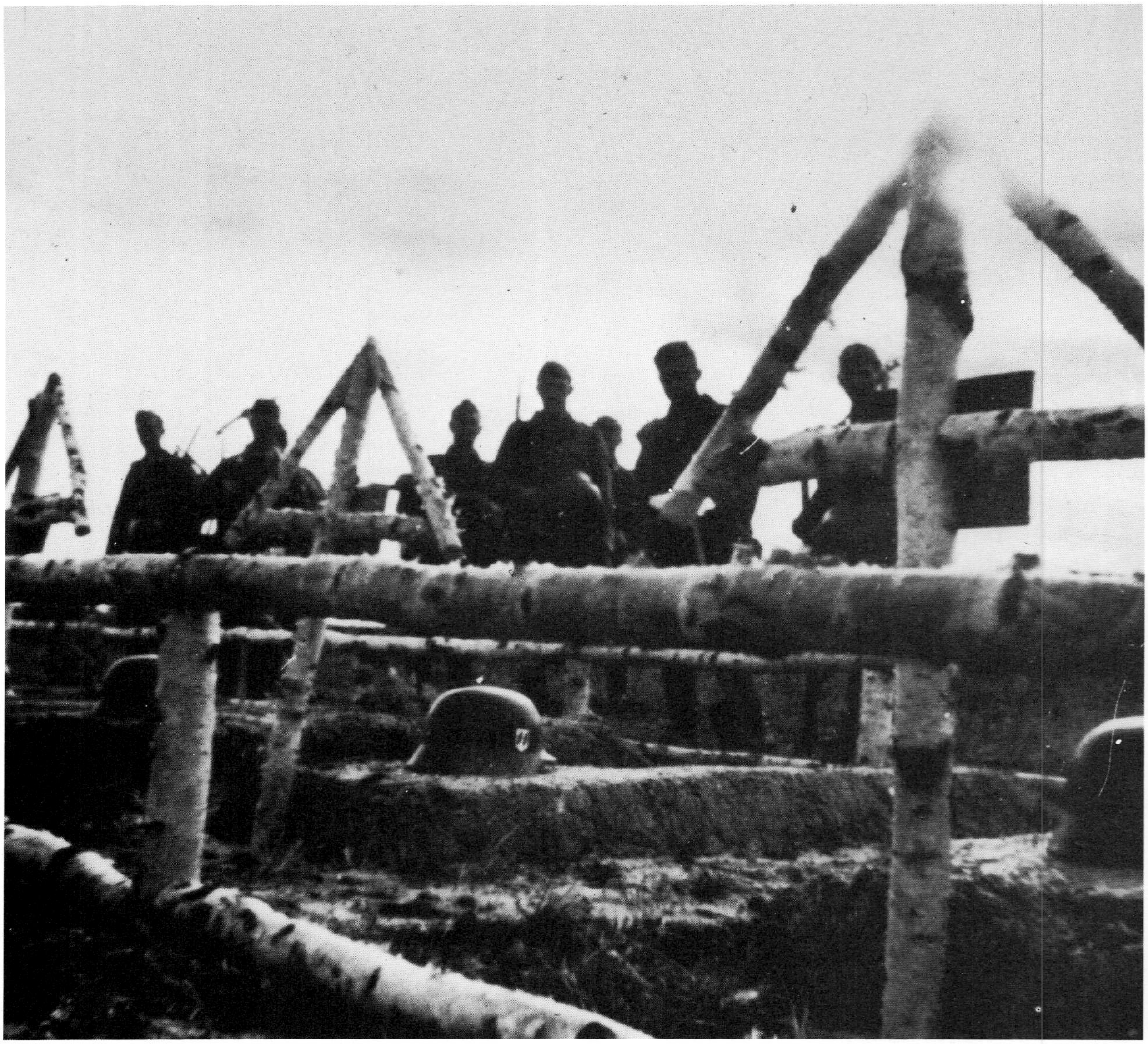

Countless soldiers of the Waffen-SS were buried in foreign soil. Far too many on both sides died during the final battles in the Reich. Those SS men who survived this six years war, faced a destiny which was no less hard.

Exhausted and defeated...the last hours of the war.

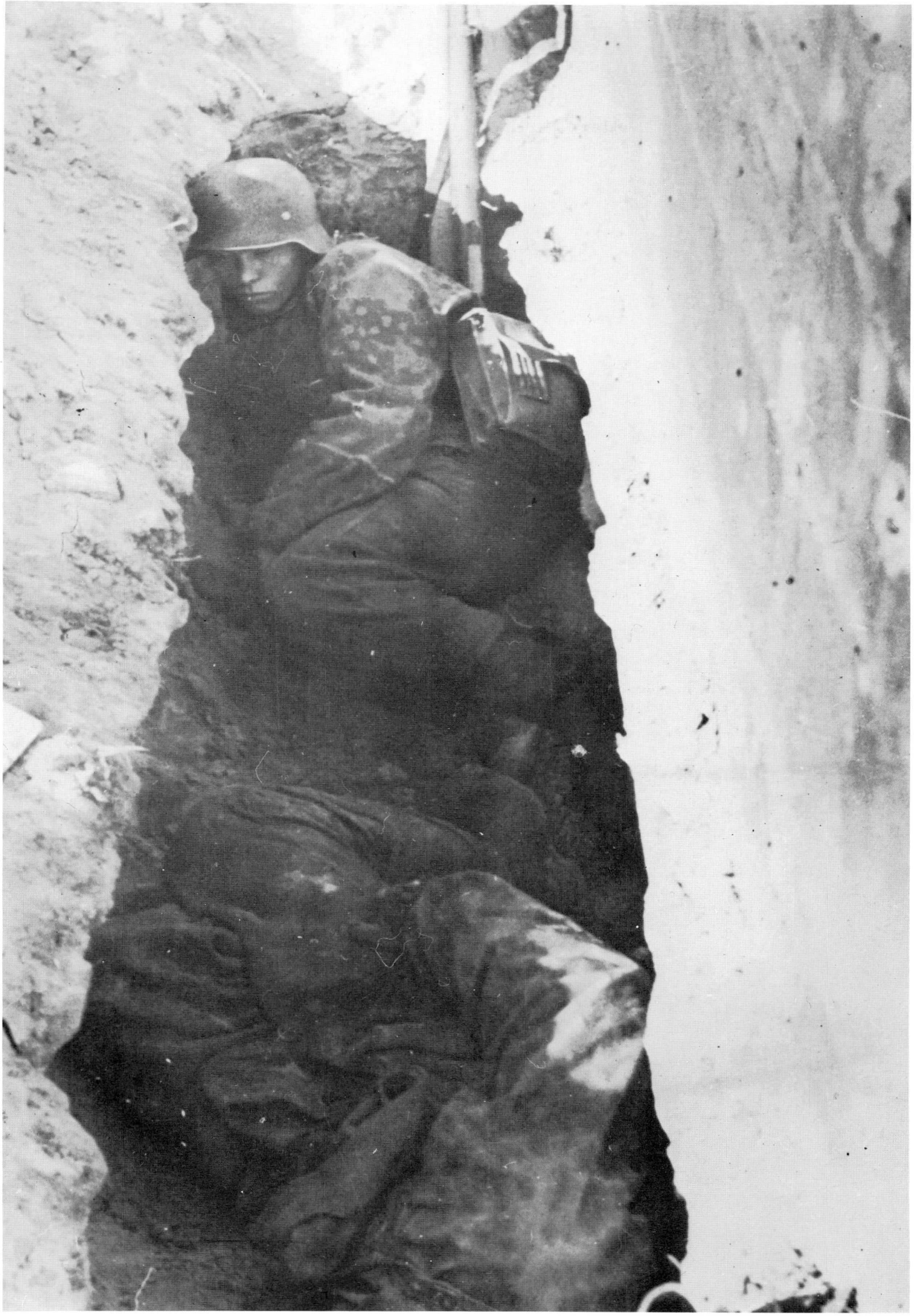

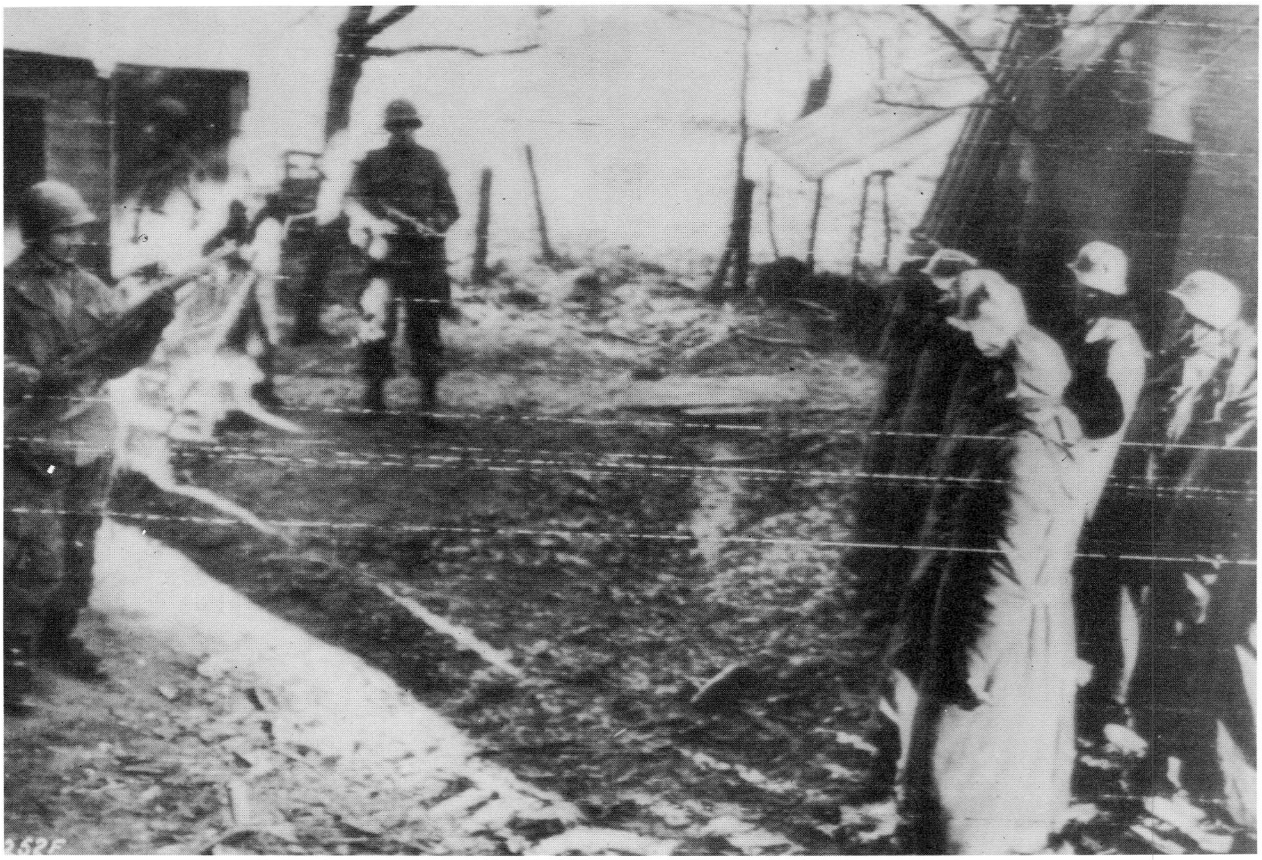

Imprisonment: In Belgium (photo above) and in Tangermünde where SS-Brigadier General Jürgen Wagner hands his unit over to U.S. troops.

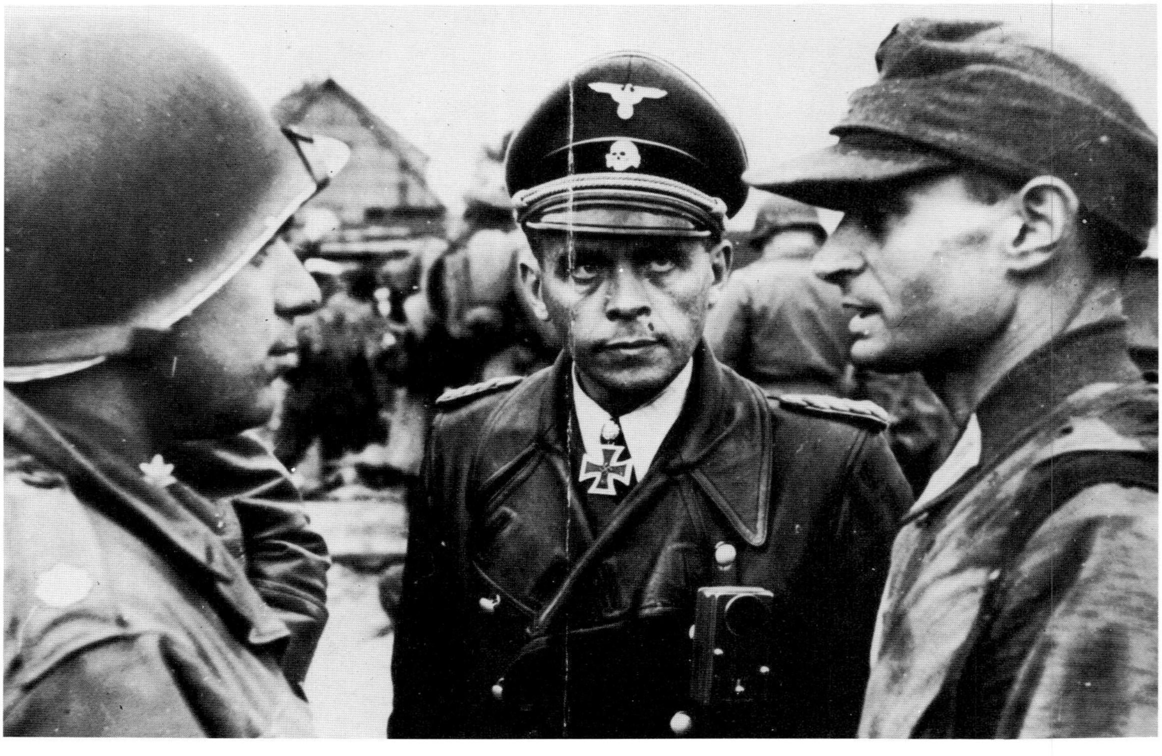

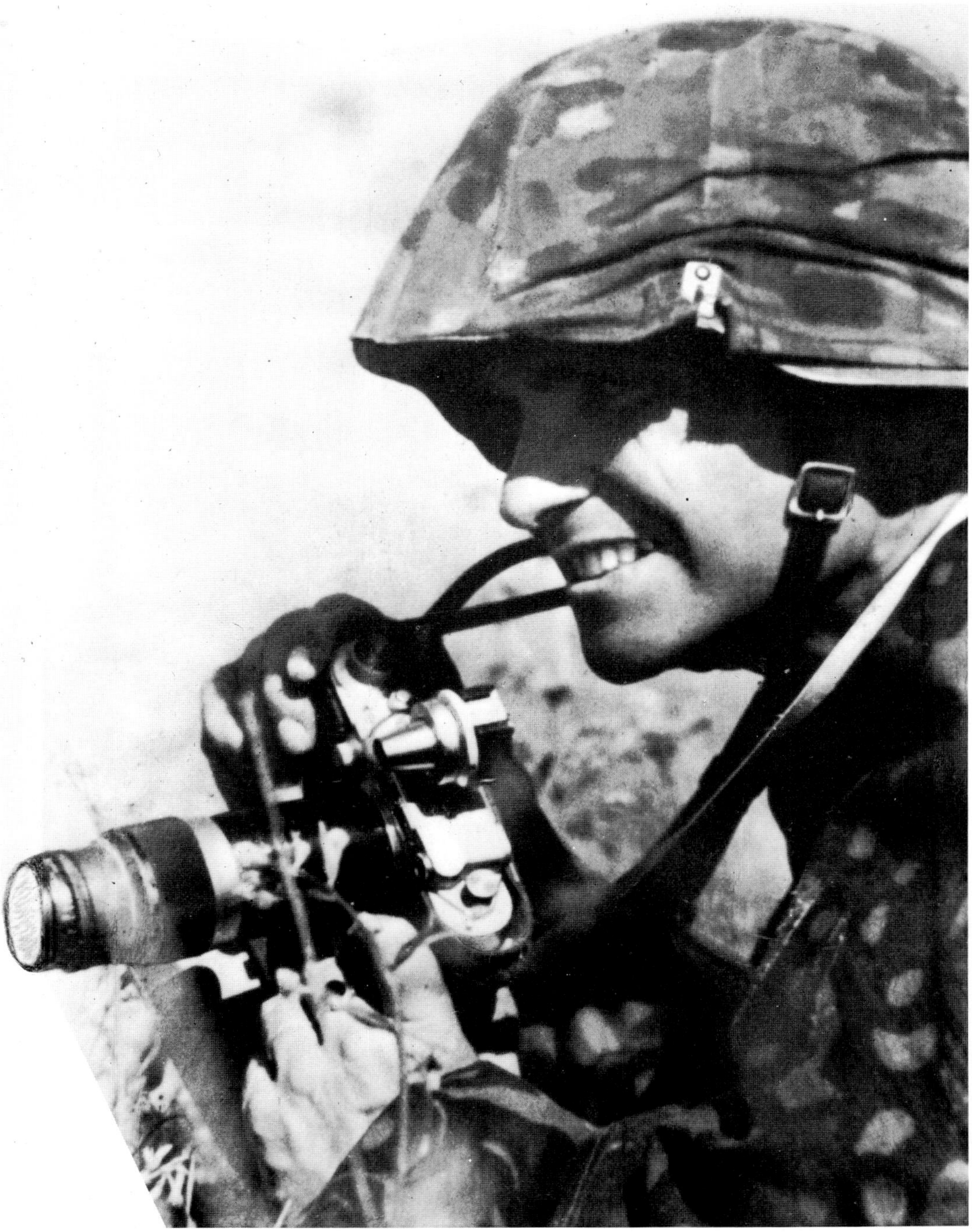

War reporters of the Waffen-SS we are indebted to them for the photographs. They didn't gad about in the bases and take pictures of only posed war scenes. If necessary, they even took up arms...

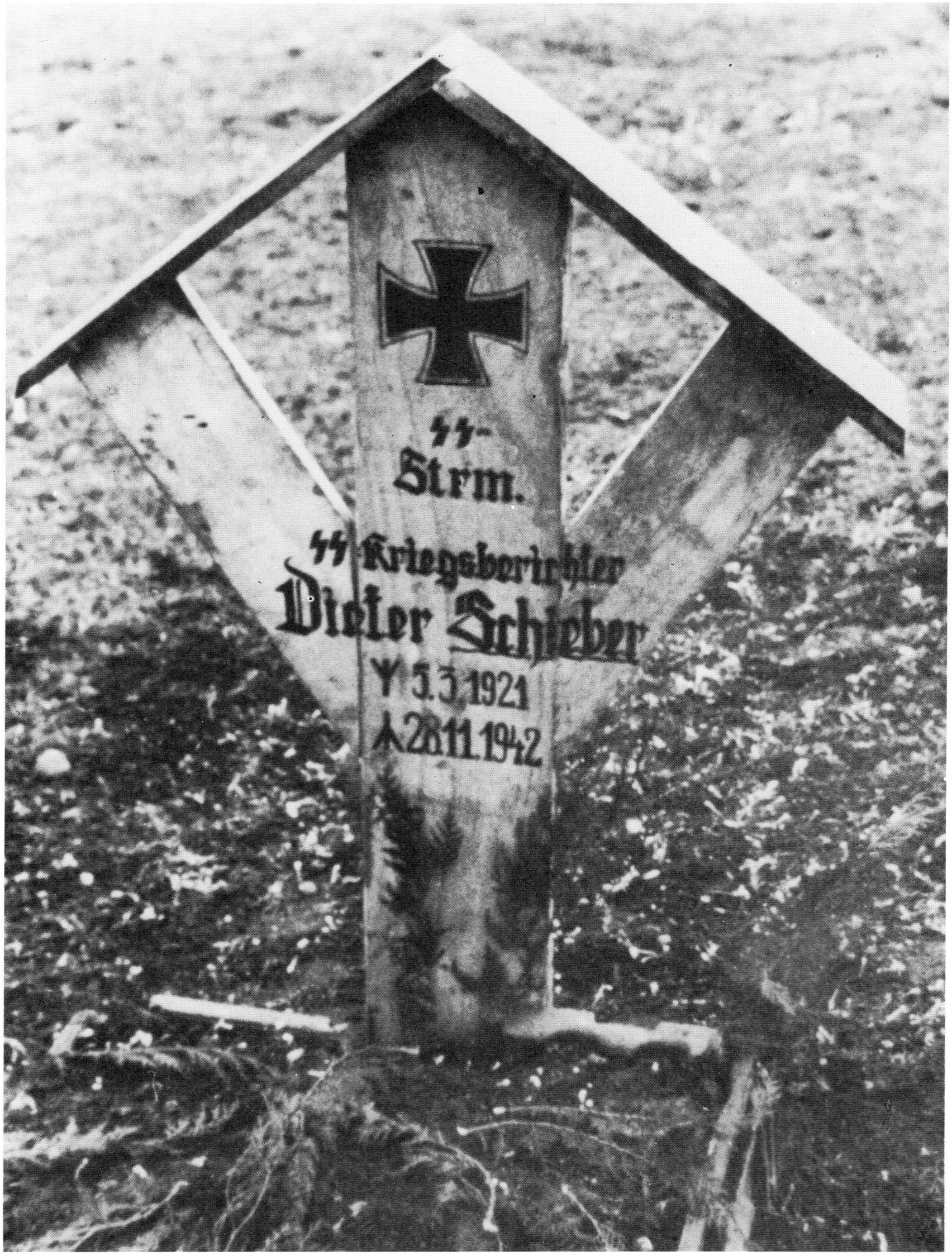
Strm.
Kriegsberichter
Dieter Schieber
5.3.1921
28.11.1942

...that is why the number of killed, wounded and missing in action among them is so unusually high.

# THE WAFFEN-SS: A WEIGHING-UP

Never before have the soldiers of any troop left their mark so clearly on the pages of military history as the men of the Waffen-SS. Demjansk, Rshew, Ladogasee, Charkow, Normandy, Ardennes, every single name is a reminder of the military achievements of a troop which enjoyed a legendary reputation, something between envious admiration and superstitious fear, that was held by both sides. But both friend and foe were at one. There was a fighting spirit among the soldiers of the Waffen-SS, such as was not excelled or even approached by any other troop.

The Waffen-SS became the personification of military steadfastness and aggressiveness. But in spite of its military successes the Waffen-SS has gone down in military history as the most controversial troop ever. Conceived as the military force of the National Socialist Party, connected in various ways to the party machine of Reichführer-SS Heinrich Himmler, incriminated with many a war crime, because of all this at the end of the war the soldiers of the Waffen-SS found themselves divested of their military ranks, put on the same level with the murder forces of the SS and the guards of concentration camps.

The commanders of the Waffen-SS corrected this distorted picture by saying they had been, "soldiers like all the others soldiers."

Individually they certainly felt this, but the true picture is far more complicated.

In the Summer of 1934 Himmler founded the Waffen-SS as an SS-special unit (VT) in order to have in his power a further weapon for the inner security of the NS-Regime. This special unit was supposed to be at Hitler's personal disposal "for special domestic policy undertakings" (according to a direction of the Reichs-wehrminister)-that is where its name came from; it was then intentionally led as a division of the NSDAP and a branch of the SS. In 1940 Hitler was still calling it a "state troop police force, with the authority to represent and to maintain the law of the Reich on all occasions."

Such a troop could not be formed without experienced professional soldiers, but military men were not keen on serving in a Party force. That is why Himmler had to allocate traditional undertakings to the VT to give it the image of a military guard troop in order to get soldiers for VT service.

This tempting picture of a new guard brought professional soldiers, especially those with the ideas of military reform to the troop. They changed it into quite a different troop such as was not originally planned by Himmler: a military elite troop of a new type, differing in its training and mentality from the army, but which, nevertheless, regarded itself as a military unit.

Even though the young VT-commanders, who were trained at the SS-cadet academies in the Hitler cult introduced a political reliability of the Nazi kind which was foreign to "only" military men such as Hausser-they all filled this special unit with a dynamic force and the consciousness of being an elite. All this soon made the guard become independent, free of all Black-Corps mysticism of the SS-command. Naturally, this irritated Himmler who had always regarded the VT as only a political instrument.

The gap between Himmler and the troop gradually grew, becoming so obvious that one day the commander of the SS headquarters exclaimed that the VT-commanders, "have never understood the policy of the Reichsführer-SS and always criticized it."

The outbreak of the Second World War destroyed Himmler's political concept altogether-the war drove the special unit onto the battlefield as a military unit, which was called the Waffen-SS-(it was enlarged)-in 1940. It was this extension of the unit that showed that the commanders of the Waffen-SS were unable to break with Himmler entirely because for a long time only he provided the troop with the necessary number of men-something which the army refused to do.

As the commanders of the Waffen-SS were so busy extending the unit they did not realize how deeply they were becoming entangled in the net of the SS empire. They accepted the "Totenkopf" units of the concentration camps whose training was meant to contrast with the real military spirit; they integrated the reinforced "Totenkopf" units which were the instruments of political terror throughout German occupied Europe. They even took on the staff from Auschwitz and Kulmhof. This infusion of elements alien to the original unit made the Waffen-SS susceptible to many kinds of inhuman warfare.

Not until the harshness and bitterness of the war in Russia was the umbilical cord torn which connected the Waffen-SS with Himmler's world, even the NS-Regime. Weakened in their faith in Hitler, doubting their victory, burdened with questionable reinforcements the army of the Waffen-SS staggered between the ideological fronts of the war. The marching columns of the SS-units followed only their own flag, led by generals, whose relations to the government had begun to totter. Stereotyped formulas of: "Führer", "Reich" and "Faithfullness" continued to pass their lips but the troop clenched up inside, it became a power molded out of itself, not SS anymore and not yet army.

The troop became the actual fatherland; the battles, the emblems and the memories of fallen comrades were woven in a mystical ribbon which kept the Waffen-SS together-to the bitter end.


Heinz Höhne

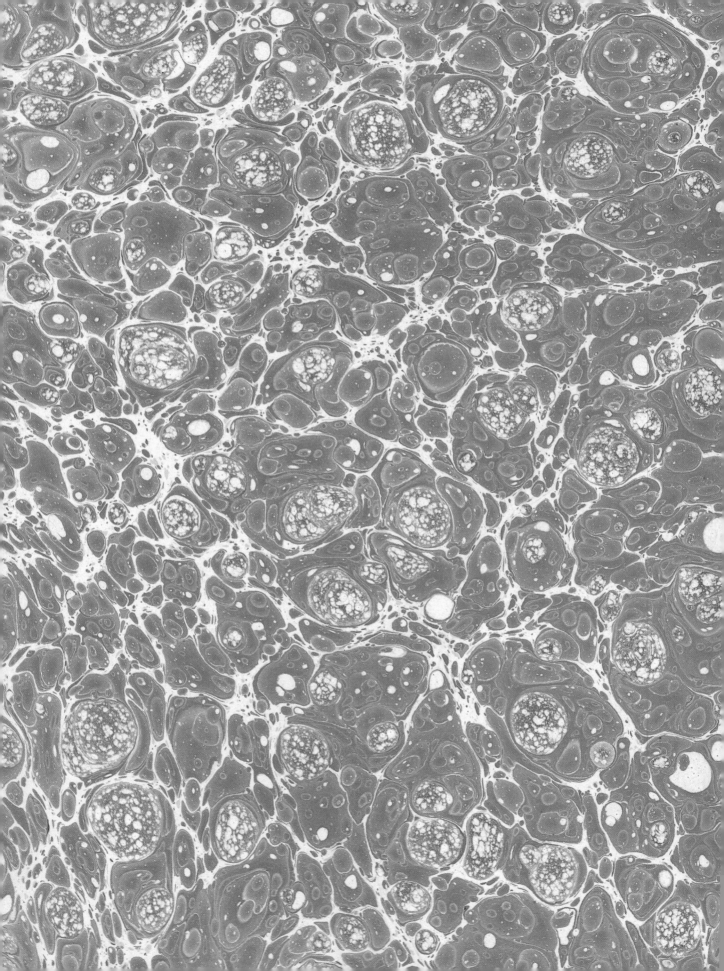